THE MEXICAN HEARTLAND

The Mexican Heartland

HOW COMMUNITIES SHAPED CAPITALISM, A NATION, AND WORLD HISTORY, 1500–2000

John Tutino

PRINCETON UNIVERSITY PRESS

PRINCETON & OXFORD

Copyright © 2018 by Princeton University Press

Published by Princeton University Press,
41 William Street, Princeton, New Jersey 08540

In the United Kingdom: Princeton University Press,
6 Oxford Street, Woodstock, Oxfordshire OX20 1TR

press.princeton.edu

Jacket/Cover design by Kathleen Lynch/Black Kat Design
Jacket/Cover art: Diego Rivera, *Friday of Sorrows on the Canal of Santa Anita, in the Court
of the Fiestas, 1924.* © 2017 Banco de México Diego Rivera & Frida Kahlo Museums Trust.
Av. 5 de Mayo No. 2, Col. Centro, Del. Cuauhtémoc, C.P. 06059, Mexico City

First paperback printing, 2021
Paper ISBN 978-0-691-22731-3
Cloth ISBN 978-0-691-17436-5

Library of Congress Control Number: 2017936621

British Library Cataloging-in-Publication Data is available

This book has been composed in Miller

For

the people of Mexico's diverse communities,
who have taught me so much about history and life

and for

my grandparents,
Anna María and Biaggio Tutino

and

Lewis and Lillian Paquin
who showed me the importance of land, food, and
family in a world ruled by factories

CONTENTS

THE MEXICAN HEARTLAND

Capitalism and Community, Autonomy and Patriarchy

THIS HISTORY offers a new understanding of the long trajectory of global capitalism by exploring how it was shaped by people working across the basins surrounding the city of Mexico—the Mexican heartland—from the sixteenth through the twentieth centuries. They were historic communities, sustaining themselves and states that rose and fell over centuries. The Mexica (Aztecs) of Tenochtitlán lived by their cultivation and craft production as they asserted power from 1350 to 1520. In the sixteenth century, facing disease and depopulation, the communities became landed republics under Spanish rule, enabling them to sustain themselves, silver mines at Taxco and Pachuca, and the city that linked them to a new empire and to global trade. At the heart of a new kingdom named New Spain, they kept land to provide for their families, gained the right to self-rule, and adapted new cultures focused on devotion to Our Lady of Guadalupe. They forged autonomies—landed, political, and cultural—that enabled them to shape a dynamic silver capitalism that marked the world until 1810.

After 1700, renewed population growth limited their ability to live on the land. They kept families and community cultures alive by complementing family production with seasonal wage work, as mining and commercial cultivation boomed all around them. Heartland republics negotiated to sustain their autonomies and limit capitalists' demands while silver capitalism soared to historic heights. Then, after 1810, insurgents focused in the Bajío, a region just to the north (where capitalist predations had not been restrained by landed republics), broke silver capitalism and Spain's empire. From 1821, while political men fought for power, heartland communities turned to the land to reinforce their autonomies. When a revival of mining and new manufacturing brought commercial pressures in midcentury, communities pushed back to defend their lands and autonomies. Then, after 1870, state power solidified while population growth mixed with land concentrations and mechanizing production, making land and labor scarce. Heartland people pressed on for decades— then joined the local revolutionary leader Emiliano Zapata after 1910 in a decade of revolution. They lost the war but won a reform that brought them more land in the 1920s. They rebuilt their autonomies, enabling them to shape Mexico's experiment in national capitalism.

The experiment seemed poised for success when, after 1950, population explosion combined with accelerating mechanization in industry and agriculture to end autonomies; production rose as chances to work and earn waned. Heartland families held on as they could. Turning to commercial cultivation brought more debt than income or sustenance. Stripped of their autonomies, people fled to scrape by in Mexico City as it spread across the heartland. Facing scarce employment, they built burgeoning urban neighborhoods with their own hands—shaping and subsidizing a new urbanizing capitalism.

After 1980 the national project collapsed, and the North American Free Trade Agreement (NAFTA) tied Mexicans to the United States and a globalizing world. By 2000, the people of the heartland made little essential to their own lives; less that seemed essential to capitalism. Many still build their own homes and neighborhoods; more depend on globalizing capitalism for the necessities of life, drawn from across the world by Walmart, its Mexican subsidiaries, and other global distributors. From the sixteenth century, people in heartland communities had made the world's money, while depending on almost nothing the wider world made. By 2000, after five centuries of struggle, they made little that contributed to their own sustenance and little deemed essential to the world. They struggle to live on insecure earnings, often in marginal neighborhoods. Globalizing capitalists now profit from the dependent poverty of heartland communities that for centuries shaped and sustained capitalism's rise.

Heartland communities shaped, supplied, and subsidized capitalism— commercial, industrial, and national—until urbanization stripped them of the autonomies that for half a millennium had allowed them to sustain themselves, the city of Mexico, mines and global trade, local and national industries. Now, people in urban barrios struggle to find work and income, dependent on a globalizing economy to survive. Capitalists profit; capitalism flourishes. The people of the heartland carry on, searching for new ways to sustain families, forge communities—and shape a world that increasingly prejudices their lives.

Capitalism: An Emerging New Vision

For 500 years, capitalism has driven expansion of global trade and concentration of wealth and power, while communities across the world have dealt with its pressures and extractions. Studies of capitalism's power, its links to changing states, its passages through war and peace, illuminate the course of modern history.[1] Its powerful, diverse, and changing impacts on lives everywhere cannot be missed. Yet we rarely see how people working the land to sustain their families and communities carried capitalism for centuries.

For a long time, the history of capitalism was seen in terms of a vision shaped by Karl Marx. His critical and influential analysis rose in nineteenth-century Europe and focused on industrial Britain. He recognized the importance of trade and the global ramifications of concentrations of capital. Still, he saw capitalism developing primarily in national units, shaped by class conflicts within. He honored the dynamism and lamented the exploitations at the heart of industrial capitalism. His vision was limited because he did not see that capitalism was not, could not be, national. The British industrial revolution that focused his thinking required commodity inputs (including slave-made cotton) from across the globe and markets for its wares around the world. Not seeing (or de-emphasizing) capitalism's global reach led Marx and others to focus on the productivity of industry and the wealth of industrial nations, and to imagine that if others followed the model, they could thrive—if they distributed benefits in socialist ways. Marx probed key economic, political, and social processes shaping industrial regions in the nineteenth century. His relevance has faded as we see capitalism as a global process that began long before industrialization, and is still dominant as industrial concentrations give way to global dispersals.

A more global vision began with Fernand Braudel. His massive *Civilization and Capitalism* explored the origins of capitalism from the fifteenth through the eighteenth centuries. Writing from the 1950s to the 1980s, as industrial capitalism faced off—in wars hot and cold—against industrial socialism, Braudel brought key emphases to the fore: that capitalism began long before the industrial revolution, that its driving force was long-distance trade in search of profit, and that it was global from its origins. He emphasized that when capitalism first stretched across the world in the sixteenth century, most people lived in communities using agriculture to sustain themselves and nearby cities and towns. Cities focused networks of trade that were becoming global—to imaginably fulfill the classic economists' vision of mutually beneficial exchanges. Braudel insisted, however, that from the start financiers, merchants, and rising large-scale producers ruled ever more complex ways of production and trade—and claimed most of the gains. He saw capitalists as predators in a world that over the centuries concentrated wealth and power, eroded the autonomies of communities and families, and created widening dependencies.[2]

Others followed Braudel's lead. Immanuel Wallerstein also saw trade at the center of an evolving world system. In four volumes dealing with the world since 1450, he could not shake the notion that power and prosperity focused in Europe from capitalism's beginnings.[3] Eric Wolf offered a powerful global vision emphasizing diverse peoples in *Europe and the People without History*—a title that revealed a persistent Eurocentrism, and kept Marx's emphasis that capitalism had awaited Britain's industrial revolution to be born. In the 1980s, Braudel, Wallerstein, and Wolf led conversations in which Europe was the center of a search for a comprehensive global history of capitalism.

The conversation quieted with the collapse of the socialist alternative in the 1980s and the turn to globalization in the 1990s. Then, as the twentieth century ended, Andre Gunder Frank insisted that we *ReOrient* to see the long primacy of Asia and the late rise of Europe.[4] As a new century began, Kenneth Pomeranz punctuated that view, emphasizing a late *Great Divergence* that led Britain and not China to rule the nineteenth-century world.[5] As more scholars added to a global history of capitalism, Ronald Findlay and Kevin O'Rourke offered *Power and Plenty: Trade, War, and the World Economy in the Second Millennium*. Emphasizing the long-term, shifting centers of power, and changing ways of production and global integration, they carried on and complicated Braudel's vision of capitalism as a long-dominant yet constantly evolving global system.

Their history of global capitalism emphasizes war and trade in changing geopolitical economies. They see four major eras: a prehistory in which trade integrated Eurasia and its neighbors while the rest of the world lived mostly apart; a global commercial capitalism from 1500 to 1800, when European empires expanded to tap the wealth of Asia and bring the Americas and more of Africa into the web; an industrial era from 1800 to 1930, when Britain centered a North Atlantic axis that ruled the world and a vast "rest of the world" sent commodities and bought manufactures; and an era of wars and depression that led to the globalization that accelerated from the 1980s, concentrating financial power while dispersing production, prosperity, and inequity across the globe.

Findlay and O'Rourke focus on Europe and Asia until the United States forced itself on the world from the late nineteenth century—the last hegemon of industrial capitalism, the first engine of globalization. They see the role of Andean silver in opening trade that linked the continents from the sixteenth century; they see how the Atlantic sugar and slave trades promoted European accumulation in the eighteenth century. But the Americas (and Africa) remain peripheral in an analytical vision focused on centers of geopolitical and economic power—which they see in Asia before 1800, then in Europe and North America with the rise of industrialism. The rest of the world lived the changing ways of global capitalism primarily as subject producers and limited consumers.

I began to challenge that emphasis in *Making a New World.*[6] It details an early rise of capitalism in the Bajío, northwest of Mexico City, where in 1500 state-free peoples lived dispersed on rich lands. Under Spanish rule an expansive mix of silver mines, commercial estates, and textile workshops generated rising flows of silver that stimulated world trade from the late sixteenth century. After 1700 the Bajío was the American engine of global commercial capitalism, ruling the world's money supply (still under a Spanish monarchy struggling in Euro-Atlantic power politics). With few landed republics, the Bajío was built to serve capitalist dynamism. Native people drawn by rising incomes and a minority of Africans forced by slavery mixed in lives of laboring dependence. They could rarely shape capitalism—until new predations became unbearable after 1780. They rose in 1810 to take down silver capitalism. In the process, they reshaped New Spain as it became Mexico, undermined China's historic economy, and opened North America to US hegemony.[7]

In *Empire of Cotton*, Sven Beckert extends understanding of the global integrations that shaped capitalism. He emphasizes that slave-grown cotton and thus planters and slaves across the US South were as essential to the industrial revolution of 1800 to 1860 as the entrepreneurs and inventors, machines and workers, of industrializing Britain. He argues that the transformation that shaped the nineteenth century came in a pivotal half-century that tied the "war capitalism" of empire and slavery to the industrial capitalism of machines and wage labor. He shows that industrial capitalism was always global and never simply European—except at the heights of power and profit.

Building on Braudel, adapting the framework synthesized by Findlay and O'Rourke, adding my emphasis on the role of Spanish-American silver in early commercial capitalism, and incorporating Beckert's recognition that slavery was as essential as machinery to the industrial revolution, leads to a new history of capitalism. The commercial capitalism of early modern times linked diverse centers of production across the globe—China and South Asia leading in manufacturing (in the literal sense of making by hand), European empires fighting to profit, and New World mines and plantations driving trade across oceans. Spanish-American silver capitalism and Atlantic war capitalism mixed to make the Americas essential to a polycentric global commercial capitalism from 1550 to 1800.

After 1750, competing European empires drove Atlantic wars. Amid battles over power and profit, promises of popular rights spread. Empires broke; nations rose across the Americas; imperial Britain fought revolutionary France for dominance. In decades of violence, revolutionary slaves took freedom and destroyed plantations in Saint-Domingue in the 1790s; after 1810, working men facing new predations took arms to destroy New Spain's silver economy. The silver capitalism that made Spain's Americas an engine of trade collapsed. War capitalism ended in Haiti, to revive as sugar and slavery expanded in Cuba, coffee and slavery rose in Brazil, and cotton and slavery drove across the US South to supply British industries. The fall of commercial capitalism and the rise of industrial capitalism came fueled by political wars and social insurgencies across the Americas.[8]

Nineteenth-century industrial capitalism concentrated mechanizing production and geopolitical power along an axis that began in Britain and later extended from northwest Europe to the northeast United States. The Americas adapted in distinct and diverging ways. Where commodity exporters found profit supplying industrial inputs and selling food and stimulants to urban-industrial societies, prosperity re-emerged—kept to the few in slave societies, better shared on Argentine pampas and US plains where free growers raised staples for industrial centers (as indigenous peoples were expelled, or worse). The industrial capitalism that reshaped the world in the nineteenth century not only emerged from the links tying British mills and workers to US plantations and slaves, it grew by tying centers of industrial production to expanding regions of commodity exports across the Americas and the world. Industrial capitalism focused power, profit, and machines in centers tied to widening regions of commodity production in an integrated world of concentrated power and dispersed poverty.

In the emerging world of industrial capitalism, Mexicans faced the collapse of silver while the United States profited from cotton and slavery. It provoked a war in the 1840s to claim Texas for cotton and slavery; California for gold and more. The North American republic divided in the 1860s to fight a deadly war to end slavery and preserve the union; it emerged to rise to continental hegemony. Mexico also found political stability and a rising agro-industrial capitalism after 1870. But locked in reduced territories, its industry faced limited markets; its exports had little space to grow. Late-century dynamism drove inequities until revolution came after 1910, peaking as Europe's powers faced off in a Great War in 1914. Russians, at the edge of the industrial world, faced a war they could not afford; they turned to revolution in 1917, seeking an industrial socialism. The United States joined the war to preserve Atlantic hegemony and industrial capitalism. A decade of war and revolution rattled an industrial world that sputtered on to collapse in the Depression of the 1930s.

As industrial capitalism dissolved in war, revolutions, and depression, people across the world (including many in European empires across Asia and Africa) looked for greater independence. Visions of national development rose, imagining that the industries that had concentrated to benefit so few could disperse to serve the many: every nation might find an industrial future. Led by Mexico and Brazil, the Americas turned to national projects during the Depression and World War II. With the great powers disabled by depression and then locked in war, dreams of development soared. They faded as the postwar years and Cold-War competition revealed the limits of national capital, markets, and resources—while populations exploded. The promise of national capitalism became a mirage by the 1970s.

Among the great powers, postwar reconstruction became a Cold War as a socialist Soviet Union disputed US capitalist hegemony, colonies struggled to become nations in Africa and South Asia, China turned to a distinct socialist revolution—and Latin Americans still dreamed of national development. The United States chose to fund a capitalist revival among its former enemies, beginning the turn to globalization. The global population explosion stressed national projects, deepening debt crises that crashed national capitalisms. The fall of Soviet socialism and the rise of a socialist China ready to join in capitalist ways turned the world to globalization in the 1990s.[9]

Communities Carrying Capitalism

This sketch of the trajectory of global capitalism focuses on half, an important half, of Braudel's understanding: capitalism's dynamism and global reach as it evolved from the sixteenth century, the expansion of empires and global trades, the rise of new ways of production in plantations and factories, the proliferation of slavery and wage labor—ultimately, the global growth of profit-seeking concentrations of capital, production, and trade tied to the expansion of laboring dependencies, free and unfree.

The other half of Braudel's vision is equally important, yet rarely emphasized. Capitalism, he insisted, has been defined, too, by concentrating powers and accelerating trades that over the centuries corroded autonomies—the independent ways of sustenance that long grounded the lives of families and communities around the world. Even when we recognize the porcelain manufactories of China and the cotton workshops in India, the mines of Spanish America and the plantations of Atlantic America, the old concentrations of workers in Mediterranean cities and new ones in the Low Countries and England—through the eighteenth century, most of the world's peoples remained on the land.

Nineteenth-century industrial and urban concentrations focused in northwest Europe and the northeast United States. Industrial capitalism drew in the products and labor of many still strong on the land, while turning against independent peoples across the interiors of the Americas, Africa, and Eurasia. Yet before 1900, the great majority of people whose lives were shaped by the long rise of capitalism still lived on the land. Many participated in capitalism's dynamism. Many resisted when states and capitalists demanded too much: indigenous peoples fought subjugation; communities defended lands and self-rule. People grounded in and defending autonomies were as important to the long rise of capitalism as the power holders who drove commercial and industrial ways and the workers, enslaved and free, who lived in laboring dependence.

Ultimately, the long, contested rise of capitalism is a history of the expanding commercialization—and thus the monetization of production and trade—of life. Spreading commercial ways created opportunities to control, channel, and profit from production, work, and trade—generating capital that consolidated concentrating powers. Those who celebrate capitalism focus on rising production and productivity—analyzed quantitatively. There certainly have been gains, yet they have come at the cost of autonomies.

The sources for the quantitative analysis of capitalism count monetized production, labor, trade, and accumulations. As more of everything became monetized, statistics that count monetized activities rise. That does not mean that more was produced or that more was gained by work. The history of capitalism in the heartland and elsewhere centered on a long process of shifting production and consumption from autonomous, nonmonetized ways focused in communities and households to commercial and monetized ways tied to spreading markets. Counts of monetized production and trade inevitably rose; they show the expansion of capitalism. The analytical challenge is how to weigh the quantifiable gains of capitalism against the benefits of autonomies, which cannot be counted.

The value of autonomies may be gauged by a very different measure: communities' historic efforts to sustain them—the focus of this history. In the process, they did not reject monetary gain. Heartland people showed a persistent readiness to sell in markets and work for wages—when their participation built on foundations of autonomous sustenance. They kept control of basic sustenance while gaining earnings. Household production complemented market integrations; communities negotiated labor relations with capitalists. In the process, communities sustaining themselves shaped and subsidized commercial production and profit. Heartland communities turned to direct resistance only when accelerating commercialization threatened the autonomies that sustained their families and enabled them to shape capitalism as they lived in its expanding web.

Yet when rural communities have found places in "big history," it has usually been as people resisting capitalism: Barrington Moore's *Social Origins of Dictatorship and Democracy* and Eric Wolf's *Peasant Wars of the Twentieth Century* led a generation of such studies. I contributed in *From Insurrection to Revolution in Mexico*.[10] Focusing on times when rural people rose to challenge prevailing powers, I explored why people in the Bajío took arms in 1810 and why Zapatista villagers turned to revolution in 1910. In those conflicts, rural people did challenge capitalism. Yet, implicit in my analysis, Bajío producers had sustained capitalism for two centuries before they fought it in 1810, and heartland villagers had shaped and carried it for three centuries and contested it for a fourth before uprising in 1910. Communities across New Spain and Mexico spent centuries sustaining, contesting, limiting, and shaping capitalism; they fought it in brief decades of violence.

Historic moments of violent opposition matter; centuries of negotiations to sustain and limit, and thus shape, capitalism matter as much or more. All must be analyzed to understand the long rise of capitalism, its changing ways—and key times of conflict. The challenge comes when we see that communities on the land in diverse regions of New Spain, Mexico, the Americas, and across the globe have lived in local autonomies and dealt with capitalism in an infinite variety of ways. Local diversities defined communities' dealings with capitalism. Most had roots on the land and relations with rulers that pre-dated ties to global trade. Diverse geographies, ways of production, social relations, and cultural visions underlay diverging histories of shaping and sustaining, limiting and resisting, the standardizing ways of capitalism. Communities grounded in local autonomies guaranteed that the rise of capitalism would not be steady, direct, uncontested—or homogeneous.

To engage the histories of landed communities within capitalism, we must grapple with shared challenges and diverse responses. In *Domination and the Arts of Resistance*, James Scott emphasized the many ways people in landed communities, at slave plantations, and in factories forged diverse understandings of lives facing power. In *The Art of Not Being Governed* he details how Southeast Asian upland peoples fended off outside powers for centuries in locally particular ways. The largest processes of capitalism must be seen in their global dimensions; its social and cultural realities must be studied in local detail.

A Mexican Heartland

I focus on the communities of the Mexican heartland, not because they were typical but because they lived five centuries of intense interactions with powerful promoters of capitalism—first commercial, then industrial, briefly national, now globalizing. Deep commitments to families grounded

MAP 1. New Spain, the heartland, and the Bajío.

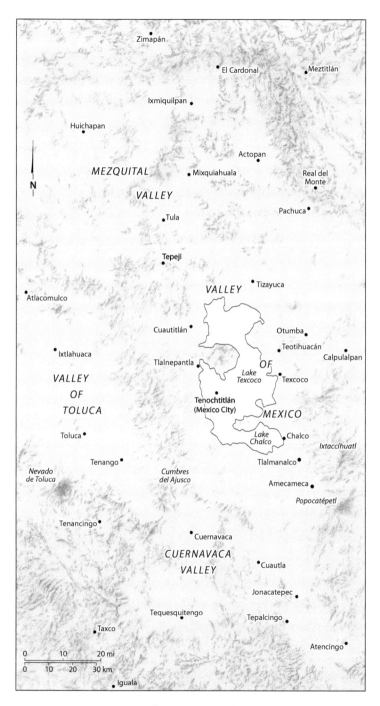

Zimapán

El Cardonal

Meztitlán

Ixmiquilpan

Huichapan

Actopan

MEZQUITAL Mixquiahuala

Real del
Monte

VALLEY

Tula

Pachuca

Tepeji

VALLEY Tizayuca

Atlacomulco

Cuautitlán

Otumba

Teotihuacán

Ixtlahuaca

Calpulalpan

Tlalnepantla

*Lake
Texcoco* *OF*

Texcoco

*VALLEY
OF
TOLUCA*

**Tenochtitlán
(Mexico City)**

MEXICO

Toluca

*Lake
Chalco*

Chalco

Ixtaccíhuatl

Tenango

*Cumbres
del Ajusco*

Tlalmanalco

*Nevado
de Toluca*

Amecameca

Popocatépetl

Tenancingo

Cuernavaca

*CUERNAVACA
VALLEY*

Cuautla

Jonacatepec

Tequesquitengo

Tepalcingo

Taxco

Atencingo

| 0 | 10 | 20 mi |
| 0 | 10 | 20 | 30 km |

Iguala

N

MAP 2. The Mexican heartland.

in autonomies on the land shaped their participations, negotiations, and oppositions. The history of heartland communities may be a limiting case. From their founding roles in silver capitalism in the 1530s to their revolutionary challenge to industrial capitalism after 1910, they were pivotally important to making a world that first included them, then marginalized them, and finally left them all but powerless, drowning in the expansion of a Mexico City they had fed for centuries.

The states, communities, and cultures that define the region rose in inland basins from 1,500 to over 2,500 meters above sea level. The city of Mexico-Tenochtitlán was founded in the 1300s on an island near the center of shallow lakes surrounded by rich cultivated lands. In 1500, it was the political capital, commercial hub, and craft center of a regime too often called the Aztec empire, better labeled the Mexica state. Devastated by smallpox in 1520, then defeated by an alliance of Spanish invaders and indigenous foes in 1521, the city revived to become the administrative, financial, and commercial pivot of New Spain's silver economies, tying the heartland, the Bajío, and regions north to Spain's empire and global trade. In 1821, the city became the capital of a nation it named. Amid struggles to build a new state and adapt to industrial capitalism in the nineteenth century, to survive a revolution and promote national capitalism in the twentieth, and now to adapt to globalization, Mexico City has endured to reign again as the largest metropolis in the Americas, the pivot still tying Mexico's peoples to the world.

The city of Mexico centers the heartland. My focus, however, is not on the city—until its explosive growth after 1950. This history looks first to communities on the land across basins bounded by towering volcanoes: the Nevado de Toluca to the west, Ixtaccíhuatl and Popocatépetl in the east. At the core is the Valley of Mexico: its highland rim blocks natural drainage; lakes, rich *chinampas* (lake-bed platforms of great productivity), and fertile plains shaped its center—until the city drowned everything. Just to the west, the Valley of Toluca is higher and drier, drained by the Lerma River that runs north to water the Bajío, then empties into the Pacific. To the north the Mezquital is drier still, while close by lie the mines of Pachuca and Real del Monte, so pivotal to the world after 1550. To the south, the Cuernavaca basin offers a tropical contrast: 1,500 meters high, its rivers run south to the Pacific; rich in sugar from the 1530s, silver mining began in the same decade at Taxco, just to the west.

The city and its hinterland together formed the Anáhuac that became the Mexican heartland. They were the center of the Mexica regime and the economy that sustained it; they remained the core of New Spain during centuries of Spanish rule and silver dynamism. When Mexico became a nation in 1821, the city became its capital; a surrounding state of Mexico included the populous and productive heartland basins. In the mid-nineteenth century, the Mezquital broke away to join a new state of Hidalgo; later the Cuernavaca basin became the state of Morelos. New regional polities did not lessen ties to Mexico City.

After 1950, the heartland reintegrated in new ways. The growth of the metropolis to twenty million people left the city more dependent on the world and ever less sustained by nearby communities, which were being buried by working suburbs and burgeoning shantytowns. In the transition, remaining rural communities sent women to serve in urban households, and men to labor in construction and public works. The metropolis has absorbed nearly all the Valley of Mexico while merging with the cities of Toluca, Cuernavaca, and Pachuca that rule the rest of the heartland. The heartland remains Mexico's core, as people struggle to remake communities, now urban, in a globalizing world of spreading dependence, marginality, and insecurity.

Capitalism, Autonomies, and Communities

As Braudel saw, communities across the world were living grounded in autonomies when expanding networks of trade drew them into more complex connections in the sixteenth century. Across much of Asia, rice farmers fed themselves and nearby towns, sustaining trades and empires; in Europe wheat growers did the same, as did maize cultivators across much of the Americas. And while population growth and land concentrations might weaken autonomies, they persisted to give communities bases of independence that enabled them to negotiate with those who ruled—and often depended on them for sustenance. This history focuses on such negotiations. Its details make it clear that autonomy is in large part about land and sustenance—while also about power and culture.[11]

I see autonomy in three dimensions: ecological, political, and cultural. Ecological autonomy exists when a family or community produces most of the essentials of survival on land or other resources it controls—or uses in open access.[12] For cultivators, cropland is pivotal, whether held by community right, owned as property, or used in tenancies. Rich fishing waters provide autonomy, as do uplands and forests. Keeping animals for transport and for meat, leather, and wool reinforces autonomy, as does building shelter with family and community resources and labor. Homemade cloth and clothing matter, too. Ecological autonomy is more than economic and about more than land. It is never complete: there are always dependencies within families and communities. But if they remain limited and local, the family or community can present a face of autonomy to nearby powers—and the world.

Ecological autonomies vary: a family or community may enjoy near complete independence of sustenance, partial means of support, or a garden and a few animals to limit dependence. And ecological autonomies change over time—as this history shows. They may change with shifts in crops and ways of production, new or lost resources, land reclamations or erosions. Most important in the heartland, they have changed in the face of demographic shifts. Families and communities consolidated the resources that sustained autonomies in the wake of the sixteenth-century depopulation; autonomies collapsed when population soared after 1950; the intervening centuries brought slow population growth that strained autonomies and stimulated efforts to defend them.

Ecological autonomy is ultimately biological: the ability to sustain human life. Yet in complex societies—and Anáhuac was complex long before Europeans tied the region to capitalism—states or similar institutions define rights to resources and adjudicate disputes over use. So ecological autonomy is also political, linked to regimes and their powers of legislation, adjudication, and more. It is important to understand when ruling powers create, protect, or threaten landed autonomies. The political autonomy of local self-rule is, simply said, even more political. Such rights are usually delegated by a state and may be limited or denied: the Spanish monarchy sanctioned community lands and self-rule in indigenous republics; Mexican liberals challenged both after independence. Political autonomy matters, yet remains a limit to dependence available only as long as negotiations with higher powers allow.

Cultural autonomy, in contrast, appears absolute and universal. People everywhere engage with neighbors, power holders, and the world as they see them—and forge their own understandings. They create and adapt visions of truth and justice, ideas of the wrong, and guides to daily life.[13] Yet cultures never evolve independently of economic powers and ecological autonomies, regime powers and political autonomies. The powerful rarely if ever force understandings on subordinate peoples. Still, power holders do constrain peoples' lives—and communities and families adapt beliefs and understandings in contexts of changing constraints. Culture is an autonomous domain enabling people to adapt to, negotiate with, and push back against economic-ecological and state-coercive powers.[14]

Thus I emphasize *autonomies*: a mix of ecological bases, political relations, and cultural constructions. Ecological autonomy proved most important to heartland villagers. They defended it for centuries. Political autonomy mattered too, but when it receded in the nineteenth century they focused on defending the land, demanding it in revolution after 1910. Throughout, they kept cultural autonomies: as power and production changed they made and remade religious and political visions focused on the justice of land rights, local autonomies, and (among men) patriarchy too—and the injustice of attempts to deny them.

Power in Communities

Long committed to autonomies, heartland communities were always structured by power within—and linked to higher powers close by and in the world beyond. Before the coming of Iberians and Eurasian diseases, Anáhuac communities were organized as *altepetl*, head towns with dependent villages. Local lords ruled backed by noble *pipiltín*, all sustained by cultivating commoners—*macehualtín*. With the consolidation of Spanish rule and the silver economy, indigenous lords lost power. *Pipiltín* became *principales* who ruled native republics through councils and governors they elected among themselves—while holding ample shares of community lands. *Macehualtín* became *macehuales*, with lands just enough to sustain their households, while they also labored to benefit local leaders and a new commercial economy.[15] Over the centuries, inequities persisted and changed—but there were always community elites engaging powers without while working to rule within. At times they served the powerful; at times they defended communities and their autonomies; mostly they worked to remain pivotal by dealing between them as circumstances changed.

Patriarchal gender relations also orchestrated power within heartland families and communities. Men ruled local politics and controlled most lands. Manhood as defined by pre-Hispanic patriarchal cultures required male control of politics, war, cultivation, and many crafts; women raised children, prepared food, made cloth and clothing, and ruled local markets.[16] Under Spanish rule, men still ruled politics and production, but military roles were denied to indigenous men; women mostly lived as before—yet with depopulation, more land came to them. After 1810, political wars and popular risings reopened military roles to diverse men as silver capitalism collapsed and national rulers threatened autonomies. Patriarchal violence culminated in revolution after 1910.

Patriarchy sustained more than dominance within households. Men ruled from the heights of power, through community notables, to cultivating families. At every level, men (and a few powerful women) privileged men below, enabling roles as intermediaries, producers, and laborers. Men above drew men below to accept subordination as the price of sustaining household rule. Hierarchies of patriarchy integrated and stabilized the unequal powers that organized heartland communities and their links to capitalism. Yet patriarchal claims never lacked challenges. As Steve Stern shows in *The Secret History of Gender*, an enduring conversation shaped patriarchal relations in heartland communities: Men asserted rights to rule wives and children—*because* they provided, *because* they delivered sustenance. Women answered that men earned the respect to rule as patriarchs *if* they provided—and that *women* would decide whether provision was sufficient or not.

Patriarchal aspirations and contested conversations shaped power within heartland communities, and the negotiations that tied them to capitalists and managers, magistrates and merchants. Heartland capitalism thrived when it sustained patriarchal families and the communities that grounded their autonomies; it faced challenges when predatory drives for profit threatened the stabilizing mix of patriarchy, family, and community autonomies. The complex links tying the profit seeking that drives capitalism to the patriarchy and autonomies that historically stabilized it in the Mexican heartland center this history.

Communities that rebuilt autonomies under Spanish rule pressed long negotiations with the regime and entrepreneurs, tying power and profit to patriarchs' ability to provide, thus to families' ability to survive—thus to men's ability to assert manhood in households and communities. When population growth and land concentrations, liberal reforms, and agro-industrial capitalism eroded autonomies, they threatened patriarchy and family survival, provoking conflicts that turned to revolution after 1910. When land reform revived autonomies set in patriarchy (only men received grants), villagers sustained themselves and the experiment in national capitalism. When population explosion and mechanized production ended autonomies, patriarchal provision became all but impossible for many after 1980. Without revolution, endemic corrosive violence persists.

Capitalist Exploitations: Symbiotic and Predatory

Capitalism exploits. It concentrates controls of production and trade, profits and property, wealth and power, in small groups of pivotally placed people and the regimes and corporations they rule.[17] Within capitalism, majorities have faced lives ranging from modest prosperity to laboring poverty to marginal exclusion. Inequities rule; yet exploitation is a blunt concept. It focuses on inequity and deprivation, with little emphasis on their complex evolutions and diverse impacts in changing societies. Patriarchy exploits women and children; yet at times it has been socially sustaining and stabilizing, while at others it operates as an exclusion that threatens families and provokes conflict.

The social exploitations of capitalism have evolved with a parallel range: at times they sustain people and stabilize capitalism's dynamism; at other times they provoke deprivations and exclusions that generate conflicts that may become destabilizing, destructive, or transforming. Capitalist (and patriarchal) exploitations may be symbiotic, sustaining power and production, producers and families, thus stabilizing their interactions. They may become predatory, driving to maximize profit while threatening the lives of producers and families, provoking destabilizing conflicts. When patriarchy profits powerful men, privileges producing men, and enables the latter to sustain families and households, it may work as a stabilizing symbiotic exploitation. When it becomes predatory, threatening working men's ability to provide and leaving families desperate for sustenance, it turns destabilizing and even violent—often first within households, later in societal conflicts.

This history of Mexico's heartland emphasizes how patriarchy came locked within larger societal exploitations that together became symbiotic to sustain silver capitalism, turned conflictive in the face of industrial capitalism, and became predatory in provoking Zapata's revolution, then destructive in times of globalization and urbanization. Symbiotic exploitations sustain capitalism when their inequities are *essential* to the sustenance and survival of producing families and communities. Predatory exploitations press producers, families, and communities toward unsustainable lives, making capitalism unstable, even unsustainable—as happened in the Bajío after 1810, and across the heartland after 1910.

In the heartland, communities grounded in autonomies negotiated land rights and labor relations to sustain symbiotic exploitations that shaped and sustained silver capitalism. Assaults on community political rights after 1821 and landed autonomies after 1870 unleashed predatory exploitations that first provoked corrosive conflicts within families and communities—and then led to revolution after 1910. In communities on the land, autonomies sustained negotiations that preserved symbiotic exploitations, sustaining and shaping families and capitalism for centuries. When predations broke autonomies, predatory exploitations led to family violence and societal conflagration.

In industrial regions where autonomies on the land are limited, labor organizations historically enabled parallel negotiations that made exploitations symbiotic, at times—also shaping capitalism while sustaining its dynamism. The end of landed autonomies and new assaults on labor organizations—both accelerating in Mexico, North America, and across much of the world after 1970—have made a globalizing capitalism ever less symbiotic. Growing numbers see it as predatory, while too many face lives of insecurity marked by endemic violence. The way forward is uncertain.

Between Capitalism and Communities: Regimes of Mediation and Coercion

The rise of silver capitalism, its collapse in the turn to industrial capitalism, the search for national capitalism, and the spread of globalization all shaped the history of the heartland in powerful ways. Communities committed to autonomies on the land negotiated and contested that history, shaping its course, limiting the subordinations that marked families' lives. Patriarchal possibilities grounded symbiotic exploitations that rose and fell at the intersection of capitalism and communities. Along the way, changing regimes worked to sustain capitalist dynamism while keeping families and communities in productive subordination. As capitalism and communities changed together, so did regimes—emphasizing judicial mediation when autonomies, patriarchy, and symbiotic exploitations held strong; turning to coercion when stabilizing ways of production gave way to predations that provoked conflict.

After armed conflicts and disease-driven depopulation took down the military states that had ruled Mesoamerica before 1520, the rise of silver capitalism and the foundation of indigenous republics grounded in autonomies on the land enabled the Spanish regime to rule primarily through judicial mediation, keeping limited military power in reserve.[18] From the seventeenth century, courts negotiated conflicts among entrepreneurs and the communities they relied on for produce and workers. A mix of economic dynamism, solid autonomies, limited inequities, entrenched patriarchy, and judicial mediation sustained communities and silver capitalism past 1800.[19]

The Bourbon regime began to strengthen militias in New Spain in the 1760s, provoking resistance that limited their effect. Judicial mediation continued to center regime rule until Napoleon's invasion of Spain led to the 1808 Mexico City coup that mobilized military units to topple a viceroy and insist that New Spain's silver flow to Seville and the fight against

Napoleon.[20] The coup closed mediations at the top of the regime, contributing to the discontent that set off insurgencies in the Bajío in 1810. Provincial elites angered by political exclusions and communities facing capitalist predations joined in armed conflicts that took down silver capitalism and Spanish rule. Politics, state power, and resistance became militarized as Mexico struggled to become a nation after 1821.

For decades into the nineteenth century, military powers ruled contests to find a national polity and a new economy—always proclaiming visions of popular sovereignty. When liberals legislated privatizations of community lands, challenging autonomies and provoking resistance, they tried to fortify state power with new police—with little success until economic expansion and political stabilization came after 1870. For a time, police and community patrols sustained power and production while autonomies corroded, inequities deepened, and patriarchal provision became difficult—and men were armed to keep the peace. They became violent at home, and then turned to revolution after 1910.

The 1910s and 1920s saw armed conflicts to claim and remake the national state in the face of armed insurgencies from below. Militarization seemed everywhere. Yet, as land reform rebuilt patriarchal autonomies, military power receded from the heights of politics. When President Lázaro Cárdenas extended patriarchal land and labor rights in the 1930s he removed the military from the heights of the regime, turning to political mediation that included rural communities and unions as it stabilized their subordination. Armed force remained, used when mediation failed to serve state interests. Still, limited coercive powers marked Mexico's midcentury regime of national development.[21]

Demilitarization proved brief. As land awarded in the 1920s no longer sustained growing populations, autonomies disappeared and patriarchy corroded. People demanded better—and faced repression.[22] As exclusions widened, labor and student protests in the 1960s faced violent repressions, shocking many who knew Mexico's recent history. When rural autonomies and national capitalism collapsed after 1980, the once-mediating regime turned hard to powers of coercion. Police proliferated and the military claimed new resources, weapons, and power—masked by a celebrated turn to democratization.

In a complex history within capitalism, community autonomies and regime coercions drove on opposite tracks. When autonomies were strong, the Spanish regime ruled through judicial mediation. When autonomies waned as Mexicans imagined a nation, regime militarization rose. When communities approached collapse around 1900, they took arms in revolution and forced a rebuilding of autonomies, enabling a brief return to state mediation. When autonomies vanished in urbanization and globalization, military and police powers came to define a state proclaiming democratization.[23]

The Rise and Fall of Revolutionary Challenges

Mexico's history in capitalism is marked by two decades of revolutionary violence, beginning in 1810 and 1910. Why a history shaped by community autonomies and struggles to keep them was punctuated by revolutions is a key to understanding Mexico as well as heartland communities' ability to shape world history. Recognizing that the recent end of autonomies ended effective revolutionary risings is equally important—if history is to inform the present. The autonomies that enabled communities to sustain themselves and carry capitalism for centuries were also pivotal to sustaining the uprisings that disciplined capitalism and the regimes that sustained it when predatory exploitations threatened communities, families, and patriarchy. The end of autonomies has closed the possibility of revolutions built upon and pressing the interests of landed communities.

To mount enduring resistance after 1810, Bajío estate dependents and heartland villagers in the Mezquital took lands, crops, and livestock, remaking autonomies to sustain families and guerrilla fighters for most of a decade. The heartland villagers who backed Zapata after 1910 did the same. Effective insurgencies require an ability to sustain families, communities, and armed resistance long enough to force change. Decades ago, Eric Wolf called the major revolutions of the twentieth century, from Mexico and Russia to China and Vietnam, *Peasant Wars*. He emphasized that their triumphs depended on communities still grounded on the land and fighting to gain more—even if the regimes they helped to power soon turned to industrial programs that assaulted those ideals.[24]

Both decades of revolution in Mexico saw communities still grounded in limited autonomies take arms to rebuild them, sustaining insurgencies that took down established regimes and ways of production. Both led to reassertions of autonomies—informally but powerfully after 1820, state sanctioned and limited after 1920. Both marked key turns in capitalism: the global shift from commercial to industrial capitalism after 1810; the fall of industrial capitalism and the rise of Mexico's national experiment after 1910.

When population explosion mixed with urbanization and a mechanizing, chemically dependent agro-industrial capitalism to end autonomies across the heartland and Mexico in the late twentieth century, no enduring popular uprising challenged the powers that drove the insecurities, marginalities, and limits to patriarchy that marked the turn to globalization. With autonomies gone and no way to rebuild them, the capacity to mobilize more than brief resistance has gone too. Mexico and its place in the world are being reconstructed again, now without the assertive participation of communities grounded in autonomies on the land. A historic era closed around 2000.

Heartland Communities Shaping a Capitalist World

Communities across the Mexican heartland built, sustained, subsidized, resisted, and changed capitalism in ways too complex to capture in an introduction. The history that follows explores three eras: first, the rise and fall of silver capitalism from 1500 to 1820; second, heartland communities in the world of industrial capitalism from 1820 to 1920; third, the revival of autonomies under national capitalism after 1920 and their collapse in urbanization and the turn to globalization before 2000.

I invert the common practice of detailing political economies of power and the ideologies that support them, while offering general—too often overgeneralized and prejudiced—summaries of work, life, and culture among the people who sustain everything. Here, chapters of synthesis offer new visions of power and production, of those who ruled, and the conflicts that rattled their powers. Detailed chapters look at production, power, family relations, community cultures, and popular insurgencies. Vignettes of everyday life aim to illuminate personal participations in contested histories.

The focus on subordinate yet never powerless people shows that the powerful mattered, yet they made history in constant negotiation with people they presumed to rule. The powerful rarely make history as they please; for five centuries, people in heartland communities did all they could to ensure that they did not.

In a history that aims to look at life within communities as they engaged changing ways of capitalism and the regimes that aimed to sustain it over five centuries, changing questions and different sources led to explorations of diverse communities and regions in a never homogeneous heartland.[25] Funded by the revenues of silver capitalism, the Spanish regime produced an array of detailed sources on population and production, estates and communities, and the conflicts they brought to court for mediation. The collapse of silver capitalism, the struggles of nation making, and the limits of state resources after 1820 mandated a shift to the private records of estate operators, clergy, and outside observers. State consolidation after 1870 brought revealing quantitative materials on population and production, crime and violence, after 1870, complemented from the 1890s by the voices of participants, often recorded by anthropologists. Parallel sources and strong historical and anthropological studies illuminate the twentieth century. Tapping varied sources, close explorations of communities facing and shaping a changing world proved most revealing.

A study of communities shaping capitalism in one pivotal region over five centuries raises comparative questions. From pre-Hispanic times, through centuries of Spanish rule and silver capitalism, to the long struggles to forge a nation as the world faced industrialization and then globalization, the heartland was unique for the enduring strength of its landed communities as they faced intense concentrations of power focused in the city named Mexico. In contrast, across the Bajío just to the north capitalism ruled a region with few landed communities, accelerating commercialization from 1600 to 1810, then provoking the early turn to insurgency that destroyed silver capitalism while most heartland communities carried on to shape counterinsurgency and the Mexican nation that followed.

In a very different contrast, communities south of the heartland negotiated centuries on the land without the nearby stimulus of silver or the adjacent presence of a city of concentrated power. The Bajío and regions north shared institutions of Spanish rule and commercial impetus with the heartland, but the dearth of landed communities there limited popular abilities to negotiate power—until insurgency exploded in 1810.[26] Regions south and east in Oaxaca, Chiapas, and Yucatán shared with the heartland institutions of Spanish rule and the enduring presence of landed communities—but faced the challenges of global capitalism in late and limited encounters. They lived distinct regional histories, with a major insurgency in Yucatán in the 1840s and a limited uprising in Chiapas in 1994.[27] Other regions of Mexico have their own variants of history built around particular encounters among regime powers, global capitalism's diverse embodiments, and locally distinct communities and cultures.[28]

Beyond comparisons with the Bajío and limited reflections on other regions of New Spain and Mexico, comparative questions gain little direct attention here. The challenge of understanding heartland communities through five centuries of capitalism proved daunting enough; a turn to wider comparative analysis would have been selective, limited, and likely misguided. My hope is that others will respond to this history with parallel studies of other regions of Mexico, the Americas, and the world, exploring how diverse communities have shaped and/or been shaped by capitalism in distinct regions. Revealing comparisons will come. In the process, we must remember and emphasize that common entanglements in shared historical processes by communities in distinct envionments, with diverse prior histories and particular economic possibilities, have repeatedly led to locally varied, often diverging political, social, and cultural trajectories— within the heartland, across Mexico, and far beyond.[29]

Still, the particular histories shaped by the varied intersections of communities and capitalism share a common trajectory: as long as communities retained even limited autonomies on the land they could and did sustain, resist, and challenge capitalism—shaping its long rise to global dominance. When autonomies collapsed almost everywhere in the late twentieth century, families and communities continued to sustain capitalists and capitalism as workers and consumers—but their ability to resist and challenge, thus to shape capitalism became sharply curtailed in a world of ever more complex dependencies. The regionally unique history of the Mexican heartland illuminates both faces of a general history essential to understanding pivotal global processes: the long era of communities negotiating to sustain, resist, and thus shape capitalism—and the new history of communities stripped of autonomies, still carrying capitalism, yet with little power to shapes its course and their own lives.

Part I explores the centuries of silver capitalism. Chapter 1 outlines the origins and trajectory of the Spanish empire in the Americas and the emergence of three distinct silver societies: Andean South America, built on remains of the Inca empire, focused on Potosí's mountain of silver, long sustained and shaped by enduring native lords and communities; Spanish Mesoamerica, set in the heartland, driven by silver at Taxco and Pachuca, sustained and shaped by indigenous republics; and Spanish North America, forged in the Bajío, driven by mines at Guanajuato and Zacatecas, and with few indigenous republics, a region thoroughly commercial from its origins, capitalist without restraint in the eighteenth century. All shared the stimulus of silver. Distinct indigenous pasts and adaptations led to differing negotiations with Spanish powers; while silver drove global trade, three different social orders rose to sustain silver capitalism.

Chapter 2 focuses on the origins of silver capitalism in the Mesoamerican heartland as communities faced depopulation, the rise of silver, and the consolidation of native republics. They adapted to shape and sustain New Spain's silver economy from 1500 to 1700, while they forged new religious cultures. Chapter 3 examines the region after 1700 as silver production soared, population rose, and autonomies waned. Communities facing land shortages sent men to work in estate fields; they gained wages that complemented family crops, creating symbiotic exploitations that sustained families, communities, and silver capitalism for another century. Chapter 4 explores a key exception: Otomí communities in the Mezquital faced population growth and land shortages in a dry basin; autonomies waned while estates offered little labor. Symbiotic exploitations that might have sustained communities and capitalism became impossible. Conflict escalated after 1800, insurgency began in 1810. Villagers assaulted local estates for five years.

Chapter 5 broadens the analysis to show how Atlantic wars rattled and militarized Spanish rule, opening the way for men facing predatory exploitations in the Bajío to rise and assault silver capitalism, joined by others in the Mezquital facing the collapse of symbiotic exploitations. Together they reclaimed autonomies, assaulted mining and estate cultivation—while most heartland communities carried on in peace and production, sustaining Mexico City and Spain's fragile regime in the fight against insurgents. Amid imperial wars, communities on differing courses sustained a violent stalemate that undermined silver capitalism and ended Spanish rule. When the military defenders of Spain's power joined entrepreneurs hoping to revive silver capitalism to proclaim a Mexican empire in 1821, a new era began.

Part II turns to Mexico's passage through the nineteenth-century world of industrial capitalism. Chapter 6 explores the fall of silver, the demise of commercial cultivation, and early experiments with industry. Men seeking power dreamed of reviving silver, some called for industry, and others argued for a turn to exports. When silver began to revive and new industries took hold in the 1840s, the United States invaded to take Mexico's northern territories. In the 1850s and 1860s, the nation faced liberal reforms, political war, French invasion, and Maximilian's empire. Only after 1870 did a regime stabilize while mining, industry, and exports expanded—fueling an economic dynamism that drove land concentrations, mechanizations, widening inequities, and corrosions of autonomy.

To detail heartland communities' route through that century, chapter 7 looks at Chalco, Mexico City's historic granary, and Iztacalco, a place of rich chinampas, as villagers asserted new autonomies from 1820 to 1845. Chalco landlords complained they could not profit and paid too much for labor; Iztacalco's priest lamented he could not rule religious life as villagers used economic independence to enforce cultural independence. Chapter 8 follows life at Chalco after the war with the United States: estates expanded irrigation and tried new crops; villagers resisted to hold autonomies. They negotiated, rioted, and finally rebelled in 1868 as liberals led by Benito Juárez retook national power. Defeated, the uprising made villagers' commitments to autonomies clear.

Chapter 9 explores life after 1870 across the southern heartland as capitalist dynamism renewed. Land privatization led to concentrations within communities as populations grew; estates mechanized wheat harvesting and sugar refining; railroads took over transport to city markets. Men became land-poor while a new economy flourished yet offered little work. Autonomies corroded; men could not provide. Violence rose within families and communities, until men joined Zapata in revolution after 1910.

Chapter 10 explores the revolution that divided Mexicans while the industrial powers faced off in a Great War from 1914 to 1918. Zapatistas and others took land by force, rebuilt autonomies, and sustained a guerrilla war in search of renewed autonomies; their Constitutionalist foes won the state with armies sustained by oil and other exports, drawing wealth from a world at war. Regime builders fought to renew capitalism and build a national culture; villagers fought to remake autonomies. Capitalists won; still, Zapata's communities forced a land reform that brought renewed autonomies—for a time.

Part III explores Mexico's attempt at national capitalism after 1920, leading to its collapse into globalization after 1980. Chapter 11 outlines the rise of a national project that first revived exports, then built industries, and along the way was forced to distribute land to calm popular pressures. After the 1929 crash closed export markets, populist politics led a turn to industry, sustained while Mexico supported the United States in World War II. After the war, population explosion mixed with laborsaving production to fuel an urbanization marked by recurring crises and rising emigration until the national project crashed in the 1980s.

Chapter 12 looks inside southern heartland communities after they fought Zapata's revolution. They gained lands in the 1920s to renew autonomies; by the 1930s population growth had begun to corrode them as the state promoted commercial ways. For once-revolutionary villagers, national capitalism brought a brief renewal of autonomies followed by decades of corrosion and conflict, social fragmentation—and the end of autonomies by the 1970s. Chapter 13 explores the lives of the people who built Mexico City after 1940. As population soared and rural lives collapsed, people streamed to the city. The regime provided little infrastructure and few services; capitalists built laborsaving industries. Soaring numbers faced enduring insecurities that fed everyday violence; to survive, struggling families built homes and barrios with their own hands.

They used work and local organization to build a city that provided jobs and infrastructure, education, health care, and other essentials in ways always late and never sufficient to the needs of a soaring population.

An Epilogue explores the triumph of globalization and the turn to democratization after 1980, focusing on the prevalence of insecurities and corrosions of patriarchy—without opening more than scarce and insecure work to most women. Waves of violence persist; state coercions rise, seeking a security that has not come; political crises continue. Yet amid those crises no popular uprising has rattled the powers that rule: Mexico has not seen a third revolution; people carry on without recourse. The end of autonomies across the heartland, Mexico, and the world, marks the end of an era. Ecological autonomies are gone; capitalist dependencies rule. Urbanizing globalization has completed the process that Braudel saw as the essence of capitalism. How people will make communities and press their needs in our new world of fully monetized dependencies remains to be seen.

There is much to learn from the historic persistence of Mexico's heartland communities. The autonomies that shaped and sustained production and adaptation, negotiation and resistance, for centuries are gone. Still, their efforts help us understand the present and enable new thinking about the future—knowing that the history of landed communities making, shaping, and contesting capitalism will *not* repeat itself.

A Note on Terminology

To write a history of the Mexica(n) heartland through five centuries and accurately portray key participants requires language that will surprise many readers of English. Mexico did not exist before 1821; the only place named Mexico before that date was the city. The North American kingdom ruled from Mexico City and reaching to New Mexico (named after the city) was called New Spain. I refer to it as such.

People of Iberian ancestry born in New Spain called themselves *Españoles*—Spaniards. Newcomers from Spain were labeled *Españoles peninsulares* or immigrants. I refer to them as such. Too often, historians impose the label "Creole" on people who knew themselves as *Españoles*. That term only came into wide use during the wars of independence. To imagine Creoles and Creole interests before 1810 is an anachronism asserting a search for independence before it was imagined.

People of power and wealth, European and American Spaniards and indigenous nobles too, used the prefixes *don* and *doña* to display their superior status during the centuries of Spanish rule—and at times after.

These were an inherent part of names, offered to announce nobility among men and women exercising power and pursuing profit—often a masking of capitalist goals (too often accepted by anglophone scholars). They are retained to illuminate those complex social and cultural usages.

I resist the label "Indian" for the native peoples of New Spain and Mexico. *Indio* was a status assigned to diverse Mesoamerican peoples; it marked subjection to tributes, rights to republics, and access to courts. *Indios'* lives were so different from the peoples called Indian in the lands that became the United States that I refuse a translation that misleads. I use ethnic identifiers when possible, "indigenous" as a general category, *indio* and *india* when useful.

Finally, Mexicans fought each other in a violent revolutionary conflict after 1910. Through two decades, popular groups fought to reclaim autonomies: Zapatistas in the heartland, Villistas in the north, Cristeros in the west. A Constitutionalist movement promoting capitalism crushed them all—forging a new state and a national capitalist project while claiming to be The Revolution. That label was a political mask, adopted uncritically by too many historians. I avoid the label to focus on the regime as it worked to defeat and then contain communities that fought for revolutionary changes.

All translations from sources cited to Spanish originals are mine.

PART I

Silver Capitalism, 1500–1820

CHAPTER ONE

Empire, Capitalism, and the Silver Economies of Spanish America

IN IMPORTANT WAYS, the first global capitalism developed in and around the Spanish empire that rose in the sixteenth century. There was no grand design. Iberians and other Europeans seeking power and profit drove outward to claim sovereignty where they could and to extend trade as far as possible. In the effort, they engaged diverse rulers and traders—and the more diverse communities that sustained them. Under Spanish oversight, American silver drew Asian cloth and other goods to global markets, in the process pulling peoples across the Americas and the world into networks of production, profit, and trade lived locally—yet driven globally.[1]

To sustain the silver production that drove commercial capitalism for three centuries, Spaniards negotiated the formation of diverse social orders in key American regions. In the Andes, silver attached to indigenous political and social foundations to boom from 1570, fall after 1640, and face native insurgencies in the 1780s. In Mesoamerica, silver built on entrenched landed communities to remain a center of financial power and enduring dynamism from the sixteenth into the nineteenth century. And in the Bajío and Spanish North America, the removal of sparse natives opened fertile lands and rich mines to European, Mesoamerican, and bound African immigrants, who together and unequally forged a new deeply commercial society that rose around 1600, soared after 1700, and collapsed in insurgency in 1810.

An understanding of the origins and development of Spain's empire and the diverging histories of its three core silver societies is essential to understand early global capitalism. While the Andes led the first silver boom and the Bajío and Spanish North America ruled mining after 1700, the Mesoamerican heartland proved the rock of stability that shaped and sustained silver capitalism for three centuries. All developed within Spain's empire, all stimulated global trade after 1550. They differed owing to their distinct geographies, indigenous legacies, and ways of incorporation into silver capitalism. Community autonomies were key: limited by a rugged ecology in the Andes, near absent in the commercial Bajío, deep and enduring in Mesoamerica.

The First Global Empire

The first empire of global reach consolidated under Spanish Hapsburg sovereignty around 1600. After a century when dueling Iberian monarchies competed to rule the expansion of European power and trade, in 1580 Felipe II took Portugal and its American, African, and Asian domains under his Hapsburg rule. Until 1640, the monarchy based in Madrid was the primary European regime in the Americas. Its domains and trades spanned the globe. Commerce in American silver, Asian silks, cottons, and spices, and Atlantic sugar and slaves all soared, enriching traders across a Hapsburg world economy and filling Madrid's coffers—which still periodically faced bankruptcies due to the costs and competitions of imperial expansion.

In 1600, silver mined by native workers at Potosí, high in the Andes, drove expanding trade. Most of this metal that was the world's primary money flowed east, profiting merchants in Seville and beyond, funding Spanish power, stimulating production and trade across Europe, and then passing through the Middle East and South Asia to eventually land in China. In return, Chinese and other Asian goods flowed toward Europe. A second stream sent silver from Potosí, Zacatecas, and other American mining centers to Acapulco, where it sailed west to Manila, the Spanish-Asian entrepôt where Chinese merchants traded Asian wares for American bullion. The silver of Spain's Americas drove trade that had encircled the globe by 1600, radically expanding the world's money supply while stimulating production across Europe, the Americas, and Asia.[2]

Meanwhile, Brazil, also under Spanish Hapsburg sovereignty, built the first large Atlantic sugar and slave society, stimulating a burgeoning slave trade, promoting sugar refining and sales in Europe along with the manufacture of goods to supply African trade. And while the silver economy and the sugar and slave trades may appear separate—silver drawing Asian silks, spices, and other luxuries to Europe and the Americas; sugar planters working enslaved Africans to supply Europeans with profit and sweet stimulants—they linked at a key junction: to purchase bound Africans, Europeans had to deliver printed cotton cloth made in India. And the price of Indian cottons was—at Indians' insistence—paid mostly in American silver. So while seemingly separate in their New World development, the silver economy and the sugar and slave trades rose as linked sectors of a burgeoning world economy under Spanish Hapsburg oversight.[3]

The rapid rise of the Iberian empires and global trades that merged under Spanish rule in 1580 is well known. Equally recognized and often emphasized, that first global empire faced a mix of attacks and emulations that challenged its hegemony in the late sixteenth century and limited its power after 1640. The Dutch rebelled to escape Hapsburg rule, creating a republic in the 1560s. They attacked Portuguese ports and trade in Asia; they took key regions of Brazil's plantation economy in the 1620s, leading the Portuguese to break with Hapsburg rule in 1640. Meanwhile, British and French monarchs saw that they could not compete for Atlantic power unless they joined the scramble for empire and trade, sending both new powers in search of colonies and profits around 1600.

What followed is the stuff of textbooks. The Dutch ruled the European economy and Asian trade through the seventeenth century. The British and French built power at home and colonies in the Americas. By the eighteenth century, they were competing to rule Europe and the Atlantic, setting Britain on course to global dominance in the nineteenth century. Spain and its empire have come to define failure. Portugal broke away in 1640 to rule an empire reduced mostly to South Atlantic domains focused on sugar and slaving. A weakened Spanish monarchy faced rebellion at home and defeat in war; 1648 famously marks its fall to secondary power in Europe. For a century and a half, those who aimed to rule Spain, Habsburgs and then Bourbons, and to revive the Spanish economy, wrote endless laments that convinced contemporaries and later historians that Spain was an entrenched calamity, its empire a crisis that would not end.[4]

For a long time this view has resonated uneasily with those who study Spain's Americas. If the silver economy slowed after 1640, from 1700 it revived and soared to unprecedented levels in New Spain. If financiers and merchants, miners and landlords, in Mexico City and New Spain complained, it was not about imminent demise, but in opposition to disruptive policies coming from reformers in Spain. While Spain faded as a European power and Bourbon rulers searched for reforms to prevent collapse, New Spain thrived—and negotiated to blunt policies imposed by distant, self-deprecating, and sometimes self-destructive rulers in Spain.[5]

It is time to understand the Spanish empire as a complex, diverse, and changing global domain that endured for more than three centuries and stimulated global economic interactions pivotal to the rise of capitalism. The empire's economic dynamism continued even while Spain faded as an imperial power. Spain's Americas were pivotal to expanding global production and trade from the sixteenth through the eighteenth centuries.

Disease, Depopulation, and Reconstruction, 1500–1600

Everyone knows that Spain's empire began in the violence that destroyed Amerindian polities: from the Inca empire that ruled across the Andes to the Mexica (Aztec), Tarascan, and other states locked in constant wars to dominate Mesoamerica. Many also know that Europeans brought diseases that devastated Amerindian peoples, setting off a continental depopulation that in a century neared ninety percent. Yet out of that violence and destruction a silver economy rose after 1550 to mobilize profit-seeking Europeans, bound Africans, and scarce Amerindians in a new economy that transformed lives across the Americas and drove unprecedented global integrations. Such outcomes do not and cannot justify origins in destruction. But if we aim to understand the role of Spain and its American domains in the origins of the modern world, we must explore how depopulation, the fall of Amerindian states, the rise of a global empire, and the creative adaptations of people across the Americas led to a new world becoming capitalist.

From the first, Iberian conquests were entrepreneurial endeavors funded by investors seeking profit, driven by men ready to use violence in search of gain, and only sanctioned by the monarchy once success seemed at hand—and revenues flowed in. Those original and enduring goals must not be clouded by the religious legitimations of Spanish rule or the creative cultural adaptations of Amerindian peoples facing new powers.[6]

And the adaptations of indigenous Americans were more than cultural. "Conquest" was never a war of Europeans against Amerindians. Before outsiders stumbled onto the Americas in 1492, the hemisphere was a vast domain of complex polities, ways of production, social relations, and cultural contests. Diverse states faced enemies within and beyond their borders; they fought rivals, resistant subjects, and contenders who challenged their rule. When Europeans intruded, the battles of "conquest" everywhere saw vastly outnumbered Europeans use the advantages of naval power, metal weaponry, firearms, and the mobility allowed by horses and hogs to ally with disaffected Amerindians against old enemies or resented rulers. Iberians claimed power backed by mostly indigenous armies.

How did outnumbered entrepreneurial conquerors emerge with claims to rule, assert the sovereignty of a distant king, and proclaim the universal power of God? Smallpox and the other diseases that drove a century of depopulation set that outcome. The first key battle of conquest proved devastating to Hernán Cortés and his men in the famous *noche triste*. Then smallpox struck in 1520, sparing Spaniards while killing uncounted Mesoamericans: rulers and commanders; priests and traders; soldiers and peasants; men, women, and children. Cultural despair exceeded physical destruction. In 1521, Cortés mobilized surviving Tlaxcalan and other native allies to defeat the Mexica, claim power for Castile, and proclaim the sovereignty of God.[7]

In South America, smallpox came overland from Panama to strike Inca domains before Europeans arrived. The disease killed the Inca emperor in 1527, setting off a war of succession while thousands died in an unknown plague. Only that context of death and division explains Francisco Pizarro's 1532 capture of Atahualpa at Cajamarca with but 168 Europeans in his company. Only the combination of that limited first conquest and the continuing disease-driven depopulation allows comprehension of the three decades of wars that followed, before Spanish rule began to consolidate in Inca domains that spanned the Andes.[8]

For decades after the dates celebrated as conquests, 1521 in Mesoamerica, 1532 in the Andes, persistent political jockeying and continuing conflicts among European factions and diverse indigenous lords and communities shaped an uncertain New World. Spaniards claimed to rule via *encomiendas*, rights to tributes in goods and work service long paid to native overlords.[9] Surviving indigenous lords often saw *encomiendas* as alliances, a sharing of rights to rule and collect tributes in communities still subject to native lords and now allied with newcomers who brought new goods, new technologies, and new beliefs along with new diseases. Even as imagined by Spaniards, *encomiendas* set European power in indigenous traditions. Conquerors gained tributes earlier claimed by native lords; they depended on native intermediaries and indigenous ways of production and work—even as they demanded radical cultural change.[10]

For a time, a few Europeans gained wealth in indigenous produce. Some mobilized native labor rights, set workers to pan for gold, and found tantalizing riches. But gold quickly panned out, and continuing depopulation undermined *encomenderos'* wealth and native lords' roles in alliances with grasping newcomers. Indigenous lords died as often as commoners, cutting claims to legitimate rule that might serve Spaniards' interests. And as population plummeted, so did *encomienda* tributes in goods and labor services. A grant of 6,000 tributary households might make a conqueror/*encomendero* rich and keep his native ally/intermediary pivotal. A community reduced to 1,000 households paid radically reduced tributes, leaving many a conqueror far from home wondering why he stayed in an inhospitable New World.[11]

Around 1550, depopulation was making colonial rule ever less promising to Iberians, surviving native lords faced the diminishing value of alliances with new rulers, and indigenous majorities struggled to sustain families and communities dying in waves of plagues. Spanish rule began to consolidate and surviving Amerindians experimented with Christianity, but the future of a New World forged in entrepreneurial conquest and devastating depopulation was uncertain.

Then in the 1550s, a surge in global demand for silver changed the course of history. From first contacts in the Caribbean in the 1490s through early decades of conflict and conquest on the mainland, gold taken from streams and surface deposits funded Spain's American enterprise and stimulated Atlantic trade.[12] Gold was not money in the precontact Americas, but did serve as a medium of valued art. Natives mined gold, delivering some to Spaniards as *encomienda* tribute; *encomenderos* sent tribute work gangs to pan for more—but returns diminished in a few decades. Americans also knew silver, again not as money but as a medium of ornamentation. Andeans and Mesoamericans refined ore by fire. Early in the 1530s, natives at Taxco southwest of Mexico City learned of Europeans' demand for silver; they increased mining aiming to profit while Europeans struggled to rule of a regime and society they barely knew.[13]

In the 1540s, as gold became scarce and Taxco made the possibilities of silver clear, Spaniards searched for new mines—meaning they pressed native allies to reveal known deposits. In 1544, they learned of rich veins at Potosí high in the Andes; in 1546 native guides showed Europeans the mines at Zacatecas, far north of Mexico City. Soon after, China stimulated new demand for silver; in the early 1550s the Ming empire mandated that taxes and international accounts be paid in silver, making it the dominant money in the world's largest, most dynamic economy. For more than two centuries China would pay a premium for silver, often twice the European price. From that historic moment China, Spain's Americas, and Europe locked together in trades that rose from 1550, waned a bit after 1640, then soared through the eighteenth century—driving the first global economy and setting the foundations of modern capitalism.[14]

Spain's Americas began in claims of conquest; they consolidated to become pivotal to commercial capitalism thanks to silver. From the 1550s to the 1620s the regime promoted reconstructions that set shrinking American populations at the foundations of a flourishing empire of silver. Regime goals reflected Europeans' vision of power. Yet economic, social, and cultural outcomes diverged in the key regions of Spanish silver production: the Andes, Mesoamerica, and the Bajío. The shared stimulus of silver and common policies of reconstruction as natives faced disease and depopulation led to diverging social trajectories in regions with distinct geographies, native political legacies, social relations, and cultural visions.

Depopulation continued as silver took hold after 1550, weakening native rulers, leaving indigenous producers ever scarcer, and vacating much land. The stimulus of silver in times of depopulation drove fundamental reorganizations of the Spanish regime, native communities, and an emerging world economy. Before silver, Spaniards exerted power by unsteady alliances with indigenous lords. Everything depended on tributes from native communities struggling to keep customary ways in the face of depopulation. As silver rose as a source of profit and revenues, the regime worked to deny the *encomienda* rights that favored the rule of conquerors, allied native lords, and their heirs. Officials took new powers, created courts, and drew tribute to the empire's treasury. The regime confirmed mining claims and distributed lands vacated as natives died. It redefined property rights and worked to monopolize justice—to stimulate silver, commerce, and the revenues mining and trade delivered to its coffers.[15]

While working to end *encomienda* rights and the power of Spanish conquerors and native lords, and promoting mining and trade, merchant profits, and regime revenues, officials joined the clergy (often the only Europeans in outlying communities) to press reconstructions of rural life. Across the Andes and Mesoamerica, surviving natives were drawn into nuclear settlements, granted lands sufficient to shrinking populations, and organized as republics ruled by native notables via local councils. The proclaimed intent was to facilitate the survival of vanishing natives and to teach Christianity to save the dying. An obvious intended outcome was to free land for Spaniards intent on building estates to supply cities and mining centers. Natives across the Andes and Mesoamerica solidified rights to community lands; indigenous governors and councilmen ruled locally, the first resort in any search for justice. The process was neither easy nor uniform: some congregations held; others saw people drift back to old settlements. But overall, as the seventeenth century began most rural families across the Andes and Mesoamerica retained land—regrounding autonomies in communities led by native notables. Numbers stabilized at low levels as people came to identify as Christians—even as many clergy doubted their beliefs.[16]

Congregated communities organized as *repúblicas de indios*—indigenous republics—became refuges of native survival and adaptation as silver soared. Local lords, governors, and councilmen dealt with nearby clergy and Spanish magistrates (often also traders). When conflict came, the republics held rights that enabled them to go to courts where they gained legal representation and access to mediating justice that aimed to keep the peace and sustain production. From the early seventeenth century, the Spanish regime in the Americas ruled native majorities with scarce military force. Everyday power relied on mediation by native leaders and colonial courts—more the former in the Andes, the latter in Mesoamerica.[17]

That was possible owing to the rise of silver in regions—long home to states and cultivating communities—suddenly depopulated. Spaniards gained profit in mining and trade, grazing and cultivation; land was plentiful, but few natives remained to labor. Most survivors lived in self-governing communities with ample land. The late sixteenth-century reconstructions solidified autonomies. No one—not aspiring Spanish miners, not entrepreneurial landlords, not native cultivators—faced scarce resources. Spaniards had enough to prosper, natives enough to survive.

Coercion receded from the center of the regime project; militias remained, most led by entrepreneurial elites, some commanded and manned by mulatto artisans or grazers. Such forces were limited, of uncertain skill and reliability, and only mobilized against native communities (and others) as a last resort. As coercion faded, it gave way to judicial mediation that negotiated the maintenance of imperial rule, commercial production, and social inequities. Military power did not return to the center of imperial rule until after 1760, a time of population growth, newly scarce resources, deepening social divisions, and growing economic insecurities.[18]

While sharing the stimulus of silver and common regime goals in an emerging Spanish empire, the Andes, Mesoamerica, and the Bajío developed notably different social relations and cultural adaptations during the first silver boom of 1550 to 1650. Their divergence reflected regional environments, indigenous political legacies, and local social relations as they engaged the prospects of silver in times of depopulation.

Diverging Silver Economies, 1550–1700

Everywhere, labor proved the key challenge facing the regime, aspiring entrepreneurs, and new silver economies. An analysis of how the Andes and the Mesoamerican heartland rebuilt communities with differing ways of local rule and sustenance, and how the Bajío built very different settlements locked in commercial dependencies, highlights important divergences.[19] If Taxco, in the Mesoamerican heartland, experimented with silver from the 1530s, the surge that made silver pivotal to the world economy focused on Potosí high in the Andes. Analysis begins there.

MAP 3. Spanish America ca. 1770.

Potosí was the world's leading silver producer from 1570 to 1640, driving global trade in the formative era of commercial capitalism as seventy percent of American bullion came from the Andes.[20] There, enduring indigenous lords, communities, and ways of labor became fundamental to silver. Why? First, the Inca empire was by far the largest indigenous regime in the Americas, arguably the most legitimate before Europeans and their plagues arrived. Inca power built on the inclusion of *kurakas*, regional lords who historically oversaw exchanges of key goods—coastal cotton, valley maize, highland potatoes, llama and alpaca—among communities in vertically distinct ecological niches. *Kurakas* soon proved as essential to Spanish rule as to Inca power.[21]

Smallpox killed the last legitimate Inca and set off a war of succession. That conflict helped Pizarro and his allies enter a world of power they barely understood. Yet the conquest of Peru proved slow as shifting factions of Europeans and Andeans sought advantage in rapidly changing conflicts. Spanish rule remained uncertain when Europeans learned of Potosí's silver in the 1540s; the regime only consolidated in the 1570s as Viceroy Francisco Toledo implemented reforms that promoted silver production, trade, and regime revenues by grounding them in the power of *kurakas* to mobilize indigenous ways of production and labor.[22]

The Incas had ruled the rugged Andes from highland Cuzco, extending power to regions now Ecuador, Peru, Bolivia, and beyond by incorporating regional lords, the *kurakas*, who linked communities in different ecological niches of the Andean landscape. *Kurakas*' key roles in the conflicts of the conquest years kept indigenous ways of production, regional exchange, and power strong into the sixteenth century. When Toledo moved to promote the silver economy in the 1570s, he saw that ruling through *kurakas* to keep local production and vertical exchanges intact, while adapting the *mit'a* labor draft to silver, could serve regime power, social stability, and labor mobility. As shrinking communities became landed republics, still dependent on exchanges across altitude, they remained ruled by *kurakas*—locally and regionally. Families cultivated for sustenance and to supply brokered exchanges, sending men drawn by the *mit'a* to dangerous work at Potosí.[23] The Andean silver economy developed by turning native ways of rule, production, exchange, and labor to sustain mining, Spanish power, and global trade.

The adaptation served Spanish power and silver production well; it entrenched *kurakas* as brokers across the Andes. Yet rule through *kurakas* to promote silver production imposed rising demands on shrinking numbers of Andean villagers expected to sustain themselves, local and regional lords, vertical exchange, new towns, and Potosí's mines. Adaptations continued.

As population plummeted, the village men who might be assigned to *mit'a* labor became less numerous and more resistant to the long treks required to undertake six-month turns working for minimal pay in dangerous mines. Wives often came along to provide support and sustenance. Over the years, growing numbers broke with home communities and the obligation to join long labor drafts. Many remained in Potosí, where men gained the skills to claim higher earnings in the risky work of mining and refining, and women took up market activities in the booming city of silver high in the Andes. After 1600, Potosí grew to 150,000 people, then the largest city in the Americas. *Mitayos* (plural of *mit'a* workers) remained important, a signature of the mix of European and Andean ways. But draft workers declined in importance as men stayed on to labor for wages if health allowed, and women joined burgeoning markets. As Spanish rulers and entrepreneurs adapted Andean ways to build a silver economy, Andean men and women made new lives.[24]

Spaniards also bought enslaved Africans and set them to work in the silver economy. As native numbers plummeted and survivors negotiated roles and remuneration, entrepreneurs saw gain in paying the high initial price and continuing costs of sustenance to bind Africans to serve. Permanent dependent workers, they learned skills, even held managerial roles, inhibited in the ability to move on and demand better lives and earnings. Too valuable to risk underground, Africans became essential to refining, to metal- and woodcraft, and to transport. They worked at the plantations Spaniards developed on irrigated lands vacated as native producers died, around Lima and other coastal towns.[25] Before 1650, the silver economies of the Andes (and New Spain) were as important as Brazil's sugar plantations to stimulating the Atlantic slave trade.[26]

The most dynamic early silver economy in the Americas rose in once Inca domains under Spanish rule, stimulated by Chinese demand. It built upon Andean ways of rule and work and stimulated trade in bound Africans to generate commercial production with global ramifications. Because of the enduring roles of *kurakas* and *mit'a* workers, Andean silver capitalism has appeared as a Spanish adaptation of indigenous ways of rule and production—and in important part it was. It is also important to recognize that as commercial ways spread, Andean ways adapted and changed. Hispanic merchants competed with *kurakas* in vertical exchanges. Andean workers and women left communities to escape *mit'a* demands, exiting domains ruled by *kurakas* to negotiate new roles shaped by Spanish employers, traders, and judges. A silver economy that began grounded in Andean ways developed commercial dynamics that eroded native powers—even as *kurakas* remained key intermediaries.

The transformation is evident when we see how the economy focused on Potosí, and the financial and administrative center at Lima reached to incorporate and transform regions once at the periphery of the Inca empire. From areas now Ecuador in the north to northern Chile and northwestern Argentina in the south, the Incas had conquered, built roads to assert power, and incorporated *kurakas* (at times called caciques by Europeans) to take tributes and rule. Spaniards tied the same regions to the new silver economy. In Quito they built *obrajes*, textile workshops where native workers made cloth to be shipped south to Lima and Potosí. Guayaquil was the center of shipbuilding for Pacific trade; African slaves and native laborers built ships that linked American ports—and sailed laden with silver from Acapulco to Manila, carrying back Chinese and other Asian wares. To the south, on interior high plains of the pampas, Spanish entrepreneurs set African and native herdsmen to tend mules and horses, sheep and cattle, all to supply mining and transport at Potosí. And around Santiago in Chile's central valley, landlords developed estates worked by Hispanic tenants and native laborers to provide an American replica of the Mediterranean diet of wheat, wine, and olive oil to those who prospered in Lima, Potosí, and elsewhere.

In all this Spaniards ruled commercial production; Hispanic merchants profited from interregional trade, and almost everywhere (the exception was livestock driven overland to Potosí) sea routes integrated exchange over long distances (as Inca roads decayed).[27] The integration of once Inca domains was steadily taken over by Spanish entrepreneurs, even as *kurakas* remained pivotal in the Andean core, still integrating vertical exchanges and sending *mit'a* workers to Potosí. Most important to communities across the core Andean highlands, the reconsolidation of land rights simultaneously reinforced autonomies—and kept them limited as vertical exchanges ruled by *kurakas* remained essential to survival. Geography and enduring lords constrained the gains in autonomy that came with depopulation. Still, Andean *kurakas* and communities carried on to shape silver capitalism for centuries.

While Andean silver capitalism built upon legacies of *kuraka* power and Inca rule, New Spain generated parallel economies in regions shaped by distinct native traditions: Mesoamerica, where militarized states took tributes from cultivating communities while trade integrated local and long-distance markets; and the Bajío and regions north, where no states ruled before 1520 and diverse hunting, gathering, and cultivating peoples had kept Mesoamerican powers away.

In Mesoamerica, regional powers sustained by communities on the land had ruled from around Mexico City south to Guatemala and east to Yucatán for millennia. If Teotihuacán integrated a dominant empire during the first millennium (CE) and Tula extended state powers northward between 1000 and 1200, when Europeans arrived after 1500 no one polity ruled Mesoamerica. The Mexica never conquered the Tarascan regime set on the shores of Lake Pátzcuaro to the west, or the Tlaxcalans to the east. After some success subduing Mixtecs and Zapotecs in Oaxaca, Mexica armies were just beginning to press into Maya zones east and south when Europeans and smallpox stopped them. And both the Mexica and Tarascans failed to assert power over the state-free Chichimecas of the Bajío and regions north.[28]

In 1519, Cortés entered a region of endemic warfare, not a consolidated imperial domain. That world at war facilitated conquest, first of the Mexica, then their foes. "Aztec" power may have found legitimacy in the capital city and among nearby allies who gained from wars that brought tribute and trade goods to the Valley of Mexico.[29] But conquered people who saw sons sacrificed by the thousand and owed tributes in labor, maize, other staples, and cloth held deep resentments.[30] Cortés learned early of the fissures in Mesoamerican society. If he faced defeat at the hands of the Mexica in the *noche triste* of 1519, once smallpox took its devastating toll in 1520 he marshaled a coalition of Mexica enemies and resentful subjects to destroy the capital in 1521. In the wake of victory and with smallpox killing natives all around, Tarascans, Tlaxcalans, Mixtecs, and Zapotecs negotiated alliances with the European newcomers, ties that Spaniards saw as subordination.

Spanish sovereignty and *encomienda* rule came early across regions that had faced and contested Mexica power. Maya Yucatán and Guatemala took longer to incorporate. When they could, Spaniards took tributes in goods and labor from city-states facing depopulation. Some entered trades long pivotal to Mesoamerican society; others sent work gangs to mine surface gold. Unlike Inca domains, where imperial and regional lords took tributes in labor and ruled redistributions labeled reciprocal exchanges, in Mesoamerica tributes taken in goods fueled active trades, local and long distance. Markets integrated Mesoamerica, as revealed by the many towns with names ending in *tenango* (market). Long-distance merchants, *pochtecatl*, traded in rare and valuable goods—including cacao beans that served as "coin" to balance transactions (and as the base of a valued drink).

With conquest and depopulation, Spaniards took control of key trades in Mesoamerica, including the acquisition of cacao from coastal Chiapas and Guatemala.[31]

Europeans were not alone in seeking profit after 1520. From the 1530s, native miners led an early silver boom at Taxco; local cultivators sold supplies and sustenance; indigenous men saw earnings in the mines as an escape from postconquest disruptions. Spaniards resented native profits and demanded exclusive rights to mine and trade in silver; but before 1560 officials had no means to back such claims. Mesoamerican lords, miners, and workers sought gain in silver when the opportunity came; early Europeans had to deal with them to acquire silver.[32]

When rising Chinese demand and prices stimulated production in the 1550s, Taxco remained a major center, joined by Pachuca and many smaller digs. At Pachuca, Bartolomé de Medina perfected the *patio* process of amalgamation with mercury that allowed refining of less rich ores. With technological innovation and mercury from Almadén in the Sierra Morena north of Seville in Spain, New Spain became a major silver producer— second to Potosí in stimulating global trade. Silver rebuilt Mexico City as the northern pivot of Spain's American power. The regime congregated native survivors in landed republics, deepening autonomies in environments that enabled communities to produce most of the necessities of life: maize, frijol, chile, and the fermented pulque that provided key nutrients. The heartland included the temperate basins of Mexico and Toluca, the dry Mezquital to the north, and the semitropical lowlands around Cuernavaca just south. All produced the Mesoamerican staples of life.[33]

The reconstruction that created republics and solidified community autonomies opened vacated lands to Spanish entrepreneurs who built commercial estates, aiming to profit from feeding the city and mining centers. Villagers still ruled the supply of native produce—maize, frijol, chile, and pulque—to Mexico City and the mines; Spaniards' estates focused on European wheat in the temperate basins, sugar in lowland Cuernavaca, sheep and other livestock in the dry Mezquital. Herding required little labor, often provided by enslaved Africans and their free mulatto descendants. To provide labor in new fields of wheat and sugar, the regime adapted the Mexica's *cuatequil* labor draft, requiring villagers to take weekly turns—now called *repartimientos*—laboring at nearby mines, cities, and estates.[34]

In the Andes and Mesoamerica, the first silver economies stimulated global trade by adapting indigenous institutions to a new commercial world. Yet there were key differences. In the Andes, *kurakas* remained pivotal to regional integrations and Spanish power for centuries; in the Mesoamerican heartland native lords saw their powers diminish after 1550 and collapse by 1600. In the Andes, the *mit'a* drove workers over long distances to serve six-month stints at Potosí; in Mesoamerica, *repartimientos* sent workers to weekly turns at nearby sites. In the Andes, *kurakas* kept control of regional exchange, limiting community autonomies; in Mesoamerica indigenous republics consolidated autonomies—nearly all they needed could be made on local lands or gained in local markets. In the Andes, *kurakas* and the *mit'a* became pivotal to Spanish rule. In Mesoamerica native power, production, and labor concentrated in local republics. They, too, would shape silver capitalism for centuries.

As the first silver boom waned in the 1640s, Mexico City consolidated as the second city in the Americas (after Potosí), the pivot of imperial power, finance, and trade for all New Spain. Across the heartland, landed republics ruled by local notables interspersed with new commercial estates. Villagers sustained themselves and sold indigenous goods to cities and mines; estates sent European goods to the same markets. Communities and estates jostled each other, disputing the best lands, contesting labor relations. The *repartimiento* draft ended in the 1630s (except on a small scale for the mines and the *desagüe* drainage project trying to divert floodwaters from the capital); village leaders negotiated the provision of seasonal workers to estates. Indigenous power, production, and cultures entrenched in communities across the Mesoamerican heartland.[35]

As population hit bottom and silver production peaked, communities remade as republics held strong as sites of economic survival and cultural adaptation. Commercial life accelerated where the stimulus of silver was strong—in the heartland and nearby regions. Estates developed early and pressed villages intensely east of the heartland in the Puebla basin—where Tlaxcalans and others had allied with Spaniards in wars of conquest. There, *obrajes*, textile workshops making woolens for the new commercial economy, came early too. In the Valley of Mexico, the bastion of Mexica power, indigenous republics held strong and estates emerged more slowly. Commercial ways flourished just south, stimulated by Taxco mines and sugar estates around Cuernavaca—yet there too, Spanish entrepreneurs had to negotiate with republics led by local notables and populated by scarce families entrenched on the land. Farther south the stimulus of silver proved weak. Across Oaxaca, Chiapas, Yucatán, and Guatemala Spaniards negotiated to rule regions redefined by landed indigenous republics, yet with limited commercial economies. Communities held strong.[36] Native republics with autonomies defined Spanish Mesoamerica.

In time, the most productive mines and the most dynamic commercial economy in New Spain rose north of Mesoamerica, in lands where Chichimecas had blocked Mexica and Tarascan rule and then contested Spanish power to the end of the sixteenth century. There, commercial life did not begin in Spanish "conquest," but with incursions of Mesoamerican peoples who pressed north to settle the fertile Bajío, while Cortés, his native allies, and smallpox took down Mexica power—and disease debilitated Chichimecas, too.[37]

In the 1530s, Otomí settlers moved north to found Querétaro, accompanied by a few Franciscans. They created an Otomí-Christian society built by irrigating very productive lands. In the 1550s, Querétaro was a transplanted Mesoamerican community consolidating as an indigenous republic when silver began to flow from mines at Guanajuato just west and Zacatecas to the north. The prospects of silver drew Europeans and Mesoamericans north to face resistant Chichimecas in wars that lasted to the 1590s. Those conflicts slowed northern mining until most Chichimecas died of disease or fled to refuge in nearby mountains or farther north.

Then, from the 1590s the Bajío and Spanish North America became the leading silver region in New Spain, second in the Americas to Potosí until the 1640s, dominant afterwards. North of the domains shaped by Mesoamerican states and cultivating communities, the Bajío silver economy could not build on adapted indigenous institutions. To generate profit and fuel global trade, newcomers expelled Chichimecas and invented a new commercial society.

Only a powerful few were European. The Otomí led agricultural settlement in the Bajío and fought beside Spaniards, Mexicas, Tarascans, and others in the Chichimeca wars that opened the region to mining, grazing, and cultivation. Spaniards and a few natives like the Tapia family (Otomí founders of Querétaro) ruled and profited. Indigenous migrants—Otomí, Tarascans, and Mexicas fleeing chaotic times to the south—came to work in mines, on the land, and in transport. Enslaved Africans came bound to labor in mining centers (again, rarely underground) and as herdsmen, artisans, and in transport. Migration accelerated with pacification in the 1590s. A region of rich mines and great agricultural potential, now cleared of original inhabitants, the Bajío developed as entrepreneurs, settlers, and workers came north: Europeans drawn by chances to profit, Mesoamericans by the opening of fertile lands, Africans by the compulsion of slavery.

Most early mine workers at Zacatecas and Guanajuato were indigenous migrants paid high wages and ore shares to do the dangerous work that drove global trade; over time, diverse natives mixed together and with

Africans to become free laboring mulattoes.[38] Cultivation across the rich Bajío sustained mining there and to the north. Otomí estate operators and family growers ruled around Querétaro. Europeans built a parallel estate economy at Celaya and regions west, where Otomí, Tarascan, and Mexica families settled as tenants and employees on estate lands. They too mixed with Africans to create amalgamating communities, often labeled as *indio*. Africans, perhaps twenty percent of the founding population of the Bajío and regions north (with Europeans never more than two percent), found ways to freedom: enslaved men fathered children with indigenous women—by law free, as were their offspring. Enslaved women gave up babies for adoption by indigenous families, separating from their children to free them.[39]

As Chichimeca wars ended, mining expanded at Zacatecas, Guanajuato, and the aptly named San Luis Potosí. The Bajío developed a mix of mining, cultivation, and cloth making to sustain Spanish North America as the leading zone of silver production in New Spain. It was a region of commercial foundations, immigrant populations, and communities built anew to serve the stimulus of silver. Beyond Otomí Querétaro, republics were few, autonomies scarce. Patriarchal dependencies defined labor and social relations; labor scarcity kept security strong.

The Bajío and regions north were also ruled from Mexico City, where leading financiers and merchants congregated. Early on, northerners bought cloth from Puebla; later, Querétaro rose as a center of textile production, first employing Otomí for salaries, later turning to bound Africans as the Otomí proved too free to sustain profit. Spanish North America was driven by silver, organized by trade, and defined by social dependencies from its beginnings—in sharp contrast with Mesoamerica, where Spanish rule and commercial ways were grounded in republics holding enduring autonomies, and with the Andes, where Spanish rule and limited autonomies depended on enduring *kuraka* power. In the Bajío, a dynamic early capitalism shaped new communities—until its unrestrained predations drove them to an insurgency that took down silver and the world it had made.

By the 1640s, Spain's Americas revolved around silver economies that stimulated global trade linked through Spain to Europe, the Islamic world, South Asia, and China—and to China and Asia directly by the Chinese merchants of Spanish Manila. England and France were beginning to build empires, in important part in response to the power and profits generated by Spain's pioneering global reach. Across Spain's Americas, silver economies rose in response to the shared stimulus of silver and the common goals of Spain's Hapsburgs. Yet by the early 1600s they exhibited diverging social organizations as silver mines and trades and Spanish ways adapted to distinct environments and indigenous precedents.

In Andean America, *kurakas* held sway over communities in diverse ecological niches, limiting local autonomies, enabling *kuraka*-mediated exchanges, making the latter essential to keeping the Inca labor draft that drew workers from communities to sustain the silver mines as commercial ways proliferated. In Mesoamerica, the power of native lords faded, Europeans entered trade, and communities reconstituted as indigenous republics reclaimed autonomies to become the base of a mixed economy that sustained Mexico City and the mines. In the Bajío and Spanish North America, Chichimecas resisted and then vanished. After 1600 nearly everyone was an immigrant, as Europeans ruled and African slaves and diverse Mesoamericans mixed to live as commercial dependents working mines, textile workshops, and estates—forging an early capitalist society all but stripped of autonomies on the land.

All three silver societies saw mines fuel global trade. Chinese demand stimulated silver while sparse populations across the Americas enabled communities to adapt and create new ways of survival and new cultural adaptations. Then everything seemed to collapse in the 1640s.

Silver fell at Potosí and Zacatecas. The European economy fell into recession as wars set Spain to struggle as a secondary power. Chinese demand for silver fell too, as the Ming gave way to the Qing in times of war and disruption. The first global economy faced the first global recession. Had Spain's Americas produced too much silver, generating inflation that inhibited Spanish economic development, undermining Spanish power while Dutch, French, and British industries gained? Had Potosí mines driven so deep that they faced unsustainable costs as ores depleted? Had silver flooded global markets, driving down its price relative to gold—still money in most of the world but China? Did Chinese demand drop as the Ming fell and the Qing began to rule? All of these challenges plausibly contributed to the crisis of the first global economy.

That time of crisis was also an era of transition that led to an eighteenth-century revival of silver in a weakened Spanish monarchy. A century of decline in Spain and depression in Europe saw the center of the Spanish imperial economy shift to New Spain.[40] Silver production never fully revived in Potosí. In New Spain, mining had shifted to new northern centers after 1640, notably Parral.[41] Stabilization and consolidation ruled—until mining soared to new heights after 1700, when renewed Chinese demand and accelerating Atlantic trade energized old mines at Taxco and Real del Monte, Zacatecas and Guanajuato, and new centers as far north as Chihuahua.

Accelerating Divergence: The Andes and New Spain, 1700–1825

During the eighteenth century, Spain faded as a European power while its Atlantic-American-Pacific empire remained pivotal to a rising global commercial capitalism. Across Spain's Americas three key developments marked the era: population growth, silver revival, and Bourbon reforms—all promoted commercial expansion, all threatened popular welfare. Native numbers grew everywhere after 1700, bringing new pressures within landed republics, limiting autonomies while providing more workers to economies in expansion. Silver revived powerfully in New Spain, which rose to produce nearly seventy percent of American silver by the late eighteenth century. Commercial growth created work at estates as autonomies waned in communities across the Mesoamerican heartland; it generated profits and deepening polarities in the Bajío, where dependent families carried on in the face of deepening insecurities. In contrast, the expansion of silver in the Andes proved limited—curtailing markets and work as autonomies corroded.[42] Meanwhile, Bourbon reforms aimed to centralize power, promote production, stimulate trade, and bolster regime revenues—backed by new military forces. They had little success strengthening Spain in Europe, proved briefly disruptive in the 1760s in New Spain, and provoked violent risings in the Andes in the 1780s.

Accelerating divergence marked eighteenth-century Spanish America. The three silver regions began with social structures and cultural adaptations built during the first silver boom. All faced population growth and Bourbon reforms after 1700. Yet, before Napoleon broke Spain's monarchy in 1808, only the Andes lived decades of violent conflict. Only the Bajío generated a decade of insurgency after 1810—destroying the Spanish empire and silver capitalism. Meanwhile, the Mesoamerican heartland around Mexico City carried on, sustaining Spain's empire and silver capitalism until both were gone. The question is *why*.

The Andes were marked by the enduring importance of *kurakas* into the eighteenth century. Communities there had kept lands sufficient for sustenance and vertical exchange as populations hit bottom after 1600. After 1700, they faced population growth that left limited resources less able to meet local needs or to make products for exchange, while *kurakas* faced rising competition from Hispanic traders. The silver economy that might have offered alternative employment and commercial openings grew with limits. Production increased from two million pesos yearly around

1700 to near seven million on the eve of the uprisings of 1780—growth at half the levels that drove commercial expansion in New Spain.[43]

In a context of population pressures and limited commercial openings, Bourbon reforms came to Andean communities as demands for higher tributes and other exactions—demands *kurakas* were expected to implement. Most resented were the *repartos*, local trades ruled by Spanish district magistrates and implemented via native lords. Knowing that most highland production remained in communities, officials and traders aimed to increase extractions of goods, profits, and revenues by pushing commercial demands backed by official power—with *kurakas* as key brokers. Magistrates delivered tools, cloth, livestock, and other goods—whether villagers wanted them or not; families owed debts they were expected to pay in cash or produce. *Kurakas* were pressed to enforce collections, with little power beyond their historic legitimacy. The new trades could not be masked as reciprocities.[44]

Villagers began to see *kurakas* as agents of oppression. Lords who had kept pivotal roles for two centuries by mediating between Spanish power and Andean peoples faced hard choices. They could tap into swelling community outrage and lead resistance to regime demands—or become targets of that outrage.[45] From the 1740s, resistance rose across the Andes in waves of violence. Some *kurakas* led rebellious communities; some faced their wrath as mining grew slowly and the majority faced heightened tribute, *reparto*, and tax demands.

In the 1770s, desperate to stimulate the Andean economy, Spanish reformers set a new viceroyalty in Buenos Aires, and opened the port to send silver directly into Atlantic trade. The Potosí mines were taken from the domain of the authorities, financiers, and traders based in Lima and shifted to those in Buenos Aires, who embraced the opening yet struggled as uncertain newcomers to silver trade and Andean complexities. In times of rising conflict, *kurakas* and communities had to await justice from new and distant authorities. Just to the north, communities long tied to Potosí remained dependent on Cuzco and Lima.

The administrative shift split the Andean highland core as regime demands and local tensions mounted. The early 1780s brought the uprising in and around Cuzco led by Túpac Amaru, a descendant of the Incas who built an alliance of *kurakas* and provincial Spaniards to raise popular communities against escalating impositions. Larger conflicts extended from Cuzco to Potosí and proved far more complex than a Túpac Amaru rebellion. If the Inca pretender aimed to lead communities in defense of *kuraka* power and community welfare, the prior, parallel, and independent uprising to the south of Lake Titicaca led by Tomás Katari fought first for community rights. The radical uprising that coalesced around Tupaj Katari near Potosí attacked *kurakas* (locally called caciques) in defense of popular demands. Rising violence split the powerful; *kurakas* divided, most provincial Spaniards returned to back the regime, while violence set angry indigenous peoples against those in power. As Hispanic elites united against native rebels, some *kurakas* led uprisings, others became their targets, still others joined the repression—and the regime began to see them as liabilities to silver capitalism.[46]

By 1784, an alliance of Spanish power and fearful *kurakas* crushed the risings in bloody violence. The Andean economy was shaken. The regime turned to a reorganization that removed nearly all *kurakas*, rebels and regime defenders, from power. They were blamed, whether they led risings or failed to prevent them, replaced by Spanish magistrates who often doubled as traders—even as *repartos* were outlawed in a clear if limited popular victory. New officials had much to learn in the Andean world, while military force took a new role in regime power. Silver production fell during the uprisings, revived in the 1790s, to fall again after 1800 as Napoleonic wars destabilized Spain's empire. Andean America stumbled into the nineteenth century, Spaniards dreaming of past economic glories that would not revive, natives wondering if dreams of reviving local autonomies and reciprocities by restoring Inca ways were but delusions.[47]

When Napoleon invaded Spain in 1808, setting off conflicts that eventually led to independence across Spain's Americas, most Andean elites froze in fears left by the uprisings and repressions of the 1780s. Andean Spaniards would not proclaim popular sovereignty, fearing that Andean peoples would claim its benefits. Native communities knew the deadly results of past uprisings; most bided their time. Independence came late and in important part from without, via Bolívar's armies. Silver revived but slowly, as Peru and Bolivia split into struggling nations.[48]

The eighteenth century was radically different in New Spain. There, silver production increased four times over, from five million pesos yearly around 1700, to hold around twelve million in midcentury, to rise above twenty million pesos yearly from the 1790s, until everything crashed in insurgency in 1810.[49] New Spain's commercial economy grew well ahead of population growth, which at most tripled. Bourbon reformers promoted silver, trade, and revenues; when their demands threatened those goals, they learned to negotiate. They could not afford to alienate the entrepreneurs who led the most dynamic economy in the Americas or disrupt the mining that sustained global trade and the remnants of Spain's power.

FIGURE 1.1. The power of silver:
Santa Prisca de Taxco, 1758.

There were summers of conflict in the 1760s. But, overall, eighteenth-century New Spain faced population growth, economic dynamism, social polarization, and cultural debates with a notable stability until Napoleon broke regime legitimacy in 1808. Then, symbiotic exploitations kept the peace in most heartland republics while thousands of Bajío estate dependents rose in insurgency in 1810, joined by villagers in the dry Mezquital. Together they took down silver capitalism.

In the heartland, mining rose before 1750 at Taxco (its stunning church shown in figure 1.1), and from the 1760s at Real del Monte near Pachuca. Mexico City boomed as the administrative, financial, and commercial pivot of soaring silver economies, nearing 130,000 in population around 1800, replacing a shrunken Potosí as the largest city in the Americas. Around the capital, the great majority remained in landed republics surrounded by commercial estates; to the south, republics still ruled rural life as small estates served small cities and towns.[50] As villagers gained immunity to conquest-era diseases, their numbers doubled from the 1680s to the 1730s, when a typhus epidemic slowed growth for a time.[51] Populations rose again from the 1770s. Both surges of growth corroded the autonomies cherished by families in native republics. Surpluses of maize, frijol, and chile once sent to cities and mines were consumed locally. New generations found their lands less and less sufficient; landless minorities began to appear and expand.[52]

Meanwhile, demand for produce rose as mining boomed and Mexico City grew. Estates that historically had raised European goods—wheat, sugar, and livestock—added native crops to commercial fields. Sugar and wheat still ruled on irrigated fields; maize expanded on rain-fed lands. Livestock left the region for pastures north as rows of transplanted maguey took over dry heartland zones, the base of a pulque industry that supplied drink to mine workers and city taverns. Mexico City estate operators profited by expanding production and offering seasonal wage work to village men and boys short of land and in need of income to support growing families. As population grew, silver boom enabled entrepreneurs to profit and villagers to survive—and remain villagers. Remnant autonomies on the land mixed with seasonal labor to make exploitation symbiotic, stabilizing indigenous republics and silver capitalism after 1700.

As autonomies waned and reliance on labor grew, disputes did escalate among villagers, and between villagers and estates, and villagers and local officials. Still, the courts mediated to keep the peace.[53] Village notables were entrenched and empowered as brokers (in the same decades that *kuraka* brokerage collapsed in violence), organizing work gangs that tied landed republics and commercial estates together. Radically unequal gains—profit for a few, survival for the many—made the links exploitative. Mutual necessity, for profit is as essential to capitalism as survival is to families and communities, made them symbiotic.

Symbiotic exploitations proved stabilizing. When insurgency spread across the Bajío in 1810, most heartland republics held loyal to an ever more tenuous Spanish regime; their people stayed at home and at work. In an exception that reinforces the comparative conclusion, in the heartland only the Mezquital and other dry zones saw deep and enduring insurgencies in native communities after 1810. Population growth drove declining autonomies after 1750, while estates with dry lands turned to pulque, generating profit with minimal labor. The result was exploitation without symbiosis—and insurgency after 1810.[54]

North of Mesoamerica, in the Bajío and beyond, silver and population grew more rapidly during the eighteenth century. Mining soared at
Zacatecas and in Chihuahua far to the north before 1750; it drove to new
heights at Guanajuato and San Luis Potosí after 1770. Old mines yielded
new ores and profits; new mines brought new bonanzas.[55] Migration from
Mesoamerican regions facing population pressure reinforced northern
reproduction to fuel demographic growth and northward expansion. The
Bajío boomed as mining, textile and tobacco manufacturing, and commercial cultivation expanded together in an economy of rising capitalist
dynamism built on social relations of commercial dependence.[56] Mining,
grazing, and irrigated planting (where streams allowed) drove north to consolidate around San Antonio in Texas, reshape Spanish-Pueblo relations in
New Mexico, and drive across California to San Francisco in the 1770s.[57]

The Bajío led an eighteenth-century expansion of silver capitalism that
stimulated global trade and Atlantic wars. Social relations rooted in commercial dependence sustained soaring production, yet proved less able to
stabilize rapidly polarizing inequities. Beyond Querétaro, most indigenous
and other working peoples lived without landed republics, without autonomies. After 1780 they faced falling wages, rising rents, and evictions with
little recourse. The Bajío became the most dynamic capitalist region of
the Americas as it generated deepening social and cultural polarizations.
Among the silver societies of Spain's America, only the Bajío lived a transforming social revolution after 1810.

Silver mining boomed at Guanajuato into the 1750s, to face a lull
caused by falling Chinese demand.[58] When Spain's participation in the
Seven Years' War of 1756–63 brought new revenue demands and militia
recruitment to mine workers at Guanajuato and San Luis Potosí, workers and artisans rioted in 1766–67. Bourbon agents learned quickly that
reforms that threatened silver production also threatened the regime and
its empire; they allied with regional entrepreneurs and militias to contain
the uprisings. Then the regime turned to promoting silver with tax concessions and subsidized mercury; mining rose to new heights after 1770.[59]
The Bajío remained at peace and in production through the 1770s and
1780s as British North Americans fought for independence and Andeans
rose against Spanish power. Bajío silver helped fund US independence
and the repression that sustained Spain's rule in a fractured Andes.[60]

Silver output soared at Guanajuato and across the north, exceeding
four times the level of 1700 by the 1790s, holding the peak past 1800.
Mining, commercial cultivation, and textile manufacturing in the Bajío
grew apace; a new tobacco factory at Querétaro drew the second largest

assembly of workers in the Americas, mostly women. The boom threatened lives locked in dependence. Mining entrepreneurs pushed to end the ore shares that had made skilled workers partners in profit; they cut laborers' wages as much as possible. Resistance forced endless negotiations as mining carried on to reach new heights. In textiles, Bourbon policy favored imports from Spain (helping new industries around Barcelona), driving large Bajío *obrajes* out of business. Local merchant-clothiers found profit pressing families in household workshops to work longer hours for less income to keep production growing. Rural estates expanded irrigation to raise wheat and vegetables for favored urban consumers; they left maize to tenants on former pastures with uncertain yields. When drought and frost in 1785 and 1786 destroyed Bajío maize harvests, unprecedented dearth set off years of famine and death.

Still, the stimulus of silver drove on. Mine operators negotiated with workers to keep production strong. After the famine, estate cultivators planted maize on irrigated fields; it proved good business as prices held high. The shift, however, led to higher rents and evictions among tenants, lower wages and food rations for workers. The economy grew, entrepreneurs profited, and working families faced falling earnings and new insecurities. With population rising, workers were no longer scarce; after 1780, evictions and falling wages undermined men's ability to provide, threatening claims to household patriarchy.

So did the employment of growing numbers of women for low wages sorting ores at silver refineries and rolling cigars in Querétaro's tobacco factory. Men struggled to provide; households struggled to survive. With the end of labor scarcities in a region of families locked in dependence, capitalists pressed hard on the people who made everything in the most dynamic region of the Americas. Without landed republics, Bajío families had little recourse. A few went to court seeking rights as republics—land, self-rule, and judicial access. Most failed. People of mixed ancestry living on private property were not indigenous enough. Patriarchal producers and their families struggled to adapt, facing mounting pressures they could not blunt after 1780.[61]

The stimulus of silver kept the economy booming and a polarizing social order at peace past 1800. Work was available, if for falling rewards, as wars escalated across the Atlantic world after 1790, disrupting trade and bringing demands for rising taxes and other revenues. When Napoleon broke Spanish imperial legitimacy in 1808, debates about rights and sovereignty escalated as people from the heartland to the Bajío faced new years of drought and scarcity. Provincial elites led by Father Miguel Hidalgo set off a mass insurgency in 1810. Thus opened a decade of revolution that transformed a region that for a century had been the North American dynamo sustaining Spain's empire, silver capitalism, and global trade.[62]

There was little insurgency at Querétaro, the one area of the Bajío where a core Otomí minority retained republican rights. There was little insurgency north of the Bajío, where population pressures were less and entrepreneurs still offered opportunities to mine workers and solid securities to rural families.[63] And there was little insurgency across the most fertile regions of the heartland, where symbiotic exploitations held in the face of broken sovereignty and famine scarcities after 1808. Only in the dry Mezquital and nearby pulque zones, where symbiotic exploitations proved impossible, did insurgents join Bajío rebels in violent pursuit of land and autonomies that broke silver capitalism and undermined Spain's rule in New Spain.

A decade of political and social violence after 1810 took down silver capitalism. New Spain's silver fell by half and stayed there until 1840. As Spanish Americans struggled to make nations, communities retrenched on the land. New Spain, China, and the world would never be the same. One lesson of this history is that capitalism requires stability to thrive in the long run, and stability requires both the generation of profits and the provision of sustainable lives to the families that carry capitalism. The communities of the Mexican heartland proved most effective in shaping and thus stabilizing silver capitalism for three centuries. A century later they would drive Zapata's revolution in a powerful assault on capitalism. Their history is worth telling.

CHAPTER TWO

Silver Capitalism and Indigenous Republics

REBUILDING COMMUNITIES, 1500–1700

AROUND 1500, the Mesoamerican heartland was a place of warring states grounded in cultivating communities working to feed and clothe themselves and to pay the tributes in goods and labor service that sustained cities and states, rulers and their wars. In 1700, the heartland remained Mesoamerican in many ways: families still raised maize, frijol, chile, and pulque on community lands, paid tributes to those who ruled, and provided labor to sustain the profits and urban lives of the powerful. Yet much had changed: war no longer plagued the heartland, rulers in Mexico City served a regime in Madrid, tribute and labor were paid in silver reales, and the local economy was tied to global trade—and to wars in distant places.

Communities rebuilt as republics reinforced autonomies on the land while they became founding participants in a new global capitalism. By 1600, Old World diseases had cut the heartland population to ten percent of precontact levels. Mesoamerican and Euro-Christian ways of engaging divine powers competed to explain the cosmos and offer assistance with the trials of everyday life. Indigenous adaptations of Christianity came to the fore. Native notables still ruled community affairs, now through councils that led republics granted lands and access to justice by a Spanish regime that pacified the heartland and tied it to global trade. And in the face of depopulation, entrepreneurs in Mexico City built estates seeking to profit by supplying the capital and the mines—dependent on labor drawn from republics staunch on the land. By 1700, communities and estates mixed across the heartland to shape and sustain silver capitalism.

Two centuries of destruction, adaptation, and creativity brought a historic transformation. Enduring Mesoamerican ways—notably, family and community commitments to autonomies—engaged the demands and opportunities of a new empire and global trade in a founding core of commercial capitalism. Two centuries of conflict and complex negotiations remade the heartland to sustain capitalism—and communities on the land.

The Mesoamerican Crucible to 1520

The heartland became the crucible of Mesoamerican civilization long before Europeans arrived and linked its peoples to a wider world. Foundational developments began in a distant past along Gulf coastal lowlands. The cultivation of maize by people in settled communities sustained the rise of new centers of power and worship. From the Gulf, early Olmec rulers pressed military power and networks of trade, helping spread maize and cities, armies and trade, inland across Oaxaca and Chiapas, Yucatán and Guatemala—and into the highland basins that would become the heartland.[1]

In the first millennium (CE), power and production began to concentrate in the basin we now know as the Valley of Mexico. Without natural drainage, its center was a series of shallow lakes, rich in aquatic life and facilitating transport in small boats. Around 200, powers rising at Cuicuilco south of the lakes and Teotihuacán to the northeast were contesting dominance over cultivating communities when a volcanic blast leveled Cuicuilco, concentrating power (and the gods' favor) at Teotihuacán. From 200, Teotihuacán rose as a city of temples and pyramids, artisans and markets. It reached perhaps 200,000 in population, sustained by stream irrigation and the lakeside platforms later called *chinampas*. Obsidian mines in nearby hills grounded economic eminence and military power; city craftsmen worked the hard stone into blades that facilitated local production, widening trade, and military expansion. The power, trade, and culture of Teotihuacán reached south to Guatemala and east to Yucatán before falling in the 600s to an uncertain but devastating mix of insurgency, economic collapse, and invasion—likely by northerners resistant to Teotihuacán's power, yet seeking its economic plenty.[2]

After a time of competition and reconstruction, around 1000 power in the heartland reconcentrated at Tula, north of Teotihuacán in the dry basin now called the Mezquital. The rise of Tula saw Mesoamerican ways of state power, religious culture, and trade extend north through the fertile Bajío and along the eastern slopes of the western Sierra Madre to reach the

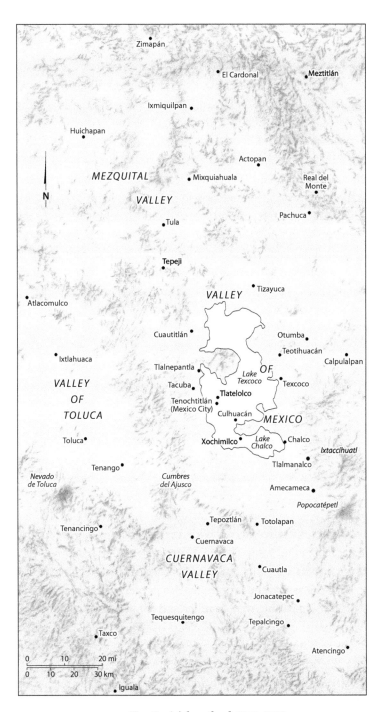

MAP 4. New Spain's heartland, 1500–1700.

upper Río Grande Valley—later named New Mexico. Trade drove north along the Gulf coast to enter the Mississippi waterway and reach Cahokia and other rising centers in the heart of North America. Tula's trade and cultural ties also stretched south to Maya centers like Chichén Itzá in Yucatán. Tula was the second great center of power in the Mesoamerican heartland, again sustained by intensive cultivation and crafts in communities strong on the land.[3]

Tula fell around 1150 to a mix of military conflict, internal uprisings, and climate change—a time of drying that prejudiced cultivation. Its fall shaped the Mesoamerican world that Cortés and his gang of freebooters entered in 1519. From the heartland through Oaxaca to Yucatán and beyond, the fall of Tula and the great Maya centers led to state fragmentation and endless wars. There would be no new overarching regime until Iberians linked Mesoamerica to a wider world. After the fall of Tula, Mesoamerica, like Europe in the same era, was a region of states at war. Its northern extensions receded southward: ties with New Mexico were few; trade with Cahokia ended. Links to the Maya world from Yucatán to Guatemala were limited, yet trade continued.

Millennia in which imperial expansion and consolidation alternated with centuries of fragmentation and conflict forged an enduring social order in Mesoamerica. The foundation unit was the *altepetl* (in Nahuatl)—a city-state with a head town led by warlords and priests (at times the same people) who took tributes in maize, cloth, and other goods produced by cultivators and artisans (also often the same people) in outlying communities. Power was military, legitimated by religious assertions— much like contemporary Europe. Cultivating families worked the land to feed themselves, trade in local markets, and pay tributes to those who ruled—and often traded across wide regions. Times of conflict brought shifting alliances and wars. The rise of an *altepetl* to superior power meant the layering of its warlords and legitimating deities over defeated neighbors, whose rulers became intermediaries in hierarchies of tribute taking. At the base of everything were families and communities on the land; they produced almost everything, while rulers used force to take surpluses that sustained cities and states at war.

After the fall of Tula ended the northward thrust of Mesoamerican states, warriors from the north invaded the heartland—the Mexica famous among them. Arriving as martial nomads, they served first as mercenaries for older states at war. After 1300 they founded the island city of Tenochtitlán; in the 1400s it became the center of a heartland still at war. The military rise of the Mexica is well chronicled, as are the religious claims that incited wars to take sacrificial victims to serve Huitzilopochtli and nourish the cosmos with human blood. Equally pivotal, Mexica military power and religious institutions depended on the produce of families on rich lands reclaimed from the lakes, and on tributes taken from conquered peoples.

The Mexica found refuge on an island near the western shore of the lake that separated—and connected—the lakeshore powers of Atzcapotzalco to the north, Tacuba to the west, and Texcoco to the east. The newcomers learned to build *chinampas* in shallow water to feed their town. They fought in Atzcapotzalco's armies; then they defeated the once-powerful city-state and allied with Tacuba and Texcoco. Meanwhile, the Mexica built dikes to separate saline water from fresh, turning salt-free marshes into vast plains of *chinampas*, opening canals linking the city to shores all around, building causeways that could be blocked in the face of invading forces.

By the mid 1400s, Mexico-Tenochtitlán was an island-fortress city surrounded by a zone of intense lake-bed cultivation and protected by lakes and dikes. It was home to rulers and their palaces, priests and their temples, diverse artisans, and rich markets, the latter expanded by the conquest-incorporation of Tlatelolco, a trading center just to the north. *Chinampas* were worked by families organized in communities led by local lords—in turn subject to great lords in the city. Families worked land ultimately held by communities; cultivators sustained themselves, traded in local squares, and paid tributes to lords and overlords—in maize, cloth, crafts, and labor. Men fought in Mexica armies; women ruled local markets. Commoners' tributes and labor sustained the Mexica regime, its temples and religious devotions, and the armies that pressed power across the basin and beyond. Tributes allowed lordly recipients to seek gain in city markets and join ventures with long-distance traders. Around 1500, the majority produced for sustenance, trade, and tribute, supporting lords, armies, priests, and religious visions—and markets that profited the powerful.[4] Family and community autonomies sustained trade and military powers.

Having defeated their overlords at Atzcapotzalco and incorporated the island emporium of Tlatelolco, the Mexica in alliance with Texcoco and Tacuba ruled the lakeshore and the surrounding valley core, and began to press outward. By 1500, the rhetoric of a triple alliance persisted, but the Mexica dominated the Valley of Mexico and asserted rising power across the large basin to the east around Cholula and Huexotzingo. They pushed south among the Mixtec and Zapotec peoples of Oaxaca. Mexica power was impressive: Tenochtitlán passed 150,000 people, sustained by nearby *chinampas* and tributes taken from conquered communities.

Yet there were limits to that power. Beyond the lakeshore, transport depended on human carriers—who could haul grain only for limited distances before they consumed more than they carried. Far conquests brought luxuries, not staples, to a growing imperial city. The people of Tenochtitlán and nearby *chinampas* along with lakeshore allies might find benefit in imperial expansion: the power to mobilize labor was essential to building the expanding *chinampa* zone that sustained so many; the same power backed trade that filled rich urban markets; thousands of outsiders taken in battle pleased Huitzilopochtli and sustained the cosmos.

People outside the center of power saw little gain. Tribute paid to Tenochtitlán limited the sustenance and power of defeated city-states. Captives were lost producers, warriors, and kin to grieving families. Subject warlords might remain intermediaries, but they ruled communities stripped of warriors, producers, and goods. As a result, the Mexica faced continuing resistance from the lords and people of Tlaxcala, who remained independent north of Cholula, and from the Tarascan federation based at Tzintzuntzán on the shores of Lake Pátzcuaro to the west. The Toluca basin just west of Tenochtitlán remained a contested borderland separating Mexica and Tarascans. With that armed stalemate, neither Mexica nor Tarascans could drive north into the Bajío, leaving its fertile lands to staunch Chichimecas—state-free peoples. The domain of states and cultivating villages ended barely 200 kilometers north of Tenochtitlán. Meanwhile, Mixtec and Zapotec city-states contested expansion to the south and Mexica power never solidified beyond Tehuantepec in the Maya zones of Chiapas, Yucatán, and Guatemala—also regions of city-states at war, grounded in cultivating communities.

When Cortés intruded, the city of Tenochtitlán-Tlatelolco had passed 150,000 people. Power and wealth concentrated within; many of the city's artisans and market vendors, along with families cultivating nearby *chinampas*, held strong attachments to the Mexica regime. Its power was essential to the water control that built and maintained their rich lakebed lands; they fought in its armies and shared a bit in the wealth that conquests brought to the capital.[5] But in regions as near as Chalco, the rich plain between *chinampa*-filled Lake Chalco and the Ixtaccíhuatl and Popocatépetl volcanoes, life was more violent and uncertain. Mexica rule was never settled there; for decades lakeside powers sent armies in search of rule and tribute, settling newcomers who jostled older communities for lands. There were demands for men to risk life in others' armies—in service of Huitzilopochtli and other gods new to local pantheons. There were heavy extractions of maize; Chalco became Tenochtitlán's granary as lake-bed *chinampas* turned to fruits and vegetables. Facing contending rulers and rising demands, Chalco villagers were as likely to feel exploited by Mexica power as honored to share in its exploits.[6]

Parallel challenges of war, resettlement, production, and tribute taking struck people in the dry Mezquital; Tula was a ruin when the Nahuas of Texcoco drove triple-alliance power over Otomí communities.[7] More uncertain incorporations spread as Mexica armies marched east and south. Farther from the centers of power, legitimacy gave way to resentments in a world of constant war. Rebellion, at times led by outlying states, at times pressed by commoners against local rulers, spread.[8]

In 1519, Europeans entered a heartland defined by a dominant city, states at war, a religion that claimed legitimacy by war and human sacrifice—all sustained by tributes taken from cultivating, self-sustaining communities. Who could have imagined at the first meeting of Moctezuma and Cortés that after a century of devastation and innovation, the survivors of that Mesoamerican world would keep communities with radically shrunken populations, still strong on the land, rebuilt as republics, and linked by silver to trade reaching Europe and China?

Invasions and Destructions, Alliances and Innovations, 1520–50

Europeans invaded the heartland in 1519; smallpox besieged the region in 1520. Europeans aimed to conquer and profit by linking Mesoamericans to the world, politically, culturally, and economically. The disease-driven devastation of native regimes and communities enabled Europeans to claim power and opened desperate native survivors to new truths. In the decades after 1520, Europeans seeking power and Mesoamericans struggling to survive faced unimagined challenges, learning about each other in times of unprecedented conflict and change.

The conflicts and transformations that began with Cortés's landing in 1519 are repeatedly called "the conquest." Yet a look beyond Europeans' claims of superiority to include the actions and reactions of Mesoamericans reveals a mix of conflicts and alliances, negotiations and adaptations—a process far more complex than simple conquest. Iberians did come with iron weapons deadlier than anything in Mesoamerica. Their horses brought advantage in battle; hogs provided mobile sustenance. Naval power delivered supplies and reinforcements from afar. Motives tying power and profit seeking to a religious mission drove them on. Still, Europeans were few: less than 500 in 1519, perhaps 1,500 in 1521 when Tenochtitlán fell to siege. Cortés's victory depended on vast armies of native allies, Tlaxcalans and others, and especially on the smallpox epidemic of 1520 that assaulted native numbers and morale among people on both sides of the battles of 1521—giving an edge to Spaniards, nearly all immune after childhood exposure.[9]

The fall of Tenochtitlán was the victory of a broad Mesoamerican alliance backed by a few powerful Europeans. Cortés quickly awarded heartland communities in *encomienda* to European comrades-in-arms. By such grants, a "conqueror" claimed rights to tribute and labor services from a Mesoamerican lord and his subjects—usually defined by an existing *altepetl*. The recipient (*encomendero*) acquired the obligation to press conversion to Christianity and provide protection from exploitation. An *encomienda* granted favored European rights to take tributes from indigenous communities. In practice, however, a "conqueror" could rule only through an established local lord—or another quickly set in place. Native lords kept shares of the tributes; Mesoamerican ways of production and work continued, as did land rights, market ways, etc. The promotion of Christianity meant pressing native lords toward public conversion and persecuting those who clung to old deities. Lords led mass baptisms, rituals publicly recognizing Spanish sovereignty and the power of a distant God. They were uncertain signs of internal commitments. (Figure 2.1 shows an early open-air chapel-amphitheater build to assemble the people at Tlalmanalco.) Ultimately, European *encomenderos* and native Christian lords allied to share tributes. The only protection offered to communities facing deadly diseases and debated truths was a limit to exploitation by other Europeans or native lords.[10]

FIGURE 2.1. Proclaiming Euro-Christian truth: the open
altar at Tlalmanalco, Chalco, 1532.

While Spaniards imagined conquest, native lords saw alliance. Unless we presume Europeans as supermen, a few thousand able to dominate tens of millions of once militant but now hapless Mesoamericans, we must recognize the decades after the fall of Tenochtitlán as a time of European-Mesoamerican coalitions. Europeans were powerful but scarce participants in new and shifting alliances, aiming to rule a society still Mesoamerican.[11] Native ways of production, tribute extractions, social relations, and cultural traditions persisted to shape life for decades after "the conquest."[12]

Yet during times of negotiated alliances and social continuities, important changes began. Christian truths challenged Mesoamerican understandings long tied to established political and social ways. The fall of Huitzilopochtli and Moctezuma and the rise of God and Carlos V in times of epidemic death could not be walled off from everyday life.[13] While *encomenderos* and native lords aimed to keep continuities in production, social relations, and ways of extraction, tribute demands strained communities as population plummeted—and new demands soon came.

The European expansion led by Iberians from the fifteenth century sought profit in trade with Asia. The goal was access to fine silk and cotton cloth, porcelains, and spices that were also preservatives—pepper, cloves, and cinnamon. Asians desired little that Europeans made and demanded payment in specie—gold and silver. If the Americas first seemed an obstacle to trade with Asia, New World gold and then silver soon accelerated global commerce. Mesoamericans had mined and worked both metals, primarily for artistic expression. Profit-seeking Europeans made gold and silver into money in Mesoamerica, too.

Gold mining proved easy within Mesoamerican ways of production and labor. Early on, armed Europeans took the metal as plunder. Soon, *encomenderos* worked with native lords to demand gold as tribute. Seeking more gold than plunder or tribute could provide, *encomenderos* sent gangs of tribute workers to pan in often distant lowlands. We have every reason to expect that native lords and commoners quickly saw the commercial value of gold, prospected on their own and sold what they found to Spaniards, who sent it into expanding trades. Gold from plunder and production stimulated trade, disrupting Mesoamerican ways only minimally.[14]

More disruptive and transforming, and setting precedents for much to come, was the early rise of silver mining at Taxco, in rugged uplands southwest of Mexico City. From the 1530s, Spanish entrepreneurs including Cortés staked claims. Early mines remained near the surface; refining came by firing in ovens. Local knowledge prevailed, capital needs were small, and natives did most mining and refining—selling ore or silver to

Europeans who sent it into trade. Spaniards might claim mining sites, as the Crown sanctioned in 1526; the regime claimed a fifth in taxes. Before 1550, as Taxco witnessed the Americas' first silver boom, Europeans took profit in trade; natives found gain in production and supply—and a new regime struggled to regulate everything and take its share in taxes.[15]

Spaniards aimed to rule and reap profits, but with limited success. They brought enslaved Africans to labor; native bondsmen taken in conquest (called slaves, though their status was not heritable) also worked the mines—as long as they survived. Villagers from the Cuernavaca basin and the Valley of Toluca came as tribute laborers, mobilized by native lords and Spaniards (including Cortés, who held rights in both basins) to work in rotating gangs at tasks from construction to transport. Mine operators' complaints and regulations written in 1542 show that, whatever Europeans' claims, natives ruled production while trading in silver; inputs like salt, firewood, and maize; and in the luxuries mining allowed.

While Africans and declining numbers of natives labored in bondage and others came in tribute gangs, uncounted native men left communities facing depopulation and disruption for a chance at the mines. They ruled excavation, extraction, and smelting. They sold ore and refined silver to Spaniards; others traded in inputs and luxuries. Europeans complained of native profiteering and demanded regulation to concentrate power and profit in European hands and reduce natives to dependent workers. The regime wrote regulations that proved impossible to enforce. In early Taxco mining, Europeans ruled links to the world market and took gain enough to stay in the silver economy. Mesoamericans, shrinking in numbers while grounded in landed communities, ruled production, supply, and sustenance—ready to take gain in the Americas' first boomtown.[16]

Meanwhile, Cortés joined other Spaniards to begin cane cultivation and sugar refining around Cuernavaca, in the lowlands east of Taxco. A sweet that made elegant confections for the prosperous and preserved fruits and their nutrition beyond days of harvest, sugar was in growing demand among Europeans at home and in the Americas. Cuernavaca was warm, fertile, and irrigated; land opened as natives died of disease. Early planting paralleled mining at Taxco: growers bought a few Africans from Atlantic and Caribbean islands to serve as skilled overseers and refiners; bound natives worked year-round; villagers drawn in rotating gangs by *encomienda* rights did the hard labor of cutting cane with machetes and feeding it into rough stone mills.[17]

From the first, sugar planters sought profit. Their primary market was the European population of Mexico City, reviving as the capital of

New Spain. Natives at Taxco mines bought sugar, too. Other fusions followed: cacao from distant Pacific lowlands produced a strong bitter drink; the beans served as coin to settle accounts in Mesoamerica. Its strong demand at Taxco in the sixteenth century suggests a slow shift from cacao to silver currency, and an early mixing of cacao and sugar to make chocolate sweet and more palatable to Europeans.

Taxco mines and Cuernavaca sugar mills made the region south and southwest of Mexico City an early crucible of entrepreneurship, native adaptation, and cultural innovation. Europeans turned quickly from tribute taking to profit seeking; bound Africans took roles in production; native bondsmen worked in profit-seeking enterprises—and diverse Mesoamericans, lords and commoners, laboring men and market women, turned early to seek gain however they could in a commercial economy stimulated by silver.[18] Cortés sought profit by linking Taxco mines, Cuernavaca sugar estates, and *encomienda* rights in the Valley of Toluca. He drew maize and labor from communities on the land to sustain his enterprises (while he and other Spaniards grazed livestock everywhere they could). Taxco became the first American silver boomtown, leading a protean silver capitalism grounded in landed communities.

All of the conflicts, continuities, and changes that shaped Mesoamerica in the decades after 1520 generated deep cultural debates. We know much about the goals of the European clergy who came to promote Christianity, little about natives' first reactions beyond the rapid end of human sacrifice, the rise of mass public baptisms, the wide collaboration of native elites with evangelization—and a few cases of resistance by men who kept old ways by retreating to highlands on the fringe of the central basins. People searched for answers to unprecedented challenges of life and death, holding to old devotions as they tried new approaches to the divine. Help in the face of disease, death, drought, and other worldly challenges was the common goal.[19]

The regions around Taxco and Cuernavaca, scenes of intense early commercial activity and cultural mixing, became crucibles of religious innovation. In 1543, at Totolapan high in the mountains separating the capital and Cuernavaca, an indigenous stranger delivered an image of Christ crucified made of native materials in a Spanish style to Augustinian friar Antonio de Roa. He pronounced the image miraculous and made it the center of self-flagellating devotions. The friar aimed to teach penitential Christianity, directing his charges to see the dying as penance for a history of sin in centuries without Christ. The people of Totolapan saw truth differently. They resisted notions of sin and saw Christ's suffering and death as divine parallels to their daily trials. Roa was soon gone, but the people of Totolapan kept the Christ as their dearest religious image. It drew the community toward Him, helping make lives of unfathomable challenge bearable, meaningful, and ultimately Christian. Theirs was not the friar's Christianity, but their own.[20]

Away from Taxco and Cuernavaca, indigenous ways of production still ruled at midcentury. Sustenance for Mexico City and Taxco came mostly from native growers who still planted maize, frijol, and chile on community lands, paying tributes in those staples and in cloth made by wives and daughters to native lords and Spanish *encomenderos*, who sold them in regional markets. Labor for urban reconstruction came from gangs drawn as *encomienda* tribute from communities still strong on the land. Producers sustained themselves and delivered tribute goods and labor without pay, at no cost to native lords and Spanish overlords.[21]

Meanwhile, Spanish settlers' preference for wheat led Europeans to plant on depopulated slopes near Tacuba, west of the capital, relying on tribute labor from nearby communities for harvesting. Old World livestock spread across the dry lands north of Toluca and the Mezquital, pressing communities already facing depopulation because of disease. Cattle, sheep, and hogs filled spaces vacated by dying humans; herding required little labor to profit Europeans.[22]

The decades from 1520 to 1550 were not a time of conquest, but an era of conflicts and alliances, destructions and innovations, bringing much that was new, European, and commercial while preserving much that was Mesoamerican in production, social organization, and culture—including communities on the land. While disease cut the heartland population in half by 1550,[23] gold and silver, sugar and wheat, imposed new work demands. Newcomers asserted power, negotiated with established lords, took tributes, promoted Christianity, and sought new ways to profit. Most of all, Mesoamericans died.

The devastating social, cultural, and emotional consequences in heartland communities can only be imagined. We know of Europeans' loud laments about losses of tribute goods and labor, prosperity and profitability. They were slow to adjust demands as population fell, raising real impositions and the survivors' sense of exploitation. By the 1540s, the promise of an enduring Mesoamerica, Christianized and tied to a wider world, was vanishing along with the majority of Mesoamericans. The deadly *matlazáhuatl* (typhus) epidemic of 1545–48 made that seem certain. European and native lords, allied in search of power and prosperity, faced falling tributes and fragile powers. The Mesoamerican majority faced dying kin, shrinking communities, and truths that could not hold. Few in the heartland around 1550 could see a promising future.

Much had changed in Mesoamerica; much had not. Mexica power and Huitzilopochtli's mandate had fallen. The sovereignty of the Spanish monarchy and of God was advancing. Yet, Spanish rule worked though native allies and God's emissaries struggled to promote Christianity as they knew it. Most production remained the province of families working community lands; their tributes in goods and labor sustained native lords and Spanish newcomers. The search for gold and Taxco silver mines added to labor demands, as did sugar and wheat harvests. At midcentury, heartland communities faced continuities in production, labor relations, and tribute exactions, and innovations promising gain to Europeans while demanding more work as depopulation made people scarce, truth questionable, and the future uncertain.

Two other developments laden with continuity and change also consolidated around 1550: the rebuilding of Mexico City and the demilitarization of Mesoamerican society. The city was shaken by the siege of 1521 and Europeans' destruction of temples they saw as dedicated to malevolent deities. As pathogens flourished in close urban quarters, depopulation was swift. From 150,000 people around 1520, a few tens of thousands likely remained in the 1530s and 1540s—plus a few thousand European newcomers.[24] Still, the Spanish regime set the *audiencia* (high court) that ruled from 1530 in the former Mexica capital. The first viceroy, don Antonio de Mendoza, came in 1535 with new fiscal and judicial bureaucracies.

Building the new capital on the remnants of the old announced that Spanish rule replaced Mexica power. The high court and Viceroy Mendoza kept the city the pivot of the heartland; they too traveled by causeway and canoe around the basin that centered power in Mesoamerica. They and their *encomendero* allies would draw tribute goods and new products to the capital by canal: fruits and vegetables, native and new, came from still flourishing *chinampas*; maize came from Chalco, sugar from Cuernavaca. New officials established a fiscal apparatus in the capital, aiming to regulate and tax mining—with limited success. The locus of power in the heartland did not change; its ways and means did as population collapsed and silver rose.

Meanwhile, warfare all but vanished from Anáhuac. The 1521 victory of the Spanish-Tlaxcalan alliance, the consolidation of ties linking European *encomenderos* to surviving native lords, the negotiated incorporation of the Tarascan regime—all conditioned by rapid depopulation— brought a profound demilitarization to a region long defined by constant wars.[25] Before 1520, the rule of Mexica and other lords combined military power and religious eminence—sustained by tributes taken from landed communities. Mexica nobility, ruling lords and their male kin (*pipiltín* in Nahuatl) claimed rights to polygamy. Multiple wives demonstrated power over women, reproduction, and society in general. At the heights of Mexica society, power was patriarchal in ways that fused the military, political, extractive, and sexual power of dominant men—all honored in religious assertions.[26]

Among commoners (*macehuales*), men allowed one wife worked the land, made diverse craft goods, and faced battlefield danger as they fought to capture foes for sacrifice and avoid capture to be sacrificed. Everyday life among commoners was also patriarchal, but men with one wife faced heavy burdens in production and tribute demands—and risked life in battle. Their roles, too, were honored in religious culture—as were, secondarily, women's efforts in production and reproduction, family sustenance and local marketing. Power and production meshed with martial roles and religious legitimations in patriarchal inequities.[27]

By 1550, as Europeans consolidated power and saw less need for armed allies, they demilitarized Mesoamerican society. Native lords might still collect tributes, oversee local justice, and lead enduring city-states; they would not command troops. Commoners would still plant crops, make craft goods, and pay tributes; they would not be warriors. The Chichimeca wars sustained martial patriarchy to the north for a time, but after 1590 disarmament accelerated while Catholic law and Spanish culture forbade polygamy. Regime and clergy worked to make marriage the union of a patriarch and one wife among the powerful and the poor.[28] The heartland stayed patriarchal after 1550, but only Europeans would carry arms.

Meanwhile, imperial officials sought new ways to rule. As population plummeted and gold became scarce, tributes became uncertain sources of wealth and revenue. In the 1540s, a series of new laws aimed to regulate tribute, end native bondage, and limit inheritance of *encomiendas* and rights to tribute. Worrying that exploitation caused depopulation, the regime sent new Spanish magistrates to oversee justice and help clergy draw surviving natives to truth.[29] Disease proved the leading promoter of Christianity: baptism promised salvation after death, and death was everywhere. Christ's compassion helped natives face epidemic death.[30]

Encomenderos resisted change, seeing no alternative way to power in a region of dying people. They were sure of their right to rule. But seeking power and profit, what might keep them in Mesoamerica as gold and people vanished? Then, amid destruction and uncertainty, a turn in the global economy drew Spain's Americas into expanding trade, opening opportunities for profit that stimulated a radical reconstruction in the Mexican heartland.

The Stimulus of Silver, 1550–1610

Silver became a key commodity-money in global trade in the 1550s. Its boom reoriented the history of the Mexica(n) heartland. A half century of New World gold mining had increased global stocks, raising the price of silver.[31] Demand for silver drove higher when the Ming empire decreed it the only money for China's internal taxation and international accounts in 1551.[32] Taxco proved the possibilities of silver in Mesoamerica from the 1530s. In the 1540s, natives introduced Europeans to rich silver deposits at Potosí high in the Andes and at Zacatecas north of Mesoamerica in the lands of Chichimecas. In the heartland, mining accelerated at Taxco and at Pachuca north of the capital.

Silver opened opportunities for profit in times of uncertain Spanish rule and rapid native depopulation. But once surface deposits depleted, mining required tunneling deep into rugged mountains; refining all but the richest ores required amalgamation with mercury, a process recently developed in Germany and adapted to the Americas at Pachuca in 1555. As most mercury came from Almadén in the Sierra Morena between Madrid and Seville, silver mining became a complex process tied to distant inputs and global markets.[33] Locally, it required large numbers of workers to tunnel underground and to refine ore with poisonous mercury. The work demanded skills gained in permanent service that came with deadly risks. Rotating tribute labor could not be the basis of silver mining; a vanishing Mesoamerican population made all labor scarce. The opportunity of silver created chances and challenges for Europeans and possibilities laden with risks for surviving Mesoamericans.

The new profitability of silver began to transform the heartland between 1551, a year of crisis at Taxco, and 1555—a time of creativity at Pachuca. In 1551, thirty-eight Taxco mine operators petitioned Viceroy don Luis de Velasco: all owned "gangs of slaves" (presumably African, though they did not say). Together, the petitioners owed 450,000 pesos and they could not feed the slaves, their greatest investment. They attributed the crisis to the dying of 1545–48. It left them without native hands and unable to buy maize to feed the workers they had, including the slaves. Meanwhile, too many merchants profiteered in essential supplies and superfluous silks. Natives came and went, taking advances, working when they wished, driving wages up; villagers demanded too much for scarce maize. Operators' debts mounted and mining faced crisis.[34]

In 1552, Spaniards learned of silver at Pachuca, north of Mexico City in mountains east of the Mezquital. In 1555, Bartolomé de Medina adapted the *patio* process there, refining by amalgamation with mercury, allowing profitable mining of midgrade ores.[35] We can thus date to between 1551 and 1555 the arrival in New Spain of the stimulus of rising Chinese demand for silver. The challenges of depopulation and labor scarcity remained. Profit seeking by all who could—Spanish mine operators and merchants, native lords, cultivators, workers, and market women—continued, such was the draw of silver. From the mid-1550s, it overcame all obstacles. (Figure 2.2 shows a sixteenth-century fortress-church at Taxco, fruit and symbol of the rising silver economy.)

Spanish American silver exports rose from under two million pesos yearly in the 1550s to average nearly three million in 1570s, then over five

FIGURE 2.2. Foundations of silver: fortress-
church at Taxco, sixteenth century.

million in the 1580s and nearly seven million in the 1590s. About a quarter went to the Crown in taxes and payments for mercury. To stimulate production, the regime lowered the price of mercury by thirty percent between 1571 and 1602 as production rose at Almadén in Spain, New Spain's primary supplier, and at Huancavelica in Peru, the source for Potosí. Three-quarters of rising silver flows entered global markets in trade.[36] A 1597 survey reported that more than fifteen percent of Spanish America's total came from greater Taxco, more than twenty percent from the entire heartland, including Pachuca. More than a third of the total came from New Spain—including Zacatecas and Guanajuato as Chichimeca wars ended and northern mining rose. Andean Potosí led, but silver from the heartland was a key stimulus to global trade (see appendix, table A.1).

Mining led a commercialization of social relations marked by labor dependencies. In 1569 at Taxco, 93 Spaniards prospered as mine owners, refiners, and merchants; 616 African slaves worked for their owners' profit; 905 natives served in gangs doing dangerous work. The report added that natives trading in local markets, including many women, outnumbered men laboring in mines and refineries.[37] By 1580, Taxco reported 150 Spaniards; 600 African slaves; 200 natives doing tribute service; and 2,300 *naboríos*, free natives laboring for wages and sustenance. Adding the nearby mines of Zacualpa, Sultepec, and Temascaltepec, there were 300 Spaniards, 1,050 slaves, 550 tribute workers, and 2,600 *naboríos* producing silver in greater Taxco.[38] Africans bought as commodities and Mesoamericans drawn by commercial incentives did the work of making money for China and the world.

In the 1570s, the Spaniards who presumed to rule and profit at Taxco still complained of native profiteering. Too many *naboríos* contracted to deliver sacks of ore to multiple mine operators or refiners; too many labored at night with little oversight and no concern for tunnel maintenance, delivering some ore to owners but keeping the best to sell in black markets. Other *naboríos* took cash advances and promised to labor for multiple Spaniards, worked a bit for one, then disappeared with cash and ore they sold to the highest bidding local refiner. Employers desperate for labor enabled such independence, repeatedly offering higher pay to men who had taken advances from another mine operator, refiner, or builder. Native *naboríos* and African slaves were said to constantly steal ore, mercury, salt, and more—profiteering in Taxco's open market. Regulations posted in 1575 called for *naboríos* to serve one employer, for advances to be repaid in work, and for markets to be public with prices regulated. Enforcement proved impossible.[39]

While Taxco accelerated the silver mining and social commercialization begun in the 1530s, Pachuca rose in the 1550s. Bartolomé de Medina pioneered mercury refining there and prospered modestly. The leading entrepreneurs at Pachuca were members of the Guerrero family, *encomenderos* at nearby Actopan, thus able to draw tribute goods and workers to subsidize early ventures. The Rivadeneyra clan enjoyed similar benefits. Without an *encomienda*, Alonso de Villaseca relied on commercial skills (and questionable dealings in mercury and more) to become the richest miner and landowner in the heartland by the 1570s. In 1556 he owned 68 of the 348 African slaves working at Pachuca. Five other entrepreneurs owned 20 to 40 for a total of 198, while ten small operators had 2 to 14 each (a total of 82). Early reliance on costly slaves in times of labor scarcity led to concentrated control of mining.[40]

By 1569, the number of slaves reported at Pachuca and Ixmiquilpan to the west had fallen to 186, far outnumbered by 1,163 native *naboríos*. When the Crown began to send rotating gangs of villagers (via the *repartimiento* draft) in weekly shifts to supplement the labor of permanent laborers in the 1570s, natives became the dominant workforce at Pachuca. In 1575, 1,108 draftees were due weekly—about equal to the number of *naboríos*. But continuing depopulation rapidly reduced draft numbers: only 692 men were due weekly in 1580 after another round of disease; a mere 250 were expected by 1610. The shift to dependent *naborío* labor was confirmed by the 1597 survey of heartland mining: 109 African slaves remained at Pachuca, backed by only 390 draft laborers, while 1,168 *naboríos* formed the core of the workforce at the heartland's second silver producer. As at Taxco, complaints of *naboríos* taking advances without working, playing one employer against another, and stealing ore and inputs and selling them for profit rose. Around 1600 in Pachuca, as at Taxco, *naborío* labor consolidated as free native workers gained cash advances against monetary salaries, food rations, and ore shares to mine silver.[41]

As native *naboríos* working for commercial incentives became primary laborers, control of mining at Pachuca dispersed: in 1584, among forty-three recipients of the 337 *quintales* of mercury, the powerful Rivadeneyra family got 70, four others gained 20 to 27, and another four took 10 to 16, while thirty-four took 10 or fewer—most of them gaining but two to five *quintales*.[42] A few men still ruled mining, but participation broadened to include more small producers and refiners—a more open market facilitated by *naboríos'* labor and negotiation of work.

Silver production grew rapidly. By 1590, 929 *quintales* of mercury were distributed at Pachuca, indicating that output had tripled there. Taxco gained 1,171 *quintales*, greater Taxco 2,794—more than half the 4,987 distributed across New Spain. Zacatecas got only 697, Guanajuato but 377 while Chichimeca wars raged. Silver mined in the heartland far exceeded that in the north as late as 1590.[43]

With pacification, mining rose in the north. Greater Taxco remained New Spain's leading producer in 1597, but its dominance fell to forty-five percent. Pachuca's share fell also, while mining at Zacatecas and Guanajuato rose to nearly thirty percent, a sign of dominance soon to come. In and around Taxco, ninety-six water-powered mills and ninety-four driven by horses crushed ore; 737 African slaves still labored, outnumbered by 1,776 *naboríos* and 931 hands drawn by *repartimiento* drafts. At Pachuca, fifty-nine water mills outnumbered the twenty-three moved by horses; slaves were few at 109; 1,168 *naboríos* dominated labor, while 394 draftees served in rotations. Early development at Taxco led to a mix of water- and horsepower—and greater investment in slaves (near the Cuernavaca lowlands where bound Africans toiled in cane and its refineries). Later development at Pachuca brought less investment in slaves, more reliance on negotiating labor with *naboríos*, and investment in water mills to crush ore for refining with mercury. In regions farther north, water mills were rare, African slaves scarce, and draft labor nearly absent in 1597; *naboríos* ruled work there—emphasizing late development and rapid commercialization (see appendix, table A.1).

After 1600, commercial ways were set at Pachuca. In 1605, only 73 slaves remained while 950 *naboríos* kept mining alive. The population reported as Spanish had risen to 744, including mine operators and merchants, craftsmen and small traders, and workers too.[44] A detailed survey for 1610 shows the population of European extraction at 764: 186 immigrants from Spain, 11 from Portugal, 9 from Genoa—and 558 Americans. Most immigrants were men—166 to 20 women. Among American Spaniards, women outnumbered men 260 to 46. Immigrants ruled mining at Pachuca and married American women; together they had produced 242 American children. If every immigrant married, there were still 20 unmarried (or widowed) American Spanish women at Pachuca in 1610, suggesting that independent women found roles in marketing, inn keeping, and more. The indigenous population had risen to 2,422: 850 men, 816 women, and 756 children. While most men labored as *naboríos*, native women joined in making and selling food and drink and trading in local markets. The number of children among Spaniards and *indios* showed that Pachuca became a settled, reproducing community.

By 1610, African slavery was ending at Pachuca: 4 men and 4 women were listed as *negros*—likely slaves. There were 168 mulattoes: 70 men, 65 women, and 33 children. Their status is not listed, but to become mulatto, many were born of free native mothers and thus were free. They joined *naboríos* in a growing population legally free and negotiating commercial lives. Only 25 (16 men, 9 women) were labeled mestizos or *castas* of mixed Spanish and indigenous ancestry, living in the same commercial world.[45] After 1600, people asserting Spanish status increased, while native *naboríos* and their families ruled labor and marketing, African slavery waned, and the descendants of earlier slaves became free mulattoes. Enslaved and drafted workers became scarce after 1600. The stimulus of silver overcame the challenges of labor by commercializing work and life at the mines.

The Great Reconstruction, 1550–1650

The rise of silver at Taxco and Pachuca created urban communities. Around 1600 mining centers around Taxco totaled about 15,000 people; those at Pachuca 10,000. Meanwhile, administrative, fiscal, commercial, judicial, religious, and educational functions concentrated in Mexico City. The entrepreneurs and merchants who tied New Spain and the silver economy to Europe and Asia lived there. Except for the metal and construction trades necessary to mining, most artisans worked in the capital, serving its markets and the mining centers. Mexico City revived to about 80,000 people in 1570, mostly Mesoamericans, while European and mixed peoples approached forty percent. By 1640, near the end of the first silver boom, the city had grown to 85,000, nearly seventy percent classed as European or mixed (see appendix, table A.2).

The mining centers and Mexico City combined to create an urban population of 100,000 in the heartland around 1600. With the rural population of the Valley of Mexico falling toward 135,000, an estimate of 250,000 for the total rural population of the heartland seems reasonable. With depopulation, a quarter of a million cultivating survivors had ample lands to sustain themselves. They had little need to supply urban centers. The constant complaints from entrepreneurs at Taxco and Pachuca—that native notables speculated in everything; that cultivators took too much for maize; that market women made everything too expensive; and that men who came to labor as *naboríos* took too much in cash advances, gave too little in work and ore, and gained too much for their efforts—show that Mesoamericans facing trying times took gain in the silver economy.

As Europeans sought profit and native numbers plummeted, producers became scarce and gained bargaining power as the opportunities of silver rose. The challenge for authorities and entrepreneurs was to slow depopulation and limit the independence of the native majority. But only the slow acquisition of immunities would end the disease-driven depopulation. To address native independence, officials and clergy congregated survivors in indigenous republics. Granted self-rule under local notables and land sufficient to sustain shrinking populations, the republics enabled native production, social integration, and cultural creativity. They became the durable foundation of the heartland silver economy by organizing indigenous independence.

The reconstruction proved complex; there was no central planning. Still, developments overlapped in a clear sequence: First, surviving Mesoamericans were drawn to compact towns given rights to local rule and lands to support local governance and religious life, notables' power and commoners' sustenance. Second, Spaniards gained vacated lands to build estates to supply mines and city markets. Third, congregated and self-sufficient natives were pressed to send work gangs to mines and estates. And throughout, courts mediated inevitable conflicts.

The clergy had long promoted the congregation of surviving Mesoamericans, aiming to facilitate oversight of a native population dying rapidly and leaving survivors scattered across the land. When the regime took up the proposal in the 1550s, congregations came with the added goal of limiting the power of native lords and Spanish *encomenderos* and solidifying regime rule. Resettlements began in the 1550s and came in waves into the early 1600s. Under the oversight of new district magistrates, clergy collaborated with native notables to draw dispersed families to towns. Notables gained rights to rule as governors, magistrates, and councilmen. Offices rotated by election among *principales*, heirs to the *pipiltín* (perhaps fifteen percent of local populations). Traditional lords—*tlatoque*, now called caciques—lost heritable rights to office, yet often ruled on for a time, moving in and out of office as governors. Depopulated city-states remade as republics gained domain over lands allocated to sustain local governance and religious life, and to sustain families according to their station. Caciques and *principales* held shares sufficient to profit as commercial growers; commoners had plots sufficient for sustenance and local trade. Crafts from cloth making to pottery carried on, as did local markets ruled by women. (Figure 2.3 shows the new church built at the center of Tlalmanalco, congregated as the head town at Chalco.)

FIGURE 2.3. Centering the indigenous republic:
the Temple of San Luis Obispo, Tlalmanalco, Chalco, 1591.

Head towns had ruled Mesoamerican city-states while families in outlying villages worked the land. With depopulation, survivors became increasingly scattered, even isolated. Congregations drew many to settle as *barrios* in and near head towns; others remained in nearby villages. Councils ruled from head towns; local officials and religious leaders led *barrios* and villages, sustained by shares of land. The new republics came laden with potential for conflict among notables and commoners, head towns and villages. They also forged solidarities in defense of land, self-rule, and cultural independence—the essence of autonomies.[46]

Inevitably and intentionally, congregations in times of shrinking population vacated vast lands. Accelerating around 1570, the regime awarded large areas to Spaniards in grants (*Mercedes*, graces) combining *caballerías* (about 40 hectares, a gentleman's portion) for crops, and grazing sites (about 800 hectares, most for sheep). Descendants of *encomenderos* and newcomers connected to viceroys built estates. As surpluses taken in tribute and work service shrank and silver promoted urban settlement, estates rose to profit elites and supply cities and mines. Land grants concentrated between 1570 and 1620. With inevitable conflicts, a great land transfer was completed by the early seventeenth century.[47]

As mining rose at Taxco and Pachuca, and Mexico City grew as the pivot of everything, estate builders met urban demand for Old World products. Basins with distinct ecological potentials raised different crops. Sugar focused in the tropical lowlands around Cuernavaca and Cuautla, where development accelerated after 1550 to draw growing numbers of enslaved Africans to work in mills and irrigated lands. The region south of Mexico City where Taxco silver met Cuernavaca sugar, both drawing large numbers of bound Africans, saw the most rapid commercialization and complex ethnic interactions. In the Valley of Mexico, the slopes of Tacuba in the west and plains at Texcoco and Chalco to the east saw estates expand after 1570 to plant wheat where irrigation allowed; the southern Valley of Toluca mixed wheat and grazing. In dry zones from the northeast Valley of Mexico around Otumba, through the Mezquital near Pachuca, and across the northern Valley of Toluca, grazing hogs, sheep, and cattle prevailed.

Political favor and the vagaries of inheritance forged a new landed elite. Some had held *encomienda* rights, others took wealth in mining and trade after 1550. Many linked in strategic marriages to concentrate landed power. The Cortés family, living in Europe by the late sixteenth century, held important sugar properties in the Cuernavaca basin to the end of the colonial era. The Rodríguez Altimarano clan, linked to Cortés and early *encomenderos* in the southern Valley of Toluca and married into the family of the viceroys Velasco, gained lands to build the rich Atengo estates there. As Condes de Santiago Calimaya, they remained the leading landed family in Mexico City through the eighteenth century. Alonso de Villaseca, the great miner at early Pachuca, built commercial estates from the northeast Valley of Mexico into the Mezquital to supply Pachuca mines and Mexico City markets. Without heirs, he left his holdings to newly arrived Jesuits, who operated the Santa Lucía properties to support city colleges for centuries.[48]

Most early estates raised Old World commodities—wheat and sugar, sheep, cattle, and hogs—to supply the Hispanic population of Mexico City, Spanish and mixed, that rose from 30,000 around 1570 to nearly 60,000 by 1640. Urban indigenous peoples—a majority of about 50,000 in 1570, a minority of 25,000 by 1640—lived on maize and other foods sold by native growers on nearby *chinampas* and in outlying republics. In times of scarce population and ample land, most rural families held land enough for sustenance and a bit of marketing, selling maize and other foodstuffs to city consumers. Native notables raised and sold ample surpluses, some on personal lands, some on lands dedicated to fund local government and religious life.[49]

The reconstruction of 1550 to 1650 created parallel agricultural economies: one based in republics producing native crops; the other at commercial estates raising Old World staples and livestock. They shared the countryside, estates jostling republics everywhere, while their produce converged in city markets. Together, they negotiated the challenge of labor in times of vanishing population. Silver and urbanization created commercial openings. Depopulation vacated land and made labor scarce. Natives with land for sustenance saw little need to work for others' profit, unless drawn by some mix of tradition, mandate, and incentive. In cultivation as in mining, the challenge was labor. In both, early mandates gave way after 1600 to commercial negotiation.

Enslaved Africans labored everywhere. They worked in mining centers, though they were too valuable to risk working underground or with mercury. They labored in urban crafts and in household service for the prosperous and the powerful. They provided supervisory, skilled, and permanent labor at sugar estates in lowland basins. They herded livestock in dry zones stretching north. Bound Africans were not "cheap labor" in the sixteenth century. The arrival of tens of thousands shows the profitability of the heartland silver economy. Their rapid incorporation into a growing population of mixed and increasingly free working people is also revealing. Most arriving Africans were men set to work among a Mesoamerican majority.

Across New Spain, in Mexico City, in mining centers, at sugar estates, and at grazing properties, enslaved African men fathered children with native women—by law free, as were their children—accelerating the growth of a population that was mixed, free, and excluded from power. Some lived with mothers in native republics. Others joined growing numbers laboring in mines, cities, and transport, and at estates. Slavery forced migration that fueled the rise of a population of free dependent workers. By 1650, most were doing the same work their enslaved grandfathers had been doing in 1570.[50] Slavery and ethnic mixing created a core of permanent, often skilled, dependent workers.

But mining, cultivation, and urban construction required large numbers of less skilled workers for labor that was usually hard, sometimes dangerous, and often seasonal. Before 1550, unpaid gangs providing tribute service to native lords and Spanish *encomenderos* drew men to such work without pay. As draft labor faded with the demise of native lordship and *encomienda* rights, Mesoamerican traditions of gang labor adapted to a commercializing world. In early native republics, men worked in communal fields to support local government and religion, and on lands of notables raising maize and for markets. At first the work was unpaid, drawn by community obligation or as tribute due to notables. Over time, Spanish clergy and officials pressed notables to pay. Unpaid work continued on lands dedicated to supporting local devotions.

Mines, city construction projects, and estates seeking harvest labor also coveted the labor of men in the republics. To mobilize work after 1550, the regime turned to the native tradition of *cuatequil*—a labor draft that called men to rotating turns in public works and other projects. With *encomiendas* ending in the heartland, with tributes limited to cash and maize, and with Spanish magistrates now in many head towns, the regime from the 1550s pressed native notables to assemble gangs to work weekly at the mines.[51] By the 1570s, as dying continued and commercial production rose, the draft was formalized to send labor to estates. District magistrates required native officials to assemble four percent of working-age men every Monday. Each worker went for three or four weeks each year (far from the six-month stints of the Andean *mit'a*) in a draft (*repartimiento*, distribution) mandating that workers earn wages—at first one real a day, later two. Men sustaining families by cultivating lands in republics were drawn to rotating labor at mines, city projects, and estate harvests. They gained cash to pay tributes and buy in markets.[52]

Producers in landed republics sent native staples to mines and city markets; they worked seasonally in mining, estate harvests, and city building. By the early seventeenth century the silver economy had grafted onto enduring native communities remade as republics. Then, after working for decades to congregate communities, found republics, grant lands, and organize labor drafts, the regime drew back after 1600 to focus on judicial mediation. Native republics provided local justice. Spanish magistrates took on disputes between communities or against estates. Unresolved conflicts went to a general indigenous court in Mexico City, where native plaintiffs gained counsel and translators. Negotiating resolutions, the courts gained growing legitimacy.[53]

Adapting to Reconstruction

The reconstruction that founded landed republics, gave land to commercial estates, and tied them together to sustain urban markets and a rising silver economy in times of depopulation seems a triumph of adaptation in the face of calamity and opportunity. Yet times of challenge and change are never simple and smooth. Personal tragedies, unconscionable demands, and conflicts over land and labor marked difficult decades. Local detail about the lives of commoners in the era of reconstruction is scarce. Where available, it is revealing.

Culhuacán lay south of Mexico City, on the west shore of Lake Chalco. Families lived by cultivating rich *chinampas* and adjacent dry lands covered with maguey that provided fiber for cordage and coarse cloth, and sap tapped to ferment pulque. The town led a city-state once ruled by descendants of Tula's Toltec kings; after Tula's fall they contended for power for a time and then fell to Mexica rule. By 1580 Culhuacán held rich *chinampas* worked by a falling population, favored by location at a junction of land and water routes converging to supply Mexico City.

We know more about lives, struggles, and beliefs at Culhuacán than for any other heartland community in the late sixteenth century, thanks to the survival of dozens of wills.[54] They show a community still facing death as an everyday devastation in the 1580s. Dying shaped everything as life became commercial, patriarchy weakened, and new religious understandings set in. Material poverty was not a major problem; survivors retained ample resources. Nor was exploitation by Spaniards a concern. Europeans were scarce at Culhuacán around 1580: a district magistrate and his kin and an Augustinian friar or two, linking the town to Mexico City and Catholic culture. A native governor, magistrates, and councilmen led the republic, plus the notary who wrote the wills that reveal a community adapting to depopulation.

The testaments show people with widely distributed lands. Prosperous and poor, they cultivated, traded, and worked in crafts from men's carpentry to women's weaving. Men and women held ample lands, mostly *chinampas* acquired by inheritance and purchase. In wills written with death in sight, they distributed land to an ever-scarcer community of the living. Women regularly inherited land, and later allocated it as they chose. Depopulation had ended patriarchal preferences in landholding, even as the republic kept office the preserve of notable men. Cultivation remained men's work (even on women's land); women wove and traded. Meanwhile life monetized, calculated in silver pesos, reales, and *tomines*. Cacao remained, but land and houses, livestock and boats, tools and clothing, even masses, had prices in silver.

Death also marked indigenous Christianity at Culhuacán. If a miraculous image drew Christ to the center of community devotion in the 1540s at Totolapan, in rugged mountains to the south, in Culhuacán's rich lowlands devotion in the 1580s had become deeply personal and notably commercial.

Dying people never willed land to the friars or to support community devotions. Instead, men and women facing death repeatedly designated lands to be sold to pay for masses in pursuit of salvation. They kept the clergy dependent on fees for sacramental service, fed a growing local land market, and showed strong commitments to a search for eternal peace. The people of Culhuacán were deeply Christian by 1600—in their own ways.

The Culhuacán testaments help resolve a great debate about heartland communities: was land held personally or by corporate communities? Sources looking from the outside repeatedly suggest that land belonged to the community, while being worked by families. Court suits pressed by native republics argue the same. Yet the Culhuacán wills show land repeatedly bought and sold, inherited and disputed—within the republic. Officials only interceded when rights were disputed, when land became vacant, or when a citizen aimed to sell outside the community.

In the reconstruction, the Spanish regime granted eminent domain to native republics; after all, they were *republics*. They settled local property disputes, reallocated land without claimant, and intervened when a citizen aimed to sell to outsiders—persons not members of the republic, not subject to its rule and review. From the outside, landholding appeared—and was—corporate. Inside, a regime of monetized private rights flourished. In the 1580s, as land became plentiful for a shrinking population, surviving women gained ample shares, silver stimulated commercial ways, and *chinampas* were bought and sold—within the republic.

The tribute obligations grounded in landholding also changed, shifting from diverse goods and labor to maize and silver—and increasingly to silver. Within communities, tribute might be collected from households or by production on designated lands. Authorities in Mexico City levied tributes (calculated by numbers of male-headed households) on communities and expected the republics to pay—by whatever means they could. The regime recognized the eminent domain of the republics in both landholding and revenue taking. Inside, diverse ways of property and production, labor and support for government and religion flourished.

The Culhuacán wills also show that in times of depopulation, surviving notables held ample lands they could not cultivate; with few heirs they regularly sold to Spanish buyers—with or without council approval. The documents on land acquisitions that created estates repeatedly show purchases from native elites or republics, deals later covered by grants from the regime. Why seek royal grants for lands already bought? In case of future dispute—and disputes did come—title under the Crown's domain would prove an advantage. In the late sixteenth century, however, as natives died, lands were plentiful at Culhuacán. They sustained families, republics, and devotions—with surpluses sold to entrepreneurial newcomers.[55]

As the people of Culhuacán adapted around 1600, those in Mexico City faced difficult times even as the silver economy prospered, entrepreneurs flourished, and the regime solidified. Rebuilt on the ruins of Tenochtitlán, the capital faced ecological challenges in a depopulated heartland. Before 1520, the city was sustained first by the produce of the *chinampas* all around, part paid as tributes, much sold as surplus in city markets. As the city grew and Mexica power expanded, tributes brought maize and other staples from Chalco and beyond.

After the siege of 1521, the city population fell from over 150,000 to settle near 80,000 around 1600. While city demand fell by half, the population cultivating *chinampas* dropped by ninety percent. As the Culhuacán testaments show, families easily sustained themselves, but provided limited surpluses. They could only produce so much with remaining hands. Meanwhile, the water-control system essential to maintaining *chinampa* production corroded. Vast drafts of labor had built and maintained dikes and causeways to protect *chinampas* from salinity and keep canals open. The population collapse and the shift of scarce labor to mines and estate harvests left hydraulic maintenance undone.

While *chinampa* cultivation diminished, the city faced rising waters. Floods struck in 1555. In the aftermath, Spanish and indigenous authorities mobilized enough native labor to rebuild the great dike that separated the saline waters of Lake Texcoco from the *chinampas* around the capital. But floods returned in 1580 and again in 1604–7. By then, it was clear that a radically shrunken population and the shift of available labor to the silver economy precluded maintaining the Mexica system of dikes and causeways. Spanish authorities turned to long-debated plans to divert the Cuautitlán River northward, draining its waters into the Mezquital through a tunnel or cut in the mountains. The wet Valley of Mexico might become drier; the capital might face less flooding; the dry Mezquital might become wetter, with more water for irrigation. The project, known as the *desagüe*, began in 1608; devastating floods in 1629 made its limits painfully clear. Work carried on for decades, in time lessening but never eliminating urban inundations. With the drainage, *chinampa* cultivation declined north of the city; it continued around Culhuacán, Xochimilco, and Chalco, preserving the canals pivotal to transport there, too. Southern *chinampa* communities carried on with shrunken populations while city markets relied ever more on maize harvested in outlying republics and wheat irrigated at commercial estates.[56]

By the early 1600s, the ecology of power in the heartland had changed. If wealth still concentrated in the city of Mexico, it now derived first from its role tying New Spain's silver economy to global trade and Spanish power. The city ruled by economic power and judicial mediation, not military force. With depopulation and the decline of *chinampa* cultivation, urban consumers depended on native republics and commercial estates, as depopulation made producers scarce in the republics and workers few at estates. The 1629 floods showed the regime's limited power over water and labor, key elements in a society still agrarian at base. Since the 1570s, imperial officials had worked through native notables to send draft labor to mines, city projects, and estate harvests. By the 1620s, scarce workers refused to serve and native governors refused to press them—not a surprise in republics facing a regime with little coercive power. In the 1630s, officials bowed to reality and ended labor drafts in the heartland—with exceptions for mining and drainage works. It was a liberation that recognized the regime's limited power.[57]

The end of the draft did not end the recruitment of men and boys from landed republics to labor at heartland estates. Rather, labor once mandated—first as unpaid *cuatequil*, then as paid *repartimientos*— became fully commercial. Local leaders continued to organize work gangs. They offered labor to mine operators, urban builders, and estate managers in return for cash—fees to labor captains and wages (generally two reales daily) for workers. Cash flowed into communities to supplement cultivation and craft production. Notables still produced surpluses sold in city markets; commoners sustained themselves: men raising crops, women making cloth and more. The earnings of seasonal labor provided workers with money to pay tributes now calculated in silver, and to spend in rising markets. Villagers bought horses and mules, sheep and chickens, candles and shoes, religious items and fine cloth, in a spreading market economy.

Population scarcity and the consolidation of landed republics enabled heartland villagers to enter the silver economy with a base of ecological autonomy. Notables prospered; commoners sustained families. Where women held ample lands, men's cultivation and cash wages kept patriarchy alive.[58] By the early 1600s, Mesoamerican communities had survived a century of depopulation, adapting to Spanish rule as indigenous republics while joining the commercial ways stimulated by silver. They sustained themselves, sold maize and other native goods in the city and mining towns, and sent workers to harvest wheat and sugar at commercial estates.

The city of Mexico remained the essential metropolis—capital of New Spain, pivot of a globally linked silver economy. Regime power concentrated there: the viceroy who represented a distant king, the audiencia whose judges offered mediating justice, the mint that turned silver into pesos, officials who claimed the king's revenues, and more. There too were the archbishop, a religious-educational establishment, and lead convents of the missionary orders. The city was home to the merchant financiers who integrated New Spain into global trade and the landed entrepreneurs who operated commercial estates, seeking to profit by feeding the city and nearby mines—from the powerful Condes de Santiago whose Atengo estates dominated the southern Valley of Toluca, and the Jesuits whose properties at Santa Lucía ruled the northeast Valley of Mexico, to many more modest growers. Yet to profit and supply the city, landlords great and small had to deal with labor brokers to gain workers from landed republics.

Because seasonal hands were landed cultivators, wages enough to pay tributes and buy goods that enhanced sustenance and provided modest luxuries sufficed. Landed republics thus subsidized estate production and the silver economy by working for wages less than the cost of sustenance. They shaped and carried silver capitalism in two ways: feeding cities and mining towns, while subsidizing profits with low wages.

Social reconstruction came with cultural creations that built on indigenous legacies to understand and facilitate lives tied to a Spanish empire, Roman Church, and global trade. Mesoamericans forged visions of the cosmos and ways of acting in the world that were new and indigenous, changing yet Mesoamerican. As shrinking city-states became republics, they built cultures of governance recorded in Nahuatl. They kept records of administration and markets, wills and land rights, in the language of the Mexica written in the alphabet of Europe. They produced *títulos promordiales*—ancestral titles to land and self-rule asserting ancient rights, independent turns to Christianity, and loyalty to Spain's monarchs. They denied subjection as conquered peopled, asserting local sovereignties in a Christian monarchy.[59]

And heartland communities created Mesoamerican Christianities. As the primordial titles insisted, there was no forced conversion. In times of unimagined plagues, unprecedented death, contested sovereignties, new economic ways, and competing truths—people adapted new understandings seeking meaning for rapidly changing lives. The fall of Tenochtitlán made the power of Huitzilopochtli demonstrably false; his demand for blood had failed to sustain Mexica power. The power of God, the eminence of Spain's monarchy, the profits of silver, and the gains of trade were demonstrably true after 1550—while heartland peoples lived devastating epidemics and the opening of a commercial world blessed by Christianity. Nearly all embraced baptism and the promise of salvation; most testators at Culhuacán sold land to pay for masses to ease a journey to eternal peace. Few Mesoamericans accepted the friars' teachings on sin and penance, as Roa learned at Totolapan in the 1540s and many frustrated clergy lamented around 1600.

Most important, as old powers and practices that had facilitated health and reproduction, rains and cultivation, came into question in times of disease, death, and ecological challenge, Mesoamericans turned to Christ, the Virgin Mary, and diverse saints for compassion, help, and protection. Two dimensions ruled emerging indigenous Christianities: first, an engagement with death evident in devotions to Christ, payments for masses for salvation, and celebrations of the Day of the Dead; second, a search for assistance with life in the world, as revealed in devotions to the Virgin and saints. In both faces of Mesoamerican Christianity, devotions led by notables and funded by republics brought communities together in unity to seek compassion and aid in festivals that centered religious lives that were simultaneously Mesoamerican and Christian.[60]

Indigenous Christianities were not uncontested. In the early 1600s, clergy worked to root out what they saw as idolatry—explicitly Mesoamerican devotions. They were active around Taxco and the southern Valley of Toluca, where they found local men and a few women offering independent ways of curing, calling for rains, and casting difficulties on enemies. Don Hernando Ruiz de Alarcón's 1629 *Treatise on the Heathen Superstitions* reads as a manual of cultivation and curing, detailing native approaches to native crops, local rains, and indigenous maladies. Notably, there were no "superstitious" ways to raise wheat or sugar, mine silver, or cure smallpox.[61] Old World challenges required Christian understandings; enduring indigenous problems kept native ways alive. Around Taxco after 1600, Christian ways and native practices fused in complex lives. Indigenous seers and curers made Spanish clergy and natives who led Christian devotions uneasy; anti-idolatry campaigns did little to limit the mixing of native and Christian devotions.

The campaigns concentrated around Taxco. The early rise of silver there and sugar nearby; the precocious presence of Europeans, Africans, and commercializing ways; and the rapid turn of indigenous peoples to seeking gain in a commercial world while facing rampant disease and death led to a contested cultural life south and west of Mexico City. It is notable that Ruiz de Alarcón led the campaign against "idolatry." He was the ordained son of a Taxco silver entrepreneur, brother of don

Juan Ruiz de Alarcón who reached the heights of power and literary eminence in Spain, sitting on the Council of the Indies and a leading dramatist of Spain's golden age. Did don Hernando's campaign against native practices come from a prodigal son's drive to purify the cultural reverberations of his father's wealth and his brother's power?[62]

Of all the Mesoamerican Christian devotions to rise in the heartland during the era of reconstruction, Our Lady of Guadalupe is best known. Just north of Mexico City, Nahuas around the Tepeyac temple long devoted to Tonantzin—a powerful mother, protector, and promoter of fertility in mothers and milpas (maize plots) in Mexica times—began to look to Guadalupe (who gave similar help to people in Extremadura in southwest Spain) soon after Europeans arrived. By the 1550s, Franciscans were opposing the natives' adoption of Guadalupe—they seemed too independent and She appeared too indigenous. Long debates among Spaniards, clergy and others, reveal widening devotions in the eastern Valley of Mexico. In the face of disease and drought, She offered cures and promised rains— and compassion when they failed. Then, in the 1640s, clergy and others in Mexico City began to promote Guadalupe. Only then was the narrative of Her 1532 appearance to Juan Diego, an indigenous convert, set to text in Nahuatl and Spanish. Did recent struggles against rising waters lead city people to Guadalupe?[63]

Guadalupe was one of many Christian powers engaged by natives across the heartland in the sixteenth and seventeenth centuries. The clergy and others in Mexico City adopted Her as the reconstruction ended. Devotion to Guadalupe was first indigenous, taken up late by the Church and the powerful. Natives ruled religious adaptations. That the clergy finally adopted Guadalupe points to the strength of indigenous devotions and a Spanish search to join, perhaps shape, the Mesoamerican Christianities that ruled the heartland in the 1640s. After a century of reconstruction, indigenous republics in control of their own production, governance, and Christian cultures sat entrenched at the base of a silver economy that fueled global trade.

Consolidation, 1640–1700

After a century of expansion, the silver economies stalled in the 1640s. Production and population at Andean Potosí plummeted; downturn at Zacatecas followed early reverses at Taxco and Pachuca. Mining carried on in New Spain with new finds at Parral far to the north. Global demand for silver slowed owing to wars and dynastic crises in Asia and Europe; costs of production rose as aging mines drove deep underground. As growth stalled in the heartland, production at Parral and other northern centers kept Mexico City important as the center of finance and trade, governance and justice, in New Spain. Its urban population and demand for produce held steady after 1650, while population numbers in heartland republics began to rise. Decades of consolidation saw silver carry on, Mexico City become the first city of the Americas, and heartland republics keep lands, self-rule, and vibrant religious cultures. A dearth of suits over land in the valleys of Mexico and Toluca from the 1620s to the 1680s indicates that in times of limited commercial dynamism and low population, heartland estates and republics carried on with limited conflicts (see appendix, tables A.2, A.3, and A.4).

Stability and scarce documentation have left the decades after 1640 little studied. Yet, key investigations have reached common conclusions about life in the heartland then. In the sugar regions around Cuernavaca, at maize-growing Chalco in the southeast Valley of Mexico, and at the Santa Lucía estates run by the Jesuits in the dry regions where the northeast basin of Mexico extends into the Mezquital, villagers still concentrated in landed communities, estates had small populations including slaves and free people of mixed ancestry, and local notables ruled republics and organized village men and boys to labor seasonally for wages in estate fields. There were frictions within the republics and between estates and communities. But stability reigned as republics and estates combined to feed the city in the middle of the seventeenth century.[64]

The northern Valley of Toluca saw different adaptations. A little-populated frontier between Mexica and Tarascan states in 1520, the post-conquest decades saw Otomí communities on arid lands face invasions by Old World livestock, parallel to the well-known developments just east in the Mezquital. Reconstruction after 1550 brought congregations of declining populations into republics at Ixtlahuaca and Atlacomulco, while Spaniards and native notables built grazing estates. Mines at Tlalpujahua, locally important if secondary to Taxco and Pachuca, brought commercial stimulus, chances to labor, and markets for community and estate produce. When reconstruction ended and silver waned around 1640, the northern Valley of Toluca mixed native republics and commercial estates like the rest of the heartland, but estates held more land and population than in more fertile zones.

Population grew rapidly around Ixtlahuaca after 1640. At first, births and growth focused on estates opening land for cultivation by irrigating the banks of the Lerma River on its way to the Bajío. Young families came to settle after the recession of mining at Taxco and Pachuca, renting land, working in estate fields, and tending livestock. After 1670, Ixtlahuaca's population continued to expand while births and growth shifted to the republics. Had estates gained all the population they needed? Had settlers learned that estate life brought dependence? Sales of staples to mines and Mexico City fell, while local markets flourished. Ixtlahuaca estates used the wool of growing flocks to employ resident natives in *obrajes* making cloth for regional markets. Spanish entrepreneurs and native notables competed for labor on the dry lands of the northern heartland; families planted estate lands and took cash advances. With their harvests in, many left before delivering promised labor. Dependence had limits in times of labor scarcity.[65]

As conflicts eased across the heartland, they peaked in Mexico City's halls of power. When Portugal broke from the Hapsburg monarchy in 1640 just as silver production and oceanic trade waned, financiers of Portuguese ancestry, long pivotal to New Spain's silver economy, were accused of Jewish practices and driven from trade. Merchants and landlords, diverse clergy, established Spaniards, and immigrant newcomers competed for eminence.[66] As silver growth subsided and social consolidation set in, pretenders for power and prestige turned on each other.

Meanwhile, an American Hispanic culture consolidated in the capital. It saw roots in the Mexica past yet found contempt for contemporary natives living in republics, ruled by local councils, strong on the land, and essential to attempts to profit. *Españoles Americanos* imagined descent from Mexica rulers, asserting ancestral rights to rule New Spain.[67] They generated intellectuals of global influence and enduring importance: don Carlos de Sigüenza y Góngora, a promoter of Guadalupe later welcomed at the court of Louis XIV; Sor Juana Inés de la Cruz, daughter of an estate manager in the Chalco uplands who found poetic eminence in a Mexico City convent and the salons of viceroys.[68] The Spanish-Mesoamerican culture that flourished amid conflicts in Mexico City adopted Our Lady of Guadalupe. Most Mesoamericans lived in landed republics, sustaining families, city markets, a slow silver economy, and indigenous Christianities.

CHAPTER THREE

Communities Carrying Capitalism

SYMBIOTIC EXPLOITATIONS, 1700–1810

NEW SPAIN'S silver drove the world economy during the eighteenth century. Production tripled from four million pesos yearly before 1700 to almost thirteen million by 1750, held steady near twelve million through the 1760s, then jumped to average over twenty-three million through the 1790s—peaking at twenty-six million pesos in 1809, before everything collapsed in a combination of imperial crisis and popular insurgency. From 1741 to 1780, New Spain produced over half the world's silver; from 1781 to 1800 its share rose to nearly two-thirds of a larger total. Given the centrality of silver to global commerce, especially to trades linking Europe and Asia, New Spain was a key engine of the world economy during a century of dynamism and transformation.[1]

That dynamism stimulated a vibrant commercial economy in the heartland. Mining rose again at Taxco before 1750 and boomed at Real del Monte, near Pachuca, in the 1760s and 1770s. Mexico City grew as the metropolis that ruled the viceroyalty and financed the silver economies of the heartland, the Bajío, and regions north—where eighteenth-century growth was even more dynamic. As the seat of government and justice, center of Church administration and education, home to the merchants who financed mining and trade and to the landed clans that ruled the heartland agricultural economy, all served by growing numbers of professionals, artisans, shopkeepers, and servants, the city grew past 130,000 around 1800.

It still drew most sustenance from the heartland basins where estates jostled republics. But through the century after 1700, growing numbers of villagers faced land shortages, as populations more than doubled while community landholdings could not expand. Meanwhile, estate production expanded to profit by supplying growing city markets. Commercial dynamism mixed with rising inequities within communities. It might have been a recipe for conflict. But the persistence of landed republics, the regime's defense of their right to land and to redress in the courts, and the dependence of commercial growers on men and boys drawn from republics to plant and harvest essential crops led to symbiotic exploitations. Estates and communities locked together in negotiated ties of inequity essential to the profits of the former and the survival of the latter. Together they sustained social stability and a rising silver economy through the eighteenth century. While social violence marked the Andes from the 1740s through the 1780s and shook the Bajío in the 1760s and again after 1810, heartland communities carried silver capitalism.

Silver Boom and Commercial Adaptation, 1680–1750

Around 1700 the political economy of the Mexican heartland seemed set: Mexico City linked New Spain to Spain and the world economy, while indigenous republics and commercial estates shared surrounding basins. Most people lived in republics; much land belonged to estates. They were linked in an economy in which natives sustained themselves and sent indigenous goods to the city, while estates hired villagers seasonally to produce Old World crops for urban consumers. City landlords and traders, native notables, and the courts integrated everything. A Hispanic Christian culture ruled in the city; indigenous Christian devotions shaped life in the republics—linked together by the Church and devotion to Guadalupe. As the new century began, the heartland was a society of parallel economies and integrated inequalities.

New challenges came soon. Population nearly doubled from 1690 to 1735. The city grew from about 80,000 to 100,000 (we lack censuses). Growing numbers called for increased food production, while the great majority still concentrated in republics that could rarely expand their landholdings. Land disputes rose in the valleys of Mexico and Toluca from 1690, to peak in 1710 (see appendix, tables A.3 and A.4). In 1692, the people of Mexico City rioted when drought made food scarce and costly. City folk believed that powerful men, including the viceroy, were profiteering while the people paid in hunger. Crowds of native women and men, soon joined by mulattoes and mestizos, burned the viceroy's palace and sacked markets. The demise of historic hydraulic works and the decline of *chinampa* cultivation had left the city dependent on rain-fed lands to

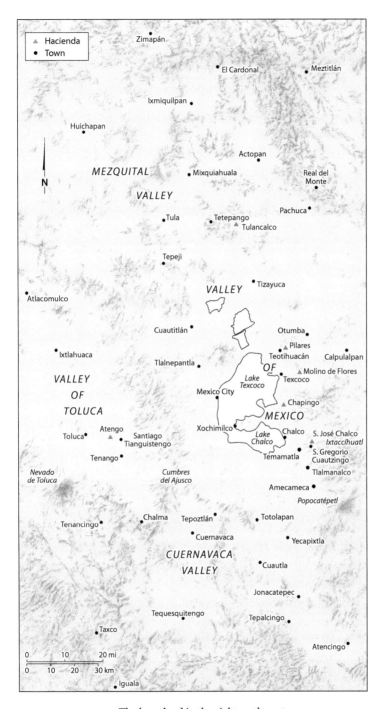

MAP 5. The heartland in the eighteenth century.

supply maize and other native staples. New population growth kept maize in the republics to feed growing families while urban needs rose. Drought brought scarcities and chances for speculators during a downturn in the silver economy. As the new century approached, speculators profited and city people rioted.[2]

Yet the pressures revealed by rural land disputes and city riots did not lead to social crisis or structural change in the heartland. Carlos II, the last Spanish Hapsburg, died in 1700 without heir. In the War of Spanish Succession that followed, France and Britain built factions within Spain and alliances across Europe to fight on Spanish soil to set a new monarch in Madrid. Yet a decade of contested power in Spain brought little conflict to New Spain. Instead, after 1700 the rising pressures revealed by rural land conflicts and urban riots were absorbed in the heartland by adaptations of established ways of life and production, sustained by a reviving silver economy.

City riots came in 1692; rural land suits peaked around 1710 and then declined into the 1740s. Rural population continued to grow until the *matlazáhuatl* (typhus) epidemic of 1738–39.[3] Pressures within the republics persisted for decades, yet land conflicts eased after 1710. The rise in land disputes in the 1680s suggests that population growth began then or earlier, before the 1692 tribute counts. The resulting limits on maize surpluses—suddenly shrunken by drought—fueled the profiteering and city riots of the same year. To officials, the riots marked the limit of urban tolerance for scarce and costly maize. Heartland estate operators saw opportunities.

Rising silver production brought expanding urban markets. Demand for staples rose while silver profits made capital available for landed investment—following the long-established path of taking wealth claimed in risky mining and trade and investing in commercial estates.[4] As population rose, village surpluses waned, and silver soared, heartland estates turned to raising native staples, notably maize and pulque, for commercial gain.

In republics established more than a century earlier, population growth left rising numbers of families short of land, thus facing declining autonomies.[5] Nahuatl-language wills left by notables and commoners, men and women, in dozens of communities in the grain-growing Valley of Toluca show how land shortages resonated in native households.[6] Notable clans continued to rule locally, hold local offices, lead community worship, and keep large areas of land they still used to raise marketable surpluses—mostly maize. Most commoner households still held lands, but they were reduced every generation and inheritance concentrated what remained. A favored heir, often an eldest son, gained the family house and lot (including garden lands) and enough outlying land for household sustenance—but rarely any surplus. Other heirs might gain a bit of land, or none. Women had been regular heirs in late sixteenth-century Culhuacán (a time of population decline); after 1700 around Toluca they gained land much less often than their brothers. In the absence of male heirs, daughters did inherit town lots, houses, gardens, and outlying lands. In new times of population pressure, women were prejudiced—not excluded. While cultivation remained men's work, women ruled production and sale of pulque and trade in local markets. Patriarchy strengthened even as some women prospered.

The heartland estates that gained lands around 1600 had focused on Old World staples: sugar around Cuernavaca, wheat in the central and southern valleys of Mexico and Toluca, livestock in the dry zones north of Toluca and in the Mezquital. After 1700, as city demand rose and native surpluses shrank, estates added commercial fields of maize and pulque. The Condes de Santiago, the greatest of landlords since the late sixteenth century, added maize to wheat and livestock grazing at the vast Atengo properties near Toluca. In the Valley of Mexico, the Jesuits acquired San José de Chalco and Chapingo near Texcoco to become major maize growers.

The transition at San José de Chalco (shown in figure 3.1), the largest cereal grower in the heartland, reveals much. Before 1700, the estate mostly raised wheat on irrigated fields, planting maize only to feed workers and hogs. Responding to new markets, from 1717 to 1721 San José harvested an average of 781 cargas of wheat and 2,126 cargas of maize. Between 1732 and

FIGURE 3.1. The hacienda as Jesuit (later liberal) capitalist enterprise: San José de Chalco, alias La Compañía, eighteenth to nineteenth centuries.

1738, wheat increased forty percent to average 1,076 cargas; maize more than tripled to averaged 6,627 cargas. The rapid rise in estate production of the native staple required a parallel increase in seasonal hands from nearby republics. The Jesuits profited in supplying city markets, funding colleges for sons of the rich and powerful. Native notables gained fees to organize work gangs. Village men and boys earned wages allowing them to remain villagers as families grew and land became scarce.[7]

A different transition led to parallel outcomes in the lowlands around Cuernavaca.[8] Sugar estates faced declining production and profitability around 1680, as decades of cane planting exhausted soil nutrients. Sugar for the capital and Taxco mines came from newer estates near Tenancingo, south of the Toluca basin, and in Gulf and Pacific lowlands. Cuernavaca estates began to lease ranchos to small growers of mixed ancestry who shifted from sugar to maize, often on irrigated fields. They too recruited villagers to plant and harvest crops that supplied Taxco mines and Mexico City markets. Irrigated lowland maize suffered less from drought; it complemented new commercial plantings in the valleys of Mexico and Toluca to meet rising demand in Mexico City. The shift to estate-grown maize held prices of the essential native staple steady at affordable levels in Mexico City into the mid-1730s.[9]

A parallel rise of estate production transformed the supply of pulque to the capital. In the northeast Valley of Mexico and the Mezquital, rainfall was sparse and irregular; early sheep grazing brought a desiccation that earned the name Mezquital—a dry land covered with sparse mesquite.[10] Otomí peoples—subject to the Mexica before 1520—inhabited most republics, holding rights to land and self-rule, adapting devotions to guide, integrate, and protect struggling communities.[11] As scarce rains and dry lands left maize harvests insecure, they tapped ubiquitous maguey to make pulque for city taverns and the mines at Pachuca and Real del Monte, where they also sold maguey fronds as combustible.

Facing population growth after 1700, villagers consumed all the maize they could raise—and much of their pulque. Meanwhile, demand for pulque grew in Mexico City and at Real del Monte, where mining accelerated from the 1730s. In the same decade, the Jesuits sent the great herds of sheep that grazed at the Santa Lucía estates to northern pastures, and began to transplant vast fields of maguey to tap for pulque. Soon, don Manuel Rodríguez de Pedroso, a Spanish immigrant merchant trading silver across the globe, bought lands to do the same.

They aimed to profit supplying Mexico City taverns, *pulquerías*. There were constraints: pulque spoiled in twenty-four hours; commercial

success required great fields tapped daily, fermented quickly—and delivered rapidly. The dry lands from the north shore of Lake Texcoco reaching
northeast to Otumba, Apan, and the southern Mezquital met the need: a
mule trip to the lake then a transfer to canoes got the drink to city taverns
on time. Estates transplanted wide fields of young plants, waited five years
for maturity, and tapped just enough daily to supply the market. Plants remained ripe for fifteen years, then the cycle of transplanting, maturation,
and tapping began again.

Maguey flourished on the driest of fields; there was no need to displace
maize. Periodic transplanting employed large gangs of workers for a few
weeks or months. But few worked during years of maturation, and production required little labor. Tapping the sap (*tlachique*) and fermenting it
into pulque employed a few skilled *tlachiqueros*, mostly Otomí; transport
required a few more men, often of mixed ancestry. By 1750, the Jesuits
and Rodríguez de Pedroso each supplied twenty percent of the Mexico
City market; their success drew others to the business. But, except during
sporadic transplanting, commercial pulque offered little labor to Otomí
villagers.[12]

After 1700, as commercial estates took on the provision of maize and
pulque to Mexico City, urban consumers were well served. Maize prices
held steady to the mid-1730s, rose modestly into the mid-1750s, and then
dropped until the 1770s.[13] Growers profited most when they could hold
crops until years of drought cut harvests and raised prices. Meanwhile,
in good years and bad, men and boys in republics earned seasonal wages,
enabling them to feed families as population grew. They mixed declining cultivation with new dependence on seasonal labor to keep solid patriarchal roles as family providers. In contrast, pulque estate operators
profited supplying Mexico City taverns while providing little labor to men
and boys desperate for income. Otomí men faced insecurities in providing sustenance and uncertainties sustaining patriarchy in struggling rural
households.

The Toluca Valley Nahuatl testaments reveal adaptations of community organization, family relations, and local devotions in times of growing
population, land shortages, and new dependence on seasonal labor. Land
sales became rare. Wills became the primary means of land transfer; local
officials became omnipresent witnesses, testifying to the republics' ultimate domain—and to testators' and recipients' rights to use.[14] Meanwhile,
there was a turn to the local in community identities and to the personal
in religious practices. The republics combining head towns and outlying
villages persisted. But many villages went to court to claim independence,

and wills show that many simply acted as if they had won.[15] Community devotions held strong, focusing more on the village than the republic. Close neighbors joined to seek protection in the face of drought and cures in times of disease, reinforcing unity under local notables' sponsorship.

There was also a new emphasis on household saints. Most families had many saints—Virgins, Christs, and others, male and female. There was a shift away from Christ—so central to natives facing the sixteenth-century dying—and toward the Virgin, who offered compassion and assistance with rains, illness, and other challenges in times of pressures on the land. Households rarely capable of accumulating lands sought aid and protection by accumulating saints. They were purchased, owned, and inherited. Saints could be reproduced; land could not. When houses were left to favored heirs—favored saints went along. When other heirs gained little or no land, they still received saints. As land became scarce and concentrated in male hands, saints served, protected, and offered compassion to those who inherited little or nothing.[16]

New relationships marked ties among republics, villages, and households. Head towns retained full councils with a governor and magistrates, sponsored major festivals devoted to patron saints, and asserted domain over lands. Villages promoted their own devotions and festivals and claimed domain over lands. Households kept usage rights to family lands, most passed by inheritance from men to men. Households also focused on personal and familial devotions.[17]

The search for independence by outlying villagers came as small but prosperous and locally powerful groups of Spaniards and others engaged in trade, crafts, transport, and other activities in head towns. They joined clans of indigenous notables, sometimes marrying in to gain roles in local governance and religion and shares of land, even as holdings shrank for the majority. Local office and landholding required *indio* status; many Hispanic newcomers married into native elite families, asserted *indio* rights, and prospered in head towns.[18] The de la Cruz clan dominated Tepemajalco, south of Toluca, to the 1750s. They held ample lands, council offices, and religious leadership. Yet the name de la Cruz often marked mulatto origins in New Spain, a dedication to Christ of children born to African men and indigenous women—free by birthright, yet of uncertain rights.[19] Had the locally eminent de la Cruz of Tepemajalco come out of the crucible of mixing at nearby Taxco and Cuernavaca to become powerful "native" notables?

As power and Hispanic outsiders concentrated in head towns, commoners looked to villages and households, personal saints and local devotions. They deepened cultural autonomy in times of declining access to land and growing reliance on wage work—labor organized by village brokers more often than by officials of the republic. As population grew and land became scarce, head towns tied the republics to the regime and regional trade, while villages and families focused on land retention, wage labor, and worship. The republics were never egalitarian; life was fraught with contradictions—that heartland peoples negotiated with skill after 1700.

Midcentury Challenges: Disease, Recession, and Resistance 1735–70

While the silver economy and hacienda production continued to expand until midcentury, people in heartland communities faced new challenges from the 1730s. After a half century of population growth, *matlazáhuatl* struck in 1736–37, followed by smallpox in 1761–62.[20] Populations declined as land disputes stabilized—to decline in the 1740s (see appendix, tables A.3 and A.4).[21] Heartland villagers again faced the grief of deadly diseases and relief from pressures on the land. The drop of rural population allowed more maize, now often harvested on estate fields, to flow to Mexico City. Prices there fell from the 1730s, and stayed low into the 1770s. City consumers gained ample, affordable supplies.[22]

New Spain's silver production passed ten million pesos yearly during the epidemics of the 1730s, rising to nearly thirteen million in the early 1750s. Commercial stimulus held strong as villagers struggled. Then, Chinese demand fell and silver production stabilized near twelve million pesos yearly through the 1760s; from 1756 to 1763 war disrupted trade and led the regime to seek new revenues.[23] After decades when population, production, and trade grew together, the heartland faced midcentury population decline, commercial stagnation, and revenue pressures.

The Mexico City archbishop ordered censuses in the 1760s that detail life across the heartland.[24] They confirm that in fertile agricultural zones—the eastern Valley of Mexico, the central Valley of Toluca, the hot lands to the south—indigenous families still concentrated in republics, mostly in outlying villages. Hispanic residents lived in head towns—and at sugar estates where slaves and their mulatto descendants formed cores of permanent workers. Native villagers cultivated as they could and sent men and boys seasonally to harvest sugar, wheat, and maize. In the uplands west of Toluca, people were more dispersed, mixing cultivation, grazing, and labor at nearby mines. On the dry northern lands around

Ixtlahuaca and Atlacomulco, about half the population lived in republics, half as tenants and workers at estates.

As heartland people faced *matlazáhuatl* in 1736–39 and then years of drought, death came punctuated by scarcity. Many villagers moved to survive: some went north to settle on estates north of Toluca or in the Bajío. Others went south seeking work at reviving sugar estates. Typhus proved less deadly in the hot country, where drought was less severe and irrigation could expand; seasonal work in cane fields and maize lands kept many alive in hard years. Meanwhile, highland estates planting maize in years of death and drought lamented labor shortages. Then, as the years of challenge passed, communities witnessed a great (re)marrying. Survivors rebuilt family households; in the 1760s population began to grow again.

During midcentury times of challenge, popular movements stirred the heartland. A deeply religious wave spread across the rich agricultural zones around Chalco and the Cuautla hotlands. While villagers adapting to shrinking landholdings and greater reliance on wage work faced typhus and drought—the enlightened, census-taking archbishop turned against indigenous Christianities. He withdrew many of the friars who had adapted to local devotions, replacing them with diocesan priests who reported directly to the Mexico City cathedral. Archbishop and clergy worked to end community devotions, especially the passion plays, common since the sixteenth century, invoking Christ's compassion for villagers' sufferings. Communities and families negotiated, resisted, and turned to household devotions beyond the clergy's reach. Villagers still sought compassion and assistance from their saints, often at home; they resisted a "rational" religion focused on sin and morality.[25]

In 1760, Antonio Pérez became a revered holy man in the uplands between Chalco and Cuernavaca—with devotees in both basins. The region was renowned for religious creativity. The uplands had spawned the Christ at Totolapan in the 1540s; after Augustinian friars took him to Mexico City in 1580, a new Christ with a wider following rose just west at Chalma. Sor Juana Inés de la Cruz grew up on an estate in the pass between Chalco and Cuautla in the mid-1600s. And there, Antonio found his calling and congregations in 1760. He had been a shepherd in the uplands, fluent in Spanish and Nahuatl. A friar introduced him to healing prescriptions linked to standard prayers, and Antonio began to innovate. He found an image of the Virgin on the slopes of Popocatépetl, the great volcano above Chalco. He became her servant, offering healing and rains, cures for a crisis set off by typhus and drought. He carried a Host of maize, sanctifying the indigenous staple. He made God and Christ into maize—and maize into God and Christ. He became priest and prophet of a native Christian revival and found receptive communities from Chalco to Cuautla and beyond. In a last prophecy, Antonio saw an epidemic and earthquake that killed all Spaniards (most American-born)—while the Devil carried off the archbishop. The heartland would belong to native villagers, free to cultivate and worship as they wished.[26]

The priest at Yecapixtla, on Popocatépetl's shoulder, captured Antonio as he preached to more than 100 devotees. Interrogations of the prophet and a dozen followers revealed 500 active participants in a region one hundred kilometers north to south, from Chalco through the mountains and across the Cuernavaca lowlands. Arrests and interrogations ended public devotions; many surely carried on in isolated uplands. Antonio and his devotees did not oppose Christianity; they revived and revised deeply indigenous Christian devotions to face hard times. Meanwhile, communities pursued resources. In 1763 San Francisco Acuautla in the hills above Chalco rioted to press a dispute with the hacienda Zoquiapan over access to the *montes*—wooded uplands that enabled families to cut wood, make charcoal, and plant small plots of maize. The jostling remained in the hills and the courts, making community needs clear and limiting estate power.[27]

Soon after villagers in the southern heartland turned to Antonio for hope, workers at Real del Monte rioted for labor rights. The 1760s brought new life to the mines. Don Pedro Romero de Terreros had taken capital gained in trade at Querétaro in the Bajío to invest in new shafts and deep drainage. Costs were high, while demand for silver dipped in the 1750s and into the 1760s. To continue the work, Romero cut the ore shares that rewarded skilled workers and reduced the wages of men facing danger underground. Hardened mine workers with essential skills faced lower salaries and ore shares. Men from outlying Otomí republics saw wages decline. In 1766 they rioted, took over the mines, killed a manager, and almost captured Romero. They returned to work only when a high-court judge backed by Mexico City militias promised better pay—and forced Romero to acquiesce. The judge mediated to resume silver production and employment.[28]

While people across the heartland struggled through midcentury difficulties, turning to religious revivals in fertile southern zones, land disputes in wooded uplands, and labor protests at Real del Monte, population growth resumed. Silver production soared after 1770 and land conflicts escalated again. Still, most found resolution in the courts (see appendix, tables A.3 and A.4). Stability returned.

Power and Inequities on the Land, 1770–1810

After 1770, populations rose steadily, intensifying pressures on families with limited lands; silver, the city, and the commercial economy boomed, generating new demand for staples and labor; a combination of frost and drought brought unprecedented famine in 1785–86. Then in the 1790s Atlantic wars created new demand for silver while shipping and trade faced repeated disruptions. It might have been the perfect recipe for social conflict and instability. Instead, life in the heartland proved remarkably peaceable and notably stable until 1810. The explanation lies in the consolidation of symbiotic exploitations—structures of inequity so essential to the profit of the few and the survival of the majority that the latter rarely challenged them.

New Spain's silver production rose from twelve million pesos yearly in the 1760s to reach twenty million yearly in the early 1780s; it dipped a bit in the famine of 1785–86 and then rose to hold between twenty-three and twenty-six million pesos annually from 1790 to 1809. It all passed through Mexico City, where the population approached 150,000—by far the largest and richest city in the Americas (see appendix, table A.2). Opportunities for profit were strong.[29] A few great entrepreneurs claimed most of the benefits in agriculture. They led Mexico City clans that over the centuries had invested the profits of mining and trade in estates operated as commercial enterprises. Some, like the Condes de Santiago, had held strong on the land since 1600. More, like the Conde de Regla who purchased Santa Lucía and other rich Jesuit estates after the expulsion of 1767, took capital from commerce and mining to secure wealth in estates.[30] A few dozen powerful clans operated about half the estates that profited supplying the capital; they focused on cereals and pulque in the heartland—leaving sugar and its higher capital costs to upstart merchants. Many operated rich properties in the Bajío and across dry grazing lands far to the north. More than a hundred lesser families struggled to compete, most also based in the capital and limited to smaller properties nearby.[31]

Among the great clans, concentrations of estates in one zone were complemented by strategic dispersals in a search for enduring profitability. The Santiago's Atengo estates ruled the central and southern Valley of Toluca; the family also held the irrigated Molino de Flores in the east near Texcoco, and developed pulque at Tulancalco in the southern Mezquital. The Jesuits dominated around Santa Lucía from the northeast Valley of Mexico into the Mezquital, leading the turn to commercial pulque in the eighteenth century. They also owned San José, the leading cereal estate at Chalco. After the order's expulsion in 1767, don Pedro Romero de Terreros claimed the Santa Lucía properties (to supply his Real del Monte mines), but not San José de Chalco. The plan of the great clans is clear: concentrate to rule a region or the market in one commodity; diversify into other crops and regions.[32]

There was a parallel mix of concentration and diversification in the larger estate economy that supplied Mexico City. A survey of estate products in the tithe district of Otumba, ranging from the fertile shores of Lake Texcoco around Acolman and Teotihuacán, through the pulque lands of Otumba, to the livestock zone around Calpulalpan to the northeast is revealing. Near the lake, where irrigation complemented good rains, estates focused on wheat, maize, and barley, yet also produced pulque and grazed some livestock. Moving inland and upland, as lands became drier wheat disappeared while maize persisted to complement a focus on pulque, barley, and livestock. Farther from the lake and city markets, maize, pulque, and barley remained while grazing ruled; hogs were a regional specialty (they walked to market).[33] Focus and diversification grounded late eighteenth-century agrarian capitalism in the heartland.

Profit was good, especially for those with large and diverse operations. An account of operations in 1782 for the dozens of estates left by don Pedro Romero de Terreros, Conde de Regla, showed profits of 8 percent.[34] Accounts for two large haciendas operated for the minor Marquesa de Vivanco from 1800 to 1805 report profits in years of changing rains and markets. At the great cereal estate of Chapingo, south of Texcoco, annual profits varied from 2.5 to 10.5 percent, averaging 6. At Ojo de Agua, a leading pulque producer north of Texcoco, profits stayed close to a six-year average over 7 percent.[35]

Profits were less for growers with limited capital and smaller, less diversified properties, often holding closer to the five percent charged by ecclesiastical bankers for the mortgage funds that struggling professionals tapped to enter the estate economy. Still, landed entrepreneurs, great and modest, profited and lived in prosperity in the capital city they sustained.[36]

Life was radically different in heartland republics. The wills from communities in the central Valley of Toluca, where villagers faced the Atengo estates of the Condes de Santiago, document a continuing concentration of lands among men and a minority of women after 1770. Family holdings shrank every generation; growing numbers inherited little or nothing. Men still cultivated—in most cases three or fewer scattered plots. Women still made and sold pulque and traded in local markets.[37] A minority of notables, often officials of the republics and religious leaders, prospered; most families struggled to get by.

Yet many republics, especially head towns, held lands not allocated to families, but used to gain income for local government and religious festivals. Some were cultivated by community labor, their produce sold to fund community affairs. Often lands were leased to Hispanic families to operate as ranchos, seeking a bit of profit while paying rents that funded local councils and their activities. A survey of the Texcoco region in 1809 indicated that four large towns gained income from land rents: Texcoco earned 1,010 pesos yearly, Tepetlaoxtoc 283 pesos from land rents alone, Papalotla gained 164 pesos, and Chiautla 80 pesos from land rents and water fees.[38]

In the Otumba jurisdiction around 1800, all four head towns reported land rents, maize sales, and pulque sales. The old head town of Otumba was not the richest in land or income. That distinction belonged to Axapusco, which annually gained 770 pesos in pulque sales, 522 pesos in land rents, and 40 pesos from maize sales, for a total of 1,332 pesos of income. Otumba claimed 236 pesos in land rents, 150 pesos in pulque sales, and only 60 pesos from maize—a total of 446 pesos. Ostoticpac collected 434 pesos, mostly from 284 pesos in rents. The poorest of the four, Cuautlanzingo, earned but 210 pesos, three-quarters from maize. The Otumba republics all used community land to gain corporate earnings, while many families were struggling to survive.[39]

Records from three of the four in 1794 show that leasing benefited Hispanic rancheros closely tied to community notables. Axapusco leased to fifteen tenants; Otumba to nine, Ostoticpac to five; they planted from less than one to nearly ten fanegas of maize and paid rents averaging ten pesos per fanega. Planting one fanega easily sustained a family, as yields were fifty to a hundred to one and a family consumed ten to fifteen fanegas a year. The majority of tenants were modest commercial growers, easily sustaining families and taking small profits in regional markets.[40] Some were members of local notable families; others were resident Hispanic families, some classed as Spaniards, others as Mestizos. Officials of the republics leased lands to themselves, kin, and allies who might soon become kin. Community elites became hispanized: they used Spanish surnames and spoke Spanish and Nahuatl (or Otomí); they produced for sustenance and for markets, hiring local men and boys on their lands—while organizing the same commoners to labor at nearby estates. Leasing corporate lands reinforced the local elites, who tied communities, their lands, and their labors into the economy focused on Mexico City.[41]

Meanwhile, inequities deepened and land shortages spread. San Gregorio Cuautzingo (its modest church shown in figure 3.2) sat next to

FIGURE 3.2. Community locked in symbiotic exploitations:
the church at San Gregorio Cuautzingo.

San José de Chalco on the Chalco plain, still Mexico City's primary granary. A court suit led to a survey of community lands, redistribution,
and a second survey. In 1790, 112 households held a total of 224 plots of
cropland. Two plots were "available" per household, plus house lots with
gardens. But generations of population growth and inheritance had led
to unequal distribution. Four favored households held five to seven plots
each, enabling modest comfort. Just over half the community, sixty-seven
households, had two to four plots. Four plots produced basic sustenance;
the three plots worked by forty families produced less than a year's food;
two plots were clearly insufficient. Five households had a house lot and
one plot—and twenty-seven had only a lot and garden. Nine families had
nothing—no house lot, no garden, no land to plant. Including house lots
with gardens, over ninety percent of the community held some land; less
than seventy percent planted croplands. Only four households had enough
for ample sustenance. The great majority had to look for supplemental
income. A large minority gained little or nothing from community lands
(see appendix, table A.5).

After the 1790 survey, the judge ordered a redistribution; there was protest and contest. An 1800 survey reveals why: San Gregorio had grown to 127 households. The new survey listed landholdings by area, not by plots, documenting how small the plots were. In 1800, no family had a full hectare of land. Seven held 0.8–0.9 hectares, about 2 acres each; two others had 1.5 to 2 acres. Redistribution led to a new concentration, or concentrating inheritances had intervened. Now, nine favored households held enough land for solid sustenance. The reallocation also led to broader sharing in the middle: in 1800, thirty-four families worked from 0.3 to 0.6 hectares; another thirty-five had but 0.1 to 0.3. The majority could raise a greater or lesser part of sustenance—never full family support. A group of thirty listed as having *poco* (little) surely held only house lots—up from twenty-seven. The descriptor *poco* shows that house lots at San Gregorio, like those near Toluca, were subdivided over the years to provide for a growing population and by 1800 allowed only small gardens. After redistribution, the landless increased from nine to thirteen households. Those with *poco* or nothing were a third of San Gregorio's households in 1800 (see appendix, table A.6).

Such surveys and redistributions were rare. The outcome at San Gregorio suggests why. The power of local notables endured. A few pressed for redistribution and they alone gained. Distribution upward led to a wider sharing of insufficiency in the middle; landlessness spread at the base. As population grew, land could not. The majority planted some maize, chile, and frijol, rarely enough for family support. Growing numbers were land-poor or landless. At San Gregorio, as across the heartland, after 1770 most families had to look beyond their lands for sustenance. Many communities had *montes*, woodlands where residents cut firewood, made charcoal, gathered a bit, perhaps planted a small maize plot. Women tapped maguey and made pulque, selling to neighbors; they made cloth to wear and sell in local markets. All this was possible thanks to community lands—however badly distributed. But community produce was rarely enough, sending men and boys to work for wages at estates flourishing all around.

Labor as Symbiotic Exploitation, 1770–1810

While estates expanded production to feed the city and take profits, the great majority across the heartland lived in republics with lands ever less adequate to growing populations. Their needs made labor available to the haciendas—labor that was flexible, affordable, and negotiated in ways that made estate-community relations symbiotic, exploitative, and generally stable.

The concentration of population in the republics is documented for four Valley of Mexico jurisdictions in 1790.[42] Ixtapalapa lay just south of Mexico City, near Culhuacán, in a zone of *chinampa* cultivation along the canal that delivered produce from Chalco and sugar basins south. There, ninety-four percent of the population (a third classed as Hispanic) lived in the town and its villages, only six percent at small estates. To the east at Chimalhuacán Chalco, between Texcoco and Chalco, ninety-three percent of a population that was ninety-four percent indigenous lived in communities. Just north at Huexotla, near Texcoco, ninety-one percent of a population ninety-six percent indigenous resided in communities. In contrast, at Calpulalpan, northeast of Otumba at the dry edge of the heartland, fewer than sixty percent lived in republics (seventy-three percent indigenous). Among the forty percent living as estate tenants and employees, sixty-three percent were indigenous.

Differing ecological conditions and economic orientations shaped the heartland. In the fertile cereal zones of the central and southern valleys of Mexico and Toluca, estate residents were few. The growers that supplied grains to the capital recruited nearly all their workers from nearby republics. In the pulque zone of the northeast Valley of Mexico and the Mezquital, estates also recruited workers from nearby republics—more sporadically and in smaller numbers. In drier areas from the northern Valley of Toluca, through the northern Mezquital, to Calpulalpan and Apan, where arable land was scarce and distance prevented selling pulque in the capital, estates focused on livestock grazing, cultivating only where irrigation allowed. There, estates recruited larger populations of residents, often tenants—yet they were still minorities. To the south, sugar estates in the warm, often-irrigated Cuautla and Cuernavaca basins also kept core minorities of resident workers, some still enslaved, most free mulatto descendants of slaves and native women.[43] The mix of cultivation and refining that made sugar an agro-industry required more permanent workers. Still, the majority of men who planted cane and provided labor in harvest and grinding seasons came from nearby republics.

Commercial cultivation required minorities of permanent employees, mostly supervisory and skilled personnel—more in sugar, few in cereals, very few for pulque. Seasonal hands did most work: men and boys hired to transplant maguey and to plant and harvest wheat, maize, and cane. Seasonal needs came in cycles of years at pulque estates, months at cereal and sugar properties. By employing workers seasonally, estates maximized profits. By paying wages to men and boys to supplement cultivation on ever less adequate community lands, seasonal labor allowed men to reinforce patriarchal claims while families still lived in the republics.

Before focusing on the seasonal labor that was the pivot of symbiotic exploitation, a look at the lives and earnings of the few long-term dependent workers at heartland estates is revealing. Estate accounts reveal three types: *sirvientes*, employees of Hispanic culture and often mixed ancestry; *tlachiqueros*, indigenous men who tapped maguey and fermented pulque; and *gañanes*, resident native day laborers often allowed to use small plots of land. They served different roles and gained differing remunerations in different basins.

Sirvientes were lesser managers, field supervisors, herdsmen, muleteers and carters, and skilled craftsmen such as blacksmiths and carpenters. The term *sirviente* does not translate as servant (household servants were *criados*). Also called *dependiente*—dependent—the closest equivalent in English is employee. They were few in numbers, decreasing as the livestock that required constant care moved north after 1700. At Pilares, a small cereal estate near Acolman, during five years in the 1790s, twenty men were employed to provide an average of seven not-so-permanent *sirvientes*. They earned salaries of three pesos monthly, plus two reales and a *cuartilla* of maize weekly, for a yearly total of fifty pesos and twelve fanegas of maize (the staple at no charge). That was basic family sustenance in the rural heartland. Yet only one man remained a *sirviente* at Pilares for the five years; the rest came for a year or two and moved on.[44]

Work as a *sirviente* was a step toward manhood among a rural Hispanic minority that worked ranchos (often leased from indigenous republics) and ran mule trains. To attract young Hispanic men, estates offered advances of salaries or maize. Holding them proved difficult, as the Pilares accounts document. Reclaiming advances was often impossible. The Santiago's Atengo properties had large numbers of *sirvientes*, dozens each on estates dispersed among Toluca basin communities. When the properties passed to a new generation in 1800, a dispute arose when no heir would accept *sirvientes'* outstanding debts. They were uncollectable and no guarantee of work, dependence, or permanence. *Sirvientes* repeatedly moved on, keeping advances that operators saw as a cost of business, borne unhappily.[45] For a few Hispanic men in the heartland, work as *sirvientes* provided steady income and guaranteed maize to sustain young families until they could find a rancho and offer transport service.

Scarcer than *sirvientes* were *tlachiqueros*, also called *sirvientes* and *dependientes*, the only indigenous men so labeled. When leading estate operators took over pulque production and marketing in the eighteenth century, they turned grazing lands in the northeast Valley of Mexico and the southern Mezquital into fields of maguey, hiring gangs of village men and boys for a few months of transplanting. They used financial power and political connections to gain a near monopoly of Mexico City *pulquerías*. Yet the skill of tapping maguey for its sap (*tlachique*) and fermenting it to make pulque remained an indigenous monopoly. Women in Nahua and Otomí communities across the heartland made pulque and sold it locally. The presumptions of Spanish entrepreneurs led them to insist that indigenous men do the work on commercial estates. They divided their holdings into ranchos, each occupying one to three *tlachiqueros* to tap maguey, ferment *tlachique* into pulque in a *tinacal*, and quickly send it to city taverns.

At Pilares, two *tlachiqueros* remained through the five years of accounts. They earned twelve reales (1.5 pesos) weekly, thus sixty-five pesos a year, plus twelve fanegas of maize. *Tlachiqueros* were indigenous, but with skills essential to the most profitable sector of the estate economy, they got cash incomes higher than most Hispanic *sirvientes*—and maize rations, too. *Tlachiqueros* were few, so entrepreneurs could afford them. In dry zones where Nahuas and Otomí faced population growth, limited lands, and few chances for earnings beyond the sporadic work of transplanting maguey, *tlachiqueros* stayed on the job while their kin in nearby villages struggled.[46]

Gañanes—indigenous workers and families permanently living at estates—were more numerous than Hispanic *sirvientes* and native *tlachiqueros* in the heartland, yet still a small minority. A 1793 census of the Intendancy of Mexico reported fifteen percent of the indigenous population as *gañanes*—but the jurisdiction reached north to San Juan del Río and Querétaro, regions of the Bajío where half the natives, most Otomí, lived on estates.[47] In the heartland, fewer than ten percent of natives lived as estate dependents, most at larger properties near upland margins or in dry northern zones.

Many, perhaps most, heartland estates had no *gañanes*. One property near Mexico City reported twenty-nine huts for *gañanes*, another forty-three; the large Chapingo and Atengo holdings included a few more. In the southern Mezquital, the adjoining Temoaya and Tulancalco estates reported twenty-five *gañan* families each, for a total of 212 native residents. In 1810, Tulancalco's *gañanes* earned 1.5 reales daily, while men recruited in nearby villages got 2; all had to buy maize at market prices; none were guaranteed year-round work.[48] *Gañanes* were a landless minority facing dependence with limited security, paid less than day laborers. Some descended from families who had sought security in estate residence long ago; others had turned to the haciendas during mid-eighteenth-century times of disruption.[49] Men with any land usually stayed in villages, cultivating as they could, taking wages seasonally.

Correspondence between Mexico City entrepreneurs and estate managers details how local notables operated as *capitanes de cuadrillas*—gang captains who organized crews and negotiated work and wages. The captains gained stipends for themselves and higher wages for workers. Their organization of seasonal labor reinforced the power and prosperity of village notables and kept villagers' wages above those of dependent *gañanes*. Many captains negotiated stable links between estates that needed workers and village men and boys who needed wages to support families and patriarchal prerogatives.[50] Those relationships were not without tensions and periodic conflicts. But before turning to those contests and negotiations, labor accounts from Pilares and Tlalteguacán in the 1790s—unique for their survival—allow a close look at estate demand for seasonal labor and how the work was taken up by hundreds of village men and boys.

From 1791 to 1795, 342 men and boys labored at Pilares, most for fewer than four weeks each year. From 1797 through 1800, 77 worked at Tlalteguacán for similarly brief periods. Labor demand was seasonal; villagers met it with flexible irregularity. In the early 1790s, Pilares hired about 150 day workers each year: 80 worked 20 days or less, 40 from 21 to 80 days, 17 from 81 to 140 days, 9 from 141 to 200 days, only 2 for more than 200 days. Adults outnumbered youths two to one. Presumed skilled heads of households, men earned two reales daily. Youths learning and supplementing their fathers' earnings were paid on a scale that began at half real daily and rose to one and then one and a half reales as they gained skill, age, and responsibility.[51]

At Tlalteguacán, with smaller plantings and fewer workers on drier lands, labor demand was parallel, as were wages. Among the average of thirty-two workers hired each year, twenty-one came for 20 days or fewer, nine labored from 21 to 140 days, only two labored more than 140 days. At Tlalteguacán, adult men provided over seventy-five percent of the labor; boys were less numerous and never hired for more than 140 days. The estates were able to use seasonal workers to meet labor needs that differed during the crop cycle. The majority who worked fewer than 20 days came only for the harvest. Those employed from between 20 and 80 days came for spring planting, weeks of cultivation during the summer, and fall harvests. Those employed more, notably the few who worked more than 140 days, joined in the full agricultural cycle and diverse building and repair projects—and were very few in number.

Varying estate labor needs allowed village men and boys to labor more or less, as family needs also varied. The few who worked year-round were landless and land poor. Those who came for a few days or weeks at harvest time gained cash to supplement solid family harvests. As family lands ranged from adequate to limited to none, village men and boys labored to earn supplements proportional to household needs.

To meet annual demand for about 150 workers, 342 different men and boys came to Pilares over five years. The seasonal workers living in villages, always paid cash wages and never offered advances that might create debts, were the only laborers called *peones* in the accounts. They came on foot—*a pie*. The largest number, 108 men and 54 boys, almost half the total, came only once in five years and only to work the harvest. They likely belonged to crews that negotiated to work at different estates over the years. Another 52 men and 25 boys also came only for harvests, but returned during two or three of the five years and worked a few more days each year. They lived in nearby communities where notables built regular ties with Pilares. So did the few who worked more of each year and came during four or five years. The more villagers labored, the more they depended on Pilares, the more they returned. Only 2 adults and 3 boys worked year-round; only the men stayed all five years. Flexibility and worker mobility ruled.

Worker remunerations are also revealing. Day laborers were paid weekly and in cash; they could use part of their wages to buy maize (at market price). Those who came only to harvest took small cash incomes (two to three pesos for men, one to two for boys) and small maize supplements (normally less than half a fanega). In contrast, the few men who worked year-round averaged fifty-five pesos per year and bought nearly twelve fanegas of maize—basic support for a rural household. The village men who worked at Pilares for more than the harvest, but less than full time, earned from twenty to seventy percent of family sustenance in cash and maize, returning for multiple years.

The accounts for Tlalteguacán from 1797 to 1800 show parallel work patterns (without detailing maize purchases). The great majority came for one harvest and gained small incomes: averaging 2.7 pesos for men, 1.5 for boys. The few who worked more of each year again returned for multiple years; a very few labored close to full time to earn incomes around 45 pesos for the year. Tlalteguacán offered less work; men who needed more than harvest wages sought more regular work at a larger estate like Pilares. Still, temporary labor, wide variations in days worked, and mobility prevailed at both properties. Such labor relations served estate needs for flexibility—and enabled village men and boys to labor as needed to supplement cultivation.

Boys' labor at Pilares tells more. Fifteen youths appeared during two or more years and progressed through two or more of the wage levels that began at half a real daily for the youngest and reached two reales with adulthood. Their work histories show patterns of growing up: boys earning but a half real daily labored nearly 150 days yearly to earn less than ten pesos—still a meaningful family supplement. As they gained age, experience, and higher wages, they cut the number of days worked. The raise to one real daily allowed boys to work just over 100 days, yet gain incomes that rose to over thirteen pesos. Further raises led to reduced days of labor—and a bit higher earnings: at one and a half reales they worked an average of 80 days to earn almost fifteen pesos; on reaching the adult wage of two reales daily, boys becoming men cut back to fewer than 60 days to earn just over fourteen pesos yearly—as they gained land, began a family, and seasonal wage work became an adult supplement. Soon, a son would start to labor for a half real daily to supplement a young father's harvest, wages, and maize purchases. The cycle of community-based, estate-linked family sustenance continued.

The record of maize purchases made by the nearly 350 men and boys who labored at Pilares shows another side of the relationship: subsistence security—for a price. The estate sold the staple to workers at market price, profiting selling maize to the men and boys who harvested it. Workers calibrated purchases as prices varied with drought and scarcity, negotiating the mix of autonomy, dependence, and security that came with mixing cultivation and seasonal labor.

From January 1791 until August 1793, rains were good, crops ample, and prices low. Pilares sold maize to workers at three reales per *cuartilla* (twelve reales per fanega). Most adults spent a quarter of their weekly earnings on maize. When rain became scarce and the 1793 harvest was reduced, Pilares raised the price to four reales per *cuartilla*. Workers responded by spending thirty-six percent of their wages on increased maize purchases, reducing their cash pay to look to the future. When rains did not come in April of 1794, Pilares raised the price again, this time to five reales. Workers paid over forty percent of a week's wages for a *cuartilla* of maize—and cut back to that basic amount. They could no longer afford to hedge against the future. Drought continued in August of 1794, confirming another harvest failure; Pilares jumped the price of maize to six reales, taking half a week's earnings to purchase a *cuartilla*. Workers cut back, spending only a third of their wages on reduced maize purchases. Had they stored enough to feed families? We cannot know. Life was difficult for villagers in months of scarcity; meanwhile Pilares and other estates profited from the maize village men and boys had planted and harvested.

Symbiotic exploitation ruled. Estates could not profit without the seasonal, flexible, and affordable labor of villagers across the heartland. Village families facing shrinking landholdings could not survive without the wages and maize gained by labor at nearby estates. The link was symbiotic: estates could not profit and villagers could not survive without each other. It was also exploitative: elites profited and lived in luxury, or at least comfort; villagers struggled in good times and faced costly, sometimes deadly, scarcities in years of drought.

Symbiotic exploitation reinforced household patriarchy. As land became scarce in the face of population growth, inheritance patterns concentrated holdings among men. As diminishing cultivation led to growing needs for wages and maize purchases, heartland estates (and village labor captains) offered labor only to men and boys. Men dominated cultivation and monopolized access to cash and maize. A recurring conversation negotiated gender relations: men asserted rights to rule wives and households because they provided sustenance; women answered that they would accept men's rule if they provided. Debates and tensions came in houses, plazas, and courtrooms.[52] Meanwhile, symbiotic exploitation brought village men to labor seasonally at estates, strengthening claims to household rule—while inequities and exploitations deepened. Relations of symbiotic exploitation negotiated by estate managers and community notables reinforced the patriarchal power (also a symbiotic exploitation) negotiated between husbands and wives, solidifying social stability in times of deepening material polarities.

Negotiating Symbiotic Exploitations, 1770–1810

The social stability that sustained silver capitalism in the heartland depended on complex negotiations. Rising conflicts over land between estates and communities and among villages went to courts that aimed to find pacifying solutions (the numbers are documented in the appendix, table A.4). When disputes could not be resolved locally, riots often sent them to the higher courts that mediated resolutions. When programs of "enlightened" religious reform threatened community devotions, priests negotiated to keep cultural peace—and their own roles and incomes.[53] Women led many riots; they were a majority in the crowds at most village protests. When men did not back patriarchal claims with solid provision or became violent, women went to family allies and local courts to seek redress.[54]

Equally important to social stability after 1770 were the negotiations among landed entrepreneurs, estate managers, community labor captains, and villagers in need of work and wages. Between everyday negotiations of household power and periodic turns to court for judicial mediation, negotiations of symbiotic exploitation sustained silver capitalism after 1770.

Negotiations often dealt with more than labor. To attract and reward village captains and workers, estates often opened access to *montes*, upland pastures and woodlands. Villagers could graze animals, favoring notables with larger herds, and gather wood to make charcoal—a source of income for the poorest. The Jesuits allowed access to the villagers laboring at the vast Santa Lucía estates in the northeast Valley of Mexico, an opening carried on by Conde de Regla in the 1770s.[55] Yet such deals could break down. Facing famine in 1785–86, Otumba sent no workers to an estate that then retaliated by denying access to the *montes*, sending the dispute to court.[56]

An effective negotiation of symbiotic exploitation is detailed for Molino de Flores, a large property near Texcoco with ample irrigated lands, a flour mill, and *montes* that extended into uplands rising to the east. The estate belonged to the Conde de Santiago, complementing his great holdings in the Toluca basin (his Mexico City home/headquarters is shown in figure 3.3). In weeks of planting and harvesting, the estate recruited one hundred or more men and boys, many from seven upland villages increasingly short of land. To facilitate village life and labor recruitment, Molino de Flores negotiated a merger of *montes*. Villagers could graze animals, gather firewood, and sow plots of maize anywhere in shared uplands; the estate grazed its own livestock, cut wood, and made charcoal there too— and gained villagers' cooperation. They could press a hard bargain. In the late 1770s, an epidemic left the estate short of workers. Labor captains demanded a raise to 2.5 reales daily.[57] The manager paid and proudly reported a successful harvest to the Conde.

In 1783 a young, less experienced estate operator challenged villagers' titles to *montes* they shared with Molino de Flores. The Conde loaned the villagers funds to hire counsel—and told his manager that he used a contact in the courts to ensure their victory.[58] Then in March of 1785, as drought and scarcity loomed, the manager reported how he kept labor peace and estate profits. He offered superior treatment, fulfilling villagers' needs for maize and never inflicting physical punishment. He always paid wages promptly on Saturday morning, never holding them until

FIGURE 3.3. Power built on the land: the Mexico City home and headquarters of the Condes de Santiago, eighteenth century.

Sunday—allowing workers and families cash to spend in the Saturday market at Papalotla (pleasing traders there). He kept good relations with villagers by treating them *como hijos*—as sons.[59] Paternalism reinforced village men's patriarchy. It worked for a manager able to pay higher wages when needed and a powerful Conde ready to defend village *montes*.

Relations between estates and villagers could also turn into years of simmering conflict, as happened a decade later at the Santiago's Atengo properties in the Valley of Toluca. There, too, villagers faced limited lands concentrating in fewer, mostly male, hands. Many depended on wage work at the estates. As usual, village leaders gained access to estate woodlands in exchange for organizing labor gangs, an arrangement periodically complemented by other deals: villagers might agree to clean an irrigation canal in exchange for use of croplands.[60] The exchange of labor for access to montes was cemented in Toluca villages by what Atengo managers called the *repartimiento de toros*: the estates annually sent bulls and other livestock to local notables, called *caudillos*—bosses—who sponsored festivals including feasts and bullfights. A *caudillo*'s account could reach 1,000 pesos, but the managers did not expect payment; the Santiago saw funding notables' power and community fiestas as a cost of business.[61]

Conflict came in the 1790s. After the death of the long ruling Conde, don Juan Lorenzo Gutiérrez Altamirano y Velasco, in 1793, the Atengo estates were leased to a provincial Spaniard, don Juan José Yrigoyen, while the estate was settled. With an eye to short-term gain, the leaseholder demanded payment for bulls and cash from villagers for the use of *montes*.[62] Several communities led by San Lucas Tepemajalco went to court claiming title to lands they had long used. The Santiagos retook control at Atengo, but the new conflicts proved hard to contain. The courts at times backed communities, noting long use and the lack of clear titles.[63]

In 1797, doña María Isabel Velasco y Ovando inherited Atengo as Condesa de Santiago. Her sister and general manager, doña María Josefa, worked to resume proven ways.[64] She opened land to villagers who sent labor gangs and ended deals with those still suing.[65] She kept allies, but foes dug in. The Condesa's sister lamented "indios in rebellion against the estate."[66] Riots injured several estate dependents, killing one. The general manager faced attack, though only his horse and dignity were injured.[67] Most damaging, the estates failed to recruit enough villagers to plant and harvest.[68] The sisters counterattacked in Mexico City courts. When a community claimed part of Atengo's *montes*, family lawyers challenged titles to all its lands.[69] They often won before the audiencia, where a kinsman, don Cosme de Mier y Trespalacios, sat as senior judge. One order sentenced any *indio* seized rioting to 200 lashes, then exile to northern presidios.[70] Such orders did little to calm conflicts between Toluca villages and Atengo estates.

The great landlords and their managers began to see that they were facing more than just adamant villagers in the fields and the courts. Behind every suit they found a provincial Spaniard.[71] Village priests urged parishioners to claim land.[72] A district magistrate did the same.[73] Local merchant-cultivators promoted suits, angling to gain use of lands for themselves.[74] Most frustrating to the Santiagos, when they won orders punishing rioters, mandating debt collection, or requiring villagers to vacate disputed lands, local officials blocked implementation. Victories won in Mexico City proved hard to enforce in Toluca communities.[75]

In time, doña María Josefa led her titled sister and family managers to accept that they had to live with simmering conflicts to maintain profitable operations at Atengo. She wrote to her general manager that although local Spanish townsmen and officials might offend him and oppose estate interests, they had to be respected.[76] A priest might be opposed in conflicts over land and labor, yet rewarded with hogs or lambs should he once act favorably toward the estate.[77] The district magistrate was considered a staunch opponent of the Santiagos, a view substantiated in many acts. Yet he was asked to aid in legal disputes and the recruitment of workers; given his close ties to community notables, only he could provide key assistance.

When the magistrate aided the Santiagos, a result they saw as all too rare, he too was showered with gifts and praise.[78]

To stabilize the confrontation at Atengo and allow production to carry on, don Manuel Moncada became the Santiagos' leading foe and essential mediator. A provincial Spaniard, merchant, cultivator, and lieutenant to the magistrate, he backed village suits claiming estate lands. He pressed villages to redistribute the lands they had, with consequences unfavorable to Atengo and favorable to Moncada. But when Atengo needed harvest workers, Moncada alone could work with the community leaders who organized labor gangs. So managers worked with him, however unhappily.[79] Rural autonomies, laden with inequities, could make the negotiation of symbiotic exploitations difficult, even conflictive.

Still, they endured. Symbiotic exploitations might operate smoothly, as at Molino de Flores in the 1770s and 1780s. They might become conflictive, as at Atengo in the 1790s and early 1800s. But across the most fertile heartland basins, they persisted to sustain profitable estate production and villagers' survival as growing populations made land ever scarcer.

Stabilizing Capitalism

New Spain's silver production increased five times over during the eighteenth century, to hold near historic peaks between 1790 and 1810. The viceroyalty remained a key engine of global trade as imperial wars and revolutions in France and Haiti destabilized the Atlantic world. Mexico City prospered as the largest metropolis in the Americas, its merchant financiers and agrarian entrepreneurs the richest in the hemisphere. City shops sold fine cloths, porcelains, and other wares from Asia and Europe. Wheat and maize, sugar and pulque, made on heartland estates supplied city markets and profited great landed families—and many lesser growers.

Capital generated by silver and global trade funded the expansion of estate production, cultivation enabled by the need for seasonal wages among villagers facing growing families and shrinking landholdings. Men and boys worked to gain sustenance and reinforce claims to patriarchy. Symbiotic exploitations stabilized economic dynamism and deepening inequities across the heartland core and the southern sugar zones. Entrepreneurs profited while republics retained lands and rights to self-rule that sustained real if diminishing autonomies, as population growth generated inequities. Local notables held on as pivotal intermediaries, brokers working between a world of prosperity and communities struggling to survive—keeping both alive.

Symbiotic exploitations reinforced patriarchy. Estate managers and village labor captains were always men; they ensured that wage labor went only to men and boys. Wages and maize purchases enabled village men to "provide" as landholdings shrank. The importance of the consolidation of patriarchy among provincial Spaniards, village notables, and native commoners was underlined by a formula repeated every time a judicial inspection surveyed lands disputed between communities and estates from Santa Lucía to Atengo. Village notables were required to attend; native women were explicitly excluded. Women, the formula insisted, rioted too often.[80] Men negotiated power through patriarchy; women too often shouted opposition, pressing family and community rights. Symbiotic exploitations reinforced power and patriarchy, stabilizing the silver capitalism that sustained Mexico City and fed global trade.

When Father Hidalgo and thousands of Bajío rebels arrived in the Valley of Toluca in the fall of 1810, most local villagers, whatever their spats with the Atengo estates, held back from insurgency. Men from communities at Amecameca in Chalco's uplands refused to march to fight against Hidalgo's rebels. Most heartland villagers stayed at home, working community lands and estate fields.[81] Two years later, when José María Morelos camped at Cuautla, in the heart of sugar country, most villagers also stood back. Landed autonomies and symbiotic exploitations kept most heartland republics loyal, sustaining Mexico City and its defense of the empire to 1821. Life was different in the dry Mezquital and nearby pulque zones. Without symbiotic exploitations, villagers there pressed insurgencies after 1810.

CHAPTER FOUR

Communities Challenging Capitalism

INSURGENCY IN THE MEZQUITAL, 1800–1815

WHILE THE MAJORITY of the heartland's indigenous peoples remained at home in republics and at work at neighboring haciendas during the decade of conflict that shook New Spain after 1810, the Otomí of many Mezquital communities pressed insurgencies that challenged estate power and the regional economy from 1810 to 1815. Aridity, scarce arable lands, and the rise of commercial pulque made stabilizing symbiotic exploitations difficult if not impossible as native populations grew during the eighteenth century. From the fall of 1810, in the wake of the risings that spread across the Bajío, villagers in the Mezquital and the pulque zones around Otumba and Apan took arms to assault estates and silver capitalism.[1]

Relations between estates and villages became increasingly conflictive in the Mezquital after 1800. Life proved exceptionally hard on villagers there during the drought that began in 1808. Many turned to insurgency in the fall of 1810. Unique sources allow close examination of rising conflicts, famine years, and regional insurgencies: letters written by the manager of the Tulancalco estate from 1800 to 1812 detail escalating labor conflicts and provide a deep local perspective on the first years of insurgency[2]; an inquiry into the drought and famine of 1808 to 1810 reveals the challenges faced by people in the heartland's driest basin; the report of a local commander detailing his fight against insurgents from 1810 to 1815 provides another view of the depth, course, and consequences of insurgency.[3] Together they allow a close understanding of an important if exceptional insurgency—the one uprising in the heartland that rattled silver capitalism.

MAP 6. The northern heartland and the Mezquital, ca. 1810.

Escalating Conflicts: Tulancalco, 1800–1810

Tulancalco developed during the first silver boom. Built by the López de Peralta family, locked in inalienable entail, and tied to the title of Marqués de Salvatierra, it was one of the grazing properties responsible for early erosion in the Mezquital.[4] By the late eighteenth century, the Condes de Santiago held the Salvatierra title and properties. As markets grew in Mexico City and Real del Monte, sheep moved north and Tulancalco turned to making pulque from broad fields of maguey, planting maize where irrigation allowed.

Don Manuel Olguín became manager in 1791. Appointed by don Juan Lorenzo, the Conde who had ruled Santiago family affairs for decades, Olguín served the new Condesa and her manager-sister doña María Josefa through the 1790s. He stayed on when the latter leased the estate in 1801. Olguín brought managerial stability as leadership changed in the powerful landed clan. Born and raised in nearby Tetepango, he knew the Mezquital.

His role was to make a profit for the proprietors by overseeing production, marketing, and labor. He succeeded for twenty years, until insurgency struck.[5] Olguín earned an ample salary and maize rations, plus access to medicines and many small luxuries sent out from Mexico City. In 1801 he gained rent-free use of a rancho large enough to harvest 400 to 600 fanegas of maize. He harvested the staple in good years, stored it, and sold for profit in times of scarcity. While serving urban landlords and taking profit himself, Olguín dealt with estate residents and Otomí villagers.[6]

While Tulancalco still grazed a few sheep for their meat and wool, and ran mule trains to Real del Monte and Mexico City, it profited most from pulque and maize. Weekly pulque sales funded ongoing operations— mostly costs of labor to plant and harvest maize on irrigated fields that yielded varying harvests and less regular earnings.

Periodically, the estate transplanted 3,000 to 4,000 maguey shoots, to await maturity and production five years later. Sales rose through most of the decade after 1800, averaging 175 cargas monthly from 1800 into 1806, rising to over 220 from April 1806 into early 1809—when drought and falling demand brought sales back to 190 cargas monthly during 1810. Earnings varied accordingly, peaking at 175 pesos monthly in 1807 and 1808, falling to 140 pesos in 1810.[7] Pulque generated regular income. Yet in 1799 Olguín lamented that Tulancalco no longer sold to Mexico City taverns: the estate produced *pulque ordinario*; city consumers demanded *pulque fino*. It lay at the northern limit of the zone able to deliver pulque in twenty-four hours; transport costs were high compared with competitors closer in. So the estate sold ordinary pulque in nearby Tetepango, Actopan, and Real del Monte, markets once supplied by Otomí women.[8] Did that displacement contribute to rising conflicts?

Selling pulque in the Mezquital kept transport costs low, but left the estate subject to the fluctuations of a regional economy dependent on scarce and uncertain rains, and on mines that struggled in times of war and trade disruptions. (Figure 4.1 shows the dry Mezquital near the end of a recent rainly season.) In May of 1802, Olguín lamented weak pulque sales caused by maize shortages and mining shutdowns at Pachuca and Real de Monte, the result of a lack of mercury from Spain. In August sales remained weak, as miners still awaited mercury. Poverty was everywhere.[9] And if sales were notably bad in some years, they always suffered from July through September as locals awaited the maize harvest in a dry basin.[10]

With aridity everyone's challenge, Tulancalco was aided by the ability to plant maize on irrigated fields. Much labor went to maintain dams, canals, and ditches. Offering some protection against crop failure, irrigation

FIGURE 4.1. The Mezquital: the dry northern heartland.

in the Mezquital relied on rain-fed streams that dried in years of drought. Tulancalco sold maize, too, in Actopan, Tetepango, and Real del Monte. Transport costs were low; there was advantage in being one of a few irrigated growers in a dry basin.[11] Harvests fluctuated: over 1,200 fanegas of maize in 1798–99, under 1,000 in 1799–1800, nearly 3,000 in 1802–3 and 1803–4, under 900 in 1804–5, over 2,500 in 1805–6.[12] Prices also fluctuated: lowest after the harvest and in good years, highest just before the harvest and in years of drought. Like all commercial growers, Olguín held the maize of good harvests to sell in times of scarcity. Maize almost always cost more in the Mezquital than in Mexico City. In the spring of 1800, after a reduced harvest across the heartland, the city Alhóndiga sold maize at twenty reales per fanega; at Pachuca and Real del Monte the price hit twenty-four. In good years city prices might fall to twelve reales per fanega; Tulancalco almost never sold below twenty.[13]

The combination of regular pulque marketing and maize sales in times of scarcity gained good earnings for doña María Josefa. Between August 1799 and November 1801, Olguín sent her 5,100 pesos. Tulancalco generated locally over 2,200 pesos per year after expenses, and there were small sales in the capital, too.[14] Dealing in the favorite drink and key staple of the native majority was good business.

The letters that passed between Olguín and doña María Josefa suggest that production and marketing of pulque was just that: business. Their exchanges were always about costs and prices, markets and profits. The same questions were always present in discussions of maize. But in dealing with the Mesoamerican staple there was always more: production, marketing, and profit came with religious meanings tied to questions of justice. It was a language of profit that reveals much about the contradictions of life in the Mezquital in the decade before 1810.

Early in 1800, as the harvest came in under 1,000 fanegas, doña María Josefa ordered a stop to all large maize sales. The price was only twenty reales per fanega in the capital and she expected a rise. Still, she directed Olguín to continuing selling in small lots at the estate granary. The goal, she insisted, was to help *los pobres*—the poor; then she noted that the continuing income would fund labor costs.[15] Charity and profit were inseparable. By July the rains were late and sparse. Olguín arranged for masses at the estate chapel, seeking aid from Santo Cristo and Santa Teresa. The goal, he wrote, was rain to assist both the estate and *los pobres*; a collection ensured that all contributed to the costs.[16] In October, a mature crop stood drying in the fields; in January it came in at 1,650 fanegas, good but not ample. The price stayed high and the estate had maize to sell. Olguín visited the Colegio de Pachuca for spiritual exercises, earning glowing praise from doña María Josefa for the good harvest and his devotion.[17]

In June of 1801, scarce rains meant that maize planted in May would have only a limited yield at harvest. Again doña María Josefa ended all sales except to *los pobres* and *indios trajineros*—native traders who sold in local villages. She emphasized that the poor would eat and the traders would sustain families with small profits. She did not state what both knew: selling in small lots kept the price high; selling only at the estate left the costs of transport, physical or monetary, to the buyer—and kept profits up. By November it was clear that scarce rains would make the harvest small; doña María Josefa repeated the order to stop sales—"but you may sell at the granary to the poor who come seeking to eat, and with good grace."[18] Selling to local traders stopped. Only the grateful poor might buy, and only in small amounts at inflated prices.

Why was profiteering in maize masked in a language of charity, even in private letters between city operator and estate manager? Maize had been the sacred sustenance of life for millennia, only recently commercialized by profit seekers. They aimed to legitimate their gains, even among themselves. The language of charity did not inhibit the pursuit of profit.

There were ambiguities in Tulancalco's relations with the Church. A deep Catholicism infused doña María Josefa's and don Manuel Olguín's letters.[19] Yet when the estate brought in its largest harvest in years in early

1803, doña María Josefa ordered Olguín to pay the tithe in cash at current low prices. The alternative was to pay a tenth of the crop—a crop that if held a year or two would double in price. Doña María Josefa ensured that she, not the archbishop, took the profit.[20] She held that crop in October of 1804 when drought and frost led to another failure. She again lamented the harm to *los pobres*—and ended all sales to maximize her profits.[21]

Maize sales were profitable, if morally problematic. And after 1800, the labor relations of maize production at Tulancalco became notably conflictive. No symbiotic exploitation tied the estate and the villagers who labored seasonally to plant and harvest the essential staple (see chapter 3). Understanding why labor at Tulancalco became conflictive after 1800 opens a window to understanding the turn to insurgency after 1810.

Olguín complained endlessly of labor scarcities. In April 1803 he had to suspend work cleaning an irrigation holding tank to have enough workers to plant maize. A year later he could not complete the same cleaning, work delayed for years. In January 1804, a labor shortage caused by disease delayed the harvest into February. In May 1807, planting was slow owing to scarce workers—no explanation offered.[22] In a basin marked by aridity, scarce arable land, growing families, and estates offering wage work and the chance to buy maize, reports of labor shortages surprise. Tulancalco could not recruit hands when it wanted and at the wages it would pay.

Labor at Tulancalco contrasted with prevailing ways in more fertile regions to the south, where symbiotic exploitations ruled. There, managers and a few permanent employees dealt mostly with workers from landed communities, making ties between estates and communities pivotal and enabling notables in key brokerage roles. Olguín never mentions labor brokers in his endless laments after 1800. Why? And why did Mezquital labor relations become so conflictive? They were simultaneously multiple, irregular, and insecure, thus unstable and conflictive.

Olguín was from Tetepango; most of his assistants came out from Mexico City, chosen for literacy, the ability to keep accounts, and loyalty to the urban proprietors. Doña María Josefa worked to keep their loyalty. During the epidemic of January 1804, she noted the illness of the steward of one rancho. She prayed for his recovery; his death would be a great loss for the estate.[23] In April 1806 she sent a new granary keeper to oversee storage and sales of maize. He could write and keep accounts; he was single and smart in rural ways, but needed to learn about pulque. He earned 150 pesos annually, plus food rations and chocolate—a luxury to set him apart from the working majority. He came with a pack mule carrying a bed and clothing.[24]

We know little about the Hispanic tenants who leased ranchos at the borders of the estate, set to buffer its lands from nearby communities. Olguín sent annual lists of tenants and rents, but none survive.[25] Tenants gave doña María Josefa income without the costs of labor recruitment; they also competed for workers at harvest time. Olguín, too, worked a rancho, rent free, enabling him to profit in regional markets for pulque and maize; his rancho competed with the estate he managed for harvest labor. Around Otumba, closer to the capital, rancheros gained land leased from communities; at Tulancalco they leased from the estate. We see a small stratum in between, some leasing from estates, some from republics—all seeking to prosper between urban landlords and landed republics. Where rancheros leased from republics they developed close ties with native elites. Doña María Josefa and Olguín drew those loyalties to Tulancalco (see chapter 3). In questions of land, they succeeded; in questions of labor, they competed.

Sirvientes meseros, employees on monthly salaries, were few. They generally earned four pesos per month, forty-eight pesos yearly, plus maize rations sufficient to feed their families without paying the costs of repeated scarcities. Security of employment and sustenance came complemented by access to food and other goods in advance of salaries, recorded as debts to the estate. They were rarely repaid in cash or work, producing income above allotted levels. Hispanic *sirvientes* were secure dependents, loyal to the estate and its manager.[26]

The Otomí men who did most work at Tulancalco divided into three categories: *tlachiqueros* who tapped maguey and fermented pulque; *gañanes* who lived at the estate, available for labor year-round; and peones—villagers who came and went. Olguín rarely noted *tlachiqueros*; they worked to his satisfaction. Few in number, essential to profit, and well paid, their favored lives surely stood out in the eyes of the Otomí majority.

About twenty-five families of *gañanes* lived at Tulancalco. Their huts were estate property; they lived rent-free and cultivated small gardens. There is no sign of access to plots to plant maize; regular purchases suggest they did not. The resident Otomí might provide up to fifty workers, fathers and sons, available year-round, but only employed as needed. *Gañanes* were always called *indios*; as adults they gained one and a half reales per day. If a man worked 200 days, a rare maximum, he earned less than forty pesos for the year. To buy ten fanegas of maize at twelve reales each, the lowest price reported in the heartland between 1810 and 1810, he would pay fifteen pesos, over a third of his earnings, to gain the staple his labor had made. In years of scarcity when maize reached twenty reales, he would give nearly two-thirds of his pay for essential maize.

Many *gañanes* brought a son to the fields; he earned less, starting at half a real per day, rising to one real as an adolescent. If the son worked 200 days, household income rose and the cost of maize became more affordable. *Gañanes* were deeply dependent. With effort, they got by—in ways that reinforced men's patriarchy. They took advances in maize and other essentials, always at levels less than favored *sirvientes*. Advances reinforced patriarchal dependence and household survival.[27] Between 1800 and 1810, Olguín reported no problems with *gañanes*. In times of population growth and rising prices, secure dependence kept labor peace among Tulancalco's residents: Hispanic tenants and *sirvientes*, Otomí *tlachiqueros* and *gañanes*.

The contrast with the escalating conflicts between the estate and the Otomí peones who came from nearby communities is striking. They were essential at times of peak labor demand: during weeks the estate transplanted 3,000 to 4,000 young maguey, when irrigation canals needed cleaning, during the planting and harvesting of maize. They were paid daily, a standard two reales for adults—twenty-five percent more than the *gañanes* who worked beside them in the fields. Peones, too, could buy maize at market rates, but only when they worked and paid cash. They gained no advances, limiting dependence, inhibiting survival in hard years.[28] Tulancalco's peones gained a daily wage that would earn them as much as Hispanic *sirvientes*, fifty pesos per year if they worked 200 days. Normally they came for only a few days or weeks, buying maize at the same price as *gañanes*, devoting less of their pay to the staple—when they worked.

Olguín reported regular conflicts with Otomí communities and scarcities of peones at key times. In 1802, local officials backed community notables in a conflict with managers over tributes owed by *gañanes*. They were registered in the republics, but village leaders could not collect on estate property. Olguín resisted and doña María Josefa backed him. They would have to pay, and then try to collect from *gañanes* already in debt to the estate. Escaping tribute had drawn many to Tulancalco. Making the estate collect, that is pay, would increase labor costs. The viceroy backed the officials, Olguín paid, and doña María Josefa joined in protests. To Olguín, Otomí notables imposed costs on the estate. They were foes, not allies or brokers.[29]

Conflict escalated in 1805. In June, a work gang recruited from Atitalaquía was locked in for the night to prevent worker flight—a practice seen as normal by doña María Josefa. A peon died. An investigation cleared Olguín of wrongdoing; there was no "excess" punishment, only the practice, said to be standard in the Mezquital, of holding villagers to ensure their service. When the harvest began in December of 1806, Olguín again locked in village workers—with the approval of the district magistrate. Doña María Josefa feared trouble.[30]

In June 1807, Olguín struggled again to recruit peones. He called the *indios* of nearby villages "most insolent" and offered an explanation. They preferred to work at the mines or the *desagüe*, the project to drain the Valley of Mexico into the Mezquital. They earned more but labored less, "they work as they please."[31] Mezquital villagers were poor and increasingly short of land, yet they had options and expected to labor when and where they chose. Work at the mines and the drainage project was dangerous and paid better. Labor at Tulancalco and other estates was seasonal and paid less, so managers locked workers in to ensure harvest hands.

There were other signs that villagers saw Mezquital estates more as adversaries. In August 1805, when maize from the previous year's small harvest was almost gone and most costly, a group of *indios* was caught butchering a cow at Tulancalco. Olguín arranged a public punishment—to discourage others, he insisted. In October 1809, as scarce rains promised a small harvest, the problem became plural. The *indios* of several pueblos stole livestock at Tulancalco and nearby estates.[32] Estate labor had not made village notables key labor brokers, had not enabled the survival of village families, and was not solidifying Otomí men's patriarchy. Some turned to proving their manhood by stealing sustenance.

Why did the Mezquital fail to develop symbiotic exploitations parallel to those that stabilized inequities in the heartland basins just south? Aridity mattered. Limited agricultural potential due to low rainfall meant that as population grew, the land remaining to Mezquital households yielded less sustenance with less regularity than was available to families with plots in more fertile regions. Aridity also mattered when estates turned to native products in the eighteenth century. In the Mezquital, estate maize was limited to irrigated fields; pulque ruled and required little labor but for irregular transplanting. Due to aridity, Mezquital villagers needed more labor and local estates offered less—and much of that went to resident *gañanes*.

Olguín complained of labor scarcities in time of peak demand. Local villagers had choices: they could work at Real del Monte just east or at the drainage project just west. Both involved tunneling and other dangers, and both were insecure: mine work depended on vagaries of financing and access to mercury; *desagüe* work depended on regime funding—all uncertain in years of long costly wars. Mezquital village men had options, but all were uncertain and laden with risks.

In a region of insecurities, Mezquital estates were able to recruit *gañanes*—resident, dependent, Otomí wageworkers and their families. Those at Tulancalco were poorly paid and spent much of their pay to buy maize. But they had regular work and access to maize, even when they could not pay immediately. *Gañanes* were a minority in the Mezquital, but they were key to production, labor relations, and rising conflicts between estates and Otomí republics. The more estates relied on *gañanes*, the less work was available to village men and boys. At Tulancalco, *gañanes* monopolized chances to labor a hundred or more days per year. That left only short stints of seasonal work transplanting maguey and harvesting maize to the growing numbers of village men and boys seeking wages to sustain families and patriarchal claims.

Estate reliance on *gañanes* and dependence on villagers only in times of peak demand inhibited symbiotic exploitations. Community notables resented the estates' offers of refuge to landless villagers—who escaped tributes while finding sustenance. Village workers did not come to transplant and harvest in numbers seen as adequate by managers like Olguín. So they locked in the workers who did come, keeping them from other chances that, if dangerous, were available—when the mines were working and the *desagüe* funded. Mezquital estates faced labor scarcities while villagers searched for earnings in a zone of widening insecurities.

The rising importance of estate production to the Mezquital economy and household sustenance reinforced patriarchy—and weakened it, too. The estate takeover of pulque curtailed native women's roles as purveyors of the favored drink. The growing reliance of native families on estate wages and maize purchases, available only to men, strengthened their rule of household sustenance. The few favored *tlachiqueros* and larger numbers of dependent but secure *gañanes* solidified patriarchal roles. But the majority of Mezquital Otomí households lived in growing communities facing increasingly inadequate and very dry lands. They relied more and more on wages and maize purchases available only to men; yet village men found access to wages ever more uncertain, while maize became scarce and costly in a dry basin facing repeated years of drought. When village men stole livestock, they took sustenance and asserted a manly provision becoming ever more uncertain.

Politics, Drought, and Insurgency, 1808–10

Turns to insurgency never come easily. The risks of violent assaults on power, property, and the people who defend them are real. The deepening poverty, widening insecurities, rising labor conflicts, and uncertainties of patriarchy that spread in the Mezquital after 1800 did not simply lead to insurgency. Two years of regime crisis compounded by deep drought and painful scarcities beginning in the summer of 1808 brought new challenges to people across New Spain. How communities across the heartland lived those years reveals much about why insurgency rose in the Mezquital and other arid zones after 1810—while villagers in more fertile basins just south, caught up in symbiotic exploitations, stayed at home and at work.

The news of Napoleon's invasion of Spain; the capture of the Bourbon kings, father and son; the rise of guerrillas and juntas in Spain; the calls for an American junta in Mexico City; and the military coup that blocked it—all came to the heartland from May to September of 1808. Claims of popular rights and assertions of armed power came to the fore in the capital.[33] Across the Mezquital, people heard those claims as they faced difficulties of production and labor, survival and patriarchy—and drought sharpened scarcities from 1808 through 1810.

In August of 1809, officials in Mexico City saw that the poor harvest of 1808 would be followed by a worse one in 1809. They ordered reports on crops and prices across the heartland, knowing that recent political debates and their own illegitimacy (having come to power in a coup) made the times fragile. By the end of the month responses detailed widespread difficulties, but the deepest challenges came in the Mezquital and other dry northern zones. On the lands of the central and southern Toluca basin, where the Santiagos' Atengo estates engaged landed republics in land conflicts and symbiotic exploitations, officials at Toluca and Santiago Tianguistengo reported good rains, good crops, and modest prices of nineteen to twenty reales per fanega. Chalco and Texcoco in the rich southeastern Valley of Mexico reported drought, reduced crops, and prices rising from twenty-four to twenty-six reales. Still, all was not lost. Chalco villagers would harvest some maize on milpas and house lots; estates with irrigated fields continued to hire workers, expected reasonable harvests, and held stocks from previous years. They would feed their workers and supply city markets as prices rose. And maize still arrived from the hot country just south. The staple was available in Chalco markets, while merchants sent it on by canal to Mexico City. Prices were high at Chalco as growers held stocks awaiting peaks in city markets.[34] Still, symbiotic exploitation, social stability, and estate production held across fertile cereal basins.

Reports from the dry Mezquital and other pulque zones painted a bleak picture. At Tula, once a great Mesoamerican capital and favored by the river of the same name, estates had brought in a good wheat crop the previous winter—thanks to irrigation. But summer maize, dependent on rain at estates and communities, was "mostly lost." The price had risen to twenty-four reales—the low price in the Mezquital equaled the high price at Chalco. Similar dearth loomed around the mining town of Zimapán in the highlands at the northern edge of the Mezquital. Only at Ixmiquilpan in the northern reaches of the basin, and where villagers irrigated their plots, was summer maize developing well. Yet the report added that most plots were too small to sustain families. They would soon need to buy maize—and none was for sale. Near Tulancalco, reports from Tetepango and Actopan stated that December would yield but a quarter of the expected harvest. No stocks were for sale, though estates still fed their workers. Prices to *gañanes* and peones were twenty-eight reales per fanega at Actopan and rising from twenty-eight to thirty-two reales at Tetepango, close by Tulancalco.[35] Threats to survival and patriarchy deepened.

The report from Apan, northeast of Otumba at the edge of the Valley of Mexico, another dry region of limited cultivation focused on pulque and stock grazing, was nearly as bleak. No more than half the expected maize would be harvested, owing to drought, frost, and hail. None was for sale at estates or in town markets. Supplies from other areas cost twenty-seven reales.[36] Contrasts across the heartland were clear: Drought brought scarcity and rising prices everywhere, but in cereal zones, from the Valley of Toluca to Chalco, wage work and maize remained available and prices held between twenty and twenty-six reales. In the dry regions to the north, maize died in the fields and vanished from markets as prices rose from twenty-four to thirty-two reales. Symbiotic exploitation held in the cereal zones; desperation deepened in the Mezquital.

Challenges worsened in 1810. In March, Olguín reported that *indios* from Tecomate were stealing cattle from Tulancalco and other estates. He saw their needs, yet added that several had been captured and should be jailed to deter others.[37] Drought struck Tulancalco's livestock, too. Its mules were too weak to haul maize to market. In May he reported the death of 450 animals, mostly sheep. In June, lack of pasturage blocked maize shipments to Actopan and Pachuca. By August, the losses of sheep to drought and theft reached 715, a third of Tulancalco's flock.[38]

Still, Olguín tried to maintain production. In May he planted maize and irrigated it with what water remained.[39] In July some rain fell and he hoped for a break in the drought. But, for the moment, the dearth of maize and deep poverty brought a steep drop in pulque markets. Sales that held around 200 cargas monthly from January through June dropped to 130 in July and 113 by September. Taverns in nearby pueblos no longer bought pulque because *indios* no longer went to taverns. Olguín shut down one rancho.[40] Meanwhile, the price of maize drove to thirty-six reales in August 1810 at Tulancalco and across the Mezquital.[41] A peon who worked full time would spend ninety percent of his earnings on maize alone—if he could find work and maize for sale.

Olguín's compassion finally equaled his frustration. As September began, he lamented that he was surrounded by "poor people" facing "much necessity." Men worked fields by day and stole livestock at night—all to survive. Knowing the animals would soon perish in the drought, Olguín sought no punishment. He was equally understanding in reporting that no tenant had paid rent; drought left them without crops, animals, or income.[42] Days before Father Hidalgo called for insurrection in the Bajío, life for many in the Mezquital had become desperate.

Insurgency: The View from Tulancalco, 1810–12

Insurgency did not originate in the Mezquital. It began in the Bajío on September 16, 1810, when Father Miguel Hidalgo called his parishioners at Dolores to arms. People across the Mezquital learned of the rising via insurgent proclamations and regime propaganda, as rebel throngs marched from the Bajío to the Toluca basin and back in October and November. Few around Toluca joined the rising; many in the Mezquital did. During the first sixteen months of insurgency, Olguín struggled to carry on at Tulancalco. Writing regularly to doña María Josefa in Mexico City, his letters offer a frontline view of indigenous insurgency, written by a manager who opposed the risings—yet never took arms to fight them.

Olguín first noted the insurgency in a letter of October 13, reporting his fear of the uprising in *tierradentro*—in the north.[43] By November 10 he knew more and feared more deeply. Calling rebels "cursed people," he took joy in their defeats. He knew of a gathering of insurgents near Toluca; other rebels held San Juan del Río, Huichapan, and Xilotepec—a line west of the Mezquital. A justice at Tula received a communiqué demanding allegiance to the rising. Olguín heard that insurgents were offering *indios* across the Mezquital four reales daily in captured royal funds, twice the prevailing wage, to join. He relayed news that *indios* had thronged to Arroyo Zarco looking for rebel leader don Ignacio Allende—only to face don Félix Calleja, who killed 2,000 to 3,000. The magistrate at Tula, several employees of the Conde de la Cortina's Tlahuelilpan estates, and many *gachupines* (immigrant Spaniards) had fled to Mexico City. Olguín sent his wife and daughter to Actopan, farther from the uprising. He sent livestock to the *montes* as estate produce and property were insurgent targets. Still, no insurgents had come closer than Xilotepec, well to the west.[44]

He did not know that Hidalgo's insurgents had fought at Monte de las Cruces, just west of the capital, and then retreated toward Arroyo Zarco—where they were defeated at Aculco by Calleja on November 6. The report of mass *indio* deaths reached Olguín within four days. What of reports that insurgents offered high wages to villagers who would join the uprising? Insurgents had sacked the great mining city of Guanajuato and taken uncounted silver. When Olguín reported that Tulancalco's pulque sales jumped from 144 cargas in October to 248 in November, it was clear that tavern goers had found new income in the days of poverty before harvest hiring began. Someone was pumping money into village economies; insurgents with captured funds seem good candidates. Pulque sales and earnings at Tulancalco peaked from November 1810 through January 1811.[45] Wary of insurgents, Olguín remained ready to profit from drinking funded by the wages of insurgency.

He continued to operate Tulancalco as rebels came closer; on November 17, 1,500 were reported three leagues (ten miles) west. Olguín's son-in-law, a *gachupín*, fled. By November 24, Julián Villagrán was leading insurgents roaming the Mezquital, holding roads around Tula. The manager at Tlahuelilpan told Olguín that all local troops might retreat to Mexico City, a flight before insurgent power. The prominent (meaning Hispanic) citizens of Ixmiquilpan fled to Actopan, leaving the northern Mezquital to the Otomí. Olguín stayed at Tulancalco awaiting the harvest.

FIGURE 4.2. Tulancalco: granary in ruins, maize triumphant.

He feared a scarcity of workers and thefts of livestock; he sold pulque in record amounts.[46]

As the harvest began, insurgents attacked the estate on December 14. Did they come to claim maize being hauled in from the fields? Olguín did not say. He reported the assault to the manager at Tlahuelilpan, who now led a counterinsurgent troop. They took quick pursuit, capturing six rebels, twenty-one horses, and five rifles; the leader and seven others escaped.[47] Across the Mezquital, rebels attacked haciendas; troops from Tlahuelilpan defended property. (Figure 4.2 shows Tulancalco's granary, now in ruins, perhaps a result of the insurgency.)

In January 1811, Olguín caught two estate employees, a cowherd and a shepherd, father and son, stealing sheep. He sent them to the new district magistrate at Actopan, reputed to be an energetic pursuer of insurgents, but the miscreants escaped before facing justice. Then came a small harvest: only 334 fanegas. Was continuing drought to blame or had insurgents taken their share? The latter seems likely—and something Olguín hesitated to report to doña María Josefa. As the manager struggled to carry on with insurgency all around, he reported difficulties such as a small harvest—but not their causes or the many compromises he negotiated. As the harvest came in, *gañanes* demanded pay in maize, not cash. Maize was their first need, more valuable than cash. Doña María Josefa saw the small harvest as a source of profits; she insisted Olguín pay cash and sell maize to workers at prevailing high prices.[48] The discussion ended there, but it appears that Olguín agreed to the *gañanes'* demand in time of insurgency. From 1811, *dar raciones*—distribute maize—meant paying workers. Maize to sustain families and patriarchy became the currency essential to maintain production at Tulancalco.[49]

By early March Olguín reported growing insurgent dominance of the Mezquital. Rebels ruled the mining town of Zimapán to the north and Huichapan to the northwest. On March 24 they attacked Tula, robbing stores and taking all the "kings money"—tax receipts. Most disturbing to Olguín, insurgents occupied the haciendas San José, San Antonio, el Marqués, Tendexé, Nextlapa, and La Goleta around Tula. Three belonged to American Spaniards, showing that insurgents assaulted landed power—not rule by immigrants from Spain. He emphasized that the rebels "destroyed" crops and livestock (surely they took them) and occupied land.[50]

Among those who presumed to rule, destruction became the term for turning profit-making property into life-sustaining resources. Olguín adopted an everyday language of counterinsurgency. Rebels were insurgents—denying them vision or legitimacy. Defenders of the

regime were patriots—claiming the legitimacy earlier asserted by political revolutionaries in British America. When rebels sacked or occupied
property—they destroyed. Insurgents took estate crops and livestock to
feed themselves and their families. Because the language of counterinsurgency required Olguín to report only destruction, we cannot know if
insurgents occupying estates around Tula in March 1811 began family production, planting maize on liberated lands. Such efforts were common in
the Bajío; surely Mezquital rebels tried the same.

Olguín emphasized that no destruction had come to Tulancalco, so he
began plowing to prepare for spring planting. He would soon settle resident workers' annual accounts, normally done in March. He then hoped
to travel to Mexico City to settle his account with doña María Josefa. But
he heard that Julián Villagrán approached Pachuca with 60,000 men (an
unlikely number; still, an unstoppable force) and that rebels ruled roads
everywhere. Olguín canceled his trip—for his safety, he said, and likely to
prevent having to share the compromises essential to survival and production in times of insurgency.[51]

In late April, he reported insurgents concentrated between Ixmiquilpan
and El Cardonal. With 500 troops, Calleja killed over 1,000 *indios* there,
losing one soldier in the fight. Troops routed poorly armed rebels. Still,
over 2,000 *indio* insurgents remained near El Cardonal, with another
3,000 at Alfajayucan.[52] By early May 1,500 rebels threatened Tulancalco
from hills above Tepetitlán. Olguín reported others in the uplands between
the Zoquital estate and the town of Meztitlán to the north. Troops killed
another 1,000 *indios* at El Cardonal.[53] The numbers reveal large uprisings
of northern Mezquital villagers, poorly armed yet little deterred by the
slaughter inflicted by the defenders of regime power and estate property.
Social conflict became deadly violence, most inflicted by troops loyal to a
regime historically sustained primarily by judicial mediation.

May and June of 1811 brought violence to Tulancalco. The nearby pueblo
of Nopala was taken over by residents led by a local blacksmith; the priest
and his vicars fled to Tula, excommunicating their parishioners. Clergy
from Huichapan also took refuge in Tula, fleeing Julián Villagrán in the
highland town west of the Mezquital.[54] In mid-May, cavalry commander
don Miguel del Campo offered Olguín sweeping powers "to secure, pursue,
destroy, or amnesty any insurgent." The manager preferred to gather news;
he did capture an insurgent emissary who revealed that the father and son
who escaped prosecution for stealing sheep in January had joined Villagrán,
and sent the messenger to raise rebellion at San Nicolás Tecomate, a village
known for labor conflicts and livestock thefts at Tulancalco.[55]

The people of Tecomate did not rise up, but trouble came to Tulancalco soon enough. Late in May fifty mounted rebels attacked. They took un-counted livestock and three resident *indios* joined the insurgents. Two nearby properties of the Conde de Regla were also invaded. San Javier lost livestock. At Temoaya, rebels sacked the great house, taking the goods and money in the estate store. There, most resident *indios* joined the up-rising, though it is not clear if they left with the rebels or just joined in the sacking. At Tesoutlapa, Hispanic employees defended the property; three died. Olguín heard rumors of insurgent *indios* from Meztitlán march-ing on Actopan. The Tlahuelilpan troop chased the rebels that attacked Tulancalco and its neighbors as they retreated toward Mixquiahuala.[56]

After the assault, Olguín left to live with his family at Actopan, going out daily to oversee production and "give rations." Still distributing maize as pay for work, he irrigated the crop in the fields in late May and hired *in-dios* to transplant maguey in June. Amid insurgency, he aimed to maintain production for the long term. Pulque sales stayed strong from January to June of 1811, averaging over 220 cargas monthly—down a bit from the peaks of early insurgency, but well above historic levels. Sales in local tav-erns earned pesos to keep production going. Rebels faced consequences. Olguín convinced the priest who said mass at Tulancalco to order the whipping of three *indios* who had joined a recent assault. To keep local peace, they were not turned over to the authorities.[57]

The summer of 1811 brought endless reports of conflict. In May the Tlahuelilpan troop attacked insurgents led by a Captain Centeno near Actopan; eight men and three women were captured, along with gun-powder and 200 animals. In the same letter, Olguín reported an attack by Calleja on El Cardonal along with rumors that "an Englishman" was leading *indios* at Aculco to the west.[58] In June, insurgents left Actopan to concentrate at Alfajayucan, where the priest had fled, and near El Cardonal, where 4,000 to 6,000 insurgent *indios* remained. As July began, 200 attacked Tepeji del Río; by the middle of the month, well-armed mounted bands held Arroyo Zarco, Xilotepec, and Tula, blocking the road to San Juan del Río and the Bajío. Villagrán's son held Zimapán while *"mucha indiada"* ruled El Cardonal. Olguín relayed all this with mounting anxiety while lamenting loyalist requisitions of Tulancalco's horses.[59]

As August turned to September, Olguín saw a region locked in conflict. Julián Villagrán led 600 armed and mounted men backed by seven can-non at Huichapan. A Hispanic insurgent challenging regime power, he may have been the least ideological of political rebels; he fought to rule his highland bastion.[60] More feared by the manager were the 13,000 insurgent *indios* who ruled Ixmiquilpan, the Mezquital republic favored with irrigated lands. The priest had fled. Alfajayucan, Tepetitlán, Chilcuatla, and Tasquila turned to insurgency, and the clergy there also fled.

While the Otomí took control of republics, expelling officials and clergy, attacks focused on haciendas—and turned increasingly deadly. When insurgents stormed the Hacienda de Batá, they took goods and money, and killed the owner, don Francisco Villaverde. The Regla family had leased the Jalpa estate, in the west near Chapa de Mota, to don Francisco Morales. Captured, he paid 2,000 pesos for freedom. A manager barely escaped at Casa Blanca, while the Salto estate lost eighty horses. Rebels looted stores at Huipustla. The commercial economy faced siege. Don Francisco Villaldea, the *conductor de platas* who shipped silver from Real del Monte to Mexico City for the Reglas, guarded 200,000 pesos at Pachuca. He could not deliver desperately needed funds to the capital while 600 armed and mounted insurgents blocked the road at Singuilucan.[61]

Early September brought polarizing conflict to Actopan. The head town, its officials, and most people remained loyal; priests and others retreated to safety there. But five nearby pueblos were taken by local insurgents. Judges at Actopan were busy, the jail full. "Actopan patriots" joined the Tlahuelilpan troop to attack rebel communities, killing 300. The rebels carried on.

So did production at Tulancalco. Thanks to irrigation, the maize maturing in the fields promised a good crop. Elsewhere, poor rains (and insurgent depredations) threatened harvests. Pulque sales declined from July through September, reaching a low of 134 cargas, suggesting that cash was scarce in towns and villages. Tulancalco had not faced attack recently, but the manager believed that "the indios in the towns close by have become insolent." Nightly they stole livestock from Tulancalco and other estates; loyal dependents captured two who were surprised rustling. Others escaped with twenty head.[62] With insurgents ruling pueblos and sacking estates, how did Olguín carry on? Irrigated maize and careful compromise. With the harvest months away, maize was scarce and expensive in September, limiting pulque sales. A search for sustenance drove villagers to take livestock at night while maize matured in the fields.

Production carried on and pulque sales turned up again, climbing to 174 cargas in October, 187 in November. Rebels ruled roads from the Mezquital to Mexico City. Insurgents took Mixquiahuala, robbing stores and the homes of leading residents. The Tlahuelilpan troop attacked 500 insurgents there, killing 5 and capturing 4. Most escaped. Insurgent pueblos still surrounded Actopan. Olguín held the annual livestock roundup, joined as always by the managers of neighboring estates to ensure that only Tulancalco's animals got the estate brand. Talk detailed losses to insurgents: San Javier had lost uncounted horses; at Temoaya rebels had taken horses, 200 pesos, and the manager's clothing—leaving him naked before his workers.[63]

On November 15, Olguín detailed another round of conflict at Actopan. Insurgents took over the pueblo of Lagunilla and burned the "the priest's home." Rebels controlled villages from Actopan to Pachuca. The next day Olguín wrote that the Casa Blanca estate, near Huipustla, had been attacked and sacked, the manager killed, his body defiled. Then Olguín heard of insurgents approaching Tulancalco. He fled to pass a worried night in the hills. No attack came. The band turned on Tetepango, sending its magistrate in flight to Actopan.[64]

Into December, conflict raged around Tulancalco. Near Tizayuca, 200 insurgents took a pack train carrying barley and straw to Mexico City; three mule trains of the Conde de la Cortina were captured; San Javier lost its last sixty horses. The haciendas Sebastián and Batá were sacked and robbed—"destroyed," wrote Olguín. Tula was attacked again, this time by a band from Zimapán. Stores, the tobacco monopoly, and the homes of leading citizens were emptied. As 1811 drew to an end, insurgents ruled north of Tula and pressed attacks south beyond Tulancalco, ever closer to the capital. Olguín asked local officials to send the two *indios* captured rustling to Mexico City. Doña María Josefa promised to seek punishment.[65] What else could the manager do? He could not take arms against the villagers Tulancalco relied on to plant and harvest maize. He worried yet remained safe; pulque sales rose; the harvest would soon begin.

Everything changed on December 10. Insurgents attacked without warning at six in the morning; finding no money and the manager away, the attackers took clothing and a few jewels. They returned three days later. Olguín and his family hid in an assistant's house. Estate residents, including *gañanes* won over by the shift to pay in maize, did not betray him. Olguín again sent his family to safety, this time at Tetepango; he went to Actopan, visiting Tulancalco to oversee the harvest and "give rations."[66] His next letter, the last to doña María Josefa, was dated January 8, sent from Actopan. He had gone to mass seeking divine support, or at least personal resolve, and was about to leave for Tulancalco to check on the harvest and distribute maize.[67]

Olguín wrote his last report on Tulancalco and insurgency on January 13, addressed to don Joaquín Echarte, a Mexico City merchant. The manager noted that insurgents daily operated as "gangs of thieves," robbing the towns of Tepeji del Río and Villa de Carbón, sacking the Batá

and Casa Blanca estates. Olguín stayed at Actopan, traveling daily to oversee the harvest at Tulancalco. Without his presence, maize would not end
up in the estate granary. He wrote to Echarte because doña María Josefa's
lease ended with the harvest; she would not renew. Olguín proposed
taking the lease himself and sought Echarte's backing.[68]

Olguín believed he had found a way to carry on amid insurgency.
Maintaining pulque production and local sales, cultivating irrigated maize,
and paying resident *indios* in maize (and villagers too; from early 1811,
there is no mention of reales, just rations)—Olguín forged a mix of secure
dependence and symbiotic exploitation. Local peace held; Tulancalco kept
producing. The estate had leased for 4,000 pesos yearly; Olguín offered
3,000, a discount for insurgency. Echarte would not offer a *fianza*, a bond,
and the Conde de Santiago would not lease without one.[69] Olguín proved
an exceptional manager amid insurgency; but neither Echarte nor the
Conde foresaw continuing success. What happened at Tulancalco after
January 1812 is unknown.

Insurgency and Counterinsurgency, 1810–15: The Tlahuelilpan Report

The persistence of insurgency and the pacification of 1815 are reported in
a source very different from Olguín's letters. In 1816, the Mezquital finally
at peace, the Conde de la Cortina and his manager at Tlahuelilpan—a set
of properties that mixed irrigated fields with grazing north of Tula—sent a
long document to officials in Mexico City. Cortina sought recompense for
the costs of defending property and the regime; don Vicente Fernández
hoped for recognition of years of risky service. These were interested views
and claims. Fernández wrote as the war seemed won, in contrast with
the immediacy of Olguín's letters. Still, the two sources, both with anti-
insurgent perspectives, converge on much about the months from 1810
into 1812, and Fernández opens a local view of insurgency from 1812 until
its end in 1815.

Writing in 1815, Fernández' long title emphasized that he led
"Tlahuelilpan Patriots" to defend "the just cause." Patriotism and justice
were with his troop. He documented the fight by Otomí insurgents who
fought officials and clerics, attacked estates that supplied silver mines, and
claimed livestock to sustain guerrillas and communities through years of
insurgency. They reclaimed autonomies to push back silver capitalism;
they imagined a future built on landed communities, and in the end
gained some success.

Fernández was proud of his efforts. He shared credit with his men, emphasizing that they were *sirvientes* of Tlahuelilpan, Ulapa, Pozos, Tenguedó, Atotonilco, and Teocalco, all property of the Conde de la Cortina and managed by Fernández from Tlahuelilpan.[70] He insisted that they had rushed to defend Fernando VII (in captivity since 1808; back in power in 1814) and holy religion: "On first news of the infernal rebellion and of the voracious fire of seduction its leaders had traitorously lit in the simple and tranquil hearts of the people of the kingdom." Hidalgo had risen to defend Fernando and true religion in 1810; in 1815 Fernández, like many loyalists, insisted that had been his role. The focus on seduction placed Otomí insurgents in dependent, female, ultimately pardonable roles, an important emphasis given the way the insurgency ended. As to the few who led the uprisings, Fernández saw things simply: "they did not work with justice or authority. . . . They persecuted Europeans to take their wealth"—a view betrayed by his own narrative and Olguín's letters.[71] That view explained little, but it legitimated dogged pursuit of leaders like Julián Villagrán and eventual pardons for most Otomí.

On October 30, 1810, Fernández began to arm and train men to defend his king and true religion: he honored "a handful of sirvientes at Tlahuelilpan" as first defenders. There is no hint that Fernández considered fleeing, as Olguín wrote at the time. Fernández emphasized that on November 10 he and fifteen troopers headed out on a "first sally," riding west toward Tepeji del Río and Villa de Carbón. They liberated two artillery wagons, several soldiers captured by Hidalgo at Monte de las Cruces, and 20,000 sheep. The soldiers returned to their units, the sheep to their proprietors.[72] Fernández took to the field after the insurgents' retreat from Monte de las Cruces and defeat at Aculco. He knew the art of the possible.

Returning to Tlahuelilpan on November 20, thirty more *sirvientes* joined the troop. They set out to warn nearby pueblos of the threat posed by the "bandits of Tepetitlán"—an Otomí community close to Tlahuelilpan where villagers had long worked at the estate and gained a reputation as bandits in recent conflicts. The parallels with Tulancalco are clear. Mezquital estates and villages had become foes—locked in exploitations far from symbiotic.[73]

For four months, the Tlahuelilpan troopers trained and raised alarms, watching as Villagrán took control at Huichapan. Fernández tried to keep insurgents out of the basin around Tula, Tetepango, and Actopan—the core of southern Mezquital. He succeeded until March 24, 1811, when rebels took Tula. He could not fight 2,000 rebels with forty-five patriots while prominent citizens fled rather than join in defense.[74] After the attack, he led his small troop toward Tula. "But we had barely marched half a league, when the rest of the sirvientes of the Conde de Cortina came shouting *vivas* and pledging to die rather than join the party of rioting." They demanded arms to serve as "faithful vassals of the king." The enlarged troop camped at Cerro de Buena Vista overlooking Tula. Fernández sent notes to priests at Atitalaquía and Tetepango, calling them to send parishioners to join his force. None came. The next day, the rebels left Tula.[75] Fernández believed they fled before his force; likely they planned to raid and retreat.

On March 29, 200 loyal troops arrived at Tula. On April 3, Villagrán attacked again, with 15,000 insurgents by Fernández' count. The Tlahuelilpan troop, forty strong, occupied the Paso del Puente, keeping another 1,500 rebels from the battle.[76] Local villagers backed Villagrán and his rebels in the second assault. The numbers were likely exaggerated, but suggest that many Otomí joined in sacking the homes and stores of the powerful and prosperous in Tula.

With Villagrán repelled—or having sacked and retreated again—a Coronel Andrade took command at Tula on April 5. Fernández provided forty of Tlahuelilpan's best horses. During April and May, the manager continued to train his *patriotas*, now eighty strong, visiting "nearby pueblos," chasing enemies "without forgetting to set right the wretched people who had been infested by the incendiary papers of our enemies." Fernández "collected a few examples, printed and manuscript."[77] While regular troops held Tula, the Tlahuelilpan patriots tried to keep Otomí villagers from joining the uprising.

On May 29, Fernández received news that "the cabecilla Centeno famous for monstrous robberies and killings, led a large band" near Actopan. Fernández set off with thirty-four patriots to fight Centeno, strong in an upland bastion with more than one hundred men. The manager-commander gloated: "We destroyed them completely. . . . The miraculous victory confirmed the strong commitments of my patriots, disabused many pueblos that had not yet decided for the just cause, filled the malicious with panic and terror, and increased considerably the number of the faithful who decided for the party of truth and justice, making Tlahuelilpan the center offering refuge to those who fled the enemy and sought security between Mexico City and Querétaro."[78]

Fernández saw the conflict in the Mezquital as a fight for the allegiance of the majority, mostly Otomí. The victory over Centeno near Actopan ensured that insurgents would not gain a quick hegemony, that head towns from Tula to Actopan would hold loyal (if subject to periodic raids), and that the southern Mezquital countryside would remain contested. Tlahuelilpan became a loyal oasis between the capital and the Bajío. That counted as a triumph in the summer of 1811. For Fernández it was a time of capturing and killing rebel *cabecillas*, returning stolen livestock to estates, and admonishing women: "I rounded up a number of women abandoned by their husbands in rebel camps and gave them liberty." Insurgent bases had become communities, including women who sustained a patriarchal insurgency. Fernández hoped the women he captured and freed would sway "their husbands, sons, and kin" to surrender and take pardons. Yet he reported that only one "Indio, cabecilla, Governor of the Pueblo of Santa María" accepted amnesty.[79] Meanwhile, Fernández forged eight cannons, bought thirty-six rifles, and made eighty lances to defend "the many decent families who came to the estate."[80]

In early fall, the troop attacked rebels led by Casimiro Gómez near Actopan, killing 150. Again, many *indias* were captured. Fernández added: "I instructed them through an interpreter." He insisted that he offered compassion and asked the Otomí women to bring "husbands, sons, and brothers" to take amnesty. This time, more than 1,000 accepted pardons and promised to live as "good patriots." The victory over Gómez came with the backing of the pueblos of Yolo and Lagunilla, bastions of *indio* loyalty.[81] Division and violence marked the Mezquital.

Beginning on the last day of October, the troop chased raiders through the pueblos of Tepetitlán, Chapatongo, and Alfajayucan, retrieving 2,000 sheep for don Ángel Puyade. In mid-November Fernández helped fortify Tula again. In December and January, as estates harvested what they could, the troop pursued *cabecillas* aiming to raise pueblos and take maize as it came in. After reporting so many priests who fled the uprising, a rebel cleric named Correa gained notice—and excommunication. From October 1811 through February 1812, as Olguín's reports ended, Fernández detailed endless pursuits and no victories.[82] Guerrilla conflict set in. Otomí majorities controlled many villages, denying regime authority, expelling priests, taking livestock. The Tlahuelilpan troop repeatedly entered pueblos, killed *cabecillas*, instructed women (by means not detailed, but perhaps more than verbal), and retrieved livestock. Few took pardons. Claiming maize harvests and livestock, Mezquital insurgents turned estate produce to family sustenance.

A violent stalemate continued, to enter a new phase in April 1812. Still patrolling pueblos and reclaiming livestock, Fernández's troop began to escort convoys carrying silver from Real del Monte to Mexico City. Mining resumed, reviving demand for labor and estate produce, creating funds for the regime. In October, Fernández led 200 *patriotas* backed by 300 *indios* from the "loyal pueblos of Yolo and Lagunilla" against insurgents around Ixmiquilpan. Many fled north to El Cardonal.[83] Similar sorties continued in 1813.[84] That summer, Fernández led 210 patriots backed by only 106 *indios* from the "most loyal towns of Yolo, Lagunilla, and Santiago," in an assault on Huichapan. The Villagráns were captured and executed, breaking the Hispanic insurgency that challenged regime power for three years. Fernández gloried in the victory, yet offered no explanation for the shift in fortunes.[85]

As often in Mexican history, disease shaped social conflict. Typhus struck Cuautla south of Mexico City during the February 1812 siege that kept the rebel band led by José María Morelos from the capital. It proved deadly among many who took refuge in the city in March 1813; it struck Cuautitlán just south of the Mezquital in summer; in October it ravaged Atlacomulco in the northern Valley of Toluca.[86] The disease demobilized insurgents and loyalists alike, while the return to mining opened chances for employment. In that context, the Tlahuelilpan troop raised a few loyal *indios* to help defeat the Villagráns. Hispanic political rebellion ended in the Mezquital.[87]

Otomí village insurgencies continued long after the Villagráns' defeat, making the independence of the popular risings clear. Only in May of 1814 did the Mezquital conflict take a new turn. Fernández led a small patrol of fifteen patriots into the insurgent bastion of Tepetitlán, offering amnesty— and the right to organize a company of one hundred mounted patriots to keep the peace and defend against attacks.[88] Otomí rebels gained sanction as an armed militia, officially to defend the regime, inevitably to consolidate local power. If this was not insurgent victory, it certainly was not defeat. If the goal was autonomy, amnesty gave the rebels much of what they fought for. Tlahuelilpan could resume production, hiring hands from a pacified Tepetitlán. Labor relations surely found a new tone as once-rebel villagers, sanctioned in arms, ruled the pueblo.

Through the rest of 1814 and into 1815, the troop offered amnesties with rights to keep militias across the Mezquital. Officially it was a victorious pacification. Myth ended the Otomí insurgency. Pueblos acquiesced in loyalist proclamations of victory; the regime sanctioned pueblo militias. Men in Otomí republics gained armed powers prohibited since the sixteenth century. The regime might rule, but pueblo autonomy (still limited by arid lands) found new strength as *indios* kept arms and gained new respect. Did they also keep the livestock claimed in insurgency? Did they gain access to estate *montes* to graze larger herds, perhaps access to lands to plant maize? Such gains were likely; Fernández would not report them to officials in the capital. People across the Mezquital negotiated new futures with reinforced autonomies and renewed access to wage work in estate fields and at Real del Monte mines. In March of 1815, insurgency ended in the Mezquital, yet persisted around Otumba and in the Bajío.[89]

To complete his report, Fernández took testimony from Spanish citizens who lived through the conflict. One saw the Tlahuelilpan troop as fighting "four years of insurrection . . . four years of bitter desolation."[90] Another stated simply that the troop controlled "rebel indios." Manuel Olguín, sixty-one years old in 1815, living at Tetepango and self-described as "Spaniard, Citizen, y Cultivator," stated that the troop patrolled the pueblos: "disabusing them, making them see the error induced in them by the rebels."[91] Olguín still saw a conflict pitting defenders of justice against malevolent rebels, competing for *indios'* allegiance. He and Fernández shared a myth that facilitated pacification: the Otomí were simple people deceived into rebellion. Olguín's letters and Fernández' report show that insurgent *indios* had visions of their own—fair sustenance grounded in pueblo autonomies. With pacification, they gained much of that.

The Costs of Insurgency: Cortina's Calculations, 1816

The Conde de la Cortina, owner of Tlahuelilpan, paid the costs of Fernández' troop and organized the report that detailed the counterinsurgent fight. Cortina wanted compensation; his bill totaled 79,750 pesos. He argued that the troop had allowed the continuation of at least limited

Table 4.1. Pulque Tax Collections in the Mezquital, 1804–15 (in pesos)

Years	Actopan and Tetepango	Tula	Total
1804–9	22,580	22,588	45,168
1810–15	17,300	10,535	27,835
Percentage decline	23	53	38

Source: VFT, fol. 77v.

Table 4.2. Tithe Collections in Actopan, Tetepango, and Tula, 1805–14

Years	Sacks of Maize	Cargas of Pulque	Lambs
1805–9	11,391	4,594	7,350
1810–14	7,442	4,016	4,400
Percentage decline	35	13	40

Source: VFT, fols. 79v–80.

estate production, pivotal to defending the regime in trying years. He added that in the pulque zones around Zempoala, Otumba, and Apan in the northeast Valley of Mexico, there had been no such defense, and there, commercial production and tax collections had ceased.[92]

To document the persistence of production in the Mezquital, Cortina used tax and tithe records showing that the estate economy had fallen nearly forty percent during the rebellion. It was a sign of destructive times that a leading entrepreneur could celebrate such a decline. His data, summarized in tables 4.1 and 4.2, suggest that the decline was real, but more complex.

Cortina's figures first compared pulque tax collections during six years before the insurgency, 1804 through 1809, and six years that included insurgency, 1810 through 1815. The decline of fifty-three percent at Tula reflected the greater insurgency there, the fall of only twenty-three percent at Actopan and Tetepango showed the persistence of production there—as confirmed in Olguín's letters. The tithe reports included three key products: maize, pulque, and sheep. Tithes were levied on harvests in the field, not earnings from sales. With indigenous growers exempt, the reports reflect commercial production. They compare collections in 1805–9 to those of 1810–14. The fall of maize harvests by thirty-five percent closely maps the fall of pulque taxes by thirty-eight percent, perhaps accurately calculating commercial decline. Of course, maize taken by villagers and insurgents was not tithed, suggesting that production did not fall as much as collections. That pulque tithes fell only thirteen percent while taxes dropped thirty-eight percent indicates that estates made large sales in small amounts in local markets (as Olguín reported)—and evaded taxes. The forty percent decline in lambs delivered as tithes after 1810 documents villagers' liberation of sheep.

The tax and tithe figures suggest that regime revenues fell steeply—thirty-five to forty percent—tithes fell less—perhaps thirty percent—and production even less—perhaps twenty percent. The difference is a measure of the transfer of produce to insurgent villagers. Limited production enabled estates and villagers to carry on through years of violent stalemate. Estates found profits scarce and the regime remained desperate for revenues while villagers took produce and reinforced autonomies. Entrepreneurs' search for profit and the regime's need for revenues help explain a pacification that conceded village autonomies in 1815. Sanctioning local rule by armed ex-insurgents proved the only way to return the Mezquital to production in support of the mines at Real de Monte and revenues for Mexico City. The Otomí kept control of communities, planted maize as they could, and labored when possible as battles waned. Communities in the Mezquital and around Otumba and Apan, where insurgency continued through 1816, forced losses on entrepreneurs invested in pulque and a regime that lived on its revenues. Villagers reinforced autonomies while weakening capitalists, the regime, and the silver economy.

CHAPTER FIVE

Insurgencies and Empires

THE FALL OF SILVER CAPITALISM, 1808–21

BEGINNING IN 1808 everything seemed to fall apart in New Spain. Napoleon invaded Spain and captured its Bourbon kings. In Mexico City, a summer of intense politics debated what to do about a suddenly vacated sovereignty: many pressed for popular rights until military powers overthrew the viceroy, proclaiming they acted as the people. In 1810, provincial elites in the Bajío rose to demand political rights—and set off a mass insurgency that challenged power and property for a decade in silver capitalism's most dynamic region. Otomí villagers in the Mezquital and nearby joined insurgencies too. The risings strangled silver mining at Guanajuato and Real del Monte. By 1811, the delivery of silver to the world was cut in half.

The powerful mobilized quickly to defend silver capitalism and an uncertain Spanish regime. Through years of conflict, the indigenous republics of the heartland's most fertile regions continued to feed themselves and the capital, sustaining the fight against political and popular insurgents through a decade of conflict. They kept the regime in place as silver capitalism limped on in times of imperial crisis, political challenge, and insurgency. Then, after a decade of violent stalemate, silver capitalism fell, Spain's rule ended, and New Spain became Mexico in 1821.

As 1808 began, New Spain remained economically vibrant, deeply unequal, and socially stable—the richest place in the Americas, the source of silver essential to global trade and European powers in a time of war, the base of Spain's attempt to remain a power while Britain and Napoleonic France fought for Atlantic dominance. In 1821, a new regime announced a Mexican empire. But silver capitalism was gone, leaving political men to debate monarchical visions, constitutional liberalism, and other ways to a political nation—while they searched for a new economy. Everything was in question when Mexico became independent in 1821.[1]

From Broken Sovereignty to Unimagined Insurgencies, 1808–10

Before May 1808, despite demands for revenue and mounting social pressures, New Spain held stable, generating silver at historic peaks while war ravaged Europe and the Atlantic world.[2] The examples of the United States and Haiti were discussed and debated, but few in New Spain imagined a war for independence; fewer foresaw popular insurgencies.[3] Everything changed after Napoleon's armies took Madrid, captured the Spanish Bourbons Carlos IV and Fernando VII, father and son, and tried to impose Joseph Bonaparte as José I, leaving a vacuum of legitimate sovereignty across Spain and its dominions. Goya's *The Third of May* painting says everything about the moment in Madrid. Spaniards resisted French rule.

The people who ruled and prospered in New Spain knew themselves as *Españoles*—most as *Americanos*, plus a few immigrants from Spain. On news of broken sovereignty and popular resistance in Spain, in August Viceroy don José de Iturrigaray and the Mexico City Council called a junta. In Hispanic tradition, sovereignty was a gift of God to the pueblos, towns that delegated sovereignty to the monarch—in return for justice.[4] Thanks to Napoleon's invasion and Spaniards' rejection of José, there was no legitimate monarch to rule or do justice in Spain or New Spain.[5] Iturrigaray and the council were strong in tradition when they aimed to call delegates from Spanish cities across New Spain (and the capital's indigenous republics, too) to meet and discuss the reconstitution of sovereignty. The viceroy represented the captured monarchs; the council represented landed elites and professionals, most American by birth, yet many linked to entrepreneurial immigrants from Spain. The proposed Junta of New Spain would assemble representatives of the powerful to discuss sovereignty in the absence of the monarch.[6]

In September, however, an alliance of military officers, judges of the Mexico City high court, and a clique of frustrated merchants, nearly all immigrants from Spain, mobilized armed men to oust the viceroy and block New Spain's chance to join in remaking sovereignty (all negotiated and imposed in the Viceregal Palace shown in figure 5.1). Coup leaders toppling the established regime by armed force while calling themselves "the people" insisted that New Spain must recognize and fund the junta in Seville then proclaiming itself supreme. Spanish power would rule backed

FIGURE 5.1. The Viceregal Palace, Mexico City: pivot of politics, 1808.

by armed power; immigrant Spaniards would dominate government and commerce. The coup aimed to ensure that the silver still flowing at peak levels would fund the fight against Napoleon. If the viceroy and the council sought unity among New Spain's elites, the coup alliance of military officers, high-court judges, and aspiring merchants put Spain and immigrant Spaniards first, at a time when no effective regime ruled in Madrid. The viceroy, the council, and their allies did not resist. The men who promoted New Spain's right to join in remaking sovereignty were not ready to fight. They stood back as armed men toppled the viceroy, blocked the Junta of New Spain, and broke the regime of judicial mediation—all to keep the link between Spain and New Spain.[7]

In a few weeks, the most basic questions of sovereignty were opened, debated, and closed in ways that left people across New Spain without participation, while they learned (with delays and distortions) that people in Spain were fighting Napoleon and struggling to build a new regime. Powerful elites, provincial notables, and popular communities across New Spain were locked in uncertainty because armed Spaniards, mostly immigrants, blocked the Junta of New Spain. The leading entrepreneurs of Mexico City, American and immigrant, acquiesced in that outcome. Silver flowed to Spain at peak levels in 1809. In the provinces, less powerful leaders who also saw themselves as Spaniards, with all the rights of Spaniards, chafed at the exclusions.

From September 1808 to September 1810, popular rights and the re-constitution of sovereignty were debated in Spain and New Spain. Political resistance and guerrilla forces across Spain generated regional juntas. The one at Seville aimed to forge a central sovereignty for the empire by calling for delegates from juntas across Spain, and allowing American kingdoms to send representatives (but not create juntas). Fourteen cities in New Spain would join to send one delegate; all could send petitions of grievance and goals. Such participation was unprecedented, yet minimal compared to the opening to resistance movements across Spain. The process of generating petitions and selecting the representative for New Spain played out during 1809.

The Junta Central had barely begun its work when French forces took Seville. In the summer of 1810, it dissolved itself, left a regency in its place, and called a *cortes*—a parliament—to meet at Cádiz, the port that linked Spain and its Americas, the last major city outside French control. Spanish councils across the empire gained increased representation. Still, the nine delegates from New Spain were far fewer than those reserved for the Spanish resistance. Had the proportional representation claimed for Spain (then mostly under French control) been allowed to New Spain, its delegates would have formed a powerful block commensurate with the silver kingdom's leading economic role. Again, the offer of representation was unprecedented—and the radical underrepresentation was blatant. New Spain's leading cities chose delegates, who were on route to Cádiz when the Hidalgo revolt began at Dolores, near the Guanajuato mines, in September 1810. When the *cortes* opened eight days later, New Spain's delegates had not arrived, and those in Cádiz did not know that everything had changed in New Spain.[8]

The political opening that led to Cádiz was limited in New Spain. Only the men of the Spanish councils in major cities gained roles. Yet Napoleon's invasion, the capture of the monarchs, the call for a Junta of New Spain, the coup that rejected it, and the promises and limits of the Seville-Cádiz project combined to create a stir that reached beyond the few called to participate. As the limits of New Spain's voice and votes became clear, provincial elites, first in Valladolid (now Morelia), then at Querétaro, sought roles in re-creating sovereignty. Seeking juntas, they followed Iberian precedent. They did not conspire for independence. Nascent juntas in both cities were revealed to postcoup authorities loyal to uncertain powers Spain. In the face of imminent arrest, outlying participants in the Querétaro movement, Father Miguel Hidalgo and militia lieutenant don Ignacio Allende, provoked the rising at Dolores on September 16, 1810.

Less political people across New Spain also faced challenges between September 1808 and September 1810. In city plazas and *pulquerías*, in town centers and village markets, the news from Spain and Mexico City caused endless talk. Ideologues and military men proclaimed popular rights, while the latter blocked their implementation. Priests announced the evil of Napoleon and called on Guadalupe to protect New Spain in dire times. Meanwhile, two years of deep drought had made maize scarce and expensive across the highlands, from the heartland to the Bajío and beyond. Struggling families lived in desperation while rich entrepreneurs (often men claiming representation) took profit from hunger. Famine and profiteering were not new; they had struck with deadly intensity in 1785–86. But 1809 and 1810 brought drought and famine, desperation and profiteering, amid a crisis of sovereignty and assertions of popular rights.[9]

The Hidalgo revolt came after two years in which sovereignty was broken, participation debated, and hunger stalked the land. Yet only provincial elites and rural communities in limited (yet strategically important) regions joined the uprising. When its vast yet inchoate mobilization was crushed early in 1811, some went home to press enduring regional insurgencies, political and popular, others found different routes through years of conflict and uncertainty. The Hidalgo revolt of 1810 began as an unplanned alliance of provincial elites demanding political rights and Bajío peoples, mixed and indigenous, most living as commercial dependents without rights to republics, newly angered by desperation imposed on their everyday lives.

Insurgencies, Political and Popular, 1810–12

The revolt that began that Sunday morning in September of 1810 surprised everyone. Hidalgo and Allende perhaps expected a few hundred to join at Dolores, a few hundred more around San Miguel. Did they imagine that by the time they captured Celaya days later they would be surrounded by thousands of angry men, a few mounted and armed, most on foot and wielding only machetes? Early on, most came from Bajío estate communities—settlements on private property without republican rights. Rebels were quick to empty estate granaries. When they took the city of Guanajuato, thousands of mine workers joined in. Heading south through Michoacán they recruited thousands more, some from indigenous republics. When the rebel mass approached Mexico City in late October it was a moving throng of over 40,000 insurgents.

As they approached the capital via the high Toluca basin, Bajío insurgents began to learn the limits of their movement. Few villagers joined them, despite long-simmering conflicts with the powerful Atengo estates. Many resented insurgent demands for food as the first good crop in two years stood ripe in the fields. In the capital, many feared the rebels. With little local support, Hidalgo sent his forces into a skirmish at Monte de las Cruces in the heights between Toluca and Mexico City, and then turned back toward the Bajío. As they retreated and faced defeat at Aculco, news of the insurgency reached Otomí communities in the Mezquital. They did not join Hidalgo, but turned on local towns and estates, beginning a long local insurgency. Hidalgo, Allende, and the survivors of Aculco returned to the Bajío, consolidated their base, and then marched west to Guadalajara, where they took the city and gained wide rural support.[10]

During the months that the Hidalgo revolt threatened the regime, a key contradiction shaped the movement. Hidalgo, Allende, and other political rebels called for rights to join in a refoundation of sovereignty— always in the name of Fernando VII, always against Napoleon and the "godless" French, always with sharp anger against *gachupines*, the immigrant Spaniards who seemed to monopolize regime posts and profitable trade—and led the 1808 coup that stymied political participation in New Spain. The insurgent masses, in contrast, sacked stores and estates, taking the necessities of life from *gachupines* and Americans alike. Allende, son of an immigrant who had left him a modest landed estate, and Hidalgo, an American priest and struggling estate operator, tried to deflect their followers from such attacks, to no avail. The uprising rhetorically assaulted *gachupines* and the French while it physically attacked the regime and its militias, the rich and their accumulations. The landed rich and the militias were mostly American.

While rebel leaders and popular insurgents grappled with their contradictions, those who expected to rule and profit rediscovered the unity that had fractured in the summer of 1808. Key participants in the Querétaro meetings that included Hidalgo and Allende, notably Corregidor don Miguel Domínguez, declared loyalty and mobilized against the insurgents. Mexico City elites who had debated sovereignty and demanded political rights saw no good in uprisings that attacked officials, took crops and livestock, and assaulted the social order. Power holders united to back counterinsurgent forces, led by don Félix Calleja and militias from San Luis Potosí, north of the Bajío. They crushed Hidalgo's rebels at Puente de Calderón, near Guadalajara, in January 1811. Hidalgo, Allende, and other rebel leaders fled north, and were soon captured, tried, and executed. The defenders of power still ruled, but the option of insurgency was unleashed.[11]

After Puente de Calderón, while a few leaders dispersed and struggled on, the insurgent majority returned home to the Bajío, often to the estates where they had long lived and worked. Many took wages to plant and harvest another crop, and then took arms to claim the food they had made. They ousted managers, took over fields, and turned to family production—taking new autonomies in a region long marked by lives of commercial dependence.[12] They fed rebel bands camped in upland strongholds fending off loyalists and raiding convoys carrying silver from Guanajuato. Meanwhile, Otomí insurgents in Mezquital villages assaulted estates near the Real del Monte mines. Popular control of the Bajío and the Mezquital threatened the mining pivotal to New Spain's prosperity and the war against Napoleon. Calleja retook Guanajuato and spent 1811 trying to contain Bajío insurgents. His failure led to long political and social conflicts.[13]

Calleja focused on the insurgents threatening silver. In 1811, New Spain's output fell to half the level sustained before 1810, to remain depressed through the decade of insurgency and long after. Two conflicts struck silver capitalism simultaneously. In New Spain insurgents inhibited mining at Guanajuato and Real del Monte, limiting investment, making supplies uncertain and expensive, forcing costly armed convoys to escort shipments across the region. In Spain, after French forces occupied most of the south in 1810, access to mercury at Almadén in the Sierra Morena was cut by the vagaries of guerrilla war. Mining declined while demand for revenue to fight the French in Spain and insurgents in New Spain rose. Capital to invest in tunnels and drainage vanished. The silver economy that sustained New Spain, Spain's fading power, and global trade became fragile as wars and insurgencies demanded revenues.[14]

The entrenchment of popular insurgencies across the Bajío and the Mezquital, along with Calleja's focus on Guanajuato, helped scattered political insurgents survive. Don Ignacio López Rayón, son of a Tlalpujahua mining entrepreneur, a lawyer, and an aide to Hidalgo, proclaimed a Junta Soberana Americana in the summer of 2011 at Zitácuaro in uplands south of the Bajío and west of the Mezquital. José María Morelos, a priest close to Hidalgo and formally loyal to Rayón's junta, mobilized resistance in the tierra caliente along rugged Pacific slopes. By the time Calleja saw his inability to root out popular insurgents in the Bajío and the Mezquital, the political rebels around Rayón's Junta and Morelos's guerrillas were enduring threats, if far from centers of power and production. They watched the process leading to the Cádiz constitution in 1812 as it offered limited rights, aiming to sustain Spain's rule in New Spain. They called for full participation by Americans, claimed power in local domains, and railed against *gachupines* and the French, accusing both of denying the people of New Spain their rights as Spaniards.[15]

Anti-*gachupín* rhetoric became the public face of political insurgency. It marked immigrant Spaniards as a powerful few, responsible for the trials of New Spain.[16] It aimed to link all born in New Spain—Spaniards, mestizos, mulattoes, and *indios*—as Americans oppressed by Spain and its *gachupín* agents. Tension between European and American Spaniards were old, yet long limited. The immigrant Spaniards favored in high regime office and imperial trade had repeatedly married American landed heiresses and left American offspring. Beneath the heights of power, silver dynamism had generated a wide prosperity that moderated tensions. The coup of 1808 created a gaping split; *gachupines* had forced allegiance to the Seville junta by toppling a viceroy who was backed by an establishment that mixed powerful Europeans and Americans.[17]

In 1810 and after, anti-*gachupín* rhetoric escalated among rebel American Spaniards—Hidalgo and Allende, Rayón and Morelos. They focused anger on immigrants, favored subjects of the regime, while officials founding liberalism at Cádiz proclaimed popular sovereignty yet offered minimal participation to Americans. The most powerful European and American Spaniards held together to fight the Hidalgo revolt and the political and popular insurgencies that followed. The populace that joined Hidalgo in 1810, and carried on insurgencies for years after, fought *gachupines* when they were local officials or usurious merchants; they also attacked the estates of powerful Americans. Loyalty to the captured Fernando VII, disgust with the "godless" French, devotion to Guadalupe, and anger against *gachupines* shaped a rhetoric that mediated tenuous ties among the political and popular insurgencies that tore New Spain apart after 1810.[18]

Social War and Peace, 1810–12

While political insurgents demanded participation in sovereignty, assaulted *gachupines*, and took refuge in isolated retreats, popular insurgencies ruled the Bajío, the Mezquital, and the pulque zone northeast of Mexico City, along with the country around Guadalajara, Gulf coast uplands, and the Pacific hot country. Most native republics in the fertile southern heartland basins and across the highlands extending south through Oaxaca to Chiapas and Guatemala, and in lowland Yucatán, refrained. An analysis of why insurgency flourished in the Bajío surrounding

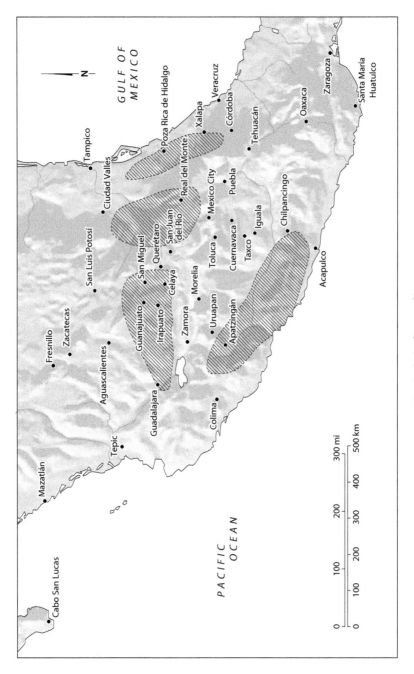

MAP 7. New Spain in the era of insurgency.

Guanajuato, but not around Querétaro, and why in the heartland insurgents ruled the Mezquital and pulque country, but not the valleys of Mexico, Toluca, and Cuernavaca, opens a window to the roots and limits of insurgency—before the option of liberalism arrived from Cádiz in 1812.[19]

Rural people around Mexico City and across the Bajío all faced deepening exploitation exacerbated by drought and famine between 1808 and 1810. They made different decisions about joining Hidalgo in 1810—and about local insurgencies in the years that followed.[20] Why? The Hidalgo revolt began around Dolores and San Miguel; the people of nearby estate communities joined in rising numbers, and after its defeat came home to press insurgencies that persisted to 1820. People around Querétaro, just east, knew immediately of Hidalgo's September revolt, but few joined— and few took arms during the years insurgents ruled all around them (in San Miguel, the Sierra Gorda, Huichapan, the Mezquital). People in the Mezquital learned of the Hidalgo revolt as it trekked west of them in the fall of 1810. Few joined Hidalgo, but many turned to local insurgencies that stretched to Otumba in the northeast Valley of Mexico and across the Apan plain beyond, risings that endured to 1815 and 1816. In contrast, people in southern heartland republics met the Hidalgo revolt when thousands of rebels camped near Toluca in October 1810, yet few joined then or later when Morelos came to Cuautla in 1812. Why did communities in neighboring regions respond so differently to the option of insurgency?

Insurgencies are violent mobilizations that challenge power and property for months, often years. They bring deadly risks to rebels and deep threats to those who presume to rule. Communities across the heartland had long traditions of rising in local *tumultos*, riots that took over plazas for a day or two, sometimes inflicted injuries and a few deaths—and then went to court to negotiate solutions. After 1810, heartland villagers still turned to *tumultos*, often hinting at links to the violent uprisings the powerful so feared—to good effect.[21] But *tumultos* were not insurgencies that threatened power and property, disrupted commercial production, or challenged the social order. More often, they aimed to restore it.

Insurgencies defined the Bajío from 1810 to 1820—with the important exception of the countryside around Querétaro. Unlike the basins around Mexico City where silver capitalism built on landed indigenous republics, the Bajío was founded anew in the sixteenth century, settled mostly by immigrants: a few Europeans, more Africans, most Mesoamericans. There were few indigenous republics, except along a southern fringe where Otomí and Tarascans gained community rights. By the eighteenth century, most Bajío towns were Spanish, most rural communities were on private lands, and most people were of mixed ancestry—including many classed as *indios*. Families lived as estate dependents without rights to land or republics.[22]

Hierarchies of patriarchy organized inequality in the Bajío.[23] Dominant men (and a few inheriting women) owned and operated the commercial estates that profited feeding cities and mining centers. They employed managers (always men) who employed the full-time workers (always men), part-time hands (always men and boys), and tenants (mostly men, plus a few widows) who worked the land. At every level of Bajío rural society, men joined in relations of unequal reciprocity, negotiating power and subordination, profit and labor, ensuring their dominance over women and children in households ranging from urban elites to the rural poor. Patriarchal hierarchies sustained silver capitalism in its most dynamic region—as long as working patriarchs gained secure access to the means to provide for dependent families.

When the famine of 1785–86 was followed by continued population growth, rising food prices, downward pressure on wages, and spreading evictions, men's ability to provide faced deepening challenges. Estate production carried on while generating widening inequities and imposing new insecurities—all driven to extremes with the return of dearth and famine during the political crisis of 1808 to 1810. Men and families in Bajío estate communities were hit hard—without land of their own, without the mediation of local notables, and with limited access to the courts.[24] As pressures heightened, men unable to provide struggled to defend claims to patriarchy—losses directly attributable to landlords and managers who cut earnings, raised rents, and forced evictions while openly profiteering in scarce grains. Patriarchy ceased to be even a minimally symbiotic exploitation. Thousands of men across the Bajío joined Hidalgo in 1810.

Families also faced challenges across the heartland. Populations grew while opportunities boomed for commercial growers. Most families there, however, lived in landed republics. When eighteenth-century population growth left community land ever less sufficient to needs, local notables organized work gangs to enable men and boys to gain wages at nearby estates, prospering as silver boomed and the capital grew. They forged symbiotic exploitations that strengthened patriarchy, relations that held to sustain production and social stability through the famine crisis of 1808–10—except in the arid Mezquital and nearby pulque zones.

Most Mesoamerican villagers remained at home and at work when thousands of Bajío men, irate in the face of dependent insecurities that assaulted claims to patriarchy, joined Hidalgo in 1810 and sustained

local insurgencies for a decade. Yet there were zones of exception in both
the heartland and the Bajío. In the latter, estate communities around
Querétaro generated little insurgency after 1810, while in the heartland
indigenous republics in the Mezquital and the pulque zones took arms
in risings that lasted years. Most Mezquital villagers and Querétaro estate residents were Otomí. But if there was Otomí exceptionalism, it led
to contrasting decisions: insurgency in the Mezquital; stability at work
around Querétaro. Why?

In the Mezquital, the Otomí majority lived in republics surrounded by
commercial estates. But in the arid strip that stretched from the northern
Valley of Toluca, across the Mezquital and the northeast Valley of Mexico,
to Apan, grazing was long the primary estate activity, with limited cultivation where irrigation allowed. If most natives lived in republics, large
minorities became estate-resident *gañanes*, who accepted dependence in
search of security. When population grew in the eighteenth century and
estates turned to seek profit from pulque, they created little demand for
labor—and most of that went to *gañanes*, leaving growing numbers of villagers struggling to survive on dry lands. Dependent *gañanes* carried on in
secure poverty. Villagers faced widening insecurities that were exploitative
without a hint of symbiosis. Conflicts between estates and villagers escalated after 1800; the drought of 1808–10 proved devastating. Community-
based insurgencies spread across the Mezquital and the pulque zone in
1810 (see chapter 5).

In contrast, the Otomí majority living at estates around Querétaro
rarely rose in rebellion. There, rural families lived and worked in geographic and economic environments little different from the Bajío basins
just west, where insurgency proved widespread, intense, and enduring.
Lands around Querétaro, as across the Bajío, were fertile and often
irrigated; estates raised the same crops in the same regional economy
supplying Guanajuato mines, Querétaro factories, and other towns. From
the 1790s, Querétaro estate residents faced the same pressures of rising
rents and forced evictions, the same limits on wages and rations, the same
jump in maize prices, the same profiteering from hunger faced by the people around Dolores and San Miguel. Yet men at Querétaro estates rarely
joined in the Hidalgo revolt or the long insurgencies that followed.

What explains the difference? Across the Bajío bottomlands from
Celaya west, diverse indigenous peoples had mixed with Africans to become *indios* dependent on estate lands[25]; in the northern uplands around
San Miguel and Dolores, Africans and Otomí mixed to make a mulatto
majority—also dependent on estate lands. Facing deepening pressures

after 1790 without autonomies or republican rights, people on the Bajío bottomlands and in its northern uplands turned to widespread and enduring insurgencies.[26]

Around Querétaro, in contrast, estate communities lived in deep internal ethnic divisions. In the city, Otomí foundations had created an enduring republic with rich irrigated huertas that sustained many families and a strong Otomí identity. There were few republics in Querétaro's countryside; estates ruled dependent communities as across most of the Bajío. But a sharp divide separated Hispanic minorities and Otomí majorities at Querétaro estates, majorities that created informal replicas of indigenous republics, with elders, labor captains, and religious leaders—but without land and without political rights. In September of 1810, the leaders of the urban Otomí republic proclaimed loyalty; like most heartland republics, they saw no gain in rising against a regime that sanctioned their lands and rights. When rural insurgencies set in across the Bajío in 1811, Querétaro estates armed Hispanic residents as militias, paying wages and rations four times prevailing rates. The stated mission was to repel insurgents; the goal was internal social control. Then, with militias in place, Querétaro estates doubled wages and made new lands available to resident Otomí men, reinforcing their patriarchy to keep the peace and maintain production. While rebels ruled across the Bajío and in the Mezquital, Querétaro estates carried on—sustaining the city as a pole of counterinsurgency second only to Mexico City.[27]

Divisive and deadly conflicts were lived through deeply religious cultures. Hidalgo carried a banner of Guadalupe. Spaniards and Otomí in Querétaro declared loyalty to Our Lady of Pueblito, the Otomí Virgin who aided their struggles of daily life. People in loyal indigenous republics in the Valley of Mexico and Toluca were also devoted to Guadalupe; Otomí villagers in the Mezquital kept local devotions that sanctioned their insurgencies. Every action, every reaction, every resistance, every loyalty was understood as religious.[28]

In years of crisis mixing social pressures, contested sovereignty, drought, famine, and profiteering in foodstuffs, families across the heartland and the Bajío faced deep difficulties. Where grievances challenged the security of families locked in commercial dependence—*and threatened patriarchy*—thousands of men across the Bajío took arms in insurgency. Men in villages across the Mezquital and the pulque zones also joined when collapsing autonomies and scarce and insecure seasonal labor blocked symbiotic exploitations—*and challenged patriarchy*. In contrast, where men retained at least limited land, and access to labor cemented symbiotic exploitations, patriarchy held and insurgency proved limited across the central and southern heartland. Where economic insecurities challenged patriarchy among estate dependents around Querétaro and ethnic division stymied early uprisings, estates raised militias, reinforced patriarchy, and delivered secure sustenance to families to keep the peace.

Rural people across the Bajío and the heartland made decisions about insurgency based on regional, local, and familial challenges, chances to gain redress by other means, and local arrays of force. Widespread and enduring uprisings in the Bajío and the arid Mezquital proved powerful enough to threaten silver capitalism. Peace and production around Querétaro and across the fertile southern heartland sustained the regime through years of violent stalemate.

Political Rebels and Popular Insurgents, 1810–12

That stalemate set in during the two years after the explosion of the Hidalgo revolt in September of 1810. New Spain lived a volatile mix of political rebellions and popular uprisings—while the process that led to the Cádiz constitution moved forward in Spain. Hidalgo and Allende were political rebels who provoked mass uprisings they struggled to lead until their defeat and execution in 1811. Afterward, Rayón led the Junta Americana at Zitácuaro, while Morelos built a political insurgency in the hot country of Michoacán that later reached the Veracruz highlands, the Cuautla lowlands south of the capital, and settled for a time in Oaxaca. The Villagrán family ruled a political movement at Huichapan in the uplands between the Mezquital and Querétaro, while José Francisco Osorno fought to hold power in the Puebla sierra.[29]

Political rebels aimed to rule locally and regionally in an empire struggling to survive while French forces controlled most of Spain. Sometimes they joined popular insurgents against common foes—from the early battles of the Hidalgo revolt to the skirmishes in which the Villagráns joined Otomí insurgents in attacks on officials, merchants, and clergy (*gachupín* and American) in Mezquital towns. But these were tactical alliances. Insurgent communities pursued deeply local goals. From the beginning, popular rebels across the Bajío and the Mezquital took maize and livestock, sustaining families and communities (and reasserting patriarchy) while denying estate profits. Many in the Bajío and some in the Mezquital took control of estate lands to expand family production— promoting autonomy, patriarchy, and family welfare in more enduring ways. Popular rebels attacked, expelled, and sometimes killed estate managers, town merchants, and local clergy—mostly American Spaniards.

Rayón, Morelos, and other political rebels fought to remake the sovereignty broken in 1808. They saw the limited participation offered from Spain as cover for continuing Spanish rule. They pressed anti-*gachupín* rhetoric, seeking unity among Americans. They offered relief from tributes and other taxes. But no political rebel supported popular insurgents' attacks on property. Political and popular insurgencies differed in their bases and goals. Still, they were mutually reinforcing. Loyalist forces struggled to fight political rebels and popular insurgents at the same time. Insurgent communities from the Bajío to Jalisco, the Mezquital to Otumba and Apan, gave strategic protection to Rayón and Morelos, the Villagráns, Osorno, and others.[30] Regime campaigns against political rebels limited moves against popular insurgents. Simultaneous wars for political power and popular autonomy kept opposition strong into 1812.[31]

Royalist control of the mining city of Guanajuato, the trading and textile city of Querétaro and its rich countryside, and Mexico City and the rich southern heartland with its estates and productive republics combined to keep the regime alive and the economy struggling on in the face of political and popular insurgencies. The regime survived, yet could not send substantial revenues to fund the war against Napoleon in Spain. The silver economy carried on at levels limiting investment in infrastructure and drainage, ensuring problems to come. Political rebels held power in marginal regions. Popular insurgents ruled strategic zones. New Spain's future was contested and uncertain as 1812 began.

Liberal Openings and the Time of Typhus, 1812–14

When news of the constitution of Cádiz arrived in New Spain in the summer of 1812, insurgencies, popular and political, continued to challenge those who ruled. The new political order confirmed Catholicism as the universal religion of a transatlantic nation, essential in a charter seeking unity against "godless" Frenchmen. New political participations began in 1813. Loyal cities gained opportunities to elect delegates to a new *cortes* that would lead imperial government in Spain. A broad electorate included adult male Spaniards, *indios*, and mestizos, but excluded men of African ancestry (aiming to hold Cuba and its rising sugar and slave economy in the empire). Complex polling in three levels limited popular influence: parish voting included most adult men; the electors chosen there were almost always men of property and literacy who dominated polling and power at higher levels. The Cádiz charter created provincial deputations, regional assemblies advising governors still named in Spain; it also offered cities and towns, Hispanic and indigenous, municipal rights without ethnic restrictions, opening new local representations.[32]

The constitution would end the separate indigenous republics that sustained so many and stabilized so much in the heartland and regions south. Councils led by native notables would give way to municipal politics open to Hispanic traders and rancheros. The republics' rights of eminent domain would end, land would be privatized under one transatlantic Spanish domain, opening all property to all people—benefiting those with the ability to buy. As councils opened to Hispanic residents, voting opened to commoners, indigenous and others. In pursuit of an egalitarian dream, Cádiz would end indigenous republics and corrode the autonomies that had long sustained native families—if the constitution was fully implemented.

Félix Calleja, now viceroy, saw counterinsurgency as his first concern. He implemented liberal programs with that in mind. He promoted provincial deputations and the tiered elections that selected New Spain's representatives to Spanish *cortes*, hoping to gain allegiance and limit political insurgency. He enabled rural municipalities, breaking exclusive indigenous rule in the republics; he allowed small communities to found municipalities, serving villagers who resented head towns. He did not privatize community lands, knowing it would threaten the autonomies that held so many loyal in times of insurgency.

The first experiments with Cádiz liberalism in 1813 came in regions free of insurgency. Still, they revealed difficulties and divisions; Calleja annulled Mexico City elections when regime opponents won. Meanwhile, people across New Spain faced typhus in the deadliest plague since the 1730s.[33] In Mexico City 20,000 died, another 40,000 across the heartland. Disease mixed with liberal openings to limit political insurgencies. Popular insurgents carried on.

The Cádiz project had little impact in the Bajío, a region of many mulattoes, few native republics, and (west of Querétaro) ruled by popular insurgents in 1813.[34] Around Mexico City indigenous republics were everywhere; every head town was a parish. Cádiz offered municipal rights to parishes with 1,000 people (and 200 adult men); smaller communities that were not parishes created municipalities too. The end of ethnic exclusions (except for mulattoes) opened local politics to all adult married men, Spaniards and mestizos, indigenous notables and native commoners. Spaniards and mestizos who had taken *indio* status to join in republican governance now faced no restriction. The politics of indigenous republics formally ended. Still, in times of conflict new municipalities kept much that had shaped the republics: common lands subject to local eminent domain, representation for ethnic barrios and outlying villages. Around Mexico City, Cádiz led to hybrid municipalities—mixing liberal openings and indigenous republican ways.[35] There, peace and production continued in the face of deadly typhus.

The Mezquital, again, proved different. Insurgency held strong in 1813, based mostly in the outlying villages of Otomí republics. Liberal participation began in many head towns. Parish elections were held in the summer of 1813 at Actopan, Tetepango, and Ixmiquilpan, while insurgents ruled nearby villages. The openings of Cádiz competed with the option of insurgency. Insurgency blocked liberal openings at Otumba, the heart of the pulque zone in the northeast Valley of Mexico. No municipalities emerged there before the liberal option closed in 1814.[36]

The pivotal year 1813 also brought an open contest between the promise of Cádiz and the political insurgencies led by Rayón and Morelos.[37] While Calleja promoted elections allowing citizens across New Spain to elect representatives to the *cortes* in Spain, Morelos called an American National Congress at Chilpancingo to declare independence from Spain on November 6. Few responded. When Morelos approached Valladolid (later named Morelia) in December, limited local support allowed Agustín Iturbide to defeat him. Political insurgency peaked and began to wane in the face of typhus, persistent popular uprisings, and the participations offered by Cádiz—liberalism in service of empire. Morelos held on in isolated zones.[38]

Restored Monarchy and Negotiated Pacifications, 1814–20

The option of Cádiz proved short-lived. In 1814, the alliance of British forces, Spanish liberals, and popular resistance ended Napoleonic rule in Spain and restored Fernando VII to the throne in Madrid. In May he annulled the constitution, ending the liberal experiment. The news reached New Spain in August. The return of Fernando and the end of Cádiz did not slow the demise of Morelos and his proposal for an insurgent-led independence. His allies wrote a first Mexican constitution at Apatzingán in November of 1814. Their vision for a nation free of Spanish rule included deep opposition to the popular insurgents challenging property across the Bajío, the Mezquital, and the pulque zone.[39] Without a strong popular base and on the run, Morelos was defeated, captured, and executed in 1815. A few political rebels held on, notably Vicente Guerrero in the hot country around Acapulco, but they could not threaten the regime.[40]

The long-desired Fernando—the imagined source of legitimacy, stability, and justice—was restored. But the imagined Fernando proved more politically adept than the real monarch. On the throne in Madrid, Fernando failed to understand that liberals had fought in his name to restore Spanish independence at home, to hold New Spain loyal, and to keep silver flowing. For a time, that mattered less in New Spain. The forces that fought insurgents, political and popular, in the name of Fernando and Cádiz, fought them after 1814 in the name of Fernando and a restored monarchy. Ultimately, their goal was to defend and restore silver capitalism. With political insurgency in decline, from 1814 they focused the fight on popular uprisings.[41]

The revived monarchy kept one key legacy of Cádiz—new taxes. The old *alcabala*, six percent collected on sales before 1810, rose to twelve and then sixteen percent. Direct taxes were levied as liberal innovations continued after 1814. Revenue collections in Mexico City and across New Spain were higher by about fifty percent from 1814 to 1820 than during the decades before 1810. To pay for counterinsurgency, the regime also continued to extract loans from Mexico City financial, commercial, and landed interests.[42] The powerful paid, aiming to restore peace and the silver economy. In the process, taxes and loans to the regime took capital out of the economy they aimed to revive, leading to pacification and economic collapse in 1820.

It took a year to pacify the Mezquital. The Villagráns and the political insurgency they led at Huichapan were defeated in the summer of 1813. Through the following year, while Cádiz offered municipal rights to indigenous republics, loyalist troops at Tlahuelilpan chased village insurgents with little success. Then, in May 1814, as Fernando returned to Madrid, the regional commander negotiated peace at Tepetitlán, one of the first insurgent communities. Former rebels declared loyalty to the regime (still Cádiz, to their knowledge), gaining rights to rule locally and remain armed as a "patriotic" militia, a hundred strong. During the next year, similar deals calmed the Mezquital. Otomí communities in rebellion for years declared loyalty (after August 1814 to the restored Fernando), gaining rights to local rule and to keep arms as militias.

Confirming local rule in restored indigenous republics reinforced established ways. Militias strengthened former insurgents, whose patriarchy gained military force. It took two more years to pacify the pulque regions around Otumba and Apan, but the process was similar. And indigenous militias were not limited to former insurgent communities. Across the heartland, as municipal rights ended and indigenous republics resumed, patriotic militias spread to defend the regime. Around Mexico City, republics reasserted autonomy as Cádiz fell, insurgencies ended, and militias reinforced local patriarchy (see chapter 4).[43] As insurgency and counterinsurgency militarized New Spain, militias brought armed patriarchy home to many families and communities.

The Bajío took longer to pacify, perhaps because it was the original homeland of popular insurgency, perhaps because insurgents there had made the greatest gains taking control of the land, perhaps because there were few republics to negotiate deals. Insurgent land taking threatened the property of once-powerful entrepreneurs. From 1818, pacification mixed military pressure with concessions granting insurgents continued use of lands they had occupied. Rebels accepted amnesties with obligations (and rights) to stay on estate lands as tenants. Some kept arms as patriotic militias charged to defend the new peace. Royalist officers boasted of triumphant pacifications. Yet they ended uprisings across the Bajío by confirming insurgents' rights to cultivate lands they had taken by force. Settlements recognized estate property while giving control of production in New Spain's richest region to tenants. Bajío insurgents did not gain property or rights as republics. Still, they gained new autonomies.[44]

Two examples are revealing: Puerto de Nieto, a large property east of San Miguel, was among the first estate communities to join Hidalgo in 1810 and the last to be pacified in 1820. After a decade of insurgency, resident families gained rights to estate lands in return for modest rents (paid only in part). Production on estate account ended. Tenant families, some prosperous, some raising bare sustenance, reshaped the community. A group of women became tenant *rancheras*, leading a third of estate households, often the most prosperous. With men away or killed, women took new control of production, roles they held through the 1820s. A search for autonomy and patriarchy had driven men at Puerto de Nieto to insurgency; pacification confirmed estate property and gave control of production to tenants, including many women.[45]

At La Griega, east of Querétaro, ethnic division reinforced by a Hispanic militia had kept the peace and strengthened patriarchy during the decade of insurgency. When pacification came to surrounding areas between 1818 and 1820, the militia disbanded. Most of the men paid so well to defend property and production left. The working men who remained, employees and tenants, saw the higher salaries and expanded

tenancies gained in years of insurgency disappear. No roles of even limited power or modest prosperity opened for women. People at La Griega
had stayed at work, gained benefits for a time, and remained dependent—
while patriarchy held.[46]

Popular insurgencies ended in the summer of 1820, except in marginal regions. The concessions that pacified the Mezquital and the Bajío
brought real gains: local rule and militias in the Mezquital, tenant production across the Bajío. Insurgency reinforced autonomies. Some women in
the Bajío found new autonomies, too. As patriarchy militarized, communities and families turned to new negotiations of patriarchy.

Insurgency and pacification proved costly to silver capitalism. After
averaging over twenty-one and a half million pesos yearly from 1801
through 1810, production plummeted to less than nine million pesos
in 1812 as popular insurgents ruled the Bajío and the Mezquital. Most
remaining silver came from Zacatecas and regions north of the Bajío,
helping keep the peace there; little reached Mexico City to pay the costs
of counterinsurgency. Production held around ten million pesos from
1813 to 1817 and the share minted at Mexico City rose back to seventy-five
percent. A rise to over fourteen million pesos in 1819 funded final pacification (see appendix, tables A.7, A.8, and A.9). Then, in the summer of
1820, as the Bajío finally quieted, the great Valenciana mine at Guanajuato
flooded—the result of years of production without investment in drainage and other infrastructure. Silver production dropped to twelve million
pesos, then below ten million in 1821. It was the popular insurgents' final
victory. Silver production would hold around ten million pesos through
the 1820s and 1830s, half the levels of the decades from 1780 to 1810. As
insurgency ended, so did silver capitalism.[47]

Monarchical Independence
and Popular Autonomies, 1821

The end of popular insurgency and the collapse of silver capitalism came
as new political challenges shook the Spanish monarchy. Early in 1820,
Colonel Rafael Riego and other officers assembled at Cádiz, readying to
defend Spain's rule in South America. They refused to sail until Fernando
reinstated the Cádiz constitution. Riego and his allies had fought to expel
Napoleon, shape a liberal regime to expand citizenship and preserve the
empire, and return Fernando to rule as a constitutional monarch. Neither
grateful nor open to constitutional ways, Fernando moved hard against
many who backed the Cádiz project. But in the face of the officers' demands,

Fernando acquiesced—showing he knew where sovereignty effectively resided. In May, people in New Spain heard the Cádiz constitution proclaimed anew. Fernando VII would rule, reluctantly, as a constitutional monarch. As silver collapsed and popular insurgents gained peace with autonomies, questions of sovereignty and liberalism reopened.[48]

Church leaders and powerful Catholics worried about a new anticlericalism rising within Spanish liberalism. No longer fighting French armies, and facing persecutions from Fernando and his clerical allies, Spanish liberals turned on the Church. In New Spain, where pacification came with economic collapse, loyalists and surviving political insurgents worried, too. Vicente Guerrero, long an ally of Morelos in the Pacific hot country, knew the return of Cádiz meant the exclusion of mulattoes from citizenship.[49] Don Agustín Iturbide, a loyalist commander, worried that the return of liberalism with anticlerical virulence would disrupt the revival of the New Spain he had fought to restore. The new liberalism of 1820 made the link to Spain worrisome among political men across New Spain—led by commanders who had fought to preserve the monarchy.

Iturbide built a coalition seeking Mexican autonomy under Fernando. The American son of a Spanish immigrant, Iturbide might have joined those seeking autonomy for New Spain after 1808—until he faced the anti-*gachupín* passions of political rebels and the attacks on property by popular insurgents. He defended the regime as it forged Cádiz liberalism, driving campaigns against Bajío insurgents. He kept Morelos out of Valladolid in 1813. He lost command in 1815 (under Fernando), accused of excessive force. In 1820 (under Fernando and restored liberalism) he earned a commission to fight Guerrero in the Pacific hot country.

Rather than fight, Iturbide negotiated, building on Guerrero's abhorrence for Cádiz's exclusion of mulattoes (thus of Guerrero and many followers). Iturbide proclaimed the Plan de Iguala on February 24, 1821; Guerrero signed on two weeks later. The program that united the loyalist commander and the political insurgent called for a Mexican constitutional monarchy. Fernando VII would remain king, invited to reign in Mexico City—until 1810 capital of Spain's richest domain. The Cádiz constitution would hold until a Mexican *cortes* wrote a charter appropriate to Mexico. Iguala promised a constitutional Bourbon monarchy without anticlericalism, and without limits on the participation of men now proclaimed Mexicans.

The plan offered three guarantees: religion, independence, and union. Religion meant Catholicism, which would keep its regime-backed monopoly. Independence insisted that sovereignty resided in a Mexican people.

Union meant that all Mexicans (American and immigrant Spaniards, along with those labeled *indios*, mulattoes, and every possible mix) would be equal—and that ties with Spain would remain via Fernando, or another Bourbon. Catholicism did unite nearly all the people now asserted Mexican. Demands for Mexican sovereignty and union with Spain introduced a blatant contradiction—as did the promise of unity among people just ending a decade fighting each other in deadly conflicts.

Did Iturbide believe Fernando or another Bourbon might accept a throne constrained by a Mexican constitution? Did he expect a sudden turn to social unity and cultural acceptance among people so recently locked in violent battles? What mattered in 1821 was to proclaim European and American Spaniards equal. Iturbide's vision of Mexico abhorred the anti-*gachupín* rhetoric that marked political insurgencies after 1810. The Iguala alliance sought reunification among Spaniards, the community of power that ruled and profited in New Spain. Promises of religion, independence, and union emphasized Catholicism; Mexican autonomy; and unity among Spaniards, European and American, loyalists and political insurgents. Iturbide orchestrated a moment of unity by a coalition of men who presumed to rule—a unity laden with contradictions.

The loyalist military centered the Iguala coalition. Forged in counterinsurgency, the army built upon old militias, expanded after 1810 at great cost. In 1820, it finally pacified the Bajío. Then, in 1821, Iturbide led it into an alliance that included regime officials, high churchmen, and leading entrepreneurs, European and American—plus a few political insurgents like Guerrero. The coalition had funded counterinsurgency, paying higher taxes and providing mounting loans to royal coffers. By 1820 the Bourbon regime owed seventy million pesos (ten years' current silver production) to Mexico City financiers. To draw them to Iguala, Iturbide committed the new regime to pay the debts of counterinsurgency and reduce taxes—as the economy collapsed.[50] No one then understood the depth of the collapse or the difficulty of revival. In times of political uncertainty, expectations of a return to New Spain's prosperity ruled. Impossible promises made by a costly army entrenched huge debts at the foundation of the Mexican empire.

Public promises of cultural and political unity masked underlying commitments to the military and its financiers. The political and entrepreneurial classes united at a historic moment to make Mexico independent. It was a coalition of the powerful and their professional and intellectual allies—men who aimed to exercise power. Professional armies proud of defeating popular insurgents led the new regime. A military staunch in defense of order and property ruled the foundation of Mexico in 1821—whatever its proclamations about sovereignty.

Iguala promoted an orderly transition to a Mexican polity. Armies marched to proclaim a Mexican empire. Neither communities nor patriotic militias were called to arms. Keeping Cádiz liberal models, popular participation in the new regime that proclaimed the people sovereign was limited to voting locally in multitiered elections. Iturbide and his allies rejected the limits set by Cádiz and Fernando on New Spain's exercise of sovereignty in the Spanish empire. They joined Cádiz and Fernando in opposition to popular insurgency and kept Cádiz's limits on the popular exercise of sovereignty in the Mexican empire. Iguala aimed to unify American and immigrant Spaniards, loyalists and political rebels. The alliance of provincial elites and popular insurgents mobilized under Hidalgo had fractured in a decade of conflict, to be lost in 1821. Iguala silenced anti-*gachupín* rhetoric in a call to elite unity. Men seeking power saw the chance and took it.

Long-insurgent communities stood aside while Iguala brought political separation from Spain. The rhetoric of Iguala promised much: independence and religion, unity and sovereignty. Why not wait to see the outcomes of those lofty goals, backed after all by the popular Guerrero? Meanwhile, those who had negotiated pacifications that confirmed local autonomies, reinforced patriarchies, and created local militias focused on rebuilding lives and communities. Again, local challenges and goals ruled popular engagements with imperial and national politics.[51] Iturbide and Iguala forged an alliance of the powerful, leaving popular communities aside. For a historic moment, they acquiesced—solid in local autonomies, old and new.

Whether independence began on September 28 when Iguala's provisional junta issued the Act of Independence, on November 2 when the empire was proclaimed in Mexico City, or when news came that the Spanish *cortes* rejected the Treaty of Córdoba (which sanctioned Iguala) and that Fernando VII refused the Mexican throne—the trajectory was clear. Mexico separated from Spain as a constitutional monarchy proclaiming popular sovereignty. On Fernando's refusal, Iturbide took the throne as Spanish rule in North America ended. The silver economy that had kept ties between New Spain and Spain strong for centuries and funded Spain's last claims to power had collapsed in a decade of international, political, and popular warfare. Insurgents from communities that had long sustained silver production, then faced predations that made lives (and patriarchy) unsustainable, took down silver capitalism and the Spanish empire.

The Iguala alliance proclaimed independence, tried to keep a monarchical link with Spain, demanded unity between European and American Spaniards, and dreamed that silver would revive. Mexico's founders agreed on that—and little else. Once the break with Spain was clear, the movement fragmented. Iturbide's Mexican empire dissolved in the face of radically divergent visions of the promises of Iguala in times of economic collapse. Sovereignty became Mexican. Would it be exercised by a central power claiming the legacy of the viceroyalty, by provinces (soon states) rooted in intendancies created in the 1780s, or by cities and towns, Hispanic and indigenous, sanctioned in Spanish traditions of the sovereignty of the pueblos? Mexican liberals pressed against clerical privileges, indigenous republics, and community properties. Republicans seeking sovereignty without monarchy allied with disgruntled military commanders to depose Iturbide in 1823. The moment of unity devolved into political conflicts, while most communities held quiet, focused on holding autonomies. Armed mobilizations, political and popular, had contested the future of New Spain beginning in 1810; they remained an option in the struggles to make Mexico after 1821.[52]

That year marked the end of Spain's global empire—even as it carried on for a few more years in the Andes, and for most of a century in Cuba and the Philippines. The silver capitalism that sustained Spain, New Spain, and global commercial capitalism had fallen. To those who would see, the years from 1810 to 1821 demonstrated the power of insurgent communities in limited yet pivotal regions: in the fertile Bajío where men locked in dependence faced predations that threatened patriarchy and family sustenance, in the arid Mezquital where men in Otomí republics saw autonomies collapse without access to labor that might sustain families and patriarchal claims. There, unconstrained predations set insurgents on fights that destroyed silver capitalism. Those willing to see might also have learned that where exploitations deepened yet remained symbiotic to sustain patriarchal families, in southern heartland republics and at Querétaro estates, people had remained at work in support Spain's rule and silver capitalism. Few proved willing to learn after 1821, as men seeking power struggled to build a nation and find a new economy. Meanwhile, communities from the heartland through the Bajío retrenched in autonomies on the land—their definition of independence. Decades of political instability, social jostling, and economic uncertainty would mark the attempts to build a Mexican nation—as the world turned to industrial innovations.

Industrial Capitalism, 1820–1920

CHAPTER SIX

Mexico in the Age of Industrial Capitalism, 1810–1910

STRUGGLING TO RECOVER from political wars and popular insurgencies, the people proclaimed Mexicans in 1821 had to invent a nation without the advantage of silver. New industrial ways linked concentrations of capital and mechanized production in Britain, the United States, and Europe to widening regions of commodity exporters and consumers.[1] China and Mexico, the historic axis of silver capitalism, slid toward marginality. In Mexico, capital was suddenly scarce while communities held strong on the land. A national state and new economy proved hard to build, bringing endless debates about forms of government and whether Mexico should build industry or turn to exports. The loss of Texas and its emerging cotton economy in 1835 closed the export option; Mexican industry began soon after. It grew despite limited markets and resources—both further constrained when the United States took vast territories in the war of 1846–48.

Only after 1870 did Mexico mix a revival of silver, industry serving national markets, and new exports. The great powers' turn to a gold standard simultaneously devalued silver and made machinery costly in Mexico, while stimulating its exports. Still, politics stabilized and the economy grew. But the regime ruled with widening exclusions as the economy delivered riches to a few and prosperity to a few more, while it generated deepening inequities and exploitations to a growing majority. Everything collapsed in revolution in 1910.

Mexico's nineteenth century is often seen as a time of failed nation making, ending in a devastating (and transforming) revolution. It is better understood as a time when Mexicans faced the collapse of the silver capitalism that had given New Spain a leading role in a world of trade.

State builders and profit seekers searched for new ways forward in a new industrial world in which Mexico held no advantage. Meanwhile, communities took advantage of a commercial respite to deepen autonomies. Among nation makers, there were long debates, political conflicts, an early industrialization, invasions by the United States and France, liberal programs that aimed to end community autonomies—and finally a consolidation of authoritarian liberalism that promoted industry and exports. Its celebrated success led to corrosions of autonomies and patriarchy in key regions—notably, the southern heartland. Revolution came in 1910.

A New Industrial Era

New Spain's silver was an essential commodity and money in global trade from the sixteenth century, arguably the most important commodity-money in the world after 1700. It drew Chinese and South Asian goods to Europe, Africa, and the Americas. As Atlantic plantation economies soared and sought rising numbers of enslaved laborers, New Spain's silver was essential to buying the Indian cotton cloth that African merchants and princes demanded as the price of slaves. Around 1750, Chinese trade fell briefly while New World sugar economies grew; then from the 1770s China drew rising quantities of silver while the slave and sugar trades drove upward, too. New Spain's silver became pivotal to Europeans' profit in world trade. Britain and France fought to claim it, helping stimulate the wars and revolutions of 1789 to 1825.[2]

Unprecedented global demand, ultimately Chinese and Indian demand, drove silver to new heights in New Spain after 1770. Mining and minting held near historic highs through the wars of the 1790s and early 1800s.[3] An enduring school of thought argues that New Spain's silver economy faced debilitating challenges from the 1790s: wartime disruptions, rising taxes, and other extractions.[4] Yet silver held strong through the decade after 1800, reaching its historic peak in 1809. New Spain's wider commercial economy showed steady growth from the 1770s to 1800, followed by stability near peak levels.[5] The peak production of New Spain's silver capitalism in the decades before 1810 demonstrates the strength and resiliency of that powerful economy, flourishing despite the disruptions of war and revenue extractions—better, stimulated by the demand created by trade, war, and rising revenue needs.

A challenge to the role of silver in the world economy began simultaneously. In the 1770s, as Britain lost dominion over the colonies that became the United States, it pressed new power in South Asia. One goal was to control the Indian cotton goods so important in global trade. But British agents struggled to rule cloth making dispersed among countless households and workshops. And British merchants needed silver to buy Indian cloth. While British traders worked to gain New Spain's silver by war and trade, British inventors and entrepreneurs began to mechanize cotton spinning and promote weaving in England.[6]

British industrialization began as an attempt to replace Indian cloth with British industrial products in African trades and beyond. Key inventions focused on spinning came in the late eighteenth century; during the wars of 1790 to 1810, British cloth output grew, but remained a small part of global trade. Silver mining in New Spain simultaneously peaked, keeping old trades and Indian production strong into years of wartime disruptions. Yet to meet the soaring demand for silver driven by Europeans at war, Indian cloth makers, and Chinese markets, entrepreneurs in the Bajío pressed falling earnings and new insecurities onto mine workers and rural producers. Global traders and local entrepreneurs profited while men who mined silver and the many who sustained them struggled—until Napoleon invaded Spain in 1808 and broke its monarchy, opening the way for the political and popular insurgencies of 1810 in New Spain that took down silver, undermined China, and cleared global markets for British industry.

New Spain's silver production fell by half in 1811, a decline reinforced by uncertain access to mercury during Spain's war against Napoleon. The historic Pacific trade sending New Spain's silver to buy China's silks, porcelains, and other wares collapsed. The flow across the Atlantic to buy European goods and on to India to purchase cotton cloth to trade for African slaves fell sharply. British traders found a new way to draw silver to India; they sold opium to China, taking silver in payment. Chinese stores of that specie that had accumulated over centuries now flowed to India in the hands of British traders. China became a source of silver, a new "mine" for the first half of the nineteenth century, profiting British dealers and Indian opium growers, sustaining South Asian cloth makers for a time. China faced a decline of manufacturing, scarce state revenues, political conflict, social polarization, and the maladies of rising opium use. Except for the last, New Spain lived parallel challenges as it became Mexico. The historic trade linking China's manufactures and New Spain's silver broke in the trans-Pacific crisis created when popular insurgents took down New Spain's silver capitalism.[7]

Britain made itself the beneficiary. An island, it never lived the destruction of the wars of 1790 to 1815 at home. It built a great navy sustained by global trade, drawing slave-made gold, sugar, and coffee from Brazil, and

slave-grown cotton from the US South to supply a rapid rise of mechanized cotton cloth production that displaced Indian textiles from African,
European, and Atlantic markets. The commercial and technical achievements of British industrialization proved transforming. They were facilitated
by Bajío and Mezquital insurgents who cut by half the silver available to
world trade, prejudicing Chinese and Indian manufacturers while privileg-
ing British capitalists who produced and exported without dependence on
silver.[8] The great rise of British cotton-cloth production and exports came
after 1810.[9] The fall of old global trades and the rise of new British industries coincided with Britain's defeat of Napoleon in 1815. Together they
opened a new era in the world economy: industrial capitalism.

Struggling to Become Mexico

The collapse of silver capitalism and the global economic transformation,
the former caused and the latter enabled in large part by New Spain's
insurgents after 1810, set unimagined challenges in the way of those
aiming to found a Mexican nation in 1821. States need revenues, which
are taken far more easily from a commercial economy taxed at key points
of production, transport, and trade than from millions of households
consuming much of what they make and dealing in small trades opaque
to state agents. The silver flow that averaged around twenty-two million
pesos yearly from 1790 to 1810 fell to eleven million pesos per year from
1811 to 1840. The commercial stimuli and state revenues tied to silver
collapsed (see appendix, tables A.7 and A.8). Iturbide's decisions to take
on the debts owed by the Spanish regime to his once-powerful Mexican
backers brought a Mexican empire founded deep in deficit. When it
failed, the first president of the federal republic, former political insurgent
Guadalupe Victoria, covered those debts and paid for his presidency by
taking loans from British bankers—deals that required opening Mexico to
a flood of British cloth imports. Victoria served his term, national debts
rose, while artisans faced displacement.

Mexican states, national and provincial, were founded and contested
by militaries built in counterinsurgency; they had to be paid. Costs of
government rose high above those of New Spain's little militarized, mostly
judicial regime, while revenues plummeted with the fall of silver capitalism.[10] Shortfalls due to the costs of the military approached forty percent
of annual revenues. As Victoria's term ended early in 1829, militarized
political conflicts drove costs and debts higher, opening an enduring
vicious cycle in which minimal revenues, military costs, and a militarized

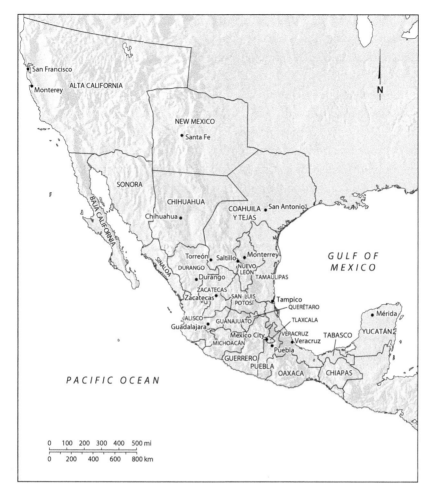

MAP 8. Mexico, ca. 1830.

politics that ensured that armies would be paid made early national regimes untenable.[11]

The revenues of silver capitalism had sustained New Spain, Spanish rule from Havana and New Orleans to San Francisco and Manila, and sent surpluses to Madrid. Taxes on silver, on trade stimulated by silver, tributes (head taxes on indigenous and mulatto men), and in the late eighteenth century revenues of a tobacco monopoly paid for the regime across New Spain's vast domains and in Spain too—as silver capitalism flourished. Then Hidalgo and Cádiz liberals abolished tributes, both aiming to offer something to an insurgent populace without touching the property of the powerful. After 1821, revenues fell with the collapse of silver; the *alcabalas* on internal sales dropped with the fall of silver's stimulus. When Iturbide's empire gave way to the federal republic in 1824, silver taxes and *alcabalas* went to the states. The tobacco monopoly struggled amid debates over who gained its revenues. The national regime was left to tax international trade, down with the fall of silver. Low tariffs on British imports kept revenues low.

The collapse of silver also, literally, disintegrated the economy that once tied New Spain's diverse regions and communities into a dynamic whole. While southern provinces from Yucatán to Oaxaca had remained aside from the trades stimulated by silver and thus deeply indigenous and autonomous, Mexico City had ruled and integrated vast regions from the heartland and extending north, tied to the world by silver capitalism. Roads leading east through Puebla to Veracruz, south to Acapulco, and north and northwest to the Bajío had set the viceregal capital as a pivot of globally dynamic trade. Along the routes, silver stimulated commercial production—stimuli that after 1770 reached into Texas, New Mexico, and California. Up to 1810, all silver was minted in Mexico City, reinforcing its power and facilitating revenue collection (see appendix, table A.7).

When insurgencies took down silver after 1810, commerce dissolved; the Bajío economy collapsed and regions north were cut off from Mexico City. Seeking new links to global markets, they turned to nearby Gulf and Pacific ports. From 1810 to 1820 mining fell by half and thirty percent was minted in the north. After 1821, silver flows held low and seventy percent fueled northern economies tied directly to the world. Independence did not reintegrate the economy that had once focused on silver, finance, and trade in Mexico City. States claimed provincial rights, promoting regional economies and new links to a changing world.

After 1821 mining carried on mostly north of the Bajío. Less than thirty percent of the output of Mexican silver (already cut in half) passed through Mexico City in the 1820s; only ten percent was minted there in the 1830s, as production hit the lowest levels since the 1750s. For decades the benefits of silver to the national regime and the merchant financiers of Mexico City were few (see appendix, table A.8). Meanwhile, production at Zacatecas doubled from the early 1820s to the late 1830s—when it mined and minted over forty-five percent of Mexico's still reduced total.[12] Zacatecas had escaped the popular insurgency that prejudiced mining at Guanajuato from 1810 to 1820. Then joint British-Mexican enterprises brought steam pumps to drain mines, innovations to tunneling, and advances in mercury amalgamation. Profit returned, providing soaring revenues to the state of Zacatecas (close to sovereign from 1824 to 1835) and high wages that drew skilled men to dangerous work.

Zacatecas's silver economy mostly served Zacatecas. The state's army backed Mexico's first experiment in liberal government in 1832–33, aiming to keep the regional autonomies (and revenues) set in the federal constitution of 1824. Without silver revenues, national liberals put in power by Zacatecas tried expropriating Church wealth to pay the soaring national debt built in the 1820s. Attacking the Church proved politically divisive in Mexico, leading in 1835 to a return of central rule. The states, including Zacatecas, lost political rights and silver revenues. And central rule accelerated the secession of Texas: provincial autonomy had covered the expansion of slavery essential to rising cotton production there after national abolition in 1829; the 1835 shift to central rule made abolition national law. Anglo-Texans mobilized to secede from Mexico. The collapse of silver capitalism brought disintegration to Mexico.

Silver prospered locally at Zacatecas through the 1830s, approaching half of a national production that rose a bit yet remained only half of the level before 1810. The 1840s saw mining finally revive at Guanajuato; national production rose to approach sixteen million pesos yearly after 1845, a stimulus to commercial life, yet only three-quarters of preinsurgency levels (see appendix, table A.9). Silver began to reclaim importance, yet was far from being the leading sector that had made New Spain pivotal to world trade. To prosper commercially in a new industrial world, Mexico would have to do more than mine silver.

An Economy of Landed Autonomies

To many Mexicans, perhaps most, the commercial collapse of the postindependence decades was not a problem, but a welcomed respite. Those who fought after 1810 to restore or create landed autonomies, and in the process brought down silver capitalism, focused after 1820 on sustaining families and communities. Bajío families gained tenancies on some of the nation's richest, often irrigated, lands. At Chalco and in other heartland regions, villagers who retained lands and refrained from insurgency after 1810 took advantage of the commercial collapse after 1820 to claim higher wages for seasonal labor. In the Valley of Toluca, villages that had disputed the lands of the Condes de Santiago's Atengo estates since the 1790s won a court victory in the 1820s—sending waves of exuberance through heartland communities and fears among struggling estate owners. Villagers across Mexico asserted autonomies in the 1820s, while commercial growers complained of collapse—meaning collapsing profits.[13]

Tithe records reporting collections before insurgency from 1806 through 1809 and then well after, from 1829 through 1832, document a broad demise of commercial cultivation. Tithes took ten percent of commercial harvests; indigenous growers of native crops did not pay. Across the new nation, collections fell fifty percent, precisely parallel to the drop in silver (see appendix, table A.10). The mean tithe income for 1806–9, multiplied by ten, indicates commercial cultivation worth twenty-two million pesos yearly—almost identical to the value of the silver produced in the final years of boom (see appendix, table A.7). Silver production and commercial cultivation both held near ten to eleven million pesos yearly in the late 1820s. The collapse of silver and commercial cropping together wracked the commercial economy. But the fall of silver was a decline in output; the drop in tithed cultivation masked a compensating rise of family production. Agriculture did not collapse; its beneficiaries shifted radically.

Commercial cropping fell by two-thirds in the bishoprics of Mexico City and Puebla, where commercial estates long mixed with indigenous republics. The Michoacán diocese saw a drop of only forty percent. It included Tarascan pueblos around Pátzcuaro and Uruapan, where estates were limited, and the Guanajuato core of the Bajío, home to commercial estates now worked by tenant families—many Hispanic and paying tithes.[14] The fifteen percent growth of tithe receipts in the diocese of Guadalajara reflects the regional strength of silver at Zacatecas, sustained by estates at nearby Aguascalientes.[15] The small decline at Durango showed continuing mining and the cultivation that sustained it. The eighty percent fall at Monterrey reveals the impact of Comanche and other incursions on life at the frontier.[16]

The demise of commercial cultivation in the central highlands led Mexico's convent-banks, long noted for investing in rural estates, to shift capital to urban real estate after 1821. During the reign of silver capitalism, convents lent mortgages to enable less wealthy estate operators to acquire or improve estates.[17] By the 1830s, seventy-five percent was in urban real estate; investment in commercial agriculture no longer paid (see appendix, table A.11).[18] Meanwhile, food remained plentiful and affordable—also in stark contrast with the last years of silver capitalism.

Across most of Mexico after 1821, commercial growers struggled to profit while families took control of cultivation and by all indicators ate well. The best series of maize prices comes from Zacatecas, not a typical region given its mining boom and strong commercial cultivation. Still, it shows staples prices holding steady from the 1820s to 1850—at levels historically low for the region and affordable to those working at mines and estates.[19] Sporadic information on prices at Chalco and the Bajío, historic granaries that fed Mexico City, Guanajuato, and the north, also indicates steady supplies and low prices, lower than at Zacatecas. And there were few postindependence reports of wide crop failures, soaring maize prices, pervasive dearth, or rising death rates—conditions that plagued so many in 1785–86 and 1809–10.[20]

The best evidence that Mexicans ate well before 1850 comes from the heights of military recruits. The army that demanded revenues, created deficits, and prejudiced the economy with political disruptions kept good records of its recruits—young men from across the nation. Their heights in the 1850s were in the middle range of men in Western Europe.[21] While commercial cultivators failed, Mexicans were well nourished from 1820 to 1850. Maize became available and affordable as estate production declined and family cultivation flourished. Tenant families ate first and marketed small surpluses in the Bajío. In the heartland, villagers pressed estates to pay more and to lease lands. Estate owners lamented village and tenant autonomies; they complained of scarce capital and scarce profits—not of scarce maize (this will be a focus of chapters 7 and 8).

Family growers led a new economy of agricultural autonomy. They ate first, held supplies to guard against years of drought, and supplied town markets only with true surpluses. The shift came in times of limited population growth: from about six million in 1810 to just over seven million by 1850. The decade of insurgency after 1810 cost uncounted lives; the typhus of 1813 took more. Mexicans faced cholera for the first time in the 1830s, and again in the 1850s. Expanded family harvests in times of low population growth kept maize available and estate profits scarce. These were not years of utopia; epidemics mixed with political and social conflicts to make life often difficult and always uncertain. Still, many claimed new autonomies and used them to eat well.

Debating Mexico's Future, 1830–32

Times defined by the collapse of silver, scarce profits and state revenues, entrenched family autonomies, and recalcitrant workers were unacceptable to men who presumed to rule and profit in a new Mexican nation. Crisis came to a head in 1829 and 1830. The British loans that kept the first republican government of Guadalupe Victoria afloat were spent and in default. The presidential election of 1828 was contested: all factions saw irregularities; all turned to military mobilizations covered with constitutional claims. A revolt in Mexico City's Acordada barracks backed by a riot that sacked the Parián luxury market in front of the National Palace brought Vicente Guerrero to the presidency. The insurgent backer of Morelos and ally of Iturbide symbolized popular power. His rise, marked by the attack on the Parián (while villagers sacked sugar estates around Cuernavaca), reminded many among the powerful of the popular assaults that challenged property after 1810.[22]

In office, Guerrero responded to city rioters, lowland cotton growers, and artisans everywhere by prohibiting imports of British cloth. He would protect Mexicans—not British bondholders and manufacturers. Self-designated *hombres de bien*—good men—ousted Guerrero late in 1829, once again with military force backed by constitutional claims. Vice President Anastasio Bustamante, an ally of Iturbide in 1821 and a leader in the art of militarized politics, took power. He began a long era in which military arbiters oversaw regimes led by diverse ministers and trying diverse programs: Bustamante alternated in the role with the more (in)famous Antonio López de Santa Ana from 1830 to 1855; after an interlude of political war and French occupation, Porfirio Díaz claimed the role from 1876 to 1911.

Bustamante led a government shaped in many ways by Lucas Alamán. They looked to limit popular participation, stabilize politics, and revive the commercial economy.[23] The success of the Bustamante-Alamán government was limited (it fell in 1832). But Alamán led a debate about the causes of Mexico's difficulties in a rapidly changing world—and how to surmount them. Born to a leading Guanajuato mining family and having experienced Europe during Mexico's decade of insurgencies, he insisted that silver would revive. He promoted a turn to industrialization linked to a renewal of commercial cultivation. Tadeo Ortiz de Ayala, a liberal serving Alamán as consul at Bordeaux, offered a contrasting liberal vision. Ortiz insisted that the way forward was to join Cuba, Brazil, and the US South as commodity exporters—an option in 1830 as Texas and its emerging cotton economy remained Mexican. Alamán and Ortiz both saw the need for political stability; both called for the demobilization of an unruly populace. They differed starkly in their prescriptions for economic change. Alamán set his views in annual Memorias published in 1830, 1831, and 1832. Ortiz first tried to shape policy with memos to Alamán. Failing to convince, he wrote a book published as the government fell late in 1832, and he sailed to serve its liberal successor in the United States.

Alamán insisted that political peace and solid government accounts would bring a "powerful impulse" to the economy. "All the mines where work has been suspended so long will return to production, giving new life to agriculture and animating internal trade." To keep stability, a rebellious populace had to be contained and property protected by "a vigorous and severe administration of justice."[24] Alamán recognized, if indirectly, that insurgents had brought down silver capitalism. Subordination would sustain recovery.

In three years of reports, Alamán imagined that political stability had arrived and mining had revived while he lamented that agriculture had fallen into a state of plenty without profit. In 1830 he wrote that "The extraction of silver and gold has increased notably in the last two years; everything creates an expectation that mining will return to the heights of its best years." In 1831 he concluded: "The sector is flourishing and advancing more every day." In 1832, Alamán touted the rise in mining at Zacatecas.[25] He did not imagine that later that year his government would fall to a liberal revolt backed by the rich state and its silver.

Alamán struggled to understand the demise of commercial agriculture. In 1830 he lamented "the last three miserable years when crops were lost and livestock died due to lack of rain." Fortunately, rains were good in the summer of 1829 and the harvest of early 1830 was ample. After three bad harvests, one good yield brought plenty. A year later he noted: "The year has been so bountiful in nearly every state that rich harvests are being offered at bottom prices."[26] Plenty was a problem.

In his 1832 "Memoria," Alamán saw the new rural order: "The irregular rains and early frosts of the previous year caused generally scarce maize harvests, but the large stocks that remained from previous years were so abundant that they eliminated all fear of a scarcity of primary foodstuffs— and removed any chance of a rise to exorbitant prices." After three years of poor harvests, two good yields, then another poor crop, food remained available and prices affordable. Such plenty "in general" might appear "a benefit." But "the low price harvests sell for in some states is ruining cultivators who cannot even regain the costs of production; the situation is also prejudicial to the morality of the people, who without a need to work lose the habit of labor, acquire bad ways, while hands become scarce in other crafts."[27] Alamán lamented plenty without profit. Commercial growers could not profit while smallholders survived without need to labor for others.

The solution was industry. Guerrero had prohibited imports of British cloth to protect Mexico's cotton growers, often mulattoes and scattered across coastal lowlands, and cloth makers, mostly household artisans dispersed across the nation. Alamán promoted a turn to the machine production pioneered in England and adopted in the US northeast. In 1830, he insisted that "the everyday cloth of cotton, linen, and wool worn by the majority of the people should be promoted by stimulating national and foreign capitalists to build factories with the machines necessary to deliver their products at a moderate price."[28] Alamán envisioned capitalists mechanizing cloth production and selling at low prices to consumers. Cotton growers might benefit; artisans would face difficult competition.

In 1831, Alamán reported good news on "industrial factories." Laws of April and October 1830 founded a Banco de Avío—a development bank—granting it a fifth of the income from tariffs on cloth imports, up to a million pesos yearly. It would fund "costly machines" and "craftsmen to show how to install them." The plan: "to promote production of ordinary cotton goods—beginning with the selection of the best seed cultivated in Texas and purchasing machines to gin the harvest, spin yarn, and weave cloth."[29]

By 1832, Alamán waxed triumphant: "A powerful impulse has come from the Banco de Avío . . . creating a new spirit of enterprise." Thanks to bank funding, "the machines and craftsmen essential to spin and weave ordinary cotton cloth are coming from the United States and everything for woolens is due from France." Plans were under way for cotton mills at Tlalpan near the capital and Celaya in the Bajío; Querétaro would gain a woolen complex; San Miguel de Allende awaited a paper mill. Funds were set; agents bought machines in New Orleans and Bordeaux; craftsmen were coming to teach industrial ways. The promise was clear.[30]

As consul at Bordeaux, Tadeo Ortiz oversaw purchases of machinery for an industrial policy he opposed. Born near Guadalajara, Ortiz held diplomatic posts for Morelos after 1810, Iturbide after 1821, and briefly for Guerrero before serving Bustamante and Alamán. He studied New Spain deeply and lived across the Atlantic world. Ortiz never found political power; he died at sea of bubonic plague late in 1832, on his way to serve a new liberal government in the United States. He published *México considerado como nación independiente* (Mexico Considered as an Independent Nation) just before he sailed.[31]

The minister and the consul differed sharply on the historical roots of Mexico's problems, shared the goal of imposing social peace on unruly people, and differed radically on the solution to Mexico's economic struggles. Alamán honored New Spain and silver capitalism, lamenting its demise in popular insurgency; Ortiz blamed Spanish rule for creating "abject people" who fell into "licentious anarchy" after 1810. Both saw popular assertions as prejudicial. Alamán would happily return to Spanish ways. Ortiz insisted that Mexico needed "the model of the United States."

A staunch liberal, he declared the people sovereign—then insisted they reform to earn the gifts of liberalism.[32]

To restrain popular assertions the minister called for severe justice. The consul proposed "the creation of a public administrative authority, above all other powers, to direct society and assure the free exercise of the rights and privileges of its members—based in the common interest."[33] Ortiz sought authoritarian power to back liberal rule. Yet he would cut the army by two-thirds and rely on hundreds of thousands of militiamen to keep the peace, arming men he found unprepared to rule. Education would solve the dilemma, backed by a penal system funded by taxes on "wine shops, pulque taverns, and the dispensaries that contribute most to the wasted years of youth, especially among the common people."[34] For Ortiz, the people were sovereign and should be armed, yet required reeducation to be liberal citizens and incarceration when they strayed—paid for in the price of their pleasures.

Ortiz differed insistently from Alamán in his prescriptions for Mexico's economic future. Early on, he sent memos calling for development of the north, especially Texas, to promote exports, mostly cotton. Military force would push back native peoples, block US expansion, and promote immigration under Mexican rule. He also called for export development along all of Mexico's coasts. US agricultural exports were more valuable than Mexico's silver, yet "we cannot compete due to the lack of hands, because happily we do not contradict humanity by holding a million and a half slaves." For the liberal Ortiz, the dilemma plaguing Mexico was how to build an export economy without slavery.[35]

Failing to convince Alamán, Ortiz wrote his book to make his case to Mexico's political classes. He insisted: "The foundation of real power in societies is agriculture, the source of life, the material base of industry, and the inexhaustible fountain of trade—together the true wealth and real force of nations."[36] Mexico had a history of rich commercial cultivation in the Bajío and wages lower than those paid free men in the United States. Mexico would thrive if silver and commercial estates would revive in the Bajío and exports develop along the coasts.[37]

In the Bajío, the problem was the tenants who had gained lands in insurgency. They did not focus on commercial sales.[38] Along the Gulf coast, Ortiz saw: "hordes of uncultured and unproductive men who live like Arabs. . . . They must be corrected by local authorities to stimulate a love of work and other pleasures, drawing them out of the state of barbarism in which they drown, so they will provide working hands for cultivation."[39] Coastal people of mixed ancestry, too long free, had too much autonomy, too much liberty.[40] Corrected (coerced?) they could sustain a prosperous export economy.

Could industry be Mexico's solution? Not until railroads integrated internal markets and cut the cost of crossing the rugged sierras between the inland plateau and coastal ports. Ortiz knew the productivity of British machines—and that they displaced large numbers of workers unless they served large markets, national and external. He called for agriculture and roads first, industry later. He emphasized "the benefits of free trade, the dismal results of prohibitions."[41] Protection could not stimulate exports, preserve crafts, or build industry. The liberal solution was free trade and pressure to promote hard work and more consumption by the people.[42]

Ortiz detailed the benefits of exports in Brazil, Cuba, and the United States, documenting the expansions of slavery at the base of their thriving economies. Mexico had abolished slavery under Guerrero in 1829. But it remained alive and expanding in Texas, still Mexican and being populated rapidly by slaveholders coming from the US South to grow cotton. They claimed provincial autonomy (state's rights) to protect the bondage essential to their prosperity. Ortiz saw the importance of Texas—and documented the necessity of slavery to export prosperity.

Relying on studies by the British parliament, he showed that Brazil, with only four million people, "almost half slaves," kept import duties at fifteen percent and imported British goods worth 6 million pounds (30 million pesos) yearly. Mexico, with (an overestimated) eight million "free inhabitants" imported only 400,000 pounds (2 million pesos). The United States, with a third more people than Mexico (about twelve million) "and about two million slaves" annually imported "an immense value of thirty-six million pounds, thanks to its liberty of commerce, its moderate rights, and its energetic civilization." Free trade, good governance, and civilization were all compatible with slave labor—and trade worth 80 million pesos or dollars (still equivalent in the 1830s).[43]

Then Ortiz turned to "Cuba that 40 years ago required four and a half million pesos sent from Mexico." Now it prospered with "free trade . . . patriotic societies, foreigners who promote agriculture and trade, and low tariffs on imports . . . with a population of 630,765 souls, more than a third slaves." With a tenth of Mexico's population, Cuba did ten times its trade. Still ruled by Spain, still importing slaves, committed to exports, mostly sugar plus some tobacco, Cuba was "after the United States . . . the most prosperous and richest market in America."[44]

Ortiz celebrated Brazilian, Cuban, and US economic dynamism based on free trade and slave labor. To finalize his argument he offered statistics generated by the United States in 1829 to prove that "men's work and free trade" were the base of productive gains—saying nothing about men's liberty. He reported US exports worth 49.5 million pesos, and listed the value of every product but cotton. The rest totaled less than 14.7 million pesos—leaving unstated but documented that seventy percent of US export earnings came from slave-made cotton.[45] Ortiz knew the role of enslaved labor in the successes of Brazil, Cuba, and the United States.

Texas was key. "The province of Texas by its location, sweet climate, fertility, fine ports, and proximity to the United States and the Antilles, producing goods indispensible to those countries—what level of prosperity it could achieve with effective programs of colonization and cultivation!"[46] Mexico could not develop its southern lowlands: "The hot ferocious climates of both coasts make unhealthy lands."[47] Exports had to come from Texas.[48] Ortiz did not say who would or should do the work.

Alamán and Ortiz offered contrasting visions of Mexico's problems and future. Alamán honored New Spain's silver capitalism, dreaming of its revival with the addition of mechanized industries. Ortiz lamented Spain's influence on Mexico, while honoring still-Spanish Cuba for its expansion of slave-made exports. They shared a belief that to prosper, Mexico must constrain its people. Neither vision, nor any containment of the people, was consolidated when Santa Ana displaced Bustamante as military strongman, backed by Zacatecas' silver.[49] Vice President Valentín Gómez Farías led an administration in 1833 that tried policies near to Ortiz's vision. Yet liberals quickly learned that an attempt to pay regime debts by expropriating Church property quickly divided a deeply Catholic country. In the same year the nation struggled with its first cholera epidemic. Was it retribution for an attack on God's Church?[50]

Santa Ana concluded that federalism was the problem, keeping states like Zacatecas rich and powerful, the national government poor and weak, and enabling the looming separation of Texas. The general found new allies, ended federalism, derailed liberalism, and moved to a centralizing constitution, the Siete Leyes—seven laws—in 1835. It claimed silver revenues for the national treasury and ended the state's rights that covered the expansion of slavery in Texas. Anglo-Texans with a few Mexican allies quickly seceded to preserve slavery. No Mexican government had the resources or the armed power to prevent it.[51]

Santa Ana's capture and surrender in Texas allowed Bustamante back as military arbiter of national government. He built a new administration without Alamán, trying to use central power to revive the economy, fill the treasury, and pacify politics. But powers centralized in a small congress so hedged the president and cabinet that they could do little. Constant talk of retaking Texas was that—talk. French forces demanding 600,000 pesos for the sacking of the Parián in 1828 landed at Veracruz in 1838, to learn that deadly lowlands were Mexico's best defense. Bustamante clung to power from 1837 to 1841 while political battles escalated.

Building a Mexican Cotton Industry, 1835–50

The Banco de Avío so proudly founded by Bustamante and Alamán in the early 1830s had barely begun to operate before Santa Ana, Gómez Farías, and their liberal allies took power late in 1832. When Bustamante returned to rule in 1835, it revived to operate as the first national development bank anywhere.[52] By the early 1840s its successes were notable. Back in government under Santa Ana in 1843, Alamán produced a survey of new industries (see appendix, table A.12). Building almost sixty mills in less than a decade, with over 100,000 working spindles and over 2,500 mechanized looms, was an achievement. Nearly eighty percent were in the departments (states under the central regime) of Mexico, Puebla, and Veracruz. The seventeen factories around Mexico City, with 23,894 spindles and 1,187 looms, pioneered an integrated cloth industry. In Puebla and Veracruz, new mills focused on spinning.

There were social consequences. Mechanization brought profit to entrepreneurs favored by the Banco de Avío; the number of workers gaining income to make cotton goods fell. Historically, spinning was women's work, done at home to make cloth for use, to support a husband's weaving, or to earn cash supplying large workshops. Mechanized spinning displaced women; mechanized weaving challenged male artisans. The integrated industry in and around the capital in the early 1840s displaced both; the spinning mills at Puebla and Veracruz mostly displaced women. Were gendered outcomes accidental? The political pressures of the late 1820s came from lowland cotton growers and urban weavers—mostly men. The industry of the early 1840s kept demand for raw cotton strong and cut the cost of yarn to weavers—benefiting men. Women faced new struggles. Most lived in patriarchal households: they bore and raised children, kept gardens, helped in the fields, and prepared meals; they spun yarn, wove cloth, and made clothing; and many earned income by spinning for money. Mechanized spinning cost them cash.

If one mechanical spindle working twelve hours daily produced what two women could spin at home in equal time, the 107,000 machine spindles of 1843 displaced 214,000 women. Most women in heartland pueblos and Bajío estate communities fit spinning into lives of childcare, food preparation, gardening, and marketing, spinning during a quarter or less of working days. Machines that would have displaced over 200,000 full-time hand spinners cost nearly a million women key supplements to family economies in the 1840s. A million women contributed to the sustenance of four million people—in a society of just over seven million. These are estimates. Still, the social impact of early Mexican industrialization was sharply gendered. While cultivation consolidated in households, new factories cut women's contribution to family economies—reinforcing patriarchy while limiting household incomes.

Alamán's reports for 1844 and 1845 confirm the secondary role of weaving in the early Mexican industry (see appendix, table A.13). The number of mills grew to sixty-two in 1844, with total spindles up six percent in a year. There was some northward expansion. By 1845, the number of operating mills fell back to fifty-five; working spindles rose by one and a half percent to total 113,814—with 15,714 listed as idle. The industry hit a plateau. Weak mills closed, others worked below capacity, a few expanded; the drive northward stalled. Still, the industry was established. Manuel Escandón at Puebla, the Martinez del Río family in Mexico City, and Cayetano Rubio at Querétaro gained fame and profit. Artisan weavers carried on. Women struggled.

A report from the early 1850s, after the war with the United States, showed that little had changed. It provides revealing detail on looms, workers, and payrolls. Total factories had fallen to forty; working spindles had risen to 120,630, up six percent in under a decade. The increase required only the activation of half the spindles idle in 1845. Mills still concentrated around the capital, Puebla, and Veracruz. The Mexico City mills became more integrated—with 15 spindles per mechanical loom. Querétaro built a parallel integrated industry on a smaller scale. Puebla all but gave up industrial weaving, with 151 spindles per loom. Elsewhere, from Veracruz to the north, the industry found a middle ground with 32 to 43 spindles per loom. There, spinning for sale to artisan weavers mixed with industrial weaving.

With 120,000 mechanized spindles prejudicing at least a million home spinners, the challenge to women remained. A small increase in mechanized weaving began to threaten artisan men. How many craftsmen did 3,393 industrial looms displace? Surely 10,000; perhaps many more. Taking the low estimates, by midcentury new industries had displaced a million women from part-time earnings and 10,000 men from full-time crafts. In that context, the total industrial employment of 11,267 is illuminating—as is the high average annual wage of 150 pesos (two to three times prevailing rural wages). Men did most factory work in Mexico; the new mills absorbed about as many male workers in weaving and spinning as they displaced from artisan weaving. Industrial profits concentrated among entrepreneurs; male workers were well paid—an emerging labor aristocracy. Patriarchy strengthened for 10,000 men; a million or more women faced new marginalities in household economies.

Violence by men against women rose at Puebla as new industries took hold in the 1840s. In a city where men remained craft weavers while machines replaced women in spinning, did struggling men resent the loss of women's earnings? In 1846, one woman refused to feed her husband, a weaver, when he came home late. He beat her with a spindle.[53] Refusal to serve a meal was the immediate issue. Was the choice of a spindle as weapon mere accident? Or had spinning mills displaced the wife, leaving the weaver to buy thread, adding cost to his workshop? In angry patriarchal eyes, had she failed doubly: not spinning to fund the household economy, not cooking to feed her husband?

The new mills of the 1840s created profit, work for men, markets for lowland growers, and cloth for consumers across the nation. Industrial capitalism came to Mexico—limited to national markets. Alamán had triumphed. Yet as Ortiz warned, limited markets meant that mechanization cut employment—losses mostly striking women. Commercial doldrums persisted; the nation's debts rose. Debates resumed.

Debating the Future Again—with Industry and without Texas, 1843–45

When Santa Ana replaced Bustamante as military arbiter in 1842, he returned Alamán to control of economic affairs. In a new series of Memorias, he documented a revival of silver as Guanajuato joined Zacatecas to generate the first expansion since 1810. He touted the success of the Banco de Avío in founding industries. Still, commercial agriculture struggled: plenty without profit endured—as did political conflict, military provocations, and empty treasuries. In a second round of debates, Alamán defended his industrial policy, liberals still pressed for an export economy—and an analyst known only as J. G. documented Mexico's limits in 1845, just before the United States turned to war to tighten those limits by taking vast northern territories.

In 1843 Alamán honored the revival of mining at Guanajuato, yet silver was far from the leading sector it had been before 1810. He defended the Banco de Avío: "The cotton industry has reached a point where it demands the full attention of the government." It needed attention because while fabric cost two-thirds less than before mechanization, without Texas Mexican growers could not supply sufficient raw cotton, and weak national cloth consumption threatened profits. The challenge was to extend planting in coastal lowlands and to expand internal markets; how he did not say.[54] A year later, Alamán insisted that "everyone knows that the only route to stimulate agriculture is by increasing industrial consumption of the fruits of our fields—which have no value if factories don't turn them into articles of trade."[55] Crops consumed by families had no value.

"With granaries already full of the harvests of years past, our farmers' fruits have suffered an even deeper fall in prices, now so low that last year's abundant harvests of maize have prevented any rise—despite the total loss of the wheat harvest in the Bajío and other regions."[56] Persistent family farming led to ample harvests and low prices. Families, rural and urban, ate affordably. If bread eaters faced high wheat prices, they turned to maize. Alamán lamented that even around the northern mines, abundant crops held maize prices low.[57] "The abundance of harvests without consumption is the cause of backwardness." The result: "estates cannot be sold, but for vile prices and with pernicious conditions."[58]

He concluded: "industry and agriculture must support each other, and together make the happiness of the nation."[59] Alamán's nation was led by industrial and landed entrepreneurs, not by villagers, estate tenants, or factory workers. The way forward was to plant cotton to supply factories. Factory owners and cotton growers would profit. If enough cotton could not be raised on the coasts, he looked to irrigation and cultivation in the northern Laguna region. Early crops there supplied new mills in Durango. Industry was the nation's first interest, "if we consider the capital invested, the products it yields, and the hands it employs." Yet industrial growth had plateaued, while machines cut the incomes of uncounted numbers of women.[60]

Mexico's liberals still opposed industrial development. They found a new voice to carry Ortiz's vision. Robert Wyllie represented British holders of Mexican bonds long in default. He wrote a long report signed in Mexico City in December 1843, published in English in London in 1844, then in Spanish in Mexico City in 1845. His report might be set aside as another statement of British goals for Latin America—until Ignacio Cumplido, publisher of *El Siglo XIX*, Mexico City's leading liberal newspaper, presented it in Spanish. Wrote Cumplido: "Wyllie's report is the victorious refutation of those who pretend that the system of free trade is not applicable to Mexico."[61] Wyllie knew that Mexico's problems had begun with the fall of silver after 1810. With silver recovering in the 1840s, he insisted that Mexico's route to prosperity and to pay its debts was through a turn to new exports: tobacco, cotton, sugar, coffee, and indigo.[62]

Mexico faced a debt crisis in the 1840s. Wyllie detailed how by 1810 two decades of Atlantic war had left obligations of 11.5 million pesos, cut to 3 million by 1823. But the costs of counterinsurgency after 1810 created new debts totaling 16.4 million pesos—most owed to internal creditors. Then the republic borrowed 3.2 million pounds at five percent in 1823, another 3.2 million at six percent in 1824. Much of the second loan paid off part of the first, and for a few years interest was paid. In 1835, the treasury owed British bondholders 5.3 million pounds. Then the cost of fighting in Texas ended payments; Mexico owed 9.25 million pounds in 1840. At 5 pesos per pound, British bondholders claimed 46 million pesos.[63] By Wyllie's calculation, customs income, the primary support of the national treasury, was 6.7 million pesos annually; expenses were 13.2 million, of which 8 million paid the military. Foreign creditors demanded 1.4 million pesos, internal creditors another 1.3 million. Debt service raised annual expenses to an impossible 16 million pesos—more than twice annual income.[64]

Unable to address the obvious point that the imbalance resulted from the costs of a military that failed to keep Texas, Wyllie insisted that Mexico stop industrializing and turn to an export economy. Industry, he claimed, only employed 3,410 people out of 7 million. Better to sell "grain, livestock, sugar, coffee, cochineal, gold, silver, and copper at the highest price possible," and buy "cloth and other manufactures at the lowest price possible." Planting cotton for national factories was not enough. Including cotton growers and workers, textiles employed only 35,000, while limits on imports cost four million in annual revenues. The bondholders' agent argued that even US industry (valued at eleven million pesos for a population of 17 million) was no more valuable than Mexican industry (valued at four million pesos for a population of 7 million). US wealth, Wyllie insisted, came from sixty-one million pesos of cotton exports.[65]

Wyllie noted another aspect of US success. The federal government earned nine million pesos yearly selling public lands from 1833 to 1840. Mexico should do the same and use the proceeds to pay down the public debt. To succeed, Mexico also must copy the United States in dealing with "the barbarous Indians of the frontier."[66] He added that US officials maintained a "notorious project" of annexing Mexican territories. Mexico must colonize its north or lose more land, opportunity for development, and the ability to pay British bondholders.[67]

In 1790 New Spain had nearly 6 million people, the United States fewer than 4 million; now with immigration and land sales, the United States had grown to 17 million, Mexico to but 7 million.[68] Wyllie added that the enslaved population of the United States had grown from fewer than 700,000 in 1790 to near 2.5 million in 1840—faster growth than the free population. Having offered cotton as the model export: "It must be said in honor of the slave owners of the United States that the progressive growth of the population of slaves would be incompatible with the harsh treatment they are accused of imposing.[69] Wyllie proposed that Mexico sell public lands and draw immigrants (and open its territory to slavery?) to pay British bondholders.

Wyllie included a letter by Alexander Forbes, a British trader at Tepic on Mexico's Pacific coast. He called for a Mexican-British colonization of California. British companies would buy land, paying with outstanding bonds. The Mexican treasury would cover debts it could not pay. California would remain under Mexican sovereignty, ruled by British developers and settlers. "The infusion of English habits of industry and morality into mixed races would be most desirable. The government would remain Mexican in name; all else would belong to the company and the colonists"—all British.[70]

The key was gold: "there are reports of a land containing gold, near a town called Los Angeles." Mining would be easy: "*placer gold* is gathered by digging the soil a bit, generally no more than a few feet, separating the gold, washing it, or where there is no water, winnowing it in the air." As mining had declined in Sonora, "people from that province, knowing the ways and work of this class of mines, could be easily drawn to Alta-California; I consider this new discovery a secure fountain of riches for this second country."[71] Forbes saw California as a new country under limited Mexican sovereignty, ruled by British companies, worked by British farmers—and Sonoran miners. Thanks to Wyllie's publication of Forbes's plan in London in 1844, and in Mexico in 1845, US emissaries in both capitals surely saw Forbes's vision of a gold-rich California and his imagined British-Mexican project.

Policy makers in Mexico City soon gained another view. The author known only as J. G. wrote to back Alamán's industrial policy and show why Mexico could not follow the export model promoted by Ortiz, Wyllie, Forbes, and the liberals of *El Siglo XIX*. J. G. asked why *El Siglo* had published Wyllie's report. Its premise "that the nation will find fountains of riches in agriculture, exporting its products," was absurd.[72] If Mexico followed Wyllie and *El Siglo XIX*: "What will happen immediately to the spinners and weavers of León, Celaya, Allende, Querétaro, and Acámbaro?" What would happen to artisans everywhere?[73]

The anonymous analyst quoted an 1843 report detailing why Mexico could not focus on exports:

> The physical nature of our land gives us a central plateau, raised more or less high above sea level, open to produce all the fruits of Europe, bounded on both sides by mountain heights that extend to the coasts of both seas—which produce all the fruits of the tropics. This configuration of our lands makes communication between the central plateau and the coasts very difficult, making the fruits of the interior impossible to export; they cannot cover the costs of transport due to distance and a nature that denies us all the means of communication linking the interior and the coasts—means so abundant in the United States.[74]

Until the Sierras could be breached, Mexico was agriculturally isolated, sustaining itself and closed to the world. The result: "a year of abundance not only does not enrich our farmers, but prejudices their business, filling their granaries with crops that have no outlets."[75] Plenty without profit still reigned.

J. G. then turned to Mexico's tropics: "Our coasts might compensate for the problem, as they produce all the fruits that nature has denied Europe, where there is such great consumption, fruits that bring prosperity to Cuba. But unique circumstances prevent our gaining those benefits. An unhealthy climate has left our coasts unpopulated," and as a result, "their fruits come in small quantities and at prices that cannot compete with the islands." J. G. knew that geography and disease blocked a Mexican export economy. The nation must mix agriculture and industry to flourish. He added with pride that most Mexicans were family cultivators or rural workers who gained incomes above the norms prevailing in "east India" or in "the United States, Brazil, the Antilles, and Asia, where workers are paid less or made to plant as slaves."[76]

And J. G. would not brook a return to slavery: "Our Republic may remain poor, but under our laws humans will not groan nor will our fruits be stained by the sweat of men who curse as they labor to produce for other men who treat them as beasts." Knowing that Texas had seceded to preserve slavery, J. G. took a phrase by which Texans had justified their secession and turned it to Mexico's honor:

> To malign us, some have taken from the Texans the saying that we are not worthy of the sun that shines upon us or the land that holds our

plants. We would be unworthy of the sun, if like Texans the sun shined upon us driving men as beasts subject to lashes; and we would be unworthy of the beautiful land taken from us by those infamous soldiers of fortune if we profaned the soil by working it with arms debased by the denial of their humanity, making fruits with the tyranny of slavery, drawing the moans and groans of desperate coerced men. May our land remain uncultivated and unpopulated, if our wealth depends on staining our selves with slavery! Let us be poor, before we consent to that.[77]

With economic, environmental, and humanitarian arguments, J. G. explained Mexico's predicament. The only course was to favor silver, the nation's only product valuable in trade. It must promote agriculture for sustenance and to supply national industries. It should protect existing cotton factories and recognize the importance of artisans in woolens and other crafts. "Our industrial system grounded in mining, agriculture, and crafts serves people in all conditions and provides for their diverse needs."[78] J. G. offered no utopia, just a clear understanding of Mexico's situation in 1845—as the United States readied to go to war and take its northern territories.

The new industrial world saw a few regions concentrate industrial power while many supplied commodities—locked together in a new industrial capitalism. In the Americas of the 1840s, only the United States and Mexico had turned to industry. But the United States had built strong industries sustained by strong commodity sectors—dependent on slavery in the cotton-growing South, and on immigrant farmers in a Midwest that fed the rest. Mexico built industries and fed itself in central highlands, but could not develop commodity exports. In 1846, the United States was seventy-five years a nation, favored by geography in the new world of industrial specialization—and living with the contradiction of proclaiming liberty while profiting from slave-grown cotton and from staples raised on lands taken from native peoples. Mexico was but twenty-five years a nation, its mines just reviving, industries just beginning, while geography and commitments to freedom inhibited exports.

At that moment, the United States mobilized for war, led by southern slaveholding interests. Its press and popular writers searched for ways to present the invasion of Mexico as liberating. They invented the idea of "debt peonage," portraying the Mexican tradition of advance payments, often overpayments and rarely constraining, as bondage equal to or worse than the slavery that sustained the US cotton economy.[79]

That construction aimed to deflect understanding of the War for North America of 1846–48 as an invasion by a powerful society profiting from slavery, aiming to take territory from a young nation seeking economic revival after ending slavery.

Postwar Mexico: Political Conflict and Economic Revival, 1850–75

The US victory and Mexico's territorial losses in the War for North America locked in the disparities evident in the debates of 1843 to 1845. The United States gained California gold, Colorado silver, and Texas cotton and slavery, creating the only economy in the world mixing industry, commodity exports, and mining wealth—all grounded in a staples sector providing internal sustenance and export earnings. Mexico carried on with a silver sector just reviving, industries limited to internal markets, and agriculture harvesting ample food at low prices.

Neither nation found postwar stability. The United States faced resistant Comanches and other independent peoples still strong on lands claimed from Mexico.[80] The incorporation of Texas added to slaveholding power, deepening the political divisions that led to civil war in 1861 and a divisive reconstruction into the 1870s. Then the United States rose to hemispheric economic hegemony. Mexicans also faced trying times from 1850 to 1870: political conflicts led to political war from 1858 to 1860, French invasion in 1862, Maximilian's imposed empire of 1864 to 1867, then years of difficult reconciliation.

The new map left Mexico geographically poor in an industrial world. After years of postwar recriminations, liberals took power in 1855 and attempted a national reconstruction. Unable to create the export economy of Tadeo Ortiz's dreams, they would liberate Mexicans from what he and other liberals insisted was a degrading Hispanic past shaped by the Catholic Church and indigenous republics. They aimed to transform by decree the nation's deep Catholic culture and its staunch communities.[81] While the United States fought a civil war to purge slavery and enable its rise to continental industrial hegemony, Mexicans fought over liberal reforms.

With the end of war in 1848, military, political, and ideological factions blamed each other for Mexico's losses. There was plenty of blame to share: provincial leaders had hesitated to send funds or troops to fight the United States; most saw a lost cause and focused on local challenges.[82] Among

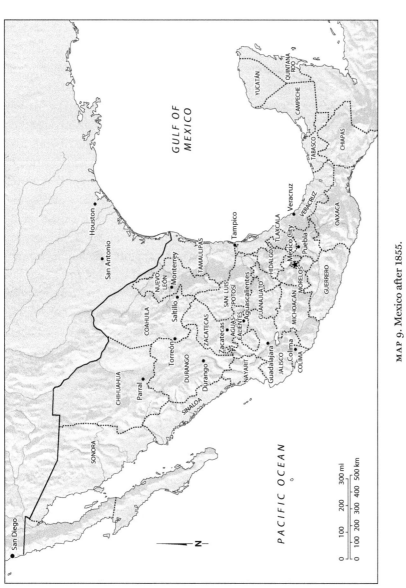

MAP 9. Mexico after 1855.

those challenges were popular pressures: most villagers and tenants stood back from a war to defend a nation that rarely saw to their interests. Native peoples in Yucatán and the Sierra Gorda saw the war years as a time to assert their own independence. Around Cuernavaca, villagers challenged sugar estates and planters looked to US troops for defense. And while the leaders who claimed to defend the nation fled to Querétaro, the people of Mexico City defended their barrios by hurling paving stones in proud if futile resistance to US marines.[83] The war showed Mexico's economic and military weakness; a united nation remained an imagined goal.[84]

In the early 1850s Santa Ana led a last government, shaped by Alamán until his death in 1853. It fell in 1854 to a rising led by Juan Álvarez, heir to Guerrero in the Pacific hotlands. Álvarez was a unique liberal. Like Guerrero, he based his power in rugged sierras and Pacific lowlands by addressing the demands of diverse peoples—including many committed to landed communities. That grounding enabled him to raise armies and march through the Cuernavaca basin to the capital. He brought a liberal coalition to power—and once there, the coalition pushed him aside. Urban liberals had no use for Álvarez and his commitments to popular communities once he had set them in power. They found backing from Santiago Vidaurri, a strongman ruling Saltillo and Monterrey, cities gaining prosperity near the border reset in 1848. Vidaurri had no interest in community rights, scarce in the north.[85]

Led by General Ignacio Comonfort, the new regime issued key decrees in 1856. The Ley Juárez, named for Justice Minister Benito Juárez (former governor of Oaxaca, Zapotec by birth, liberal by education), ended the separate justice enjoyed by the clergy and the military. Mexico would have one judicial system. The law aimed to cut Church power and military independence.

The Ley Lerdo decreed uniform property rights. Only persons would own property; no corporation, no Church institution or native community, would hold real estate, urban or rural—except for institutional use. The goal was not expropriation. Church institutions would transfer ownership of city houses to tenants, who would pay long-term mortgages to support religious activities. Rural estates would be auctioned, the Church gaining the proceeds. The law imagined a less propertied but not less funded Church. Many city residents would become homeowners, ideal liberal citizens dependent on a liberal government for their new property.

The call to privatize community lands aimed directly at village autonomies. Land subject to community domain would become personal property subject to state domain (for the cost of surveys and titles).

Notables who held larger shares would gain them in property; families who worked small plots would become proprietors too. To that point, there was no expropriation. But the commons (*montes*) that provided pasture, woodlands, and more to many of the poorest would be auctioned to the highest bidder, the proceeds going to community treasuries. Whether *montes* went to a local merchant or an outsider, many of the poorest would lose access to land essential to survival. Lands leased or worked to generate community income would be auctioned too, the proceeds going to local treasuries. Village notables or outsiders might gain ownership. As the locally powerful gained their lands as personal property, they would lose interest in defending community lands. A liberal law promising to make proprietors and mobilize property would break the cohesion that defended community domains and fuel land markets that would surely concentrate holdings to benefit the prosperous and prejudice the poor.

Why were Mexican liberals determined to privatize community lands? The 1812 Cádiz charter had recognized indigenous people as full citizens and called for privatizing community lands. Men would gain personal political rights; the corporate rights that grounded landed autonomies would end. In a time of popular uprisings, authorities had refrained from privatizations in 1813. The precedent remained. In the 1830s, Tadeo Ortiz blamed Mexico's economic difficulties on indigenous backwardness. By the 1850s, liberals had congealed a new and deeply denigrating vision of native peoples. Landed communities became irredeemable obstacles to progress. Native resistance to commercial ways and national power led midcentury ideologues to a new racial construction of *indio*: refusing progress, *indios* became obstacles to the Mexican nation.[86]

Midcentury liberals blurred the diversity of native peoples: they fused people in former republics that had sustained silver capitalism with Apaches and Comanches fighting subjugation to any state. All were seen as like the Maya who promoted bloody "caste wars." Independent people and republican villagers merged in the liberal mind as savage barbarians: recalcitrant obstacles to progress. Minus the racist edge, the liberals were not wrong: Comanche and other independent northerners did block Mexican northward expansion. People in former republics clung to autonomies and production for sustenance, making the plenty without profit that so bothered Alamán. The Maya of Yucatán and natives in the Sierra Gorda did rise up amid the war with the United States. All this frustrated liberals—still determined to reform indigenous ways.

The Juárez and Lerdo laws, politically and socially transforming in intent, generated deep opposition. Conservatives backed by the Church pressed the War of Reform from 1858 to 1860. In 1859 President Benito Juárez nationalized Church properties; in the face of war, liberal authorities would sell them and take the proceeds, expropriating the Church. The war prevented wide implementation of community land privatization, while most communities stood aside from deadly conflicts among political factions. Liberals led by Juárez won in 1860 thanks to their control of the port of Veracruz and most of the north, and regime revenues.[87] A rapid sale of Church properties followed, creating new proprietors beholden to liberal rule.[88]

Desperate conservatives looked to Europe. Britain, France, and Spain still had large financial claims against Mexico and the liberals would not pay. Napoleon III retained his famous uncle's dream of imperial power grounded in the wealth of New Spain, now Mexico. He built a coalition of French, British, and Spanish forces on the pretense of collecting debts; when the intent to invade became clear, his allies departed— leaving French troops alone to face defeat on May 5, 1862, at Puebla. A year later, reinforced French armies drove Juárez from Mexico City; in 1864 Maximilian of Hapsburg came to take a throne backed by French force, Mexican conservatives, and others desperate for peace. Maximilian did not return properties to the Church (he could not repay buyers); he lavished public concern on native peoples—and kept the Ley Lerdo. He ruled as long as French armies remained; when they went home to face Prussian threats in 1867, he stayed to face capture, trial, and execution.[89]

Maximilian led a government of conservatives and moderate liberals, previewing the authoritarian liberalism built by Porfirio Díaz after 1876.[90] In 1867, Juárez regained the presidency and saw a mandate to resume liberal programs. The nationalization of Church property was complete, so he pressed the privatization of community lands—provoking a round of resistance from communities that had stood aside from the political conflicts of 1858 to 1867. Many rose up to defend community rights in regions as near the capital as Chalco and the Mezquital, and as distant as Nayarit and Chiapas. Liberals even pressed privatization in the Sierra de Puebla, where communities had been pivotal to the Cinco de Mayo—Fifth of May—victory and the long fight to oust the French. Again, resistance led to negotiation and limited implementation. On retaking power in 1867, Juárez and the liberals learned that they lacked the means to transform communities. They did not revoke the Ley Lerdo, but left implementation to provincial initiatives.[91]

The trajectory of the Mexican economy during the decades from 1845 to 1875 is little studied. Silver mining rose during the 1840s, uninhibited by the war of 1846–48 or years of postwar recriminations, when output reached 16.5 million pesos yearly. Why the revival? Most mines had returned to Mexican control. British pumping technologies were adapted to Mexican ways of production with Mexican workers. British capital remained important: the merchant-financiers Manning and MacIntosh (MacIntosh was British consul general in Mexico) controlled most mints to 1850 and all but monopolized exports to London. From there, British merchant-bankers ruled exports to China, which rose sharply from the mid-1850s. The outflow of silver that had drained China from 1810 to 1850 stopped; with Mexico's midcentury revival China again became a leading importer of the precious money. But now, instead of selling fine porcelains and silk cloth to the world, China sent tea and raw silk to England, joining the world of commodity exporters sustaining British industry in trades again fueled by Mexican silver.[92]

The late 1840s and early 1850s saw bonanzas at La Luz, above Guanajuato, and Real del Monte, northeast of Mexico City. Success brought challenges. Workers had to be attracted by offering the ore shares so important in Spanish times. When production rose operators turned to ending shares and cutting labor costs—provoking, as in Spanish times, labor conflicts. Output dipped under sixteen million pesos yearly during the wars of 1855 to 1864, rose to eighteen million under Maximilian and the restored republic, and hit twenty million in the early 1870s (see appendix, table A.9). Political conflict did not block mining revival.[93]

Meanwhile, the textile industry soared between 1850 and 1880. While silver rose fifty percent, textile capacity more than doubled: the forty factories, 120,000 spindles, and 3,400 looms of the early 1850s increased to ninety-nine mills, 261,000 spindles, and 8,800 industrial looms in 1880. Industry (and the challenge to household spinners and artisan weavers) expanded in established industrial regions around Mexico City, Puebla, and Veracruz, and from the Bajío to Jalisco. It showed new growth in the north and beginnings in the south (see appendix, tables A.14 and A.15). The restoration of mining and the doubling of industrial textiles led a midcentury commercial revival.

Mexico City remained the nation's largest urban center; new industries concentrated in nearby suburbs. Factories went out to tap water power, while the center retained vibrant artisan communities: carpenters and other building trades; shoe makers, hatters, and tailors; printers, silversmiths, and diverse others. Spinners and weavers were few in the city after 1865, displaced by workers in outlying mills. The latter lived a revealing evolution. In the 1850s, most industrial workers were married men, joined by a few young single women. By the 1870s, the number of single men equaled married men; women remained a minority. As a working class rose in Mexico City's industrial suburbs, a turn to younger workers cut labor costs—and worker incomes.[94]

During decades of political conflict and mining revival, the textile industry expanded while artisans held strong—precisely J. G.'s vision. In the 1870s, tailors' shops began to import sewing machines—labor saving on a personal scale. In the coming years, they would be taken up by women for household use, making family clothing and gaining a bit of income too.[95] Printing shops bought mechanized presses—limiting workers and skills. Hat makers turned to divisions of labor that cut demand for skilled workers. Commercial dependencies rose in artisan workshops—and in households buying sewing machines on credit. Conflicts heightened, often in shops owned by European immigrants resented after the ouster of French troops and Maximilian's empire. The liberal governments of Juárez and Sebastián Lerdo from 1867 to 1876 aided artisan education, backed mutual aid societies, and allowed the emergence of an artisan-worker alliance in the Gran Círculo de Obreros Mexicanos. They hoped to tap artisan political support by negotiating limited demands. When workers in outlying factories turned mutual aid societies into unions that pressed strikes in the 1870s, Lerdo backed mill owners in repression.[96] Artisan politics and labor conflicts marked a growing urban-industrial sector.

From 1850 to 1875, agriculture remained contested. Heartland estate operators pressed commercial production and liberals legislated privatizations of community lands; community cultivators pressed back, sometimes claiming estate lands in court, often defending village lands in fields and courts.[97] Stalemate ruled: villagers fed themselves by cultivating community lands and plots leased on shares from struggling estates; estates employed villagers to grow commercial crops when markets promised profit. Neither gained a clear upper hand before 1875.[98]

In the Bajío, as textile industries expanded at Querétaro and mining regained historic heights at Guanajuato, most cultivation remained in the hands of tenants. They fed themselves and nearby cities, keeping landlord profits limited.[99] At Zacatecas, after holding low for decades, maize prices peaked from 1850 to 1854, doubling the level of the 1830s (they had been low owing to disease, drought, and a local downturn in mining). Prices returned to steady low levels during the wars of 1855–64, peaked in 1865–69, then held low again in 1870–74; silver production held strong from 1860 to 1874.[100] Midcentury decades brought reports neither of widespread scarcities nor of excess production and low prices. Had family croppers and estate growers found a new equilibrium, sustaining themselves, their on-going stalemate, and growing mining centers and textile industries, after 1850? That seems a fair hypothesis based on limited knowledge.

An export opening in Gulf lowlands led native communities to adapt liberal privatization to take gain in Atlantic markets. The Totonacs of Papantla in northern Veracruz were long marginal to the commercial econ-omy focused in interior highlands. They held ample lands in communities that were heirs to colonial republics, most used for shifting agriculture along with hunting and gathering. Vanilla grew wild in the forests. When export markets grew around 1870, merchants funded increased gathering. To protect community lands and raise production, Totonac leaders orga-nized *condueñazgos*: joint stock companies in which community members gained shares in proportion to lands they held. Native notables worked with immigrant merchants to promote exports; commoners cleared, planted, and harvested shifting milpas while earning cash gathering and drying vanilla. For a time in Papantla, it seemed that the liberal dream of exports, privatization, and native welfare could be real.[101]

The midcentury decades mixed postwar conflicts, political wars, for-eign occupation—and a revival of silver, a doubling of industrial produc-tion, and the promise of exports. Still, communities remained staunch on the land across the heartland and southern highlands while tenants ruled the fertile Bajío. The acceleration of industrial capitalism in Mexico awaited two key developments: privatizations that corroded community autonomies, and railroads to integrate internal markets and link Mexican producers to the United States and the world.

Industrial Acceleration: Silver, Industry, and Exports, 1870–1910

Mexico's long era of political conflict ended in 1876, when a coup installed General Porfirio Díaz as president, the last military arbiter of nineteenth-century politics. He used military power to stabilize the regime—and in time limit military costs, which were taking over sixty percent of the national budget when Juárez retook power in 1867, then fell below fifty percent as Díaz ended his first term in 1880.[102] Regime stability often gains credit for the economic expansion that transformed Mexico—until everything collapsed in revolution in 1910. The political peace of Díaz and decades of capitalist expansion were mutually reinforcing.[103] Just as the collapse of silver capitalism underlay the political instability of the decades after 1820, the revival of silver and the expansion of industry from the

1840s brought profits to entrepreneurs and revenues to the regime, setting foundations for political consolidation after 1870. Mexico's per capita
gross national product, commercial production divided by the number of
the population, in 1870 regained the level of 1800–1810.[104] Commercial
life had grown during midcentury decades of war and conflict, while family production and community autonomies held strong. After 1870, continuing expansions of silver and industry came with railroads and new
export sectors. Mexico finally fused its historic role as a silver producer
with internal industries and commodity exports.

In the 1870s, Mexican silver production, as measured in pesos, finally
regained the levels of 1790 to 1810, holding above twenty million pesos
yearly. As population had risen fifty percent, the gains remained limited.
But rapid growth followed. National silver production reached seventy to
eighty million pesos yearly from 1900 to 1909, while population rose only
another fifty percent.[105] The silver boom of the late nineteenth century
was a real stimulus—measured in pesos. It stimulated profit and export
production far more than the common welfare. Rural wages held steady:
the two to four reales daily of the late eighteenth through mid-nineteenth
centuries were comparable to the twenty-five to fifty centavos daily of the
late nineteenth century. Soaring silver production towered over the earnings of a growing population—both measured in pesos.

How could silver expand so much without generating at least limited
wage and welfare gains? The boom of 1875 to 1910 came as the value
of silver and of the Mexican peso plummeted in the world economy. In
1873 the ratio of gold to silver in global commodity-currency markets
was sixteen to one. By 1902 it approached forty to one.[106] The 20 million
pesos of silver produced annually in Mexico around 1875 was worth about
1.25 million gold-backed dollars; the 70 million silver pesos of 1905 was
worth but 1.75 million gold dollars. While silver production tripled in
pesos, valued in gold it increased only forty percent—less than the growth
of the Mexican population. The demand for Mexico's primary export
rose while its value dropped. The result was economic boom and social
polarization. The shift began not with Díaz's political consolidation, but
with the industrial powers' consolidation of a gold standard in 1873.

Britain had turned to a gold standard after the Napoleonic wars.
Historically, close ties to Portugal had brought Britain favored access to
Brazilian gold, while it struggled (with some success) to gain New Spain's
silver. After 1808, direct trade with Brazil kept gold coming, while alliance
with the Cádiz regime fighting to liberate Spain brought access to New
Spain's silver—until its collapse in 1810. Britain's turn to gold after the wars

was unique, linked to its equally unique rise to industrial eminence. The rest of the world remained either bimetallic or tied to silver. The United States and Mexico shared the silver peso/dollar as currency through the 1840s; China still required silver and struggled as it flowed out to buy opium from British India. Californian and Australian gold rushes in the 1850s brought rising stocks of that money-metal. The United States gained California gold and Colorado silver before, during, and after the civil war—a time too fragile to change the money system. But in 1873, the United States and Germany, both unified after years of conflict, joined Britain on the gold standard. The industrial powers made gold their primary money.[107]

The value of silver in international trade plummeted; demand rose as silver remained money, ever less valuable, in most nations, including Mexico. Commodities made in regions using silver became cheap in industrial societies using gold. The global division of labor, in which a few regions dominated finance and heavy industry while the rest of the world sold commodities, defined the world of industrial capitalism. Commodities cheapened; industrial goods could be exported thanks to laborsaving machines and economies of scale. Machines became costly outside the industrial cores; capital made in gold found easy entry in nations struggling with declining silver. Capital and industry consolidated among the powerful. Commodities and poverty entrenched across the world.

The consequences for Mexico proved both energizing and polarizing. US investors came south to build railroads—backed by Mexican government subsidies accounted in gold. Many floated bonds in London to gain capital; Mexico was back (via the United States) in London financial markets. The 1870s saw railroads tie Mexico City to the port of Veracruz; the 1880s brought trunk lines linking the capital to the US border. If investors aimed to favor exports, a network centered on Mexico City also integrated internal markets. Thanks to Díaz's funding of US capitalists, railroads finally surmounted the constraints to Mexico's incorporation in commodity markets now focusing on the United States. With the construction of regional connectors, the 6,000 kilometers of railroads in 1884 became 20,000 by 1910.[108]

US investment followed the railroads, taking hold in silver, copper, and after 1900 in oil. To produce rising quantities of silver as its value plummeted, investors brought labor and cost-saving machinery: industrial smelting and cyanide-based refining separated silver, gold, and lead from the same ore.[109] Mexican gold production rose to over forty million pesos yearly after 1905 (twice the value of the silver mined around 1800; half the value of silver produced in the early 1900s). With great smelters at Aguascalientes and Monterrey, the Guggenheim family and their American Smelting and Refining Company (ASARCO) ruled silver production, exports, and profits after 1900. The Cananea copper mines just south of the Arizona border, founded by William Greene and famous for his repression of labor conflict of 1906, ended up part of the Phelps Dodge mining empire by 1910. Profit flowed to New York, while laborsaving ways ensured that little gain went to Mexican workers. While production soared from 1897 to 1907, mining employment held near 120,000 (in a population of 12 million). Wages were at best steady and often pressed down (leading to conflict at Cananea). Mexicans finally saw a mining boom. Metals and profits went to the United States; the few Mexicans involved gained limited prosperity.[110]

The decline in the value of silver relative to gold made imports of manufactured goods from industrial centers on the gold standard expensive for Mexicans paid in silver.[111] The difference protected the consumer industries that had served internal markets since the 1840s, enabling continued expansion after 1870. Textile mills still focused around Orizaba in upland Veracruz, at Puebla and nearby Atlixco, and in Mexico City's industrial suburbs—as well as in the Bajío and Jalisco. Railroads facilitated access to wider national markets and cotton produced in the Laguna (taking pressure off disease-ridden lowlands). While capitalists based in the United States ruled railroads and mining, immigrants often from France and based in Mexico City led internal industry and mass marketing. Foreign capitalists and immigrant entrepreneurs differed: all tapped international capital and imported machinery, but foreigners took profits and capital home; immigrants and their profits stayed in Mexico. In a dual industrialization, foreign capitalists led export industries in silver, gold, copper, and petroleum, mostly in the north; immigrants ruled textiles and other consumer industries in the center.[112]

The sectors fused in Monterrey. Long a frontier town surrounded by grazing lands, after silver's collapse its marginality was reinforced by Comanche raids. The War for North America pressed the Comanche back north and brought the US border to the nearby Rio Grande. The 1850s saw the beginning of a textile industry, buying cotton from the Laguna just to the west. The US Civil War brought new chances; Monterrey merchants profited bringing slave-grown cotton across the river, marking it Mexican, and selling it in Britain and the US North. The trade built capital and entrepreneurship in Monterrey. Mexicans (notably the Madero family) and immigrants (Irish Patricio Milmo, among others) built industries and founded banks to spur commercial growth.[113]

The 1890s brought a second round of opportunities. Rails linked Monterrey to Texas and the United States, to the Bajío and Mexico City, and to Torreón and the Laguna, Chihuahua, El Paso, and Zacatecas. Monterrey capitalists expanded consumer industries from textiles to beer, its glass bottles, and cardboard cases. At a key junction in an expanding rail system, with access to coal and iron ore, Monterrey investors built the first iron and steel mill in Latin America. The Guggenheims built their greatest smelter, drawing ore from across Mexico's north, refining silver, lead, and gold, and sending them to the United States. The mix of consumer industries, rails and other metal products for Mexican transport and industrial markets, and mineral processing for export created a unique economy at Monterrey. An urban dynamo, it drew migrants from all around after 1890, centering an industrial society that transformed Mexico's north.

Railroads and the declining value of silver also fueled Mexico's first agricultural export boom after 1880. Crops produced by workers paid in silver earned gold in US and European markets. Still, diverse products generated differing social outcomes in different regions. Three examples illustrate. Vanilla exports continued at Papantla into the 1880s. Totonac leaders joined merchant exporters to press a second round of privatization, breaking the land into lots based on shares that had concentrated in the previous decade. The prosperous gained land; the comfortable carried on; the poor were marginalized; the landless excluded. While exports held strong, most found ways forward; when recession hit in the 1890s, uprisings challenged local leaders. Backed by the Porfirian state, they held on—as did the liberal order of privatization and polarization.[114]

Mexico also became a major coffee exporter in the 1880s. Along Gulf foothills in Oaxaca and Veracruz, and Pacific uplands from Oaxaca through Chiapas, privatization facilitated coffee planting on properties of diverse sizes. Most growers were Mexican; European immigrants ruled exports that grew from around ten million kilograms yearly near 1890 to twenty million around 1900 and fifty million in 1907—before the crash. Earnings did not grow in parallel. Growing global harvests led by Brazil glutted markets, while trees that yielded beans for fifteen years kept producing.[115] Still, coffee generated profits for merchants and growers in regions long marginal to commercial life. Processing machines limited labor and the cost of readying beans for export. Harvesting—labor-intensive yet seasonal—fit into the life of cultivating communities in often stabilizing ways.

Coffee came to coastal foothills after 1880 as population rose in nearby highlands. Milpa cultivation was seasonal; so was coffee picking. Growers recruited upland villagers, often with wage advances, for weeks of picking that did not disrupt family harvests. Men, women, and children all picked (for unequal pay), reinforcing patriarchal ways. There were disputes over everything: land, work, pay, and more—all signs of economic expansion; still, coffee zones created new symbiotic exploitations tying villagers to commercial growers. Coffee expanded; villagers stayed villagers while gaining income. Local officials organized workers and mediated disputes to maintain production and stability; coercion came when mediation failed.[116]

A very different export economy rose on the dry plains of northwest Yucatán, long home to Maya communities that scratched maize-based sustenance from difficult soil. When the United States developed the industrial agriculture that enabled the rich lands of the Mississippi basin, cleared of native peoples, to feed its cities and much of the world, harvesting machines needed twine to bind crops. Yucatán was a short sail from New Orleans, its lands home to henequen cactus, long stripped of fibers used in many ways by Maya families. On the promise of export profits, Yucatán elites mobilized political power and liberal laws to build plantations. US financiers backed railroads and funded imports of processing machinery. Privatizations and population growth pushed many Maya to become plantation residents and permanent hands.

Most stayed near home, family, and community, drawn to transplant henequen shoots in rows across vast fields, then to the rough work of cutting fibers from huge fronds. Transplanting was periodic; production was constant, requiring many hands to cut, haul, and process fibers. As population grew, many had little option but move onto estates. Plantations offered advances to draw men to lives of labor. When they married, estates advanced the cost of a simple wedding; when children came, advances paid for baptisms and other needs. Gaining earnings beyond low wages, men found it hard to leave—in part because survival depended on estate labor, in part because wages and advances reinforced patriarchy, and in part because rising export earnings backed new state powers that helped planters enforce worker debts. When estates were sold, debts were sold with them. The long Mexican tradition of advance payment and obligated labor began to resemble the debt peonage imagined by US slaveholding imperialists in the 1840s.

In 1910 John Kenneth Turner told readers of *Barbarous Mexico* that slavery defined Yucatán.[117] Deep exploitations ruled; they differed from slavery in key ways: people were not property; Maya had rights as citizens, if hard to enforce; and debts consolidated patriarchal families, a contrast with slavery, which often inhibited such ties. Henequen was labor-intensive and exploitative, but Maya workers were not slaves.

An industry financed from the United States and serving US markets depended on obligated, often coerced, Maya workers. Their efforts were essential to US agro-industrial expansion: laborsaving US farmers depended on labor-intense henequen estates. Bread on US tables was affordable thanks the labor of landless and indebted Maya.[118]

While henequen plantations drew thousands of Maya to labor in support of mechanized cultivation in the US heartland, after 1900 a new petroleum economy began to rise along Mexico's northern Gulf coast around the port of Tampico. The cutting edge of industrial capitalism came to Porfirian Mexico. As petroleum became the energy source driving the industrial world, discoveries in Texas led Edward Doheny to nearby Mexico, soon followed by British magnate Weetman Pearson. For a decade, they paid Mexican landlords and indigenous cultivators for the rights to explore. Most drilling sites were near tar pools that Huastec guides revealed to foreign prospectors. Landlords lived high on ample fees; indigenous families cultivated in traditional ways as men took wages to guide prospectors and clear drilling sites. Oil promised wealth to the prosperous and work to the native poor—until gushers came in rapidly between 1908 and 1910. Doheny and Pearson saw the promise of black gold; they brought experienced drillers and other hands from Texas; Mexican landlords continued to receive ample payments; the Huastec majority saw their lands cleared and polluted, relegated to the least paid labor while their lands degraded. Oil began to flow profitably in 1910, as revolution began.[119]

Mexico finally had the exports dreamed of by Ortiz and other early liberals. Vanilla gathered in northern Gulf coast lowlands, coffee harvested on Gulf and Pacific foothills, and henequen grown on the dry plains of Yucatán claimed profits for international traders and Mexican growers, delivering revenues to local, regional, and national governments. Silver and copper generated profits and revenues—yet little labor. Oil promised more of the same. Drawn into the commodity circuits that sustained industries and cities around the world, growing numbers of Mexicans faced diverse exploitations and chances to labor. Only Totonacs knew vanilla; highland villagers were necessary to coffee harvests; without Maya men, henequen exports were impossible. Huastec people found income and labor in petroleum exploration.

Exploitations, conflicts, coercions, and degradations were everywhere—they defined the dynamism of industrial capitalism. But Totonac gatherers mixed shifting cultivation with vanilla gathering to carry on; Oaxaca and Chiapas villagers took income picking coffee, creating new symbiotic exploitations sustaining exports and village life; Maya estate dependents found work and patriarchal securities, sustaining families while they supplied twine to the most mechanized agricultural economy in the world. Huastec people around Tampico faced discrimination and hard labor, but up to 1910 traditional cultivation carried on while new cash came in. The powerful profited; US and European economies gained products subsidized by Mexicans' poverty; Mexicans labored on. Totonac families, Oaxaca and Chiapas villagers, Maya henequen workers, and Huastec oil laborers rarely turned to revolutionary uprisings after 1910.

Nor did most people in the mill towns of Veracruz, the industrial suburbs of Mexico City, the capitalist dynamo at Monterrey, or the copper mines at Cananea. They negotiated and sometimes struck to gain rights and remunerations. Yet they too adapted to industrial capitalism and rarely turned to revolutionary mobilizations—until rural revolutionaries in two key regions, the southern heartland and the northern borderlands, undermined commercial ways. The industrial labor conflicts of Porfirian Mexico were not precursors to revolutionary uprisings.

After 1870, Mexicans lived times of sustained commercial growth: per capita domestic product rose 3.9 percent yearly from 1877 to 1892, jumped to 5.1 percent from 1893 to 1902, then slowed to a still strong 3.2 percent annually from 1902 to 1910.[120] Commercial growth came with deepening inequities, often accompanied by declining material welfare. Mexicans' nutrition and physical stature declined from 1850 to 1910.[121] Yet revolution did not come simply from poverty and polarization, exploitation and exclusion. Only where capitalism corroded community and family autonomies, ended symbiotic exploitations, and blocked young men's chances at patriarchy did revolution explode and persist for a decade in the southern heartland. Only where financial collapse suddenly blocked the opportunities promised by rising commercial dependencies along the northern border, again threatening men's patriarchy, did Pancho Villa raise the armies that drove a northern revolution. A 1907 economic downturn deepened pressures in the north; drought and scarcity in 1909 challenged life in the heartland; political conflicts brought Díaz's fall in 1911—all opening the way for popular uprisings focused in the borderlands and the southern heartland. In the latter, communities clinging to historic autonomies negotiated nineteenth-century challenges until an agro-industrial acceleration corroded those autonomies and threatened men's patriarchy after 1870. They turned to revolution after 1910.

CHAPTER SEVEN

Anáhuac Upside Down

CHALCO AND IZTACALCO, 1820-45

IN THE NEW nation struggling to emerge after 1821, Anáhuac became Mexico's heartland. Mexico City still ruled; rural people still lived in communities claiming lands and self-rule; estates still supplied the capital and nearby mining centers. Yet much had changed. With the fall of silver, capital was scarce and landed entrepreneurs struggled. At Chalco, Mexico City's historic granary, political men tried and failed to profit as commercial growers. Priests became pivotal intermediaries, sometimes serving political landlords, sometimes operating their own estates, always in close contact with villagers quick to press their interests in times of commercial struggles and political conflicts. Communities around Cuernavaca pushed back against sugar planters; Toluca villagers won a court victory gaining lands long sought in struggles against the Condes de Santiago's Atengo properties.[1]

Heartland estates still required village men's labor; villagers retained lands, claimed higher wages, and worked only when it served their interests. For decades after 1821, estates rarely profited; they blamed recalcitrant workers for their difficulties. At Iztacalco, a *chinampa* community on the canal from Chalco to Mexico City, villagers ruled production and cultural life. Meanwhile, some priests became anticlerical liberals while liberal leaders honored Guadalupe—the people's powerful protector. Across the heartland, communities retrenched on the land and found ways to better sustenance, higher wages, market gains—and cultural independence. Social inversions marked the heartland as villagers consolidated autonomies and women found new openings, too. To those who presumed to rule and profit, the world seemed upside down.

Chalco Upside Down

Chalco estate operators still lived in Mexico City, aiming to profit by feeding its people; population still concentrated in communities with limited lands, unequally held; village leaders called *capitanes* still led work gangs called *cuadrillas* that labored for wages in estate fields. But during and after the wars that took down the silver economy and led to national independence in 1821, their interactions changed: landlords faced financial constraints; managers and *capitanes*, local priests and town traders, found their powers increased, yet always contested. Villagers pressed gains; estate operators pushed back. Profit stayed scarce as tensions simmered.[2]

After 1821, indigenous republics no longer existed in law, eliminated by the Cádiz constitution, replaced by municipalities that carried on under the state of Mexico within Mexico's federal republic after 1824. Formally, local government was no longer a native preserve. The Cádiz charter also called for the privatization of community lands, but no power dared implement that assault on autonomies during years of insurgency or after. Community landholding persisted, formally subject to municipalities. Indigenous self-rule carried on in most villages. While Lorenzo de Zavala,

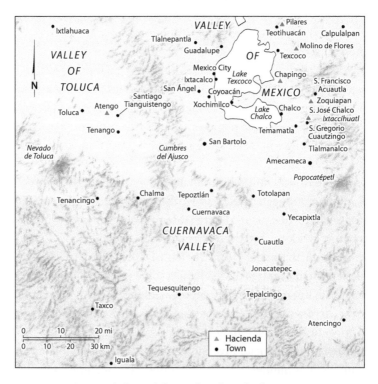

MAP 10. Chalco and the southern heartland, 1820–70.

a liberal ally of Vicente Guerrero, ruled the state of Mexico in 1826, the lands won from the Atengo estates by Toluca communities were taken into traditional corporate tenure.[3] Villagers celebrated while estate owners worried.

Estate ownership became unstable at Chalco during the decades before 1821: among forty properties, only four were advertised for sale in the 1790s, seven from 1800 to 1810, then ten from 1811 to 1821 as civil wars disrupted commercial ways and insurgents to the north brought down silver production. The social origins and financial capacity of Chalco estate operators also changed, radically. When silver flourished, leading estate operators were usually members of landed clans that drew capital from mining and trade to purchase estates and finance operations. Profit required paying for labor and other costs of production, then holding crops for years until drought brought scarcity, rising prices, and peak profits. After 1810, the fall of silver made capital scarce; holding crops to profit from scarcities became less possible and less profitable—as Alamán lamented.

By the 1820s, military men and political actors ruled estate operations at Chalco. The great San José de Chalco property, first built by the Jesuits, was the leading cereal grower in the region. After the 1767 expulsion, Spanish authorities leased it to merchants who could fund profitable operations. In 1819 Agustín Iturbide took the lease—before he led the drive to independence. When the short-lived emperor fell in 1823, Vicente Guerrero leased the estate, then known as La Compañía, until his death in 1831.

Guerrero was a muleteer and trader in the hot country around Acapulco before he joined Morelos in insurgency, then survived to back Iturbide in the 1821 Plan de Iguala. He continued to run mule trains linking Taxco, Tixtla, and Acapulco, once key routes in the silver economy and Asian trades. As Iturbide fell and republicans wrote the Federal Constitution of 1824, Guerrero turned to building a landed empire in regions where he traded—and had political aspirations. He bought Platanillo, a sugar estate near Taxco, in 1824. In 1829, while president, he leased Tierra Colorada, a cane property near Acapulco. Both had suffered in years of insurgency; while Guerrero rebuilt machinery and markets, he leased nearby grain lands. And in 1824, he leased La Compañía from new republican authorities. Did they aim to hold the popular insurgent loyal to the new regime?

Guerrero tried to profit while awaiting a chance at power. He leased La Compañía for 6,550 pesos yearly—an enormous sum in uncertain times. He bought a dock and storage depot on the Chalco lakeshore to ease deliveries to Mexico City, where he ran a bakery. He profited through the 1820s—by never paying rent to the government for La Compañía or to the Tixtla sodality that owned Tierra Colorada. There were advantages to being a former insurgent and then president. After Guerrero's ouster in 1829, followed by his rebellion, capture, and execution in 1831, Guerrero's widow owed the government, Alamán's government, 63,511 pesos, and large sums to many others. She paid nothing, yet the government attempted no new lease. In 1833, the liberal regime of Santa Ana and Gómez Farías offered a deal. Guerrero had held years of harvests at La Compañía, awaiting peak prices that never came. The liberals forced his widow to sell; the proceeds paid all but 13,063 pesos owed the government (a boost to the treasury). Then officials leased La Compañía to Mariano Riva Palacio, Guerrero's son-in-law, for nine years at 6,990 pesos yearly, plus installments to pay the rest of Guerrero's debt.

Riva Palacio was a native of Mexico City, growing up while insurgencies swirled all around. Studying law as national politics began, he married Guerrero's only daughter, Dolores, and served on the Mexico City Council while his father-in-law was president. After Guerrero's death and Alamán's fall, Riva Palacio was a deputy in the liberal congress of 1833 that attempted to expropriate Church properties—and provoked its own demise.

Meanwhile, Riva Palacio turned to landed entrepreneurship at Chalco. Facing large lease payments and low staples prices with little capital, he entered a partnership with Atilano Sánchez, chief notary of the Mexico City Cathedral's mortgage bank. In 1830 Sánchez had bought the Moral estate, near La Compañía and once owned by the richest of merchants, don Antonio de Basoco. Riva Palacio and Sánchez merged estate operations; when that did not bring profits, Sánchez leased Moral to Riva Palacio in 1834. When Riva Palacio rarely paid the rent, Sánchez sold Moral for what he saw as the absurd price of 110,000 pesos. The new owner took on Sánchez's debts—and ended Riva Palacio's lease.

The government soon revoked the latter's lease of La Compañía. By 1838, unpaid rents exceeded 7,000 pesos. Riva Palacio begged for time, insisting that climate damage to crops precluded profits. Estate operators historically took profit when drought drove prices high. Now Riva Palacio could not hold crops and had little to sell when crops failed. The government, again led by Bustamante, took back La Compañía in 1840. Guerrero and Riva Palacio ran the great estate for nearly twenty years, backed by political clout, not capital.

Riva Palacio lowered his expectations and turned to smaller Chalco estates. In 1842 he bought the combined Asunción and Archicofradía properties for 4,000 pesos, plus the obligation to pay large debts accumulated by the former owners. Riva Palacio served the creditors.

In 1853, he bought San Juan de Dios for 28,000 pesos from José María Tornel, a political general close to Santa Ana. By the 1850s, Riva Palacio was an established estate owner. How he survived reveals much about Chalco and the contested relations between estates and communities after the fall of silver capitalism.

Without access to capital from mining and trade, Riva Palacio and other Chalco estate owners turned to city grain merchants and bakers for operating funds in the 1820s and 1830s. Early each growing season, they agreed to provide from 100 to 300 pesos weekly to pay labor and other costs; estates agreed to deliver a set quantity of grain at a predetermined price. Most men financing Chalco estates worked with one or two growers; operators of larger estates, including Riva Palacio while he leased La Compañía and Moral, needed funding from more than one lender. Estates kept planting: any profits of scarcity went to financiers. Years of dearth left estate operators owing grain they could not deliver.

Facing such pressures while living in Mexico City's political vortex, Riva Palacio relied on agents and intermediaries at Chalco. From 1824 when Guerrero took over the lease at La Compañía to 1840 when Riva Palacio lost it, José Antonio Caballero managed the estate, adding Moral when the estates merged from 1834 to 1839. Responsible for production and marketing, labor recruitment and village relations, in 1835 Caballero earned 36 pesos weekly, an annual salary just under 2,000 pesos. The manager gained more from Chalco estates than either Riva Palacio or Sánchez. He was served by forty-five full-time assistants, overseers, and specialists—all men. Their earnings ranged from over 400 pesos yearly for a mayordomo (site manager), nearly as much for a secretary-bookkeeper, to 250 pesos for the granary keepers who accounted crops at each estate, and 100 pesos yearly for lesser employees, including a teacher. All gained secure incomes for serving estate interests. They received maize rations at no cost, access to education for their children, and medical care when needed. Many received wage advances—rarely repaid and never inhibiting a move to another employer. While political estate operators struggled, managers and permanent workers at Chalco estates prospered. They linked in a favored community of patriarchal dependence by ties of *compadrazgo*, ritual kinship forged when the owner or manager sponsored marriages, baptisms, and other family milestones.

For the essential work of planting and harvesting, Chalco estates still relied on villagers recruited seasonally. Community labor captains remained pivotal, but the brokerage roles held by district officials under Spanish rule gave way to local priests in the 1820s. Political power had become unstable, making political officials unreliable brokers. Priests remained everywhere—and open to entrepreneurial possibilities. They mixed religious roles and trade, often in service of the haciendas. Crop sales and labor recruitment ruled the correspondence between the pastors at Temamatla and Amecameca. Merchant-clerics sold livestock, foodstuffs, and cloth to parishioners, took a fee, and returned profits to the estates to pay operating expenses—mostly wages paid to villagers the priests helped recruit. *Compadrazgo* also linked local priests to estate operators and managers.

Juan Antonio de Germán, pastor at San Gregorio Cuautzingo in the early 1830s, traded in the several villages of his parish. He often earned over 300 pesos weekly to help finance Riva Palacio's estates—limiting reliance on Mexico City dealers. The priest sold corn and livestock to villagers he persuaded to work at Moral and La Compañía. If wages were delayed, he complained to Riva Palacio: villagers knew their spiritual guardian provided payroll funds and he had begun to lose respect. Father Germán's demise shows the dependence of the merchant priest. Early in 1834, his debts to Riva Palacio passed his ability to pay. Pressed by the landlord, the cleric begged for time; but his deal with La Compañía ended. Unhappy with the loss of a local market and uncertain access to labor, Riva Palacio arranged Germán's transfer. The political estate operator, with his own debt problems, then recruited a new priest, Mariano Olmedo, formerly at Culhuacán.

Caught between scarce operating funds and low crop prices, Riva Palacio and other Chalco entrepreneurs competed to control costs and raise earnings. They kept mule trains to transport wheat to mills and corn to lakeside docks, which many bought to limit transfer costs as indigenous boatmen still carried staples to Mexico City. Guerrero began buying molasses around Cuautla and distilling it into cane brandy at La Compañía—an operation continued by Riva Palacio. The business never became profitable. Nearby Miraflores built one of Mexico's first textile mills after 1835. No other Chalco estate followed its lead.

Wheat and maize remained the primary business of Chalco estates. The great majority of the region's people lived in communities still distributing lands, depending more or less on day labor in estate fields. An 1845 census of two key Chalco parishes, Tlalmanalco on the fertile plain and Amecameca in arable uplands, counted ninety-three percent of residents living in towns and villages, only seven percent at estates—a number inflated by the 433 workers at the Miraflores textile mill.

Estates depended on villagers to plant and harvest. Village clergy helped fund and facilitate that employment—and took income. Village labor captains still ran work gangs. Every Sunday, managers visited nearby communities, offering cash payments to captains. Crews from San Lucas, San Gregorio Cuautzingo, San Martín Cuautlalpan, Huexoculco, Tlapala, and other communities regularly labored at Moral and La Compañía. Times of estate financial weakness gave new bargaining power to villagers. Labor bosses demanded cash before sending any workers; groups traveling more than short distances demanded pay for travel. In May of 1835, during weeks of planting, only 50 workers appeared at La Compañía one Monday, while 124 labored the rest of the week; all were paid for a six-day week. The estate also paid youths who accompanied the gangs to deliver food. Caballero called the outlays dead wage. If they were not paid, no workers would appear.

Two weeks of accounts from January of 1835, the peak of the maize harvest, report villagers working at both Moral and La Compañía—the largest employers at Chalco. From January 18 to 24, they hired 338 village men and youths; from January 25 to 31, they recruited 375. During the first week, 11 men earned three reales daily; during the second week 13 men gained that high wage—all likely gang captains, suggesting an equal number of crews, averaging about 30 workers each. The first week, 94 were youths, earning one or one and a half reales daily (the low wage of half a real, long paid to the youngest boys, was gone); the second week, the number of youths rose to 123. The majority were adult men; a few gained two reales daily (the standard before 1810), most two and a half. Wages had risen twenty percent since the eighteenth century while maize prices held steady or fell.

Managers complained constantly that villagers chose when to labor: they would not work during community fiestas; they would not work when village crops needed attention. Villagers attending to their own fields first repeatedly delayed estate work. Late planting shortened the growing season; late harvests increased vulnerability to frost. Yet even after taking cash advances, villagers came only when they were ready. After 1821, estate operators, priests, and managers lived comfortably; community notables and labor captains prospered; village men and boys mixed cultivation and seasonal work to sustain families. Higher wages and labor independence brought new gains for villagers.

Priestly Business and Politics: Axalco, 1825–40

Guerrero's and Riva Palacio's struggles to operate estates from the 1820s into the 1840s reveal the limited powers of political men trying to profit as landed entrepreneurs. Facing financial challenges and resistant workers,

FIGURE 7.1. The church at Temamatla: Manuel López Escudero's parish, 1825–39.

they profited by not paying rent to governments that honored or feared their power. Less powerful men also found politics essential to estate operations. Manuel López Escudero was pastor at Temamatla (his church is shown in figure 7.1), near La Compañía, from the 1820s to his death in 1839. He also owned and operated Axalco, a small estate nearby. He survived by mixing priestly income, credit, and political juggling.[4]

With three sisters, he inherited Axalco in 1813 from his mother, doña Antonia Marta Pérez de las Cuevas. Her legacy included furniture, clothing and jewelry worth 9,000 pesos, 3,500 pesos of gold and silver, "*varios efectos*" (miscellaneous items) worth 6,700 pesos, and a Mexico City house valued at 9,300 pesos: the ornaments of city life totaled 28,500 pesos. Axalco was valued at 43,000 pesos in July of 1812, just after the loyalist triumph in the siege of Cuautla, but only 32,640 pesos in October of 1813 while insurgency raged in the Bajío and the Mezquital and typhus ravaged the highlands. After debts, the heirs shared property worth 34,240 pesos.[5]

López Escudero ran the estate. To deliver the maize essential to recruit village workers, in 1826 he received 1,500 fanegas of maize valued at three pesos each from don José María Palacios of Mexico City, backed by a lien on Axalco, to be repaid in maize or cash after future harvests. Like Mezquital villagers during the insurgency, Chalco villagers demanded maize—sustenance—as the price of their labor in the 1820s. By 1829, López Escudero had not repaid Palacios. The priest insisted he was not a "*pícaro*"—a rogue; the times made payment impossible: "More is lost day after day." Drought plagued the region, and he could not plant because

FIGURE 7.2. The parish house at Temamatla,
López Escudero's warehouse, 1825–39.

villagers would not work without rations. López Escudero sold 1,000 fanegas at two pesos each, a low price in times of drought. It did not cover half
the 4,500 pesos he owed. Hoping for higher prices, he ordered his manager
to halt sales, except the "wages needed to hire workers."[6] The landlord-
priest struggled (his parish residence and warehouse are shown in figure
7.2) while villagers demanded maize to work.

By March of 1831 he owed Palacios over 5,000 pesos. He tried to sell
crops in deals facilitated by another priest, Cristoval Martínez de Castro,
living at Guerrero's country house near the capital while the old insurgent
and deposed president was in the south, in rebellion against Bustamante
and Alamán. As Guerrero faced capture and execution in October,
creditors closed in on López Escudero. Martínez de Castro proposed
that López Escudero try "flight" followed by "obstinate resistance"—to be
aided by Riva Palacio.[7] The priest kept Axalco. Late in 1831, he borrowed
12,000 pesos at ten percent interest (twice the rate before 1810) from the
Quintanilla family, promising to pay 400 pesos interest every four months.
In 1833, López Escudero borrowed another 1,100 pesos to pay wages.

In July, Martínez de Castro lamented "the difficulty of the times, the
sluggishness of all business, and our lack of skill to find a peaceful settlement." He lived at the "country house at Mixcoaque," now Riva Palacio's.

The cleric lamented "this Babylonia"; he longed for "the peace we so desire; without it we cannot live." The lawyer Riva Palacio and the priest Martínez de Castro were caught up in Gómez Farías's liberal project, while López Escudero struggled to evade creditors. In December, the priestly estate operator sent a food delivery to Martínez de Castro—who wrote with thanks, adding that "doña Jesusita la Rubia" insisted on visiting Xochimilco and Chalco for the holidays. "We live in liberty as a family." The liberal political priest would celebrate Christ's birth with doña Jesusita at the landlord-priest's estate.[8]

Into 1834, Martínez de Castro was "drowning in the wearing work of the Congress." In May he protested that "repugnance for the laws to reform the Church has brought our opponents to arms . . . today more than ever our country is challenged by exalted passions . . . we will face war without end." He envied López Escudero's life at Chalco.[9] Yet 1835 brought the latter more demands from creditors; a political turn sent Martínez de Castro in flight to Zimapán in the northern Mezquital; Josefa López Escudero became her brother's city agent. In 1836 Martínez de Castro was back to help fend off creditors.

They defended Axalco into 1839.[10] After López Escudero died in that fall, Martínez de Castro worked with Riva Palacio to untangle accounts. They reveal how the Chalco priest carried on for three decades. Income from several chaplaincies paid him 850 pesos yearly; rent from the Mexico City house another 200. Mostly, López Escudero, like Guerrero and Riva Palacio, did not pay debts. He had redeemed only 2,000 of 12,000 pesos owed the Quintanillas, only 5,500 of the 9,600 pesos due as 10 percent annual interest. The interest he did pay was the equivalent of 5.5 percent over eight years, a solid return. The Quintanillas gained the city house in the final settlement, avoiding any major loss.[11]

As long as he lived, López Escudero's ties to President Guerrero, the lawyer Riva Palacio, and the priest Martínez de Castro, political men all, offered protection in uncertain economic times. Why did they defend the landlord-priest? López Escudero's role as pastor at Temamatla made him essential to Chalco estate operations—including La Compañía and Moral. Amid unstable politics, uncertain markets, scarce financing, and unpaid debts, estates faced one constant: the need to pay wages and maize to village workers. If not paid and delivered maize, they did not work; if they did not work, there were no harvests of Chalco maize—and the capital did not eat. A power inversion ruled in times of plenty without profit.

Entrenched community autonomies grounded that inversion. López Escudero's letters confirm that by a conspicuous silence. Neither he nor any of his correspondents ever mentioned priestly activities or local worship. Yet the people of Temamatla kept the devotions and festivals that marked local Christianity and family life. Riva Palacio's managers could not recruit workers when festivals focused villagers. Father Germán complained that when La Compañía failed to pay wages and rations, he lost respect as a priest; López Escudero's silence suggests that he paid his parishioners, delivered maize, and let them worship as they pleased. Cultural autonomy held strong.

Iztacalco: An Angry Priest in an Autonomous Community, 1831–32

Iztacalco lay just south of Mexico City, in the recently created federal district. Like Culhuacán, Xochimilco, and lakefront towns at Chalco, Iztacalco lived by cultivating fertile *chinampas* to supply local families and urban markets. They also kept taverns to serve city folk who came by canal for weekend and holiday retreats. Assigned as pastor in 1831, Manuel Espinosa de los Monteros quickly became angry with parishioners who refused to support him economically or heed his religious teachings. In desperation, he kept a long diary detailing their economic ways and cultural lives.[12]

He came to Iztacalco near the end of a long career. Born in Mexico City in 1773, his roots reached to communities at Ecatepec, north of the capital, Tula in the Mezquital, and Tlalmanalco at Chalco. His grandfather served an estate near Ecatepec; his father worked salt beds near Apan in pulque country; his mother ran a tobacco shop in the city (an outlet for the royal monopoly after 1775). She centered the family while Manuel studied for the priesthood, first at the Franciscan College at Tlatelolco, then at the ex-Jesuit seminary at Tepozotlán. Ordained in 1800, he was certified to preach in *mexicano*—Nahuatl.[13]

Such ancestry, studies, and skills suggest indigenous roots, urban experiences, and the priesthood as a way forward for a favored son. Once ordained and certified in *mexicano*, he gained posts as vicar at Nextipac, near Iztacalco, then at Coyoacán just south. In 1806, he was pastor at Tlanchinol, in the sierra north of the Mezquital, a poor, rugged parish where most spoke Otomí, not *mexicano*. Espinosa de los Monteros was miserable there, leaving in 1810 just before insurgency spread across the Mezquital. He went to Chiautla near Texcoco, then moved in 1814 to Ixtapaluca, between Texcoco and Chalco, regions of peaceful production while insurgency raged to the north. In 1819 he went to Acolman near the Teotihuacán pyramids. He stayed until 1830, his longest and most successful posting. Did he join in dealings that kept estates like nearby Pilares operating?[14]

At Iztacalco he became alienated from his parishioners. His first baptism brought antipathy: "They are continuously drunk, grossly ignorant, with no lack of propensity to lie."[15] After a year his view had not changed—and he was certain his parishioners would not change: "Ignorant and undisciplined people cannot be expected to reform their ways."[16] His diary is filled with complaints: they avoided sacraments, they resisted confession, too many ignored chastity before marriage. Most of all, neither local officials nor parishioners would pay the fees Espinosa de los Monteros believed his due. From January to July of 1831, he received 308 pesos. Then the community cut him off.[17] Priest and parishioners were completely alienated.

He continued to record irreligion and document life in the community (often relegated to peering down from the windows in his parish residence, shown with the church in figure 7.3)—to prove he could be paid and show why he was not, in the effort detailing a very independent community. Iztacalco was a place of rich *chinampas*, close to the capital on the canal to Xochimilco and Chalco. Locals supplied city markets with fruit and vegetables and offered city residents weekend recreation. Community resources sustained the economy; *vecinos* (citizens) ruled political and religious life. With no estate production, there was no place for a priest's

FIGURE 7.3. The church and attached residence at Iztacalco: Manuel Espinosa de los Monteros's refuge, 1831–32.

brokerage. There were inequities, exploitations, and conflicts—but they operated within a community that kept Espinosa de los Monteros out.

He found documents from 1821 showing that the barrio of Santa Ana had seventy-five *vecinos* and 333 *chinampas*. One man controlled 100, four others but 1 each. Still, seventy shared 230 *chinampas* (unequally). In 1831 the entire Iztacalco community worked 2,000 *chinampas*. Concentrations persisted: one man held 300, another 100. Still, in a community of 1,800 people in 1830, fewer than 450 households lived independently if unequally on 2,000 *chinampas*.[18] The prosperous hired the poor—and wages at Iztacalco had risen to three reales daily, plus ample food rations, higher than the remunerations also rising at Chalco. Locals did not provide enough workers to serve the few with many *chinampas*, so families came from Mexicalcingo, Tláhuac, and elsewhere to live and work without rights as *vecinos*.[19]

How prosperous were Iztacalco's *chinamperos*? Espinosa de los Monteros believed "monopolists" profited by 50 to 100 pesos monthly selling produce in the capital.[20] If middling *chinamperos* gained 10 to 20 pesos monthly, they earned 120 to 240 pesos yearly—in addition to family sustenance. Those who worked at *chinampas* for wages earned three reales daily (plus full sustenance); 200 days of labor would bring 75 pesos yearly (plus sustenance). Families with very few *chinampas* sent men and boys to labor on their neighbors' more ample holdings—a bit of in-community symbiotic exploitation. The rich few among Iztacalco *chinamperos* profited as much as (and more regularly than) operators of small Chalco estates; the majority mixed cultivation of a few *chinampas* with labor for their prosperous neighbors to average 80 to 100 pesos yearly income—in addition to food. And *chinampa* production was supplemented by other earnings of the lush water environment: reeds from local marshes were woven into baskets and *petates* (sleeping mats); ducks, frogs, and small fish taken from canals and marshes were sold in city markets and local eateries; men shuttled canoes from Iztacalco to the capital, delivering produce and bringing city couples to local taverns.[21]

There was more. The municipality owned *potreros*, corrals rented out as pasture, and *ciénagas*, marshes leased for duck hunting. The priest believed town rents approached 8,000 pesos yearly—and suspected that local officials profited while denying him a stipend. He learned that the municipality had placed a loan of 7,500 pesos with "un fulano Ochoa" in Mexico City, collecting 350 pesos annual interest (the standard five percent). He later learned that the council paid 38 pesos yearly from its rental income to every *vecino*—adult male.[22] Nearly 400 households thus gained a fifty percent boost in annual earnings, suggesting why they honored local officials' rule—even if the big men profited far more.

Espinosa de los Monteros was angry that local leaders accumulated *chinampas*, profited, ruled the community, ignored his preaching, lived as they pleased—and refused to pay. In that anger, he detailed their powers. He knew that origins as an indigenous republic meant that lands, *chinampas*, corrals, and marshes, were community domain. He knew that rights to *chinampas* went to indigenous *vecinos*; that rights to participate in the council belonged to *principales*—notables. As long as the republic endured, there were reasons to be *indio*: it was necessary for a family to work *chinampas* or a man to hold office.

Espinosa de Monteros also knew that by the eighteenth century, notables in republics around Mexico City, including Iztacalco, were often of mixed ancestry and Hispanic culture. A man might come to trade in *chinampa* produce or operate a tavern; he married a local woman, through her gained *chinampas*, and if politically savvy claimed a seat on the council—asserting status as an *indio principal.* Like community lands across the heartland, marshes and corrals were leased to generate income for local government and religious festivals, while milpas and *chinampas* operated as private property, passed by inheritance and sale among resident families—within the community. Inequality grounded in autonomies marked life in Iztacalco.

The end of indigenous republics and their replacement by municipalities ended the mandate to be *indio* to hold office. But whatever Cádiz's and Mexican liberals' goals, they did not end the requirement to be a *vecino*, a citizen of the community, to hold *chinampas* and participate in local politics. Politics did change: indigenous republics held pivotal roles in the judicial politics of Spanish times; there is nothing about courts in Espinosa de los Monteros's diary—and much about politics and militias, even a proposal for police.

José María Vázquez rose as local commander of a patriotic militia formed to defend the Spanish regime after 1814; in the 1820s he led a civic militia backing Vicente Guerrero and Lorenzo de Zavala. Some said he led men from Iztacalco to join the Acordada revolt and Parián riot that brought Guerrero to power in 1828. When Espinosa de los Monteros came in 1831, Guerrero and Zavala had been ousted. Vázquez remained town treasurer. Wrote the priest: "From my balcony, many times I heard him say: *the law says; the law orders.* With such claims the huckster fools the clods of the town, making himself boss of a faction. . . . He is a loud charlatan. . . . Some one told me that he meddles violently in town affairs, trying to dominate everything. . . . He is more feared than loved by the vecinos. Certainly, he is no indio."[23] Peering from a balcony and listening to gossip, the priest saw militia power and a politics of exclusion fueled by pulque during election seasons.[24] He may not have been wrong, but that power defended unequal prosperity grounded in local autonomies.

Early in 1832, Espinosa de los Monteros proposed reforms he imagined would improve life at Iztacalco—and for himself as priest. The key question was: "Who should be called *vecino*, who a resident? The towns have communal holdings: grazing lands and fishing sites, croplands and hunting grounds, even quarries for building stone. They provide house lots, corrals, and orchards to families; pastures graze live-stock, other lands serve the parish to support the sacraments and provide burial grounds. By agreement and custom, they are used for free or for very small fees. They say that no person holds dominion over communal lands and goods, only rights of use. Dominion belongs to the community, administration to the council." The ways of the indigenous republics persisted in the Mexican republic: the community held land in eminent domain; *vecinos*—citizens of the community—gained rights of use. The one change was that administration shifted from republics exclusively indigenous, however porous the category, to councils open to all *vecinos*. Who qualified as a *vecino* mattered, and Espinosa de los Monteros proposed new qualifications:

"First: single, married, and widowed adult men are vecinos." Patriarchy came first.

"Second: those who pay municipal taxes and other public levies are vecinos and gain communal rights." Patriarchal citizenship came with obligations.

"Third: vecinos are given lands in usufruct to maintain their families and nothing more, never with an excess that would disturb equality; with excess comes opulence and damage to others of equal worth." The patriar-chal bargain of household rule grounded in family sustenance came first; land concentrations threatened equality.

"Fourth: If by skill and ambition a man becomes opulent by gaining more land than others, he will pay double, triple, or quadruple taxes in proportion to his possessions." If land concentrations were inevitable, the rich should pay more to the community.

"Fifth: Single women over 25 and widows, if locally born and living in town, are *vecinas*." Women had long held community lands; Espinosa de los Monteros would limit that right to locally rooted widows and single women over twenty-five.

Vecino status and land rights could be lost: moving away, taking *vecino* rights elsewhere, not paying taxes, having no "honest means of sustenance." The latter, the priest argued, should lead to expulsion. He aimed to put Iztacalco to work. Yet outsiders who came to work would not gain citizenship and land rights: "Those from other municipalities who come to rent or buy a house . . . to exercise a craft, trade in commerce, or serve another in his house, his business, or on his lands will be classified a resident"—without rights to land or political participation. Espinosa de los Monteros accepted one exception to the limits on newcomers, recognizing a longstanding reality: "the outsider who marries a vecina born locally will become a vecino."[25] Unions between entrepreneurial newcomers and propertied women remained the way in and upward in communities transiting from indigenous republics to municipalities.

With powerful notables entrenched on rich *chinampas*, the angry priest saw only one route to reform: "The solution is armed force. With that to back me, in a year I would turn them all into saints, and gain a decent living too. The community has natural resources and productive potential. But without coercion there will never be order, health, good customs, learning, or religion. I have lived for 30 years in such towns and have seen them advance in nothing. People act as if they have just come down from mountains where they live as barbarians to inhabit a place next to Mexico City—yet proximity and trade have not polished their ways."[26] Too autonomous, heartland villagers were barbarians to their priest; the solution was coercion.

Espinosa de los Monteros also imagined economic improvement. His utopia sought neither mechanized industry nor export commodities. He wanted productive families in a community benefiting an entrepreneurial priest: "The council should promote the arts of carding, spinning, and weaving wool and cotton—first to employ the many lazy men and women who live nearly naked with their children, and second to stop the flow of money to the other more dedicated people who make and sell cloth." The angry priest did not oppose patriarchal family autonomies; he would redistribute lands to make them more egalitarian, and add cloth making to household economies. Espinosa de los Monteros believed the community should build more *chinampas*, not saying where it would find the labor for dredging and reclamation. He also proposed recruiting skilled carpenters to help local men build boats to shuttle between Chalco and Mexico City. He dreamed of an egalitarian community grounded in patriarchal autonomies—and supporting its priest.

He lamented that too many lived as "idlers" in chronic "drunkenness."[27] He despised Iztacalco's economy of weekend diversions (a tavern just

FIGURE 7.4. Tavern on the Iztacalco plaza: focus of Espinosa de los Monteros's anger.

across the plaza from the church is shown in figure 7.4). People at nearby Zacahuisco recruited a "music master" to professionalize a cultural economy the priest found despicable: "For what? So vecinos and visitors from the city can add a bit of music to their diversions. The rabble of Iztacalco, men and women, love to sing; the rabble love to dance—not the few good men and women. With resident musicians festival days, Mondays, and even Tuesdays will become days of idleness and drinking for local machos and girls. And many more will come from the city to visit and spend nights partying."[28]

Iztacalco was rich in *chinampas*, on a waterway that made marketing in the capital easy—and offered easy recreation to its people. The priest sought more intense production better shared across the community; he despised the culture of recreation that brought local people and city folk together in festivities. "Today in Iztacalco alone there are nine pulque taverns. Don Antonio Ayala runs a mule train to bring fourteen barrels of cane brandy weekly from the hot country." Ayala's canal-front tavern belonged to "the Mexico City merchant Yermo." Beyond selling pulque and cane brandy: "there is nightly gambling, run by local big shots."[29] The men who ruled local politics and monopolized *chinampas* also profited from taverns and gambling.

The priest was especially angered by an "idiotic diversion" called "The Hanged Man," performed annually at Iztacalco. Watching from his balcony: "I observed that a bum wore a robe mimicking a disguised friar. Another followed dressed as a woman. On climbing the stairs to the sham gallows, the friar embraced and kissed the woman, with that indecency provoking howls from more than 300, even 500 spectators." Did the people of Iztacalco know the liberal priest Martínez de Castro and his companion Jesusita "la Rubia" as they passed by on the canal on their way to Chalco? The spectators certainly gloried in the theatrical skewering of the unsanctioned ways of the clergy who aimed to teach them to live sanctioned lives of sacraments and work.

Espinosa de los Monteros ignored that obvious lesson. He emphasized that the annual performance of "the indecent farce" continued because "so many vecinos (even councilmen) profit as visitors buy drink and meals, rent rooms, and pay for canoe rides out from the city."[30] Irreverent public theater was good business at Iztacalco, bringing income (unequally) to those who also prospered (unequally) from the *chinampa* economy.

Ecological autonomies enabled cultural entrepreneurship, and together grounded an adamant religious independence, angering Espinosa de los Monteros. Infants were baptized and marriage was common enough, though rarely with chaste antecedents. He despised his parishioners' refusal to confess, even as he offered to listen in Spanish and *mexicano*. In his view, "Much can be achieved from the pulpit, so much more in the confessional"—if people came with true penitential intent. Unfortunately, "I fear that these vecinos have in the past had ministers that offered confessions at a gallop, causing a lack of appreciation for the sacrament of penance and its disuse." Lax priests—like López Escudero at Temamatla—accepted villagers' distaste for the confessional, enabling people to live by "drunkenness, lewdness, robbery, and scandal while setting bad examples. They avoid mass, waste money in vices, lose time in idleness, yet work on holy days."

The angry priest saw his chance when "people are attacked by a grave illness. These moments of fear are precious and the priest must take advantage to reprimand them, even scare and confuse them, if the sickness makes it possible." Still, confessions remained rare. Why? "People are in danger of perverting their faith when they get involved with others suspicious of religion. Local big men and town officials have become perverted; sin is everywhere—shadowed by city magnates of ill fame. All is consumed in spiritual ruin."[31] All Iztacalco's evils were linked: strongmen ruled, profiting from the weekend pleasures of city folk; they drew locals into the business of entertainment—perverting religion.

Iztacalco lived a transformation Espinosa de los Monteros could not comprehend: "there are elder men and women who barely understand Spanish; for them it is essential to know doctrine in their own tongue. Even those who know Spanish talk among themselves in their own language." The priest certified in *mexicano* saw only loss in a turn to Spanish: "those who speak Spanish can't learn; those who know mexicano forget." He lamented: "To know that these people don't understand Spanish it is enough to talk with them for two minutes on any vulgar subject."[32] A local schoolmaster did little: "The teacher earns twenty pesos monthly, a ruinous salary." And "few boys go to school. Keeping customs from the past, parents send them to find firewood for cooking or take them to the chinampas to work." Household economies took precedence over literacy in Spanish. "Few go to school and the rest do not know how to read or write, nor know Christian doctrine." Again, local big men gained blame: "The mandarins of the towns, whether called republics or municipalities, are the same in this America. We need new ways to promote learning."[33]

Beyond anger and frustration, there is irony in the priest's language. In the late 1700s enlightened clerics tried to reform local religion—and the notables who ruled the republics frustrated everything. Now nation builders aimed to educate—and the men who ruled municipalities blocked everything. Double irony: to Espinosa de los Monteros, local big men were "mandarins" and "satraps"—just as real Chinese mandarins and South Asian satraps found their powers challenged owing to the fall of the silver economy that also entrenched local autonomies across Mexico.[34]

The cycle of local popular festivals carried on, some drawing the entire community, some particular to barrios and villages. Espinosa de los Monteros knew little of the details; the people kept him at a distance: "On festival days, once mass is done the people quickly disappear and the church remains empty all day." Why? "Because they are ruled by the opinion that the priest is but a paid servant of the people, even that they are the owners of the church." The priest provided sacraments while being excluded from directing religious life: "the priest is a servant consulted about nothing."[35] People married in the church, baptized children, and saw the mass as essential to opening their festivals. They did not negotiate morality in confession. Festivals, the core of religious culture, belonged to the community.

The excluded priest knew Guadalupe's power and tried to use Her to draw women to the sacraments: "To draw at least the girls to the sacraments, I began in each village a group dedicated to Our Lady of Guadalupe. A few joined and confessed in San Juanico; two or three came in Santa Ana; none in Iztacalco."[36] Women looked to Guadalupe for help with ills and childbirth; families sought Her aid with rains and fertility. Espinosa de los Monteros tried to convince girls that She called them to confession. They stayed away. He confessed to himself at the end of his diary: "It appears that most of my parishioners have not confessed in more than ten years. Many have not done so since they married."[37] Opposition to confession and moralizing priests went back to the sixteenth-century consolidations of indigenous Christianities; it would not change for Espinosa de los Monteros.

The festivals of integration forged in the same era carried on. Excluded, the angry priest could only list them, lamenting that he gained no fees while offering glimpses of autonomous, integrating, and redistributing devotions. "On All Saints Day there was a mass in Santa Ana, one in Iztacalco, another in Magdalena, another in San Juanico that should have paid me two pesos each. . . . Two Spaniards and one india took communion." After mass, the community took over the tower bells, ringing them constantly, "proving that their heads are made of cement." At one in the morning: "I saw several gangs of men walking the town, singing boastfully in rude voices." In San Juanico "they tell me that being single, they go in gangs demanding offerings; to bully their victims, they steal hens and hogs from houses that give nothing." He added that "on most moonlit nights, the mandarins walk rounds; but on All Saints night, so dark and foggy, I saw no one on rounds."[38] Local officials skipped patrols to allow redistributions. Negotiations lurked within inequalities.

Espinosa de los Monteros's solution: "do away with so many masses, so many fiestas, so many displays of the host, so many processions, so many disputes over rights, so much ringing of bells, so much spending on powder for infernal fireworks. What is needed is more preaching and more confessions."[39] He would end the religion of festivals and integrations, replacing it with sermons and confessional morality.

In December of 1831, the priest noted that the people of Iztacalco and San Juanico had journeyed together to "Guadalupe's sanctuary," where they paid 60 pesos for a "a mass with three priests, a sermon, and I believe a procession." In addition to the fees delivered to Guadalupe's priests, they paid two pesos each to local men who organized the pilgrimage,[40] an annual event that linked community devotions to Mexico's protecting Virgin. Espinosa de los Monteros knew little about its organization, aims, or meanings. He remained excluded from local religious life—and the fees it produced.

He missed the dark irony when he recorded in his diary on March 8, 1832, that he had won a chair in moral theology and "mexicana language" at "the College of our Lady of Guadalupe."[41] He gained an honored position to promote morality among "Mexicanos" under the gaze of Guadalupe. In his joy at escaping Iztacalco, did he think that the next December he would again meet the parishioners he despised—returning to Guadalupe to worship in their own ways for their own purposes?

The Ambassador's Wife Finds Heartland Communities, 1839–41

Both Manuel López Escudero, the priest who ignored religion at Temamatla on the Chalco plain, and Manuel Espinosa de los Monteros, the priest who despised social and cultural practices at Iztacalco, the *chinampa* community near Mexico City, documented community autonomies, landed and cultural, in the 1830s. Neither left detailed descriptions of the festivals that focused local Christianities. Others did.

Frances Inglis (Fanny) Calderón de la Barca was born in Scotland and migrated to Boston and then Staten Island, where she met and married Ángel Calderón de la Barca. A Spaniard born in Buenos Aires and veteran of Spain's war against Napoleon, he later joined Spain's diplomatic service. Named minister to the United States in 1835, he served as Spain's first ambassador to Mexico beginning in 1839. Fanny Calderón kept a diary and copies of many letters: in 1843 she compiled them in a book, *Life in Mexico*.[42] Mexican Catholicism was an early and enduring interest. Her first public appearance was a mass at the Mexico City Cathedral. Within a week of arrival, the ambassador and his wife joined an excursion to "the cathedral of Our Lady of Guadalupe" led by two great landlords, don José Adalid and the Conde de la Cortina, and the latter's wife, Paulita. Fanny knew Paulita's devotion, told the story of Guadalupe's appearance as "a tissue of the greatest absurdities," and saw a church "crowded with people of the village, especially the ragged poor."[43] A skeptical Protestant, Fanny Calderón saw that Guadalupe linked the powerful to the pueblos.

In April of 1841, she and the Adalids joined many of the capital's aristocrats in Holy Week festivities at Coyoacán. Local clergy joined the community in a religious theater that drew prosperous visitors. Calderón set the scene: on Holy Thursday the church was "magnificently illuminated, ornamented with loads of flowers and fruit (especially oranges), and thronged with the ragged poor and blanketed Indians." Outside, aristocrats took seats in the shade: they were observers, not participants. For four days, priests preached, at times eloquently said Fanny, while villagers performed the passion from Judas's treason, to Pilate's sentence, to Christ's crucifixion and resurrection. Villagers stayed throughout; aristocrats came and went. Local women sold fruit, drinks, and meals. "If ever there was a patient, good-natured, *laissez-aller* mob, this was it."

The Scottish observer saw priests repeatedly turn to the Virgin, set in several side altars, to ask Her intercession in the world. Popular worship focused on the Virgin; She was as central as Christ in Coyoacán's Easter theater. The clergy had adapted to the people. All seemed orderly and honorable as aristocrats, priests, and villagers mixed in honoring Christ's sacrifice and Guadalupe's service, until a pickpocket and a few horse thieves served themselves with redistributions.[44]

Days later, Fanny joined an excursion from San Ángel to the highland village of San Bartolo, seeking a retreat, refreshing springs, and a view back to the capital. She began to see a gendered picture of villagers. "San Bartolo is a small, scattered Indian village with a church, and is remarkable for its beautiful spring of water . . . and for the good looks and cleanliness of the Indian women, who are forever washing their long hair." Many younger women "were laughing and talking at a great rate in their native tongue." In contrast, "The men looked as dirty as Indians generally do."[45] Was this gender bias, or did men face hard, dirty, and debilitating tasks while women kept family and community in another inversion?

Fanny reflected on indigenous devotions. "All these festivities of the church, their fireworks and images and gay dresses, harmonize completely with their childish love of show, and are in fact their greatest source of delight. . . . Attempts have been made by their curates to persuade them to omit the celebration of certain days, and to expend less in the ceremonies of others; but the indignation and discontent which such proposals have caused have induced them to desist in their endeavors." Acknowledging insistent autonomies, she turned to indigenous character: "Under an appearance of stupid apathy they veil a great deal of cunning. They are grave and gentle and rather sad in their appearance, when not under the influence of pulque. But when they return to their villages in the evening, and have taken a drop of comfort, their white teeth light up their bronze countenance like lamps, and the girls especially make the air ring with their laughter, which is very musical."[46] While Mexican clergy saw pulque as debauchery, the Scottish observer saw its liberations. Fanny began to find depth and beauty among indigenous women.

Such discoveries deepened in a visit to the San Xavier estate, just north of Mexico City near Tlalnepantla. Escaping political turmoil in the capital during September of 1841, Fanny saw "waving fields of corn." Arriving at the great house she saw a reservoir, well-kept gardens, and tree-lined paths to nearby villages. The estate had been part of the Jesuit's Santa Lucía complex, later held by the Condes de Regla, now owned by the "Señoras de Fagoaga"—women of a family who once ruled mining finance in New Spain.

Fanny saw Tlalnepantla as "a small village with an old church, ruined remains of a convent where the curate now lives, a few shops, and a
square where the Indians hold market (*tianguis*, they call it) on Fridays.
All along the lanes are small Indian huts, with their usual mud floors,
small altar, earthen vessels, and collection of daubs on the walls (especially
of the Virgin of Guadalupe), with a few blest palm leaves in the corner—
occupied when the men are at work, by the woman herself, and her sturdy
scantily-clothed progeny." Had Espinosa de los Monteros ever ventured
into such a home? He had no sense of women of poverty so dedicated to
devotion and family.

The next day, "a shower drove us for shelter to a farmhouse, where
we entered a sort of oratorio attached to the house: a room which is not
consecrated, but has an altar, crucifix, holy pictures, etc." Household devotions held strong at Tlalnepantla in the 1840s. "The most remarkable
object of the rancho is its proprietress, a tall, noble-looking Indian, Doña
Margarita by name, a mountaineer by birth, and now a rich widow pos-
sessing lands and flocks, though living in apparent poverty. The bulk of
her fortune she employs in educating poor orphans. . . . She takes them
into her house, brings them up as her own children, has them bred to
some useful employment, and, when they are old enough, married. If it is
a boy, she chooses a wife from amongst the girls of the mountains, where
she was born, who she says are 'less corrupted' than the girls of the village." She aimed to replicate her own social trajectory among the twelve
to twenty orphans usually in her care. Many were "maimed and sick . . .
nevertheless, we saw various healthy, happy-looking girls, washing and
ironing, and sewing, whose eyes gleamed when we mentioned her name,
and who spoke of her with a respect and affection that it was pleasant to
witness." No such people inhabited Espinosa de los Monteros's Iztacalco.
"The remainder of her fortune she employs in the festivals and ceremonies
of the church—in fireworks, in ornaments for the altars, etc."[47] The angry
priest did know such devotions at Iztacalco, and aimed to end them.

Fanny Calderón, seeking to understand Mexican Catholicism and
indigenous people, saw positive devotions linking the powerful and the
populace—especially women. She saw that in times of political conflict,
commercial challenge, and community autonomies, rural men found
ways to sustain families by hard and debilitating work. In community
cultures that presumed patriarchy, she saw women with space to rule
households, local markets, and religious devotions. In their daily lives,
they appeared happy and bound together—while men carried on. To the
increasingly appreciative Scotswoman, village households were centers

of devotion run by women invisible to priests and powerful men. Had an inversion of patriarchy begun within the inversion of power in heartland communities?

A Liberal Rediscovers Community Cultures: Looking Back at 1830–45

Manuel Payno was a leading Mexican liberal who late in life tried to see the personal religious lives of heartland women and the Guadalupan devotions that linked the powerful and the people of heartland communities. Born in Mexico City, Payno had a long career in government service culminating in terms as treasury minister in the late 1840s and the 1850s. Later, Porfirio Díaz honored Payno with posts of distant exile. While consul in Barcelona in 1888, the elder statesman wrote the episodic tales that became *Los bandidos de Río Frío* (The Bandits of Río Frío) for serial publication in a local newspaper.[48] Distance of time and place from the political conflicts and social contests of the 1830s and 1840s brought perspective; the need to engage Catalan readers mandated detail. Like Fanny Calderón, Payno could not presume his readers knew life in Mexico.

Like so many, Payno opened by condemning the people he aimed to portray: "for years and years life was ruled by pernicious customs and practices . . . a kind of barbarism that everyone tolerated."[49] Having announced his liberal credentials, Payno's first episode turned to a rancho just outside Tlalnepantla. Had he read Calderón? Did he aim to open with his own view of rural life and women? If so, he offered a different, not contradictory vision. Payno's tale focused on Pascuala, the Hispanic illegitimate daughter of a provincial priest, and her husband, Pascual, a "ranchero indio." They lived outside Tlalnepantla, while joining in the festivals that integrated the community.

Payno's tale took a revealing turn when Pascuala faced a difficult pregnancy. She went to the capital seeking the best of city medicine. Science failed, so Pascual proposed that she consult "the witches," two indigenous women, "curanderas" recommended by "the Canon Camaño." They lived on the road to Guadalupe, in a village "fully composed of those called macehuales . . . that is those who work the land . . . yes, the lowest class . . . conserving its poverty, ignorance, superstition, commitment to old customs." The villagers raised maize, gathered firewood, and worked at nearby estates for cash and more maize. Like many villagers in the 1830s, they retained autonomies and links to estate economies; to the liberal Payno: "thus they live, or better said vegetate."

On local religion: "Neither the parish priest nor any other has taught them Catholic religion; they do not know how to pray or read; they speak their Aztec language, and Spanish only badly; they even keep a bit of their ancient traditions and religious ways; of things modern they only know and adore the virgin of Guadalupe."[50] It was a portrayal worthy of Espinosa de los Monteros in its denigration of community life, except the priest at Iztacalco blamed local big men, while Payno blamed priests. Both saw devotion to Guadalupe—an indigenous worship, adopted by the powerful—as modern.

As Payno detailed the women healers' lives and practices, they became professional and entrepreneurial: "the two Marías . . . had a vocation for things botanical. Dedicated to collecting plants, they studied their therapeutic benefits, experimenting on the vecinos of the Santa Ana barrio and the muleteers who filled nearby inns." Scientific women got their start serving neighbors and passing muleteers. They remained deeply religious: "curing began with certain ceremonies. . . . They lit a blessed candle they always carried and asked the patient to pray an Our Father, a Hail Mary, and to commend himself to the virgin of Guadalupe while the healer quietly said a few words in her Aztec language. Then the medicines were administered."[51]

Over time the *curanderas* gained fame and a bit of fortune. They served a region from the city to Guadalupe; they built a large house in the village, they bought new clothes, they learned a bit of Spanish. They established a "*consultorio*," a practice, in the heart of Mexico City. In another inversion, indigenous *curanderas* brought religious medicine to the capital: "There did not pass half an hour when they were not surrounded by the servants of the neighborhood, and sometimes from far away, for all knew that their array of herbs, like no other, had a selection beyond imagining. . . . They competed with physicians, costing them visits. . . . The crowds not only of servants, but of men in capes with fur collars and women in fine skirts and shawls, were so large that it was often impossible to obtain an herb in less than an hour—and for good reason, as they had cures for every known illness."[52] They remained dedicated to Guadalupe, visiting her on the twelfth of every month, bringing candles, buying medallions. When the pastor at the Virgin's sanctuary faced intractable illness, he too turned to Matiana María, who cured the distinguished cleric.[53]

Having recognized the deep connections linking communities and *curanderas* to Guadalupe and her priests, Payno turned to the great public celebration of the Virgin: "The twelfth of December is the most solemn day of the year in Mexico, the day of the Virgin of Guadalupe, Patron of Anáhuac. The entire government attends the religious event. The President of the Republic . . . leads the march . . . behind come ministers of state and Mexico City councilmen in new and luxurious coaches. . . . Every family, rich and poor, goes to la Villa on December 12." On arrival "the abbot in his cape of gold cloth followed by a chorus of canons in long robes of black silk and carrying fine inlaid staffs, receive the first magistrate of the nation and his ministers, blessing them with holy water." Inside, "The sermon is delivered by the cleric of greatest fame . . . the Apparition is the required topic . . . it concludes with these words: Obey faithfully the Holy Virgin of Guadalupe. Her will is sovereign and must be served."[54]

Then all joined in a great meal, enacting Guadalupe's service to sustenance: "The government men ate as if for three days, even the masons with claims to be freethinkers; they fraternized with the canons while all praised the cooks and the Virgin of Guadalupe." Then the men of power returned to the city—and the people took over: "The indios and the people were left to rule the Villa's field; the fiestas and banquets really began." People paraded before the Virgin, addressing Her in *mexicano* and Spanish, asking Her help, leaving what they could for the priests who served Her—and Her people. "Outside the temple, the movement was immense. The hill and the streets were full of indios and city people lunching on richly filled tortillas, savory sauce, and fine pulque—most families in the open air." Guadalupe provided sustenance. Her priests had to serve the people. The government, however liberal, had to bow before Her—at least in public ceremony.[55]

After the fall of silver, as political men struggled to forge a Mexican nation, commercial ways collapsed, and instability reigned, heartland communities held strong. At Chalco commercial elites gave way to political men as landed entrepreneurs. Desperate for financing, they struggled to profit. They had to pay higher wages to the villagers who raised their crops—and guarantee maize rations, even when it meant taking debts to draw grain from Mexico City. Chalco villagers made real gains from 1820 to 1845. At Iztacalco, rich *chinampas* sustained economic and cultural independence. There are hints that women across the heartland found gains as well. Life was not easy; inequities were everywhere, but so were autonomies—and Guadalupe's protection.

CHAPTER EIGHT

Commercial Revival, Liberal Reform, and Community Resistance

CHALCO, 1845–70

AFTER 1821, struggles to found an imagined nation and to rebuild a lost economy favored heartland villagers: they reinforced local autonomies, claimed higher wages, and pressed religious independence. Then, beginning in the 1840s, Mexicans faced decades of international invasions, political wars, and popular insurgencies. Equally important, silver began an expansion that continued to 1870, while textile manufacturing also grew. War and political instability mixed with commercial growth from 1845 to 1870. In the heartland, commercial growers tried to revive estate agriculture while communities defended land and local autonomies. Simmering conflicts kept a social stalemate.

Around Cuernavaca, cane planters pressed expansions in the 1840s— to face staunch resistance from entrenched communities.[1] At Chalco, a parallel turn to innovation and expansion by estate operators provoked resistance in the fields and the courts, proposals to create police, and laws to privatize land. There, conflicts culminated in months of armed rebellion in 1868 as Benito Juárez led liberals back to power in Mexico City.[2] The rising was contained, its leaders punished. Still, it showed that Chalco villagers would take arms to defend autonomies. Community uprisings against Juárez's liberal regime followed in the Mezquital, just east around Puebla, and in distant regions from Tepic to Chiapas in 1868 and 1869.[3] Chalco's time of commercial revival and political assertion, community resistance and regional rebellion, reveals an era when capitalists pressed for advantage, liberals pushed transformations in service of capitalism—and people on the land pushed back to keep their definition of independence.

An Estate Offensive, 1849–56

The crisis that followed Mexico's losses in the War for North America made a commercial revival (and the state revenues it might generate) essential to entrepreneurs and political leaders. Silver and manufacturing growth created market stimuli. Chalco estate operators saw an opening. They tried new techniques and new products; they looked for profitable new ways to raise maize and wheat; they tried dairying on newly irrigated fields of alfalfa. They aimed to raise yields and revenues, and in the effort provoked conflicts with Chalco communities quick to defend lands and autonomies.

Experiments with seeds had been rare among estate cultivators in colonial New Spain; every year they planted seed saved from the previous harvest. In the late 1840s, Chalco growers began to plant wheat, maize, and vegetable seed or seedlings from harvests reporting high yields in other regions.[4] Fertilizing had been limited in times of silver boom and postindependence difficulties: a British visitor in the 1820s found Mexican growers little interested in manuring. But in the 1850s it became an obsession among Chalco estate managers. They expanded flocks of sheep to obtain more waste; they mixed manure and maize stalks to stretch fertilizer supplies.[5] Imported plows that turned deeper soils became common; a few estates invested in winnowing machines to separate wheat grain from chaff (and reduce labor).[6] Facing commercial openings after decades of struggle, Chalco estate growers were ready to innovate to raise traditional crops.

They also tried new products. In the late 1840s at least six Chalco estates turned to dairying. They purchased cows and developed alfalfa pastures, which required new irrigation and more manure.[7] Dairying could surmount shortages of operating funds. Milk delivered by canal was sold daily in Mexico City; it generated regular income that could cut reliance on grain merchants and bakers for scarce and expensive credit.[8] The promise was great; the outcome limited. By 1857, so many Chalco estates produced milk that they saturated the market; prices fell and much could not be sold.[9] Plenty without profit continued.

To raise yields of old crops and create a dairy industry, Chalco estates worked to increase control of the water in the streams that flowed from the snow-covered heights of the great volcanoes. When Asunción expanded dairying in 1849, it built a dam and irrigation ditches to water fields of alfalfa. Similar works came at Buenavista.[10] At Zoquiapan, dairying led to an elaborate new irrigation system. A foreign engineer, Mr. Alan, designed and directed construction of a series of catch basins in the highlands above the estate, along with canals to distribute water across its fields.[11] The Asunción and González estates drilled artesian wells. Another foreigner led the search for groundwater; however, Mr. Bener proved unfamiliar with local water tables and Riva Palacio and other growers were unfamiliar with the cost of imported innovations. Drilling brought little water and long contract disputes.[12]

All the expansion and innovation (except the winnowing machines) increased labor demands. Building dams and irrigation canals required many hands, as did planting and manuring extensive alfalfa fields. Chalco estates needed more day laborers, yet recruiting villagers remained a challenge.[13] In 1849, the harvest was delayed again at Asunción when villagers at Temamatla and other communities would not come until their own crops were in.[14] Then cholera struck for a second time in 1850. The manager at Asunción reported eight residents stricken; two died. At the nearby Zula, fifty were ill and at least seven died. Similar challenges were reported across Chalco and the heartland. Managers could not find enough workers to cultivate crops; weeds invaded estate fields; harvests were reduced.[15] The people of nineteenth-century Chalco still lived the grim paradox of agrarian life: disease that reduced their numbers preserved bargaining power with estates. In the face of estate water claims and rising labor demands in the late 1840s and 1850s, villagers moved beyond local negotiations to protest in the courts and the fields.

Community Counteroffensive

The 1840s were a time of rising indigenous and community mobilizations to defend autonomies and fend off challenges from landowners and their state allies. Early in the decade, Juan Álvarez mobilized indigenous communities in the south of the state of Mexico (now Guerrero) in defense of their rights and his political project.[16] During the War for North America, Maya in Yucatán, Zapotecs at the Isthmus of Tehuantepec, and diverse people in the Sierra Gorda northeast of the Bajío asserted independence, while national armies struggled against northern invaders.[17]

In the basins around Mexico City, the late 1840s and early 1850s brought estate assertions and community resistance that at times became violent. Protesting communities and irate estate operators all cited the decades-old precedent of Toluca communities' legal victory over the Atengo properties.[18] Beginning in 1848 in the Mezquital, around Otumba and Teotihuacán, and near Xochimilco in *chinampa* country, villagers threatened or used violence in disputes over land, water, taxes, and local office.[19] After decades of negotiating autonomies with weak estate operators and a fragile state, heartland villagers began to press their interests more assertively.

Mobilizations were intense in the Cuautla and Cuernavaca lowlands south of Chalco. There, villagers rose up repeatedly, beginning in 1849, to challenge sugar estates' claims to lands. Protestors might be led by a local priest, joined by local merchants, and even backed by local militias. There were many stimuli: old disputes over land and labor; US troops' defense of estates in 1848—then their departure. In 1849, the state of Mexico passed a law calling for the privatization of community lands—legislation it could not enforce in times of rising conflicts. Still, it announced intentions that threatened community autonomies. The Cuernavaca district of the state of Mexico (later the state of Morelos) remained a hotbed of politicized agrarian conflict from 1849 into the 1850s.[20]

In the face of community challenges and local uprisings across the heartland, landed politicians from the liberal Andrés Quintana Roo to conservative Francisco Pimentel developed a siege mentality. They saw villagers threatening property and state power: communities ignored court decisions, refused to respect property, and neglected to pay rents; men worked poorly when they worked at all; insubordinate villagers assaulted legitimate property and regime power.[21] Communities around Cuernavaca and at Chalco, of course, believed they were challenging illegitimate properties and powers. In 1851, officials at Amecameca, in the Chalco uplands on the road to Cuautla, demanded resolution of an old land dispute, again citing the Toluca precedent. They threatened violence in the fields, then went to court in a dispute that continued to 1855.[22] Most protests at Chalco, however, responded directly to the new estate offensive.

When Riva Palacio built a dam to expand irrigation at Asunción in 1849, it flooded community lands in the jurisdictions of Chalco and Temamatla. Villagers threatened to break the dam; a local official wrote to Riva Palacio seeking compromise: he could not stop rising discontent. When the project was completed, it was clear that newly harnessed waters would irrigate lands held by the village of Cuicingo. The estate claimed them and villagers rioted. Riva Palacio convinced officials at Temamatla to offer alternative lands to the dispossessed. Angry villagers answered by building a makeshift dam blocking the river above Riva Palacio's new structure, draining his irrigation system. A court ordered the destruction of the villagers' dam; local officials reported they could not enforce it without setting off violence. No final resolution is known, but in 1850 Asunción was cultivating irrigated fields at Cuicingo.[23] Expanding irrigation led to encroachments and disputes—and not all resolutions favored estates. To plant alfalfa, Tomacoco usurped waters long shared with nearby villagers. The communities went to court and won.[24]

The most intense, enduring, and violent dispute at Chalco in the 1840s and 1850s set San Francisco Acuautla against the hacienda of Zoquiapan, owned by the Villaurrutía family, heirs to the former Marqueses de Castañiza. Disputes between Acuautla and Zoquiapan over uplands and other resources went back to the middle of the eighteenth century.[25] In 1849 the estate began to build a new irrigation system to capture water in the highlands and channel it to estate fields. Conflict came quickly. The people of Acuautla, in uplands northeast of Chalco, lost cropland, pastures, and woods to new irrigation works.

The community hired a Mexico City lawyer, Luis María Aguilar, to represent them. He visited Acuautla in early October. To protect himself from the political costs of helping a community fight an important landed family, Aguilar wrote to Riva Palacio. His letter reveals as much about a liberal's view of rural villagers as about the conflict at hand.

The community greeted Aguilar with fireworks and festival music. He saw self-degradation that he blamed on rural priests who treated parishioners as beasts of burden. Aguilar's solution: eliminate the distinction between *gente de razón* (people of reason) and *indios*. The lawyer proclaimed that all people, even *indios*, shared reason. They should be assigned Spanish surnames, useful for contracts, taxation, and militia recruitment.[26] People at Acuautla would have been pleased to know their lawyer believed they shared in human reason; his interest in taxation and militias would have distressed them. They might have smiled at his presumption that their deferential greeting revealed self-denigration. When Aguilar failed in court, the people of Acuautla showed abundant courageous self-esteem.

In early 1850, a court ruled in favor of Zoquiapan. Only a small fraction of the lands in dispute went to Acuautla; the estate got the rest. The ruling would be implemented by a judicial survey in the fields, described by the estate manager:

> During the morning there were no problems. And although the towns-people came en masse to claim they were due twice the land allotted them, the judge told them that given the participation of their repre-sentative, they could have no role in the proceedings. . . . The survey resumed and the indios returned home.
>
> But in the afternoon a community leader arrived and told the judge that if the survey continued, he could not control the consequences, given the volatility of the townspeople. The judge said he lacked power to suspend the survey, as he was executing a court order. He barely finished answering when the community arrived, advancing in close formation, armed with stones and sticks. Unarmed, the judge and his aides found it prudent to retire to Chalco and suspend the proceedings.
>
> The attack made the indios the masters of the fields and left the au-thority that is supposed to instill respect in them in a sorry predicament. I believe that the judge will ask for assistance to complete the survey and impose respect with armed force—the only recourse remaining. As you are aware of the precedents to this event, and you know the people of Acuautla, excuse my repeating another example of their insubordi-nation, and of the losses they have imposed on the estate. But you will agree with the need to limit their continued impudence. Thus I implore you to take the steps necessary so they will not do away with us all.[27]

Early in March of 1850, the prefect of Texcoco sent fifteen armed men who stood guard to enable completion of the field survey.[28] But the dis-pute did not end. The people of Acuautla returned to court, winning a more favorable ruling early in 1851, gaining an additional two *caballerías*, about 210 acres. They remained angry, and perhaps emboldened by the court's shift in their favor. Implementation of the second resolution re-quired fifty armed guards. The villagers attacked with sticks and stones, but could not prevent its completion. The commander of the guard con-cluded that the people of Acuautla "will never accept any resolution that is not to their liking."[29]

The dispute continued. After the second resolution, construction of the irrigation works resumed. The villagers responded by blocking workers and taking tools; armed guards reclaimed tools and allowed work to resume. In May of 1851, conflict came to a violent head. Villagers obstructed work while continuing to gather wood and graze animals on disputed lands. Managers began to seize villagers' livestock. Tensions escalated, leading the estate owner to use his influence to persuade defense minister Mariano Arista to send troops to quell what was now labeled an "Indian riot."[30]

The owner went to Zoquiapan a few days ahead of the troops. As he arrived, two leaders from Acuautla were with the manager, demanding the return of livestock. When the manager refused, a fight erupted in which he was wounded by several machete blows. He later died. Other estate employees answered with firearms, holding off the villagers until a larger militia force arrived near nightfall and forced them back to Acuautla. The next morning, fifty men of the Chalco National Guard—mostly armed estate employees—went to Acuautla, capturing one of two leaders and thirty-five other presumed protestors.

The armed conflict ended before the cavalry arrived from Mexico City. Still, Zoquiapan's owner remained apprehensive. The people of Acuautla had become too bold, only subdued by the National Guard—a process that took time and disrupted estate operations. He wrote to Riva Palacio demanding quick and severe punishment of the "rebels" and police to protect property rights.[31]

Two weeks later, people from Acuautla again threatened Zoquiapan. The owner offered a solution. He would pay the community for the lands it claimed—if the villagers could move to another part of the state.[32] Did the offer show a lack of confidence in estate land claims, despite court victories? Did it reflect doubt in the state's ability to enforce court rulings? It certainly showed ignorance of community values. Cash and forced relocation would not compensate for the loss of traditional lands and separation from cherished shrines. The dispute between Zoquiapan and Acuautla then fades from Riva Palacio's correspondence. When a wider uprising erupted in 1868, men from Acuautla led their neighbors in attacking estates and demanding land.

The State's Solution: Rural Police

The conflicts that began in the late 1840s made it clear that the stabilization once sustained by silver dynamism, symbiotic exploitations, and judicial mediation was gone. The unequal interdependence of estates and communities remained. But with the collapse of silver in times of political instability, estate commercial power waned while community autonomies remained. When new commercial opportunities enabled estate expansion and innovation in the 1840s, communities mobilized to defend lands and autonomies—and learned they could not rely on national-era courts for mediated resolutions. The courts and states mostly backed estate operators, who were often powerful political actors. Yet while the courts favored proprietors, the state had little means to enforce decisions. As estate operators pressed gain, the state revealed enduring weakness. It was a recipe for conflict.

Chalco landlords and leaders of the state of Mexico, fused in the person of Riva Palacio, saw a solution in police powers. New forces of coercion had been imagined in conversations among the powerful for decades. In the late 1840s, states across Mexico began to found rural police.[33] In the state of Mexico, legislation came in October 1849 as conflicts rose across the heartland. In December, the Chalco subprefect called a meeting of estate operators to implement the law.[34] He aimed to forge an alliance of commercial growers and state powers.

By early 1850, a small force was in place at Chalco, well below the desired strength. Tax receipts were low and officials could not fund the full unit. The detachment was armed with fifty rifles sent by the Ministry of Defense. Later that year a second "proprietors meeting" sought funds to increase police personnel.[35] Meanwhile, a reserve would deputize the "armed dependents" of local landholders. Police would be agents of entrepreneurial interests. And still, estate operators' financial problems kept the force below strength. In December 1851, another proprietors' meeting sought funds for police—with little result.[36]

In 1855, renewed local disturbances, most intense around Cuernavaca but evident across the heartland, led the subprefect to try again to fortify police at Chalco. He imagined a mounted patrol, but his treasury could not fund it. So he turned again to estate operators, calling them to contribute horses or the money to buy them. They liked his proposal, but pleaded cash shortages; most did not pay their quotas. Early in 1856 the patrol was only partly manned and supplied; the subprefect threatened fines against landlords who did not contribute. He learned that the 4,800 pesos annual cost of twenty armed and mounted men could not be extracted from Chalco estate operators.[37] Chalco entrepreneurs wanted police to protect them from villagers quick to challenge land and water claims. Financial difficulties, sustained by community resistance, blocked funding. The problem—community autonomy—prevented the solution: police in service of landed power. Stalemate ruled as liberals took national power in 1855.

National Liberals' Solution: Privatize Community Lands

The goal of ending community property rights—the eminent domain rooted in historic indigenous republics and described by Espinosa de los Monteros at Iztacalco in the 1830s—had marked Hispanic liberalism since the 1812 Cádiz constitution. Attempts to legislate privatization in several Mexican states in the 1820s and again in the late 1840s came to little. Either they failed in legislatures fearful of raising discontent, or they proved unenforceable by states with limited powers. Even Santa Ana's last government of the early 1850s debated such legislation.[38] For decades, Mexican liberals had announced the goal of undermining community autonomy. Privatization would break the primary link uniting local notables and cultivating commoners in defense of rights and resources. It would open lands long subject to sale and accumulation within communities to new concentrations—with outsiders free to participate. Chalco villagers understood this, as they saw the state weakness that blocked implementation. They were ready in 1856 when national liberals made privatization national policy.

There was a paradox in the liberals' rise to power. They took the government in 1855 thanks to the ability of Juan Álvarez, political heir to Vicente Guerrero, to mobilize forces from Pacific foothills through the Cuernavaca basin, building on a famed history of backing community land rights. Once in office, however, national liberals, many landlords and urban professionals, ousted Álvarez—clearing the way for privatization.[39] The Lerdo Law of June 25, 1856, decreed that all "rural and urban estates" held by civil and Church corporations would be "adjudicated in property to the renters." It gave tenants and occupants three months to claim holdings before they would be auctioned.[40] Follow-up rulings made it clear that the intent was to end communities' eminent domain.[41]

Chalco villagers understood and quickly organized to resist. On August 19, the subprefect reported that in upland Amecameca and at San Gregorio Cuautzingo, close by La Compañía, "there are secret meetings of indios, it appears to oppose the implementation of the laws of June 25 past, and to take by force some lands of the haciendas."[42] Villagers were ready to defend community rights; they set forth rumors of a counteroffensive against estate lands. Early in September, the manager at Asunción wrote to Riva Palacio: "Last night I was in Temamatla and was told the following in great secrecy: that don Francisco de Sales on several nights, when the citizens have retired so that no one could observe his activities, has brought together in his house people from Chalco, Zula, Cocotitlán, San Gregorio, Tlapala, Chimalpa, etc., to discuss a war of castes . . . that one of these nights at a designated hour, they would attack the *familias de razón* in the towns and at the haciendas." Plotting had begun six weeks earlier and the planned uprising awaited only the purchase of arms—it was time to move beyond defense with stones, sticks, and machetes. The manager asked for rifles to defend the estate; he found the news so threatening that he did not tell estate employees, who would bear the brunt of any attack.[43]

No attack came. The threat worked. While a few properties leased to generate town income did pass to tenants in 1856, there was no general application of the Lerdo Law at Chalco. Villagers did not claim their plots as private property; no outsiders were ready to denounce community holdings after the three-month limit passed. Chalco is all but absent in the lists of properties alienated in the state of Mexico in the last six months of 1856.[44]

Community opposition and threats of violence were not limited to Chalco.[45] By fall, Lerdo recognized that most villagers were ignoring the reform law. He believed they were misled; he also saw that most could not pay the costs of surveys, titles, and taxes. He issued a new rule: lands valued at less than 200 pesos would pass automatically to the occupants with no tax, no survey, no title. His goal was "public peace, the welfare of the most destitute classes, and the implementation . . . of the rules dictated for the mobilization of property."[46] The rule ended the need to implement the Lerdo Law as applied to community smallholdings. The regime could announce completion of the reform; villagers could carry on as always. Yet problems would come: villagers would continue to hold and work their milpas; the state could consider them private property and refuse to recognize community titles—and families would have no titles to their plots.

Lerdo's October ruling also stated the regime's goal in privatizing community lands: to mobilize property. To liberals, mobilization promoted commercial expansion; to villagers it threatened autonomies. Property being open to sale and inheritance only among *vecinos* had protected the subsistence bases (however limited) of rural families, and forged a common interest among local notables and commoners. Despite inequities, they all depended on and defended community lands. Privatization would widen inequities and allow outsiders to buy pastures, woodlands, and the properties leased for income. And it would limit local notables' interest in defending community rights. The liberal reform would weaken the ability of villagers to stand together in defense of autonomies against estates and the state.

What Chalco entrepreneurs expected from the Lerdo Law is revealed in a letter sent by an estate operator to Riva Palacio in April 1857. He complained that community lands had not been divided and privatized and pressed for rapid action. He insisted that only the end of community rights would end conflicts between communities and landholders.[47] Politicized entrepreneurs could share in correspondence what they could not state in public: the goal of privatization was to undermine community autonomy and cohesion—to facilitate commercial expansion under entrepreneurial control.

The Lerdo Law was included in the liberal constitution of 1857, which Riva Palacio and his son Vicente helped write. There was little debate, and a vote of seventy-six to three.[48] The new charter provoked widespread opposition—focused on its attacks on Church powers and properties. The dearth of debate on community privatization showed it as a reform that found a broad consensus among the powerful. Political men and their landed allies did not defend community rights. The liberal ideology of economic individualism complemented landed entrepreneurs' desire to limit community autonomies. The privatization decreed in 1856 aimed to strengthen the state and promote commercial agriculture by weakening communities' cohesion while opening their lands to market accumulations.[49]

Still, the political division provoked by the liberals' attack on the Church made implementation of the Lerdo Law difficult in the face of community opposition. Liberals also knew the solution: they began to build national rural police.[50] Yet again, political division, state weakness, and limited revenues blocked implementation. Villagers at Chalco and beyond saw political entrepreneurs challenge their autonomies while revealing little capacity to rule. National leaders turned away from the judicial mediations that had sustained Spanish power; they preferred police they could not fund. When political war began in 1858, communities were left to their autonomies.

Political Wars and Estate Crisis, 1857–67

The liberals who decreed the Lerdo Law and wrote the constitution of 1857 imagined they were leading transformations that would stabilize Mexican politics and strengthen commercial life. Instead, they set off a decade of political wars: the War of Reform between liberals and Church-backed conservatives from 1858 to 1860; a liberal victory that brought a brief respite; then a French invasion backed by desperate Mexican conservatives that led to liberal triumph on May 5, 1862, French occupation in 1863, and Maximilian's French-backed, conservative-supported, and liberal-contested empire of 1864–67. Silver production and textile industries continued to grow during the decade of political warfare; the estate economy at Chalco returned to disarray.

As political conflict began in April of 1857, Chalco estate operators and managers saw a way to increase social control: a gathering of "the most honorable and wealthy citizens" compiled lists of the region's "most pernicious inhabitants," to be drafted into liberal armies.[51] But the war soon escaped their control—social or political. As battles approached Chalco, landholders, officials, estate managers, and town merchants fled to Mexico City.[52] For two years, Chalco communities were left to themselves; they reinforced autonomies while factions of the powerful fought deadly battles.

When liberals returned in 1859, they saw "banditry" everywhere. The response of the government headed by Benito Juárez was, again, to build rural police. Chalco estate operators promised cooperation, but once again weak revenues made funds to recruit, arm, and pay police scarce.[53] Social coercion was the goal; effective coercion remained impossible. Community autonomies continued.

During 1861, a year of political peace before the French landed, Juárez's government looked to commercial projects. In April, it granted "los Sres Abreu," a charter to raise 2 million pesos (selling 2,000 shares worth 1,000 pesos each) to build a railroad from the capital to Chalco. The government would buy 200 shares, thus invest 200,000 pesos, a tenth of the cost, paying with funds from the sale of Church properties. The route would pass from the city to Mixcoac, through Coyoacán and Tlalpan, to Chalco.[54] The goal was better transport and travel from the capital through the *chinampa* communities to Chalco. Yet that route already had the most efficient transit in the Valley of Mexico, thanks to historic canals and the indigenous boatmen whose canoes moved goods and people easily and cheaply. Rail service might make transport a bit faster, unlikely cheaper; it would displace boatmen at Iztacalco, Xochimilco, and Chalco, while profiting rail entrepreneurs.

In August 1862, a revised charter reset the route to pass west through Tacubaya, then south through Mixcoac and San Ángel, until reaching Tlalpan and extending to Chalco.[55] Had boatmen in canal communities protested? The new route passed through favorite weekend retreats of the capital's leading families while taking longer to reach Chalco. Serving the comfortable and limiting conflicts with native boatmen, the shift served two purposes. A weak economy and an empty treasury delayed construction.

Political conflict and social instability resumed with the French invasion of 1862. When the invaders took Mexico City in 1863, they followed Mexican liberals in seeing police as the solution to social unrest. They too called landholders' meetings at Chalco, seeking funds for police and equipment.[56] Arguably, there were only two policies that all political men agreed on in the 1860s: land privatization to weaken communities, and police as the way to enforce privatization and other policies on resistant communities.[57]

Unable to implement either policy in times of political wars, estate difficulties deepened at Chalco from 1857 to 1867. In October 1857, the owner of Tomacoco faced debts that forced a quick sale to satisfy creditors. No buyer appeared, so he offered parcels to neighboring estate owners.[58] In June 1858, the Villaurrutía clan had to lease Zoquiapan—with payment going directly to creditors.[59] The people of Acuautla surely delighted in the bankruptcy. Meanwhile, warring factions saw Chalco estates as sources of scarce funds. During 1860, liberals levied forced loans that cost a major proprietor 1,000 pesos.[60] Many could not or would not pay, whether demands came from political friends or foes. A liberal commander embargoed one estate for failure to pay 500 pesos.[61]

Two cases of proprietor crisis illustrate the collapse of profit during the decade of turmoil at Chalco. Three Garrido sisters, all minors, inherited Atoyac in 1855. They had leased out the property, but when the contract ended in 1859 the tenant quit, citing the impossibility of profit. Riva Palacio, the sisters' guardian, sought a new tenant. None came, so he leased the estate to his son Vicente. That deepened Riva Palacio's troubles, so they tried a partnership with the resident manager. No gains came: in 1855, 1859, 1861, 1862, and 1864, expenses rose an average of 1,000 pesos yearly to pay special taxes, forced loans, and the costs of redeeming Church mortgages. Riva Palacio saw no option but to sell the estate in 1864, a moment of peace as French power settled in and Maximilian began to rule. One buyer bid, buying Atoyac at the bargain price of 40,000 pesos.[62]

Atilano Sánchez faced similar problems. Once chief notary of the Mexico City Cathedral mortgage bank, he used favored access to credit to buy haciendas. In the 1830s he owned Moral while helping finance other properties. Unable to survive commercial and community challenges, he sold Moral and bought Buenavista, near Apan in the pulque zone to the northeast. To increase its value and profits during the commercial opening of the early 1850s, he borrowed 10,000 pesos for improvements. He could not repay when wars and commercial disruptions returned after 1857. He tried to sell the property, valued at 125,000 pesos, but found no offer above 115,000 pesos. He held on, hoping that French occupation would bring stability and profit. Disruptions and exactions continued; he lost 7,000 pesos yearly. He sold livestock and implements to pay operating expenses—village workers had to be paid. Finally, he sold Buenavista in 1866 for only 103,000 pesos to a member of the Martínez de la Torre family. Sánchez considered the sale a theft. The once-prominent banker and estate owner was left to live on 330 pesos monthly from the new owner. That might have funded a quiet retirement, but Sánchez owed 180 pesos monthly to creditors. The remaining 150 pesos was less than the manager of a small estate might earn at Chalco. Sánchez lost his place among the landed few.[63]

Adaptation to Crisis: Sharecropping

Facing political disruptions, financial exactions, and communities retrenched in autonomies, estates at Chalco and across the heartland turned to sharecropping. They aimed to cut costs while maintaining production; tenants, often villagers, took over planting and harvesting and gained half the crop. Estates might profit for little expense; villagers gained new control of production—reinforcing autonomies. In times of instability and commercial uncertainty, sharecropping kept estate production and community life going—and linked. New instabilities came to already-stressed ties of symbiotic exploitation.

Sharecropping was rare at Chalco and across the heartland during eighteenth-century times of silver boom and the early adaptations to collapse. The first reference to the practice there came in 1856—before the Lerdo Law—when the manager at Asunción reported that sharecroppers planted part of the estate's maize and all its labor-intensive beans and chickpeas. In 1858, the manager at Buenavista gloated that he had avoided capture by political opponents by posing as a sharecropper.[64] At Asunción in 1867–68, as the liberals resumed national rule, sharecroppers planted half the estate's maize, but harvested only a fourth of its crop. Riva Palacio kept irrigated fields for estate cultivation, allocating rain-fed plots to village sharecroppers. Scarce rains left them with small yields. All the estate's beans and chickpeas remained with sharecroppers. Most revealing, share deals were done not with individuals, but with communities and brokered by local leaders.[65] Sharecropping reinforced notables' power, increased villagers' plantings and autonomies, potentially strengthening symbiotic exploitations.

The great Jalpa estate north of Mexico City, owned by heirs of the Conde de Regla, also turned to sharecropping in the midcentury crisis. In a long report to Riva Palacio, then overseeing Regla family affairs, the manager at Jalpa detailed how the estate lacked funds to hire hands to plant and harvest in a timely way. Men in nearby villages would not come without immediate cash payment. The result was a self-reinforcing cycle of unprofitability. Riva Palacio understood; he had seen it all at Chalco. The manager at Jalpa tried leasing maize lands to cash tenants in the 1850s. But uncertain rains and weak markets led tenants to feed families first. By 1865, they owed 4,406 pesos in back rents. The year before, sharecroppers had raised fifty-eight percent of Jalpa's maize; by 1866 they planted seventy-two percent.[66]

In contrast with Chalco estates, Jalpa contracted for shares with individuals, not communities. There, sharecropping dispersed costs, difficulties, and potential profits among diverse dependents—and a few villagers.[67] An 1866 inventory lists ninety-eight men: fifty-one employees and forty-seven sharecroppers, with twenty holding both roles. A group of fifteen were managers and major croppers: nine gained salaries of 200 to 300 pesos yearly; thirteen harvested from 200 to over 2,000 fanegas of maize, delivering half to the estate, keeping the rest for sustenance and sale. They were commercial growers supplying local markets and Mexico City. Salaries as managers funded crops; with good rains they might prosper.

Less favored but solidly comfortable was a group of fifty-five men and boys, including twenty-eight employees and thirty-nine croppers who gained salaries of 40 to 100 pesos yearly and harvested 50 to 250 fanegas of maize. Most were part of clans mixing multiple employments and share tenancies. Jalpa's fifty-five leading sharecroppers planted maize that would yield 13,000 fanegas in an average year—the croppers keeping half, the estate gaining the rest to market at little cost. The general manager and leading sharecropper gained an ample salary, 25 fanegas in annual maize rations, and kept 1,000 fanegas from most harvests. Again, the manager gained more than the owner in difficult commercial times.

Few of the favored croppers were villagers. A group of eleven men based in nearby communities did plant maize that would bring in 25 to 100 fanegas; most harvested 50 to 70. Their shares would average 25 to 35 fanegas; after families consumed 10 to 12 they had a bit to sell in local markets. Another small group retained a scarce security at Jalpa. They were not sharecroppers, but employees: six adults gained 48.5 pesos yearly and 12.5 fanegas of maize rations; six boys got 24 pesos and 6 fanegas. Descendants of *gañanes*, they remained estate dependents (none had surnames in 1866; all other estate employees, croppers, and villagers did, a sign of hispanization). The ex-*gañanes* were six fathers and six sons; six patriarchal households each earned nearly 75 pesos plus over 18 fanegas of maize—solid sustenance in the rural heartland, a rare security in trying times.

The 1866 Jalpa inventory documents a dispersal of maize production that brought commercial opportunity to a few and solid sustenance to more. It does not detail labor relations. Fewer than a dozen villagers gained lands in shares, while the labor needs of planting, cultivating, and harvesting 13,000 fanegas of maize remained large and seasonal. Inevitably, village workers still came to plant and harvest. Were they still organized in gangs led by local captains? A semblance of symbiotic exploitation held on. But the shift from one major employer to dozens of share tenants dispersed and complicated labor relations in ways we cannot see. Before, one employer recruited in many villages; now there were more employers than communities and labor gangs. Did labor power shift to favor villages with lands and cohesion? The dispersal of planting brought new potential for conflicts among sharecroppers competing for labor and communities pressing for advantage.

Estate financial difficulties and the shift to sharecropping brought gains to many communities. At the same time, instabilities rattled ties of symbiotic exploitation and land conflicts persisted. At Amecameca, in the Chalco uplands below Popocatépetl, one suit dates to 1744, then pitting a community facing population growth against the hacienda San Antonio Abad and the rancho San Pedro Matrir in the years that estates began commercial cropping of maize.[68] In 1833, local families protested the cession of *montes*, wooded uplands, to the estates by the *regidor decano* (senior councilman) at Amecameca. Details are hazy, but the councilman and landlords surely aimed to gain amid the commercial difficulties in the 1830s.[69] The estates and the disputed lands passed in 1855 to Diego Arróyave and his brothers in another debt adjudication. Then, in 1860, amid the waning conflicts of the War of Reform, villagers entered the *montes* to cut firewood and make lumber. The Arróyaves' manager demanded "repression of the abuses"; new officials at Amecameca declared the lands "community property."[70] In new times of community assertion, villagers invaded lands and local leaders backed them. (The maize lands and parish church at upland Amecameca are shown in figures 8.1 and 8.2, respectively.)

The proprietors won in court in March of 1860. Fearing resistance, the Amecameca council, the state of Mexico, and the local *jefe político* joined to block implementation. The Arróyave brothers returned to court and won an order confirming their rights in August of 1865— under Maximilian. Still unable to enforce their claim, they published the original sentence and its reaffirmation. They called their opponents "the so-called community of Amecameca." The town could not hold the

FIGURE 8.1. Maize in the Chalco uplands.

FIGURE 8.2. The church at Amecameca: center of the Chalco uplands.

lands because no community legally held land in 1865. Yet in the verdict, the judge described the plaintiffs as "the community and citizens of the pueblo of Amecameca." Even as he ruled against it, the judge recognized the community as a rightful participant in the suit. In 1865, the right to community property remained unsettled and Amecameca kept the *montes* the judge had awarded to litigious landlords.

The law and the courts might deny Amecameca and other communities' rights to lands; on the ground, Chalco villagers kept community holdings and expanded production by sharecropping fields the estates could not make profitable. Community autonomies were reinforced (despite liberal legislation); symbiotic exploitations linking estates that needed workers and villagers who needed wages persisted. They also destabilized as entrepreneurs lacked cash to pay wages and villagers increased planting in share deals.

Rebellion, 1868

In June of 1867 liberal armies retook Mexico City, soon followed by Juárez and his government. Occupying the capital did not guarantee effective rule, even in regions as close as Chalco. Political conflicts calmed with the departure of French armies, the ouster and execution of Maximilian, and the marginalization of conservatives. Liberals led the regime with little opposition. Still, communities at Chalco, across the heartland, and beyond challenged the restored republic and its vision of liberal reform.

Liberals in power remained convinced of the need to privatize community lands. Should villagers resist, and liberals knew they would, police power would respond.[71] As political wars waned, the restored regime focused on social control. Still, the forces of coercion remained limited. When in their last drive to power liberals levied a final forced loan on Chalco estates, struggling operators again insisted they could not pay—likely true.[72] As liberals again revealed their staunch goals and limited powers, Chalco communities took arms to challenge local estates as 1868 began.

Planning began at Acuautla. Early meetings were in the home of Viviano Anaya, a leader of the earlier protests against Zoquiapan's land-taking to expand its irrigation, and said to be responsible for the death of the estate manager in 1851. Old grievances were clearly in play. So were new participants and ideologies. A proclamation issued on February 2 by Julio López made that clear. Declaring himself a "true liberal and patriot," he had fought for the liberal cause. Claiming no grievance against the regime, he called for rebellion against Chalco estates.[73] López had been an estate employee near Texcoco, joined the liberal army to oust the French, and then allied with radical activist Plotino Rhodakanaty, an exile from Europe's social wars. He promoted anarchist visions easily seen as taking liberalism to its logical end of stateless freedom.[74] The French occupation was a project of Napoleon III, his power forged in the revolutionary cruci-ble of 1848—conflicts that generated Marxism and other radical visions.[75] In 1868 France's occupation had ended; radical dreams remained.

They found fertile ground in Chalco communities.[76] Historical con-flicts in defense of lands and autonomies drove grievances. López brought new organization. A report sent to Riva Palacio on February 4, two days after López's first proclamation, told of "terrorists" numbering sixty or seventy men, backed by villagers from Coatepec to Huexoculco in the uplands east of Chalco. Acuautla was the heart of the uprising (the view from its *montes*, communal uplands, is shown in figure 8.3). The report concluded by noting surprise at the lack of pillaging and violence.[77] López's proclamation emphasized support for the liberal regime, calling it to mediate between Chalco communities and estates. By February 18, authorities in Mexico City had rejected the invitation, sending fifty troops to pursue the rebels.[78] Four days later the manager at La Compañía reported that the active rebels remained a small band of leaders plus a few bandits. The *gente de a pie*—the men who came on foot to labor—had not taken arms.[79] Limited numbers enabled guerrilla mobility that proved frustrating to the troops.

On February 23, López issued a second proclamation calling communities to unite to regain lands usurped by predatory estates. He argued that the long custom of looking to the courts only led to unfulfilled

FIGURE 8.3. Acuautla's uplands: defended against liberal assaults,
1845–70 (now invaded by metropolitan sprawl).

promises—while communities lost time and money.[80] The same day, he sent a warning to the troops, ordering them to leave the region or face dire consequences. Rebels and printed broadsides circulated through towns, villages, and estates across Chalco, offering land to those who took arms or provided sustenance, threatening death to all in opposition. The manager at La Compañía reported that his employees feigned illness or fled. He called for more troops.[81]

With the military patrolling Chalco, López found many sympathizers but few ready to take arms. His mobile band was reduced to fewer than twenty men as February ended. Confident the rising was waning, the troops left. The first days of March were uneasy for estate managers. They heard rumors that General Miguel Negrete, a radical liberal, directed the rising, though there was no evidence. Troops gone, rebel ranks rose again, responding to offers of estate lands. Most worrisome, the insurgents remained model rebels: there was no vandalism, no random violence. They were well sustained by sympathetic villagers.[82]

The troops returned, led by battle-tested liberal General Rafael Cuellar. On March 6, leaders at Acuautla issued a proclamation of grievances and proposed solutions. They detailed their long conflict with Zoquiapan; they had repeatedly produced titles to disputed lands, but "justice always favored the powerful." As recently as 1862, under liberal rule, four village leaders had taken claims to court—to be arrested and drafted into the army. They were sure that if President Juárez knew the facts, he would disapprove. A special court should review Chalco land titles; estates must present their documents first; during the review neither estates nor villagers would use disputed lands.[83] The people of Acuautla called for judicial mediation, a memory from times of silver boom and landed republics.

López backed their call on March 7. As "representative by unanimous vote" of the pueblos of Chalco, he insisted that rebellion was necessary only because local judges had become landlord agents. His claim to election was likely true: a gathering of two delegates from each Chalco community had met on March 4.[84] The authorities again turned to force.

Skirmishing between rebels and troops continued, with few direct confrontations and few casualties. On March 12, Cuellar met with López, offering guarantees if the rebels would lay down arms in surrender. López asked for twelve hours to consider the proposal, and at the appointed hour marched on Tlalmanalco with 150 armed men. Cuellar's troops answered with fire and most of the rebels turned in retreat, firing at random as they dispersed into the uplands.[85] A few Chalco villagers were ready to take arms; more supplied the rebels. But with limited training and few weapons, very few were ready to face hardened troops. Guerrilla resistance continued, sustained by local communities.

Recognizing his weakness, on March 14 López again proclaimed that he had no quarrel with the government, only Chalco estate operators. The regime recognized no such distinction. With little room to maneuver, on March 19 López and twenty-five men surrendered in exchange for safe-conduct passes and the right to return home.[86] Three days later a group of communities issued a proclamation. They blamed López for the uprising, but added that he gained support because of the "misery and misfortunes" imposed by "ambitious landlords who possess the lands of the towns in which we were born, community water supplies, and woodlands and pastures that are ours." Landlords had been enabled by "the tolerance and ignorance of our fathers and grandfathers" who had wasted years working in legal channels ruled by landlords. Community leaders insisted they opposed the uprising, yet argued that the only way to avoid violence was for the government to lead an impartial examination of land titles followed by a survey of Chalco properties. They demanded a mediating state.[87]

The town leaders said nothing about privatization. Did they believe that with a fair recognition of community land rights, privatization was acceptable, perhaps favorable to local notables who would gain title to ample shares?[88] Chalco was calm in April and May. Officials and estate managers believed the troops had frightened most villagers. One official toured communities, reprimanding them for rebel sympathies. And a few local merchants began to claim lands under the Lerdo Law.[89] What landlords, officials, and merchants did not see was that rebels took the amnesty so villagers could plant. Sustenance came first.

With planting completed—on village milpas and estate fields (gaining villagers cash incomes)—López rose up again on May 29. Officials in Mexico City were deluged with pleas from estate owners, managers, and officials for troops.[90] Seeking wider support, López turned to communities on the plain. Villagers there lived close by the richest haciendas and depended on them for land and labor. Few had risen up earlier. Now, people at Zula near Asunción and San Gregorio Cuautzingo by La Compañía joined. Managers got messages from López declaring pastures and woodlands community property; villagers would no longer pay rents.[91] The *montes*, last resort of autonomous sustenance, focused the conflict.

By June 4, López led forty mounted rebels and an equal number on foot. Officials and managers were certain they gained support and sustenance from villagers. Estate owners and managers began to pack valuables and head to the city.[92] National officials took no chances when they sent troops on June 7. By June 13, there were 400 in the region, another 150 on the way. From June 9 to 18, they chased rebels across the uplands separating Chalco from the Puebla basin to the east. For a time, the chase favored López; his rebel band passed 100 men. They knew the woods; in early skirmishes, they left behind a few casualties and retreated into the mountains. Then on June 17, seasoned troops captured 50 insurgents near Acuautla. López escaped, but the rebel force never recovered.[93]

Communities that had backed the uprising turned to seeking lenient treatment. On June 26, leaders at Acuautla, Coatepec, and San Pablo proclaimed their people "peaceful and hardworking men" caught in a judicial dispute with the Zoquiapan estate. They had been attacked by troops and did not deserve severe punishment. The government ignored their pleas. Captives presumed rebel supporters were forced into the army. Leaders and armed fighters, including one woman, faced exile to Yucatán.[94] On July 7, López was captured. After quick consultation with Defense Minister Ignacio Mejía, he was executed without trial. Two weeks later, the same fate befell Adelaido Amaro, who had tried to carry on. Villagers appealed sentences to military service and labor in Yucatán to President Juárez; he upheld nearly all; those sentenced to Yucatán sailed in October from Veracruz.[95]

The Chalco uprising of 1868 found wide support in communities facing simmering grievances as liberals returned to national power. Still, the rebel force never exceeded 150. A government free of political wars sent troops sufficient to crush the uprising after six months. And military force was not the rebels' only powerful opponent. The summer of 1868 brought a drought that promised months of scarcity to Chalco villagers.[96] In the face of armed power and looming scarcities, most turned to the daily challenges of survival.

Troops stayed at Chalco to the end of the year. Early in 1869, having taken pay for harvesting at La Compañía, villagers at San Gregorio Cuautzingo rose up again to claim lands held by the estate that shadowed their lives. Symbiotic exploitation had broken. Their neighbors did not join and defeat came swiftly.[97] Chalco stayed calm in the fall of 1869, when communities in the new state of Morelos just south, in the Mezquital to the north, and across Puebla just east, rose up to attack haciendas. They too had ideological leaders; Francisco Islas proclaimed a "communist plan" in the Mezquital. Troops restored order by January 1870.[98] The liberal regime became a state with the power to impose its rule.

The rebels of 1869 shared key grievances with the Chalco villagers who rebelled a year earlier; the second wave extended across wider areas of the heartland. The difference lay in their timing in the agricultural cycle so central to community life. Called by López just after completing the 1867–68 harvest, Chalco rebels faced both government troops and drought in the summer of 1868. The wider uprisings of 1869 came after the scarcities of 1868 had heightened the challenges of village life—and as the good crop of 1869 stood in the fields, ripe for taking by rebels.[99] The second round of heartland uprisings proved longer and more threatening. The cycles of an uncertain nature still shaped life on the land; the state and its troops eventually prevailed. Still, heartland uprisings begun at Chalco in 1868 convinced the liberal regime to slow and negotiate their program of privatizations.

Victories in Defeat

Since the collapse of silver capitalism, estate financial woes had kept profits scarce, reinforcing community autonomies, forcing higher wages and guaranteed maize rations—all inhibiting estate attempts to return to profitability. Innovating in search of profit from the 1840s, estates claimed community lands, closed uplands, charged for their use, and sought police protections they could not fund; liberals aimed to weaken communities by privatizing community lands, hoping to enforce the program with coercions they too could not fund. The courts, key mediators in earlier times, became agents of landed proprietors; communities demanded a return to fair mediation. The labor relations tying estates and villagers together persisted through the middle of the nineteenth century, reinforced by new sharecropping. It was the threat of privatization and the end of state mediation that turned communities to direct resistance. They failed in 1868, yet made their interests clear.

The 1868 uprising kept estates in financial difficulties—a small victory. In the years that followed, as mining rose and industries expanded, bankrupt Chalco estate owners offered properties for sale. Many found no one willing or able to buy, offered to sell parcels, and still found no buyers. Landowners unable to pay taxes saw the state that had fought to protect their estates take them to auction—with few bidders into the 1870s.[100] The uprising prolonged and deepened the long nineteenth-century crisis of estate operation at Chalco.

Soon the crisis claimed its most prominent victim: Mariano Riva Palacio. With mounting debts and sparse income, in 1870 the aging liberal patriarch sold the estates centered at Asunción to Felipe Berriozábal, once their manager. With little capital, Berriozábal became the owner by paying only 4,000 pesos, while recognizing 78,000 pesos owed to Riva Palacio and another 38,000 pesos due the Garrido sisters. The new owner took on a huge debt, while dealing with communities quick to press their interests.

Early in 1871, Berriozábal complained that his small earnings could not cover the debts owed Riva Palacio and the Garridos; the new owner hung on until 1873 and then defaulted. The courts would auction the estates; if bids were low, as Berriozábal expected, the properties would revert to Riva Palacio—who did not want to regain their liabilities. Berriozábal pleaded for a deal.[101] That is the last reference to Chalco estates in the Riva Palacio papers. By 1890, all the properties once owned by Riva Palacio belonged to a new generation of entrepreneurs who bought estates cheaply after 1870, to find profit in times of political stability and commercial opportunity under Porfirio Díaz.[102]

Did Chalco villagers find satisfaction in the fall of Riva Palacio? An 1890 survey of Chalco landholding revealed two greater triumphs. First, estates had increased their holdings little over the course of the nineteenth century. Many gained a bit to expand irrigation, but overall boundaries changed little. And lands portrayed as community domain still surrounded every estate.[103] Liberal privatization was the law; Chalco villagers retained most of their once-community domains. What the boundaries did not show was that privatizations led to concentrations within communities as populations grew. Landless men searched for work as estates turned to mechanization. A new and different crisis would lead many to revolution after 1910.

CHAPTER NINE

Carrying Capitalism into Revolution

MAKING ZAPATISTA COMMUNITIES, 1870–1920

EVERYTHING SEEMED to change at Chalco and across the southern heartland after 1870. Political peace set in under Porfirio Díaz; commercial ways energized. In an apparent continuity, villagers still mixed local cultivation and estate labor in ties that for a time appeared to revive historic symbiotic exploitations. Yet after 1910, Chalco villagers joined their neighbors in Morelos and the southern Valley of Toluca in violence without local precedent—conflicts reminiscent of the insurgencies that rattled the Mezquital and transformed the Bajío a century earlier.

How did political stabilization and capitalist dynamism lead to Zapata's revolution? Population grew, privatization concentrated land within communities, and mechanization limited chances to labor. With land and labor scarce for growing numbers, symbiotic exploitations eroded, as did men's chances to provide as patriarchs. Families and communities struggled while facing corrosive internal violence, including a rising tide of infant deaths plaguing newborn girls. When the commercial crisis of 1907 came followed by subsistence crisis in 1908–9 and political crisis in 1910–11, the violence rising in families and communities turned outward against those who ruled—landlords and the regime that sustained them.

When we understand patriarchy as the social cement that historically organized production and inequalities in heartland communities, we can see the complex changes that provoked violence within communities after 1880 and fueled revolutionary conflicts after 1910. Zapata's men fought for land, autonomies—and patriarchy. A moral utopia of landed communities legitimated revolutionary uprisings; men fighting for that goal presumed patriarchy a birthright. Contradictions defined the revolution that challenged agro-industrial capitalism in Mexico's heartland. The insurrection famously led by Emiliano Zapata began in sugar-growing Morelos; it expanded to raise men and sustenance in nearby highlands, across Chalco, and in the southern Valley of Toluca. Economic dynamism drove social polarizations; communities and families struggled to sustain growing numbers while land concentrated and work became scarce. A plague of social violence struck southern heartland communities until men turned to revolution. In the end many gained land and a renewed patriarchy; autonomous communities proved harder to build.

Porfirian Peace and Liberal Capitalism

Many indigenous men and communities across the heartland supported Porfirio Díaz when he took arms to claim power in 1876. The celebrated general had led the fight to oust the French; he promoted commercial development and promised municipal autonomy; he demanded "effective suffrage, no re-election." His promoters in the state of Mexico, mostly military men, promised that Díaz would fix injustices in land privatization; some claimed he would redistribute estate lands. They knew how to raise support in the rural heartland. Once president in 1877, however, Díaz turned against the radicals who had helped bring him to power and away from the promises of autonomy and land redistribution that had mobilized community support.

The late 1870s brought new political conflicts. Díaz worked to consolidate liberal programs and exclusions while many former supporters—generals, ideologues, and communities—demanded that he back liberties, municipal autonomies, and community rights to land and legal personality. They organized leagues of communities pursuing a hybrid vision of sovereignty and justice that might be called liberal communalism—reminiscent of Juan Álvarez's earlier vision. Landlords and Díaz maligned it as communism. Officials saw rebellion and threats of "caste war." Violence came as pre-emptive repression by local and state powers.[1]

By 1880 Díaz had consolidated a regime at once liberal in economic goals, authoritarian at the heights of power, yet ready to negotiate locally to keep order and seek capitalist prosperity.[2] The state promoted market production and private investment, Mexican and foreign; it subsidized railroads, privatized public and community lands, and promised education. By the 1880s, success seemed everywhere: rail lines drove across the landscape, industry and laboring communities proliferated, commercial cultivation boomed. Mexico City and provincial towns reveled in urban improvements: new shops, services, and schools.[3] The community resistance of the 1860s and 1870s was contained by state power, local negotiations, and economic revival.

Commercial openings and political stability returned the heartland to peace and production, for a time. After 1880, entrepreneurs, growing urban middle sectors, rural big men, and some factory workers found new prosperity. In heartland communities, the regime pressed privatization. In the state of Mexico, as elsewhere, many of the lands that sustained family crops were privatized between 1868 and 1880, with or without formal titles. Legally, communities could no longer defend lands in dispute; only individuals could go before the courts—though to keep the peace the restriction was negotiated. A second round of privatizations after 1880 turned uplands and forests long open to community use into private holdings subject to restrictions and fees for access. The outcome almost everywhere was the concentration of cultivatable lands and uplands as property of village big men, limiting access to both as population grew.[4] A new generation of local notables began to find profit serving nearby estates. Rather than defend community lands in court, they accumulated private property; they profited by renting land to the landless and by taking fees for access to uplands once open to all. The republics that had organized community life to sustain silver capitalism to the end of the eighteenth century were stratified within, but local notables' power and prosperity required defense of community lands and village laborers. After privatizations, stratification deepened while big men gained lands and profit, and at times became agents of estate interests.

Morelos: Sugar and the Search for New Symbiotic Exploitations

Morelos focused on sugar, the most labor-intensive and industrial of crops. Cane required eighteen months from labor-intensive planting, through long weeks of irrigation and cultivation, to a more labor-intensive, often maiming harvest—the last driven by the need to get cane to the mill quickly, to begin an intense process of refining. The need for skilled workers to oversee a complex process and run the mills demanded a core of permanent hands: early on often enslaved Africans, later their free mulatto descendants. The large numbers of seasonal workers needed to

MAP 11. The southern heartland, 1870–1920.

plant, water, cultivate, harvest, and transport cane were historically drawn from communities in the basin and nearby uplands.[5]

With the collapse of silver and commercial cultivation after 1810, sugar growers and villagers across Morelos began decades of jostling that planters saw as assaults by unruly and too-independent communities.[6] With the peace of Porfirio after 1870, Morelos communities lived with concentrations of privatized lands and accelerating population growth, while sugar production surged—sustained by expanding irrigation and new mechanization. An agro-industrial boom remade relations with Morelos villages, stabilizing in a new facsimile of symbiotic exploitation until everything collapsed in revolution.[7]

Land planted in cane increased from 3,500 hectares in 1869 to 10,000 hectares by 1909; sugar harvests grew five times over. The increases did not come from radical extensions of estate landholding, but from new irrigation to plant cane in fields earlier sown with maize. Estates did gain land to extend irrigation, often by purchasing privatized community properties, sometimes by usurpation. The increased production came from new water control and new ways of mechanized refining, incorporating US technologies first proven in Cuba. Rail links built in the 1880s cut delivery costs to Mexico City. The collapse of Cuban sugar production in the 1890s during its war for independence (and US intervention) opened export markets for planters on Mexico's Gulf coast, leaving Morelos growers dominant in the interior.

Cane cultivation boomed as machines took over much of refining—saving labor—and railroads took over transportation—saving labor. The populations of estate *reales* (communities of permanent workers) declined twenty-five percent, while Cubans were recruited to bring skills to new refineries (and a few Japanese came to tend gardens for mill owners). The need for permanent workers paid secure earnings, always limited, shrank while the call for seasonal hands to do the hardest and most dangerous work rose. The challenge was to keep them available and affordable when needed—and alive and nearby when not.

The population of Morelos, most living in communities, grew from 120,000 in 1870 to 180,000 in 1910, generating growing numbers of potential workers. The privatization of village lands brought concentrations in the hands of local merchants and moneylenders, leaving more men land-poor or landless, increasing their need for seasonal labor. Yet Morelos planters did not simply prey on desperation. Recalling the local protests in the 1840s and 1850s, the Chalco uprising of the 1860s, and the persistent banditry of famous highland *plateados*, they engineered new symbiotic exploitations. They leased lands not open to cane to village big men, who allotted them in share tenancies to village men in need of land and maize. They made local big men and many of the poor dependent on estate lands, the former to profit, the latter to survive.[8]

Growing numbers of land-poor and landless men and boys might serve estates as essential seasonal hands—but to be available, flexible, and affordable (meaning poor and cheap) they had to stay in the villages. For the estates, the solution seemed easy: lease lands to village big men, who added the title *arrendatario* to roles as merchants, lenders, and political bosses. They sublet to village men who became *patrones de la milpa* (patriarchs of the cornfield), who in turn took on adult *gañanes* and young *peones* who labored for shares of the crop.

A new hierarchy of patriarchy tied villagers directly to estates, consolidating the rule of local big men, allowing maize plots to growing numbers of men and boys, keeping the latter available for estate labor on demand. Estates took half the maize crop for no cost; sold in Mexico City, it was the second source of profit after sugar. Local big men gained maize to sell in local markets (at times in the capital, too): they gained direct shares from the *patrones*, they leased plow teams (grazed on former community lands) for additional shares, they advanced maize to *patrones*, *gañanes*, and peones during the months of scarcity before the harvest—and took double in return. The new hierarchy of sharecropping brought estates maize and profit—and kept workers dependent and available. It served village big men by diversifying their profits and bolstering their power— and tying them to the estates. It gave a generation of *patrones*, often retaining some privatized land, access to more. It provided *gañanes* and peones, usually landless fathers and sons, access to land and maize—a remnant of autonomy to sustain families and community ties.

It was a new, patriarchal, symbiotic exploitation—with a fundamental difference. During centuries of Spanish rule and silver capitalism, notables and commoners had cultivated lands that were community domain. Notables ruled councils that organized community religious and political life; they held ample areas of land they planted to profit; they organized gangs to labor seasonally at nearby estates. And they led communities in defending their lands, rights, and autonomies in the courts. Before 1810, notables' powers were grounded in the republics, sanctioned and facilitated by a regime that recognized their rights and roles. They could operate as brokers in service of autonomous communities.

With independence in the 1820s, municipal councils were no longer the exclusive domain of indigenous notables. With the privatization of lands after 1870, they accumulated property free of community constraints—and of obligation to defend community domains. They accumulated land and livestock and local market controls to serve themselves; they took roles as *arrendatarios* to serve themselves and estates. The new symbiotic exploitation offered villagers becoming landless a chance to cultivate maize, feed families, maintain communities, and labor for minimal wages in cane harvests. They survived, subsidizing estate profits with cheap labor and free maize. But it was a symbiotic exploitation bereft of community autonomies on the land, stripped of community political rights, and weak in access to courts—built to serve estate power. It generated profit and social stability as long as sugar markets held strong. When Cuban exports revived around 1905 (ruled by US producers and favored in US markets), followed by the Mexican recession set off by the US panic of 1907 and the drought of 1908–9, markets for Morelos sugar shrank. Harvests fell seven percent from 1909 to 1910, bringing unemployment and insecurity to a growing generation of landless men.

Growing Up Landless: Rosendo Rojas, Pedro Martínez, and Filomena, 1890–1910

A new generation of men and women came of age in Morelos around 1900. Few had claims to family lands; access to estate land on shares had become scarce. Growing numbers competed for labor at sugar estates— where mechanization kept demand low and seasonal, and shrinking in the crises after 1905. The new century brought new pressures on young lives; accommodations mixed exploitations and insecurities, as three life histories show.

Rosendo Rojas was born in Tlayacapan, in the highlands between Morelos and Chalco, in 1875. His father held two plots of land that he cultivated with four sons. Far from the sugar fields below, Tlayacapan kept more land than most communities, with some irrigation. Rosendo's family raised maize to eat, fruit and chile for market. But the family land would not provide for four adult sons. In 1900, Rosendo, then twenty-five, married Heliodora, ten years younger. Unable to support a new household by helping his father, Rosendo headed to the hot country in search of work in the cane, because "the best local plots—most formerly community property—were in the hands of the local rich." At first he found work as a day laborer paid by the task. When he worked, the estate paid *tlacualeros* to carry tortillas from wives at home. When he did not work, Rosendo had to pay. Struggling with that insecurity, Rosendo signed on as a *gañan*, gaining access to land, a team, and maize on shares. A more secure dependence brought basic sustenance and kept him in the lowlands for weeks on end.

With patriarchy stretched to its limits, geographically and economically, Heliodora took advantage of a life often alone in Tlayacapan to claim a new role. She began to buy, roast, and grind coffee raised in neighbors' house lots, selling first in a corner of the plaza, then in a market stall. She earned enough to buy a plot of land from an uncle without heirs. Mixing lowland sharecropping and labor with highland marketing and cultivation (thanks to Heliodora), the couple struggled on to 1910.[9]

Pedro Martínez (a pseudonym) was younger, born in 1889 at Tepoztlán, a community nestled in a narrow valley where the Sierra de Ajusco meets the Morelos lowlands. He told in the 1940s how he had grown up landless and without a stable family, struggling to survive before 1910.[10] Pedro's father died three months after his birth; his mother left with another man when Pedro was but eighteen months old, leaving him in the care of her mother and sister. Pedro's grandfather, father, and uncles made tiles; they spoke *mexicano* (Nahuatl). "They didn't plant because they had no land." His grandmother and aunt "provided for me out of what they had," until they sent him at three to live with his godmother because "she was a little better off." His grandmother was a midwife and healer, giving massages at childbirth, cures when needed. She found a little income grinding maize for families with absent mothers. His aunt gathered fruit and mushrooms she sold to survive. All the women who cared for him saw men come and go.[11] Patriarchy was an ideal for Pedro—but not a reality in his early life.

Looking back, he understood the powers that limited his life: "There was much hunger in those days because the rich didn't allow the poor to plant on the communal hillsides. The rich [men] who lived in the center were called *caciques* because they were the kings here. Only the *caciques* planted the good valley land. When the destitute ones who had no land began to make clearings in the hills, the *caciques* said, 'We can't allow the poor to have their own cornfields, because then we won't have *peones* to work for us.'" Pedro faced concentration of once community lands, leaving village big men powerful and prejudicing others' lives. The caciques paid miserable wages and kept people alive by lending small sums in trying times, dependence Pedro resented.[12]

At seven he went to live with cousins, caring for oxen. Later, his mother came, "well dressed, with shoes and everything." She took him to live with a stepfather at Yautepec. There, he went to school (insulted as an "Indian") and began to work in the fields. He began making eighteen centavos daily; older boys made thirty-seven. Over the years he worked at Oacalco, Temixco, Chiconcuac, San Gaspar, and Hospital; with age, experience, and some Spanish he earned fifty centavos daily. He only finished one year of school, but did learn to read. Life taught him hard lessons.[13]

"In the *tortillería*, where my mother made *tortillas*, I noticed that many women, and men too, came there and got together. They whispered to each other and made signs and stroked each other, and then a couple would go to a room and lock the door, or they would go outside." Work at the *tortillería* earned his mother one and a half pesos a day; his stepfather gained only thirty-seven centavos daily in the fields—when there was work. The impositions of the *tortillería* and uncertain employment in the fields at Yautepec led them back to Tepoztlán. There, Pedro noted with pleasure that he ceased to be an *indio* and became a ladino—thanks to good Spanish and the ability to read.[14]

Neither brought secure work or solid income. Shortly after returning to Tepoztlán, a labor recruiter asked Pedro to join a crew heading to San Gaspar. On the road, he learned that the gang aimed to steal 8,000 pesos at the estate. Pedro fled and headed to work at another estate. At seventeen he got access to a small plot to plant maize; meanwhile "I worked hard at the haciendas and gave all my money to my mother. . . . In 1910, I began to look for a bride." It was time to become a man.[15]

Yet 1910 brought promise laced with difficulties. "My stepfather and I were planting our own corn for the first time, on a hillside belonging to the hacienda de Atlihuayán. Many of us who worked as *peones* on the *hacienda* asked to plant on unused land." But the land was an eight-hour walk from town, keeping men away all week, only coming home on Sundays. Still it was an opportunity opened just as Pedro's mother died. He met Esperanza, equally poor. She reported: "My papa was a field hand; my mother worked at gleaning fields." On marriage, "I took responsibility for everything in the house." Pedro recalled differently: "My wife didn't know how to do anything, not even to cut a piece of clothing. . . . Esperanza couldn't cook either, or even sweep . . . I showed her how."[16]

Pedro presumed to be patriarch, yet spent much time away from home. "I worked on my *tlacolol* (hillside plot) and became a *tlacolero*. It was harder work to plant on the hillside than to work at the hacienda. But I liked it very much." He cherished the chance to raise maize. He was home enough to father a child, who came as news arrived of revolution in the north. Pedro's stepfather went to work at Yautepec, leaving Pedro and Esperanza to face uncertain times.[17]

Filomena was born around 1900 in a village in Guerrero, just south of Morelos. In her telling of her early life, while men faced the breakdown of patriarchal provision, women endured worse. Her father died when she was three, leaving a wife and two young daughters small plots of land and a few animals. Filomena's mother sold them, adding to concentration in the community. In Filomena's eyes, her mother "used the money to run around and have a good time, to go to Acapulco." A single mother in a collapsing community engaged in serial relationships with men to sustain herself. Young Filomena passed from family to family; she remembered repeated beatings as she learned to sustain herself; beginning to work at eight, she got one and a quarter pesos monthly by rising at two in the morning to grind maize so others could have their daily tortillas. Her mother came in and out of her life; later a brother offered refuge while he tried to reclaim their father's lands—a last chance at household patriarchy. For Filomena, life before 1910 was a time of insecurity, family breakdown, violence, and a search for autonomy. While her mother turned to men to survive and her brother sought a piece of land, Filomena focused on grinding sustenance.[18]

Rosendo Rojas, living in upland Tlayacapan, came of age before 1900 and juggled cultivation and labor to sustain a young family—in good part thanks to Heliodora's marketing. Pedro Martínez, from Tepoztlán on the edge of the lowlands, lived more insecure struggles to survive and form a family as 1910 approached. Filomena, a girl without a father and with a mother dealing with many men, faced beatings in many households while she tried to find a way to live. Their personal trials reflect social trajectories that were prejudicing lives across the southern heartland.

Chalco and Tenango del Valle: Corroding Autonomy and Patriarchy

The high plains at Chalco and Tenango del Valle, just north of Morelos, remained Mexico City's granaries, supplying wheat, maize, and more. There, too, great majorities still lived in communities after 1870 as populations grew, land concentrated, and estates began to mechanize. Villagers faced agro-industrial transformations parallel to those in Morelos. Lives of landlessness, insecurity, and threats to patriarchy drove a common search for labor that brought heartland men and boys together searching for work in Morelos before 1910—and in revolution soon after.

A modernizing state of Mexico compiled statistics that documented commercial boom, corrosions of patriarchy, rising violence within families and communities, and an escalation of infant death that mostly struck newborn girls—all accelerating around 1900.[19] They detail the consequences of capitalist accelerations on community life at Chalco and Tenango del Valle, regions of strong Zapatista uprisings.[20] The recollections of people who lived liberal development and then revolution at Xalatlaco, in the uplands between Tenango and Morelos, bring the mix of economic concentrations, family struggles, and escalating violence into vivid focus.[21]

Sustained population growth underlay everything; it expanded markets and laboring populations—and made land scarce for growing numbers. From 1870 to 1900, the population of the state of Mexico grew forty-four percent, the Tenango district forty-six percent, and Chalco forty-nine percent.[22] The great majority remained in rural towns and villages: at Chalco ninety-four percent in 1877, still ninety percent in 1900. Towns grew larger, but the largest, the district seat, barely exceeded 8,000 residents in 1900. The population living at estates fell from five to four percent in the same years. Two factory towns, the textile center at Miraflores and the paper mill at upland San Rafael, included four percent of Chalco's people in 1900. Chalco remained a place of villagers in 1900.[23] Tenango was similar, with but one small factory. Across the southern heartland, people in small towns and smaller villages faced a nearly fifty-percent increase in population in the decades before 1910.

Meanwhile, privatization concentrated once community lands across the state of Mexico, too. Local notables gained property in their ample shares of community holdings; they and others bought lands once leased as income properties. Over time, the market accelerated concentrations as prosperous men bought poor neighbors' lands—or took them for debt. By the 1880s, arable lands were widely privatized, sometimes with surveys and titles, often without them. Land concentrated in ever fewer hands. Late in the century, the upland pastures and woodlands that served as resources of last resort for the poorest and the landless also became private, some claimed by local big men, others by estates. Access required payment—hardest on the poorest.[24]

Meanwhile, rapid growth in Mexico City drove market production across the heartland. In 1877, the federal district included 327,512 people, a doubling since independence, still half the state of Mexico's 650,653. By 1900, the city had grown to 541,516, almost sixty percent of the surrounding state's 939,140. In 1910, the metropolis reached 720,753, nearly seventy-five percent of the state's population. Heartland villagers struggled to feed their own families while estates and community big men looked to profit by feeding surging numbers in the capital.[25]

At Chalco, while lands concentrated within communities, the expansion of estate holdings on the plain was limited; there, too, it focused on water to enable irrigation for commercial crops. Protests continued, yet accomplished little in the face of the Porfirian state.[26] Thanks to growing markets and rail connections, Chalco's historic estates emerged from the plague of debts that had crippled them for decades; from the 1880s, well-capitalized newcomers took over—the purchase of La Compañía by Spanish immigrant and Porfirio Díaz ally Iñigo Noriega a clear case. The only major expansion of estate lands at Chalco came in the mid-1890s when Díaz granted Noriega rights to drain Lake Chalco, creating a vast new property with rich lands and privileged easy access to city markets.[27] Away from the lakeshore, landlessness came from the mix of privatization, population growth, and concentrations inside communities as big men accumulated.

Local accumulations were remembered sharply at Xalatlaco. There, in the highlands between Tenango and Morelos, families raised maize and barley and worked the forests to make charcoal and shingles. The goal was sustenance—and sales to gain what they did not produce. Local traders and muleteers carried grain and wood products to sell in Morelos. They returned with vegetables and *aguardiente*, cane brandy. Local men who ran stores and mule trains accumulated wealth and much of their neighbors' land.[28]

Natalio Lorenzana remembered Dolores Reynoso: "The biggest of the *caciques*. . . . He had many hectares; most of the town was his farm." He kept stores and ran mule trains; he sold on credit and took land when customers could not pay. Natalio went on: "Don Dolores did not dress like a *charro* [a Mexican cowboy], but in slacks, with a hat like a rich man, and I heard he carried a pistol. . . . He was very respected; all the big shots were respected in those days." Reynoso kept ties to other big men: "The rich also threw parties. . . . They invited friends and allies from Toluca and other big towns. Dolores Reynoso had a friend and trading partner from Tacubaya [near Mexico City]. He gave Dolores the resources to set up his store, bakery, and butcher shop."[29]

Leonardo Ceballos offered parallel memories: "It was in the years that Dolores Reynoso, a rich man, ruled. . . . He had many lands; he had more than twenty plow teams, many more." Having accumulated sixty hectares of land, Reynoso also accumulated women. The boss kept five women and their children in five households. "In addition, he had a pulque tavern in his house; he had a mill powered by gasoline to grind maize for torti-llas . . . he was the richest man in town."[30] Memories of Reynoso's wealth also came from within his family. His nephew Margarito Gaspar recalled: "my uncle Dolores Reynoso had a lot of money, so much there was no place to put it. . . . he had a store, he had a dry goods store, he had a bakery, he had a pulque tavern."[31]

The people of Xalatlaco, struggling while Reynoso accumulated wealth, land, and power, found an explanation for his sudden gains: a pact with the Devil. Leonardo Ceballos's memories were clear: "his riches did not come from work, but from 'the Other.' Later, when he distributed his land among his sons, they all died in sadness, because the riches came from the Other." Ceballos added, "Dolores had poor men who worked for him, he had a lot of workers; because he had money, he deceived them. It was clear to me he made a pact with the Devil, and that poor men worked for him because they needed his wages, they needed work. But it is clear that he sold them, that they too went to the Other."[32] Margarito Gaspar knew his uncle was not alone in dealing with the Devil: "they say that the Pastranas, from the town of Coatepec, enjoyed money they got from pacts." He also knew how the Devil delivered money: "There are people in San Agustín who tell how at midnight a wagon descended, all illuminated and amid thunder; it brought money from the hill named Cuahuatl and deposited it in town."[33]

Was the diabolical explanation absurd? The privatization of community lands, a liberal policy, and the acceleration of market production, a liberal goal, together fed accumulations like Reynoso's. Those liberal programs came linked—by liberals—to the privatization of Church properties and the separation of Church and state. Clerics and conservative ideologues protested that liberal programs attacked religion and God's work in the world. While most Mexican liberals saw themselves as Catholics, they aimed to end Church temporal powers, its sway over education, and beliefs they saw as superstitious. Ironically, while big men like Reynoso took advantage of privatization and the market to accumulate wealth and property, they joined arrangements that assigned sodality lands supporting local worship to private owners (often women), enabling communal support of festivals and other worship.[34] People at Xalatlaco heard liberalism equated with an assault on religion, on God. They tied liberal programs, market acceleration, and land concentration to the Devil. They understood clearly—in their own religious idiom.

Populations grew, big men accumulated, and land became scarce in communities at Chalco and Tenango del Valle. Commercial production soared. Chalco led the way. Canals still linked its fertile plains to the metropolis; it also lay on the rail line built in the 1880s to bring Morelos sugar to the city. The Chalco plains were ideally situated to supply wheat and maize to Mexico City's burgeoning population. The challenge was to expand production. Estates had claimed most lands open to irrigation in Spanish times; they took more in the market opening of the 1840s and 1850s, more still after 1870. Still, the gains were limited until Noriega's drainage of Lake Chalco created a vast well-watered plain of nearly 10,000 hectares, increasing by more than ten percent the lands held by Chalco estates around 1900. Adding Xico to La Compañía, the Noriega family dominated production of cereals for the capital—while displacing lakeshore villages, their productive *chinampas*, and their historic reliance on aquatic life. They protested in court, but could not win.[35]

Noriega and other Chalco growers also mechanized, buying planters, harvesters, and threshers from the United States—demonstrating modernity and the knowledge that machines increased profits. They also reduced demand for labor, thus production costs, while market demand soared.[36] Yet the turn to machines came not in the face of scarce workers; the mix of population growth and land concentration left growing numbers desperate for work and wages. A survey of 1893—the railroad complete, mechanization beginning, the drainage at Xico not begun—reported that Chalco estates employed 1,454 workers year-round and 9,747 seasonally to plant and harvest crops.[37] Day wages ranged from thirty-one to thirty-seven centavos. In a district approaching 70,000 people, perhaps 6,000 lived by permanent estate labor, another 40,000 gained partial sustenance from seasonal labors. How did the majority survive?

Alternatives were limited. The Miraflores textile mill, built in the 1830s, employed 150 men, 150 women, and 50 children—paying adult men and women a peso a day, the children twenty-five centavos. Two new small mills hired a few more: Tomacoco employed 60 men, 10 women, and 35 children—paying eight-five centavos daily to the men, fifty to the women, thirty-five to children; El Caballito offered work to 30 men at a peso daily and 4 women who earned from twenty-five to seventy-five centavos. The nearly 500 people working at textile mills created a local "labor aristocracy" (among adults). They added to those gaining regular employment in the region, bringing the total at estates and mills to near 2,000 regular workers, sustaining perhaps 8,000 people—just over ten percent of the district's growing population. In the 1890s, the San Rafael paper mill opened in highlands above Chalco, using the rapid fall of the Tlalmanalco River to generate hydroelectric power and tapping the vast forests on the flanks of the towering volcanoes.[38] Papermaking created limited permanent work and San Rafael recruited skilled workers outside the region—housing them in company barracks, taking their money back in a company casino (see the plant, barracks, and casino in figures 9.1, 9.2, and 9.3, respectively). The plant did hire local men to cut and haul timber, a source of irregular income for growing numbers without land. When Noriega's Xico entered full production after 1900, it employed but 128 permanent workers to plant 9,827 hectares of grain.[39] Seasonal work surely expanded—but insecurities marked new dependencies in communities long grounded in *chinampa* cultivation and aquatic gathering in lakes and marshes now gone.

FIGURE 9.1. The San Rafael paper mill, 1890s.

FIGURE 9.2. The San Rafael workers' bathhouse (*right*) and barracks (*left*), 1890s.

FIGURE 9.3. The San Rafael casino, 1890s.

A survey of nonagricultural activities in 1900 revealed 376 stores and shops, many the basis of the local wealth of the few who accumulated village lands. There were 176 artisan shops, with shoemakers, carpenters, blacksmiths, and tailors most numerous. They brought modest prosperity to a few families. And there were 150 "industrial" establishments, most small except for San Rafael and the three textile mills. There were 91 shops making pulque to supply local taverns, 14 bakeries, and 11 candlemakers.[40] An estimate that 650 small stores and shops employed five persons each suggests that town activities supported 3,200 workers—more than permanent work at estates, textile mills, and San Rafael combined.

What sustained Chalco's population passing 70,000 around 1900? Combining the 2,000 workers permanently employed by estates and mills and the 3,200 sustained by town stores and shops suggests that over 5,000 men took regular sustenance from the commercial economy, supporting families totaling 20,000—just over a quarter of the district's people. If 2,000 found irregular work cutting wood for San Rafael, then adding them to the 10,000 finding seasonal work in estate fields indicates that nearly 50,000 gained earnings from that booming sector—but rarely enough for family sustenance. Did men contracted to deliver wood to San Rafael use access to the *montes* to plant *tlacolol* in clearings (as Pedro Martínez did just south at Tepoztlán)? They might gain maize, but insecurities remained.

Men struggled to support families by combining cultivation on shrinking remnants of community lands, seasonal labor at estates, and cutting timber for San Rafael—caught in a tightening vise created by population growth, land concentration, and estate mechanization. How did they carry on into the early twentieth century? The railroad building of the 1880s created a brief boom in demand for hard labor—followed by the laborsaving impact of rail transport and mechanized harvesting. In the 1890s, the drainage of Lake Chalco brought another surge of labor demand—followed by more mechanized production and mostly seasonal labor demand. Did the sharecropping that balanced estate production and community needs during the midcentury decades of commercial crisis and community assertions continue, providing a mix of sustenance and labor parallel to the system strong in Morelos, just to the south, to the end of the century? Perhaps, but such attempts to rebalance symbiotic exploitations are not reported for Chalco after 1870. Young women did leave in uncounted numbers for household service in Mexico City. And after 1900, young men from Chalco left seasonally for the difficult work cutting cane in Morelos.[41] The people of Chalco found ways to survive, but they proved increasingly irregular and insecure. They began to separate family members, challenge patriarchy, and threaten community cohesion.

Were there no protests? The people of the lakeshore tried to resist the drainage that took their *chinampas* and marshes, to little effect thanks to Noriega's ties to Díaz.[42] A zone famous for protests from the 1840s to 1868 offered little public resistance to transformations undermining family survival and patriarchal norms. Why? Government consolidated nationally and in the state of Mexico; the spaces that political conflicts opened for popular resistance in the middle decades of the century closed with Díaz's mix of authoritarian rule and negotiated stabilization. And his regime promoted two programs of social control: education and police.

Mexican liberals had long promised education to cure "indigenous backwardness," blaming limited results on political conflict, clerical resistance, and natives' reticence.[43] With the return of liberal rule in 1867 and after the uprisings of 1868, the state of Mexico made a concerted effort to build schools and increase enrollments. At Chalco the thirty-two schools and 1,595 students of 1870 grew to seventy-three schools and 4,328 students in 1877. Girls' schools rose from four to ten, enrollments from 196 to 988—real gains that showed a strong preference for educating boys. Schools and enrollments concentrated in larger towns. And in a telling transition, as Díaz consolidated rule the number of schools at Chalco increased to eighty-five in 1878, but enrollments dropped to 3,793. Girls' schools increased to seventeen, but enrollments fell to 834. Boys' enrollments rose by 200.[44]

Educational offerings at Chalco paralleled those across the state. The number of schools increased from 439 in 1870 to 1,050 in 1877; enrollments rose from 24,640 (3.8 percent of population) in 1870 to 52,201 (7.5 percent of population) in 1877. Then they fell throughout the Porfiriato. By 1907, there were only 995 schools in the state; the number of students fell to 47,357—while population increased by nearly 100,000—leaving enrollments under 5 percent.[45] An analysis of education statewide reveals loud commitments to the promise of education, a concentration of schools and teachers in populous and prosperous head towns, laments that rural families failed to respond to the promise, and grudging recognition that lives of poverty and insecurity led too many to bring children to the fields. Beyond that, outlying villagers resisted paying taxes for schools their children could not attend—with curricula they could not control.[46] Liberal education reinforced the concentrations and exclusions already dominant in economic life.

The state proved better at policing—long desired by the powerful, left unfunded in earlier times of commercial difficulties. After the uprisings of

1868, Chalco had a mounted force of only 16 men in 1870. The Porfirian state found an alternative. It created civilian patrols called *veintenas*, mobilizing 20 men nightly in every subdistrict, more when emergencies rose. In 1890 they enrolled over 4,700 men across Chalco. By 1900, the patrol—renamed the Second Reserve of the Army—enlisted 11,153 men at Chalco (more than found regular work). They were subject to periodic drills and monthly patrol duties, mobilizing 378 men daily. They carried personal weapons, saving the state of the cost of arms.[47] A majority of adult men at Chalco participated (sixty-five percent). The (re)militarization of patriarchy that began in insurgency and counterinsurgency after 1810 and persisted through political conflicts and rebellions after midcentury gained sanction and organization under Díaz. While growing numbers struggled to assert patriarchy as providers, the state sanctioned manly violence in service of social stability.

Parallel developments ruled at Tenango del Valle, though commercial life was less vibrant there. For 1890, the state estimated transactions at just over 200,000 pesos, fifteen percent of activity at Chalco. A rail line crossed the sierra to connect Toluca to Mexico City in 1882, but it continued west, providing little access for producers at Tenango and south. Industrial and commercial development concentrated along the line running through Toluca, stimulating textile mills, breweries, and hydroelectric plants that gained tax exemptions to encourage investment and mechanization.[48] In the Tenango district, a small cloth factory operated at Santiago Tianguistengo in 1890, at first employing but 8 men, 5 women, and 5 children. Industrial wages were low, ranging from eighteen to thirty centavos daily.[49] That left the district's growing population dependent on subsistence cultivation (as lands concentrated) and work at eight haciendas and twenty-five ranchos. Estates offered regular work to only 463 people, leaving 13,908 to seek seasonal labor (at eighteen to twenty-five centavos daily).[50] Morelos became a last chance. Seasonal sojourners to cut cane were so common they earned a label at Xalatlaco: they were *morelianos*. Apolonio Flores remembered: "Tradition says they liked going to work in the cane."[51] Necessity was surely the primary impetus.

Facing the vise of land concentration and population growth without even the limited expansion of labor brought by factories, rail projects, and land drainage at Chalco, people at Tenango found other adaptations. After 1900, as more men became *morelianos*, women took seasonal work in local fields—a shift reported only at Tenango.[52] Families split for months. Patriarchy persisted as a goal among men. It was challenged by men's lack of prospects, by separations, and by women's wage work. As patriarchy corroded, crime records reported a rising tide of violence among men, and by men against women—often their wives.[53]

The Involution of Social Violence

The statistics gathered by the state of Mexico show that the rising tide of violence reported at Tenango marked the wider highlands.[54] Clear trends appear.[55] Deadly violence dipped after 1870, held low in the 1880s and early 1890s, to rise again around 1900. Nonlethal violence rose from 1870 to 1885 as Porfirian development began, and held near that high level to 1900. Total violence followed the same pattern. Sexual crime showed a steady decline—suggesting a limited state interest. Property crime held steady—until it too began to rise around 1900. Across the state, an escalation of crime began with the acceleration of liberal development, held high as it endured, and began a second rise as disruptive social impacts took hold around 1900.

At Chalco crime mirrored state trends with anticipation and acceleration.[56] Crime was high and rising after the rebellion of 1868; pacification did not end social conflict but turned it inward. Crime declined in the 1880s and early 1890s, as rising market demand, railroad building, and the opening of San Rafael created work for a time. Then from the 1890s, as land concentrated, Lake Chalco was drained, population continued to rise, and mechanization took hold, crime, notably violent crime, drove toward historic peaks.

Tenango del Valle saw a distinct trajectory.[57] In 1870 levels were low. Then violence and property crimes rose to peaks far above levels across the state and at Chalco by 1885. Tenango saw population growth and land concentration without a parallel development of even temporary labor for men struggling to sustain families and patriarchy. Crime soared. Then, the late 1880s and 1890s brought a sugar boom in Morelos, drawing Tenango men to long absences of hard labor as *morelianos* while women went to local fields to take low wages planting and harvesting grain. Separations of men and women, along with women's new income, challenged patriarchy. Overall crime at Tenango declined from 1885 to 1900; still, while property crime fell, violence held above the levels of 1870. Tenango judicial records reveal that violent crime, mostly by men against men but also by men against women, rose again from 1900 to 1910, concentrated among an indigenous majority struggling to survive.[58] Did roles in armed patrols facilitate and implicitly sanction violence by village men, even as they limited property crime?

Xalatlaco lived that manly violence. A powerfully remembered conflict linked trade with Morelos, concentrating wealth, banditry, manhood, and police patrols. Margarito Gaspar narrated:

> The *retablo* [sculpted altar] in the chapel of Santa Teresa tells of a battle between muleteers and robbers in 1892. Up there in the high woods robbers blocked a mule train. The leader of the muleteers, at the head of the train, was don Juan Medina from the San Francisco *barrio*. He sent for help from the chief of the *veintena*, what we later called the patrol. They took their weapons and went; they marched into the woods. As they got to where the muleteers were blocked, the bandits and their chief called out: "Who goes there?" "*Sus padres*," answered the men of the patrol, who then called back: "Who goes there?" The bandits and their chief shot back: "*Sus padres*." Then don Irineo Sánchez, chief of the patrol from the *barrio* San Agustín, had the luck to mortally wound the bandit chief. They carried him off like an animal, tied hand and foot and hung from a branch.
>
> Arriving at the town hall, they dropped the bandit and the other prisoners and shouted victory. The men of the patrol trembled with courage. Hearing the racket, everyone came to see. One person saw the wounded bandit in front of the town hall and taunted him, "Ah, this son of who knows, how far he has fallen," and kicked him. The bandit raised his head with a glare of hate and vengeance, but could do nothing.[59]

The prisoners were paraded in chains through upland towns on the way to face justice at Tenango del Valle. There "the bandit chief died, and they sent him back home; they say he was a *sacristán* [vestryman] from Amecameca, because he carried a big ring of keys."[60]

There is much to contemplate. Bandits aimed to claim gains made in trade with Morelos. The Xalatlaco patrol mobilized to stop them. Both groups boasted of manliness—each were the other's "*padres*." The patrol won, asserting dominant manhood while defending a trade that allowed a few to accumulate while many struggled (including men in the patrol). The battle forged an identity linking the lead muleteer, the head of the patrol (both honored as *don*), and local patrolmen (anonymous in memory). A patriarchal alliance in defense of property integrated a community dividing between a prosperous few and a struggling majority. The triumph of manly unity was sanctified in a *retablo*, set prominently in a local chapel. The defeated became "boys," easily kicked. The bandit leader died. He was an outsider from Amecameca, a prosperous town between Chalco and Morelos. Men in the uplands bordering Morelos competed violently for the scarce spoils of the booming sugar basin.

At Xalatlaco the battle of 1892 gave way to ritual conflicts, often bruising, sometimes maiming, in the years before 1910. Natalio Lorenzana remembered: "We fought battles; we fought here in Tzati against the boys from San Agustín. I remember that our leader was named Rocha, I don't remember who was leader in San Agustín. We fought every afternoon. On Sundays it was earlier and there were more people. The battles between barrios were fought with rocks and clods of earth; sometimes there were injuries. The authorities did not intervene. We also fought battles with boys from Tilapa. All of this was an omen of war, of the cruelty of war." Félix Quieroz added: "we had a war with the Otomí from Tilapa, with slings, *chinga* with stones. We fought battles near Ocotenco, fifteen on each side. All this fighting we knew, but it was nothing compared to what came later."[61]

Combats to test manhood pitted bands of youths from rival barrios of Xalatlaco against each other; bands from Xalatlaco fought the nearby town of Tilapa, remembered as ethnically other, as Otomí. As it became ever more difficult for young men to claim patriarchy as providers, men fought each other. Local officials let them fight combats recalled as precursors. Manhood and violence linked in banditry, state-sanctioned patrols, locally honored combats, and rising tides of crime, while liberal development made household patriarchy a distant ideal for a new generation.

Meanwhile, patriarchal families began to break.[62] In 1885, ninety-two percent of births across the state were recorded as legitimate, the product of a married couple. The percentage was a bit higher at Tenango, ninety-five percent, significantly lower at Chalco, only seventy-eight percent. By 1900, only sixty-two percent of births statewide were recorded as legitimate; at Tenango legitimacy fell to seventy-eight percent; at Chalco it plummeted to thirty-eight percent. As men struggled to find land and labor that might allow them roles as heads of household, marriage became less and less common.

At the same time, reproduction increased. At Chalco, where most men remained in the region while struggling to find ways to claim patriarchy, total births increased more rapidly than across the state—while marriage collapsed as a dominant institution. Men resisted marriage, yet engaged energetically in sex, asserting manhood by fathering rising numbers of children recorded as illegitimate. At Tenango, where local opportunities were scarce and insecure, and absence in Morelos common, births increased less (near state averages). Marriage remained common too; nearly eighty percent of infants were registered as legitimate in 1900. While

Tenango men spent much of each year in Morelos and women worked local fields, marriage held strong and reproduction lagged. Did men's absence strengthen marriages while limiting conceptions?

For Xalatlaco, Gregoria Camacho González recalled with pain how she learned the necessity of a patriarch to family survival. Her father was jailed, falsely she insisted (he was found with a piece of cloth made by a murdered shawl maker): "Who would support us? My parents had seven children, but two died and only five, all girls remained; there wasn't even a little man to help. My father left a little land and my mother tried everything to feed us."[63] Her desperate memory presumed that a man was essential to family sustenance.

Meanwhile, for many across the state of Mexico girls became unwanted, expendable, as the social insecurities of liberal capitalism proliferated. The state recorded a rising rate of infanticide as the nineteenth century ended.[64] Numbers were small, even when combining crimes classed as infanticide and those labeled "clandestine burial" (used when an infant was found buried and parents could not be identified). Medical professionals saw an infanticide problem and offered two solutions: education and criminalization.[65] They would not imagine that rising infant deaths might be linked to the social impact of the development they celebrated as the essence of progress.

Birth records confirm the sharp increase of female infant deaths at Tenango, Chalco, and across the state of Mexico. Normally, slightly more males than females are born, a ratio reversed in maturing populations as women die owing to complications of childbirth. Yet late nineteenth-century birth records show a growing predominance of boys, documenting selective deaths among newborn girls.[66] In 1885, deaths of infant girls were rising across the state, accelerating at Chalco, but not evident at Tenango. By 1900 female infant deaths were rising everywhere; registrations indicate that over 1,600 newborns girls died that year across the state, including over 200 at Chalco and over 100 at Tenango. The trajectory of infant girls' deaths paralleled liberal development—accelerated at Chalco, limited at Tenango, and widespread across the state.

And female infant deaths linked in complex ways to an accelerating breakdown of patriarchal families.[67] Statewide in 1885, the emerging excess of male births, thus of female infant deaths, concentrated among the great majority that remained legitimate—the children of formally married couples. The few births among unmarried women reported a female majority: single women kept their daughters. The pattern at Chalco in 1885 was parallel, but more extreme. Female deaths were greater and concentrated among married couples; single women delivering children outside marriage were more common—and they kept their daughters. At Tenango in 1885, marriage ruled and daughters lived—while many men were away working in Morelos.

By 1900, the death of female newborns generated a ten percent excess of males statewide—and girls born to unmarried mothers died at the same rate as those recorded as legitimate. Growing numbers of single mothers were no longer able to save their daughters. At Tenango, where men and women lived more separate lives and births increased less rapidly, female infant deaths among married couples rose to statewide levels and began to appear among single mothers. At Chalco, where insecurities proliferated and men faced challenges claiming patriarchy, formal marriage became an option for only a minority, while birth rates rose; female infant deaths dropped among the married minority to rise among the new majority born outside wedlock. Marriage was most common among the prosperous; people who could pay for weddings kept their daughters. Among the majority, over sixty percent, of infants born to unwed mothers at Chalco, female infant deaths soared. Did single mothers face lives of such desperation that they constructed cultural ways of denying their daughters sustenance?[68] Were unmarried mothers linked to men who were so insecure they resisted marriage, fathered growing numbers of children, then imposed pressures that led to escalating female deaths? Both were possible; with available sources we cannot know.

The utopian promises of liberal capitalism became lived realities for small minorities at Chalco and Tenango del Valle, as across the states of Mexico and Morelos. The privatization of land and the commercialization of production benefited powerful minorities nationally; a few prospered in local towns. For the rest, privatization and mechanizing agro-industries intersected with population growth to generate social insecurities lived by men as challenges to patriarchy and women as new desperations. Family breakdowns came with rising violence among men, by men against women, and by one or both (actively or not) upon newborn daughters.

Liberal privatization, agro-industrial capitalism, and social violence were linked—they occurred in the same communities at the same time, lived by the same families. To join the medical professionals of Mexico City and claim that the rising tide of violence, including what they labeled infanticide, resulted from lack of education and criminal tendencies— while people were losing control of their lives, struggling to survive, and facing challenges to patriarchy—is to join in bigotries constructed and promoted by the few who profited from liberal development.

From Involution to Revolution

The celebrated boom of Porfirian agro-industrial capitalism generated social corrosions that deepened across the southern heartland after 1900. The attempts to re-create symbiotic exploitations across Morelos reached a limit when there were no lands to share with a new generation of landless villagers—who competed with men and boys from Tenango del Valle and Chalco for day labor. Patriarchal families became hard to create and harder to sustain. Violence rose in communities and families, and began to focus on newborn girls—a desperate destruction that might limit population growth, the only aspect of the social vise in villagers' control. Men unable to claim roles as providers turned to a violent manhood that preyed upon neighbors and kin, wives and daughters—the social payoff of progress across the southern heartland.

After 1910, the social violence that progress had spawned and order had turned inward to plague struggling families and communities began to turn outward to challenge the powers that ruled and profited while people faced desperation and violence. The turn was neither automatic nor spontaneous. The process that turned deepening grievances into revolution mixed global crisis, national politics, and drought. The particulars in Morelos are well known.[69] The years after 1907 brought recession linked to a financial panic on Wall Street; sugar harvests fell as Cuban mills revived to serve US markets. Seasonal chances to labor declined as needs rose. Then drought struck in 1909, heightening searches for wages to buy maize.

Meanwhile, state elections in 1908 set a local candidate against an outsider tied to Díaz and the sugar planters. The campaign inflamed issues of local rights and uncertain justice, until Díaz imposed his chosen ally. In the same years, local land conflicts at Anenecuilco, a village surrounded by sugar estates, brought Emiliano Zapata to prominence as a defender of community rights. He was an outlaw in 1910 when Francisco Madero, rebel son of a powerful landed industrial and banking family from the north, challenged Díaz for the presidency. Díaz engineered another re-election, Madero rebelled, and Zapata led Morelos villagers in demands for land and justice.

Pedro Martínez recalled the opening to revolution in Tepoztlán: "In 1910 the Revolution came." He knew political conflicts had begun with the elections for governor in 1908, when Díaz imposed his candidate. He also knew that "In 1910 the action was still in the north. It was still possible to work, then. So once again I went to the haciendas looking for work. But the foremen didn't do anything to us anymore. They were afraid." Men desperate for work gained from the challenge to Díaz's power. Pedro added, "In those days it was the *caciques* in our own villages who oppressed us most. They had the money and rode fine horses and were always the officials. They took advantage of the poor girls." While estates offered work and backed off harsh treatment, town big men still ruled, imposing themselves on poor women.[70]

Pedro recalled that the first revolutionaries rode into Tepoztlán on March 17, 1911 (facing the historic church seen in figure 9.4). "They shouted 'Long Live the Virgin of Guadalupe! Long Live Francisco I. Madero!' and rushed to the palace and began to burn it." Villagers saw: "It's the *caciques* they are after. They all ran away, all the *caciques*." The revolutionaries' first strike aimed to topple local big men. Divisive violence followed. In 1912 and 1913 there was no work at the haciendas, so Pedro made rope, a product useful in revolution, while working his *tlacolol* maize plot in rough uplands. "That was my whole life now, planting *tlacolol*." (See the rugged uplands shown in figure 9.5.) He heard about Zapata in 1913, learning that his father had been a modest cultivator, cut from his land by the Tenextepango estate. When the chance came, Pedro went to the hills to meet Zapata, on the pretext of delivering tortillas. "I joined Zapata and was with him through 1914,

FIGURE 9.4. The church at Tepoztlán.

FIGURE 9.5. The Tepoztlán highlands: home to survival by *tlacolol*.

1915, and 1916. . . . My wife stayed behind." He added: "Now we knew what we were fighting for—Land, Water, Forests, and Justice."[71]

Esperanza lived a different revolution. "The government soldiers, and the rebel soldiers too, violated the young girls and the married women." She gave tortillas on demand to Zapatistas and government troops, adding: "the government men were the ones who behaved the worst and did us most harm."[72] Filomena, living the revolution in Guerrero uplands, added gruesome detail:

> In 1915 my dear grandfather died of hunger. There was such great need. . . . I used to go hiding with the girls in the caves and fields. Once we went to hide in a church and the government men found us. We did not know what to do so we began to pray. . . . Once we slept in the trees so they wouldn't find us. They had stolen some twelve-year-old girls to have as wives. . . . Government men stole not only daughters, but the wives of just anyone. Once they stole one of my girlfriends, who died after eight days of being constantly screwed. Then they threw her dead body into her house. . . . Many children were born of unknown fathers to girls who had been raped.[73]

If many Zapatistas fought to reclaim patriarchy, many federals fought back with sexual violence.

Meanwhile, Pedro fought in a band loyal to Zapata, at times coming down from the hills to visit Esperanza. In the key fights of 1914, he passed through Toluca, reached Tula in the Mezquital, returned to Coyoacán, took a trolley to Xochimilco, then camped at Milpa Alta to hold the Ajusco uplands above Tepoztlán and the Zapatista heartland. He fought at Tizapán in 1916: "That was the last big battle . . . I finally had it." Pedro fled south to Guerrero to survive years of Zapatista demise. When he returned to Tepoztlán in 1919, "there was nothing here."[74]

Pedro, Esperanza, and Filomena lived violent times across Morelos and the southern heartland. If the revolution began in politics, it was fueled by social corrosions and family violence. While Madero demanded Díaz's removal, fair elections, and abstract justice, insurgents in Morelos villages attacked estates and towns, pressing south into Guerrero and northeast toward Atlixco in the state of Puebla. Their threat to property and power in the heartland prevented Díaz from focusing his armies on northern political uprisings. Stuck in a military-political vise, the aging authoritarian who had overseen decades of capitalist boom negotiated a transfer of power that aimed to preserve the regime, defend property— and allow Madero to claim the presidency.[75]

But when an interim president and then Madero refused Zapata's demands for land, and the federal army waged scorched-earth campaigns against people expecting justice from a reformer they had helped to power, in the fall of 1911 Morelos became home to an expanding community-based insurgency demanding land and local autonomy. If the corrosions imposed by capitalist progress gave villagers reasons to seek change, the deadly and destructive violence inflicted by defenders of power (as they promised democracy and justice) left insurrection the only viable response. During 1911 and 1912, and into 1913, insurgency spread among Morelos villagers—early in hotland communities squeezed for lands, slower in the east where sharecropping kept many alive and at work. Some estates struggled to raise and mill cane during the early years of conflict— owners seeking profit, workers finding wages, insurgents taking taxes to arm their uprising.[76]

In the fall of 1911, after Madero's refusal to recognize villagers' right to reclaim historic lands by force of arms, Zapata issued the Plan de Ayala—asserting that right and rejecting the capitalist democrat who offered vague promises of justice. Zapata's revolution kept Madero weak: the elite reformer could not pacify Morelos, proving to Mexico's capitalists that he could not rule the nation in their interests. After a coalition led by General Victoriano Huerta (aided by the US ambassador) ousted and killed Madero early in 1913, most national and international capitalists backed Huerta's militarized regime in defense of property while Morelos villagers escalated the uprisings that turned national political conflicts into a regional social revolution.

A generation of young men, most under thirty, unable to gain lands to cultivate or find work steady enough to provide for families, took arms to assert rights to land and autonomies. From late 1913 through most of 1916 they ruled Morelos as a league of agrarian communities. While young men and many boys fought as guerrillas, older men and many women took control of lands and production as they could, limiting the planting of cane while expanding harvests of maize to feed families and guerrilla bands. A few mills still ground a bit of cane; with an eighteen-month growing cycle, much stood in the fields as planters and managers fled the basin. But when Zapata asked for more sugar to fund and arm his men, villagers insisted that their revolution was about land and autonomy—maize, not cane. Zapata acquiesced in a compromise that made his revolution a force that could not win the national state—yet would not lose the communities' allegiance.[77]

Revolution came later to the state of Mexico. There, the gubernatorial election of 1908 proved a quiet affair. Fernando González, son of former president Manuel González and owner of the Chapingo estate north of Chalco, was re-elected by a united oligarchy. Madero's campaign for effective elections in 1910 found little resonance in the Toluca basin. At Chalco, where Díaz and his allies were a stark presence after Noriega drained Lake Chalco to create Xico, Madero raised hope and found support in struggling towns. Still, the fall of Díaz and the resignation of Governor González in 1911 led to change more apparent than real. The state oligarchy quickly "elected" Manuel Medina Garduño—a landed entrepreneur, textile mill owner, and hydroelectric producer on lands west of Toluca—as governor. A quiet beneficiary of the Díaz regime, Medina had sat out of politics, more Catholic than the liberal authoritarians who ruled. He took power in 1911 backed by Catholics, Maderistas, and some Porfirians. He aimed to keep business strong and Zapata away.[78]

Elite politics kept the state of Mexico quiet while insurrection gained strength in Morelos. But people at Chalco faced deepening insecurities, uncertain patriarchy, and escalating social violence in communities, caught between political conflicts in Mexico City and insurgencies in Morelos. On the rail route from the sugar basin to the capital, Chalco dissidents looked to Madero and Zapata in 1911, provoking conflict with those backing Díaz and local entrepreneurs. With the old authoritarian gone, villagers pressed for land and justice. They focused outrage on Xico, Díaz's gift to Noriega, stark evidence of a liberal economy that favored a few and marginalized many.

Conflict escalated after Madero's ouster and death. Chalco became a Zapatista stronghold in the fight against Huerta in 1914; it held strong against Carranza and the Constitutionalists into 1915. Defenders of power often held town centers; federal and Constitutionalist troops protected Xico—essential to feeding the capital. Villagers on the plain and in the uplands reaching toward Morelos demanded land and justice, with Zapata an inspiration. Landlords complained that they destroyed estates— meaning they took the land, planted maize, and fed families, and guerril- las too.[79] The social violence that had plagued Chalco communities and families turned outward in revolution.

Revolution also came to Tenango del Valle and the southern Valley of Toluca soon after it gained strength in Morelos, just east. Early correspondence among officials shows that they understood underlying grievances: privatizations concentrated once community lands while a growing generation faced dependence on estate labor that was increasingly seasonal, insecure, and scarce.[80] A government of men who profited from those processes did nothing to reverse them.

Revolution came first to Tenancingo, south of Tenango del Valle. Hacienda development was limited there, owing to distance from rail lines. Still, a few estates, notably La Tenería, became important wheat growers; some owners lived in Tenancingo; others (including several German immigrants) lived in Toluca. They helped bring telegraph and telephone services to the region, and hydroelectric power for lighting, too. There were water-powered mills to grind flour sent to outside markets; nixtamal mills to save town women the work of grinding maize to make tortillas; a textile mill employed a hundred workers, limiting women's chances to earn by spinning. With estate lands limited, there was little overt conflict with communities before 1910.

There were escalating insecurities. Local wheat production peaked to hold near three million kilograms a year from 1901 through 1903, creating demand for seasonal labor. Harvests then slid to two million by 1908, cutting work by a third. A spike to three million in 1909 (when drought sent prices soaring), then a drop to two million in 1910, revealed that declining wheat harvests would likely endure. The fall in production came as harvests at newly drained Xico rose to supply the nearby capital. The decline of labor around Tenancingo as population grew, land privatized, and machines limited women's incomes generated tensions that pitted outlying villages against town centers where estate owners, merchants, local officials, and capitalist modernity concentrated.[81]

Zapatista bands came to Tenancingo in the middle of 1911. Estate managers' and town merchants' descendants remembered an imported revolution, not a response to local issues. Yet they describe conflicts that began in 1911 and deepened in 1912—when Zapata came to lead a pilgrimage to honor Christ at Chalma, making clear his commitments to community lands and local devotions. For the rest of the decade, local defense forces held Tenancingo and other town centers; outlying villages became Zapatista strongholds. Estates were attacked and sacked, and then abandoned by owners; locals took land to reclaim autonomies in a decade of armed conflicts. As owners fled, the uplands from Xalatlaco near Tenango del Valle, through Zumpahuacán east of Tenancingo, to Malinalco farther south became bases for Zapatista guerrillas led by Genovevo de la O. Communities provided sustenance and supplies, while town centers lived under siege.[82]

Conflict intensified just north at Xalatlaco in 1913 as Zapatistas pressed for land and Huerta militarized the regime.[83] The turning point came in July. Federal troops led by General Alberto Rasgado chased four rebels into town, killing two in a firefight in front of frightened villagers. The next morning, Rasgado took over the community, jailed local leaders, and sent people in flight.[84] Again, federal repression turned rebel sympathizers into active revolutionaries. People at Xalatlaco later recalled their revolution in stark detail. Gorgonio Zacarías told of an early Zapatista raid, linking industry and revolution: "On the 24th of September of that year 1912 the revolutionaries burned Santiago [Tianguistengo] and its factories. . . . They pulled out the spinning machines. Many from Xalatlaco had worked in the mills. Ciriaco Mendoza had lost an arm in the machines. Three Mendoza brothers later became Zapatistas: Hilario, Sixto, and Julio."[85] Industry maimed—and led to revolution.

Brígida Flores Monjardín set patriarchy at the heart of the conflict:

> I was a poor little girl; I never knew my mom and dad; I lived with my aunt. . . . My aunt married me off so I would have someone to defend me, so I would have the help of a man. My aunt feared for me because the Zapatistas and the Carracistas were bad; they seized girls and took them off, they stole them; that's why she married me to that man.
>
> From what I know, the revolution began because of Zapata's little sister, because the girl went to buy a little maize from the *hacendado*

[landowner], and because she had no money to pay him the boss got mad, slapped her face and took back the maize, leaving her to run home. The little girl ran crying. Zapata got angry and said: "Let's go to war so they can't slap our sisters, so their tears will not run any more." So the war began.[86]

Brígida's aunt saw destructive assertions of patriarchy in all combatants; a girl needed a husband to protect her. Still, Brígida remembered Zapata as driven to war to defend the protections good patriarchs provided sisters, wives, and daughters.

Francisco Medina Mayo recalled that in 1913: "Zapata promised that if he won, the poor would no longer pay taxes. So they followed him and became Zapatistas. From the beginning they killed *riquitos* [little rich men]." Díaz gave tax exemptions to rich investors. Zapata promised them to the poor. Yet the revolution began by killing "*riquitos*," local big men, not the great men who ruled and profited at a distance. Medina also remembered Rasgado's raid: He "came trying to draft boys twelve to fourteen years old. So my *patrona* [woman boss] dressed me as a girl."[87] The general turned boys into regime soldiers; to prevent unwanted manhood, Medina dressed as a girl.

Félix Bobadilla remembered Zapatista promises of land: "Francisco Pacheco, under the command of Genovevo de la O, announced, 'I am going to distribute lands.' The people liked that, because in Xalatlaco ten rich families monopolized a lot of land."[88] Liberal capitalism concentrated land and corroded patriarchy in a generation of poor and insecure young men and women. Zapata's revolution promised land to the poor—and a chance to reclaim patriarchy.

Men struggling to rule in Tenancingo, Toluca, and Mexico City imagined a revolution brought to the state of Mexico by bandits from Morelos. People in Xalatlaco knew a revolution from within led by Regino Vega, made a general by his neighbors. Natalio Lorenzana recalled:

The Vallejo boys made Regino Vega a General. They were the first to join, not as leaders, but just like any other fighters. They gave the lead to Regino. The other fighters said to him, "You'll be the leader, and let's go." Regino did not want to lead because he did not know much, but . . . well, they made him. So they named him and that's how it went. . . . The Vallejos were from here, from the San Agustín barrio; they worked the fields; they worked for the *riquillos* [the local rich], not always, but at planting and harvest time. The rest of the time they worked the forests.[89]

Marginal men from a barrio that had joined ritual battles began the insurgency and chose their leader, pressing Vega to become the people's patriarch.

Leonardo Ceballos, of a prosperous family that lost everything to the revolution, knew: "Regino Vega was a general from here, from the town of Xalatlaco, the real Regino Vega was from here, born and raised in the town. Manuel Camacho, Valentín Camacho, Benito Muciño were also Zapatistas; Feliz Navarrette also went along. They were authentic revolutionaries; their carbine rifles were bigger than they were, because they were poor and very small. Their camp was up there on the hill they call Vinatero."[90] Ceballos resented the revolution, yet took pride in local revolutionaries. Sympathizers honored an uprising linking people in town and rebels camped in hills above. Natalio Lorenzano offered detail: "I visited all the camps, because the people were in touch, connected. They were united as if they were a family, understand me? Non-combatants visited; so did Emiliano Zapata's troops. The camps were like little towns, like villages, complete, complete villages, except they planted nothing and had to go to town to get supplies to eat. Yet they had hogs, chickens, and turkeys. Everyone ate together. There was not so much selfishness; if you needed anything, here came help; if some one had nothing to eat, others gave part of what they had, so there was no hunger."[91]

The sharing contrasted with the acquisitive individualism of earlier years. Lorenzano continued: "In the camps there was also justice. The captains did it, the colonels. The general told them, 'I may not be here, but you are.' If some one came to complain of something, they did justice. They also held weddings, because the young people married, and where would they marry if they could not go to the other side? They also registered newborns there; a secretary did that. Religious weddings were done when the *padrecito* came by."[92] Xalatlaco's revolutionaries worked to reconstitute autonomy, community, and patriarchal families. There were also renegotiations of patriarchy. Again, Natalio Lorenzana remembered: "There were also revolutionary women from Xalatlaco, like Margarita Miranda. First they were Maderistas, later they came as Zapatistas. The women were also brave; see, not all of them just left; they rose up, and see. Now among the fighters, now they chose a partner; now he was only their friend and helper as it were, and he was the one she cared for. Margarita ran almost everything, yet each one had her people. It was like a family."[93] Margarita and other women refused to marry, joined rebel troops, and chose the men they would sustain in time of war. They limited traditional patriarchal roles, surely remembering the violence earlier done by frustrated patriarchs on women and daughters. Rebel women made assertive contributions to renegotiated revolutionary families.

For years, communities in Morelos, Chalco, and the southern Valley of Toluca took arms to reconstitute autonomies, families, and communities—undermining agro-industrial capitalism in the southern heartland. At Chalco and around Tenango del Valle, including at Xalatlaco, rebels faced defeat in 1915 at the hands of northern factions that mobilized the resources of global capitalism to claim power for a regime that proclaimed itself Constitutionalist. Campaigns of repression took longer in Morelos and around Tenancingo, continuing after the 1917 constitution promised rights to land. Deadly influenza weakened resistance in 1918. The same year eleven women near Tenancingo faced arrest for running food and clothing, arms, ammunition, and information to rebel camps.[94] Destructive repression came to Morelos in 1919, leading to the assassination of Zapata. The last battles depopulated and dispersed communities that had fought for a more just world grounded in landed autonomies, coherent communities, and enduring patriarchy. A military regime took power by devastating communities in Morelos, Chalco, Xalatlaco, and beyond.[95]

CHAPTER TEN

Capitalism Constraining Revolution

MEXICO IN A WORLD AT WAR, 1910–20

AFTER 1910, men from southern heartland communities took arms to challenge the Díaz regime and the capitalists, great and small, who ruled and profited while so many faced the mix of landlessness and scarce labor that threatened family sustenance, community autonomies, and patriarchal ways. They pressed demands for land and visions of a just (and patriarchal) society into conflicts over state power and Mexico's place in a capitalist world as, in 1914, it faced its greatest war in a century. Mexico's revolutionary conflagration proved simultaneously destructive and creative—and laden with contradictions. Victorious Constitutionalists claimed the state and promoted a more national capitalism. Heartland communities rose up with Zapata to demand land and autonomy. They aimed to limit capitalism, learned they could not take state power, yet succeeded in forcing new national powers to deliver land to rural peoples.

The conflicts that reshaped Mexico after 1910 had parallels with those that remade New Spain after 1810. Both were social wars that came while the world faced transforming military conflicts: in 1810, Napoleonic wars rattled Europe and Spain's empire, opening the way for uprisings that took down New Spain's silver economy—and global commercial capitalism; after 1914, Europe's powers pummeled each other in a Great War as Mexico's revolution hit a conflictive peak—and Russians began a socialist challenge to industrial capitalism. The Mexican conflagrations of 1810 and 1910 both mixed conflicts over regime power, the nation's place in the world, and the role of communities in that world. Both led to regimes that struggled to establish power, enabling communities to rebuild autonomies and limit commercial impositions—for a time.

There were also key differences between the two revolutions that shaped Mexican history. In 1810 New Spain was a dynamic region fueling a global commercial capitalism with soaring flows of silver, ruled by a Spanish regime with limited coercive power. In 1910, Mexico still struggled for a place in the world of industrial capitalism, mixing industry and exports under a national regime that had emerged from long political wars just decades earlier. The communities that rose up to demand autonomies differed too. After 1810, insurgency focused in the Bajío, the deeply commercial region at the core of silver capitalism, where community rights were scarce and most people lived as commercial dependents. Facing challenges to incomes, security, and patriarchy, men took the occasion of Napoleon's assault on Spain to take land, rebuild communities, sustain guerrilla bands, and take down silver capitalism. After 1910, it was heartland communities built as landed, self-governing republics under Spanish rule, then threatened by liberal reforms, that rose up to reclaim autonomies and patriarchy. Amid political wars, they took land and drove an insurgency that took down the agro-industrial powers that sustained Mexico's capital.

And while both decades of revolution led to renewed autonomies on the land, after 1810 they were claimed locally, never sanctioned in policy or law—yet endured for decades. In contrast, after 1910 the autonomies demanded in revolution by heartland communities were blocked by a regime that insisted only it could deliver land. It distributed land reluctantly, while promoting a national capitalist acceleration that eroded autonomies. The conflicts of 1810 to 1820 destroyed the Spanish regime and silver capitalism, leading to long struggles to build a national state and find a new commercial economy, enabling decades of community independence. The conflicts of 1910 to 1920 rebuilt a national state committed to capitalism. Despite loud commitments to land reform, the postrevolutionary regime drove policies that led quickly to the demise of autonomies.

Contradiction layered on contradiction in Mexico's twentieth-century revolution. Heartland villagers fighting to reclaim autonomies and constrain capitalism faced complex alliances and conflicts with northerners deeply grounded in capitalist ways. In the key conflicts of 1914–15, while war consumed Europe, Zapatistas allied with Pancho Villa, the leader of powerful armies based in northern borderlands, forces that depended on exports, promoted national industry, and promised to limit landed power. Zapata and Villa fought against Constitutionalists led by Venustiano Carranza, also based in the borderlands, who tapped the wealth of exports, notably the petroleum made valuable in time of war, and committed to an externally linked capitalism while promising land and labor rights in a search for popular support.

Sustained by oil and other exports, the Constitutionalists won the state in 1915. They proclaimed nationalism, promoted capitalism, and did all they could to block the land and labor reforms they incorporated in their 1917 constitution. Nationalists sustained by export capitalism ruled. Zapata's communities could not. Still, regrounded on the land, they did not cede the battle to define the nation. Rulers proclaiming themselves "the Revolution" promoted capitalism, while struggling to contain the demands of Zapata's communities. The contradictions that shaped Mexico's revolution brought a last brief reconstruction of landed autonomies.

Falling Apart

The breakdown after 1905 of the political peace and capitalist dynamism that had marked Porfirian Mexico since 1870 is well known: the 1905 turn to the gold standard by the Americas' leading silver producer rattled everything; the US panic of 1907 deepened Mexico's economic downturn; the drought and scarcity of 1908–9 brought greater difficulties to popular communities, urban and rural—all fueling the political succession crisis that rose as Díaz approached his eightieth birthday. Many worried about his ability to keep juggling national politics. In that context, Francisco Madero—son of one of Mexico's richest landed, industrial, and banking families, with holdings in Monterrey, Saltillo, and the Laguna—called for effective suffrage and no re-election, reviving a slogan that had served Díaz in his rise to power in the 1870s. Madero raised hopes among powerful clans outside of Díaz's ruling circle, among middle classes expanded by his policies yet excluded by his politics, and among the rural poor, thanks to vague promises of landed justice.

Díaz jailed Madero, engineered another re-election in 1910, and felt so confident that he released the dissident, who fled to San Antonio, Texas. There, he called for an uprising to topple the aging president. A mix of skirmishes and negotiations followed in the north, focused on Juárez, across from El Paso. Pancho Villa joined early, building on a life of cattle wrangling, muleteering, and smuggling—perfect credentials for a guerrilla. Zapata, from a family of muleteers and traders and famed as a horseman, led villagers in Morelos in a second front south of the capital. Díaz chose to resign and go into exile in early 1911, leaving his army and cabinet to an interim president, who oversaw the inevitable election of Madero.

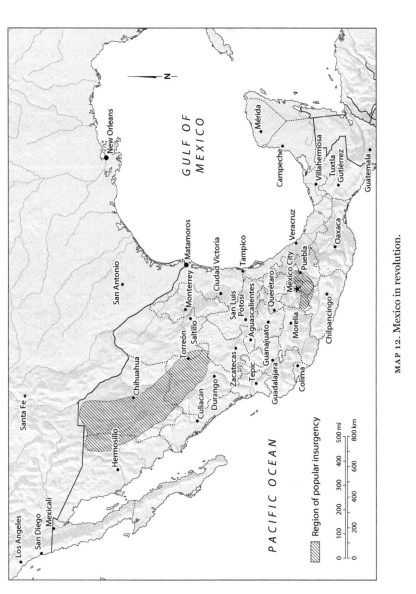

MAP 12. Mexico in revolution.

In office in the fall of 1911, Madero kept the federal army and the political backing of reformers. He pressed Zapata to disarm his fighters, asking Morelos villages to await a process he would design to study land rights. After helping Madero to power on his promise of landed justice, they felt betrayed. In November, Zapata issued the Plan de Ayala, disavowing Madero and demanding immediate recognition of community lands. The coalition that had brought down Díaz broke. Heartland villagers returned to fighting for the land; entrepreneurs who expected Madero to broker social peace, while protecting their power and properties, saw a failing reformer. The year 1912 brought deepening polarization.[1]

As 1913 began, Mexico lived an impasse. The powerful saw Madero as powerless, the populace saw him fail to deliver on commitments to land and justice. Complaining that the democratic idealist failed to maintain order, powerful interests combined to oust him in February. Joining the coup were General Bernardo Reyes, long a confidante of Díaz, once strongman in industrial Monterrey, he had refused to lead opposition to the aging patriarch in 1910; Félix Díaz, the old ruler's nephew who aimed to be his political heir; General Victoriano Huerta, who stayed in the federal army under Madero, led scorched-earth campaigns in Morelos, yet found the reformer too accommodating of popular demands; and Henry Lane Wilson, US ambassador with long ties to the Guggenheim mining interests that nearly monopolized Mexican silver refining and exports as the revolution began.

After ten days of duplicity and bombardment that devastated urban neighborhoods, Huerta arrested Madero and had him shot—a killing the US ambassador insisted he had never imagined. Reyes died in the conflict, leaving Huerta a military strongman leading the federal army. It was quickly clear, however, that he did not rule the nation. Nor did he have the backing of key international powers. Ambassador Wilson had acted under Republican President William Howard Taft; Woodrow Wilson, a reforming democrat, had already been elected and would take office on March 2. President Wilson felt much in common with Madero (both democratic idealists), and found his ouster and assassination unconscionable. So after a US ambassador had helped him to power, Huerta faced the opposition of a new US president. Huerta expected British backing via the power of Weetman Pearson, who gained riches from port, rail, and drainage contracts let by Díaz, and then became one of Mexico's leading oil entrepreneurs. But as war loomed in Europe, the British government told Pearson to follow the United States' lead— and the United States found Huerta unacceptable.[2] It never recognized

Huerta, turning to cold neutrality in the summer of 1913, then to blunt opposition in 1914. In February it opened its border to arms sales to Huerta's opposition. In April, President Wilson found a pretext to occupy Veracruz, denying the port and its revenues to Huerta.[3]

Within Mexico, staunch opposition from a US government could bolster legitimacy in times of rising nationalism; such sentiments helped Huerta for a time. With waning international backing while grasping the mantle of nationalism, he tried to build a regime of militarized power. It proved a difficult task. Opposition spread and intensified among heartland villagers; if Madero had hesitated on land rights, Huerta led brutal campaigns against Morelos communities. Opposition also rose across the north: Villa honored Madero and found his assassination despicable; resistance in northwestern Sonora formed around mechanic, teacher, and entrepreneur Álvaro Obregón; in Coahuila, the heart of Madero family interests, former Porfirian senator, landlord, and reformer Venustiano Carranza declared himself first chief of a Constitutionalist coalition that refused to recognize Huerta.

While Huerta held the capital, led the federal bureaucracy, found backing among entrepreneurs (landed and industrial; Mexican, immigrant, and foreign), and commanded the federal army, his regime was but one of several factions fighting for power in 1913. Rhetoric aside, neither effective suffrage nor community land rights interested his regime, except as challenges to be overcome.

Huerta backed landlords in local conflicts, provoking wider rural resistance; he could not crack Constitutionalist resistance across the north. So he turned to building military capacity, aiming to strengthen his armies by two means: conscription, and pressing landlords to arm their dependents in defense of property and the regime. Conscripts were at best reluctant soldiers. Many men facing Huerta's draft chose to join local rebels. They preferred to risk life fighting under local leaders pursuing local interests, thus avoiding becoming targets in the ranks of a reactionary regime. And draftees had to be paid, the price of minimal loyalty—a price increasingly difficult to meet as Huerta's army grew while economic disruptions cut tax collections.[4]

Unlike poor conscripts, landowners might gain from Huerta's protection. But in the widening regions where villagers rose up in violent insurgencies, landlord activism invited retaliation. Few proved ready to take that risk for Huerta. Only where local uprisings were limited did landlords field significant forces.[5] Entrepreneurs facing village uprisings after 1910 expected a militarized state to protect them—but would not (or could not) commit the resources to sustain a regime of uncertain power and limited legitimacy.

Mobilizing Revolution

From February 1913 to July 1914, Huerta claimed to be president of Mexico. At best he led the most reactionary of the several factions fighting for power. Opposition seemed everywhere, yet concentrated in communities south of the capital and near the border with the United States. The Zapatistas began in the communities of the Morelos hotlands and spread to Chalco, the southern Valley of Toluca, and nearby areas; they proved the most persistent and consistent revolutionaries. We have seen their historic commitments to community, landed autonomy, and patriarchy, and the challenges that led them to rise up after 1910. Their strategic position, adjacent to a capital that depended on food they made, set their power in conflicts to reshape the nation. The hot-country communities that rose up first with Zapata negotiated with Madero, the landlord reformer, then rebelled against him when he did not deliver. They remained in arms against Huerta. His scorched-earth campaigns proved he would never sanction their rights to land. After the coup of 1913, the Zapatistas maintained a widening presence around the capital—keeping a regime aiming to protect the powerful from focusing on rebels mobilizing far to the north.[6]

As they consolidated control of Morelos, the southern heartland, and adjacent zones in 1913, the Zapatistas retrenched in ways of life and war that kept them strong at home, yet limited their ability to take the state. They took control of land to reinforce communities and rebuild patriarchal families. When Zapata took over the great irrigated estates of Morelos in 1913, he proposed maintaining sugar production to earn cash to buy arms. He knew enough to consult among villagers; village after village confirmed that their support depended on turning land from sugar to maize. Zapata acquiesced and kept the staunch loyalty of the people of Morelos. He would lead a movement of defensive power, adamant demands for lands and autonomy, and limited ability to assert force beyond the heartland.[7]

Defensive strength was reinforced by an inability to tap the world economy. Deep in the interior highlands, the primary market for Morelos sugar was Mexico City. Exports could not compete with coastal growers or Caribbean producers. And while Zapata sent emissaries seeking recognition and aid from a United States proclaiming support for democratic rights in 1913 and 1914, a revolutionary movement grounded in communities demanding land and autonomy found no allies there. US representatives, like so many Mexican elites, saw Zapatistas as "Indian" bandits, destructively fighting to return to an atavistic, barbarian past. Racist constructions fueled opposition to a movement fighting to limit the capitalist ways at the heart of the imperial vision driving an expanding US role in the Americas.[8] With a commitment to community autonomies reinforced by geographic and diplomatic isolation, Zapatistas held strong in the fight to redefine a Mexico they could not rule.

The heartland communities loyal to Zapata were the most adamant agrarian revolutionaries. They were not alone in the fight for landed autonomies. Across Tlaxcala, east of the capital, villagers demanding land also rose up to back Madero in 1910. They too gained little once he was president. When Huerta promoted a landlord reaction in 1913, Tlaxcalan villagers fought back, some allying with Zapata, others with distant northerners. All demanded "land to the villagers," sharing Zapata's goal.[9]

The other major movements that arose in 1913 to challenge Huerta in the fight to remake Mexico emerged in the north, along the US border—a very different Mexico. Community rights and landed autonomies were scarce there; commercial ways had long driven northern expansion.[10] The 1840s War for North America set a new border and limited Mexico's northern territories. Then, after decades of midcentury conflicts, the borderlands became regions of opportunity in times of Porfirian peace and commercial growth. Livestock sold in the north to supply expanding US markets; Sonoran entrepreneurs ousted long-resistant Yaqui, taking their fertile homelands to begin cultivation for US and Mexican markets via new rail lines. The Laguna, near the rail junction of Torreón, saw irrigated cotton fields expand to supply Mexican industry. Monterrey became an industrial city: Mexican, immigrant, and foreign capitalists ran textile factories, steel mills, breweries, glass works, and a great silver smelter in a transnational economy. Bernardo Reyes, the Maderos, the Guggenheims, and others negotiated conflicts and opportunities among themselves and with a growing working population after 1900 (see chapter 6).

With the important exception of the Yaqui, remnants of the Apache and other native peoples, and older settlers displaced or worse by the march of Porfirian capitalism, the north seemed to rise in an unequal collaboration among entrepreneurs and producers drawn to a frontier of opportunity. Mining investors profited and mineworkers found work; estate developers expanded in Sonora, the Laguna, and elsewhere—and settlers came as tenants and workers to find land and income not available in the heartland.[11] In Monterrey, capitalists built industries and workers found work and wages above national norms; employers responded to profitable opportunities and labor scarcities with high wages and a bit of paternal care. The north promised ways to unequal prosperity (except among dispossessed native peoples)—until everything began to crumble in 1905.

Mexico's turn to the gold standard that year ended a key advantage of Mexican exports in US markets. The panic of 1907 that began in New York cut investment in Mexico and US markets for its exports. Profits tumbled, production and employment dropped; opportunities for people who had come north to build new lives seemed to vanish. Many northern entrepreneurs—like the Maderos, who had prospered outside Porfirio Díaz's inner circle—blamed the aging ruler, who had demonetized silver while integrating Mexico into the US economy. Workers, cultivators, and cowboys blamed landed and industrial entrepreneurs who joined Díaz and US interests to drive the boom that suddenly collapsed to leave so many facing desperation. While the corrosions that fueled Zapata's uprising took decades to develop, the borderlands lived opportunities that seemed to crash in a moment. Heartland communities and borderland capitalists and professionals, workers and cultivators, became revolutionaries at the same time—for very different reasons under very different leaders. Zapata's drive for community contrasted with the visions of Madero and Villa, Carranza and Obregón—all seeking variants of a capitalist future.

Díaz had consolidated power in the borderlands, as in other regions, by placing allies in power and ousting entrenched local clans from politics— while allowing them to profit from the boom that came with railroad development and integration with the United States. The Maderos lost power in Coahuila, as did the Terrazas in Chihuahua and the Maytorenas in Sonora. Then, around 1900, Díaz shifted path—in some states: the Terrazas were allowed to reclaim rule in Chihuahua; the Maderos and Maytorenas remained excluded. Resentments rose.[12]

But they were only resentments, until collapse hit the borderlands after 1905 and the succession crisis rattled the Díaz regime. Then, Francisco Madero, the idealist son of a powerful family long marginalized by Díaz, led the national movement and northern revolt that toppled the general, but kept his army. Madero's inability (or refusal?) to understand heartland communities and the depth of their outrage led to the stalemate that undermined his reform project. His fall led to wider and more diverse uprisings across the north.

Where local power holders had backed Madero against Díaz, as in Coahuila and Sonora, the uprisings of 1913 were grounded in state governments and the reformers that ruled them—notably Carranza in Coahuila.

In Chihuahua where the Terrazas had backed Díaz against Madero, and Maderista Governor Abraham González was killed after Huerta's coup, upstart Pancho Villa led a mobilization that was more independent, complex, radical, and populist. The Constitutionalist uprising that coalesced in opposition to Huerta across the north mixed leaders building on state powers, including Carranza and Álvaro Obregón who soon dominated mobilization in Sonora, and movements pressed by more popular radicals led by Villa. All depended on a borderland economy that continued to supply US markets, generate tax revenues, and fund arms purchases in the United States. As long as Huerta was their common enemy, the northern coalition kept an uneasy alliance with Zapata.

The northerners shared a broad ideology that was liberal, statist, nationalist, and populist. It was liberal in promoting a capitalist future—insisting on private property, social individualism, and a limited role for the Church. It was statist in demanding a regime that promoted a capitalist economy. It was nationalist not by seeking to isolate Mexico, but in demanding more Mexican control of Mexico's involvement in the world economy. And it was populist in insisting that the state should look to the well-being of the majority. Not all was unity: Carranza was more a liberal capitalist, Villa more the reforming populist.[13]

Organized as alternative states tied to export economies, the northern movements developed strengths and weaknesses exactly the opposite of Zapata's. Northerners built paid armies funded by expropriating opponents' lands to gain export earnings. Their forces moved on rail lines to assert offensive power. Command structures facilitated war and limited popular assertions. Carranza insisted that his Plan de Guadalupe, the charter of Constitutionalism, make no mention of agrarian reform. The poor would participate as producers, taxpayers, and soldiers, awaiting reforms designed by leaders. In that, he was a true heir to Madero. Carranza and his allies proclaimed that they fought for the nation. It soon became clear that they fought to become the state and to rule the nation.[14]

Villa led a more complex northern movement: like the Constitutionalists in northern origins, export dependence, and state organization, like the Zapatistas in seeking popular bases. But most northerners sought private properties, seeking sustenance and commercial prosperity, more individualist in their search for rights still adamantly patriarchal. Villa found his most enduring support among expropriated rancheros, tenant farmers, and cowboys in western Chihuahua, and among struggling sharecroppers and workers in the Laguna—cotton producers struck hard by economic dislocations after 1905.

Villa had a devoted rural base with visions of justice that included rights to land and better labor conditions. But with goals focused on patriarchal welfare in a capitalist world, Villa also drew support from entrepreneurs and professionals, even powerful US interests. The Hearsts had large landholdings in Chihuahua; the Guggenheims kept major mining and smelting interests across the north. Villa worked with them to generate resources for his movement. He also rejected the loud anticlericalism that marked Constitutionalist rhetoric. Accommodation with the Church separated Villa from Carranza and helped ties with Zapatistas, whose only uniform was an image of Guadalupe pinned in their hats.

A mix of popular mobilization, entrepreneurial allies, state organization, and export earnings enabled Villa to build the most powerful military force in Mexico in 1913 and 1914. He recruited the largest armies by promising land, justice, and immediate pay. They moved by rail, sustained by an effective supply service and mobile medical corps. In essence, Villa mobilized the contradictions of Díaz's liberal capitalism to build a revolutionary army: he tapped entrepreneurs and the export economy for funds; he raised armies driven by deepening discontent—and he paid steady wages. As a result he lacked a clear ideology and juggled deep contradictions: to generate the resources essential to his movement, he could not malign powerful interests; to keep armies in the field he had to promise social justice.

He became the ultimate populist sustained by revealing, and for a time effective, contradictions. He expropriated the vast landholdings of the Terrazas and other powerful foes. While his generals operated the estates in service of the movement while conflicts continued, Villa promised that the lands would be broken up and distributed among his soldiers and their widows and orphans—after victory. Armies were funded, generals rewarded. Soldiers were paid, their aspirations for land kept alive. The policy worked as long as the movement seemed en route to victory; when defeats later mounted—everything fell apart.[15]

Villa's vision of landed justice was the inverse of Zapata's. Heartland villagers demanded land as family plots in community domains, taken immediately—and Zapata acquiesced. Villa promised private ranchos and insisted that soldiers and families wait for victory to gain their reward. Soldiers and their families would benefit—if Villa won. The consequences also proved contradictory: Zapatistas kept a staunch defensive strength long after the movement faced defeat; Villista power faded once the war turned against it.

In the fight to become the state that made Mexico a battleground from the summer of 1913 to the summer of 1915, state-building Constitutionalists first allied with and then turned against Zapatistas grounded in heartland communities. The Villistas began as a key part of a larger northern alliance, mediating between neighboring Constitutionalists and distant Zapatistas, winning the key victories that ousted Huerta in the summer of 1914. Then Villa tried to work with Zapata to consolidate a state that could tap a vibrant export economy in time of Atlantic war, while serving diverse communities, landed and industrial. It proved impossible. In the end, Carrancistas and their export-oriented, state-making allies would rule; Villa and Zapata faced defeat. Zapata's villagers could not win— and would not lose. They forced victorious Constitutionalists to make a revolution of contradictions.

Revolutionary Confrontation

When Huerta took power in February of 1913, he had the advantage of controlling the national state and commanding the federal army. Most entrepreneurs—commercial, landed, and industrial—favored his rule, as did the British government. He did not rule in Morelos, just south of the capital, nor along the northern border, and he faced the rising ire of the United States. It took time for opposition to organize and mobilize, but by the spring of 1914 Villa led armies marching south, taking the key rail junction at Torreón in April, the same month the US navy occupied Veracruz. From that moment, Huerta's months in office were numbered— and divisions began to fracture the Constitutionalist coalition.

As long as ousting Huerta was the shared goal, Carranza, Obregón, and Villa kept a coordinated march southward, while Zapata occupied federal troops defending the capital against his guerrillas. After Villa's victory at Torreón and Huerta's loss of Veracruz and its revenues, Carranza began to fear that Villa would take the capital and ally with Zapata in an alliance of northern populists and southern communities.

With Huerta gone in July, Villa and Obregón met in Torreón to plot a way forward. Villa insisted on land reform and that Carranza be named interim president—blocking him from a full term leading a new government. Obregón took the proposal to Carranza, who rejected it. He would neither commit to land redistribution nor limit his political ambitions. Obregón backed Carranza.[16] A fragile unity held as revolutionaries converged on the capital. Though Villa's armies had won the deadly battles that decided the campaigns of 1914, Carranza ensured that forces loyal to him reached Mexico City first, in August. After Villa paused to consolidate his northern bases, Carranza's allies blocked Villa's route to the capital, while US officials at El Paso cut his access to coal to power his trains. A de facto alliance linking Carranza and the United States against any Villista-Zapatista coalition began to take shape. When Carranza loyalists entered Mexico City, they sent federal forces that had served Huerta to hold the capital's southern flank, blocking any advance by Zapata. Carranza could join Villa and Zapata to oust the remnants of the Díaz regime. But as that regime crumbled in the summer of 1914, the Constitutionalist leader worked to marginalize Villa and defeat Zapata. Popular revolution was not Carranza's agenda.[17]

Once in the capital, Carranza learned that he, too, did not rule Mexico. Villa held strong across the north, Zapata ruled south of the capital, and the US navy still occupied Veracruz and its customs house. In September, Zapata made recognition of the Plan de Ayala and the immediate return of land to communities the basis of any union with the Constitutionalists. Carranza refused, and revolutionary unity broke definitively.[18]

Still, no leader and no faction wanted a turn to violent confrontation among the forces that had just taken Mexico City. They called a convention at Aguascalientes, far from the capital held by Carranza and the heartland communities backing Zapata—and not far from Villa and his armies. None of the three key leaders attended. Weeks of fiery rhetoric and backroom talks could not forge unity among factions all claiming to be revolutionary. There were strong sympathies linking many of Villa's and Zapata's commanders, often grounded in popular communities and committed to radical reform. But Zapatistas insisted on reform to rebuild communities, while Villistas understood that in the north, land must promote family ranchos. And while land and community autonomy for villagers were the essence of Zapata's program, Villa also dealt with entrepreneurial allies—many backing General Felipe Ángeles, a former federal commander who had joined the revolution seeking a more just and democratic route to a capitalist Mexico. Villistas and Zapatistas negotiated a limited alliance, downplaying differences in their bases and goals.

Their agreement proved unacceptable to Carranza. Even rhetorical calls for land reform remained anathema to the Constitutionalist leader in the fall of 1914. Obregón tried to persuade the first chief that a promise of reform was essential to any coalition that could end the fighting. Carranza refused, and Obregón again acquiesced. By late November the revolutionary factions had split: a tenuous Villista-Zapatista alliance kept the name of the Convention, promised radical reforms, and controlled the highlands from south of Mexico City to the northern border; Constitutionalists led by Carranza and Obregón held the capital, Sonora in the northwest, and parts of the northeast. Carranza left Mexico City and headed to Veracruz—which the United States evacuated as the factions split in November.[19]

As 1914 ended, the balance of power in Mexico favored the Villista-Zapatista coalition—if it could integrate bases and programs grounded in heartland communities and northern commercial ways. Others had to choose a side. The movement led by the Cedillo brothers in San Luis Potosí backed Villa. In Tlaxcala, Domingo Arenas led an agrarian force that backed Zapata; his rival Máximo Rojas turned to Carranza.[20]

In the face of impending defeat, Carranza, counseled by Obregón (and desperate reality), turned to a new strategy: In January of 1915 he proclaimed programs of land reform and labor rights; then he turned to tap key resources of the world economy as war escalated in Europe. It was a strategy of hypocrisy tied to realism. Constitutionalists promised land and justice to groups fighting to limit capitalism within Mexico, while working to claim the revenues of global capitalism to rise to power.

Capitalism and Revolution

In the early years of revolutionary conflicts, the commercial economy had recovered from the downturn of 1905–10. The social conflicts of 1911 to 1913 focused in Morelos, and even there sugar production carried on at a reduced level. The first years of political conflict in the north did not radically disrupt the economy there; successful mobilizations depended on continued export earnings. Arguably, the commercial revival made Madero's reform project imaginable. Nationally, sugar production held steady to 1912, to then plummet; textile manufacturing, concentrated from Mexico City through Puebla to Orizaba in Veracruz, supplied by cotton from the northern Laguna, grew seven percent from 1910 to 1911 and held that higher level through 1913. Iron and steel at Monterrey jumped forty percent in 1911, indicating strong demand for rails, and that few expected a long disruptive conflict; in 1912 it fell back to the levels of 1910.

Export products did better in the early years of conflicts that were mostly political (outside of Morelos): gold and silver held steady from 1910 through 1912; copper grew nearly twenty percent; petroleum more than quadrupled. Henequen in Yucatán, far from political spats, rose by more than forty percent. Mexico's exports to global industrial capitalism held strong as conflicts began.[21]

The great mobilization of 1913–15 brought fundamental changes: as Zapatista communities took sugar land for maize, sugar production fell, though it survived in coastal enclaves. Mobilizations and battles that disrupted internal markets and transport brought a decline in textile production and collapse to Monterrey's iron and steel. Gold and silver fell by seventy to eighty percent, a near collapse. Mining was spread across the north, from the Bajío to the borderlands; ore was shipped for refining to the Guggenheims' industrial operations at Aguascalientes and Monterrey, before export to the United States. Such capitalist complexity could not survive revolutionary disruptions. Copper faced similar challenges, but strong demand kept the decline to only fifty percent. In contrast, henequen exports rose twenty percent from 1912 to 1916 as US agriculture geared up to sustain Europe at war. And Mexican oil production doubled from 1912 to 1915, to rise another twenty percent in 1916.[22] The wealth of export enclaves would shape the outcome of the revolution.

The fall of the commercial economy in 1913 hurt Huerta most. His rule depended on entrepreneurial favor and commercial revenues. It hurt Zapata least; a shift from sugar to maize and a focus on local consumption was his faction's driving goal. Northern rebel armies grew as economic disruptions helped recruit fighters paid with revenues from continuing livestock exports and armed with guns bought in return. In time, the mobilization begun in 1913 undermined the internal economy that mixed industry and commercial cultivation across the highlands. It reinforced the autonomies that allowed villagers to contest commercial ways—and often defined their aspirations.

That left the balance of power to the export sectors imagined by liberals in the 1830s and energized under Díaz after 1880. The northern factions, Constitutionalists and Villistas, depended on exports, but the borderland staples—from cattle, to copper, to silver—all faced declines. Two enclaves built under Díaz and set in coastal regions away from revolutionary uprisings, henequen and oil, flourished from 1913 to 1916 and became pivotal to the outcome of the conflicts that shaped Mexico's twentieth century.

Yucatán's henequen economy rose in the late nineteenth century, making cordage essential to the mechanical harvesting that enabled expanding grain production with limited labor across the US Midwest and Great Plains. Henequen was labor-intensive, and many Maya saw autonomies vanish as they were drawn to lives of dependent labor. Yet they gained the security of sustenance grounded in patriarchy, at times backed by coercion. There were skirmishes as Maya communities lost lands to expanding plantations. But no uprisings before or after 1910 threatened growing production or exports. As war rose in Europe in 1914 and US grain became pivotal to the allies fighting Germany, henequen production, exports and earnings held strong.

The Mexican petroleum industry rose after 1900 along the Gulf coast around Tampico. US and British entrepreneurs, notably Edward Doheny and Weetman Pearson, ruled production and local refining—which only gained importance as revolution began in 1910. Despite conflicts with local landlords and Huastec peoples over payments for land and labor, and in the face of environmental degradations, oil output rose as it became the preferred energy for war and production in the capitalist world. Revolutionary disruptions cut internal Mexican demand after 1913, but US and European needs soared from 1914. Mexico became the world's leading oil exporter.[23]

Facing elimination from the fight to rule Mexico in the fall of 1914, Carranza fled the capital toward Veracruz. Did he contemplate following Díaz and Huerta into exile? Perhaps. But when the United States evacuated in November (long after Huerta's fall), commanders ceded the port and large supplies of arms and ammunition to Carranza's allies. In the months before the marines departed, the United States had not removed military supplies; instead it stocked warehouses with war materiel left for the Constitutionalists.[24]

Had the US government decided to back the Constitutionalists, despite their loud anti-Yankee nationalism? Earlier, the United States had blocked arms shipments to Villa, while allowing a free flow to Carranza's backers. The Wilson administration had no interest in supporting Zapata, seen in the United States as a bandit leading "Indian" rebels. Nor would it easily ally with Villa, despite his ties to US business interests and promotion of northern exports; Villa had been a bandit, or at least a smuggler (an honored occupation of transborder free enterprise), and his features revealed roots in northern Mexico's mulatto majority. Could the leader of Jim Crow America back such a commander? Beyond reluctance to back ethnically other and socially radical Mexican revolutionaries, Wilson heard voices offering Carranza as the most capitalist of Mexican contenders— coming from political allies in Houston.[25] Whatever Wilson's reasons, he armed Carranza. Was the Constitutionalist's loud nationalism a cover for a turn to US backing?

In November of 1914 the Convention coalition collapsed, the United States delivered Veracruz and arms to Constitutionalists, and Carranza's movement took control of Tampico, where oil was refined and shipped to Atlantic markets. US arms, plus oil revenues, began the Constitutionalist revival. With control of oil, Carranza escalated rhetoric demanding subsoil rights for the nation; disputes over royalties and taxes took the headlines. The goal was revenue to enable the Constitutionalists to become the state.[26]

Having tapped US arms and oil revenues, Carranza turned back toward the capital in January 1915. With armies campaigning across the Puebla-Tlaxcala basin, he faced a key decision. He had arms and export revenues; he lacked a popular base in the central regions where power was most contested, community demands for land were strong, and Zapata ruled his base. Carranza's generals captured the two state capitals—Tlaxcala on January 1, Puebla on January 5. Then his leading political adviser and military strategist, Obregón, and his leading ideologue, Luis Cabrera, convinced the first chief to promise agrarian reform.

On January 6, 1915, the day after occupying Puebla, Carranza issued decrees calling for field commanders to return disputed lands to communities—reserving confirmation to the national executive, Carranza. The first chief insisted that reform be state controlled, not community engineered as Zapata allowed. Key commanders, notably Francisco Coss, set about sanctioning village land claims and winning allies across Puebla and Tlaxcala in January and February of 1915. The January decrees were politically astute; they drew rural support where Constitutionalist armies sanctioned local claims. Carranza's allies took the Puebla basin and retook Mexico City in February of 1915.[27]

In the capital, Carranza, still counseled by Obregón and Cabrera, broadened his populism to address industrial workers. The downturn that had afflicted the commercial economy since 1913 favored villagers living on the land, strengthening Zapatistas and making Carranza's turn to agrarian promises essential. Declining industrial output left workers unemployed and in search of sustenance. The challenge of urban survival in time of revolution was clear in February of 1915, when Zapatistas cut water and food supplies to the capital. Villagers demanding autonomy on the land and workers dependent on a complex urban-industrial economy faced distinct challenges in times of revolution.

The Constitutionalists saw that the workers of Mexico City, Puebla, and Veracruz, Mexico's industrial core, did not share the Zapatista vision. Carranza promised labor rights to organized workers and found some support. A few joined "red" battalions in exchange for promises and pay; many offered political support, or at least labor peace. Those who labored for immigrant or foreign industrialists appreciated Carranza's nationalist rhetoric; others saw a soldier's wage as a risky necessity.[28] Could they count on Carranza's promise to back strong unions, better wages and working conditions, and even strikes? That was uncertain—but where else could workers turn?

By February 1915, the Constitutionalists were building a populist coalition linking entrepreneurs, urban workers, and agrarians not allied with Zapata. Oil revenues and promises of reform sustained an uneasy coalition. To bolster his faction, in March Carranza sent 6,000 men by sea to occupy Yucatán and its vibrant henequen export economy, led by Salvador Alvarado, a loyal Sonoran. He proclaimed that revolution had come to Yucatán, expropriating henequen lands in the name of Maya communities. But export production still ruled. Planters kept the machines that extracted fiber. Carrancista authorities monopolized exports to gain revenues rising in time of war. Planters still profited; Maya workers remained workers, paid better and honored as revolutionary producers; the Constitutionalists gained a second revenue stream in a world economy at war.[29]

In March, Carranza again evacuated the capital; it was hard to hold and not the key to victory. Zapata retook the metropolis and responsibility for supplying urban markets, while Carrranza consolidated his bases along the Gulf coast and Obregón turned north to face Villa—then building a new coalition to challenge the Constitutionalists' new export-linked and rhetorically populist alliance.

In January 1915, the Convention had met in the capital as a Zapatista-Villista congress. Zapata pressed for immediate land redistribution, implemented by villagers. Villa insisted on delayed and state-implemented land reform; immediate redistribution would limit his armies and cost resources essential to the fight. Zapatistas sought a parliamentary state—weak at the center to allow for regional and community autonomies. Villistas saw a strong state as essential to a capitalist and populist future. These were not petty differences but conflicts grounded in regionally distinct bases: Zapata's heartland villagers and Villa's northern alliance of entrepreneurs, tenants, rancheros, and cowboys.

Unable to shape a common program as Constitutionalist armies approached and Carranza promised land reform, in late January the Zapatistas returned to Morelos with the remnant of the Convention. Villa named his own government and headed north. The alliance linking Villa and Zapata was not broken, but it had weakened. When, in March, Obregón abandoned the capital to prepare for battle in the north, the Convention returned, still debating whether land reform should be immediate or delayed, village run or state ruled. Preparing to face strengthened Constitutionalists, Villistas and Zapatistas both complained that the other did not provide support. Both were right: Zapatistas with local bases, defensive strength, and limited offensive capabilities could not send major armies to the north; Villistas marching toward northern bases left Zapatistas to defend the heartland. The limits of their alliance were real and grounded in their bases.[30]

Still, Villistas and Zapatistas shared deep opposition to Carranza. As key battles shifted north, Zapatistas harassed Obregón's rear guard with guerrilla attacks.[31] The distance, geographical and political, separating the popular movements did not cause the Constitutionalist victory of 1915. Villa did not just retreat north, he went north to build a coalition linking his popular base and military power to industrial Monterrey.

Villa and General Felipe Ángeles had a vision that might tie their movement to Mexico's most dynamic capitalist sectors: Monterrey and the petroleum that might energize its industries. Late in December of 1914 they sent troops to contest Carranza's control of Tampico's oil—starting a long battle at El Ébano that continued into May of 1915. Meanwhile, they forged an alliance with key members of the Madero family, who retained important banking and industrial interests in Monterrey. Could petroleum and its revenues revive industries facing decline amid revolutionary disruptions? Iron and steel had all but collapsed, as had silver mining, refining, and exports; textiles were down, as were beer and production of bottles to contain it (though revolutionary armies sustained demand for both). The Maderos had been rivals to Carranza in northeastern politics; Villa had fought for Francisco Madero and broken with Carranza. The alliance grounded in Villa's control of Chihuahua and the Maderos' power in Monterrey, brokered by Ángeles, also disdained the anticlericalism so strong among Constitutionalists and generating resentment in a Catholic population. The Villista-Monterrey coalition aimed to claim Tampico and its oil revenues, revive Mexico's most dynamic industrial city, and tie them to the northern movement with the deepest popular support—all to counter Constitutionalists strong in export earnings and loud in populist promises.[32]

The attempt soon demonstrated the fragility of the industrial city in times of revolutionary warfare. To be industrial, to generate products, profits, and revenues for entrepreneurs and a state—or a faction fighting to become a state—Monterrey required energy and access to complex networks drawing raw materials in and sending finished goods to national and international markets. Villa, Ángeles, and the Maderos understood that. Their first effort was to contest Constitutionalist control of Tampico and the oil fields. The long battle at El Ébano began in March of 1915 and continued in months of deadly trench warfare (much like battles ongoing in Europe). Had the Monterrey coalition won Tampico, a mix of oil, export revenues, and revived industrial production and revenues linked to Villa's popular base (with potential ties to Zapata) might have led to a very differ-ent regime—less export dependent, more grounded in a mix of industry, oil, and agrarian populism (in regional variants), and much less anticlerical.

But El Ébano proved a stalemate; the Constitutionalists kept the oil enclave and the revenues it took from the Great War. That allowed Carranza's northeastern allies to wage guerrilla campaigns across an arid countryside, cutting the rail links that brought coal and iron ore, silver ores and raw cotton, and other inputs to Monterrey and delivered industrial products to regional and US markets. By May of 1915, the Constitutionalists had proved that a war funded by export revenues could strangle the industrial city, leaving it a place without production, work, or promise—a place of desperation.[33] The stran-gulation of Monterrey, a close outcome based on the stalemate at El Ébano, forced Villa to return south to face Obregón in the Bajío, first at Celaya, then at León—often seen as the key battles of the revolution, with Obregón cred-ited the better general. Previously and more decisively, El Ébano and the strangulation of Monterrey set the Constitutionalist victory.

In the pivotal conflicts of 1915, three ways of being Mexico—all present in the debates of the 1830s and 1840s—contended to rule the nation's twentieth-century future. The Zapatistas and their allies demanded community autonomies, a vision founded in the historic indigenous republics that had carried silver capitalism for centuries. Rebuilding landed communities in revolution, Zapatistas gained defensive power, but lacked the offensive capacity to capture and shape a militarized state. The Constitutionalists, in contrast, built a movement and armies grounded in export enclaves, fueled by adamant anticlericalism, and framed by a rhetorical nationalism mixed with populist promises of shared welfare. They were almost perfect heirs to the nineteenth-century liberals.

The Villista-Madero alliance that forged the Monterrey-based coalition to contest the last battles of the revolution followed Lucas Alamán's vision of Mexico: silver (and now oil) to take wealth in global markets, industry to serve national markets, agriculture with commer-cial emphasis, exports when and where possible. The mix of industry and exports promoted by Alamán had shaped Mexico from 1870 to 1910. But in time of revolution and European war, the Constitutionalist strategy of tapping export enclaves, strangling the industrial city, and contain-ing agrarian communities by a mix of armed force and populist prom-ises prevailed. In 1915, a revived nineteenth-century liberalism won the state by tapping dynamic exports, devaluing and destroying industry, and proclaiming a divisive anticlericalism—while announcing a populist nationalism promising gains to all.

Revolutionary Contradictions

Key battles won, in the fall of 1915 Carranza led the Constitutionalists back to Mexico City, isolating Zapata in Morelos and Villa in Chihuahua. He gained de facto recognition from the United States in October, confirming the backing that supplied his armies a year earlier. Zapatistas held strong in commitments to land rights and local autonomies. Villa, having lost the chance to rule the oil fields at El Ébano and facing the collapse of Monterrey and defeat by Obregón in the Bajío, returned to his bases in Chihuahua and Durango. He began to address the demands for land that drew so many into his armies, turning to expropriations that helped the powerful see him more as a bandit, and less a statesman.[34]

Also in October of 1915, a remnant Convention met and finally generated a common program. It promised to deliver lands to those who worked them, allowing for community holdings to meet Zapatista demands and private properties to serve Villista expectations. It called for government built on autonomous municipalities, coordinated by a parliamentary regime responsive to local and regional interests. Armed militias would replace the military (imaginably replicating the patriotic militias that had reinforced local autonomies after 1810).[35]

The program revealed the potential for a Villista-Zapatista alliance based on shared recognition of land rights, with different implementations in differing regions. The call for municipal rights backed by popular militias showed the impossibility of the alliance as long as Villa joined Felipe Ángeles and northern entrepreneurs to build large professional armies. The goal of a limited state grounded in landed autonomies remained broadly popular; it could not prevail in a world of capitalism orchestrated by strong states.

Shared commitments to landed autonomies and limited states helped Zapatistas and Villistas carry on in home regions for years after their defeat in the contest for national power. Villa, irate at what he saw as US betrayal when it recognized Carranza, invaded Columbus, New Mexico, in 1916, drawing the Pershing expedition, which chased him for months across northern Mexico. Its failure showed Villa's local power and popular bases. Carranza sent waves of destructive military incursions into Morelos, wasting communities and remnant estates and forcing guerrillas into the hills, before he orchestrated Zapata's 1919 assassination. Villa was killed under Obregón in 1923. Both lived on as martyred heroes.[36]

With victory, the Constitutionalists returned to core priorities. Carranza backed away from land reform. He assured landowners of his support for property rights; he drew many into his regime. In Morelos, he returned estates first claimed by rebel villagers and then sacked by Constitutionalist armies to their owners. In the Puebla-Tlaxcala basin, where Constitutionalist commanders had sanctioned community land claims since January 1915 to recruit rural support, confirmation rarely came—or delivered small parts of community claims. Carranza continued to talk of land reform, but shifted to favor estate production. His was not the communities' agrarian reform.[37]

He simultaneously backed away from promises to labor. He made it clear that in his vision of capitalism, workers would return to the factories, back the regime, build mutual aid societies, and await economic improvement. When workers returned to traditions of political independence and assertive unions, demanding reduced hours, better pay, and safer working conditions, then mounting strikes during 1916, Carranza cracked down with force.[38] His populism offered limited reform; it brooked no independence from below.

Yet Carranza did not always get his way. He called a constitutional convention in the fall of 1916, aiming to revise and update the liberal charter of 1857. All delegates were Constitutionalists (no Zapatistas or Villistas allowed). Many, however, were commanders who knew that promises of reform had brought them to power and had to be kept—or at least to be set in the constitution. Obregón led those who insisted that the rights of communities to land (article 27), of labor to organize and gain fair pay and working conditions (article 123), and of the nation to control subsoil deposits (also in article 27) be included in the text. Yet while rights were set in the charter, Carranza ensured that implementation awaited enabling legislation, making acquisition of land and labor rights a long and contentious political process subject to state power. The constitution of 1917 set the contradictions of Constitutionalism at the heart of the post-revolutionary regime.[39]

The constitution did not settle the revolution for Zapatista communities. Many still worked lands taken in insurgency; others negotiated to plant on shares as estates reclaimed fields. Reviving sugar was not an option, so maize cultivation ruled—a small victory in trying times. Deaths from revolutionary battles and Constitutionalist invasions, along with flights to escape both, reduced the population on the land. Zapata held on with guerrilla forces based in impenetrable uplands.

As Mexico's uncivil revolutionary wars ended, the Great War among capitalist hegemons continued in Europe. The United States joined actively (led by General John Pershing) in 1917. Across Mexico, textile and other internal industries revived, while exports continued to rise. When the Great War ended in 1918, henequen earnings fell but oil rose to new heights that peaked in 1921. Years mixing export earnings and industrial renewal sustained Carranza and the Constitutionalists as they worked to consolidate state power. Yet all was far from well. The influenza of 1918 (maligned as Spanish) caused at least half of the deaths that cut Mexico's population by a million between 1910 and 1921.[40] Once again, epidemic disease became a pacifying force in times of social contradictions and continuing conflicts.

Carranza, head of state from 1915, ruled as president from 1917 to 1920; Zapata kept a staunch regional following until he was killed in 1919; Villa held on in isolated regions of Chihuahua. As the first chief's term neared an end, a decade of revolution had brought adamant popular assertions, promises of radical transformation, the revival of capitalist ways—and a new regime committed to promoting those ways. Álvaro Obregón, the general most responsible for the populist project that brought the Constitutionalists to power, credited with ensuring that the new constitution was at least open to agrarian and labor reform, left Carranza's government soon after the charter was completed. He went home to Sonora to build an export-oriented landed empire. He knew that to sustain Constitutionalist rule, agrarian and labor promises would have to be kept—at least in Zapata's heartland and key industrial centers. Obregón understood the contradictions of the revolution.[41]

At the end of his term in 1920, Carranza tried to impose a protégé, then ambassador in Washington, as his successor. All but Carranza's closest allies knew that Obregón had brought the Constitutionalists to power, winning key battles and negotiating pivotal conflicts and coalitions. He was the essential next president. Obregón built a coalition of Constitutionalist factions to oust Carranza—who fled toward Veracruz and exile, to be captured and executed en route. To consolidate power without Carranza's allies, Obregón turned to surviving Zapatistas, led by Gildardo Magaña. Obregón knew that heartland villagers could not be defeated; they had to be accommodated. He likely also saw that the mix of industrial revival and export boom led by a soaring petroleum sector made a revival of cane in Morelos unnecessary to the national economy and improbable after years of social war and military destruction. He offered a deal giving Zapatistas positions in his government and promising agrarian reform as a national program.[42]

The Obregón-Zapatista alliance of 1920 (without Zapata) set the course of postrevolutionary Mexico. Heartland communities had not won—yet certainly had not lost. They worked the land for sustenance first; Morelos sugar estates were all but destroyed; cereal properties at Chalco and in the southern Valley of Toluca barely operated. Villagers did not rule—but men they trusted held cabinet seats and local offices. Nothing came easily or automatically in the years to come. But the right of villagers to land would be part of every conversation, every negotiation, local and national, in decades of reconstruction.

PART III

National Capitalism and Globalization, 1920–2000

CHAPTER ELEVEN

Mexico and the Struggle for National Capitalism, 1920–80

THE AGE OF industrial capitalism, in which power and industry concentrated along a North Atlantic axis and the rest of the world supplied raw commodities and bought finished goods, faced challenges in war and revolutions after 1910, to collapse in the depression of the 1930s. Mexico's decade of revolution rattled the power of those who ruled the nation and many of the landed, industrial, and commercial capitalists who had profited during the decades after 1870. The postrevolutionary regime first pursued an export model that began to fail in the middle of the 1920s, prompting a shift to industry. When the US economy and the globally integrated industrial capitalism it led broke in 1929, Mexico was already turning toward a national capitalist experiment. It accelerated through the 1930s and into the 1940s, leading the hemisphere toward what came to be called national development—trying to make the productive potential of industrial capitalism serve national economies and societies, aiming to bring manufacturing and more equitable participation to societies long focused on agriculture and commodity exports. Mexico became a laboratory case: during the global depression of the 1930s and World War II in the 1940s, the national project seemed full of promise; later—in the face of an unprecedented population explosion and renewed US hegemony in capital, technology, and global power—it proved impossible.

Mexico had advantages in the turn to national capitalism. Core regions from the heartland through the Bajío and regions north had been pivotal to global capitalism since the sixteenth century. After the collapse of silver, from the 1830s Mexico saw the rise of mechanized industries serving national markets, complemented by commodity exports after 1870. No one had to teach Mexicans how to seek profit as capitalists, nor how to negotiate life and labor in a capitalist world. Still, Mexico's participation in industrial capitalism after 1870 revealed sharp limits and deep contradictions. Industries serving limited national markets generated products and profit while limiting employment. Agro-industries in the heartland promoted profit and production while curtailing employment, thus helping stimulate the community-based revolution that shook Mexico's core after 1910. The rapid incorporation of its northern export sectors into the westward expansion of the United States after 1880 seemed more promising, until a US panic became a Mexican recession and a then borderland crisis, generating a very different revolution there beginning in 1910.

During the decade of violence, heartland communities retrenched in economies of sustenance to sustain guerrilla forces, constraining agro-industries around the capital. Textile industries faced disruptions and reduced markets; the integrated industrial center at Monterrey learned how devastating revolutionary disruptions could be. Meanwhile, the demand created by war in Europe helped key exports flourish, notably the petroleum and henequen pivotal to the Constitutionalists' rise to power in 1915. Carranza, Obregón, and the Constitutionalists proclaimed a loud nationalism, yet took power dependent on exports. Their commitment to capitalism never wavered.

Carranza ruled from 1915 to 1920, backing capitalists, especially export earners, while blocking land reform and labor rights.[1] When Obregón took the presidency in 1920, he understood the need to mix export promotion, industrial revival, workers' rights, and land reform—always tying rights and reforms to the state, thus limiting the autonomies at the heart of Zapatista communities' dreams.[2] Twentieth-century Mexico would be defined by the contradictions of its revolution. Mexico's experiment in national capitalism promoted capitalist ways and contained community goals while the world faced serial crises.

The experiment, with all its internal conflicts, seemed promising from the 1920s into the 1950s. Then, as the United States consolidated an alliance to revive capitalism cross the northern hemisphere, rebuilding Germany and Japan to counter Soviet socialism in a war that was not always cold, Mexico faced a population explosion. Accelerating mechanization of industry and agriculture promised solutions to sustain growing numbers. But while production rose, industrial employment lagged and agricultural labor vanished. While population soared, landed autonomies collapsed. Soon enough, the national project collapsed too.

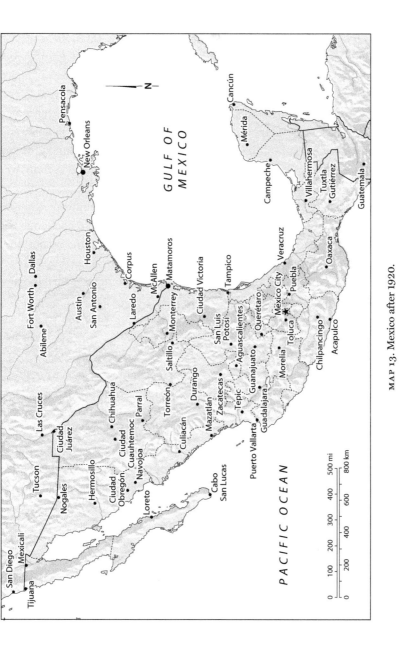

MAP 13. Mexico after 1920.

Struggling to carry on from the 1950s, government agencies and diverse enterprises imported capital and technology—building debts while limiting labor. Serial debt crises plagued the nation while laborsaving ways widened social exclusion. Rising populations in rural communities faced land scarcities and vanishing access to labor. Chances to sustain household patriarchy disappeared—again, fueling violence in families and communities. Men and women left, in the heartland most often to Mexico City—where industry concentrated yet never offered enough employment, leaving newcomers to find income and build neighborhoods by their own wit and sweat. Many others went to the United States to labor in fields and factories, sustaining families and home communities. In time, growing numbers stayed in El Norte—regions once Mexico's north, taken by war into the United States—rebuilding families and communities in the face of prejudice. As autonomies, communities, and national capitalism collapsed together after 1980, no third revolutionary rising came to challenge the powerful and their projects. Men who had led the regime of national capitalism to failure engineered a turn to globalization shaped by NAFTA in the 1990s. The gains for the majority of Mexicans, in the heartland and beyond, remain scarce.

Regime Building and the Fall of Export Capitalism

An enduring political narrative presents Mexico in the 1920s as consolidating the regime that won the revolution: Obregón ruled from 1920 to 1924, followed by his Sonoran ally Plutarco Elías Calles—who aimed to return power to Obregón in 1928. Obregón was assassinated just after his re-election; Calles stepped in to rule as *jefe máximo*—maximum chief—exerting power behind three interim presidents until he handed the regime to Lázaro Cárdenas, who beginning in 1934 consolidated both the regime and national capitalism. If focus is restricted to the heights of state power, there is reality in that narrative. But if Mexico's rapidly changing role in a disintegrating world economy comes into view, revealing complications arise. And if the diverse interests and goals of Mexican capitalists and generals, workers and communities, enter the narrative, a history emerges that is more complex, often conflictive, at times violent, and certainly not the history of a singular trajectory that might be called "the Revolution."

The export boom that helped Carranza to power sustained his rule from 1915 to 1920. Henequen peaked in 1918 and petroleum in 1921, when Mexico remained the leading oil exporter in the world. The dollar value of export earnings in 1920 had reached historic heights, having doubled that from 1916. Internal industries and commercial cultivation (outside the Zapatista heartland) also revived.[3] The return of lands to estate owners and the backing of industrialists in labor disputes helped commercial recovery and revealed Carranza's underlying goals: to defend property and promote profit in support of regime power, to promise land and labor rights as tools of pacification—and implement them as rarely as possible. Promising reforms while blocking them, the Constitutionalist state remained a military regime masked by Carranza's refusal of a military title. In 1920, 100,000 men at arms claimed sixty-five percent of the national budget.[4]

Obregón took power in a 1920 coup, taking a role as military arbiter of national politics reminiscent of Bustamante, Santa Ana, and Díaz. Like them, he aimed to hold power while working to stabilize a regime. Like Díaz, he promoted economic growth while aiming to end political conflict and contain popular pressures. Obregón took over at a moment of boom and saw little need to alter the export-led revival. But Zapatista survivors had helped him take power, so he began a targeted reform delivering lands to Morelos communities. The goal was to pacify them, and to make them dependent on the state.[5] They had fought to reclaim ancestral lands; Obregón insisted that the state would give land to groups of petitioning men. He made postrevolutionary agrarian reform a state-building project. Any gains to local autonomies would have to be negotiated in that context.

Riding an oil-export boom while facing the collapse of henequen earnings, Obregón opened negotiations with the United States that gained him recognition via the Bucareli Accords in 1923. The nation kept rights to subsoil silver, copper, oil, and more, as set in the 1917 constitution. Obregón agreed to implement those rights only by taxes and royalties.[6] Export-led growth, targeted land reform, compromise with the United States, and military power sustained Obregón. Rhetoric aside, there was no early turn to a more national capitalism.

Like so much in Mexico's history, the shift came in unscripted encounters with global market forces. Even as Obregón negotiated to calm US worries about expropriation, Mexican oil production entered a steep slide: from 193 million barrels in 1921 to 140 million in 1924. Revenues dropped proportionately. Why? The question has long been debated—but the trajectory is clear. While US and British producers drove exploration and production to a peak during years of revolutionary conflict, they worried about the threat of expropriation implicit in article 27 of the new constitution. They knew the new regime depended on oil revenues. They worried about the arrival in the oil fields around Tampico of a generation of exiled European radicals organizing to demand rights and earnings for diverse workers—increasingly Mexican. Pressures for higher government revenues and worker earnings backed by the threat of expropriation sent the oil companies to Venezuela, where they found new deposits without the challenges of regime nationalism or worker radicalism. They shifted exploration, let Mexican wells produce until dry—and moved on. State revenue pressures and worker demands mattered; the promise of new fields in a nation with a compliant regime and less radical workers mattered, too.[7]

Obregón gained US recognition as export revenues plummeted. He began to favor industry and faced a rising tide of labor conflicts.[8] As his targeted land distribution helped pacify the Zapatista heartland, landlords elsewhere worried that they could be next. They were not wrong. Communities in regions that had not risen up in arms between 1910 and 1920 saw that land went to those who had threatened the regime. In Michoacán, Veracruz, and elsewhere, men took arms in the 1920s to demand what the new constitution promised but Obregón gave only to pacify Zapatista communities.[9]

Amid all this, Obregón worked in 1923 to deliver the presidency to his Sonoran ally, General Plutarco Elías Calles. A coalition of opposing generals quickly formed around Adolfo de la Huerta—also from Sonora and not a general—aiming to block the succession. Facing more than half of the military in rebellion, Obregón and Calles saw one way to victory: mobilizing factions (mostly outside the heartland) that would take arms in return for promises of land reform. Obregón (who aimed to keep land distribution to a limited program of pacification) and Calles (who opposed land reform) escalated promises of land distribution to fight the rebellion led by de la Huerta (who also opposed land redistribution). Obregón and Calles prevailed—and entrenched policies they opposed at the heart of the regime. Calles doubled land distributions and extended them to wider regions during his rule from 1924 to 1928.[10]

Calles took over as exports fell, all but forcing a turn to internal industrialization. Given his route to office, he could not curtail land reform. To promote industry, he set a pact with Luis Morones and the CROM (Confederación Regional de Obreros Mexicanos), promising political access and limited gains in wages and benefits in exchange for labor peace. Strikes plummeted[11]; strong growth marked 1925 and 1926.[12] Then Calles pressed anticlerical policies that provoked new violent and disruptive resistance.

Why Calles turned on the Church is debated. Personal anticlerical views fueled a goal of making the state the prime educator in the nation. Did a need to appear radical while accommodating US interests, seeking closer ties with capitalists, constraining labor, and pursuing land reform only as a political necessity come into play? In June of 1926 he issued laws that sharply cut the number of clergy, enclosed all worship inside churches, and mandated secular education. In July, Mexico's bishops answered with a cessation of sacramental services. They expected to force negotiations with Calles, struggling to rule a country of diverse Catholics with divergent views of the clergy.

In the rural heartland, people had long focused on community devotions, less dependent on the Church and its priests (Iztacalco was a typical if extreme case). In Michoacán, Jalisco, and other regions of west-central Mexico, more people lived devoted to Christ in deeply religious and proclerical communities. Many saw the closure of their churches and the denial of sacraments as an assault on truth, and on the Hispanic ranchero communities they had built in the nineteenth century, grounded in family properties and often led by priests. Fearing that a politicized land reform might take their ranchos, they saw Calles deny them access to priests and the sacraments. They took arms in 1927 and pressed violent resistance into 1929—while gaining only rhetorical support from the high clergy and little material aid from Catholic elites, who defended the cause from safe urban refuges. Cristero communities with their own visions of truth took arms to defend autonomies against a state that aimed to remake their lives.[13]

To fight them, Calles again turned to agrarian promises. He promised (politicized) land reform in home regions to Saturnino Cedillo of San Luis Potosí, and to others who would mobilize forces to back the segments of the army loyal to Calles. Together, they slowly contained the Cristeros, who were never clearly defeated. In 1929 the bishops negotiated a settlement that reopened churches and resumed sacramental services, yet left many Cristero communities feeling abandoned by state and Church. Once again, a popular mobilization led the regime to accelerate land reform; Cristeros fighting to defend ranchero properties and Catholic-clerical community cultures forced Calles to make concessions to ambitious men who could mobilize people seeking community land and their own visions of truth— often grounded in a less clerical community Catholicism. In the late 1920s, the men aiming to rule Mexico faced people ready to fight for divergent visions of community and cultural autonomy.

A radical Catholic assassinated Obregón in 1928, preventing his return to rule for another term as president and military arbiter. Calles could not continue as president, given the Constitutionalist commitment to no re-election—proposed and ignored by Díaz, then proclaimed by Madero, the one principle shared by all who claimed to be revolutionaries after 1910. The year 1929 proved pivotal: Cristeros remained at arms while conflict rose within the military to determine who should succeed Calles.[14] He had set up Emilio Portes Gil as interim president; a Calles loyalist, Portes Gil had mediated labor conflicts in the oil fields and promoted land distribution to consolidate power in Tamaulipas. After Portes Gil took office in December 1928, Calles announced a new National Revolutionary Party (PNR) early in 1929. It was an alliance of regional forces assembled to support Calles's power and Portes Gil's rule, far from hegemonic in contested times.[15] Portes Gil authorized land recipients to form armed guards to protect their gains and defend the government. He made 1929 the leading year of land distribution since the program had begun. In March, General Gonzalo Escobar rebelled, backed by a third of the military. Thanks to support for Calles by Cedillo in San Luis Potosí, Lázaro Cárdenas in Michoacán, and others building power by distributing land, Escobar faced defeat in May (at a cost of 2,000 lives). In September, with the regime finally entrenched, the bishops signed a settlement that restored worship and left many Cristero rebel communities feeling abandoned.[16]

The PNR consolidated as a coalition of Calles allies in diverse regions (including Carlos Riva Palacio in the state of Mexico), loyal military commanders, agrarians like Cedillo, and negotiators like Cárdenas. Escobar's defeat and Cristero containment both depended on agrarian mobilizations backed by promises of land distribution. Afterward, Calles worked to demilitarize the heights of power; he cut standing forces back to 52,000 men, dropped the military share of the budget to twenty-five percent, and dispersed key units and commanders across the country. They should serve the regime, not threaten it.[17]

The year 1929 brought pacification—and a new threat to Mexico's role in the world economy. Through the late 1920s exports had continued to fall. Oil production dropped to forty-five million barrels in 1929, less than a quarter of the peak of 1921. Other exports faded too, in bulk and value. Mexico's role as an exporter in the world of industrial capitalism, the role that had brought Constitutionalists to power, was collapsing. Meanwhile, rises in the textile, iron and steel, and cement industries brought modest economic growth from 1926 to 1929. The Monterrey capitalists Carranza and Obregón had crushed to take power in 1915 revived to lead key sectors in Mexico's economy.[18] While Cristeros fought and generals jockeyed for power, Mexico moved unplanned toward a more national industrial capitalism.

Global Depression and the Search for a National Economy

It often appears that the depression set off by the Wall Street Crash of November 1929 changed everything everywhere. In the United States, finance, industry, agriculture, and employment collapsed together in what seemed an economic apocalypse. The nations of the Americas that had built their prosperity, however limited, by selling exports to the industrial powers of Europe and North America faced sudden reckonings. Elsewhere, the crash confirmed developing trends. The European industrial powers had assaulted each other in war from 1914 to 1918 and struggled to regain dynamism in the 1920s. Germany's economic, political, and social troubles were already deep when depression hit. The Soviet Union was on the road to socialism, which it continued to pursue after 1929.[19] And in Mexico, a rhetorical search for national capitalism during the decade of revolution became a real pursuit in the 1920s as exports fell. The crash came as a jolt because of still-close ties to US finance and markets. Yet it was a jolt that accelerated a turn to national industrial capitalism already under way.

The sudden drop in US demand cut Mexican exports already in decline. The dollar value of Mexican trade fell by two-thirds from 1929 to 1932; government revenues fell 35 percent as the internal economy proved more resilient. Manufacturing fell only 8.8 percent yearly; cultivation rose 0.6 percent, enabling the gross internal product to decline only 5.4 percent annually in the first three years of the depression.[20] The land reform done so reluctantly as a political necessity by Obregón, Calles, and Portes Gil sustained production and work that cushioned Mexico's way through the depression. When the crash hit, 667,000 recipients had received over 7 million hectares of land, averaging more than 10 hectares each. Presuming families of four, nearly 2.7 million Mexicans gained sustenance in a population under 17 million.[21] Cultivators kept planting to feed families.

Yet the waning of the Cristero conflict, the defeat of Escobar, and the success of Calles and the PNR setting up Pascual Ortiz Rubio as president brought a radical cut in land reform in 1930. Mexico began an early commercial recovery in 1932, well before the US turnaround. A shift from the gold standard (that tied Mexico to the United States) and to increasing issues of silver-backed paper currency raised the money supply. Gold, silver, and oil exports rose, if only to the low levels of 1929. Industry resumed a steady growth that made it a leading sector. The depression downturn and turnaround showed the Constitutionalists an industrial route to national capitalism.

The same years brought escalating labor conflicts and new demands for land, as Calles and presidents Ortiz Rubio and Abelardo Rodríguez revealed staunch preferences for profit, labor control, and minimal land reform. New popular challenges, however, forced the regime to relearn the lessons of the 1920s: a postrevolutionary state committed to capitalism must engage the demands of workers and rural communities.[22]

While Calles and Rodríguez ruled and limited land distribution and labor rights, a reform faction used the 1933 PNR national convention to call for their acceleration—and to gain Calles's backing for the nomination of Lázaro Cárdenas for a six-year term as president to start in 1934. The *jefe máximo* saw the need to make reform promises and to nominate a reform candidate he presumed to constrain once in office. Land distribution rose during the campaign, reaching a level only exceeded in 1929, the year of pacification. Accelerating reform made Cárdenas popular and he took office in December of 1934 with an aura of promise—and saddled with a cabinet of Calles's allies. During 1935, he accelerated land distribution, increasing the area granted to many recipients. Shoring up his base, he ousted Calles's allies from the cabinet and drove the *jefe* into exile in 1935.

By 1936, Cárdenas ruled the regime and the party—and knew he had to address the popular demands that enabled his rise. He took land reform to new peaks. Almost 400,000 recipients gained nearly ten million hectares in 1936 and 1937 alone, nearly a quarter of all beneficiaries and a third of all lands distributed from 1915 to 1940. He built power in much of rural Mexico, in part because grateful recipients turned to working their lands, in part because politicized distributions set off local conflicts that consumed political energies.[23]

Meanwhile, Cárdenas promoted industrialization. Under Carranza, capitalists had formed national chambers of commerce (CONCANACO) and industry (CONCAMIN). In 1936, while regime-mediated strikes peaked, Cárdenas gave the chambers direct links to his Ministry of the Economy.[24] They gained a sanctioned voice in policy planning. He built roads to integrate markets; he brought energy and infrastructure to the capital, focusing industry there. He favored national capitalists. Yet when Monterrey industrialists aimed to force workers into company unions, Cárdenas threatened expropriation. They backed off, and carried on to flourish in iron and steel, beer and glass, and other industries. He also welcomed US manufacturers who would build plants in Mexico, employing

Mexicans to serve Mexican markets. He knew that national capitalism could not be fully national.[25]

Cárdenas pressed cultural policies he called socialist education. Born and raised in the heart of Cristero country and Governor of Michoacán while that conflict raged, he knew the depths of popular resistance to Calles's anticlericalism. He eased direct attacks on the Church, but promoted state schools and secular curricula that deeply religious people saw as assaults on truth. In heartland communities and other regions that welcomed land reform, complex negotiations worked to limit teachers' ability to challenge religious cultures. Where land reform was less welcome or provoked divisions, teachers and socialist education focused rising conflicts.[26] Cárdenas imagined socialist teachers making a modern citizenry. His educational projects fueled divisions that inhibited the regime consolidation that his land reform and other programs aimed to promote.

Cárdenas's land distribution culminated a Constitutionalist agrarian reform that did not fulfill the goals that the heartland communities had fought for after 1910. It was a program of pacification, tying recipients to the regime, hoping they would feed themselves and generate surpluses to feed the cities. From Obregón to Cárdenas, Constitutionalists knew the power of demands for land. Focused on building a regime, they never accepted the goal of reconstituting autonomies; a necessity of political stability, land reform—they hoped—might open a smallholder route to commercial cultivation. When Luis Cabrera pressed Carranza to consider land reform before 1915, he knew that community lands complemented labor at neighboring estates. He argued that limited redistribution would reset a balance that provided limited autonomy to families and communities—and send cheap labor to commercial growers. Carranza acquiesced in the agrarian law of January 1915 to serve pacification and profit.[27] He blocked implementation before 1920, but Cabrera's vision of land reform as a route to pacification and support for commercial-industrial development lived to influence Obregón and his successors.

People across the heartland and wider regions of historic landed communities dreamed of regaining ancestral lands to rebuild local autonomies—in production, politics, and religious culture. The regime offered ejido grants, new constructs dependent on the national state, ruled by local committees dependent on national powers. And ejido lands went to male heads of household. The land reform promoted patriarchal autonomies in cultivation—and dependence on the regime. Reformers hoped that recipients would honor the regime and send produce to feed city people and industrial workers. They soon learned that ejidatarios pursued their own visions: feeding families first and only selling true surpluses that were always limited.

Expropriated estates retained core lands, water, and machinery— yet could rarely revive production at levels that provided meaningful wage supplements to former seasonal workers now holding ejido lands. Recipients often retrenched in household economies and sent little food to the cities. Reformers saw failure. Cárdenas pressed ejidatarios toward market production, offering credit to fund commercial cropping. But credit-dependent farming was just that—dependent. For men seeking patriarchal autonomy as providers, credit and market dependence meant uncertainty and insecurity—not the goal of their revolution. Villagers and reformers locked together in an experiment, while pursuing conflicting goals. Through the 1930s, many villagers turned the reform to their own purposes. Cárdenas, like Zapata before him, learned not to push back too hard.

In key commercial crops like sugar, cotton, henequen, and citrus, Cárdenas saw a solution in cooperatives. Ejidatarios at Zacatepec in Morelos, in the Laguna far to the north, in Yucatán, and in the hot country of Michoacán gained land as communities organized to grow commercial crops for mills and processors. In complex systems mixing industry, cultivation, and labor, producers did everything but generate their own food. With strong government backing, several cooperatives carried on for years—exceptions in a nation of land-reform recipients focused on sustenance. Did Cárdenas see a necessary failure? Land distribution was essential to pacification and regime stabilization. Recipients sustained themselves, in that way carrying the national project. But by the late 1930s, it was clear that they could not and would not feed the cities and the industries focused there.

Recognizing the limits of land reform as support for his industrial vision, Cárdenas cut distribution by forty percent in 1938, twelve percent in 1939, and another forty percent in 1940.[28] The reformer and regime builder concluded that continuing land reform was not Mexico's way forward. Yet political necessity had made it Mexico's way of the moment. By 1940, nearly half of the nation's arable land was held by ejidatarios, over 1.7 million recipients, most focused on sustaining families and communities totaling nearly 7 million of Mexico's nearly 20 million people. The postrevolutionary reconstruction left Mexico again locked in a contradiction tying capitalism to communities.

As the turn away from land reform revealed, 1938 was a pivotal year in Cárdenas's search for national capitalism and regime consolidation. He had linked leading capitalists to his state as favored groups earning consultation; he began to limit land reform and constrain strikes and workers' demands. And as 1938 began, he called for a reconstruction of the national party. From the loose coalition of regional powers and parties in the PNR since 1929, it would become the Party of the Mexican Revolution (PRM), built on a new corporatist organization of land recipients, labor unions, and the military. The goal was not to empower those groups, but to control them. As land distribution plummeted, recipients would join a National Peasant Federation (CNC), formed to limit demands and channel support to the regime. A Mexican Workers Party (PTM) would contain strikes and direct labor support to Cárdenas. The military, little threat to the heights of power since 1929, gained honor as a party sector as it turned to serve political and social control.[29]

Groups that had contended for power since 1920 faced constraints. Ejidatarios were to cultivate, sustain themselves, feed cities, and support the regime. Workers would join in a state-mediated populism that promoted industry and promised benefits to laborers within state-mediated limits. The military would provide force to back the regime and its allies across the nation—the coercive base essential to all industrial states.[30]

While working to reconstruct the party and the regime, Cárdenas faced his greatest challenge and won his most famous success. After negotiations with the international oil companies broke down, union workers pressed a suit in the supreme court seeking new rights, better wages, and benefits. The companies, led by Standard Oil of New Jersey, resisted. Mexican production had fallen to 33 million barrels yearly in 1932 and 1933—a true crash in the context of its 1921 peak of over 193 million barrels. Growth had resumed to hold near 40 million barrels yearly from 1934 through 1936, then to near 47 million in 1937, giving new hope for profits to companies, for income to workers, and for revenues to Cárdenas. The companies and the unions disputed those gains, real and potential.

The supreme court found for the unions on March 1. After a brief negotiation with Cárdenas, the companies rejected the decision. Refusing to recognize the supreme court, they denied Mexican sovereignty. After consulting advisers, Cárdenas nationalized the oil companies on March 23, 1938—a key date in the construction of Mexican nationalism. If the expropriation was provoked by labor conflict and the companies' denial of the supreme court's jurisdiction, implementation was conditioned by Cárdenas's understanding of the importance of oil to the United States and the world as they moved toward another great war—as he and Franklin Roosevelt recognized in the negotiations that followed.[31]

While the US companies protested, backed by allies in Roosevelt's administration, the two presidents negotiated a resolution that accepted Mexico's right to expropriate—with fair compensation. They understood that oil was more important than company profits in a world headed to war. In a brilliant ploy, Cárdenas offered compensation based on 1937 Mexican tax filings; when the companies insisted that the filings undervalued their holdings, Cárdenas answered that they were welcome to refile for the last decade, pay back taxes, and claim higher compensation. The companies accepted the low compensation, which Mexico still struggled to pay. A nationalist celebration framed a call for popular contributions to redeem oil—and national sovereignty.

The oil nationalization often appears as the pivot of a turn to national capitalism. Powerful global companies faced expropriation, Mexico took ownership of energy pivotal to an industrial world—and the United States acquiesced. Still, in negotiating with Roosevelt, Cárdenas agreed that Mexico would continue to welcome US investment and technology. In 1939 he raised tariffs to protect consumer goods made in Mexico—while enabling imports of equipment and machinery for energy and manufacturing.[32] Nationalization of oil, electricity generation, and railroads gave the state control of key sectors. Manufacturers in Mexico would employ workers and sell consumer products in Mexico—while the nation remained in a world shaped by US capital, technology, and power. National capitalism, better, nationalist capitalism, proved to be a way to navigate the crisis of global industrial capitalism. It was not a break with US power or global integration, as became clear when the 1940s brought the war Cárdenas and Roosevelt expected.

World War, North American Integration, and the Limits of National Capitalism

Having backed away from land reform, turned against labor independence, and nationalized oil in pursuit of industrial growth, Cárdenas named Miguel Ávila Camacho as successor and ensured his election in 1940. Ávila Camacho announced himself a Catholic believer and limited anticlerical policies. Only in that did he break with Cárdenas, who surely knew it was coming. At the inauguration in December, Vice President Elect Henry Wallace represented the United States. His father had built Pioneer Seeds; Henry had been secretary of agriculture—and he saw a solution to Mexico's agricultural challenges.

Cárdenas was disillusioned with the results of land distribution: recipients focused on sustenance and did not generate commercial surpluses.

Wallace proposed a program of mechanized, chemically sustained, scientific cultivation to feed the cities. He returned home to consult Nelson Rockefeller, whose family ruled the recently expropriated Standard Oil and whose role in Creole Petroleum in Venezuela helped make him a key Roosevelt adviser on Latin America as war loomed. He backed Wallace's proposal and led the Rockefeller Foundation to fund a US-Mexican program begun in 1943, seeking a new agriculture for Mexico. It would be productive, commercial, and laborsaving—profitable for Mexican growers and US makers of hybrid seeds and farm machinery, herbicides and pesticides. A new transnational agricultural capitalism would come to Mexico.[33]

While Ávila Camacho continued to promote an urban industrial Mexico and planned a new agriculture to sustain it, a year after his inauguration Japan attacked Pearl Harbor. The United States joined the war in the Pacific, and soon in Europe too. Mexico, led by Cárdenas—who entered the cabinet as defense minister—was ready to back the US war effort. It supplied copper and other strategic metals; it sold cotton and other agricultural goods; it sent workers to replace US men drawn to war. The two governments negotiated the *bracero* program, sending men north with permits aimed to guarantee fair wages and paid travel both ways. Others went informally, notably to Texas, removed by the Mexican government from the official labor program in protest of working conditions. Mexicans picked crops, maintained rail lines, and worked in cities and towns across the United States; 500,000 Mexican citizens fought in the US armed forces during World War II—to face the highest casualty rates.[34]

In Mexico, war stimulated economic growth and industrial expansion. Industry was only 12 percent of Mexico's economy in 1929; it rose to nearly 20 percent in the 1940s. More important, the war enabled a mix of strong exports and internal industrial growth. Not only did copper, other minerals, and petroleum exports grow, so did sales of cotton cloth to the United States and Central America. From 1939 to 1942 in the run-up to the war, Mexican exports rose 8.3 percent yearly; during the war they soared 15.6 percent yearly as the United States bought more and Mexican manufacturers sold in markets vacated by US manufacturers. While Mexico imported machinery to increase production in support of the war effort, strong exports brought mounting dollar reserves to the Banco de México—from 41 million dollars in 1939 to 328 million in 1945. Mexican government revenues rose a healthy 3.2 percent yearly in the run-up, a stronger 4.1 percent yearly during the war.[35]

Ávila Camacho, backed by Cárdenas, put those resources to use in revealing ways: from 1941 to 1946, 779 million pesos went to roads, 168 million to railroads, and 261 million to electricity generation—all in support of industrial acceleration; 626 million went to irrigation projects for the new "scientific" agriculture; 143 million went to credit for ejido producers—most to cooperatives. Only 42 million pesos funded school construction; 38 million built hospitals and medical facilities; 84 million paid for potable water systems and 68 million went to sanitation systems.[36] The regime invested to support industry, mechanized agriculture, and market expansion. Social investment lagged far behind.

The decade from 1935 to 1945 brought Mexico's pivotal turn from a primarily agricultural economy to a focus on industry.[37] The shift came in a sequence that began with Cárdenas's populist reforms and continued with his turn to favor industry (with nationalized energy), support for the US economy in the run-up to war, and then the mix of export growth and industrial expansion in wartime—as the United States needed diverse imports and could not supply consumer goods. Once more, a pivotal shift in Mexico's role in capitalism came not by plan, but from politicized responses to social pressures, national political challenges, and the constraints and possibilities of a changing world economy. By 1945, a decade of dynamic growth had moved Mexico toward an industrial capitalism ruled by a nationalist regime, led by national capitalists (and key international collaborators), worked by Mexican workers, and serving national markets. National capitalism seemed at hand.

As the war ended, new political-industrial interests were entrenched in Mexico. They held massive credits in dollars redeemable in the United States, available to fund new industries and technologies, fueling a continuing industrial advance. But Mexico remained tied to the United States and the global economy, and after the war both changed radically. Mexico faced new constraints. The promise of 1935 to 1945 gave way to deepening contradictions.

The war ended with the United States unleashing nuclear weapons on Japan, while the Soviet Union occupied Eastern Europe and the German capital at Berlin. A new era began. As the Soviets began to spread industrial socialism, the United States aimed to revive a northern axis of industrial capitalism, including its recent foes Japan and (western) Germany. Justified as essential to pacification and to prevent a return to war (among capitalist powers), the goal was to revive a world of capitalism to counter Soviet power and the socialist alternative.

As the Soviets kept military forces across Eastern Europe (justified as necessary to prevent another German invasion) and pressed reconstruction via industrial socialism, the United States turned to reconstruction in Western Europe and Japan, mixing military occupation with infusions of capital via the Marshall Plan, and promises of integrated markets that would benefit all within capitalism. Over the years, Europe and Japan revived within a capitalist world centered on the United States. The Soviet-centered socialist world carried on. Both sides in an escalating Cold War proclaimed universalizing goals beneficial to all humanity; both built nuclear arsenals threatening universal annihilation. As the threat became a mutual deterrence that both cowed and protected populations in the contending powers and their allies, wars of mass mobilization ended in the old industrial heartlands. Anticolonial conflicts seeking variants of national development (sometimes capitalist, sometimes socialist) proliferated across collapsing colonial empires in Africa, the Islamic world, and South Asia. China, a US ally in the recent war, fell into a civil war that became an independent Communist revolution, in time promoting industry imposed upon a rural majority in the world's most populous nation.[38]

Mexico faced a new world, locked within capitalism and tied to the United States. Before Germany surrendered to Russian occupation in early May and Japan relented after the nuclear bombings of Hiroshima and Nagasaki in August, the United States called a meeting of hemispheric allies in Mexico City early in 1945. It gained a treaty of mutual defense and began to press visions of free trade that Mexico, Brazil, and others resisted. Having built new industries protected by depression and then the war, they knew that open trade and the revival of US industry would bring dislocations. As the United States did when it first turned to industry during Napoleonic conflicts and the War of 1812 and then protected it with tariffs in a postwar world ruled by Britain, so Mexico insisted on protecting its industries after World War II. When a 1947 meeting in Havana led to the founding of the GATT, the General Agreement on Tariffs and Trade that looked toward a capitalist world of free trade, the United States, Canada, and their European allies signed—Mexico, Brazil, and the rest of Latin America refrained. Signing on would return the region to reliance on the commodity exports that had collapsed in the depression. Could such economies sustain growing populations?

Tariffs and other protections enabled Mexico to maintain its industrial drive after 1945. For a few years, it spent the credits acquired in wartime support for the United States to purchase machinery and other technology essential to industrialization. When credits ran out, the only recourse was costly loans—while the United States subsidized capital and technological assistance to rebuild its recent foes. In the postwar world, Mexico had no exports sufficient to pay for its dependence on US capital and technology.

The protection essential to sustain industries made Mexican goods costly at home and uncompetitive abroad. Cycles of debt financing followed by currency and debt crises began to mark Mexico's economic life, heightening political challenges while social polarities deepened.

As 1946 began, in his last year in office, Ávila Camacho brought a last reorganization to the party that sustained the regime. The renaming was significant: the PRM, the Party of the Mexican Revolution, became the PRI, the Institutional Revolutionary Party. In 1938 Cárdenas, turning away from radical reform, renamed the party to assert that it remained the embodiment of revolution—however debatable the claim. In 1946, Ávila Camacho saw a revolution institutionalized. He advertised stability; radical reform was in the past. The name became an emblem for the contradictions that marked Mexico after 1946. Mexicans and others asked: Can revolution be institutionalized? Can a regime be revolutionary? Debate continued while Mexicans searched for a national capitalism.

The party changed in more than name. The agrarian (CNC) and labor (PTM) sectors remained two of three key sectors. The military left the party, announcing regime confidence that the army now served as the coercive arm of the state.[39] It was replaced by a popular sector (CNOP) that aimed to represent (and control) the diverse middle classes proliferating in Mexico City and beyond, as the nation became more industrial and urban. Bureaucrats dependent on the state for education and employment formed the core of the new sector.[40] The renamed party continued to focus on political control in rural regions, and on negotiating power and programs with the professionals and industrial workers it aimed to favor—within the limits of national capitalism.

Capitalists remained most favored in the nation, operating outside a party focused on political control. Their long-established organizations, CONCAMIN promoting industry and CONCANACO backing commerce, were joined by COPARMEX (a league of entrepreneurs begun in Monterrey) and the more recent CANACINTRA (National Chamber of Industries of Transformation, established under Ávila Camacho in 1941 by new industries seeking national protection)—all favored with regular access to the heights of power. They jostled to promote policy preferences while capitalism ruled the way forward.

With a political system locked in to favor capitalists and control peasants, workers, and middle sectors, the immediate postwar years under proudly capitalist president Miguel Alemán (1946–52) brought a boom fueled by imports of machinery paid for with wartime credits. When credits ran out in the late 1940s, problems arose. Industry operating in

Mexico, employing Mexicans, and supplying national consumers was the heart of the model. A mix of Mexican industries in cloth and other consumables and international subsidiaries in automobiles (Ford and more) and other durables (General Electric and others) made real gains. But Mexico did not produce the machines and other technology essential to industrial production. With wartime credits gone, how would Mexico pay for essential imports?

It had no exports sufficient to the task. Nationalized oil (and electricity) provided subsidized energy for internal industries, a key support for the national project. Both Cold War hegemons, the United States and the Soviet Union, were major energy producers, while Venezuela and the Middle East sent oil to supply a reviving Europe and other markets. Petroleum exports were not an option, even if the industry could be revived. Mexico's other exports could not begin to pay for its needs for imported capital and technology. While the United States provided aid and subsidized credit to rebuild Western Europe and Japan in a northern-hemisphere capitalist core, it left Mexico (and other Latin American nations) to seek funds in costly and uncertain financial markets. Credit was available and would fund industrial and infrastructure development for decades to come. It never funded growth sufficient to repay its costs—principal plus interest usually over 6 to 8 percent yearly—or to fulfill its promises: growth (celebrated as it averaged 6 percent over 1950–62), employment (which rose less than 3 percent annually in the same era), and rising industrial wages (which increased but 2.2 percent yearly—in a favored sector).[41] While Alemán and his successors ruled and entrepreneurs profited, monetary, balance-of-payment, and debt crises plagued Mexico while inequities spread to define lives in times proclaimed a development "miracle" after 1950. Perhaps the miracle was the regime's ability to sustain a system structured by deepening polarities and widening exclusions.

Miracle Development, Green Revolution, and the Crash of National Capitalism

Most analysts of Mexican (and other Latin American) economic development after World War II have focused on disjunctions between the need for capital to build industry and infrastructure, limited expansion of production and markets, and repeated debt crises.[42] Others emphasize uncertain property protection, politicized courts, and low taxes that fueled concentrations while limiting infrastructure and social spending that might serve the general welfare and social distributions.[43] Political analysts debate the ability of the PRI regime to sustain its power and national stability through decades of economic growth and political exclusion—some focusing on mediations, others on coercions, the best on their fusion.[44] All deal with key questions. But they deflect focus from the fundamental processes that generated dynamic growth tied to widening exclusions, making deepening inequities the defining essence of Mexican capitalism after 1945: a long history of laborsaving capitalism intersected with a new acceleration of life-sustaining capitalism—in medicine and agriculture; their triumphant fusion generated economically profitable and socially debilitating exclusions.

The industrialization that shaped the capitalist world after 1800 made laborsaving machinery the core of its economic dynamism—as so many have emphasized.[45] It concentrated production and profit in key regions, using machines to increase worker productivity. In the pioneer industrial zones of Europe and the United States, in time and after reform campaigns and fights for unionization, new working classes gained sufficient benefits, leading some to see "labor aristocracies," others "vanguard proletarians" who might lead the world to a more just socialism.[46] Of course, early mechanized industries and their workers were linked to slaves growing cotton in the US South and others—some coerced, some just desperate—working to make key commodities for little gain across the globe.[47]

Equally important, mechanization allowed some shared growth in nineteenth-century England because its core of workers set to machines produced for markets across the globe (by combinations of trade, imperial pressure, and force). By drawing income from across the world, the first industrialists could reluctantly share prosperity with English workers in times of world dominance.[48] After 1870 in the United States, industries that concentrated in the northeast served markets and took produce and profit from across an expanding continental nation (cleared of native people and settled by immigrants fleeing Europe). Again, in the United States, mechanization could generate shared growth when industries served markets beyond home regions—and organized workers and farmers demanded a sharing.[49]

When mechanization accelerated laborsaving production in Mexico, it came to a very different context. In a nation with limited resources (thanks to the war of 1846–48), a dense and growing population, limited internal markets, and little prospect of exports, machines could not create shared prosperity. Instead, they generated production, concentrations, and exclusions—in agriculture and industry simultaneously.

As the 1940s began, Mexico remained an agricultural nation, its historic focus confirmed by the postrevolutionary agrarian reform. Mexico City had doubled in size—from under a million people in 1920 to nearly two million by 1940—evidence of a rising urban-industrial society focused on the capital. The national population grew more slowly, from under fifteen million to nearly twenty million in the same two decades. As Cárdenas learned, land reform could pacify and help sustain rural communities; it did not provide for growing cities. Then, after 1940, a surge of national population growth accelerated urbanization. The turn to mechanized, chemically fed cultivation proposed by Henry Wallace, backed by the Rockefeller Foundation, and later celebrated as a "green revolution" aimed to feed growing cities. It succeeded—while cutting labor needs and corroding autonomies across rural Mexico and sending migrants in growing numbers to Mexican cities and the United States.

Two unquestioned social goods, a suddenly healthy and growing population and a newly productive agriculture to sustain it, merged to generate profits and social exclusions in a nation defined by limited resources and plagued by capital shortages and periodic debt crises. The triumphs of health, industrial acceleration, and green revolution are honored; their merger to fuel social crises and national calamity is rarely analyzed. The forces that fueled the catastrophe—medical capitalism, agricultural and in-dustrial mechanization, and urbanization—remain central to the promise of globalization since the 1980s. An inquiry into the contradictions that drove and undermined Mexico's national project is essential.[50]

If a disease-driven radical depopulation shaped heartland communi-ties' roles in the origins of silver capitalism, facilitating autonomies they cherished and fought to protect, explosive population growth beginning in the 1940s drove the collapse of autonomies in the heartland from the 1960s and across Mexico by the 1980s. What caused the surge? Land distribu-tions from the 1920s enabled families to feed children better, and children worked to increase production on new lands. As families ate better, populations grew, accounting for modest rural demographic expansions into the 1940s. Then something radically different began. After Mexico's population, still mostly rural, grew from 15 million to 20 million from 1920 to 1940, it jumped to 35 million by 1960, 67 million by 1980, and nearly 100 million by 2000—a fivefold increase from 1940 to the end of the century.

State health programs and potable water and sanitation systems contributed to improving health and longer lives. Still, the key was the rapid spread of inoculations and especially of antibiotics. Penicillin and other medicines were perfected to keep soldiers alive during World War II.

After the war, an expanding pharmaceutical industry saw potential for sales and profits across the world. In Mexico, by the late 1940s and early 1950s every city neighborhood, small town, and soon every village had a pharmacy, or a store that sold antibiotics. Parents turned to medicines that stopped infections and kept children alive, a joyous triumph of medical capitalism. Healthy children worked to sustain families facing limited opportunities; they cared for parents facing longer times of old age. Only after it was clear that most children would live to become healthy adults did parents limit childbearing in the 1980s—as the national economy collapsed. Yet, by then, expanded numbers of healthy adults were having children. Decades of population explosion gave way to continued population growth.[51]

Healthy families were celebrated. The industrialization under way in the 1940s promised production and employment to sustain growing numbers. Yet by relying ever more on laborsaving technologies that increased productivity (a good to every capitalist), industries increased employment very slowly—and wages even less. Industrial workers became a favored sector, economically and politically, but the favor had limits. The prophets of development proclaimed that, in time, industrial growth would generate employment for Mexicans. Laborsaving production ensured that time never came.

While Mexico remained grounded in landed communities, the rising productivity with limited employment that characterized industry generated profits and consumer products—while growing numbers sustained themselves and national capitalism on the land.[52] The demographic explosion broke an always-tenuous balance. A "green revolution" came in time to feed soaring urban populations. But its vaunted ability to make increasing harvests with ever fewer hands drove contradictions that destroyed rural autonomies and undermined national capitalism.

The rise of the green revolution in Mexico is well known. After Henry Wallace's 1940 state visit, by 1943 a research program was underway, centered at the National Agricultural School (at the old Chapingo hacienda shown in figure 11.1), funded by the Rockefeller Foundation and directed by leading US agricultural scientists, famously Norman Borlaug who won a Nobel Prize in 1970 for his work. They adapted to Mexico the system of cultivation based on hybrid seeds, chemical fertilizers, herbicides, pesticides, and machines that had brought great gains in productivity to a land-rich and sparsely populated US Midwest. To flourish in arid Mexico, irrigation was essential—literally to create new agricultural zones in a land-poor nation. To profit—and the green revolution was an agrarian

FIGURE 11.1. Chapingo: historic hacienda, school for land-
reform surveyors, laboratory of green revolution.

capitalism—machines and chemicals had to displace labor in a nation of
soaring population desperate for work and income. The project focused
first on wheat, an urban staple. The goal was to feed the cities and the
prosperous within. Government planners knew that villagers and land-
reform recipients, focused on maize, would resist a system that required
credit to buy seeds and chemicals, irrigation they rarely had, tractors they
could not buy—and access to markets others ruled.[53]

While scientists tested seeds, herbicides, and pesticides, the government funded dam and irrigation projects—most in the north, far from
land-reform communities. The goal was to favor "small proprietors." They
were not the old haciendas, holding thousands of hectares; nor were they
villagers or ejidatarios with plots under ten hectares—and shrinking every
generation. The chosen growers would work fifty to a hundred irrigated
hectares (120 to 240 acres). They could gain credit, buy machines, and
take advantage of scientific cultivation to profit and feed the cities. On its
own terms, the program succeeded. From the late 1940s Mexico had two
agricultural systems: one in communities of smallholders struggling to
feed families, the second led by commercial growers prospering by increasing production (first of wheat, later of maize and other crops) to feed
the cities. Together, they kept food available and prices low, subsidizing
industrialization. To the prophets of capitalism it was a green revolution
worth celebrating—and spreading across the globe.

Urban benefits came with social costs that struck rural communities
first, and then reverberated back upon urban centers. The chemicals

essential to productivity and profit passed on to poison consumers; when Rachel Carson's *Silent Spring* (1962) led to consumer resistance in the United States, producers shifted to chemicals that mostly poisoned workers in the fields—as those workers became mostly Mexicans.[54] The few still working in a mechanized agriculture gained minimal earnings, paid seasonally, too often at the cost of their health. On a larger scale the green revolution enabled Mexico to rebuild a flourishing capitalist agriculture to feed its cities, while employing fewer and fewer hands—a good, given the poisons in play. Gains in productivity were celebrated; poisonous impacts on land and water, consumers and field hands, were slowly addressed. The displacement of labor as population soared pushed families to migrate, mostly to Mexican cities through the 1960s, increasingly to the United States from the 1970s.[55]

While the green revolution generated rising production but minimized work in the new capitalist agriculture, old communities and land-reform recipients faced rising populations on limited lands. Family holdings split into smaller and smaller plots, often eroded by constant cultivation in desperate search for sustenance. Fertilizers and other chemicals became essential to growing maize; yet they had to be bought, forcing reliance on credit and sales of already limited harvests. Population explosion, erosion, and market dependence forced rising numbers off the land in old communities, adding to migrant streams. When the national population hit thirty-five million in 1960, Mexico City had grown to five million; when the nation reached sixty-seven million by 1980, the metropolis exceeded thirteen million.

Yet cities pursuing laborsaving industrialization could not begin to employ the rural population "freed" from labor by population explosion and green revolution. Work in the capital focused on building a new center and spreading neighborhoods of desperation. Much of that work was minimally paid, and too often informal and unpaid as migrants built their own barrios. A "Mexican miracle" fed by "green revolution" in times of population explosion drove deepening contradictions. Production and productivity, industrial and agricultural, soared; employment and income lagged far behind, incapable of sustaining a soaring population concentrating in cities. Concentrations of power and profit, deepening polarities, and spreading marginalities, rural and urban, marked Mexico after 1950.

Powers sustaining production and profit, poverty and exclusions, underlay rising political conflicts, serial economic crises, and streams of migrants searching for new lives. In the heartland, the movement led by Rubén Jaramillo in the 1940s and 1950s claimed the mantle of Zapatismo while demanding a better deal for cane growers and refinery workers at the government's Zacatepec mill cooperative. Jaramillo was assassinated in 1962.[56] In the 1950s too, railroad workers seeking independent unions organized, struck, and faced repression.[57] Middle classes that grew with urbanization faced political frustrations that culminated in the student protests and deadly repression of 1968.[58] Political blockages led to guerrilla fights led by Genaro Vázquez and Lucio Cabañas in Guerrero, just south of the heartland, in the late 1960s and into the 1970s, leading to the deaths of both leaders.[59]

Political challenges persisted in the cities and the countryside through the 1970s; the PRI regime adapted, negotiated, and sometimes repressed to carry on. The commitment to national capitalism mixing industrial urbanization and agro-industrial mechanization also continued, provoking booms and crises managed by the regime.[60] There is endless debate about whether the regime operated as a brilliant negotiator, mediating conflicting interests, co-opting opposing forces to serve the powerful—or was increasingly coercive. It was both: mediating when it could, turning to repression when political tools failed to produce desired results—meaning PRI rule, capitalist concentrations, limited benefits to urban middle sectors and favored industrial workers, and acquiescence in marginality by the many in dying rural communities and burgeoning city barrios.[61]

Following the crisis of 1968, visible because it killed hundreds of students in the capital on the eve of the Olympics, the early 1970s saw attempts to accelerate development based on more international borrowing, rapid industrialization, and rural mechanization, now combined with new education, social service, and infrastructure spending and an attempt to revive land reform—all covered with President Luis Echeverría's populist rhetoric. Debts rose to new heights as many benefited, many more struggled, and migrants increasingly left the nation. The impossibility of the national capitalist model seemed clear when the 1973 OPEC (Organization of Petroleum Exporting Countries) oil embargo brought a spike in global energy prices that for a time stressed Mexicans' lives more—and then enabled an imagined solution.

New offshore drilling promised to make the nation a major petroleum exporter again. International capital surged in via US banks, funding exploration and production, aiming to add non-OPEC supplies to the world market—and to bring prices down. From the mid-1970s, mounting international debts funded a broad-based boom that left many believing that Mexico's time had come.

Then, in the early 1980s, rising flows of new oil from Mexico's Gulf fields and the North Sea did bring down global prices. The United States and industrial nations benefited. Mexico faced huge debts contracted on the premise of soaring prices—with the explicit goal of bringing prices down. With that success, Mexico could not pay. Global capital markets closed to a nation dependent on global capital. The 1980s became Mexico's great depression, a lost decade punctuated by the earthquake that devastated Mexico City in 1985. The dream of national capitalism, laden with contradictions since the 1950s, became untenable—impossible even—in the 1980s.

A new world of globalization, a new era of capitalism, rising across the northern hemisphere since the 1950s, drew Mexico in. Urbanization continued; industrialization collapsed, then turned to supply US markets; agro-capitalism did the same. The focus on laborsaving technologies of production and integration accelerated while population continued to rise, leaving Mexicans facing the collapse of rural autonomies and widening urban marginalities to struggle for new ways to live—and to head to the United States in unprecedented numbers.[62]

The trajectory of the Mexican economy during the search for national capitalism is illuminated in revealing ways by changing emphases in production. In 1921, the rural economy (including cultivation, livestock, and forestry) remained the largest sector, exceeding twenty-two percent of gross internal product; booming petroleum exports led a sector (including mining) that exceeded twelve percent; industry (including manufacturing, construction, and electricity) held at eleven percent; while the commerce that integrated everything was just over thirty percent—a level it would hold to 1980. By the 1940s, the rural economy had fallen to nineteen percent, petroleum and other extractions to five percent, while industry had almost doubled to nearly twenty percent. Through the 1950s, rural production fell to under seventeen percent, extraction held near five; while industry rose to twenty-four. In 1971, as political crisis fueled a new populism, the rural economy was but twelve percent, extraction only two and a half; while industry neared thirty. Then, in 1981—as Mexico's second oil boom busted—rural production fell under nine percent; extraction, including oil, had risen to but three and a half percent; and industry was up to thirty-two percent, nearly a third of the national economy.[63]

Through six decades of difficult change, Mexico had become an industrial country. Industry was by far the dominant productive sector. Agriculture shrank radically and became industrial—that is, mechanized and chemically dependent. Both were defined by growing productivity, agriculture by vanishing employment as population soared—leaving growing numbers to live in commercial and service sectors shaped by informality, marginal earnings, and endless uncertainties. Mexico's search for national capitalism brought profit to capitalists, comfort to middle sectors, and secure earnings to minorities of favored workers. The nation and its soaring population were drawn into lives of market and machine dependence; when national capitalism crashed in the 1980s, a new globalization limited production, labor, and incomes, leaving Mexicans dependent on global capitalists for the means to live. The Stock Exchange (shown in figure 11.2) set near the US embassy on the great Paseo de la Reforma became the symbol and center of power as Mexicans faced the new world of globalizing neoliberalism.

The people of the heartland lived the decades of national capitalism and the turn to globalization in diverse local ways. Once-revolutionary

FIGURE 11.2. Global power in Mexico City: Stock
Exchange on the Paseo de la Reforma.

rural communities gained lands and struggled to rebuild autonomies as industrialization rose—to see dreams of independence, long tarnished, vanish as population soared. Displaced people fled to Mexico City in search of new lives in a metropolis that concentrated profit and limited employment, offering comfort and services to some, only marginality to many. People locked in dependence and insecurity had to negotiate the turn to globalization in the 1980s, incorporation in NAFTA in the 1990s, and the electoral opening celebrated as democratization in 2000. Lives defined by profit for a few, prosperity for a few more, insecurity for most, and exclusions for too many persist. Autonomies are gone. Powers built on dependencies rule a new urban heartland.

CHAPTER TWELVE

After Zapata

COMMUNITIES CARRYING NATIONAL
CAPITALISM, 1920–80

THE MEN WHO fought alongside Zapata during the decade after 1910 risked everything—life, family, and community—in desperate hope that they might reclaim the land and rebuild families and communities grounded in patriarchal ways of provision. The women of Morelos and nearby communities lived years of fear and dislocation, physical deprivation and sexual predation. When the conflict ended with the assassination of Zapata in 1919 and alliance with Obregón in 1920, people faced a region broken by war and depopulated by half—because of death, disease, and departures. However noble the goals of many, social war in times of industrial-military technology proved deeply destructive.

The decades that followed began with promises of land reform—which Zapatistas expected would restore autonomies. Land came not in restorations of ancestral rights, but as gifts of a regime that aimed to rule and limit autonomies. Land distributions to pacify rural communities and consolidate regime power began under Obregón and focused on Morelos early in the 1920s. They culminated nationally in the 1930s under Cárdenas, who promoted an agrarian capitalism that pressed communities toward market production. Morelos villagers saw population grow, conflicts escalate, and autonomies corrode. By the 1970s, the only remnant of their revolutionary aspirations was a Zapatista myth used by the regime to cover capitalist concentration and political exclusion.

Morelos was the heartland of community revolution after 1910, the center of the drive for landed autonomies and the focus of outsiders' assaultive destruction. It was the first region to gain a thorough land reform and to face the political conflicts it engendered. Morelos communities were also among the first to live the mix of population explosion, land scarcity, chemical cultivation, and commercialization that ended autonomies by the 1970s. The people of Morelos led the heartland and the nation in a twentieth-century history that began in a revolution that demanded autonomies and culminated in their final destruction as Mexico and the world turned to globalization. It is a history worth knowing.

It can be explored in depth and detail thanks to a confluence of exceptional sources. Precisely because of the dreams promoted by the Zapatista uprisings and the difficulties that followed, Morelos communities became the focus of studies by leading anthropologists from the 1920s through the 1980s. They detailed production, politics, social relations, and religious culture in diverse ways. Most were drawn to historical perspectives— surely because of the weight of history on the people of Morelos. For a historian looking to understand the trajectory of a difficult and transformative twentieth century, they are exceptional sources. The authors report their experiences and observations, at times backed by quantitative materials and often illuminated by the voices of local people, men and women.

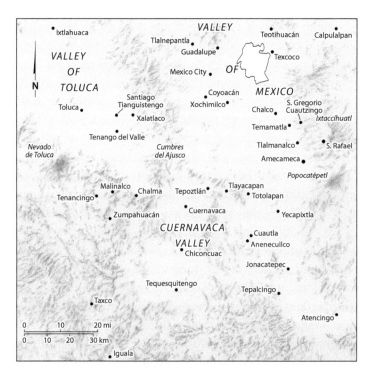

MAP 14. The Zapatista heartland after the revolution.

As with any source, the anthropologists and the people they recorded must be engaged critically. All reflect the times they lived, the problems they addressed, and their own perspectives. Still, they offer unique windows into once-revolutionary communities living decades of change.

Divisive Autonomies: Land Reform
and Local Politics in the 1920s

While Zapatista men fought landlords and outside armies, from 1913 through 1915 communities took rich bottomlands to raise maize. When Constitutionalist troops invaded in waves, beginning in 1916, villagers fled the bottomlands for uplands where many survived by *tlacolol*, hard yet productive slash-and-burn cultivation. The deaths, dislocations, and departures of revolution came followed by a Constitutionalist "pacifica-tion" and the "Spanish" influenza of 1918. By 1920 the population of the Morelos was reduced by nearly half.

When surviving Zapatista leaders allied with Obregón to end armed conflict and join the regime, autonomies on the land were real for many survivors. Obregón named Antonio Díaz Soto y Gama, a former Zapata secretary, to run agrarian programs. They understood that to keep the peace and set regime power in Morelos, they had to distribute rights to the lands people were already working. From 1921, they elicited petitions; by 1923 they had approved most as preliminary grants; it took until 1929 for most to become definitive by presidential decree. A key difference separated petitioners from reformers. Villagers sought land in restitution, in recognition of ancestral rights. The reformers, noting the complexity of old titles and conflicts among claimants, insisted on making new grants.

That decision accelerated the preliminary grants that sanctioned immediate use. It also politicized land rights. In the indigenous republics that organized communities under Spanish rule, the political republic held domain over all land—creating a unitary political-landed domain that could deal with conflicts within and challenges from without. The liberal reforms that culminated in the 1857 constitution, to be implemented by Juárez and Díaz after 1868, broke the link between local governance and landholding, while privatizing and concentrating lands. Revolutionary communities dreamed of reuniting local political and landed auton-omies. In the 1920s, the regime claiming to be revolutionary insisted that ejido grants be awarded via local committees distinct from munic-ipal authorities—and dependent on national powers. Local politics and community land rights were formally separated. Endless conflicts fractured communities as they gained lands.

Despite deals that welcomed ex-Zapatista leaders Gildardo Magaña, Genovevo de la O, and Antonio Díaz Soto y Gama to high office, local Zapatistas were often blocked from municipal office. The committees that petitioned for land were separate from municipal powers—and often based in local factions. In Tepoztlán, one petition came from residents in exile in Mexico City. As it became clear that gaining land depended on access to officials in the capital, frustrations rose. Arturo Warman, a Mexican anthropologist who completed historical research and extensive interviews across eastern Morelos in the early 1970s, concluded: "the Agrarian Law of 1915 and the Constitution of 1917" were "cheap demagogic tricks." By the 1920s it was clear that for Morelos villagers "everything had been lost . . . the new regime was a ferocious reincarnation of the Porfiriato."[1]

Still, villagers facing new authorities took the land as they could and turned to cultivating maize for sustenance. With old sugar mills destroyed, lands across Morelos—irrigated former cane fields in the lowlands, rain-fed lands in temperate zones, and cool uplands, too—were sown in maize. Villagers fed families first, selling surplus maize and other crops only as supplements. The turn to maize and autonomy was made possible by the revolution, the land reform, and the small population of survivors, joined slowly by the return of some who had fled and the arrival of newcomers.

Through the 1920s landed autonomies sustained families and communities across Morelos. Still, they were not easily gained or held. Pedro and Esperanza Martínez lived the decade in and out of Tepoztlán. They recalled the struggles that marked a politicized land reform: Pedro had lived landlessness and the collapse of patriarchal family ways before 1910; he joined Zapata from 1914 to 1916, fled to escape Constitutionalist repression—and returned in 1919 to find Tepoztlán a shambles. The good news: "There were no more *caciques*. They had all gone to . . . Mexico City." The bad news was that there was no work and no money. "Then we learned that Obregón had become a *Zapatista*. . . . After that things began to change." Pedro and others took to the *montes*, now open to all, to plant *tlacolol* and make charcoal to sell locally and in the city. Caciques returned and tried to take over the business, bringing men from Toluca. They were turned away. Pedro was elected barrio leader. Men labeled bolsheviks began to organize charcoal makers, including Pedro: "I went to plant corn on the hillside. I also worked as a plowman for others." No one could pay, so he took a share of the crop.[2]

Pedro also:

> [planted] the saint's *milpa*. This land was put in my stepfather's name, but it belonged to the saint of the *barrio*. My stepfather got it from the *barrio*; they entrusted it to him because the saints were no longer allowed to own land. Later, it was passed on to my name and I paid the head tax . . . but it was really the saint's. From 1919 on, I planted the saint's *milpa* to buy whatever the chapel needed. The others in the *barrio* cooperated. Those with money bought the cloths, others cleaned the cemetery or worked on the *milpa*, or decorated the chapel and the cemetery at festival time, all laboring for the saint.[3]

In the early 1920s, the big men gone and locals in charge, Pedro and his neighbors returned to plant maize to support families, the saints, and community festivals.

After years of cultivating without interference, "The Agrarian Reform came in 1925." The government sent two "young boys," surely agronomy students full of ideals, to survey local estates and distribute land to villagers. Pedro received one hectare—2.4 acres—and began to plant. Finally, he could make maize without hiking to difficult highlands. But men linked to the CROM and Calles had organized charcoal makers. Pedro aimed to make charcoal and plant his new ejido plot; the CROM opposed the Agrarians—in national politics and local life. The agronomists were killed, followed by a "massacre in the plaza." Pedro fled to Yautepec and then to Mexico City, surviving as a fruit vendor. The politics of reform opened chances to grow maize and make charcoal—and blocked Pedro from both.[4] Said Esperanza: "I don't like politics. It just serves to bring together a bunch of thieves who steal everything." On life in the city: "I liked Mexico City very much, with its cars and trams; what I did not like was that it all cost money."[5]

While Pedro and Esperanza scraped by in the city, new conflicts arose in the southern Valley of Toluca. Tenancingo had held loyal to government forces—Diáz, Huerta, Carranza, and the Constitutionalists. But outlying communities had welcomed Zapatistas, taken lands, and worshipped Christ at Chalma. Local women were arrested as late as 1918 for supplying rebels. They continued to sustain communities in the 1920s. At Xalatlaco, Victoria Nava Carmona remembered: "Once we returned to the town, we began going to Mexico City to sell. Women did a lot to revive the community." Teodora Salazar recalled carrying jars of pulque down to Tenango del Valle, trading for fish and meat brought back to the town. Men raised maize and cut firewood, hauling both to sell in Morelos and in Mexico City.[6] An economy of sustenance and trade rose in the once Zapatista community.

People also remembered a local bandit, Rafael Galicia, as an honored Robin Hood. All knew he stole livestock and more outside Xalatlaco—but never locally, where he was honored for hiring young men. Galicia's widowed mother was said to rule at the upland rancho that centered their activities.[7] The struggles to rebuild patriarchal autonomies in the 1920s came with real openings for women. The same decade brought a new priest, born in the region, educated in Rome during the revolution, sent to Xalatlaco to purify worship and help local development. In local memory, he was as honored as the bandit Galicia—despite drawing some into the Cristero conflicts of the late 1920s.[8]

Those conflicts proved intense around Tenancingo. The prosperous families living in town and focused on sacramental worship had fought after 1911 to contain rebel villagers devoted to Christ at Chalma. From 1927 to 1929, the factions allied in an uprising to defend the Church and religious autonomies against Calles's intrusions. Zapatista revolutionaries and Cristero rebels defended autonomies, the former focused on the land, the latter on religion. Times and threats might change; the drive for autonomies held strong. The regime pacified Cristeros by ending restrictions of public worship; then it distributed ejidos around Tenancingo, delivering lands that promised autonomies and politics that proved divisive.[9]

When Pedro and Esperanza returned to Tepoztlán in 1929, Pedro had lost his ejido land. "They had already given it to some one else." He went back to planting *tlacolol* in the mountains, gathering fruit and making pulque as well. The family ate; Pedro sold a bit, too. He made it his cause to defend the *montes*, the uplands still open to community use.[10] He led the *tlacololeros*, men without ejidos planting on hillsides—until the Forestry Department came in the 1930s to save woodlands it claimed as a national park. To plant maize or make charcoal, villagers needed a permit from national officials. At first, many got permission; then came the order for "no more cutting."[11] Pedro learned that a regime promising to restore autonomies could take them away in politics focused on national power.

Still, amid the conflicts provoked by state-building politics, many in Morelos realized key goals in the 1920s and into the 1930s. Warman captured revealing memories: "Land and corn, conceived as a single unit, were capable of serving as support of the autonomous persistence of the peasant family unit." Together, they "permitted partial and modest realization of the ideal for which the peasant had fought so much: the possibility of producing and surviving independently."[12] Amid politicized struggles, many found autonomies in the postrevolutionary decades.

New Pressures: Population, Politics, and Commercialization, 1930–50

Across most of Mexico, the 1930s brought Cárdenas's acceleration of land reform in pursuit of regime building. In Morelos, where land reform was completed earlier, the decade brought population pressures, regime building, and commercialization—processes that continued into the 1940s, as the nation grappled with the opportunities and limits brought by World War II. Broad trends are clear: the state population fell from 180,000 to just over 100,000 in the decade of revolution. By 1929, the regime had distributed nearly 200,000 hectares, forty percent of the land; the haciendas were destroyed. By 1940, the population of Morelos had grown back to 180,000, including 40,000 newcomers who saw opportunity in the land of land reform.[13] And thanks to improved nutrition, land reform brought population growth, straining the ability of the lands gained in reform to sustain growing families.

Villagers consumed their maize and other produce first, sending shrinking surpluses to city markets. The regime saw failure; its agents pressed commercial projects. In 1937, officials saw communities below Xalatlaco in need of water for drinking and irrigation. Without consultation, they began to divert the ample flows from the springs at Xalatlaco to communities below. The people of Xalatlaco saw an assault on autonomies and occupied the plaza; in an armed confrontation several soldiers died. María Trinidad Reyes Lara recalled: "it was a Sunday when the people suddenly turned violent; it was because of the water they wanted to take from us and the people would not let them—especially the women. The leader was Juana Reyes. She jumped to lead, put herself in front; they did not let them take our water." Soldiers died, but more came. Xalatlaco had to send water to communities below—gaining small payments to its treasury.[14] Women held strong in defense of autonomies as they waned at the hands of state projects.

In Morelos in the 1930s, state agents pressed ejidatarios with irrigated former cane lands to plant rice: a staple mostly consumed in the capital. It required great work and care to earn cash from local merchants who sold it in the city. And the pursuit of cash created dependence on merchants and markets. So those with small plots on irrigated bottomlands and others in temperate uplands began to plant rice on the former, maize on the latter, hoping to feed families and prosper too.[15]

In the late 1930s, Cárdenas decided it was time to bring cane back—a sure sign that his goals were not the same as most villagers'. No estate mills had operated in the 1920s; in the 1930s a few struggled to revive, dependent on cane grown by ejidatarios on irrigated bottomlands. But milling required machinery and large harvests to profit, plus a core of skilled workers, complemented seasonally by throngs of harvest hands. Cárdenas aimed to revive sugar with a government-built mill at Zacatepec, presented as an ejido cooperative but operating as a state enterprise.

Built between 1935 and 1938, the "radical" years of Cardenismo, the new mill aimed to make sugar from cane raised on thirty-two ejidos, with 19,000 small growers holding 13,000 hectares of irrigated land. Most would plant less than a hectare in cane. The mill would employ

FIGURE 12.1. The Zacatepec sugar mill:
honoring Zapata, crushing his legacy.

400 permanent workers, the skilled recruited from outside, others hired locally for heavy lifting. Advised by a council of ejidatarios, the mill began production in 1938 run by a manager appointed in Mexico City. The goal was to maximize production and sell sugar at the lowest price possible in the capital. The enterprise would use the latest techniques of agro-industrial capitalism to cultivate cane with fertilizers, herbicides, and pesticides, and refine it with the most efficient machinery (see figure 12.1), all saving labor to keep costs low—capitalist goals, but for the mandate to sell low.[16]

A capitalist enterprise ordered not to take profit saw endless profiteering among managers, suppliers, and others who could. Legislating against profit could not change capitalism; it could make the enterprise dysfunctional, shaped by internal conflicts. Ejido growers, celebrated as Zapata's heirs and the true owners (landed shareholders?) of the cooperative, grated under a system in which they had no control over production, faced state-mandated costs, and gained minimal pay for their cane. A few got administrative roles, a few more worked in the mill, others added to what the mill paid for cane by laboring for wages planting and harvesting fields they "owned." In times of maximum labor demand, the cane fields needed workers far beyond those available among ejidatarios, their families, and communities. Throngs came seasonally from Guerrero and Oaxaca to the south, drawn from poor communities, paid less than Morelos villagers demanded.[17]

This was not the vision of those who fought with Zapata, however much it was proclaimed such by regime planners. During the founding years, while Cárdenas presided, his populist political touch worked to gain the support of ejidatarios who hoped for modest profits and others who saw chances to earn wages. Famously, Rubén Jaramillo first backed Cardenas's plan for the mill and ejidatario participation, to later become a hard opponent of the mill and the regime.[18] Born to a mine-working father in the state of Mexico in 1900, he came to Morelos in 1904 with his widowed mother and six siblings, then joined Zapata in 1915. He honored the movement's ideals, but was not of the communities that sustained it. After the conflict, he settled in Tlaquiltenango in the bottomlands, raised rice and became a Methodist pastor; he studied regime politics and its opponents' radical visions. He backed Cárdenas in founding of the mill, aiming to make it serve ejidatario growers. As frustrations mounted, he turned to opposition in 1943.

The Zacatepec mill could not fulfill the goals of Zapata's communities; Cárdenas aimed to draw ejidatarios to grow cane to feed the mill and provide for urban consumers. Jaramillo collaborated until he saw that the promise of prosperity was a mask, the claims that the cooperative served the ejidatarios was false—and that managers and the regime took profit from their lands and labors, while they struggled to survive.

Jaramillo rarely defended the rights and earnings of the migrants who came from Guerrero to cut cane. The cooperative made ejido cane growers shareholding pensioners in a project that paid them little, yet required that they pay others for the back-breaking work cutting cane. The movement did not mobilize seasonal hands, in part because they came only seasonally, in part because ejido growers' and cutters' interests conflicted. For the cutters, the Zacatepec mill revived a Porfirian hacienda, with ejidatarios layered in to struggle between management and labor. The postrevolutionary revival of sugar at Zacatepec made very complex conflicts. Nothing promoted or enabled autonomies.

The turn to rice on the bottomlands of eastern Morelos and the return of sugar at Zacatepec combined to drive a turn away from autonomies on the most productive of lands in the Zapatista heartland. State credit agencies and agricultural advisers promoted rice; the state built Zacatepec and mandated cane among ejidatarios in the cooperative. Some prospered a bit. Many still raised maize in uplands to feed families. A few asked why they could not return to maize; mill managers could not allow it. As the 1940s began, maize-based autonomy was collapsing on the bottomlands; a 1942 strike by mill workers and ejido cane growers was crushed. Jaramillo took arms in 1943. Having helped implement Cárdenas's vision of land reform turned to capitalism, then seeing it marginalize growers and workers, he radicalized. With allies, he moved between negotiation and resistance for decades. They gained little but fame and frustration until Jaramillo was killed in 1962. His efforts and death revealed a rising dilemma: how to negotiate gains or press opposition in communities stripped of autonomies as national capitalism took hold and the regime that promoted it consolidated power.

Not all was lost in Morelos communities. Away from the bottomlands, villagers kept autonomies. Life in Tepoztlán, detailed by Oscar Lewis from 1943 to 1948, reveals the strength and limits of those efforts. Set just north of the bottomlands, the town and its villages held limited lands open to plow culture and larger areas for *tlacolol*, grazing, and woodcutting in *montes* rising toward the Ajusco range separating Morelos from the capital.[19] The town croplands, long community domain, had been privatized in the late nineteenth century and, as everywhere in Morelos, saw concentrations that favored the merchants who served as intermediaries leasing lands and recruiting workers for sugar estates. The bosses had used control of the municipality to close uplands to *tlacolol*—pressing men to join the work gangs sent to cut cane.

During the revolution, the bosses fled and many returned to *tlacolol*—as Pedro and Esperanza reported. In the 1920s, with population cut in half, a mix of privatized plots and open uplands allowed sustenance to most. New politics helped Tepoztecos living in Mexico City (not including Pedro) to gain ejido grants, confirmed in 1929. Plowland increased by 200 hectares, uplands by 2,000. Yet soon after agrarian officials confirmed the ejido, forestry authorities ordered the end of planting in forested uplands. Conservation would be served, *tlacolol* blocked, except by permit. A decade of conflict culminated in marches in Mexico City that gained open access in 1938—another case of Cárdenas's populism.

Meanwhile, population grew. Postrevolutionary authorities sent teachers who saw literacy, national culture, and health education as key concerns. They promoted hygiene and inoculations that joined with the wide access to sustenance to lower death rates by a third. A town population near 4,000 before 1910, which fell to 2,000 around 1920, rose to 3,200 by 1940, then to exceed 4,000 by 1947. Thanks to health care and better nutrition, land adequate to sustenance in the 1920s fell short by half in the 1940s.[20]

When Lewis and his team arrived in the mid-1940s, they found 833 families living in 662 households—most nuclear, a few extended. Among the 833 families, 202 held private plots, 153 had ejido lands, while 109 benefited from both. Lewis counted 384 families, forty-six percent, with no land, private or ejido. The reform had brought new areas to plant and new concentrations within. Surveys showed that thirty-six percent of families with land held less than a hectare; thirty-two percent one to four hectares, while ten percent had ten hectares or more. Most holdings were less than half cultivable, the rest open to gathering and grazing.[21] Access to uplands and *tlacolol* became ever more essential as population grew.

Lewis saw that "the family is the cooperative unit of production," and that "the biological family seeks to be independent and self-sufficient." Family autonomy in a community context remained Tepoztecos' goal. What Lewis called a biological unit remained a patriarchal construct: Men "supported" families by raising maize and taking resources in the forests; women "cared for" families: preparing meals, making clothing, gardening, marketing, and more. Both were essential: men insisted that they provided; women delivered necessary care.[22]

For a man to produce maize, chile, and frijol, the classic Mexica(n) diet, he needed land. As ever fewer had plowlands, growing numbers depended on *tlacolol*. Lewis learned (with apparent surprise) that though it to his eyes seemed primitive, *tlacolol* was more productive than plow cultivation. After cutting and burning trees and brush, the ash proved exceptional fertilizer. In the first year, most *tlacolol* produced far greater yields of maize than plowed lands—with ample chile and frijol too. In the second year, yields fell to about the same as plowed fields—to then plummet. The land had to lay fallow for six to eight years, allowing new brush to grow, enabling the cutting, burning, and planting to begin again.

Tlacolol was very productive if a grower had access to four times as much land as he needed to plant each year. It required little capital beyond an axe, machete, and hoe, but much more labor than plowed fields, where oxen pulled metal plows and fertilizers were coming into use. These helped production with less labor—but cost money, requiring access to credit followed by market sales to pay it back. Plow culture pressed men toward market dependence; *tlacolol* sustained autonomies, as long as land was ample. As population rose in the 1940s, men and boys were ready to work but land became scarce. Men cut, burned, and planted too soon; yields fell while erosion corroded the land—and autonomies too.[23]

As population growth continued, the overuse of *tlacolol* eroded the uplands while increased reliance on plowlands pressed people into markets, limiting the autonomies Lewis recognized as central to life at Tepoztlán. Increasingly, commercialization brought a doubling of the cost of oxen and the price of maize from the 1930s to the mid-1940s. Those who bought maize to eat paid more, those who rented oxen to plant paid more— only those with maize to sell earned more, and they were a minority. Of the 14,000 cargas of maize harvested in good years, only 1,000 were sold. Meanwhile, shortages of land and maize were exacerbated by the collapse of charcoal in the 1940s. For decades, men like Pedro had worked uplands to mix *tlacolol* with charcoal burning. But the expansion of electricity and petroleum power in Mexico City and Cuernavaca brought down charcoal markets, helping air quality in the cities, undermining autonomies and incomes in Tepoztlán.[24]

Lewis reported five percent of Tepoztecos as prosperous, fifteen percent as subsistent, and eighty percent as poor—including ten percent truly destitute.[25] Commercialization drove concentrations. In 1927, Robert Redfield reported fewer than 70 persons gaining income from activities beyond cultivation and labor. In 1944, Lewis counted 273—mostly men, though there were 5 woman storekeepers, 10 teachers, 9 corn traders, and 23 healers. Among the 273, 186 held private or ejido lands. As storekeepers and teachers, butchers and bakers, accumulated land, incomes concentrated as autonomies waned.[26] Adding to commercial gains while saving women's labor, sewing machines came to prosperous households, while mills began to grind corn for women who could pay.[27]

Lewis was less perceptive about politics and religious life. He saw that politics made unity difficult, and that much conflict came from the need to engage powers in Mexico City. He saw that a key division set Zapatistas against caciques as the latter imported "revolution" from the city. Those committed to land, community, and autonomy were being pressed aside by men tied to the regime and committed to the commercialization of life.[28]

The anthropologist struggled to understand local religious ways. He saw that nearly all identified as Catholic, yet few (mostly women) attended mass. Beyond baptisms that welcomed newborns to the community, the sacraments were ignored—as were Church rules about sex before and during marriage. He saw, vaguely, the continuity of community Christianity: all were baptized; women annually took the seed their husbands would plant to be blessed in the church; barrios still organized festivals that brought community integration and sought divine aid with rain and crops, curing and fertility.[29]

Lewis noted that while many did not marry by Church or state, most couples stayed together. There might be other partners, especially among men, but core family households endured—even as unions without formalities of Church or state could be broken by either partner.[30] Crime, notably violent crime, held constant as population grew, political conflicts continued, and autonomies waned. In six years of reporting from 1920 to 1943, no more than two homicides were recorded in any year.[31] For all the challenges faced by Tepoztecos, the continuing mix of plow culture and *tlacolol* enabled pursuits of autonomous sustenance that made family unity and community sociability keys to survival. Population pressures and commercial ways threatened autonomies—but before 1950, family, community, and integrating religious festivals held the center of life at Tepoztlán.

Struggling on the Bottomlands in the 1950s

Life was radically different at Chiconcuac, on the bottomlands near the Zacatepec mill, when Lola Romanucci came to live and study in the late 1950s.[32] The village was not a historic community formed as an indigenous republic with rights to land and self-rule. Before 1910 it was a *real*, the residential compound at the Chiconcuac sugar estate. Older residents mixed African and indigenous ancestry, reflecting the historic roles of enslaved Africans in the estate's core labor force. As the revolution began,

Chiconcuac became a federal garrison; later, Zapatistas took control. Many local people fled; those who stayed recalled hard conflicts and few heroes. By 1920, the estate was devastated; only 250 residents remained in 1928. After cultivating maize by necessity during years of revolution, they gained a small ejido in 1924, to later see some of the land reallocated to a nearby community. As the 1920s ended, the estate held 90 hectares; the former *real* had 120—enough for a small population on rich irrigated bottomlands.[33]

Chiconcuac drew immigrants as residents planted maize, then added rice, seeking earnings in city markets. Among 800 residents in 1960, only 119 adults were born in the village, 79 elsewhere in Morelos, 151 in Guerrero, 41 in the state of Mexico, 19 beyond.[34] Gaining land required political contacts; political bosses rose and fell; conflict spread, often pitting original residents descended from estate managers against those who came after the revolution. When Zacatepec opened in 1938, Chiconcuac was required to plant cane for the mill, a crop still supplemented by rice. By 1940, maize cultivation was all but gone, as were any remnant autonomies. The village was tied to Cárdenas's agrarian capitalism.[35]

Beside newcomers who came to live and work, others arrived to experience the promised revolution within capitalism. The famous "revolutionary" artist Diego Rivera (who spent the decade of conflict in Paris) built a retreat on the edge of Chiconcuac; he rested among people he imagined revolutionary Zapatistas, employing a few as servants and gardeners. Schoolteachers came out from the city, too, aiming to lead the community to a new future. They taught literacy, basic math, and a heroic national history. They helped build a new village square in the late 1930s (shown in figure 12.2, shadowed by a old estate irrigation aqueduct); they petitioned for potable water in 1937 (not gained until 1960); they called for electricity in 1947 (delivered in 1955). Paved roads trucked cane to Zacatepec, then linked the village to Cuernavaca.[36]

Slowly, Chiconcuac gained the trappings of modernity. With autonomies gone, lands limited, and population growing, prosperity proved harder to claim. Political conflicts persisted: the bosses who gained lands for favored allies in the 1920s were pressed in the 1930s by others tied to teachers and promises of services from Mexico City— and later by men linked to managers at Zacatepec, who held out hope of favored treatment from the mill that ruled cane production. All the bosses profited from their efforts to rule; a few served the community as they could. The revolution made in the city and promoting agrarian capitalism mostly served the politically connected few.[37] Through the 1940s and

FIGURE 12.2. Chiconcuac: community in the industrial cane.

1950s, conflicts pitting Rubén Jaramillo, mill workers, and cane-growing ejidatarios against managers at Zacatepec carried on nearby, little noted in memories at Chiconcuac.

Meanwhile, the small community with limited lands and no autonomies lived decades marked by social violence and family breakdown—if family meant traditional patriarchal households. As a woman living in Rivera's former retreat, Romanucci proved adept at gaining local women's insights. They saw men failing to claim the historic role of provider. The few who did might be desirable as husbands, heads of durable households; most men could not take steady earnings from small cane or rice plots and scarce chances to labor. They fell into a macho culture: drinking in bars, shouting manliness, fighting to protest small slights, pursuing women while knowing they would rarely find a steady partner. Romanucci saw couples in constant flux, leaving women the effective heads of most families, the link between mother and son the most enduring bond— remnant of a dying patriarchy becoming macho violence done by men most often against men, but striking women, too. A state "de-pistolization" campaign aimed to take firearms from men and give social control to police backed by the army. Murders declined, but maiming violence persisted, intensifying in the eyes of many women.

Life for all was an endless search for sustenance and companionship; women and men had multiple partners; men with dreams of patriarchy aimed to produce children—and opposed birth control; women dreamed of access to new ways of family planning and kept using old ways of abortion to limit families and the need to provide sustenance men did not deliver. Women and men found sex and companionship in fluid relationships; with few formal marriages, either could end a relationship. Often, couples split because a man failed to provide, leaving a woman alone to feed their children. Many turned to serial links with diverse men, themselves struggling to earn what little they could. Mothers and sons kept a semblance of family alive.[38]

The political conflict that defined and divided the village during Romanucci's visit from 1958 to 1961 is revealing. A new boss promised to get permits in the capital to link community lands and forests to build a *balneario*—a bathing resort offering spring-fed pools to people coming out from Mexico City. The boss-developer would prosper; his wife, a curer who gave penicillin injections, helped legitimate the plan. But the project would tie up villagers' rights to woodlands and the springs, while most would gain at best low-wage work serving wealthy vacationers. The plan failed, and outsiders soon built the *balneario*—benefiting villagers even less. The imagined vision of a Zapatista utopia that drew Rivera

FIGURE 12.3. The chapel at Chiconcuac: private retreat in an industrial cane community.

(and perhaps Romanucci) to Chiconcuac soon brought tourists; villagers survived as service workers. Without autonomies, facing family fluidity and simmering violence, the people of Chiconcuac served prosperous weekenders out from the city—often to marry in the refurbished hacienda chapel (shown in figure 12.3).[39]

The End of Autonomies: Morelos
in the 1960s and 1970s

Autonomies corroded early in the cane-growing bottomlands around Zacatepec, driving political conflicts over who controlled and gained from a mill proclaimed a cooperative but run by government favorites—the only ones who profited. At nearby Chiconcuac, weak autonomies collapsed in the regime-sponsored shift to cane and rice, underlying the dissolution of patriarchal families that fueled social violence and local political fissures through the 1940s and 1950s. In upland Tepoztlán, autonomies grounded in maize production persisted to sustain a majority through the 1940s— but they corroded in the face of population growth and as the *montes* essential to *tlacolol* eroded. Then, as population soared and commercial ways spread across Morelos in the 1960s and 1970s, political conflicts continued and autonomies vanished as families, communities, and cultures faced corrosive pressures.

After access to land and improving nutrition brought the population of Morelos back to 180,000 by 1940, continuing maize production, new potable water systems, access to inoculations, and especially penicillin more than doubled that number to 386,000 by 1960. Then reproduction by growing numbers of healthy, well-nourished women brought a population of 600,000 by 1970.[40] The lands distributed to just over 100,000 people in the 1920s had provided sustenance and a chance at autonomy. In 1940, as population grew and lands became scarce and eroded, cornfields "ceased to give"; they required twice the work to generate sustenance.[41] By the 1960s, Warman reported that the irrigated lowlands across eastern Morelos were fully committed to commercial crops, as Romanucci found at Chiconcuac to the west. Where cane mills operated at Zacatepec and in small private operations at Oacalco and Casasano, ejidatarios grew cane. Elsewhere, they turned to rice, onions, and in uplands to tomatoes—everywhere pressed by the government and its credit banks. They promised cash, yet it rarely came in amounts sufficient to pay loans and interest, or the costs of seed, fertilizer, herbicide and pesticide, or harvest workers. Lenders and merchants, often the same people, took profit; ejido growers faced enduring debts.[42]

As population growth continued and made everything more difficult into the 1970s, those who dealt in the market to gain small incomes
continued to plant maize to feed families. Arturo Warman and Guillermo
de la Peña (working simultaneously yet separately: the former in eastern
zones ranging from irrigated lowlands through cold highlands; the latter
in Tlayacapan, a municipality with highland and lowland ejidos) reached
parallel conclusions. While government pressures, growing needs, and
market enticements drew more and more into the market, those who
could kept raising maize.

They split small ejido plots between market crops and foodstuffs;
they planted *tlacolol* in uplands when necessary. Ejido plots were legally
indivisible, but families shared them to provide sustenance to as many as
possible. When repeated cultivation of *tlacolol* and plowed lands led to soil
exhaustion, many applied fertilizer bought for commercial crops to maize
fields. Yields fell on both while maize fields eroded. Yet those who could
continued to sow maize. The commercial crops favored by government
agents, lenders, and local merchants yielded sparse earnings and growing
debts; the maize, chile, and frijol harvested for sustenance kept families
alive and let men provide.[43]

The anthropologists who documented this time of deepening
challenges for families and communities saw how the persistence in maize
cultivation was pivotal to the vaunted success of the Mexican miracle—
the national capitalist project. To quote de la Peña: "the agrarian reform
and the capitalist enterprise are not enemies, but traveling companions."[44]
Warman argued: "Peasant autonomy is the philosopher's stone of
economic growth, the essential condition for the flourishing of dependent
industry." Many have seen how the agrarian reform was essential to
rural pacification, thus to the politics of national development. Most add
that the low productivity and limited commercial orientation of ejido
cultivators inhibited commercial growth. Deeply engaged in communities
struggling to survive in postrevolutionary, post-land-reform Morelos, de
la Peña and Warman saw that families caught between growing numbers
and scarce lands raised cane, rice, tomatoes, and other produce at low
cost for city consumers—while giving endless labor to feed themselves
on eroding plots. National capitalism generated population, produce,
and unemployment; Morelos villagers' drive to keep autonomies on the
land through the 1970s occupied "surplus" hands to sustain burgeoning
families at the margins of survival. They subsidized national capitalism for
decades. When they could carry it no longer, it collapsed.

By the early 1970s the effort was reaching, perhaps passing, a breaking point. Across eastern Morelos, Warman found that seventy percent of adult men then had no legal claim to land—private or ejido. Fathers and sons split plots into fragments to sustain as many as possible, accelerating overcropping and erosion. Some paid the little they could for fertilizers and pesticides. Yields fell and debts soared—but men sharing land in family bonds kept kin groups together (except when conflicts erupted). Bosses who had ruled by renting lands and plow teams gave way to merchant-lenders tying local growers to Mexico City markets. Land and harvests commoditized, especially in lowlands where poor cultivators had to buy inputs and hire migrants from Oaxaca to harvest rice, onions, and tomatoes. When possible, they kept maize for family consumption; when they labored for neighbors, they asked for maize rather than cash. As commercialization accelerated, men saw maize as their one hedge against desperation. The family could eat.[45]

Conflict escalated. As the merchant-bosses were resented, the army came to assert control with new frequency. Families that had held together in nuclear households and extended networks into the 1960s began to fragment: men stayed to cultivate, labor, and face political conflicts. In a new generation, more began to leave. In families with resources, young men and women left to seek education; among growing numbers facing scarce lands, women left for household service in Cuernavaca and Mexico City. As families fragmented, those holding to lives grounded in land, family, and community kept barrio devotions alive. After all, the historic role of Guadalupe and the saints was to integrate communities, bring good harvests, and keep families healthy. Meanwhile, new clergy arrived devoted to justice in a capitalist world, uncertain if Guadalupe could lead the way forward.[46]

Guillermo de la Peña lived in upland Tlayacapan in the early 1970s. Like Warman he pursued a historically grounded analysis detailing the sociocultural conflicts and changes that were rapidly fragmenting families and communities. The people of Tlayacapan lived a highland variant of the pressures and changes that transformed life across Morelos in the middle decades of the twentieth century. Underlying everything was population growth: after falling to 5,000 in 1920, numbers grew to 11,000 in 1950, then past 17,000 by 1970. Vaccines, antibiotics, potable water, and health clinics brought healthier families.[47]

And at Tlayacapan as elsewhere, population growth corroded landed autonomies and generated poverty, dependence, and insecurity—pressing migrations that fragmented families. Still, the local process was complex and in ways unique. Autonomies strengthened during the revolution. Under the Zapatista peace that began in 1914, men just took land to feed their families. The 1915 harvest proved abundant. As conflict ended, estates offered lands on shares, while villagers petitioned for ejidos beginning in 1920. They gained provisional grants in 1923 (in the face of the de la Huerta rebellion) and presidential confirmation in 1927 (as Cristero conflicts escalated). Yet as the regime granted land, it blocked Zapatistas from local office—fueling political conflicts. And as estates lost lands, labor to gain wages became scarce. Ejido grants could not revive the once-stabilizing ties of symbiotic exploitation forged by laboring at nearby haciendas.[48]

In the 1930s, the revival of small cane mills at Oacalco and Casasano brought regime pressures and credit incentives for those with ejidos in the irrigated lowlands to grow cane. Most at Tlayacapan who gained bottom-land plots also held uplands to plant maize. They raised cane for the mills and maize for sustenance. The majority with only uplands planted maize for consumption. Remembering Zapatista pasts, lowlands mills including Zacatepec refused to hire men from Tlayacapan even to cut cane; they preferred cheaper, less political hands from Guerrero and Oaxaca.[49]

Tomatoes came to Tlayacapan in the 1950s. People recalled that an Italian immigrant who settled in Cuautla leased lands in the highlands, developed a mix of seed, fertilizer, pesticides, and herbicides that flourished, found markets in Mexico City—and drew locals to a crop that promised profits at a time maize yields were falling. Through the 1960s and into the 1970s, the crop flourished more than most local growers. Local merchants saw good business lending money (at rates near ten percent monthly), selling inputs, and accumulating the harvest (often by a debt for a fixed-price contract) to sell in the capital. They got officials to build paved roads linking the highlands to markets: by 1970 merchants' trucks delivered crops to Cuautla in thirty minutes, Cuernavaca in an hour, the capital in two. The same year, it cost 450 pesos cash to plant a hectare of maize (as families never counted their labor as a cost), 10,700 pesos to raise a hectare of tomatoes (paying for credit, commercial inputs, and harvest laborers—mostly men from Oaxaca).[50]

Few earned enough to sustain families, so most kept raising maize, an economically losing proposition that subsidized tomatoes. In 1950, ninety percent of arable land across Tlayacapan was planted in maize, valued at sixty-four percent of the annual harvest; six percent was in cane, generating thirty-one percent of harvest value; one percent was in rice that brought three percent of value. By 1965, sixty-four percent of the land remained in maize, but it produced only eighteen percent of harvest value; cane dropped to two percent of land planted, three percent of value (as local mills closed and Zacatepec was too distant); rice replaced cane in irrigated fields, planted on eight percent of the arable land, yielding twelve percent of market value. Tomatoes claimed nineteen percent of Tlayacapan's lands to yield fifty-nine percent of market value.[51]

The regime and its economists saw the value of tomatoes and wondered why people at Tlayacapan did not accelerate commercial planting. They taught de la Peña why: the rising commercial value of the tomatoes was nearly all taken as profit by lenders, input sellers, market accumulators, and transporters—often the same people. Cultivators who turned shrinking areas of land and undervalued labor to tomatoes gained little but debts. Continuing to plant maize was a commercial catastrophe essential to feed families.[52]

Once again, maize sustained families—and capitalists' profits. But with accelerating population growth in Tlayacapan and burgeoning market demand in nearby Mexico City, the moment proved brief. As tomatoes and profits flowed to the city and held men on the land, growing numbers of women left for the city, usually to labor as household help for the prosperous. As local mills ground maize for small fees, women's labor became less necessary to sustain families; inexpensive premade clothing had a similar impact. A commercialization of sustenance decreased women's household work and increased the need for income, rarely available to women in Tlayacapan. The metropolis was made closer by roads built to deliver tomatoes. So women left—some to return, others not—fragmenting families and challenging patriarchy in ways different from the breakdown reported by Romanucci for Chiconcuac a decade earlier. Women would not lead families at Tlayacapan.

The departure of women contributed to social fragmentation. So did a parallel fracture of sociocultural unity. The growth of contacts with the city—by market selling, migration and return, and the import of urban goods—completed a postrevolutionary shift to Spanish as a first language and the loss of *indio* identities. The people of Tlayacapan became Mexicans, looking down on Oaxacans who picked tomatoes as *indios*.[53] The end of indigenous identities was claimed a success by merchant-bosses, and teachers too. Neither joined or funded the religious festivals that historically integrated community life.[54]

The people of the barrios kept the festivals alive to the extent they could in the face of opposition from new clergy who came to liberate them. Families still organized festivals devoted to Christ, Guadalupe, and the saints, marking the cycle of cultivation, calling on divine grace to ensure good rains and ample harvests. They kept faith with protectors who helped with fertility and childbirth, cures and family relations. They sanctioned public use of masks and alcohol, openings to free expression that might be leveling for a liberating moment.[55] The festivals promoted the survival of communities grounded in landed autonomies, even as autonomies collapsed. By drawing migrants back from the city, they kept families linked—even as they fragmented.

Merchants and political bosses, teachers and clergy, opposed the festivals—for different reasons. Merchants did not want to pay; bosses and teachers were committed to national culture; and priests came in the 1960s and 1970s devoted to a liberation theology that promised justice, yet too often condemned local culture. Sergio Méndez Arceo became bishop at Cuernavaca in 1953, leading the diocese that oversaw Morelos communities until 1983. In 1961, he backed Ivan Illich in founding CIDOC, a center for language study and learning for social engagement that aimed to limit the influence of the United States, capitalism, and conservative Catholicism in the region and across the Americas—in the shadow of Cuba's revolution and against claims of the Alliance for Progress. Morelos became a center of liberation theology and Christian base communities in the 1960s and 1970s. Most of the clergy were committed to radical social visions. Most analysts saw them as challenging the Church and the Mexican regime to become at one with the communities they served.[56]

Warman and de la Peña learned quickly that people in the communities saw the new clergy as another group of outsiders coming to tell them how to live and worship. Radical clerics saw old devotions and festivals as at best outdated, often as wrong superstitions. A few attempted coexistence while promoting the new theology; many condemned ways of worship that had sustained communities for generations, alienating their parishioners. In a revealing episode, the people of Totolapan (in Tlayacapan's jurisdiction) told Jennifer Scheper Hughes of the time Méndez Arceo came to bring the religion of liberation: villagers forced him out of his car outside town, insisting he walk to pay homage to the Christ they had worshiped—and who had served them—since the sixteenth century.[57] In Tlayacapan, some priests came to reform and found themselves outsiders; others came with more openness and resources to help community projects—and found more positive receptions. The overall outcome was a rise of fissures dividing priests and parishioners, creating factions among clergy that overlay political splits already separating teachers from communities they aimed to educate.[58] The people of Morelos still aimed to control their own cultures.

Multiplying fragmentations fueled conflicts in politics, in trade, in community affairs, in religious culture, and in family life. Conflict resolution became all but impossible within Tlayacapan: disputes went to courts at Yautepec, where contacts and the resources to pay them favored those at the intersection of regime power and the market. Living in the community for years, de la Peña saw escalating conflicts as "always tied to the everyday context of competition for scarce resources."[59]

The mix of population growth and commercialization that undermined autonomies, fragmented families and communities, and challenged local cultures in Morelos also transformed the southern Valley of Toluca. By the 1970s, autonomies were vanishing there too, capitalism ruled to profit a favored few, the state intervened more and more, and communities and families faced escalating pressures.[60] At Xalatlaco, by the 1970s, lands cultivated communally to support the saints had been "donated" by local officials to support public works: schools, libraries, and health clinics, along with a town auditorium and municipal parks.[61] Resources long devoted to protecting saints were given to the state to support social services. Had power and truth shifted from saints to the state? Or did officials transfer the land to promote state services without the consent of the community?

Meanwhile, the once Zapatista community of Villa Guerrero, west of Tenancingo, lived transformations parallel to those in Morelos. In the 1920s and 1930s it gained ejidos; its small but growing population first planted maize for sustenance, then added avocados and plums to gain cash in Toluca and Mexico City. Then, in the 1950s, the shift from sustenance to capitalist cultivation took a radical turn. A group of Japanese immigrants came, a few with capital to buy land, more with the skills of floriculture— the commercial cultivation of flowers. At first, the Japanese focused on flowers while their neighbors kept to maize, plums, and avocados. Then, in the 1960s (as tomatoes took off at Tlayacapan), the wider community at Villa Guerrero turned to flowers. Again, lenders and merchants profited; ejidatarios became dependent workers subject to credit and market contracts, paid to labor on their own lands. Facing new competition, the Japanese left; but flower culture ruled at Villa Guerrero. Communities once mobilized to fight for land and autonomies gained lands in a government-ruled reform, faced population growth in times of commercialization, and lived a sequence in which maize ceded to plums and avocados, until flowers ruled the fields. Sustenance depended on cash from nonconsumable crops. Capitalism ruled another corner of the Zapatista heartland.[62]

Guillermo de la Peña concluded: "Local drives for power and office cannot be separated from local economic ways shaped by a growing necessity for money, and by the spread of risk and uncertainty. . . . Local political impotence is tied to economic impotence. The dependence of local political leaders on outside patrons parallels the dependence of local cultivators on banks, mills, moneylenders, wholesalers, truckers, sellers of imported technology—and exporters, too." The result: "National society is built on pyramids of power—patron-client relations that concentrate power at the top."[63]

In the terms used here, the end of autonomies of sustenance combined with the concentration of political power in the capital generated a commercialization that locked people in dependencies defined by risk and insecurity. Hierarchies of patriarchal power consolidated dominance at the top, leaving men on the land searching for ways to sustain families, to provide. The historic heartland of communities grounded in autonomies of production, local rule, patriarchal households, and community religious cultures was gone.

A New Morelos, 1960–80

The people of Morelos remained. As population continued to grow, many migrated to the capital and elsewhere. As landed autonomies vanished, a new Morelos emerged. While agriculture persisted to supply cane to Zacatepec and other mills, new ways of life developed around two poles: industrialization at Cuernavaca and combinations of tourism and suburbanization across much of the state. The latter began in the 1920s when Plutarco Elías Calles, a president with no commitment to land reform, built a weekend retreat in Cuernavaca, joined by political cronies who came to play at an elegant casino. Diego Rivera, the muralist dedicated to honoring revolutionary people, built a retreat at Chiconcuac, ironically (and likely unknowingly) setting himself in a community built on a sugar estate and home to families that had not joined Zapata. Cárdenas, who could be a populist and a puritan, closed the casino in the 1930s, but tourists kept coming.[64]

We have seen the *balneario* proposed and finally built at Chiconcuac; others came to Oaxtepec and other former haciendas. They served as symbols of wealth and places of luxury, as Zapatista dreams faded to become comforting myths among the powerful. When paved roads cut the drive to Mexico City to a few hours, the prosperous built weekend homes—a trend beginning at Tepoztlán when Lewis visited in the 1940s, flourishing at

Tlayacapan when de la Peña worked there in the early 1970s. Inexpensive land in beautiful settings (with revolutionary pasts) just hours from the city drew growing numbers. With new superhighways in the 1980s (and despite tolls) Tlayacapan, Tepoztlán, and even Cuernavaca became suburbs to Mexico City—as the capital city drove up the slopes of Ajusco.

A new veneer of modernity came to Morelos, shaped by visitors and residents who derived wealth and prosperity elsewhere. It marked hotels, spas, restaurants, and shops catering to the needs of those who could pay. Cultivation might carry on in limited ways, but it supported few men and households; women could stay in home communities as work in service of Mexico City families came to Morelos. To work in service, men and women needed basic education and good health; the state began to provide both better than previously. Many came from the city with resources and a social conscience that led to good treatment and adequate pay, even the provision of education to a promising youth. The visible signs of indigenous ways were banished to craft shops and festivals for tourists, as the people of Morelos lived in a commercial Mexican world—and Mexico was drawn deeper into global integration.[65]

Are villagers who serve the powerful and the comfortable in homes, resorts, shops, and restaurants more or less prosperous than their ancestors who worked the land for sustenance, always searching for a little extra money? It is an unanswerable question, or one with many answers. Incomes are surely higher, but everything to sustain a family must be bought. Gains in medical care, technology, education, and communications are real—for those who can afford them. One thing is clear: however prosperous or poor, the people of Morelos have lost all semblance of landed and political autonomy, as de la Peña insisted. They keep cultural autonomies, striving to understand the new world that shapes their lives. They are bombarded with images and information from across the globe, while pressed to be ever more Mexican. What that means remains debated and subject to change.

While rural communities negotiated the fall of autonomies and the turn to service after 1960, burgeoning industries drove a new urbanization in Cuernavaca. Of course, industry was not new to Morelos. The mechanizing sugar refiners of the late nineteenth century built industrial operations substantial for their times, employing meaningful numbers of permanent, often skilled, laborers. After the revolution, private operations gave way to the massive mill at Zacatepec, officially a cooperative, in reality a state industry employing hundreds of mill workers, thousands of small cane growers, and larger numbers of seasonal hands, most from Guerrero.[66]

Urban industrialization began with the development of the Ciudad Industrial del Valle de Cuernavaca industrial park outside Cuernavaca in the 1960s. The goal was to disperse industries concentrating in Mexico City, sharing the demand for infrastructure and services that came with rapid urban growth. First came locally owned textile factories; in 1966 Nissan opened its first full assembly plant outside Japan. Skilled workers often came from Mexico City and other established industrial centers; the unskilled came in growing numbers from rural Morelos, Guerrero, and Oaxaca. Those with skills and union protections gained high wages, benefits, and life in barrios with good services and schools. The many from rural communities and arriving with little education and few skills settled in old Cuernavaca barrios or nearby villages, scraping by as they could. They jostled with established residents, competing for housing, work, and income, seeking to join religious festivals—that were soon rejected by Méndez Arceo's clergy and their new theology.[67]

During the 1960s and into the 1970s, the gains of industrialization for those drawn to Cuernavaca outweighed the struggles and disruptions. Old families and newcomers merged in industrial communities to build new lives. After 1975 (as autonomies collapsed across rural regions) the industrial city faced a surging population without employment to sustain it—even as the nation entered the oil boom (that no one knew was the last gasp of national capitalism). Claudio Lomnitz-Adler found spreading informalities and insecurities linked to proliferating drug use and surges of crime in barrios of marginality. He saw fragmentations of community, family, and politics, while power concentrated above and outside. When he returned in the early 1980s after the boom had crashed, the crisis of barrio life deepened. Atomization ruled; individuals struggled, often fought, for personal gain, while culture retreated from the barrios into households searching for meaning in a decade of collapse.[68]

By the 1980s, an urbanization defined by dependencies, inequities, and insecurities was taking over the heartland. The Mexico City metropolis spread into Morelos from Tepoztlán to Tlayacapan and beyond. Cuernavaca urbanized from within, encroaching on nearby bottomlands. People across a basin that had risen up with Zapata in pursuit of autonomies faced a world of urban dependencies. So did their neighbors in the capital's burgeoning neighborhoods of marginality.

CHAPTER THIRTEEN

Building the Metropolis

MEXICO CITY, 1940–2000

IN PIVOTAL WAYS, Mexico City defined the history of the heartland. Power focused there from Mexica times through centuries of silver capitalism and during long struggles to build a nation. In 1500 and again in 1800 it was the largest city in the Americas; in 2000 it was among the largest in the world. City people led judicial, administrative, religious, and cultural activities, living among traders, artisans, and industrial workers, and many floating poor. The city was a place of power, production, and consumption—dependent on sustenance sent by rural producers. And into the twentieth century, the great majority of heartland peoples lived, worked, and worshipped in rural communities. Zapata's revolution was famously agrarian.

Then, from the 1940s, Mexico experienced surging population growth that drove an unprecedented urbanization. A heartland and nation mostly rural when the twentieth century began were overwhelmingly urban when it ended. While rural people struggled on the land, surging numbers went to the capital. They worked to build new lives in a metropolis that never provided enough employment, education, infrastructure, health care, or other services. So city people turned to self-help, mobilizing families and neighbors to build homes and communities while organizing to demand services from urban authorities. Locked in dependencies that too easily became exclusions, city people built popular barrios with their hands. They worked to gain more viable lives, while facing enduring dependence and deep social challenges in a metropolis growing beyond imagination.

The Century of Urbanization

The twentieth century brought radical change to the demographic structure of Mexico and the heartland. As the century began, Mexico City was a capital with half a million people, four percent of a nation of fourteen million. By 1940, as Cárdenas completed the agrarian reform, industrial acceleration, oil nationalization, and the promotion of education and health services that enabled him to consolidate the regime, the national population approached twenty million, growing forty-five percent in four decades of conflict and reconstruction. Gains in nutrition, resulting in part from a land reform that allowed recipients to focus on feeding families, stimulated population growth.[1] Meanwhile, industrialization and a new more bureaucratic regime drew growing numbers to the city.

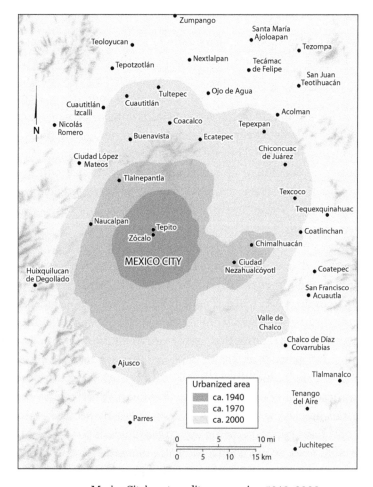

MAP 15. Mexico City's metropolitan expansion, 1940–2000.

While national population rose less than fifty percent from 1900 to 1940, the population of Mexico City more than tripled to 1.8 million.[2]

The turn in the 1940s to laborsaving, chemically dependent ways of agriculture drove further urban growth. New ways of cultivation generated rising harvests while employing ever fewer hands, feeding the cities while sending people without land or work in rural areas to seek new lives there. When, after World War II, the government promoted vaccinations while global pharmaceutical makers found profit selling antibiotics to Mexicans, population growth soared and further concentrated in the cities. From 1940 to 1980, the national population more than tripled from twenty million to nearly sixty-seven million; the population of the Mexico City metropolis broke the bounds of the federal district, spilling across fields and communities in the state of Mexico, to rise from under two million to thirteen million—multiplying seven times in four decades. By 1980, metropolitan Mexico City was home to nearly twenty percent of all Mexicans.

The increase of both the national and the metropolitan populations began to slow—just a bit. Parents saw more newborns live while facing the costs of sustaining and educating children in a city of uncertain employment and limited services. They began to have fewer children. Still, longer lives kept populations growing.[3] From 1980 to 2000, the metropolis grew by forty-two percent to over eighteen million; the nation increased by forty-eight percent to reach ninety-nine million. Toward the end of the century, the nation grew faster than the metropolis. Why? The 1980s began with an economic collapse, saw the 1985 earthquake that devastated much of the capital, followed by a shift to globalization that undermined many of the city's industries and the more secure, better-paid employment they provided to a favored minority. Struggles for work, income, and community marked the metropolis as the millennium ended.

The slowing expansion of the metropolis after 1980 did not slow urbanization in the heartland. While Mexico City's sprawl filled the Valley of Mexico, Toluca lived an urban expansion just over the mountains to the west. The state of Mexico's capital reached 1.5 million in 2000, nearly 2 million by 2010. In Morelos, Cuernavaca and nearby Cuautla together expanded from nearly 1.1 million to over 1.3 million in the same decade. In Hidalgo to the north, the capital of Pachuca joined Tula in the Mezquital and Tulancingo to the east to drive urban population to over 700,000 in 2000. As the twenty-first century began, the 25,493,122 people living in the heartland (the federal district, and the states of Mexico, Morelos, and Hidalgo) totaled more than 25 percent of Mexico's population—concentrated in but 2.5 percent of the nation's territory.

In the basins that focus this history, 21,683,968—85 percent—lived in urban agglomerations.[4] A heartland long defined by landed communities became thoroughly urban. Lives defined by autonomies and the struggles to defend them gave way to lives locked in dependencies, leaving people searching for new ways to negotiate with concentrating powers and a globalizing capitalism they still carried.

The City Before the Urban Explosion

The expansion of Mexico City began amid the political conflicts and liberal reforms of the mid-nineteenth century. From the 1840s to the 1870s the capital grew from 150,000 to 200,000 people, the federal district to 300,000 as mechanized textile mills spread across the slopes south and west of the center to tap hydraulic power. The city became a metropolitan complex as manufacturing suburbanized, while artisans making cloth, clothing, shoes, and more remained in the center and Tacubaya joined San Ángel as a suburban refuge for the rich and comfortable.[5]

As liberals consolidated power after 1867, privatizing Church and community properties, a land market rose in the city. Rich investors bought clerical properties, building wealth and loyalty to liberal rulers. The end of corporate land rights in San Juan Tenochtitlán and Santiago Tlatelolco, the capital's populous indigenous republics, proved profitable and problematic. By the liberals' design, house lots would become property of their residents; plazas and streets would pass to the city; open space would be auctioned. But no one surveyed lots or gave the poor titles to homes on once community lands. The city lacked funds, while liberals insisted that privatization could not wait. So privatizations accelerated both a formal urbanization that served the rich and comfortable and an informal urbanization that forced the poor to live in legal uncertainty.[6] Facing privatization without legal guarantees and urban expansion without city services, barrio residents organized. They claimed homes and lots; defended plazas, streets, and markets; and fought claims by outsiders— with limited success. Workers in suburban industries and downtown craft shops created political associations and mutual-aid societies, demanding better pay and working conditions, and periodically striking. Workers and barrio residents organized to claim better lives in a growing city.[7]

When politics stabilized under Porfirio Díaz, the national economy diversified and grew rapidly, and Mexico City continued to expand.[8] Railroads reaching to the Gulf at Veracruz and the US border at Laredo and El Paso reinforced the centrality of the capital and ties to a world increasingly ruled by US capital. Industrialization and export development benefited Mexico City entrepreneurs and their political allies. The population of the city more than doubled; the federal district that included growing industrial suburbs tripled. There were signs of modernity and prosperity: palatial homes and public buildings near the center; neighborhoods of comfort stretching west along the boulevard named Reforma to honor liberal progress. Horse-drawn trolleys integrated the center in the 1880s, replaced by electric trolleys around 1900.[9] Factories moved downtown as steam and electricity allowed location near markets and workers. The best neighborhoods got pavements, water, sewers, and lighting.

Another Mexico City spread north, east, and south of the center. There, subdivision and settlement preceded planning; legality was uncertain, informality inevitable.[10] In the indigenous barrio of Tepito just north of the center, privatization came after 1868 without surveys or titles. Entrepreneurs bought lots at low cost from residents with uncertain titles. Developers obtained city permission to draw streets and plazas, set new lots, and sell them with title to buyers. The city promised to pave streets; questions of water, sewers, and lighting were set aside. Land was privatized, entrepreneurs profited, and residents got titles—a basic legality. The streets were never paved (the city claimed lack of funds); water came from a few wells drilled in public spaces; unpaved streets doubled as sewers; there was no public lighting.[11]

Neighborhoods of uncertain legality and few services shaped the working city. Limited employment, low wages, and scarce services left growing numbers struggling to live. In Tepito, rents were cheap and vendors everywhere, as poor as their customers. Informal insecure work and sales kept growing the numbers in marginality. By 1900, Tepito was famous for open markets: food was cheap; clothing and shoes were made, sold, and repaired. Tools and household goods were on every street corner; with prices so low, who asked if they were used or stolen? Tepito was a community of informality—condemned from without, a way of life within. Informal, unhealthy, and often illegal, its cheap housing, sustenance, and wares subsidized the formal economy, keeping the poor alive, allowing those who paid pittance wages to profit and proclaim modernity.[12]

The expansion of industry created new chances for some. As struggling households needed multiple earners, employers drew women to labor. Their work helped keep all wages low—while they faced condemnation by the prosperous for "abandoning" the children they worked to feed. City life brought enduring insecurities to women and men at the margins of the middle class, among workers, and those struggling for a bit of profit in uncertain markets. A downturn, unemployment, or an illness that left an adult without work could threaten family life. Pawning became a way of survival when all else failed. Cheap jewelry, clothing, utensils, and other housewares were left for cash—hopefully to be redeemed when times improved.[13]

The social response was to organize. When women and men in shops and factories built mutual-aid societies, they were honored. If they turned to charity they found small rewards. When they struck to demand rights and higher pay, condemnation came quickly.[14] In the face of persistent poverty, structural inequities, and enduring insecurities, informal struggles allowed small gains. Local markets and petty service economies kept families alive, helping stabilize city life while low wages subsidized a formal economy that profited a few, sustained the regime, and kept the city growing—while marginality spread. The powerful flourished; a small but growing middle sector of managers, merchants, and professionals found new comforts. The majority struggled in neighborhoods north, east, and south of the center, far from monuments, with few services except the canals that flushed the city's effluent by the new penitentiary at San Lázaro.

When politics opened in 1910 and the regime collapsed in 1911, many in the capital hoped to gain new rights, while they worried that rural rebels might deny them food. Most city people stayed at home and at work, uncertain observers as social battles surrounded them and political warriors descended from the north. Mexico City's diverse people survived the revolution, trying to shape it as they could. They organized, petitioned, rioted, and struck. Dependent on wages, they could not make insurgencies to compete with Zapatistas, Villistas, and others grounded in rural autonomies. Like the people of industrial Monterrey in the north, they could not make revolution.[15]

Years of revolution did heighten political conflicts, along with economic and social insecurities. Between 1910 and 1921, while the nation lost a million people to revolutionary violence and the deadly influenza of 1918, the capital added 200,000 residents as people sought refuge.[16] The Constitutionalists who ruled the city from 1915 courted city workers, even mobilized them to fight when possible. But Carranza, Obregón, and their allies aimed first to consolidate a new regime; they promised much to workers—and delivered as little as possible.[17] In 1916, engineer and intellectual Alberto Pani saw a city plagued by polarization and disease; he blamed "the sickening corruption of the upper classes and the destitution of the lower classes."[18] In power, the Constitutionalists crushed strikes that aimed to limit destitution.

The 1920s brought continuing political conflict, the revival of the export economy, and a slow turn toward industrialization. The city continued to grow, still without resources to provide basic services. Chapultepec Heights— later the Lomas de Chapultepec—became an elegant new neighborhood for "revolutionary" elites, with parks, paving, and the best electricity, water, and sewerage services. Elsewhere, new subdivisions for the throngs seeking a chance in the city profited those who sold the land, usually without services. The poor continued to adapt by self-help, competing for the limited resources offered by a "revolutionary" regime. As the decade ended, the city approached a million people—most still struggling to get by.[19]

While so many struggled, national leaders offered the city as capital of a revolutionary nation promising gains for Mexicans, a model to many seeking a global transformation—but not a turn to communism. Intellectuals, writers, and artists drew global dreamers to the city. They imagined a world of justice grounded in idealized rural communities they rarely visited—while villagers faced a regime promoting reforms in service of capitalism. Radical dreamers rarely saw the struggles in Tepito and other city barrios. Through the 1920s and 1930s, the world saw a city of hope in a nation of promise, while urban and rural Mexicans struggled.[20]

In 1930, depression cut export production as global markets collapsed; external sources of capital dried. Led by Lázaro Cárdenas from 1934, Mexico turned toward industrialization for national markets. He accelerated land distribution to pacify rural communities and press them to produce surpluses for urban industries and consumers. He drew new factories to the capital; he favored industrial workers with union rights and rising wages in return for political support.[21] He built a regime authoritarian at the top; corporatist in confederations of peasants, workers, and entrepreneurs; inclusive in its goal of drawing every major interest into a state-mediated domain where goals were negotiated and oppositions balanced in controlled ways.

Cárdenas's political consolidation succeeded. Villagers gained land, organization, and a limited voice in the regime. Industrial workers gained rights, benefits, better wages, and union representation. Capitalists got support for industrialization—as they faced the limited constraints needed to pacify peasants and benefit workers. In Mexico City the regime offered fragmented participation. With no independent government in the federal district, politics focused on the national authorities. Entrepreneurs found representation through their chambers; so did organized industrial workers via unions and the Confederation of Mexican Workers (CTM). The unequal participation of industrialists and workers facilitated industrial development and a limited address of worker concerns. Middle sectors grew and concentrated in the capital, dependent on the state for education and on the regime and new industries for employment.[22] Too many others lived in marginal barrios facing little economic opportunity and less voice in politics.

Surviving the City, 1940–60

After 1940, everything appeared to change—except commitments to national capitalism and accelerating urban growth. The political system built by Cárdenas had provided limited participation and often-effective mediation while he worked to consolidate power. His successors focused on promoting industry, and using the regime to control rural communities and industrial workers. In the capital, the regime favored entrepreneurs while limiting gains to organized labor. When middle sectors grew in the 1950s, the PRI's popular sector served their interests in limited and controlling ways. Meanwhile, the green revolution that fed the city drove throngs left landless and unemployed to its barrios, where they found little political voice.[23]

The regime consolidated, participation constrained, and a new agriculture begun, the push to a national industrial capitalism accelerated. Capital and resources for urban infrastructure were always scarce. To save costs, the regime concentrated industry in the capital city. The national transportation network focused there, a legacy of nineteenth-century rail construction reinforced by twentieth-century road building. Energy focused on the city, with petroleum piped from the Gulf coast to a suburban refinery at Atzcapotzalco. People, too, concentrated in the capital. From 1940 to 1970, permanent migration to Mexico City paralleled temporary migration to the United States. By 1970 the capital included nearly half of Mexican industrial production and related services. Almost sixty percent of transportation activities focused there, easing access to national markets. With twenty percent of Mexico's population and forty percent of industrial investment, output, and services, Mexico City became an industrial behemoth dominating an urbanizing nation.[24]

For the majority in the burgeoning city, life remained a series of everyday challenges. Employment lagged far behind industrial growth. The prevalence of mechanized, laborsaving techniques ensured that. A national combination of laborsaving cultivation and laborsaving manufacturing created a booming economy of growing production and productivity—guaranteed to lag behind in creating employment.

Agriculture offered mostly seasonal, badly paid, insecure work; new industries generated well-paid, more secure employment far short of the needs of a surging urban population. Scarce employment and low incomes beyond the middle sectors and industrial workers limited markets for manufactured goods. A cycle of growth with inherent constraints locked the city in structural inequities as it expanded to incorporate soaring numbers. A few profited, more prospered in middle roles, and industrial workers found steady work, solid wages, and new benefits—surrounded by marginal populations seeking to survive and sustain families any way they could. The capital city, the industrial city, the informal city, and the desperate city grew together.

From 1940 to 1960 the city grew from under two million to over five, drawing many migrants from rural communities. They came from the heartland and beyond, leaving communities facing population growth, land shortages, political fragmentation, and family dissolution. Most went to old neighborhoods like Tepito where aging housing and scarce services stretched to accommodate newcomers short on chances. In the mid-1950s, Oscar Lewis recorded detailed life histories of five members of the Sánchez family (a pseudonym), most living in a *vecindad* (tenement) in Tepito. They told of lives of deep poverty, endemic insecurity, family fragmentation, and regular violence—among men, by men against women, and among women too. Published in the early 1960s, *The Children of Sánchez* was widely read and often controversial.[25] Lewis aimed to reveal lives locked in a "culture of poverty." Many US readers saw self-destructive lives and presumed they reported "Mexican culture." Promoters of Mexico's national project saw prejudice in the selection of histories Lewis opened to the world.

Read more than a half century later, the Sánchez narratives offer the voices of people clinging to expectations rooted in rural communities, cultures of family patriarchy, yet learning every day that their goals were impossible to achieve in the city. The patriarchy by which men expected to provide for families and women expected (or were expected) to sustain households, preparing meals, making clothing, raising children, and trading in local markets—proved impossible in the city. There, only cash could sustain households, and it proved scarce in Tepito. Men struggled to provide; women struggled to feed, clothe, and raise children. Children, always uncertain about daily tortillas, with worn shoes, tattered clothing, and dim prospects, rarely obeyed at home or in school—where they rarely stayed. The ways of autonomous sustenance and family integration that had kept families together in landed communities for centuries (and corroded after 1870), collapsed in the city. Equally powerful in the Sánchez narratives was that patriarchal expectations persisted as they became impossible. The mix of expectation and impossibility made lives insecure, desperate, and too often violent.

Jesús Sánchez came closest to living the patriarchal ideal, as he insisted and his children agreed. Born in a village in the state of Veracruz, son of a muleteer merchant, as a boy he moved to a nearby town where his father opened a small store—to see it sacked in revolutionary times. His parents separated, his mother died, he fled his father to work in cane fields and grain mills in postrevolutionary Veracruz. Struggling to eat, he left for Mexico City, settled in Tepito, and took work as a food buyer for a restaurant. He went daily to the Merced food market. Building ties with dealers there, he began to raise and sell birds and then hogs to vendors. In the 1950s, he bought a lot (with few services) in one of the new outlying barrios where he built a small house and kept a few animals. He rented and later bought a corral at Ixmiquilpan, in the Mezquital north of the capital. He mobilized knowledge gained as a youth in the country to link the rural world to the city. He never profited, yet always gained more than most in Tepito. He insisted that his goal was to provide for a family made by relationships with a series of women who bore numerous children (including the four Lewis interviewed).[26]

Early on Jesús stated his patriarchal goals clearly: "I respect my boss. . . . He is like a father to me." He added: "All I do is work and take care of my family. . . . For me there are no parties, no outings, no nothing—only work and family." He understood the cause of the endemic conflicts lived by his family and neighbors: "In most homes, arguments and tragedies have an economic base because if you have fifty *pesos* a day expenses and you don't have the money, it bothers you and you worry and quarrel with your wife."[27] His children recalled that Jesús always provided something—a room, food, a bit of cash, clothing, shoes—but never enough. They lived lives of insecurity laced with conflict, linked to a father who at least tried to provide their only enduring relationship—a tie defined by a mix of respect and distance.

As boys, the sons Manuel and Roberto spent little time in school, gaining only basic literacy while constantly searching to find a little income—small jobs, petty trades, little thefts. Manuel understood: "But *papá* couldn't make enough for so many of us." His response: "I'm from Tepito, and we don't take crap from anybody."[28] As the boys grew older, regular work proved scarce—Manuel jumping from job to job, Roberto often turning to theft. Both chased women and fathered children; never able to provide, they never forged enduring relationships and could never claim a patriarchal role. Both left the city at times: Manuel worked in the United States as a bracero; Roberto tried Veracruz, then joined the military and was assigned to Guadalajara. Nothing endured and they always came home to Tepito, dependence on their father, relations with multiple women, and struggles to be fathers to their children. Violence began in gang fights in the tenement and shaped their lives in conflictive family relationships.[29]

Manuel tried the old ways: "My *mamá* and all her family went to Chalma regularly," and he went along as a boy. Later, when he began to court his first love, "my relations with Graciela were insecure." He went to "the Sainted Christ of Chalma. He seemed to be receiving me alone, and that gave me a wonderful feeling, because I had much faith at that time. I asked the Saint to give me strength, to show me the way to earn enough money to marry Graciela, and not to let me betray her." It did not work out, with Graciela or any other woman. Relationships came and went; children came and struggled to live, often dependent on very insecure mothers while Manuel could never provide.[30]

Rural ways remained an ideal for Roberto. His memory of David, a cousin from near Córdoba, Veracruz, may be the only positive portrayal of a man in the volume: "He was big, a giant, and when he shook hands, what a grip he had. . . . David lived with us and my father got him a job. . . . David always behaved well and we all liked him." Roberto told of a time when a married woman tried to seduce David—and he refused. "David later returned to Córdoba on some pretext," likely the lack of work in Tepito. In the late 1940s, he returned to visit with his mother and they took Roberto back to the village. "I liked it very much there. I stayed with them for a month, and I didn't want to leave. It didn't have the comforts my father supplied, but I was healthy and happy. I prefer country life. It is calmer and quieter, and one can breathe tranquilly. You feel the honesty even in your elbows. They are a different type of people, more respectful and upright. Here in the city I have always to be alert, ready for anything from anybody."[31]

Struggling to live by violence and theft and with insecurity in the city, Roberto imagined staying in the village. "I wanted to be a farmer and I learned the work while I was there. Olivia's husband [David's stepfather] taught me everything, how to plant sugar cane, corn, beans, and rice." Yet he left. The family could use Roberto's help and teach him to cultivate. Yet they had no land to share. So Roberto enjoyed his time, learned rural ways, and returned to Tepito. Still, the month in the village "was useful to me later, because when I traveled about, I worked in the fields."[32] A city youth could dream of a rural life; he could not make one.

Consuelo, the elder daughter, reported different memories of life in Tepito. As a girl she tried to help an aunt grinding maize for a festival meal. "I tried but I couldn't. My aunt said '*Ay* child, what are you going to do when you get married? What if you get a husband who is very demanding, like my first one? I had to get up in the morning to grind five *cuartillas* of corn to make tortillas for his breakfast. And when at first I couldn't do it, he beat me to make me learn.'"[33] Men who did not cultivate and struggled to provide cash expected women to do hard labor to turn crops into meals. Consuelo learned the lesson. She completed primary education, pursued jobs to gain her own income, and for years avoided men who could not provide. Schooling helped her find jobs; few paid well and none endured.

Her young sister Marta gave in to men early on. She learned what Consuelo feared: men pursued her for sex with promises of sustenance; they failed, disappeared, or both in the face of family obligations. Said Marta with blunt clarity: "Do you know what kind of a man he turned out to be? One of those who like to have a wife and children, but without being responsible for them." She appreciated her father, long widowed: "My *papá* was still free—he wasn't tied down by any law, only by his own sentiments. If he had been different, he would have abandoned us a long time ago. But there he was, taking care of everybody."[34] Still, Marta and her siblings reported that while Jesús always provided something—a place to sleep on the floor, a bit of clothing, some cash—he never provided a secure sustenance to any of his many children.

Marta tried to respect her father. She also found a female ideal:

> Of all the women I know, my Aunt Guadalupe was the one I most admired. She was the kind of woman who knew how to suffer. I wish I had her courage to go on, to never let trouble conquer and to be resigned to whatever happens. True, she complained a lot about money and was always worrying about paying the rent but she was so resourceful that no matter how little she had, she managed to cook enough for everyone there. She would buy fifty centavos worth of pork, 20 centavos of bruised tomatoes, a few centavos of oil, dried up onions and garlic and make a casserole.[35]

Like Jesús, Guadalupe had come from the country, in her case from Guanajuato. She accepted that a woman's role was to feed the household; she had the skills to succeed—if someone provided the pesos needed to buy staples.

Marta could not replicate Guadalupe's life, hard as it was. The youngest Sánchez told of a life among women with many men, more pregnancies, potions to induce abortions, and more children than the men could or would support. She too trekked to Chalma to ask Christ for help, or at least hope. "I asked Him to send me a good job, but He never did." She gave up on men as providers, so she asked God to enable her to provide. Nothing ended her life of struggles. With every child, she visited Guadalupe at her temple, giving thanks and asking help—to little effect. She lamented: "My heart went out to my poor little daughter, because even before she was born, her father did not recognize her."[36] It was hard to be a mother in Tepito.

Manuel, the eldest, ended his narration with a dream: "I would be proud to set up a modest home, to educate my children, to save my money. I would like to leave something behind me so that when I die everyone will remember me with affection. It sounds laughable."[37] The dream of patriarchy lived—to become a joke. Roberto faced jail in Veracruz, worked in Mexico City factories, and never found a solid income or family life. Yet he too kept the dream: "To my way of thinking, a man who only produces children without accepting the obligations that go with them, doesn't deserve to live."[38] He condemned himself, without recognizing that it had become impossible for the many crushed in barrios like Tepito to live the patriarchal ideal.

Consuelo, with the most education, a drive to independence, and dreams of wearing white to marry a supportive husband, resisted informal relationships and the children they produced for a long time. Eventually she fled to Monterrey with a man who promised a better life. On arrival, all but alone in a city she did not know, she became pregnant and faced the same dilemmas as her sister and so many other women: lack of commitment, lack of support. Her father came and brought her back to Tepito, where she too went from man to man, job to job. After striving to be an independent woman in a world of urban marginality, she felt despair: "I try to quiet the pain and anxiety I feel in my breast and look with indifference on the four children I have loved so much. It wasn't right for me to expend all my moral and physical strength to offer them a better life," only to fail. "I have no job any more and that gives me a powerful defense." She ended sadly: "Like the rest of the people ... [I] will adapt to reality."[39] Marta also understood the urban dilemma: "The trick of having children is not just to bring them into the world, but to feed them and send them to school." She condemned her brothers for their failures and her lovers for making it impossible for her to succeed. As her story ends, she was awaiting another child, dreaming of something better, knowing it would not come.[40]

In a final reflection, Jesús asked himself why he tried so hard to sustain his children to such little effect. He wondered why they always worked at something, never got ahead, and rarely showed commitments to their children. Yet he knew the answer: "There is not enough money, not enough work, and everything is so expensive; prices went up again today. For example, take a family with eight, or six mouths to feed. How are you going to support them on a wage of eleven *pesos* a day? True, they've raised the minimum wage a *peso* a day. What does a *peso* amount to if the stuff you buy has gone up three or four times? Well that's the way it is." Still, Jesús had a dream. He bought a lot in the new barrio: "That's my ambition, to build that little house, one or two rooms or three so that each child will have a home and they can live there together. . . . Just a modest place that they can't be thrown out of. I'll put a fence around it so no one will bother them. It will be protection for them when I fall down and don't get up again."[41]

Having despaired of the four children who shared their painful histories, Jesús built a house for the three he fathered with his latest companion. Having learned in Tepito that food and family depended on money, he saw that the only way forward in the city depended on work and the land to build a house. He bought a lot to build a home—that would be his patriarchal legacy.

Building the Metropolis, 1960–80

From 1960 to 1980, the Mexico City metropolis grew from five million to thirteen million, adding eight million people in two decades. If the decades from 1940 to 1960 saw migrants and the larger population of the urban poor focused on survival in older neighborhoods crammed with growing numbers, the decades from 1960 to 1980 were shaped by an outward surge in which more rapidly growing numbers drove people to build new neighborhoods and homes, and organize to demand services, schools, and more—still facing scarce economic prospects. Before 1960, the Sánchez children focused on survival in Tepito, where they faced insecurities that fueled fragmentation and conflict; after 1960 growing numbers followed Jesús's example and turned to building homes in new barrios.

While employment, income, and services remained scarce, many turned from adaptation to action. Real gains came. In many ways, the marginal majority built the burgeoning city. By hard effort they subsidized the regime, urbanization, and the industrial economy. People used the little they had, access to a lot and hard labor, to build homes, barrios, and the metropolis. When done, many were better off—in an urban world still defined by insecure dependencies, scarce income, family struggles, and uncertain futures.

After 1960 industry boomed, employment lagged, and marginality spread. An entrenched alliance of entrepreneurs and national powers ruled the city, keeping taxes on profits, wealth, and income low.[42] With revenues far below the needs of a rising metropolis, the city invested in industry and the neighborhoods of the rich and comfortable. Production boomed, the prosperous flourished, and the infrastructure of urban life lagged. Water and drainage, electricity and education, and health services, too, remained scarce in the barrios that were home to growing numbers of workers, vendors, domestics, and the migrants who joined them.

People pouring into the metropolis competed for ways to live, dependent on cash income and the market to survive. Their poverty subsidized industry and urban projects with low wages and self-help initiatives. With concentrated power, industrial production, and social polarity locked in place, the challenge of building a metropolis growing to thirteen million was enormous. The regime knew the importance of providing neighborhood services: water, sewers, paving, electricity, schools. It funded infrastructure and services—but never at levels that kept pace with explosive expansion. Officials insisted that failures and delays were due to lack of funds. Critics answered that politicized powers made choices. Ultimately, national and city officials made politicized choices with always insufficient financial resources.

There were economies of scale and real savings in focusing economic and infrastructure investment in the metropolis. That drove an enduring cycle in which industrial-commercial expansion concentrated in Mexico City, drawing a burgeoning population and creating escalating needs for work, infrastructure, and services. But the regime had few resources left to fund urban infrastructure. So it planned, promised, and fulfilled promised plans in limited ways. A metro rail system was built, water and sewerage works came sooner or later, funded by loans that led to soaring debts in the 1970s. The promise of petroleum revenues brought more borrowing for urban projects. More infrastructure was built; barrios gained schools and services—before everything collapsed in the 1980s.[43] Ultimately, the project of capital-scarce, debt-dependent national capitalism generated profit, industrial production, and urban expansion, while limiting employment, income, and consumption. It drove a metropolitan explosion grounded in marginal neighborhoods—in large part built by their inhabitants.

The powerful few and the marginal many negotiated life in the city they shared. The national regime, authoritarian at the top, corporatist in organization, inclusive within limits, and participatory in controlled ways, ruled a federal district that included Mexico City—the metropolitan core. The president appointed the head of district government; powerful men pressing favored interests and barrio movements demanding basic services all addressed national officials. Chambers of commerce and industry promoted entrepreneurial interests. The national labor confederation (CTM) represented industrial workers. No formal organization addressed neighborhood needs for employment, infrastructure, and services.[44]

The popular sector (CNOP) organized in the 1950s gave corporate representation to a growing middle class of government bureaucrats and some professionals. Most depended on the state for education and employment. The city's professional and commercial middle sectors benefited from mid-century developments, even as many struggled to remain middle class. They depended on the government and its model of national capitalism, they sought consumer ways modeled on the United States—yet out of reach. Many, too, held Catholic principles that cut against the secular ways promoted by the regime.[45] In a city of constant organization, negotiation, and mediation, limited resources flowed to industry and powerful interests first. People striving to become and remain middle class and others laboring in industry gained a little. The throngs in barrios shaped by poverty and insecurity were left mostly to their own devices. They responded by building their own city—subsidizing the urban heart of the national capitalist project.

Sprawling new communities were built with sanctioned illegalities— that is, by developers who gained rights to land at the edge of the city, sold lots with or without clear title, drew lines for streets they rarely paved, promised electricity that came late at best, and waited for the authorities to provide schools and clinics—that also came late and in limited ways. Such communities were defined by economic insecurity and shaped by informalities in housing and services that made self-help a way of life—the base of political mobilization, negotiation, and pacification that shaped the chances of millions. While the Sánchez family's struggles in Tepito revealed the persistence of patriarchal expectations and the impossibility of achieving them in the twentieth-century city, those who joined Jesús in the move to outlying barrios showed that traditions of organized effort also endured to claim important if limited successes in struggles to build new urban communities—without altering the underlying dependency, insecurity, and marginality that marked so many city lives.

The growth of Ciudad Nezahualcóyotl in many ways defined metropolitan expansion in the 1960s and 1970s. Neza (in popular talk) occupies a vast expanse of the drained bed of Lake Texcoco, east of the airport, just outside the federal district in the state of Mexico.[46] Settlement began informally in the 1950s; perhaps 30,000 people were squatting there by 1960. The state set regulations requiring subdivisions to provide basic services: paved streets, water, sewers, and electricity. In 1963 Nezahualcóyotl became a municipality. Politically connected entrepreneurs gained rights to survey large subdivisions. They sold lots to people desperate for a stake in the city and the population exploded. Former residents of the city center and migrants from outlying regions came in rising numbers. In 1970, Neza had over half a million residents, by 1980 more than a million.

New subdivisions were sanctioned but none built legally mandated services. Residents bought lots on streets that were literally lines in the sand. A few wells provided water; electricity was scarce and irregular, sewage removal informal. Everything flooded in the annual rainy season. Uncertain titles came from developers who did not live up to the terms of their ownership rights. Lots changed hands informally. The construction of Nezahualcóyotl was the essence of state-sanctioned illegality. People came in astonishing numbers. Sanctioned illegalities led to neighborhoods and lives shaped by the entrenched informalities of street markets, small shops, and labor for wages that were a mere pittance. Informal ways offered at least marginal opportunities for people facing lives without secure work, regular income, essential services, or access to regime powers.[47]

For millions, neighborhoods like Nezahualcóyotl became a solution. There, one could buy a lot for very little and build a house with family labor and neighbors' help, using material bought or scavenged as circumstances allowed—Jesús Sánchez's last dream. The constant arrival of newcomers created economic openings, however small: a woman could make food to sell to neighbors building makeshift homes; others could make or repair clothing, or help with childcare for the few with regular jobs. A small entrepreneur could sell tools and hardware; another could repair cars that barely ran; others could tap electricity lines for themselves and neighbors. Building a city without formal services, a city of structural and sanctioned illegality and widespread informality, allowed desperately poor, insecure, dependent people to use the little they had—a lot, work, self-help, neighborly assistance—to build new lives.

In new settlements like Nezahualcóyotl people facing dependence, poverty, and insecurity mobilized to improve desperate lives. In Tepito, the old *vecindades* were built; the challenge was to pay rent and survive crowded within. In Neza and other new communities, settlers had to build shacks while dreaming of homes, in the face of scarce incomes and services. Cooperation to build homes and barrios led to organizations pressing the city, new suburban municipalities, and the developers they sanctioned to live up to obligations to provide pavement and drainage, electricity and lighting, water and sewerage services, education and health care—and title to lots, the one piece of autonomy available to city people. The rise of informal organizations demanding services is well known.[48] When effective in organizing struggling neighbors and skilled in engaging local authorities and the party-state, they gained benefits for the neighborhood: new pavement or better water service, longer electricity lines, even a school or clinic—always an improvement, never sufficient to resolve underlying deficiencies. Many an organizer found a job in the party or the government, usually away from the neighborhood he or she had organized. Communities gained limited services; the regime rewarded and constrained their leaders.

Barrio politics of organized informality brought real gains—just enough to keep focus on fights for limited improvements and away from challenges to the regime and the model of national industrial capitalism. Sanctioned illegalities and entrenched informalities are usually portrayed as problems of urban development. They are—in imagined worlds of shared decision making, widespread sustaining employment, plentiful resources, and commitments to use them for the common good. In the real world of Mexico City, as it faced an urban explosion structured by the inequities of national capitalism, illegalities and informalities provided entrepreneurs ways to profit, government officials ways to negotiate popular discontent, and millions of struggling city dwellers ways to use what little they had

FIGURE 13.1. Ciudad Nezahualcóyotl: a working city built by community hands.

to make life a bit better. Informality, family self-help, and community organization became defining characteristics of the megacity facing limited resources and constrained economic opportunities. They enabled families to build homes, communities, and in time a new metropolis. By the early 1980s, Nezahualcóyotl was becoming a city with services and a settled, if poor, population (shown in figure 13.1), while new marginal neighborhoods sprang up farther out—as economic and political crisis struck the nation and the metropolis.

Collapse and Globalization, 1980–2000

The crash of the brief petroleum boom of the late 1970s brought debt crisis, deep recession, and challenges to every aspect of Mexican politics and development in the 1980s.[49] Mexico City's metropolitan difficulties contributed to the crisis. Funds borrowed internationally to build metro lines and water and sewerage projects could not be repaid; new projects became impossible. People across the city had lived an underfunded, unequal, informal, and often marginalizing urban development for decades; they faced widening unemployment, declining wages, and delayed services in the lost decade of the 1980s. They turned again to informal ways of production, trade, and politics; street vendors hawking anything and everything appeared everywhere. The 1985 earthquake assaulted the city. Apartments, schools, and hospitals in the historic center, in prosperous enclaves like Condesa and Roma, and in working barrios east and south collapsed. Tens of thousands died; many more became homeless and unemployed, living in tents and rough shelters in parks and boulevard medians. The self-built, low-rise barrios all around the center suffered less—perhaps because they had less to lose.

In the face of economic and geologic destruction, the responses of the national regime and the city government it controlled were blatantly inadequate. The people who had built so much of the city by self-help did not hesitate. Young men came to crawl through rubble and rescue survivors. Neighbors provided food, clothing, and shelter to those without. Every local, national, and international observer concluded that the regime had failed. Its development model was condemned. Informality and self-help were honored as the response that allowed the people to show strength and solidarity—and save their city.

Much infrastructure the regime had built, pressured by neighborhood organizations to be sure, did survive the quake, enabling the celebrated informality that led responses to destruction and the beginning of reconstruction. The metro (built to survive earthquakes) kept running under crushed neighborhoods and collapsed medical centers. Electricity, water, and sewerage services faced disruptions, but continued in most of the city. The response to the quake mixed popular action and public infrastructure— the way that barrios had been built during decades of struggle.

The party-regime and the model of national development lost legitimacy in the face of the 1981 crash and the 1985 quake—as the United States led a rush to globalization.[50] There were pressures toward a democratic opening from within and without the regime. But, led by Carlos Salinas de Gortari, dominant minister in the cabinet of Miguel de la Madrid from 1982 to 1988, the regime held strong while it led Mexico into the General Agreement on Tariffs and Trade in 1985, ending the dream of national capitalism and opening a weak and deeply indebted economy to the competition of world trade and the power of international capital. Unemployment, poverty, marginality, and public debate spread; the regime stayed closed. It blocked the challenge of Cuauhtémoc Cárdenas (Lázaro's son) in 1988, guaranteeing the "election" of Salinas as president in 1988, enabling him to break unions and end the right of villagers to ejido lands in 1992. He proposed NAFTA and brought it to fruition as 1994 began. The North American trade bloc aimed to free capital to go where profits seemed most promising, goods to go where markets promised the best prices. People were to stay at home—locking Mexicans in poverty and low-wage jobs, and where they were lacking, in enduring marginality.

What did globalization via NAFTA bring Mexico City and its people? Low-wage labor was Mexicans' new "comparative advantage." Nationally, that led to another vicious cycle: rural poverty deepened as subsidized US grains invaded; devastated rural communities sent more people to Mexican cities—and to the United States, with and without documents. Migration north had continued in waves through the twentieth century; it jumped during the uncertainties of the 1970s, rose more in the collapse of the 1980s, to more than double as Mexico entered NAFTA in the 1990s.[51] Decades of national capitalism had limited employment, corroded autonomies, and made patriarchal family ways all but impossible. The crisis of the 1980s and the turn to globalization expelled people. Mexico's people searched for new ways and places to live.

Within Mexico, low wages were not Mexico City's comparative advantage. Industry had concentrated there when its role was to produce for Mexican consumers. While unions held strong, the city's industrial workers gained solid pay and remained important consumers—a minority among a struggling urban majority. In the neoliberal model, the city lost industry and the secure, well-paid, union jobs it sustained. The industry that survived in Mexico had to serve export markets; *maquiladoras*— factories assembling imported inputs for quick export—stretched along the US border employing young women in high-tech assembly plants for low wages, few benefits, and without union rights. The assembly of automobiles and other heavy goods for US and hemispheric markets survived, and in time expanded—focused outside the capital metropolis: at Toluca, Cuautitlán, and Cuernavaca in the heartland; in Puebla just east; and from Silao and León in the Bajío, through Aguascalientes just north, and a northern strip from Hermosillo to Saltillo and Monterrey. Hi-tech, increasingly robotic production kept the benefits of relatively well-paid automobile labor to a few, as union power eroded.

Mexico City continued to grow while it deindustrialized—the unmistakable sign of the end of national capitalism in the national capital. The metropolis turned to a service economy focused on government, finance, and commerce. A very few profit enormously; more struggle to hang on to middle-class lives of comfort marked by insecurity; growing numbers face entrenched poverty, insecurity, marginality, and exclusion. Dependent service defines life in government offices, international banks, educational institutions, medical centers, and other places that reward skill with relative comfort. It defines employment in retail stores, restaurants, and shops that provide less income and little security. The household service that keeps so many women alive is the definition of dependence—with security dependent on obedience. And as the twentieth century closed, growing numbers in the great city lived in a burgeoning informal sector of self-employment and street vending—the definition of marginality and insecurity.

The metropolis grew from thirteen to over fifteen million in the 1980s decade of crisis, to more than eighteen million as globalization set in during the 1990s. The city had to accommodate five million new people as its economy shifted to low-wage, insecure, and often informal ways of production.[52] People struggling to survive began to have smaller families. But small families were ever more numerous and reinforced by continuing arrivals from a countryside that kept expelling people.

Amid a celebrated shift away from national development and authoritarian rule, and toward neoliberal globalization and electoral democratization, the metropolis continued to expand and concentrate wealth, power, and comfort; expanding middle sectors with the skills to serve the transnational economy gained a little; skilled industrial labor earning good wages and solid services all but vanished. Marginality and informality spread outward, leaving desperate families to continue building neighborhoods through local organization, political mobilization, and constant self-help at the edge of legality. The histories of Ajusco in the 1980s and Valle de Chalco in the 1990s illuminate life at the metropolitan margins in times of globalization.

The Sierra de Ajusco rises majestically at the southern end of the Valley of Mexico. In the 1970s, urban development filled the plain below with universities, businesses, and shopping malls, along with rich, middle-class, working, and marginal neighborhoods. Ajusco loomed just beyond, a last unsettled space in the federal district, a forested upland close to chances for work and transit links to the wider metropolis. Everyone coveted Ajusco: the air seemed cleaner, the forests refreshing, the views spectacular. People rich and poor were ready to invade or buy lands held by ejido communities or the heirs of estate owners. The law prohibited sales of ejidos, yet many were ready to profit as urban sprawl neared lands of little agricultural value. District officials opposed expansion into Ajusco. It would be difficult and costly to bring roads, water, and sewers to rugged highlands; with new environmental concern they argued that settlement would cut forests that made oxygen for an oxygen-thin basin and disrupt the recharge of aquifers needed to sustain the metropolis. Ajusco was set aside as an ecological preserve.[53]

Once more, law proved a basis for negotiations among the regime, the powerful, and the desperate poor. Early settlements and attempts to enforce environmental restrictions came in the late 1970s during the debt-driven oil boom that fueled a sense among officials and the populace that anything was possible. Private landlords and ejido officials sold land to settlers, who received titles that were at best uncertain and often fraudulent. The rich bought official acquiescence and essential services. The destitute banded together to build homes, rough streets, and schools, to string electric cables, and truck in water. They organized against government attempts to restrict their settlements, arguing that the ecological ban aimed to keep Ajusco for the rich. They knew the history of city settlements: politically connected developers with uncertain rights sold land with minimal services to desperate buyers; once profits were taken and settlers came, they mobilized to defend their occupation and build houses and neighborhoods. Sooner or later, usually later, authorities "regularized" land titles (often doubling profits to developers, who were paid a second time to create clear titles). Officials responded slowly to local demands to pave streets; to bring electricity, water, sewerage, and drainage services; to build schools and medical clinics. In long-contested processes, neighborhoods finally consolidated as exhausted residents demobilized.

When oil boom turned to debt crisis in the early 1980s, the sequence played out again in Ajusco—with a new environmental language shaping public debates, and little else. Neither a struggling national regime nor city officials had the resources or the political power to change a now-standard process: titles were regularized, often allowing landlords to sell a second time. Settlers stayed in ecological preserves; minimal services slowly came. The government staffed settler-built schools; city programs offered work with political constraints to once-independent community leaders; a slow provision of services came punctuated by festivals celebrating national heroes. As the regime turned to neoliberalism and city officials faced earthquake damage, Ajusco saw developers profit from illegality while settlers built communities, again, by mobilizing informalities. One key difference marked Ajusco: the wealthy also coveted its uplands; they too negotiated crisis, illegality, and informality to set their own, often gated, communities near entrenched marginal neighborhoods. They look down together at the city below, sharing a unique vantage as neighbors in a polarizing metropolis.

As Ajusco consolidated, in the 1990s settlement surged east toward Valle de Chalco.[54] A first survey would suggest they were very different metropolitan fringes. Ajusco was an upland forest coveted by people prosperous and poor; Valle de Chalco was a dried lake bed southeast of the city, a remnant of Noriega's once prosperous Xico estate, long since left to desiccate, open to the desperate because no one with resources would settle there. Still, there were parallels: both began with uncertain, often illegal land sales; both led to mobilizations that demanded legal titles and services; both were built mostly by settler sweat; in the end, both gained just enough state support to consolidate marginal lives and demobilize popular pressures.

The last major settlement in the metropolis in the twentieth century, Valle de Chalco grew in revealing ways. As national and metropolitan population growth slowed, a majority came from already urbanized zones, including Nezahualcóyotl, where infrastructure and services were finally in place—making rents too high for the poorest families. In Valle de Chalco they could buy a lot; they could own a piece of the city. They knew they would begin without services, without schools, and far from employment and transit. But they could build a shack with discarded materials and hard work. They could demand water, electricity, and schools from a government promoting privatization and promising to benefit every Mexican, even those in new slums in a lake bed along the highway to Puebla, a very visible site in a politicized nation.

Men and women building families went to work; often both joined the economy—a few traveling outside to gain employment, many entering informal trades that grew again to serve the poor in a fringe city approaching 300,000 in the early 1990s. They wanted land, work, and schools. Again, parents endured hardships for a chance at education for their children. It was the only way ahead in a deindustrializing metropolis. Their visibility and their mobilizations got the attention of Salinas as he promoted NAFTA in the early 1990s. Promising a new Mexico, he insisted that private enterprise would bring a prosperity he knew would not reach Valle de Chalco any time soon. So he created National Solidarity, a program targeted at the most desperate communities, with Valle de Chalco its demonstration site in the metropolis.

Solidarity brought electricity, water, schools, and medical clinics more rapidly than usual, but not pavement or sewers. Employment came more slowly. Most survived in informal sectors; family members worked long hours, juggling childcare and endless toil on a dusty plain that flooded dangerously in 1996 when rain came in torrents. Valle de Chalco, like its predecessors, got just enough services to stabilize marginality. Organizations pressing for services waned later in the 1990s, as political activity refocused on electoral openings in an urban municipality in the state of Mexico—then the edge of a metropolis. The new politics proved fragmenting; families struggled on, hoping that education would offer their children a road forward. In time, too, Valle de Chalco would become a settled, still poor urban community (shown in figure 13.2), built in large part by its settlers' sweat.

FIGURE 13.2. Valle de Chalco: an edge city built by community hands and solidarity.

Their struggles, once again, were marked by gendered violence: young fathers raised to patriarchal presumptions but living without means to provide for families hit wives struggling to contribute to household income (thus challenging patriarchal presumptions). Sometimes wives and mothers hit back; too often, fathers and mothers struck children. People locked in marginal lives at the edge of the metropolis, lacking economic opportunities and effective political openings to better their prospects, lived daily violence in households struggling to survive.[55] From Tepito in the 1940s to Valle de Chalco in the 1990s, families faced marginality laced with insecurities and too much violence. Beginning in Nezahualcóyotl in the 1960s, they used self-help and local organization to build minimally sustainable lives in a long process of urban community self-construction. In the long run, they built the city—again, carrying capitalism. Along the way they paid a heavy price.[56]

There have been meaningful gains, notably in health and longevity. A death rate that held at 34 per thousand in 1900 fell to under 13 in the 1950s, when antibiotics began to have their effect. It had fallen below 5 per thousand by 1995. The infant death rate fell from 400 per thousand live births in 1900 to 22.5 in 1995. Infants lived, and people lived much longer—accounting for most population growth since 1950. Once it was clear that children would live, women had smaller families. Women averaged six children in 1970, two or three in the 1990s. Population growth held over 5 percent annually from the 1940s to the 1970s; it fell to 1.4 percent after 1995. Migration from the countryside keeps the city growing—at much slower rates. Meanwhile, basic education has become widely available: boys in the city on average complete ten years, girls nine—well above the national averages of seven and a half and seven years.[57]

Life-preserving medical care, mostly through easy access to pharmaceuticals, remains real for city people. Educational gains have been more modest, but real too. Authorities have struggled to provide water and sewers, pavement and electricity, and education to serve burgeoning numbers. Yet, over time, in response to popular mobilizations and with subsidies from residents' self-help efforts, most of the metropolis has gained basic services. Given the enormous growth and dispersal of the metropolitan population, the accomplishment is impressive.

Politics and family relations continued to change in the burgeoning city as the century ended. Near the National Autonomous University of Mexico, on plains shadowed by Ajusco, Santo Domingo began in land invasion—founded in illegality, forged in years of self-help, set in poverty while surrounded by prosperity. As lives became more settled, families became smaller. In continuing struggles to sustain them, men and women adapted patriarchal ideals: women worked outside the home to gain income, more men devoted more time and care to children—especially their sons. Through the 1980s and 1990s, the people of Santo Domingo, like so many others, demanded services and democratization. They made real gains for their neighborhoods, their children, and the city.[58]

Gender norms have evolved across the metropolis. As the economy turned from industry to services, middling and poor families had to send multiple earners to work. More women work for income; among the poorest, so do children. As the Sánchez family learned in Tepito in the 1940s, dependence on cash and the need for multiple earners challenged the fundamental bargain that historically sustained patriarchy: men would provide; if they did, women and children would serve. Such patriarchy was always stronger where men held land and the autonomies it sustained; it was always weaker in cities marked by commercial ways. By 2000 it was all but impossible anywhere in Mexico, especially among the poor. In middle sectors, where women with education earn money that makes everyday life better and increases children's opportunities, men—especially younger men—have begun to accept more egalitarian households. In families scraping by day to day, where women's earnings are small, often informal, and always insecure, men—even younger men— adapt reluctantly. They see the necessity of women's earnings yet aim to keep patriarchal prerogatives. Among the desperate, as in Valle de Chalco in the 1990s, violence against women remains too common in families struggling to make lives in the city.[59]

In the late 1990s as neoliberalism took hold, unemployment proliferated, marginality spread outward, and democracy remained an uncertain promise, a wave of violent crime took the streets of Mexico City. Muggings, robberies, and kidnappings reached new heights, fanning rising fears in a city long famous as a place that, for all its polarities, one could walk without fear. As a first wave abated, armed guards seemed everywhere, employed to protect others' property and prosperity. With democratization in the federal district in 1996 and nationally in 2000, followed by a new time of economic expansion, crime seemed to wane in the metropolis.

Still, subsequent waves of prosperity and collapse have brought new times of crime—and new forces of security that struggle to contain it. During decades of challenge, marginal people across the metropolis mobilized self-help and community pressures to build neighborhoods and make lives minimally sustainable. Their efforts made their neighborhoods and the city livable—while never threatening the powers that sustain and deepen polarities that have not abated. In the emerging world of globalizing capitalism, can resilient people locked in urban dependencies find ways to shape more secure, prosperous, and less violent lives in a more sustaining, egalitarian, and just city? That remains uncertain in a thoroughly urban heartland.

After the Fall (of Autonomies)

GLOBALIZATION WITHOUT REVOLUTION

SINCE 1980, the people of Mexico and the world have lived deepening challenges that have radically changed political systems; ways of production, work, and trade; and the social relations and cultural visions tied to them. Mexico's heartland became urban as agriculture all but ceased and industry left the region. The city remained a pivot of government, financial power, and commercial exchange—tying people in one of the world's largest metropolitan conglomerations to a globalizing economy. In those key sectors, a few people found wealth and more took comfort. The metropolis is also a center of health and education—the former keeping millions alive, the latter offering the skills to compete for scarce opportunities in a polarizing city. Beyond those sectors of power and prosperity, most of the city's more than twenty million people work to build and maintain the city: housing and transportation, food and sales—formal and informal. To the global economy, most were consumers—very poor consumers. Celebrated political openings have not led to effective participation or greater justice. Corrosive violence spreads in waves, while governments militarize social control in a quest for "security" that rarely comes.

How did that happen, in a region that for centuries saw landed communities sustain mines and a city pivotal to silver capitalism, then dispute a nineteenth-century turn to industrial capitalism and carry Mexico's twentieth-century experiment in national capitalism? Much of the answer is clear: if the radical depopulation of the sixteenth century allowed communities the landed autonomies to sustain the heartland and capitalism for centuries, the radical overpopulation of the twentieth century undermined everything in a destruction deepened by profit-seeking

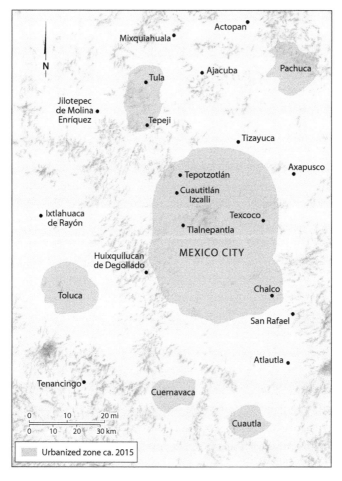

MAP 16. An urban heartland, ca. 2010.

commitments to laborsaving ways. The vise set by population explosion and laborsaving production was already driving urbanization and making national capitalism untenable when everything collapsed in the 1980s.

From National Capitalism to Globalization

Still, political processes tied to a changing world economy shaped Mexico's turn to globalization. In the 1970s, a nation facing rising debts that stymied growth saw salvation in oil exports. After brief gains, oil proved a bubble that burst in the early 1980s, leaving the regime without means to pay the greater debts contracted in a last attempt to keep national capitalism alive. An inability to access international capital except to repay the international banks ensured that the 1980s would be a decade of deep recession marked by falling and then stagnant production, declining and then low earnings, and spreading marginalities as growing numbers juggled informal ways of life. The regime responded by opening Mexico to global trade, entering the GATT early in 1985. Later that year, a devastating earthquake took down Mexico City neighborhoods, hospitals, schools, and more. The authorities struggled to cope; the people of the city led rescue efforts.

Soon the PRI regime faced internal conflicts that became national challenges in the 1988 presidential elections. Carlos Salinas de Gortari had ruled economic policy under President Miguel de la Madrid. Already leading the effort to open Mexico's economy to the world, Salinas became the designated successor. Cuauhtémoc Cárdenas, son of the populist who consolidated the regime in the 1930s, broke away to lead a Democratic National Front (FDN) in opposition, hoping to salvage some of his father's nationalist legacies and social programs. Manuel Clouthier led the National Action Party (PAN) from religious opposition to become a coalition promoting fair elections and market openings. In voting most saw as fraudulent, or at least tainted, Salinas claimed the slimmest of majorities. A year later, Clouthier died in a car crash that his supporters and many others saw as deeply suspicious.[1]

In office, Salinas kept the structures of authoritarian power to engineer a rapid transition to globalization. He used a regime and party that had depended on powerful unions for decades to break the labor power that had favored core industrial workers, ensuring that Mexico's opening to the world would come with declining earnings to the majority.[2] Salinas won a constitutional reform ending communities' right to land in 1992. The amendment did not prohibit community landholding (as liberals did in the nineteenth century); it did open ejidos to privatization, division, and sale—by local option. People seeking profit or facing desperation, the former powerful, the latter prevalent across rural Mexico around the 1990s, were pressed to join the world of open markets. Ejido communities did not open as rapidly as the regime desired, but change began.[3]

The regime justified breaking union power as necessary to allow Mexican workers the "flexibility" to adapt to export industries expanding along the northern border, and promising to spread in a globalizing world.[4] It ended ejido protections, so that a new round of privatizations would allow smallholders to take advantage of new commercial openings.[5] Both "reforms" came amid an economic collapse that hit industrial labor, the last hope for prosperity among workers, while rural peoples faced land scarcities and market ties that built debts, fragmented communities, and pressed many to migrate. Salinas's reforms ended state defense of workers' rights and villagers' lands. They also attacked the unions and ejidos that sustained key sectors of the PRI.

In that context, Salinas proposed, negotiated, and implemented NAFTA. With authoritarian powers intact while rural autonomies collapsed, urban marginalities spreading and poverty laced with insecurities defining so many lives, he promised that opening trade and capital flows with the United States (and secondarily Canada) while keeping Mexicans at home in Mexico (NAFTA was a trade pact, not a social union) would bring economic growth and shared prosperity. He negotiated the deal with Republican President George H. W. Bush; it was ratified under Democrat Bill Clinton and took effect on January 1, 1994.[6]

That day, as officials in Mexico City, Washington, and Ottawa prepared to celebrate, they awoke to news that rebels calling themselves Zapatistas had risen in far Chiapas, demanding land and justice, democracy, fair wages, education, and social services. The movement was armed, and based in eastern lowlands; insurgents quickly occupied the state capital of San Cristóbal de las Casas—named for the sixteenth-century defender of native rights. They claimed the world's attention as Mexican authorities mobilized a military response that produced a stalemate within a week and led to long, difficult negotiations. The rebels soon saw that their focus on rights for all Mexicans gained limited traction; they shifted to emphasize the rights of indigenous peoples, their base in Chiapas. Years of advocacy enabled by globalized communications brought negotiations that won limited gains for native communities, most in Mexico's impoverished south. The second wave of Zapatistas generated little for Mexico's urban majority.[7]

The rising contained, Salinas readied one more round of PRI-orchestrated national elections. His designated successor, Luis Donaldo Colosio, was assassinated in March; a replacement candidate, Ernesto Zedillo, won in August to hold the presidency for the PRI. Soon after, an assassin killed PRI secretary-general José Francisco Ruíz Massieu, Salinas's brother-in-law and expected to lead the next Chamber of Deputies. Then, as Zedillo was inaugurated in December, the overvaluation of the peso engineered by Salinas to provide cheap imported goods to those who could buy them, thus to promote the benefits of NAFTA, led to a sudden devaluation and an economic collapse deeper than that of the 1980s. Employment and earnings plummeted again, marginality and violence spread; the impact of NAFTA became clear. To salvage future prospects, the United States arranged a financial rescue for Mexico's government and US banks. Mexico's economy limped forward.[8]

After the calamities of 1994, consensus spread among political leaders that it was time to "democratize." NAFTA locked Mexico by treaty into globalizing circuits of capital and trade, favoring US power and the powerful in Mexico while deep divisions and violence wracked the PRI. After the financial bailout, the United States pushed for democratization, meaning elections—its solution for everything. Under pressure, Zedillo began a steady process. Cuauhtémoc Cárdenas became the first elected mayor of Mexico City in 1997; a national elections board worked to limit PRI control of national elections. In 2000, Zedillo stood back and allowed a groundswell to elect the PAN's Vicente Fox, in a vote as much about ending PRI rule as backing Fox. For many among the powerful, Fox was a bulwark favoring capitalists and capitalism and blocking a presidency of Cuauhtémoc Cárdenas, still preaching nationalism and popular rights. Fox would brook no limit to globalization, no revival of union power, no return to community land rights.

Many celebrated 2000 as the triumph of democratic capitalism in a Mexico locked to the United States in a globalizing world. For a time the economy flourished, thanks to the US hi-tech boom that stimulated border jobs in Mexico and drew many Mexicans to the border and beyond. In that context, Fox worked with George W. Bush, whose foreign policy experience as governor of Texas focused on Mexico, to imagine a larger union—perhaps allowing freer movement of people across borders. Might more Mexicans find greater prosperity? Could US citizens not lose if Mexicans gained?

Those questions remained open when September 11, 2001, turned the United States and the Bush administration to xenophobia, closed borders, and military adventurism. NAFTA and Mexico remained foundations of US prosperity, a base of its power as during World War II. Yet anti-Mexican sentiment grew in the United States, while another disputed Mexican election held the presidency for the PAN in 2006. The United States government pressed new President Felipe Calderón to start a war in Mexico against drugs consumed in US cities, suburbs, and towns. In US political and media eyes (with a few exceptions), Mexico became the cause of the drug problem, a neighbor mired in violence. Armed force, of course, could not stop drug supplies or violence while US demand held strong, sending profits and weapons south to Mexico.

Still, NAFTA began to bring new industries and trades to parts of Mexico, mostly regions from the Bajío north—once the dynamic core of silver capitalism. Automobile and aircraft assemblers, electronics makers, and more settled there, creating work and some prosperity, modestly shared. Southern and coastal zones gained little, surviving with economies mixing export agriculture (thus seasonal labor), resorts that proffered lives of dependence for low pay, and drug cartels that profited a few while proliferating violence.

Mexico and a World without Autonomies

The acceleration of globalization under NAFTA, followed by an opening of elections proclaimed democratization, has not brought wide benefits to Mexico's majority.[9] Global capital found new openings and trade expanded, while Mexicans faced election contests that proved a theater of money and media that gave them little influence in a politics they know rarely serves their interests. Autonomies gone, rural communities across Mexico faced family fragmentation that deepened as so many men, women, and children left for the United States during the 1990s.[10] In Mexico's burgeoning cities, below the globally and politically connected few, people in the middle negotiated endless insecurities while growing numbers dealt with marginal lives surrounded by endemic corrosive violence.[11] For working men expecting (and expected?) to provide, work sufficient to patriarchal provision is scarce and insecure; women hear calls for their liberation but face scarce opportunities to gain income and few openings to social mobility, while expected (and expecting) to keep houses and raise children with or without the fathers' help or provision.[12]

Parallel challenges mixing political conflicts, economic pressures, social insecurities, corrosions of patriarchy, and widening social violence had led to widespread and enduring insurgencies in the Bajío and the Mezquital in 1810, and to the Zapatista revolution across the southern heartland and beyond in 1910. Yet no powerful and enduring uprising from below has come during the long crisis that has mixed deep economic uncertainties, unresolved political contests, enduring social dissolutions, dissolving patriarchy, and endemic social violence since the 1980s. Simply said, no third revolutionary insurgency has come with the power and persistence to give people and communities a say in transformations that have spread social insecurities and pervasive violence.

The question is why. The brevity and limited impact of the 1994 Zapatista uprising, for all its inspiration among those dreaming of better lives, is the best evidence that Mexico had changed irrevocably in the second half of the twentieth century. Its quick containment demonstrated that the end of autonomies brought the end of revolutions as Mexico and most of the world had known them.[13]

I argued in *From Insurrection to Revolution in Mexico* that threats to autonomies were pivotal to provoking insurgencies in landed communities, and that political conflicts were key to breaking established power and opening the way to widespread uprisings. Now it is clear that remnant autonomies—and the ability to reinforce them—were essential to insurgents' abilities to sustain opposition long enough to threaten power and force change (if never quite as they sought). Reconstituted autonomies sustained rural insurgents during the decades after 1810 and 1910. The collapse of autonomies and the spread of urbanization made enduring challenges grounded in landed communities—the essence of Mexico's historic revolutions—impossible after 1980.

With that realization, the rise and fall of landed, that is ecological, autonomies become central to the history of the heartland, Mexico, and the world. Braudel argued that the history of capitalism is defined by an expanding commercialization that enabled growing concentrations of power, and that together steadily eroded the autonomies that long sustained families, communities, and even world regions. This history emphasizes that while capitalism did steadily erode autonomies, along the way communities grounded on the land also sustained and shaped capitalism—and defended autonomies. Communities carried the capitalism that in the long run destroyed them. When capitalist predations assaulted autonomies (and men's patriarchy), and political conflicts opened opportunities, communities took arms to challenge the powers that threatened them. Into the twentieth century, they rebuilt autonomies to sustain communities and guerrilla forces—and compel change.

Now, the end of ecological autonomies in a mechanizing, urbanizing, globalizing world had ended the capacity of communities to sustain themselves. In a telling example of Mexico's transformation, at Tehuacán—east of the heartland, where archaeological studies have traced the most ancient origins of maize—rural families have all but abandoned the cultivation of the historic staple. A few among the elderly raise maize for *elotes*—the Mexican variant of corn on the cob, a delicacy. Their children see no future in the historic staple. They look for labor locally, in Mexico City, or the United States. They know that the world of their ancestors will not return.[14] With little hope for gain from political participation, people seek solutions in personal and family adaptations. They can carry on in rural towns, build city barrios, or migrate to seek new opportunities. They petition and demonstrate. But they cannot press the powerful with enduring insurgencies. People fully subject to markets can defy power only as long as incomes and store supplies last. Whatever their grievances, whatever the political openings, the people of our urbanizing world cannot press insurgencies long enough to rattle power and claim gains.

Since the 1990s and the transformations accelerated by NAFTA, Mexico has faced a parallel loss of autonomy as a nation. Mesoamericans had invented maize, one of the great cultivated staples that sustained New World peoples before 1500, and soaring numbers across the globe in more recent centuries. All along, Mesoamerican and then Mexican families and communities had harvested maize to sustain themselves and a rising global capitalism. After 1950, as soaring populations and green-revolution cultivation undermined family and community autonomies in the heartland and across Mexico, the new "scientific" agriculture had served to sustain a time of national food autonomy.

Then NAFTA blocked tariff protections for Mexicans' maize while allowing the United States to subsidize corporate farmers who flooded Mexico with cheap mechanically raised and chemically fed staples. Transnational corporate agro-industries then led Mexico to shift to using its scarce irrigated lands (created by government-funded projects) and still cheap, often desperate, laborers to produce designer fruits and vegetables—strawberries and tomatoes, avocadoes and broccoli, and more—for comfortable US consumers.[15] Mexico lost independence of basic sustenance—while Mexicans sustained North American capitalism as buyers of maize and producers of specialty crops made affordable by their low wages. Lives of dependence still carry and subsidize global capitalism.

Meanwhile, in rural villages, provincial towns, and city barrios families searched for viable social adaptations—to find marginalities laced with insecurities. There is no dearth of violence in contemporary Mexico—or in our world. Household violence remains endemic and deeply corrosive. Lives of crime, major and petty, prey on the existing economy. Drug cartels endure because they profit in capitalist markets, buying arms to act like states and defend their business. But thieves, profit-seeking kidnappers, and cartels have little incentive to pursue social change, even as some bandits may appear as Robin Hoods, taking from the rich to give to the otherwise poor (themselves), and cartel leaders are sometimes honored in popular music for challenging power—and thriving. Predatory kidnappers, too often killers, gain no such praise. All take redistributions; all offer income to the few open to dealing in death and deadly risk. Crime and cartels are not ways to social, economic, or political change. Violence marks contemporary Mexico in too many ways; it has not found a route to challenge established powers, to promote justice, or to press redistribution. Endemic violence persists as an enduring corrosion. The end of landed autonomies and the triumph of urban lives locked in dependency, and too often in marginality, have stimulated corrosive violence while precluding revolutionary uprisings. The capacity to sustain revolution is gone.

Urbanization and the End of Revolutions

A historic parade of scholars have documented how the revolutionary conflicts that challenged the regimes and ways of production that came with capitalism were repeatedly grounded in communities on the land. When they faced threats in times of crisis, they mobilized to challenge the powerful—and to demand land and justice. They rarely claimed state power; they repeatedly forced negotiations on men aiming to rule. Barrington Moore's *Social Origins of Dictatorship and Democracy* and Eric Wolf's *Peasant Wars of the Twentieth Century* set the agenda in the 1960s; in the 1970s, Jeffrey Paige gave us *Agrarian Revolution* and James Scott focused on Southeast Asia in *The Moral Economy of the Peasant*; Theda Skocpol's *States and Social Revolutions* deepened the comparisons in the 1980s, when I added *From Insurrection to Revolution* to bring Mexico into the conversation; in the 1990s the vision broadened with Jack Goldstone's *Revolution and Rebellion in the Early Modern World*. During the recent crisis of globalizing capitalism, in 2009 James Scott gave us new depth in *The Art of Not Being Governed*.

With different emphases and perspectives, all these works saw the pivotal importance of communities on the land to the revolutions that contested and shaped capitalism and states for centuries. It is time to ask what the end of landed autonomies means for the possibilities of revolution, state making, economic change, social reform, and communities and families, too, across the globe. The last revolutions grounded in rural communities to succeed in establishing new states came in China in the 1950s, and Vietnam in the 1970s.[16] The conflicts that wracked Central America in the 1980s saw attempts to mobilize communities with remnant autonomies—to be crushed by regimes backed by the United States. The victors promised democracy and built export capitalism. Autonomies rarely revived.[17] Life since has been marked by pervasive insecurities and corrosive violence, sending fractured families to join displaced Mexicans in the United States.

As population explosion and urbanization mix to drive globalization everywhere, autonomies vanish. Lives of dependence, marginality, and insecurity proliferate.[18] Violence seems everywhere: inside families and communities, urban and rural; via cartels that profit in trades made illegal;

in diverse conflicts too often lumped together as terrorism—and in state (and private) responses aiming to contain all of this and more. This history of capitalism and communities in Mexico's heartland suggests that to understand the turn to endemic corrosive violence that now plagues so many lives without stimulating social reform, more sustaining ways of life, or effective political participation, we must explore the impact of the end of autonomies on families, communities, economies, and polities across the globe.

Most notably, popular mobilizations have been transformed—and sharply limited. People frustrated by dependency, insecurity, and marginality lead demonstrations, they mobilize on the internet, they disrupt transportation, and they seek political favor.[19] Some attack the local rich, or neighbors seen as vulnerable; people seen as different, often godless, are held responsible for a world gone wrong. Protests and assaults live by tapping the wealth and communications of the globalizing capitalism they challenge. None has delivered enduring gains to popular communities, rural or urban. The most destructive acts often reinforce the power of the powerful, locking the privileged and their prosperous dependents inside security perimeters, locally and nationally—ready to pay people recruited from among the poor to restrain or attack dispersed opponents. While so many face poverty, marginality, and social insecurity, others retreat to live in fear, acquiesce in losses of freedom, and lament their own insecurity.

Popular movements are everywhere. Diverse groups organized to demand the opening of the PRI regime in Mexico in the 1990s; their efforts contributed to the triumph of democracy in 2000. The lack of fundamental social change as elections became media circuses, inequities deepened, and justice remained a dream now contributes to a culture of disillusion.[20] Across Latin America new social movements have also organized to claim limited gains, yet they have generated few deep transformations. A celebrated Arab Spring brought down despised dictators, demanded democratization, and dreamed of justice. After brief openings, little of the promise endures. In the United States, movements from Occupy Wall Street to the Bernie Sanders presidential campaign brought months of hope, followed by frustrations as the limits of public protests and electoral processes become clear. Donald Trump appealed to people facing dependence, insecurity, and imagined losses of privilege to win the presidency, while angrily dividing people, white, black, and Latino, who share underlying struggles. In the heartland of global capitalism, too, electoral theater constrains popular participation.[21]

No movements in recent decades, nonviolent or violent, have begun to derail the concentrations of wealth and power detailed by Thomas

Piketty in *Capital in the Twenty-First Century*, the spread of insecurities explored by Zygmunt Bauman in *Liquid Times*, or the marginalization that plagues so many, as detailed in Mike Davis's *Planet of Slums*. Many struggling in dependent insecurity, caught between the powerful few and a desperate many, cling to the promises of the powerful. A few turn to violent destructive assaults on those they can hit—rarely the truly powerful. Most, seeing no clear road forward, focus on making the best they can for the families and communities they have.

Piketty documents capitalism's historic trajectory of generating soaring commercial production while concentrating wealth and property in ever fewer hands. He details how such concentrations ruled in Europe and the United States, while they dominated the nineteenth-century industrialization that spread commercial ways.[22] He shows how from 1910 to 1970—decades shaped by wars hot and cold, revolutions, and a global depression—concentrations gave way to limited yet meaningful distributions toward the many in the old industrial cores, and in regions pursuing national development, too. And he details how globalization has brought new and unchecked concentrations of wealth across the globe.

Piketty recognizes that soaring concentrations are socially corrosive, likely, sooner or later, to generate resistance that will undermine the productivity of the world economy. He challenges capitalists and their allies to see that deepening inequities will eventually destabilize everything and threaten their ultimate interest—the capitalism that generates profits and prosperity. Piketty documents that concentration is the normal dynamic of capitalism. History suggests it is unlikely that capitalists will recognize a need to limit short-term gain in pursuit of long-term stability, at least not until they face challenges that threaten their immediate interests.

This history of Mexico and the global studies of the agrarian bases of revolutions suggest an addition to, better a complication of, Piketty's vision of capitalism. During industrial capitalism's long run of concentrations in Western Europe and the northeastern United States from 1815 to 1910, it faced few wars and revolutionary challenges. The decades from 1910 to 1970 were precisely decades of wars, revolutions, and depression, along with anticolonial uprisings linked to cold-war conflicts across the globe. As Piketty shows, capitalism's turn to redistribution came in response to violent challenges, wars among states, and social mobilizations that were often linked. Many social revolutions came in response to threats to autonomies, enabled by rural peoples' capacity to rebuild autonomies, carry insurgent challenges, and demand social justice. Since the 1970s, the end of autonomies across the globe has sheltered globalizing capitalism from challenges beyond brief demonstrations and violent destructions that spread fear, yet rarely provoke change. Concentrations carry on.

Piketty, an economist, seeks a solution in fiscal policy. He argues that state powers, the guarantors of the property rights that sustain capitalism, must find a way to moderate excesses and distribute benefits. Knowing that an attempt by any one state will only send capital and the few jobs it creates elsewhere, Piketty proposes a global tax on capital to limit concentrations and share gains. But no global polity exists to design and implement such a program. Others who see the challenges to globalizing capitalism inherent in mounting concentrations and limited participation call for national reforms to defend property and promote justice, both grounded in the rule of law.[23] A global tax promoting redistribution and national reforms making property rights, politics, and justice more transparent and fair would do much good. There is little sign they are coming—globally, or in nations where concentrations and exclusions are extreme and deepening.

The intersection of Piketty's emphasis of the normality of concentrations and the historical understanding that popular movements grounded in landed communities (and, in industrial centers, labor movements built on strong unions) have been the primary ways people have long pressed the powerful to negotiate, leads to different questions: Can organized popular power revive in a world of globalization without autonomies— and in which global dispersals of production inhibit organizations of workers? If redistributions engineered by the political allies of those who profit most seem improbable, can new ways and means of popular assertion rise to press the powerful? Electoral political openings matter, as do organizations promoting human rights and welfare. Still, they have had little impact in bringing effective justice or meaningful redistribution. In an overpopulated urbanizing world, a return to autonomies on the land is improbable.[24] That is the world we have lost.

Can new ways of empowering communities to serve families (as they rapidly change) develop in a world structured by fragmentation, insecurity, and dependence? Perhaps the efforts of so many to mobilize self-help and local organizations to build more viable neighborhoods in Mexico City— and, in the effort, to build a metropolis—suggest ways forward. Without autonomies, people must organize to press their interests. That too is the lesson of movements for workers' rights within industrial capitalism. Still, the organizations that built Mexico City neighborhoods exhausted themselves in the effort, first co-opted by PRI power, then diverted to electoral theater. Labor organizations were broken by state power in the turn to globalization—in Mexico, the United States, and Britain. Their persistence in Europe deserves thoughtful consideration. The question remains: How can people in communities stripped of autonomies, defined by dependencies, and shaped by everyday struggles for survival organize to press their interests?

In the search for answers, one point demands emphasis. This history has detailed the patriarchal organization of families and communities grounded in landed autonomies, and shown how threats to autonomies, lived as challenges to patriarchy, sent men to violence, first in families and communities, then after 1810 and 1910 to challenge the powers that ruled. The fall of autonomies has undermined patriarchy—first in assaults on men's ability to provide, then by movements demanding women's rights and equality. After centuries of primacy, the patriarchal family is collapsing in Mexico and across the globe. Its inequities and exploitations are clear; patriarchy need not revive. That emphasized, the challenge for our times is to find new ways to organize and sustain changing families and communities that are more equitable—and secure in enduring ways. For many women of prosperity, challenges to patriarchy have brought new opportunities, though still limited; for too many women struggling to sustain themselves and families, the fall of autonomous ways of provision and the patriarchy it brought has led to demands to work for income, serve households, and care for children in the face of endemic insecurity—and too often corrosive violence. A nonpatriarchal world needs to be open, secure, and sustaining.

Are there ways to forge families free of patriarchy in communities capable of providing secure sustenance in a world integrated by globalizing inequities? States facilitate the global operation of great banks, industrial corporations, and commercial behemoths. They are legally sanctioned transnational organizations. Meanwhile, people who produce, consume, or just struggle to survive live linked together in a world economy of unprecedented complexity—while their attempts to organize are inhibited locally and blocked internationally. Can people find ways to strengthen local communities, organize to promote their goals, and link across borders to press common agendas?

At present, states facilitate global movement of capital and goods while working to lock people inside nations. Nationalist, too often xenophobic, politics promote the restriction of people as a solution to poverty, dividing those who might organize together to demand shared prosperity—within their borders and in the wider world. That world is globalizing power and production while politics remain insistently national, autonomies vanish, and communities fragment. People face constrained mobility and limited ability to organize in polities restricted to national domains. Can diverse, more gender-equal families and communities find ways to effective participation, new security, and shared prosperity? Can they organize locally, integrate nationally, and extend beyond borders to promote common needs? Efforts have been under way for decades; their energies are impressive, their commitments clear—their impacts uncertain.[25] Questions and uncertainties with no clear answers must end this long history of Mexicans negotiating lives within capitalism. Their and our current difficulties in an integrated yet divided North America are reasons to worry; their enduring resilience in the face of so many obstacles gives reason for hope.

Postdata: Mexico's Heartland, 2016

In October 2016 I joined two Mexican friends, a historian and a linguist-photographer, in a tour seeking photos of the mining centers, estates, and communities that long sustained Mexico City and global capitalism, and now are drowning in a huge expanding metropolis. We learned much that punctuates this history and sharpens its emphases. Taxco remains a prosperous center of silver production—focused on making and selling jewelry to Mexican and international visitors, employing more people in service than in mining. No longer sending capital to stimulate world trade, Taxco

FIGURE E.1. Funding silver tourism at Taxco: Banamex-Citibank, 2016.

depends on global banks to finance tourism, entertain the prosperous, and keep the populace in service. The Banamex branch shown in figure E.1 is a subsidiary of Citibank.

Meanwhile, urbanization has driven beyond the drained Lake Chalco to the historic Chalco plains—Mexico City's historic granary. The San José de Chalco estate (shown in figure 3.1), built by Jesuits and later operated by the Emperor Iturbide, President Guerrero, and liberal reformer Mariano Riva Palacio, now houses a secondary school serving the youth of San Gregorio Cuautzingo. The old village has become an urbanizing town in which the discount store Bodega Aurera (owned by Walmart) dominates the landscape more than the local church (shown in figure 3.2). The haciendas' once vast fields now mix formal housing developments (see figure E.2) for the modestly prosperous and shacks built by families taking a piece of the land to claim a place at the edge of the metropolis. High above, on the shoulders of the volcanoes that still dominate the landscape (when clouds and smog clear enough to see), the San Rafael paper mill offers a few low-paid jobs in new buildings beside historic ruins announcing past prosperity—also kept to a few. On a cliff above the mill, families take bits of hillside to build shacks clinging to the edge of globalization—flying Mexican flags to show

FIGURE E.2. Living on the lands of San José de Chalco
(La Compañía), 2016: tied to the city by car, to the world by dish.

FIGURE E.3. Clinging to the cliff, flying the flag: San Rafael, 2016.

national pride (see figure E.3). A modern church dedicated to the Virgin shows that people still seek her help in the face of marginal lives.

Remnants of rural ways persist. Beyond Tlalmanalco, where a sixteenth-century church centers a modern town (see figure 2.3), and on the way to Amecameca (shown in figure 8.2), fields of maize persist (see figure 8.1), most worked by truck- and tractor-driving men; still, a few cling to remnant autonomies, using horses to cart crops home and to market. To the north in the Mezquital, the Tulancalco estate threatened by insurgents after 1810 is now an ejido where poor men work fields of maize surrounding a ruined granary, which once held a noblewoman's crops awaiting times of scarcity to profit (see figure 4.2). Homes are self-built; trucks tie families to markets via a new road; the old *casco* (operations center) is a ruin; a school centers the town. The hacienda that held off insurgents is gone; maize holds strong as families seek chances for their children (see figure 4.2).

In the historic sugar basin around Cuernavaca, home of the insurgency that rattled the Mexican state and agro-industrial capitalism after 1910, sugar still rules across lowland plains, some planted by ejido cooperatives, much by private growers; all is refined in huge mechanized mills, the state-built factory at Zacatepec (see figure 12.1) complemented by new private enterprises. Sugar reigns where the mills still grind; trucks are everywhere; autonomies are gone. Mill workers live in small but solid homes; rural growers endure in small, often self-built, shacks.

Finally, fast highways (for a fee) have made Tlayacapan and Tepoztlán suburbs for the prosperous escaping city smog and congestion. The old church still stands at the center of Tepoztlán (see figure 9.4), now surrounded by weekend tourists seeking fresh air, cafes, arts and crafts. Local people who clung so long to maize to keep sugar capitalism at bay now serve the prosperous few who serve global capitalism. Inequities, dependencies, and insecurities define a globalized urban heartland. Some profit and growing numbers prosper. Still, lives of secure sustenance, equity, and justice remain but dreams for most—even as they continue to carry capitalism by spending at Walmart to buy the necessities of life drawn from US farmers, Asian manufacturers, and others dispersed in unprecedented networks of dependencies across the globe.

THE BOOK BUILDS on, revises, and integrates research and analysis I began in the 1960s, always in conversations with scholars in Mexico and the United States. The need for acknowledgments is endless. Every listing in the notes and bibliography is a recognition, inevitably insufficient, as I cite only works that directly shaped my analysis. Many more have contributed to my understanding of Mexico and the world. Colleagues and students everywhere I have been have taught me much and changed my views. Those at Georgetown opened new worlds. John McNeill led two seminars bringing colleagues together to read and improve the volume, one early on, one near the end. They made this a better book.

There are so many others. In the beginning I read John Womack to learn how Zapata's revolution mattered; Octavio Paz showed me that Zapata's revolution, a revelation of Mexico's deepest being, had to be seen in a long historical vision; then Charles Gibson opened a window into the histories of the communities of the Valley of Mexico. This book is a long-developing response to their visions and questions. In graduate studies, I first used the Mariano Riva Palacio papers to study Chalco in 1972 (a foundation of chapter 7), guided by Nettie Lee Banson, who also taught me Mexican history. I studied capitalism and the industrial revolution with Standish Meacham; Richard Graham helped me think across oceans; Richard Adams led me to see power in the long term. James Lockhart taught me about Spanish America and social history, and then mentored the dissertation that grounds chapters 3 and 4.

Friedrich Katz invited me to a working group on rural resistance in Mexico, leading to chapter 8; Eric Van Young shared sources essential to chapter 4. Mark Wasserman was a reader for my first book; he invited me to write an essay precursor to chapter 10 here, then asked me to contribute to the journal *History Compass*—leading to analyses key to chapter 9. Recently, Bryan McCann reminded me of the importance of *The Children of Sanchez*, making chapter 13 much more insightful. Bill Taylor, Steve Stern, Pat Carroll, and Brian Owensby have had deep and enduring influence on my understanding of Spanish imperial times; Sue Cline and Catarina Pizzigoni opened Nahuatl wills as windows into family and community cultures; Vera Candiani set a new vision of the changing ecology of the Valley of Mexico. Jon Brown, Alan Knight, Mary Kay Vaughan, Emilio

Kourí, and Myrna Santiago shaped my thinking on the national era. Harry Cross's unfortunately unpublished dissertation opened new visions of the nineteenth century. Recently, Jennifer Scheper Hughes taught me about local devotions from the sixteenth century to the present. Marty Melosi and all our colleagues in the working group on New World Cities brought me into the world of twentieth-century urbanization. Part III could not have been written without their collaborations.

In Mexico, I have been welcomed into scholarly conversations as I tried to learn: Enrique Florescano opened his office and analytical mind to an unknown neophyte; Jan Bazant soon did the same. Thanks to the Katz group, I got to know and learn from Leticia Reina, and Arturo Warman too. I met Guillermo de la Peña when we visited during the same year in Austin. Arturo's and Guillermo's essential works shape chapter 12. Leticia introduced me to Elisa Servín, bringing me into the *Cycles of Conflict* project that taught me so much about the long term. I met Enrique Cárdenas more recently; chapter 11 could not have been written without his unmatched analyses of Mexico's economic history. Beyond that core, I have learned from Tomás Jalpa and Teresa Jarquín; José Enciso Contreras and Gilda Cubilla Moreno; América Molina del Villar and Gerardo Lara; Alfredo Ávila and Erika Pani; Romana Falcón, Felipe Ávila, and Alejandro Tortolero; Luis Fernando Granados and Adolfo Gilly. Antonio García de León and Aurora Gómez Galvarriato are pioneering a Mexican history of capitalism focused on the Gulf state of Veracruz. Brian Connaughton made the voice of the angry priest of Iztacalco available to the world.

As the above acknowledgments note, much of the work presented here developed from research undertaken since the 1970s and shared in various publications. Most of the chapters are fully new texts built on that work. A few, while revised, reflect earlier publications more directly. Chapter 5 offers a substantial revision, rewritten in English, of "Soberanía quebrada, insurgencias populares, y la independencia de México: La guerra de independencias, 1808–1821" (*Historia Mexicana* 59, no. 1 [2009], 11–75). Chapter 6 includes sections, again substantially revised and rewritten in English, of "El debate del futuro de México: Buscando una economía nueva; encontrando desafíos y limites, 1830–1845" (*Historia Mexicana* 65, no. 3 [2016], 1119–92). Both are included here by permission of El Colegio de México. Chapter 8 is a radically revised version of "Agrarian Social Change and Peasant Rebellion in Nineteenth-Century Mexico: The Example of Chalco," published in Friedrich Katz, *Riot, Rebellion, and Revolution*. It is included by permission of Princeton University Press.

I must also recognize the doctoral students who have worked with me on Mexico: Theresa Alfaro-Velcamp on migration to Mexico, Luis Fernando Granados on indigenous peoples in Mexico City—the heart of the heartland, Emilio Coral on Mexico City's middle classes, Ben Fulwider on roads and transport, Rodolfo Fernández on Monterrey and revolution, Fernando Pérez Montesinos on Purépecha communities and liberal programs, Larisa Veloz on migration to the United States, Adrienne Kates on Maya chicleros and global capitalism, Hillar Schwertner on water and the Tijuana-San Diego metropolis. All have shaped my understandings of the heartland, Mexico, and the world.

This book was possible in great part thanks to the resources of the Benson Latin American Collection Library at the University of Texas at Austin. I was introduced to its treasures—manuscripts, periodicals, and books from everywhere (especially works from provincial Mexico, unavailable elsewhere)—by Nettie Lee Benson herself. The Collection grounded my graduate studies, and I have returned almost annually over the years to tap its unmatched resources. So much here is based on the personal papers, state compilations, and rare books held at the Benson— and kept so easily accessible. Its staff and directors, from Miss Benson (as we called her with a mix of fear and respect) to Julianne Gilland, have earned my endless gratitude.

Bringing this volume to press has been an odyssey: Norris Pope saw promise and offered encouragement and a contract early on. Brigitta van Rheinberg drew the volume to Princeton and challenged me to write Part III on the twentieth century; her assistant Amanda Peery worked hard to help me focus at the end; the production and editing team of Jenny Wolkowicki, Maia Vaswani, and (again) Rodolfo Fernández have brought me closer to clarity. Margaret Chowning was three times a reader, always positive, also pressing me to clarity. Bill Nelson has again produced essential maps.

Three colleagues who are also friends brought visual illumination to the volume. The photos came during days of exploration shared with Alfredo Ávila and Dinorah Pesquiera. Our mix of historians' and photographers' eyes proved revealing. What I learned during those days led to analytical revisions—and the Postdata at the end of the volume. Beyond acknowledgment, they earn abrazos. And when gaining permission to reproduce on the cover the Diego Rivera image that reveals so much about community proved daunting, Catherine Mayo—transnational scholar, writer, novelist, historian—showed the way. She gains the deepest thanks from me and Princeton University Press.

Ultimately, this book and my life are about family. Jane remains my essential partner. We met just after I read Womack; she gave me Gibson's *Aztecs under Spanish Rule* as a college-graduation gift. We lived and learned together in Mexico City during all of 1973; while I plumbed archives, she cared for children in the intensive care unit of the National Pediatric Institute (IMAN). We return together regularly. She shaped and shapes every conversation by insisting that the work and welfare of everyday people is always what matters. In that, the book is a testament to her vision. We share an ever more Mexican family that illuminates our lives and understanding: Gabriela and María, Israel and Pilar. And yes, María, I still go to school—happily and almost every day.

Finally, the people to whom I dedicate this book earn a bit more acknowledgment. The people of Mexico and its communities have inspired me for decades—since our first encounters in 1965, just after I graduated from high school. They have carried on through a long history that threatened much, destroyed many, and offered little—keeping family and community together as they could, always with an eye to new ways forward. Their resilience continues to inspire me, as they face new challenges and live in new communities across Mexico and North America. We "gringos" need to learn from them, not denigrate them.

Late in life, I recognized that my grandparents, Biaggio and Anna María Tutino, Lillian and Lewis Paquin, were the first to teach me the value of community and sustenance as they lived hard transitions from lives on the land to dependence on industrial work. They were different in important ways: Biaggio and Anna María crossed oceans; Lillian grew up an orphan. Biaggio and Anna María labored in a woolen mill; Lewis worked in a machine shop. Anna María was a midwife, bringing Italian village ways to a New England mill town. Biaggio and Anna María were Catholic; Lillian and Lewis Congregationalist Protestants. Still, they shared much: Biaggio and Lewis kept rich gardens as long as they lived, certain that the food they grew was better than anything they could buy; Anna María and Lillian made weekly feasts, drawing families together. During years of school and summer vacations, I lived with them, learning to appreciate lives of labor and the value of homemade food. On endless Sundays we shuttled to join in both feasts, one Italian, the other old New England. From my grandparents I learned what the people of Mexico's heartland always knew: the essential importance of family and food—and the value of even remnant autonomies.

ANALYSES OF LAND and labor, capital and production, family, crime, and violence essential to several chapters are based on analyses of quantitative materials. When those materials have been presented and discussed in previously published texts, I cite those publications rather than include tables here. When quantitative materials have not been published, they are presented here and discussed in the relevant chapters.

Table A.1. Production and Labor at New Spain's Silver Mines, 1597

	Silver in Pesos	Water Mills	Horse Mills	African Slaves	Native *Naboríos*	*Repartimiento Indios*
Taxco Region						
Taxco	421,658	36	45	266	834	406
Zacualpa	219,411	23	3	117	304	126
Huautla	178,679	3	23	178	244	200
Temascaltepec	169,380	17	0	46	172	133
Sultepec	110,713	17	23	130	222	66
Total	**1,099,841**	**96**	**94**	**737**	**1,776**	**931**
North Heartland						
Pachuca	262,548	59	23	109	1,168	394
Tlalpujahua	88,774	6	13	4	137	113
Total	**351,322**	**65**	**36**	**113**	**1,305**	**507**
Spanish North America						
Zacatecas	670,489	0	65	130	1,014	0
Guanajuato	248,957	2	44	42	415	166
Total	**919,446**	**2**	**109**	**172**	**1,429**	**166**
New Spain total	*2,370,609*	*163*	*239*	*1,022*	*4,510*	*1,604*

Source: Calculations are based on Cubillo Moreno, *Dominios de la plata*, 253, fig. 1.

Table A.2. Population Estimates for the Valley of Mexico, 1520–1800

	1520	1570	1640	1800
Mexico City				
Indios	250,000	50,000	25,000	30,000
Spaniards		15,000	30,000	70,000
Mixed		15,000	30,000	50,000
City total	**250,000**	**80,000**	**85,000**	**150,000**
Urban total	**(400,000)**			
Provinces				
Indios	1,250,000	275,000	125,000	250,000
Spaniards and mixed		5,000	10,000	50,000
Provincial total	**1,250,000**	**280,000**	**135,000**	**300,000**
Rural total	**(1,100,000)**			
Valley total	***1,500,000***	***360,000***	***220,000***	***450,000***

Sources: Estimates are based on data in Gibson, *Aztecs under Spanish Rule*, 137–44, 377–81; de Urrutia, "Noticia geográfica," 68–127; and Reyes García, "Estado general de tributos."

Notes: The urban total in parentheses for 1520 aims to account for the population of outlying cities such as Texcoco; the rural total in parentheses for that year subtracts that estimate from the valley total to account for the rural population. The estimate of 150,000 for Mexico City in 1800 aims to balance census counts from the 1790s that hover near 100,000 and counts from 1810 that approach 170,000.

Table A.3. Indigenous Tributaries in Three Valley of Mexico Jurisdictions, 1570–1800

Year	Chalco	Tacuba	Texcoco	Total
1570	13,050	9,900	19,400	42,350
1644	2,910	2,430	2,074	7,414
1692	2,689	2,916	2,711	8,316
1735	5,369	5,293	5,906	16,568
1742	5,071	3,965	5,969	15,005
1764	5,180	3,571	4,793	13,544
1782	6,373	5,210	7,540	19,123
1790	7,182	5,951	6,847	19,980
1800	8,623	6,561	7,547	22,731

Sources: Gibson, *Aztecs under Spanish Rule*, 142–43, table 10; figures for 1735 are from Cook and Borah, *Essays in Population History*, vol. 2, 227–28, table 2.7.

Table A.4. Suits Over Land in the Valleys of Mexico and Toluca, 1556–1805

Decade	Total Suits	Suits at Santa Lucía
1556–65	26	
1566–75	20	
1576–85	29	5
1586–95	46	2
1596–1605	34	4
1606–15	32	2
1616–25	20	2
1626–35	12	0
1636–45	16	3
1646–55	17	2
1656–65	13	0
1666–75	24	7
1676–85	34	2
1686–95	84	2
1696–1705	134	1
1706–15	236	12
1716–25	220	9
1726–35	201	8
1736–45	209	9
1746–55	185	10
1756–65	245	5
1766–75	304	
1776–85	394	
1786–95	375	
1796–1805	362	

Sources: Total suits are based on Colín, *Índice de documentos*; suits at Santa Lucía are calculated from Konrad, *Santa Lucía*, appendix B, 365–69.

Table A.5. Distribution of Land in San Gregorio Cuautzingo, 1790

Number of Plots	Number of Families	Percentage of Families
7	1	1
6	1	1
5	2	2
4	11	10
3	40	36
2	16	14
1	5	4
House garden only	27	24
No land	9	8
Total cultivated plots: 224	*Total families: 112*	

Source: AGN, Tierras, vol. 1912, exp. 1, fols. 22–24, April 13, 1790.

Table A.6. Distribution of Land in San Gregorio Cuautzingo, 1800

Hectares per Family	Number of Families	Percentage of Families
0.81–0.90	7	6
0.71–0.80	1	1
0.61–0.70	1	1
0.51–0.60	11	9
0.41–0.50	11	9
0.31–0.40	12	9
0.21–0.30	23	18
0.11–0.20	12	9
0.01–0.10	6	5
Little	30	24
None	13	10
	Total families: 127	

Source: AGN, Tierras, vol. 1912, exp. 11, fols. 51–56, February 13, 1800.

Table A.7. Silver Minted in Mexico City, 1741–1810

Decade	Silver Minted Annually
1741–50	10,664,000
1751–60	12,385,000
1761–70	11,507,000
1771–80	16,903,000
1781–90	18,804,000
1791–1800	22,235,000
1801–10	21,562,000

Source: Calculated from Ministerio de Fomento, *Anales del Ministerio*, 5–17.

Note: Figures for silver minted are given as mean, in pesos.

Table A.8. Silver Minted in Mexico City and Northern Mints, 1811–53

Years	Mexico City	%	North	%	Total
1811–20	8,103,000	71	3,306,000	29	11,409,000
1821–30	3,068,000	28	7,725,000	72	10,793,000
1831–40	1,060,000	10	9,108,000	90	10,168,000
1841–47	1,816,000	14	11,409,000	86	13,225,000
1848–53	2,310,000	13	14,805,000	87	17,115,000

Sources: Calculated from Ministerio de *Fomento, Anales del Ministerio*, 5–17.

Notes: Figures for silver minted are given as mean, in pesos.

The leading northern producers changed over the decades:

From *1811 to 1820,* Zacatecas averaged 2,000,000 pesos yearly, Durango 650,000.

From *1821 to 1830,* Zacatecas minted about 4,500,000 pesos yearly, Guanajuato about 2,000,000, and Durango and Guadalajara 650,000 each.

From *1831 to 1840,* Zacatecas held around 4,500,000 pesos yearly, with Guanajuato still near 2,000,000. San Luis Potosí rose to average over 1,000,000 pesos annually, with Durango and Guadalajara still about 650,000 each.

From *1841 to 1847,* Zacatecas rose to mint about 4,700,000 pesos yearly while Guanajuato rose more, to average 3,700,000 pesos annually. San Luis Potosí held just over 1,000,000 pesos yearly, and Durango and Guadalajara remained near 650,000 pesos each.

From *1848 to 1853,* Guanajuato soared to lead with over 7,000,000 pesos minted yearly, while Zacatecas fell to 3,800,000 pesos. San Luis Potosí rose to 1,400,000 pesos, Durango to 700,000 pesos, and Culiacán on the Pacific coast to 650,000 pesos yearly—while Durango fell back to near 500,000 pesos annually.

Table A.9. Minted Silver Production, Mexico and Zacatecas, 1820–79

Years	Mexico	Zacatecas	Zacatecas Percentage
1820–24	9.33	2.75	29
1825–29	9.28	3.77	41
1830–34	11.39	5.11	45
1835–39	11.63	5.34	46
1840–44	12.56	4.59	37
1845–49	15.93	4.53	28
1850–54	16.59	3.53	21
1855–59	16.31	3.71	23
1860–64	15.66	4.14	26
1865–69	18.07	4.71	26
1870–74	19.49	4.61	24
1875–79	24.44	5.05	21

Source: Cross, "Mining Economy of Zacatecas," 32, table I-C.

Note: Figures are given as annual mean, in millions of pesos.

Table A.10. Tithe Incomes Before and After Independence

Diocese	1806–9	1829–32	Percentage Change
Mexico	582,501	184,593	−68
Puebla	476,899	157,487	−67
Michoacán	512,256	306,450	−40
Guadalajara	192,142	221,640	+15
Durango	167,357	138,761	−17
Monterrey	158,208	30,457	−81
Oaxaca	105,938	47,295	−55
Chiapas	11,086	5,349	−52
Total	*2,206,387*	*1,092,032*	*−51*

Source: LAM, 1843, Estado no. 2.

Note: Figures are given as annual means, in pesos.

Table A.11. Mexican Convent-Banks, ca. 1835

Diocese	No.	Nuns	Props.[a]	Rents	Capital	Interest	% Earned	Total Income[b]
Mexico	24	831	768	383,404	2,452,881	88,687	3.6	472,093
Puebla	12	355	507		1,606,905			166,075
Michoacán	8	231	19	2,684	1,009,623	48,318	4.8	51,002
Jalisco	7	251	144	36,700	357,266	17,697	5.0	54,397
Oaxaca	5	128	137	8,978	177,589	15,703	8.8	24,681
Chiapas	1	13			74,975	1,950	2.6	1,950
Yucatán	1	36	18	100	12,800	525		625
Total	*58*	*1,845*	*1,593*		*5,692,039*			*770,823*

Source: José María Luis Mora, "México y sus revoluciones" (1836), as tabulated in RWM, table F.

[a] Props. are income properties; by their low mean rents, they are mostly urban residences and shops.

[b] Total income combines rental earnings with interest collected on capital; the report on Puebla had already combined those earnings, so the interest earned on capital could not be calculated.

Table A.12. Mechanized Cotton Factories, 1843

State	Factories	Spindles	Looms	Spindles per Loom
Center				
Mexico	17	23,894	1,187	20
Puebla	21	37,396	530	71
Veracruz	8	22,856	366	62
Greater Bajío				
Querétaro	2	5,400	112	48
Guanajuato	1	500		
Jalisco	4	8,900	220	40
North				
Durango	5	5,560	140	40
Sonora	1	2,198	54	41
Total	*59*	*106,704*	*2,609*	*41*

Source: LAM, 1843, Estado no. 5.

Note: The listing only includes mechanized spindles and looms; hand looms are excluded.

Table A.13. Mechanized Cotton Factories, 1844, 1845

State	Factories 1844	Spindles 1844	Factories 1845	Spindles 1845	Spindles Idle 1845
Center					
Mexico	17	26,077	10	21,868	5,648
Puebla	21	38,094	20	42,812	68
Veracruz	8	18,353	8	19,807	4,866
Greater Bajío					
Querétaro	2	4,566	3	4,800	1,200
Guanajuato	1	800	2	1,592	
Michoacán	1	1,530	1	1,688	
Jalisco	4	13,056	4	11,588	3,076
North					
Durango	5	5,560	5	5,520	856
Sonora	1	2,198	1	2,198	
Coahuila	2	1,960	1	1,960	
Total	*62*	*112,194*	*55*	*113,833*	*15,714*

Sources: LAM, 1844, Estado no. 1; 1845, Estado no. 4.

Table A.14. Mechanized Cotton Factories, ca. 1853

State	Factories	Spindles	Looms	Spindles per Loom	Workers	Payroll[a]	Pay per Worker[a]
Center							
Mexico	6	21,622	1,406	15	2,786	456,170	164
Puebla	14	40,448	268	151	1,437	340,824	237
Veracruz	6	22,034	509	43	1,082	326,680	302
Greater Bajío							
Querétaro	1	7,500	500	15	3,000	250,000	83
Guanajuato	1	900			65	9,000	138
Jalisco	5	18,292	427	43	1,767	226,702	128
North							
Durango	5	6,600	183	36	645	66,846	103
Sonora	1	1,924	60	32	157	42,720	272
Coahuila	1	1,300	40	33	180	19,200	107
Total	*40*	*120,620*	*3,393*	*36*	*11,119*	*1,738,142*	*156*

Source: Ministerio de Fomento, "Estado de las Fábricas . . . ," in Anales del Ministerio.

[a] Payroll and pay per worker are in pesos. The small number of workers and exceptionally high pay in Sonora are likely due to the California gold rush, which drew migrants from Sonora and created demand there. The high pay in Mexico City and Puebla seems anomalous; perhaps the total payroll included payments to independent weavers not listed among workers. Perhaps the two reports are exaggerated, or just in error. The rest seem reasonable.

Table A.15. Mechanized Textile Factories, ca. 1880

Jurisdiction	Factories	Spindles	Looms	Spindles per Loom
Heartland				
Federal district	8	32,788	1,302	25
State of Mexico	5	21,418	793	27
Hidalgo	4	2,034	90	23
Heartland total	17	56,240	2,185	26
East Center				
Puebla	21	67,130	2,002	34
Tlaxcala	3	4,800	85	56
Veracruz	5	26,200	609	43
East center total	29	98,130	2,696	36
South				
Guerrero	1	2,500	80	31
Oaxaca	2	19,000	580	33
Yucatán	1	700	20	35
South total	4	22,200	680	33
Greater Bajío				
Querétaro	3	10,000	600	17
Guanajuato	4	6,668	287	23
Michoacán	3	7,200	175	41
Jalisco	10	24,800	510	49
Colima	2	3,750	170	22
Greater Bajío total	22	52,418	1,742	30
Near North				
San Luis Potosí	1	2,500	126	20
Zacatecas	1	500	15	33
Aguascalientes	1	750	25	30
Sinaloa	3	6,200	400	16
Near north total	6	9,950	566	18
North				
Durango	7	5,030	305	16
Sonora	1	900	30	30
Coahuila	7	6,550	210	31
Chihuahua	3	4,600	340	14
Nuevo León	3	3,100	95	33
North total	21	20,180	980	21
Mexico total	***99***	***259,118***	***8,849***	***29***

Source: Emiliano Busto, *Estadística de la República Mexicana* (Mexico: Ignacio Cumplido, 1880); reported in Ramos Escandón, *Industrialización*, 337–46, fig. I.

Note: Tabulations and calculations are my own. Listings include cotton and wool factories; the latter were few—two in the federal district, one in the state of Mexico, one in Puebla; a few others report both cotton and wool production. The great preponderance in mechanized cloth production was in cotton.

ABBREVIATIONS USED
IN CITATIONS AND BIBLIOGRAPHY

AGN: Archivo General de la Nación, Mexico

AHH: Archivo Histórico de Hacienda (within AGN)

BLAC: Benson Latin American Collection, University of Texas at Austin

BRF: Payno, *Bandidos de Río Frío*

CIESAS: Centro de Investigaciones y Estudios Superiores en Antropología Social, Mexico City

CMCH: Colegio de Michoacán

CMEX: Colegio de México

CNSE: Colegio Mexiquense

CSL: Lewis, *Children of Sánchez*

CUP: Cambridge University Press

DUP: Duke University Press

FCB: Calderón de la Barca, *Life in México*

FCE: Fondo de Cultura Económica

HAHR: *Hispanic American Historical Review*

HM: *Historia mexicana*

INAH: Instituto Nacional de Antropología e Historia

JG: J. G., "Industria nacional"

JHU: Johns Hopkins University Press

LAM: Alamán, Memorias, cited by year (see Bibliography)

MCX: González Montes and Patiño, *Memoria campesina*

MEM: Espinosa de los Monteros, *Miscelánea*

MLE: Manuel López Escudero Papers, BLAC

MRP: Mariano Riva Palacio Papers, BLAC

PCR: Papers of the Condes de Regla; PCRb, bound volumes; PCRun, uncataloged items, Washington State University Library

PML: Lewis, *Pedro Martínez*

PUP: Princeton University Press

RWM: Wyllie, *México*

SUP: Stanford University Press

TOM: Ortiz, *Mexico*

UCP: University of California Press

UNAM: Universidad Nacional Autónoma de México

UNC: University of North Carolina Press

UNM: University of New Mexico Press

UNP: University of Nebraska Press

UOP: University of Oklahoma Press

UTP: University of Texas Press

VFT: Fernández, *Testimonio . . . 1816*

Introduction

1. Modern studies begin with Braudel, *Civilization and Capitalism*, and culminate in Findlay and O'Rourke, *Power and Plenty*.

2. This emphasis is clear in Braudel, *Civilization and Capitalism*, vol. 2, *The Wheels of Commerce*, 229–30.

3. Wallerstein, *The Modern World-System*.

4. Andre Gunder Frank, *ReOrient*.

5. Pomeranz, *The Great Divergence*.

6. Tutino, *Making a New World*.

7. On the ramifications of the Bajío revolution, see the essays in Tutino, *New Countries*.

8. See Tutino, "Rise of Industrial Capitalism."

9. See Tutino and Melosi, *New World Cities*, for explorations of twentieth-century urbanization.

10. Tutino, *From Insurrection to Revolution*.

11. See Tutino, *From Insurrection to Revolution*, and "Revolutionary Capacity."

12. Tutino, *Making a New World*, links ecological foundations, political coercions, and cultural constructions.

13. On moral legitimacy, see Tutino, *Making a New World*, and Scott, *Domination and the Arts*.

14. Tutino, *Making a New World*, 44–62.

15. See Gibson, *Aztecs under Spanish Rule*; Lockhart, *Nahuas after the Conquest*.

16. See Clendinnen, *Aztecs*.

17. Piketty, *Capital*, is the most recent and powerful statement of this truth.

18. On early regimes, see Strayer, *Medieval Origins*, and Collins, *Early Modern France*.

19. See Owensby, *Empire of Law*; Sánchez de Tagle, *Del gobierno*; and Lempérière, *Dios y el rey*.

20. That pivot to military power is detailed in Tutino, *Mexico City, 1808*.

21. See Córdova, *Política de masas*, and Hamilton, *Limits of State Autonomy*.

22. Rath, *Myths of Demilitarization*.

23. See Tilly, *Coercion*; North, Wallis, and Weingast, *Violence and Social Orders*; and on state and coercion in twentieth-century Mexico, see Rath, *Myths of Demilitarization*.

24. Wolf, *Peasant Wars*; Tutino, "Revolutionary Capacity."

25. Primary, often archival, research grounds chapters 3, 4, 6, 7, 8, and 9. Chapters of synthesis and studies of communities in the sixteenth and twentieth centuries build on the research of historians, anthropologists, and economists too. Interpretations are mine.

26. That is the focus of Tutino, *Making a New World*.

27. On Yucatán, see Farriss, *Maya Society*; Rugeley, *Yucatán's Maya Peasantry*; Wells and Joseph, *Summer of Discontent*. On Chiapas, see García de León, *Resistencia y utopía*, and Womack, *Rebellion in Chiapas*; for long-term studies that parallel this book on the Mixtec regions of Oaxaca, see Rodolfo Pastor, *Campesinos y reformas*; Ruíz Medrano, *Mexico's Indigenous Communities*; and Smith, *Roots of Conservatism*.

28. On Michoacán, just west of the heartland and south of the Bajío, a region of important yet less intense encounters between capitalism and entrenched landed communities, see Rodrigo Martínez Baracs, *Convivencia y utopía*; Castro Gutiérrez, *Tarascos*; Pérez Montesinos, "Poised to Break."

29. That is the emphasis of the studies brought together in Tutino, *New Countries*.

Chapter One

1. Many surveys cover this; I prefer Kamen, *Empire*; my exploration of silver capitalism began with Tutino, *Making a New World*; on Asia's key role, see Giraldez, *Age of Trade*.

2. Giraldez, *Age of Trade*, provides a powerful synthesis of silver's global reach.

3. Understanding colonial Brazil begins with Schwartz, *Sugar Plantations*. On the world economy, see Findlay and O'Rourke, *Power and Plenty*. For the role of silver in gaining the cotton goods necessary to sustaining the African slave trade, see Parthasarathi, *How Europe Grew Rich*.

4. Stanley Stein and Barbara Stein, in *Silver, War, and Trade* and *Apogee of Empire*, engage the many laments.

5. My critique of enduring understandings of Spain's empire reflects Tutino, *Making a New World*.

6. See Lockhart, *Spanish Peru*, and Lockhart and Otte, *Letters and People*. On indigenous adaptations, see Lockhart, *Nahuas after the Conquest*.

7. Alfred Crosby made this key point long ago in *Columbian Exchange*.

8. Crosby, *Columbian Exchange*; Lockhart, *Men of Cajamarca*.

9. Early Spanish attempts to govern Mesoamerica are explored with a clear and critical eye in Ruíz Medrano, *Reshaping New Spain*.

10. Indigenous-Spanish alliances were first emphasized in Stern, *Peru's Indian Peoples*; that reality, despite Spanish rhetoric, is evident in works ranging from Gibson, *Aztecs under Spanish Rule*, to Spalding, *Huarochirí*; Farriss, *Maya Society*; García Castro, *Indios, territorio y poder*; and Rodrigo Martínez Baracs, *Convivencia y utopía*.

11. See Lockhart, *Spanish Peru*, and Gibson, *Aztecs Under Spanish Rule*.

12. On gold, see Vilar, *History of Gold*.

13. On early silver mining at Taxco, see Enciso Contreras, *Taxco*.

14. On Chinese demand and silver trade, see Flynn and Giráldez, "Born with a 'Silver Spoon'," and "Cycles of Silver."

15. See Spalding, *Huarochirí*, and Stern, *Peru's Indian Peoples*.

16. For New Spain, see Tutino, "Urban Power"; on the Andes, see Mumford, *Vertical Empire*.

17. Taylor, *Drinking, Homicide, and Rebellion*; Borah, *Justice by Insurance*; Owensby, *Empire of Law*.

18. On Spanish power, see Cañeque, *The King's Living Image*; on the late rise of the military, see Archer, *Army in New Spain*, and Vinson, *Bearing Arms*.

19. The very different history of the Bajío and Spanish North America is detailed in Tutino, *Making a New World*.

20. Brading and Cross, "Colonial Silver Mining." The estimate of seventy percent is on p. 571.

21. The emphasis on the continuities of *kuraka* power from pre-Incaic, through Inca, to Spanish times is a key contribution of Spalding, *Huarochirí*.

22. Crosby, *Columbian Exchange*; Lockhart, *Spanish Peru*; Hemming, *Conquest of the Incas*.

23. See Bakewell, *Miners of the Red Mountain*; Spalding, *Huarochirí*; Stern, *Peru's Indian Peoples*; and Mumford, *Vertical Empire*.

24. Mangan, *Trading Roles*. For mining and labor beyond Potosí, see Zulawski, *They Eat*.

25. Bowser, *African Slave*. On the Andean economy in the age of silver, the place to begin is Assadourian, *Sistema de la economía*.

26. See Curtin, *African Slave Trade*.

27. Again, see Assadourian, *Sistema de la economía*.

28. See Hassig, *War and Society*.

29. Clendinnen, *Aztecs*.

30. Padden, *Hummingbird and the Hawk*; Hassig, *War and Society*.

31. Clendinnen, *Ambivalent Conquests*; Gibson, *Aztecs under Spanish Rule*; Lockhart, *Nahuas after the Conquest*; MacLeod, *Spanish Central America*.

32. See Enciso Contreras, *Taxco*.

33. Sanders and Price, *Mesoamerica*, long ago emphasized the importance of adjacent temperate and tropical basins in centering historic power in the heartland since the rise of Teotihuacán.

34. The classic analysis is Gibson, *Aztecs under Spanish Rule*. Chapter 2 builds on Gibson and newer sources.

35. Lockhart, *Nahuas after the Conquest*, emphasizes the republics' creative adaptations.

36. On Puebla see Grosso and Garavaglia, *Región de Puebla*; on Cuernavaca, Martin, *Rural Society*; for Taxco, see Enciso Contreras, *Taxco*; and on Oaxaca, the classic study is Rodolfo Pastor, *Campesinos y reformas*, now complemented by Terraciano, *Mixtecs of Colonial Oaxaca*, and Yannakakis, *Art of Being*.

37. This analysis of Spanish North America synthesizes Tutino, *Making a New World*.

38. Tutino, *Making a New World*; Bakewell, *Silver Mining and Society*; Guevara Sanginés, *Guanajuato diverso*.

39. Again see Guevara Sanginés, *Guanajuato diverso*, and Tutino, *Making a New World*.

40. Lynch, *Spain under the Hapsburgs*.

41. West, *Mining Community*.

42. Brading and Cross, "Colonial Silver Mining," 576–79.

43. See Jacobsen, *Mirages of Transition*, 43, fig. 2.1.

44. Serulnikov, *Revolution in the Andes*, emphasizes the disruptive impact of the *repartos*.

45. See Spalding, *Huarochirí*, and Stern, *Resistance, Rebellion, and Consciousness*.

46. See Stavig, *World of Tupac Amaru*; Charles Walker, *Smoldering Ashes*, and *Tupac Amaru Rebellion*; Serulnikov, *Subverting Colonial Authority*, and *Revolution in the Andes*; and Sinclair Thomson, *We Alone Will Rule*.

47. On silver, Jacobsen, *Mirages of Transition*, 43, fig. 2.1; on the broader aftermath see Charles Walker, *Tupac Amaru Rebellion*, and especially *Smoldering Ashes*; Sinclair Thomson, *We Alone Will Rule*; and Serulnikov, *Revolution in the Andes*.

48. See Tutino, "Rise of Industrial Capitalism," and Chambers, "From One Patria."

49. Tutino, *Making a New World*, 550, appendix D, table D.1.

50. This summarizes chapter 3; see the citations there.

51. Molina del Villar, *Nueva España*.

52. All this is detailed with citations in chapter 3.

53. See Taylor, *Drinking, Homicide, and Rebellion*.

54. The Mezquital and its exceptional insurgent communities are the focus of chapter 4.

55. See Hadley, *Minería y sociedad*; Langue, *Los señores de Zacatecas*; and Brading, *Miners and Merchants*.

56. This final section on the Bajío and Spanish North America again summarizes my *Making a New World*.

57. See Barr, *Peace Came*; Ross Frank, *From Settler to Citizen*; and Ortega Soto, *Alta California*.

58. Flynn and Giráldez, "Cycles of Silver."

59. See Castro Gutiérrez, *Nueva ley y nuevo rey*, and chap. 4 of Tutino, *Making a New World*.

60. See chap. 4 of Tutino, *Making a New World*.

61. The gendered nature of Bajío social polarizations focuses part 2 of Tutino, *Making a New World*.

62. Tutino, "Revolution in Mexican Independence."

63. On social relations and the limits of insurrection north of the Bajío, see Tutino, *From Insurrection to Revolution*.

Chapter Two

1. Hassig, *War and Society*.

2. See Millon, Drewitt, and Cowgill, *Urbanization at Teotihuacán*, and Sanders and Price, *Mesoamerica*.

3. See López Austin and López Luján, *Mexico's Indigenous Past*, and Florescano, *Orígenes del poder*.

4. See Padden, *Hummingbird and the Hawk*; Clendinnen, *Aztecs*; Hassig, *Trade, Tribute, and Transportation*; Palerm, *Obras hidráulicas prehispánicas*; and Berdan, *Aztecs of Central Mexico*.

5. In *Aztecs*, Clendinnen emphasizes that Mexica society was integrated and legitimate in the capital, not beyond.

6. This vision of Chalco before 1520 builds upon Jalpa Flores, *Sociedad indígena*.

7. Cubillo Moreno, *Dominios de la plata*, 49–71.

8. On Mexica power, see Hassig, *Trade, Tribute, and Transportation*; on rebellions, see Katz, "Rural Uprisings."

9. See the classic analysis in Crosby, *Columbian Exchange*.

10. See Simpson, *Encomienda in New Spain*; Silvio Zavala, *Encomienda Indiana*; Himmerich y Valencia, *Encomenderos of New Spain*; Gibson, *Aztecs under Spanish Rule*; Lockhart, *Nahuas after the Conquest*; García Castro, *Indios, territorio y poder*; and Jalpa Flores, *Sociedad indígena*.

11. Early attempts to build a European regime, constantly negotiated, are the focus of Ruíz Medrano, *Reshaping New Spain*.

12. See Rodrigo Martínez Baracs, *Convivencia y utopía*, and Andrea Martínez Baracs, *Gobierno de indios*.

13. The classic study is Ricard, *Spiritual Conquest of Mexico*. See also Burkhart, *Slippery Earth*, Clendinnen, *Ambivalent Conquests*, and Tavares, *Invisible War*.

14. See Vilar, *History of Gold*, and Miranda, *Función económica del encomendero*.

15. On early silver mining at Taxco, in "Organización económica-espacial," Margarita Menegus Bornemann saw ties to the Toluca basin; in "Our Suffering," Robert Haskett saw links to Cuernavaca; Enciso Contreras, *Taxco*, looks at Taxco from the perspective of local mine operators.

16. This is my reading of Enciso Contreras, *Taxco*.

17. On Cortés and early sugar, see Barrett, *Sugar Hacienda*, and G. Michael Riley, *Fernando Cortés*.

18. On indigenous adaptation to commercial stimuli in Potosí, see Mangan, *Trading Roles*.

19. See Ricard, *Spiritual Conquest of Mexico*, complemented by Gruzinski, *Man-Gods*, 1–62.

20. This is my synthesis of the analysis in Hughes, *Mexican Crucifix*.

21. Hassig, *Trade, Tribute, and Transportation*; Miranda, *Función económica del encomendero*.

22. Melville, *Plague of Sheep*; Crosby, *Columbian Exchange*.

23. The most detailed studies of the depopulation are in Cook and Borah, *Essays in Population History*. Many have challenged particulars, but dispute focuses on whether the fall was ninety or ninety-five percent, devastating by either result.

24. Mundy, *Death of Aztec Tenochtitlan*, emphasizes indigenous continuities in the city.

25. On Tlaxcala, Andrea Martínez Baracs, *Gobierno de indios*; on Michoacán, Rodrigo Martínez Baracs, *Convivencia y utopía*.

26. This is detailed from different perspectives in Padden, *Hummingbird and the Hawk*; Clendinnen, *Aztecs*; and Berdan, *Aztecs of Central Mexico*.

27. This is explored sympathetically in Clendinnen, *Aztecs*.

28. See Tutino, *Making a New World*, chaps. 1 and 2.

29. These changes are discussed in Simpson, *Encomienda in New Spain*, and Gibson, *Aztecs under Spanish Rule*. For a recent analysis, see Ruíz Medrano, *Reshaping New Spain*.

30. This is a key emphasis of Hughes, *Mexican Crucifix*.

31. This is detailed in Vilar, *History of Gold*, 39–75.

32. Flynn and Giráldez, "Born with a 'Silver Spoon.' "

33. Vilar, *History of Gold*, 103–18.

34. Enciso Contreras, *Taxco*, 101–4.

35. Cubillo Moreno, *Dominios de la plata*, 22–23, 133–34.

36. Cubillo Moreno, *Dominios de la plata*, 135, 152–54.

37. Enciso Contreras, *Taxco*, 24, 46.

38. Enciso Contreras, *Taxco*, 39.

39. Enciso Contreras, *Taxco*, 115–31, 134–45.

40. Cubillo Moreno, *Dominios de la plata*, 87, 98, 122–25, 137–39, 189.

41. Cubillo Moreno, *Dominios de la plata*, 161–62, 174–81, 198–210.

42. Cubillo Moreno, *Dominios de la plata*, 137–39.

43. Enciso Contreras, *Taxco*, 147.

44. Cubillo Moreno, *Dominios de la plata*, 265, fig. 5.

45. Cubillo Moreno, *Dominios de la plata*, 266–67, fig. 6.

46. For the Cuernavaca basin, see Haskett, *Indigenous Rulers*; on the Toluca see Wood, "Corporate Adjustment," and "Evolución de la corporación indígena"; for the heartland in general, see Lockhart, *Nahuas after the Conquest*.

47. Gibson, *Aztecs under Spanish Rule*, 257–99; Menegus Bornemann, *Del señorío a la república*.

48. On the Valley of Mexico, see Gibson, *Aztecs under Spanish Rule*; on the northeast, Konrad, *Santa Lucía*; on the Mezquital, Melville, *Plague of Sheep*; on Cuautla and Cuernavaca, Barrett, *Sugar Hacienda*, and Martin, *Rural Society*.

49. This is clear in works ranging from Gibson, *Aztecs under Spanish Rule*, to Lockhart, *Nahuas after the Conquest*.

50. On slavery in sugar, see Barrett, *Sugar Hacienda*, and Martin, *Rural Society*. For a mixed agricultural and grazing property, see Konrad, *Santa Lucía*. On Mexico City, see Velázquez Gutiérrez, *Mujeres de origen africano*.

51. See Haskett, "Our Suffering," and Menegus Bornemann, "Organización económica-espacial."

52. The key source on the *repartimiento* remains Gibson, *Aztecs under Spanish Rule*, 220–56.

53. Borah, *Justice by Insurance*; Owensby, *Empire of Law*.

54. This is my interpretation of the exceptional research and analysis of Cline in *Colonial Culhuacan*.

55. On the mix of purchases and grants in Spanish land acquisitions, see the sources in note 46. On depopulation and village lands, see Osborn, "Indian Land Retention."

56. See Israel, *Race, Class, and Politics*; Hoberman, *Mexico's Merchant Elites*. Humboldt called the *chinampas* he saw around 1800 the most productive fields he found anywhere. See Humboldt, *Ensayo político*. On floods, the drainage, and the persistence of *chinampas* in the southern basin, see Candiani, *Dreaming of Dry Land*.

57. Again, it is Gibson, *Aztecs under Spanish Rule*, 246–48, who is the key source on the collapse of the draft, then its abolition.

58. This pivotal shift is evident in many sources. See Gibson, *Aztecs under Spanish Rule*; Konrad, *Santa Lucía*; Martin, *Rural Society*.

59. See Lockhart, *Nahuas after the Conquest*, and *Nahuas and Spaniards*; Haskett, *Indigenous Rulers*, and *Visions of Paradise*; Wood, *Transcending Conquest*;

Schroeder, *Chimalpahin*; Cline, *Colonial Culhuacan*; and Horn, *Postconquest Coyoacán*.

60. In addition to the studies in note 32, on religion see María Alba Pastor, *Crisis y recomposición social*, and *Cuerpos sociales, cuerpos sacrificiales*; and Taylor, *Shrines and Miraculous Images*, and *Magistrates of the Sacred*.

61. Ruiz de Alarcón, *Treatise on the Heathen*, 9–12.

62. Tavares, *Invisible War*.

63. See Poole, *Our Lady of Guadalupe*; Sousa, Poole, and Lockhart, *Story of Guadalupe*; Brading, *Mexican Phoenix*; and Taylor, *Shrines and Miraculous Images*.

64. See Martin, *Rural Society*; Jalpa Flores, *Sociedad indígena*; and Konrad, *Santa Lucía*.

65. This synthesizes Islas Jiménez, *Real de Tlalpujahua*, and Velasco Godoy, *Ixtlahuaca*.

66. Many of these spats are detailed in Israel's classic *Race, Class, and Politics*.

67. Brading develops this thesis in *First America*.

68. See Paz, *Sor Juana*.

Chapter Three

1. Silver production is in Tutino, *Making a New World*, 550, appendix D, table D. 1; the global percentages are from González Reyna, *Riqueza minera*; New Spain's global import is confirmed in Giraldez, *Age of Trade*.

2. See Silva Prada, *Política de una rebelión*.

3. Molina del Villar, *Nueva España*.

4. See Tutino, *Making a New World*, 159–227; On Taxco, see Pérez Rosales, *Minería y sociedad*.

5. On the Valley of Toluca see Kanter, *Hijos del Pueblo*.

6. The wills are analyzed with great skill in Pizzigoni, *Life Within*.

7. On San José de Chalco, see James Riley, *Haciendas jesuitas en México*, especially the table at 103–4; on Chapingo see James Riley, *Haciendas jesuitas en México*, 49, and González Marín, "Chapingo," 19; on San Javier, see Konrad, *Santa Lucía*, 300; on Atengo, see Kanter, *Hijos del Pueblo*, and Tutino, "Creole Mexico," chaps. 5–7.

8. Martin, *Rural Society*, building on Barrett, *Sugar Hacienda*.

9. Florescano, *Precios del maíz*, 130–34, 137, graphs 10, 13.

10. Melville, *Plague of Sheep*.

11. Taylor, *Shrines and Miraculous Images*, 63–94, explores such devotion and its links to Mexico City.

12. Konrad, *Santa Lucía*, 100–103. On Chapingo, see González Marín, "Chapingo," 18.

13. Florescano, *Precios del maíz*.

14. Pizzigoni, *Life Within*.

15. Gibson, *Aztecs under Spanish Rule*, shows pursuits of legal independence; Pizzigoni, *Life Within*, presumptions of independence.

16. Pizzigoni, *Life Within*.

17. Again, this is my synthesis of materials in Pizzigoni, *Life Within*.

18. This is documented in Tutino, "Creole Mexico," chaps. 5–7, and Molina del Villar, *Diversidad socioétnica*.

19. On Mexico City, Velázquez Gutiérrez, *Mujeres de origen africano*; on the Bajío, Tutino, *Making a New World*.

20. Molina del Villar, *Nueva España*.

21. This section relies on Molina del Villar, *Diversidad socioétnica*.

22. Florescano, *Precios del maíz*, graphs 10, 13.

23. These pressures are examined in Tutino, *Making a New World*, 229–60, chap. 4.

24. The reports are analyzed in Molina del Villar, *Diversidad socioétnica*.

25. See the detailed analysis in Lara Cisneros, *¿Ignorancia invencible?*

26. See Gruzinski, *Man-Gods*, chap. 5.

27. Tortolero Villaseñor, *Notarios y agricultores*, 201–11.

28. Couturier, *Silver King*, and Ladd, *Making of a Strike*.

29. On commercial life, see Tutino, *Making a New World*, part 2.

30. Tutino, "Creole Mexico," 20, table 1.1.

31. Tutino, "Creole Mexico," 30, 41, tables 1.3, 1.8, chap. 1.

32. Tutino, "Creole Mexico," 48–86. On the Bajío and the north, see Tutino, *Making a New World*, 263–99.

33. Tutino, "Creole Mexico," 304, table 6.1.

34. Tutino, "Creole Mexico," 78–79, 169, tables 2.5, 3.10.

35. Tutino, "Creole Mexico," 171–73, tables 3.11, 3.12.

36. The economic and social lives of Mexico City entrepreneurs are detailed in Tutino, *Mexico City, 1808*, chaps. 2, 3.

37. Again, see Pizzigoni, *Life Within*.

38. AGN, AHH, vol. 397, exp. 3, 1809; the report is in Tutino, "Estructura agraria," 511, fig. B.2.

39. AGN, AHH, vol. 376, exp. 4; vol. 386, exp. 4, 8, 1791–94; vol. 440, exp. 4, 1787–89; the totals are in Tutino, "Estructura agraria," 514, fig. B.3.

40. The full list is in Tutino, "Creole Mexico," 266–67, table 5.7.

41. Tutino, "Creole Mexico," chaps. 5–7; Martin, *Rural Society*; Pizzigoni, *Life Within*.

42. AGN, AHH, vol. 672, exps. 1, 9, 1792; vol. 675, exp. 11, 1793; the full counts are reproduced in Tutino, "Estructura agraria," 510, fig. A.3.

43. This is documented in Martin, *Rural Society*, and Molina del Villar, *Diversidad socioétnica*.

44. The Pilares and Tlalteguacán accounts are in AGN, vínculos, vols. 53–55; the *sirvientes* work records and earnings are analyzed in Tutino, "Creole Mexico," 308–10.

45. This synthesizes the detailed discussion in Tutino, "Creole Mexico," 306–13.

46. Tutino, "Creole Mexico," 308–10.

47. See Tutino, *Making a New World*, especially chaps. 1 and 7.

48. See the detail and sources in Tutino, "Creole Mexico," 312–16.

49. Molina del Villar, *Diversidad socioétnica*.

50. Tutino, "Creole Mexico," 319.

51. Again, the accounts are in AGN, Vínculos, vols. 52–54; the analysis summarized here is presented in greater detail in Tutino, "Creole Mexico," 319–36, tables 6.2–6.6.

52. This is detailed in Stern, *Secret History of Gender*.

53. William Taylor details judicial and clerical mediations in *Drinking, Homicide, and Rebellion* and *Magistrates of the Sacred*.

54. Women's activism is detailed in Taylor, *Drinking, Homicide, and Rebellion*, and Stern, *Secret History of Gender*.

55. James Riley, *Haciendas jesuítas en México*, 267–68; on the transfer to the Conde de Regla, PCRun, "Posesión de San Javier . . . 1777."

56. AGN, Tierras, vol. 2381, exp. 3, fols. 1–4, 1785.

57. PCR, vol. 75, September 23, 1775; vol. 78, September 15, 1776; vol. 81, December 7, 1777; vol. 88, May 31 and December 22, 1779; vol. 101, April 1 and October 22, 1784.

58. PCR, vol. 97, June 16 and October 9, 1783; vol. 101, November 9 and 14, 1784.

59. PCR, vol. 105, March 30, 1785.

60. PCR, vol. 121, fol. 68, May 28, fol. 91, August 12, and fol. 102, September 1, 1800; vol. 123, fols. 73–74, September 30, 1801.

61. The *repartimiento* and negotiations with *caudillos* are detailed in letters in PCR, vols. 118, 121, 123, 1799–1800.

62. "Ayuntamientos, Alcaldes, y Ciudadanos, 1826."

63. PCR, vol. 118, fol. 21, March 29, fol. 27, April 23, fol. 64, July 17, fols. 84–85, September 11, and fol. 110, December 14, 1799; vol. 121, fol. 58, May 7, 1800.

64. For an analysis of the Condesa and her sister's rule, see Tutino, "Power, Class, and Family."

65. PCR, vol. 118, fol. 27, April 23, and fol. 36, May 29, 1799; vol. 121, fol. 58, May 7, fol. 83, July 23, fol. 85, July 30, and fol. 88, August 9, 1800; vol. 124, fol. 7, January 30, 1802.

66. PCR, vol. 121, fol. 83, July 23, 1800.

67. PCR, vol. 123, fol. 6, January 17, 1800, fol. 9, January 24, fol. 43, March 27, and fol. 44, March 30, 1801.

68. PCR, vol. 121, fol. 77, July 9, fol. 80, July 12, and fol. 82, July 19, 1800; vol. 123, fol. 55, July 4, fol. 91, November 20, and fol. 93, November 28, 1801.

69. PCR, vol. 121, fol. 21, March 20, fol. 62, July 17, and fol. 110, December 14, 1799.

70. PCR, vol. 121, fol. 84, July 30, 1800.

71. PCR, vol. 121, fol. 93, August 16, 1800; vol. 123, fol. 8, January 24, and fol. 48, June 13, 1801; vol. 124, fol. 7, January 30, fol. 87, October 27, and fol. 90, November 13, 1802.

72. PCR, vol. 123, fol. 50, June 17, and fol. 86, November 4, 1801.

73. PCR, vol. 118, fol. 116, December 1799.

74. PCR, vol. 121, fol. 75, July 2, fol. 77, July 9, fol. 82, July 19, fols. 85–86, August 2, fol. 87, August 6, and fol. 129, October 19, 1800.

75. PCR, vol. 123, fol. 41, May 13, and fol. 75, October 10, 1801; vol. 124, fol. 2, January 13, 1802.

76. PCR, vol. 121, fol. 30, March 5, 1800.

77. PCR, vol. 118, fol. 9, January 29, and fol. 52, June 26, 1799; vol. 121, fol. 90, August 12, 1800; vol. 123, fol. 76, August 10, and fol. 78, October 17, 1801.

78. PCR, vol. 123, fol. 3, January 10, fol. 24, March 14, fol. 27, March 19, fol. 50, June 17, fol. 77, October 17, and fol. 91, November 20, 1801; vol. 124, fols. 2–3, January 13, 1802; vol. 125, fol. 7, February 9, 1803.

79. PCR, vol. 121, fol. 25, February 21, fol. 35, March 8, fol. 59, May 14, fol. 75, July 2, fol. 77, July 9, fol. 82, July 19, fol. 85, July 30, fol. 86, August 2, fol. 87, August 6,

fol. 101, August 30, and fol. 129, October 19, 1800; vol. 123, fol. 12, February 4, and fol. 14, February 7, 1801; vol. 127, fol. 12, August 22, fol. 13, August 29, and fol. 14, September 12, 1804.

80. PCRb, "Posesión de la Florida, 1777," fol. 2; "Posesión de San Javier, 1777," fols. 3–4, 39–40, 75–78; PCR, vol. 121, fol. 104, September 1, 1800. The roles of women in local riots is documented in Taylor, *Drinking, Homicide, and Rebellion.*

81. Tortolero Villaseñor, *Notarios y agricultores,* 212–30.

Chapter Four

1. On rioting at Cuautitlán and Atlacomulco see Van Young, *Other Rebellion,* and "Of Tempests and Teapots." On insurgencies in the pulque zones around Otumba and Apan, see Guedea, *Insurgencia.*

2. Olguín's letters are in PCR.

3. VFT. Eric Van Young brought this key report to my attention.

4. The subject of Melville's now classic *Plague of Sheep.*

5. See Tutino, "Power, Class, and Family."

6. On Olguín's roles and remunerations, see PCRun, "Autos 1810," fols. 7, 24, 59, 1791; PCR vol. 123, 38, April 28, 1801; PCR vol. 138, December 16, 1809.

7. My compilation and calculations based on reports in PCR, vols. 121, 125, 127, 137, 138, 141, and 143, 1800–1811.

8. PCR, vol. 118, 59, July 10, 1799; vol. 124, 24, April 21, 1802; vol. 124, 83, October 16, 1802; vol. 124, 95, December 23, 1802; vol. 126, October 18, 1803; vol. 127, 7, May 9, 1804.

9. PCR, vol. 214, 32, May 12, 1802; vol. 124, 71, August 11, 1802.

10. PCR, vol. 143, August 4, 1811.

11. PCR, vol. 118, 83, September 11, 1799; vol. 121, 14, January 29, 1800; vol. 121, 59, May 7, 1800; vol. 121, 96, August 20, 1800; vol. 124, 88, November 3, 1802; vol. 125, 19, August 10, 1803; vol. 125, 24, November 9, 1803; vol. 129, 2, March 2, 1805; vol. 132, 16, October 8, 1806.

12. PCR, vol. 118, 4, January 12, 1799; vol. 118, 39, January 5, 1799; vol. 121, 61, May 14, 1800; vol. 123, 10, January 28, 1803; vol. 125, 6, February 2, 1803; vol. 127, 2, February 15, 1804; vol. 127, 19, December 22, 1804; vol. 129, 1, January 9, 1805; vol. 132, 2, January 22, 1806; vol. 132, 4, February 12, 1806.

13. PCR, vol. 118, 70, August 7, 1799; vol. 118, 71, August 7, 1799; vol. 121, 59, May 7, 1800; vol. 129, 5, May 29, 1808.

14. PCR, vol. 118, 76, August 24, 1799; vol. 121, 69, May 28, 1800; vol. 121, 31, October 22, 1800; vol. 123, 71, September 23, 1801; vol. 123, 83, November 4, 1801.

15. PCR, vol. 121, 14, January 29, 1800.

16. PCR, vol. 121, 80, July 16, 1800.

17. PCR, vol. 121, 128, October 15, 1800.

18. PCR, vol. 123, 49, June 17, 1800; vol. 123, 83, November 4, 1801.

19. PCR, vol. 125, 24, November 9, 1803; vol. 127, 11, August 15, 1804; vol. 141, July 14, 1810.

20. PCR, vol. 125, 6, February 2, 1803.

21. PCR, vol. 127, 16, October 3, 1804.

22. PCR, vol. 123, 31, April 1, 1801; vol. 124, 15, March 6, 1802; vol. 124, 20, April 1, 1802; vol. 127, 1, January 25, 1804; vol. 127, 3, February 21, 1804; vol. 134, May 2, 1807.

23. PCR, vol. 127, 1, January 25, 1804.

24. PCR, vol. 132, 7, 8, April 30, 1806.

25. PCR, vol. 141, July 14, 1810.

26. They caused Olguín little concern. See PCR, vol. 141, March 5 and 12, July 14, and August 4, 1810.

27. PCR, vol. 124, 71, August 11, 1802; vol. 129, 4, May 8, 1805; vol. 138, November 11, 1809; vol. 141, January 20, February 3, March 12, and August 4, 1810.

28. See the reports on labor in note 31, plus PCR, vol. 127, 3, February 15, 1804.

29. PCR, vol. 124, 40, April 2, 1802; vol. 124, 43, June 5, 1802.

30. PCR, vol. 129, 6, June 12, 1805; vol. 132, 18, December 23, 1806.

31. PCR, vol. 134, 6, June 1807.

32. PCR, vol. 129, 8, August 19, 1805; vol. 138, October 21, 1809.

33. This is the focus of Tutino, *Mexico City, 1808*.

34. AGN, Intendentes, vol. 73, exp. 9, fol. 10, August 25, 1809; fol. 22, August 1809; fol. 37, August 26, 1809; fols. 71–72, August 31, 1809; exp. 5, fols. 15–20, October 25, 1809; fol. 52, November 5, 1809.

35. AGN, Intendentes, vol. 73, exp. 9, fol. 17, August 26, 1809; fol. 49, September 1, 1809; fol. 52, August 31, 1809; fol. 73, August 31, 1809; fol. 92, August 31, 1809.

36. AGN, Intendentes, vol. 73, exp. 72, fol. 10, August 25, 1809.

37. PCR, vol. 141, March 12, 1810.

38. PCR, vol. 141, March 12, May 9, and August 4, 1810; PCRun, "Autos 1810," fols. 40–42, June 2, 1810.

39. PCR, vol. 141, May 26, 1810.

40. PCR, vol. 141, July 7 and 14, 1810; plus pulque reports January to September: my calculations.

41. PCRun, "Autos 1810," fols. 40–41, June 2 and August 31, 1810.

42. PCR, vol. 141, September 3, 1810.

43. PCR, vol. 141, October 13, 1810.

44. PCR, vol. 141, November 10, 1810.

45. PCR, vols. 121, 125, 127, 137, 138, 1800–1809; PCR, vols. 141, 143, 1810 and 1811: my calculations.

46. PCR, vol. 141, November 17 and 24, 1810.

47. PCR, vol. 141, December 14, 1810.

48. PCR, vol. 143, January 5, 19, and 26, and February 5, 1811.

49. PCR, vol. 143, May 24 and December 14, 1811, and January 13, 1812.

50. PCR vol. 143, March 2, 9, and 30, 1811.

51. PCR, vol. 143, March 30, 1811.

52. PCR, vol. 143, April 26, 1811.

53. PCR, vol. 143, May 4, 1811.

54. PCR, vol. 143, May 4, 1811.

55. PCR, vol. 143, May 18, 1811.

56. PCR, vol. 143, May 22 and 24, 1811.

57. PCR, vol. 143, May 24, June 1 and 22, 1811; and pulque reports: my calculations.

58. PCR, vol. 143, June 1, 1811.

59. PCR, vol. 143, June 1 and 22, July 13 and 30, 1811.

60. On Villagrán, see Hamnett, *Roots of Insurgency*, and Van Young, *Other Rebellion*.

61. PCR, vol. 143, August 31, 1811.

62. PCR, vol. 143, September 5, 1811; pulque reports, July–September, my calculations.

63. PCR, vol. 143, November 2, 1811.

64. PCR, vol. 143, November 15–17, 1811.

65. PCR, vol. 143, December 7, 1811.

66. PCR, vol. 143, December 14, 1811.

67. PCR vol. 143, January 8, 1812.

68. PCRun, "Autos 1810," January 13, 1812.

69. PCRun, April 10 and May 8, 1812.

70. VFT, fols. 52v–53.

71. VFT, fols. 53–54.

72. VFT, fols. 53v–54.

73. VFT, fol. 53v.

74. VFT, fol. 54.

75. VFT, fol. 54.

76. VFT, fol. 55v.

77. VFT, fol. 56.

78. VFT, fols. 56v–57.

79. VFT, fol. 57.

80. VFT, fol. 56.

81. VFT, fol. 58.

82. VFT, fols. 58v–59v.

83. VFT, fols. 60–64.

84. VFT, fols. 65–66.

85. VFT, fol. 66.

86. Molina del Villar, "Santa María de Guadalupe."

87. VFT, fols. 66v–67.

88. VFT, fol. 68.

89. VFT, fols. 68–70v.

90. VFT, fol. 1.

91. VFT, fols. 18–19.

92. VFT, fol. 71v.

Chapter Five

1. The best short analysis of these years is Ávila, *En nombre*; Rodríguez, *True Spaniards*, offers more detail and often differing interpretations.

2. On the wars of the 1790s and the crisis of 1808–10, see Barbara Stein and Stanley Stein, *Edge of Crisis* and *Crisis in an Atlantic Empire*.

3. This analysis of 1808–10 synthesizes Tutino, *Mexico City, 1808*.

4. Lempérière, *Dios y el rey*.

5. On conflicts in Spain, see Cayuela Fernández and Gallego Palomares, *Guerra de independencia*.

6. On events of 1808 to 1810, see Benson, *Spanish Cortes*, and recent works such as Guerra, *Modernidades e independencias*; Ávila, *En nombre*; and Breña, *Umbral de las revoluciones*.

7. This is detailed in Tutino, *Mexico City, 1808*.

8. On the Cádiz process, the pivotal work is Breña, *Primer liberalismo español*.

9. On the origins of the insurgencies of 1810, see Tutino, *From Insurrection to Revolution*, and *Making a New World*.

10. See Tutino, *From Insurrection to Revolution*, and Herrero Bervera, *Revuelta, rebelión y revolución*.

11. Hamill, *Hidalgo Revolt*, remains essential.

12. Tutino, "Revolution in Mexican Independence."

13. Tutino, "De Hidalgo a Apatzingán."

14. On mining during the decade of insurgency, see Romero Sotelo, *Minería y guerra*.

15. Lemoine, *Morelos*, remains essential. On Rayón's roots, see Islas Jiménez, *Real de Tlalpujahua*, 40–41.

16. Guardino, *Time of Liberty*, details Morelos's occupation of Oaxaca in 1812.

17. Brading, *First America*, details divisions; Tutino, *Making a New World*, and *Mexico City, 1808*, emphasize the integrations of power before 1808.

18. See Hamill, *Hidalgo Revolt*; Lemoine, *Morelos*; Tutino, *From Insurrection to Revolution*; Hamnett, *Roots of Insurgency*; and Van Young, *Other Rebellion*.

19. Indigenous republics across Oaxaca and Yucatán pursued political autonomies within the possibilities of Cádiz liberalism. See Guardino, *Time of Liberty*, and Caplan, *Indigenous Citizens*.

20. On the Bajío, see Tutino, *Making a New World*, part 2; on more indigenous regions, see Van Young, *Other Rebellion* and "Of Tempests and Teapots."

21. Van Young, *Other Rebellion*; Herrero Bervera, *Revuelta, rebelión y revolución*.

22. Tutino, *Making a New World*.

23. This view is developed in Tutino, "Revolution in Mexican Independence" and *Making a New World*.

24. Tutino, *Making a New World*.

25. Granados, *Espejo haitiano*.

26. Tutino, *Making a New World*.

27. On Querétaro in the decade of insurgency, see Tutino, "Querétaro."

28. Van Young, *Other Rebellion*; Taylor, *Magistrates of the Sacred*; and Tutino, *Making a New World*.

29. Hamnett, *Roots of Insurgency*; Van Young, *Other Rebellion*; and Guedea, *Insurgencia*.

30. The best case study is Guedea, *Insurgencia*.

31. Tutino, "De Hidalgo a Apatzingán."

32. This section relies on Ávila, *En nombre*; Guarisco, *Indios del valle*; and Annino "Two-Faced Janus" to outline the Cádiz project and its application in rural regions.

33. Studies by America Molina del Villar and Juan Ortiz Escamilla presented in 2008 at the Colegio de México revealed the impact of the 1813 typhus epidemic. See also Molina del Villar, "Santa María de Guadalupe."

34. Tutino, *Making a New World.*

35. Guarisco, *Indios del valle.*

36. Ávila, *En nombre,* 128–29; Guarisco, *Indios del valle,* 131–50.

37. Detailed for Oaxaca in Guardino, *Time of Liberty.*

38. Lemoine, *Morelos*; Ávila, *En nombre.*

39. Tutino, "De Hidalgo a Apatzingán."

40. Serrano Ortega, *Sexenio absolutista,* delivers important new studies of politics in long neglected years.

41. Ortiz Escamilla, *Guerra y gobierno.*

42. On taxes during the years of counterinsurgency, see Sánchez Santiró, *Alcabalas mexicanas,* 29–62; on loans and the debt at independence, see Hernández Jaimes, *Formación de la hacienda,* 35–66.

43. Guarisco, *Indios des valle,* 151–69.

44. Tutino, "Revolution in Mexican Independence."

45. Tutino, "Revolution in Mexican Independence."

46. This previews Tutino, *Remaking the New World.*

47. Romero Sotelo, *Minería y guerra.*

48. This sections relies on Ávila, *En nombre,* and on Arenal Fenocchio, *Modo de ser libres.*

49. On Guerrero and the hot country, see Guardino, *Peasants, Politics.*

50. Hernández Jaimes, *Formación de la hacienda,* 51.

51. Van Young, *Other Rebellion* and "Of Tempests and Teapots."

52. On Iturbide, see Anna, *Mexican Empire.* On the empire's fall, see Ávila, *Para la libertad.* Annino, "Two-Faced Janus," explores early disputes over sovereignty. On federalism, see Benson, *Provincial Deputation,* and Anna, *Forging Mexico.*

Chapter Six

1. This is the key emphasis of Beckert, *Empire of Cotton.*

2. I analyze this transformation in "Rise of Industrial Capitalism."

3. The post-1775 peak of Chinese demand for silver is detailed in Lin, *China Upside Down*; on the simultaneous peak of New Spain's silver production, and the polarizing social consequences, see Tutino, *Making a New World.*

4. Grounded in the work of David Brading, John Coatsworth, and Carlos Marichal, this view is ably synthesized in Cárdenas, *Largo curso,* 38–75.

5. Cárdenas, *Largo curso,* 38.

6. This is a key contribution of Parthasarathi, *Why Europe Grew Rich.*

7. In *China Upside Down,* Lin details how silver drought brought China's economic, political, and social crises and the opium trade. The link to parallel developments in Mexico is my addition to her pivotal interpretation.

8. Parthasarathi, *Why Europe Grew Rich,* details British industrial displacement of Indian cloth in global markets.

9. Allen, *British Industrial Revolution,* emphasizes the technical achievements of 1780–1810—and shows that global hegemony came only after 1810.

10. Mexico's post-1821 fiscal collapse is analyzed brilliantly by Hernández Jaimes, in *Formación de la hacienda.*

11. Cárdenas, *Largo curso*, 99.

12. Cross, "Mining Economy of Zacatecas." This is a key work, unfortunately unpublished.

13. See Tutino, "Hacienda Social Relations," and "Agrarian Social Change." I generalized in Tutino, *From Insurrection to Revolution*, and detailed popular gains in Tutino, "Revolution in Mexican Independence." Paul Hart, *Bitter Harvest*, shows estate decline and community gains in Morelos.

14. This shift is detailed in Tutino, "Revolution in Mexican Independence."

15. This too is detailed in Cross, "Mining Economy of Zacatecas," 287–375, chap. 8.

16. See Hämäläinen, *Comanche Empire*, and Delay, *War of a Thousand Deserts*.

17. See Tutino, *Making a New World*, among many sources.

18. I calculate total capital of 20,000,000 by estimating the total income of 770,823 as a 4 percent overall return. Estimating at 5 percent would lower the total to 15,000,000. Either way, only 24 to 33 percent was invested at interest, the great majority placed in rental properties. For Mexico City, we know that 2,450,000 pesos of invested capital gained 89,000 pesos interest—3.6 percent; presuming that the 383,000 pesos of rental income was 4 percent of the properties' value, the latter totaled 9,580,000 pesos. There, where the convents were richest, thanks to the concentration of wealth in the eighteenth-century silver boom, by the 1830s they retained about 12,000,000 pesos of wealth—80 percent in city real estate, only 20 percent in investments at interest. The exceptional revival of estate profits in the state of Michoacán in detailed in Chowning, *Wealth and Power*.

19. Cross, "Mining Economy of Zacatecas," 153–79, chap. 4, and 287–375, chap. 8.

20. See Tutino, "Hacienda Social Relations," "Agrarian Social Change," and "Revolution in Mexican Independence."

21. The heights and analysis are in López-Alonso, *Measuring Up*. López-Alonso takes pains to show that military recruits came from wide and representative regions, and that heights serve as a fair reflection of nutrition.

22. My analysis of the politics of this period is guided by Andrews, *Espada y la Constitución*, which offers a persuasive new vision.

23. See Andrews, *Espada y la Constitución*, and Guardino, *Peasants, Politics*.

24. LAM, 1830, 166–67, 172–84.

25. LAM, 1830, 207; 1831, 282–84; 1832, 372–73, 428.

26. LAM, 1830, 203; 1831, 275.

27. LAM, 1832, 363.

28. LAM, 1830, 206.

29. LAM, 1831, 277–78.

30. LAM, 1832, 365–70, 408–27.

31. TOM. The details of Ortiz's career are in a brief preface to the reprint; his knowledge of studies of New Spain is demonstrated in the text: 173–256.

32. TOM, 11–12, 27, 30, 41, 47–48.

33. TOM, 50, 71, 86.

34. TOM, 448–50, on military and militias; 112–18, 159–64 on education; 273–74 on the penal system.

35. TOM, 537–38, 544–52 on colonization; 572–73 on exports and slavery.

36. TOM, 280.

37. TOM, 284–85.

38. TOM, 309–10.

39. TOM, 297–98, 305–6.

40. On coastal peoples, see García de León, *Tierra adentro*.

41. TOM, 337–46 (quote 337).

42. TOM, 349, 355.

43. TOM, 357–58.

44. TOM, 360–62.

45. TOM, 371.

46. TOM, 429–30.

47. TOM, 459.

48. TOM, 441–42, 444–50.

49. See Andrews, *Espada y la Constitución*, and Cross, "Mining Economy of Zacatecas."

50. Stevens, "Temerse la ira del cielo."

51. That Texas's secession was ultimately about cotton and slavery, debated in a language of citizenship and states' rights, is clear in Lack, *Texas Revolutionary Experience*.

52. On the origins of the bank, the classic study is Potash, *Banco de Avío*.

53. Lipsett-Rivera, *Gender and the Negotiation*, explores a vast set of court cases involving violence against women to detail the enduring culture of patriarchy that shaped often-conflictive family relations in and around Mexico City and Puebla from 1750 to 1856. Not focusing on change during that century, she shows that core presumptions persisted. My interest in how changing economic ways altered families' abilities to implement and negotiate those established values led to a rereading that indicated rising violence aimed at women who failed to honor traditional patriarchy from the 1830s to the 1850s, notably at Puebla.

54. LAM, 1843, 22–26 (quote 24).

55. LAM, 1844, 89.

56. LAM, 1844, 92.

57. LAM, 1844, 127–30. For eighteenth-century prices, which rarely fell below six reales per fanega, see Florescano, *Precios del maíz*, and Tutino, *Making a New World*.

58. LAM, 1844, 93.

59. LAM, 1844, 98, for the quote; the analytical emphasis, of course, is mine.

60. LAM, 1844, 98–100.

61. RWM, 247.

62. RWM, 266, 268, 271.

63. RWM, 286–91, 312.

64. RWM, 317–27.

65. RWM, 353–62.

66. RWM, 369.

67. RWM, 370–71.

68. RWM, 377–80.

69. RWM, 330.

70. Forbes, in RWM, 381–82.

71. Forbes, in RWM, 383.

72. JG, 414–16.

73. JG, 417.

74. JG, 417.

75. JG, 417.

76. JG, 419.

77. JG, 420–21.

78. JG, 421.

79. The invention and its ideological uses are detailed in Streeby, *American Sensations*, and "Imagining Mexico."

80. See Hämäläinen, *Comanche Empire*, and Tutino, "Globalizing the Comanche Empire."

81. Pani, *Serie de admirables*, analyzes midcentury ideological and political conflicts.

82. Vázquez, *México al tiempo*.

83. Indigenous resistance during the war is sketched in Tutino, *From Insurrection to Revolution*; the rising in the capital is detailed in Granados, *Sueñan las piedras*; on landlords and US troops, see Paul Hart, *Bitter Harvest*, 42–44.

84. See González Navarro, *Anatomía del poder*, and Escalante Gonzalbo, *Ciudadanos imaginarios*.

85. This is detailed in Guardino, *Peasants, Politics*.

86. This was documented long ago by González y González in *El indio*.

87. This is an important emphasis of Pani, *Serie de admirables*.

88. Jan Bazant, *Alienation of Church Wealth*.

89. Dabbs, *French Army in Mexico*.

90. This is clear in Pani, *Mexicanizar el segundo imperio*.

91. On early privatizations, see Powell, *Liberalismo y el campesinado*; for an overview, see Tutino, *From Insurrection to Revolution*; the essential analysis is Falcón, *Naciones de una república*. On the Sierra de Puebla, see Mallon, *Peasant and Nation*, and Guy Thomson, *Patriotism, Politics*.

92. Lin, *China Upside Down*, 71–114.

93. This sketch of midcentury mining synthesizes Velasco Ávila et al., *Estado y minería*, 113–252.

94. On those ideals, see Lipsett-Rivera, *Gender and the Negotiation*.

95. See Beatty, *Technology*.

96. Illades, *Hacia la república*; Trujillo Bolio, *Operarios fabriles*.

97. González y González, *San José de Gracia*; Purnell, *Popular Movements*; and Pérez Montesinos, "Poised to Break."

98. See Paul Hart, *Bitter Harvest*.

99. Miller, *Landlords and Haciendas*.

100. Cross, "Mining Economy of Zacatecas," 168, table IV-C.

101. Kourí, *Pueblo Divided*.

102. Cárdenas, *Largo curso*, 184.

103. Guerra, *México*.

104. Cárdenas, *Largo curso*, 106.

105. Velasco Ávila et al., *Estado y minería*, 274, graph XIII.14; my analysis depends on their fine synthesis, 253–424.

106. Velasco Ávila et al., *Estado y minería*, 403, fig. XVIII.3.

107. My analysis is based on Velasco Ávila et al., *Estado y minería*, 286–312.

108. On railroad building, see Pletcher, *Rails, Mines, and Progress*; Coatsworth, *Growth against Development*; and the synthesis in Cárdenas, *Largo curso*, 189–291.

109. Beatty, *Technology*.

110. The literature on Porfirian mining for export is synthesized in Velasco Ávila et al., *Estado y minería*, 253–424.

111. Cárdenas, *Largo curso*, 202–3.

112. On Porfirian industrialization see Haber, Razo, and Maurer, *Politics of Property Rights*.

113. This vision of Monterrey synthesizes Fernández Martínez, "Revolution and the Industrial City."

114. On the second round of vanilla boom and land privatization, see again Kourí, *Pueblo Divided*; on the conflicts of the 1890s, see Reina, *Rebeliones campesinas*, and Ramírez Melgarejo, *Política del estado mexicano*.

115. On the late nineteenth-century commodity chains, see Topik and Wells, *Global Markets Transformed*.

116. See Chassen López, *Liberal to Revolutionary Oaxaca*, and Fowler-Salamini, *Working Women*.

117. Turner, *Barbarous Mexico*.

118. See Joseph, *Revolution from Without*; Wells, *Yucatán's Gilded Age*; and Wells and Joseph, *Summer of Discontent*.

119. This is explored in brilliant detail by Myrna Santiago in *Ecology of Oil*.

120. Cárdenas, *Largo curso*, 204.

121. Again, López Alonso, *Measuring Up*, is pivotal.

Chapter Seven

1. See Paul Hart, *Bitter Harvest*, and Kanter, *Hijos del Pueblo*.

2. This section summarizes and revises Tutino, "Hacienda Social Relations." The analysis there and here is based on letters and documents in the Mariano Riva Palacio Papers (MRP).

3. On these changes, see Salinas Sandoval, *Política y sociedad*, and Kantor, *Hijos del Pueblo*.

4. López Escudero's letters and records (MLE) survive because Riva Palacio served as executor of his estate.

5. MLE, file 6, account of testament, copy dated December 4, 1839.

6. MLE, file 1, letters 1826–29.

7. MLE, file 2, letters 1831.

8. MLE, file 3, letters 1833.

9. MLE, file 4, letters 1834.

10. MLE, file 6, letters 1835–39.

11. MLE, file 7, testamentary accounts 1839–40.

12. MEM.

13. This family and career history is in Connaughton's fine "Estudio introductorio," especially 49–53.

14. Acolman was not a famously peaceful place: see Tutino, "Provincial Spaniards," on conflicts in the 1790s.

15. MEM, 87.

16. MEM, 261.

17. MEM, 224.

18. MEM, 233, 259–62.

19. MEM, 269, 391.

20. MEM, 169.

21. MEM, 267–68.

22. MEM, 199, 333–34, 381.

23. MEM, 214, 373–74.

24. MEM, 169.

25. MEM, 366–69.

26. MEM, 246–47.

27. MEM, 220–21.

28. MEM, 220.

29. MEM, 170, 264.

30. MEM, 378.

31. MEM, 105–7.

32. MEM, 201–2.

33. MEM, 203–4.

34. See the dual reference in MEM, 189.

35. MEM, 228, 221, 351.

36. MEM, 201.

37. MEM, 389.

38. MEM, 241.

39. MEM, 257.

40. MEM, 316.

41. MEM, 375.

42. I use the edited and annotated version compiled by Howard and Marion Hall Fisher: FCB.

43. FCB, 120–23.

44. FCB, 435–41.

45. FCB, 443.

46. FCB, 444–45.

47. FCB, 505–7.

48. BRF.

49. BRF, "Prólogo," xiii.

50. BRF, 6–12.

51. BRF, 13–14.

52. BRF, 15.

53. BRF, 16–17.

54. BRF, 21.

55. BRF, 23.

Chapter Eight

1. Mallon, *Peasant and Nation*, and Paul Hart, *Bitter Harvest*.

2. This chapter revises Tutino, "Agrarian Social Change." It is based on the Mariano Riva Palacio archive (MRP), cited by document number and date. See Dabbs, *Mariano Riva Palacio Archive*.

3. Tutino, *From Insurrection to Revolution*; Falcón, *Naciones de una república*.

4. MRP, 5915c, June 4, 1856; 7079, October 12, 1857.

5. Bullock, *Six Months' Residence*, 277; MRP, 5871, March 10, 1856; 5915h, July 13, 1856; 5915k, August 19, 1856; 5915n, September 9, 1856.

6. MRP, 5915k, August 3, 1856; Basave Kunhardt, "Algunos aspectos," 241–42.

7. MRP, 5915L, August 26, 1856; 8019a, n.d.; 7113, October 27, 1857.

8. MRP, 3254, October 9, 1849; 3334, October 23, 1849; 3446, November 12, 1849; 3507, November 28, 1849; 3540, December 4, 1849; 3801, January 30, 1850; 3912, March 5, 1850; 4254, June 5, 1850; 4285, June 10, 1850; 7445, February–March 1862.

9. MRP, 6646, August 27, 1857.

10. MRP, 3080, July 31, 1849; 3417, November 6, 1849; 3546, December 4, 1849; 3912, March 5, 1850; 4254, June 5, 1850; 6446, April 26, 1857.

11. MRP, 5051, February 6, 1851; 5177, May 13, 1851.

12. MRP, 5683, March 15, 1855; 5685, March 27, 1855; 6556, May 12, 1856; 6627, June 4, 1857.

13. MRP, 3183, August 26, 1849; 5915b, May 20, 1856; 5915c, June 4, 1856; 5915g, July 6, 1856.

14. MRP, 3447, November 12, 1857; 3507, November 28, 1849.

15. MRP, 3875, February 24, 1850; 4281, June 9, 1850; 4284, June 10, 1850, 4332, June 19, 1850; 4384, June 10, 1850; 4398, July 3, 1850.

16. Díaz Díaz, *Caudillos y caciques*; Reina, *Rebeliones campesinas*; Guardino, *Peasants, Politics*.

17. See Tutino, *From Insurrection to Revolution*.

18. González Navarro, *Anatomía del poder*.

19. MRP, 3986, March 18, 1850; 4091, April 29, 1850; Reina, *Rebeliones campesinas*, 61, 63, 123.

20. Reina, *Rebeliones campesinas*, 157–70; Paul Hart, *Bitter Harvest*, 48–59.

21. González Navarro, *Anatomía del poder*, 162–65; Pimentel, *Raza indígena de México*.

22. MRP, 5484, October 16, 1851; 5683, March 15, 1855.

23. MRP, 3046, March 5, 1849; 3080, July 31, 1849; 3721, July 13, 1849; 3723, January 14, 1850; 3912, March 5, 1850; 4252, June 5, 1850.

24. MRP, 7113, October 27, 1857.

25. Tortolero Villaseñor, *Notarios y agricultores*, 201–11, 230–43.

26. MRP, 3270, October 11, 1849.

27. MRP, 3804, January 31, 1850.

28. MRP, 3902, March 4, 1850.

29. MRP, 4955, January 10, 1851.

30. MRP, 5015, February 6, 1851; 5023, February 8, 1851; 5172, May 10, 1851; 5178, May 13, 1851.

31. MRP, 5177, May 13, 1851; 5178, May 13, 1851; 5023, May 11, 1851; 5207, June 2, 1851.

32. MRP, 5189, May 23, 1851.

33. González Navarro, *Anatomía del poder*, 123–24.

34. MRP, 3575, December 10, 1849.

35. MRP, 3902, March 4, 1850; 4452, July 13, 1850; 4718, October 10, 1850; 4815, October 29, 1850.

36. MRP, 5207, June 2, 1851; 5543, December 2, 1851.

37. MRP, 5701, June 15, 1855; 5807, October 2, 1855; 5869, March 6, 1856; 5870, March 8, 1856; 7255a, January 10, 1859.

38. González Navarro, *Anatomía del poder*, 142–43; Fraser, "Política de desamortización"; Huitrón, *Bienes comunales*; Menegus Bornemann, "Ocoyoacac."

39. Guardino, *Peasants, Politics*, details the key role of Álvarez in the liberals' rise to power.

40. Lerdo de Tejada, *Memoria de la Secretaría*, 3–6.

41. Lerdo de Tejada, *Memoria de la Secretaría*, 4–5, 25, 70–71, 324–89; Fraser, "Política de desamortización," 632–34; Powell, *Liberalismo y el campesinado*, 140.

42. MRP, 5915k, August 19, 1856.

43. MRP, 5915m, September 2, 1856.

44. Powell, *Liberalismo y el campesinado*, 71; Lerdo de Tejada, *Memoria de la Secretaría*, 324–89.

45. Lerdo de Tejada, *Memoria de la Secretaría*, 113–16, 156–61.

46. Lerdo de Tejada, *Memoria de la Secretaría*, 58–59.

47. MRP, 6421, April 13, 1857.

48. Powell, *Liberalismo y el campesinado*, 82.

49. Powell, *Liberalismo y el campesinado*, 87–89; Fraser, "Política de desamortización," 627; MRP, 6350, March 28, 1857; 6435, April 18, 1857; 6458, April 24, 1857.

50. Vanderwood, *Disorder and Progress*.

51. MRP, 6473, April 27, 1857.

52. MRP, 6718, July 4, 1857; 7007, September 23, 1857; 7079, October 12, 1857; 7098, October 19, 1857; 7102, October 21, 1857; 7108, October 24, 1857; 7113, October 27, 1857; 7175, January 4, 1858; 7228, September 2, 1858; 7232, November 3, 1858; 7237, November 12, 1858; 7241, December 2, 1858; 7242, December 3, 1858; 7243, December 6, 1858; 7246, December 18, 1858; 7248, December 31, 1858; 7252, January 8, 1859; 7253, January 8, 1859; 7254, January 9, 1859; 7256, January 10, 1859.

53. MRP, 7255a, January 10, 1859; 7256, January 10, 1859; 7260, January 16, 1859; 7262, January 21, 1859; 7265, January 22, 1859; 7288, May 16, 1859; 7306, December 22, 1859; 7307, December 1859; 7402, May 25, 1860; 7419, August 12, 1861; 7422, September 3, 1861; 7441, January 22, 1862; 7457, April 21, 1862. See also Vanderwood, *Disorder and Progress*.

54. *Estatutos de la Empresa*, founding charter, April 26, 1861, 3–5.

55. *Estatutos de la Empresa*, revisions and additions, August 1862, 7–15.

56. MRP, 7526, February 5, 1863; 7527, February 7, 1863; 7528, February 10, 1863; 7531, February 25, 1863; 7533, March 11, 1863; 7543, March 25, 1863; 7555, May 13, 1863; 7558, May 24, 1853; 7559, May 25, 1863; 7597, August 16, 1863; 7605, December 3, 1864; 7613, January 27, 1865; 7679, July 6, 1866.

57. See Pani, *Serie de admirables.*

58. MRP, 7113, October 27, 1857.

59. MRP, 7212, June 8, 1858; 7217, July 19, 1858.

60. MRP, 7331, June 22, 1860; 7336, July 11, 1860, 7352, November 30, 1860.

61. MRP, 7440, January 21, 1862; 7712, January 4, 1867; 7712a, January 5, 1867; 7712b, January 6, 1867.

62. MRP, 7313, March 1, 1860; 8019c, n.d. [1864].

63. MRP, 7682, July 20, 1866.

64. MRP, 5915a, May 5, 1856; 5919c, June 4, 1856, 5919d, June 10, 1856; 7175, January 5, 1856.

65. MRP, 7920, 1868.

66. MRP, 7595a, May 23, 1864; 7594b, June 18, 1864; 1795c, June 21, 1864; 7612, January 8, 1865; 7670, May 28, 1866.

67. The inventory is PCRun: "Inventario de los ensures y muebles de la Hacienda de Jalpa . . . Agusto de 1866." See Tutino, "Family Economies," 266–67, for a detailed tabulation of sharecropping.

68. Zubieta, *Sentencia definitiva.*

69. Tortolero Villaseñor, *Notarios y agricultores,* 243–45, also explores this conflict.

70. Zubieta, *Sentencia definitiva,* 8–9.

71. Powell, *Liberalismo y el campesinado,* 131–32; Fraser, "Política de desamortización," 652.

72. MRP, 7721, March 28, 1867; 7723, April 15, 1867.

73. Reina, *Rebeliones campesinas,* 71.

74. The classic analysis of Rhodakanaty and López is in John Hart, *Anarchism.*

75. This is emphasized in Pani, *Serie de admirables.*

76. Tortolero Villaseñor, *Notarios y agricultores,* 230–43, offers an analysis of the uprising, with different emphases.

77. MRP, 7824, February 4, 1868.

78. Reina, *Rebeliones campesinas,* 66.

79. MRP, 7833, February 18, 1868.

80. Reina, *Rebeliones campesinas,* 72.

81. MRP, 7836, February 24, 1868.

82. MRP, 7480, March 1, 1868; John Hart, *Anarchism,* 34.

83. Reina, *Rebeliones campesinas,* 72–74.

84. Reina, *Rebeliones campesinas,* 74–75.

85. MRP, 9852, March 13, 1868.

86. Reina, *Rebeliones campesinas,* 66–67.

87. Reina, *Rebeliones campesinas,* 75–76.

88. There is much evidence of this from Michoacán in Pérez Montesinos, "Poised to Break."

89. MRP, 7855, March 17, 1868; 7859, March 19, 1868; 7872, April 24, 1868; 7873, April 25, 1868.

90. Reina, *Rebeliones campesinas*, 67; MRP, 7886, June 2, 1868.

91. MRP, 7887, June 2, 1868; 7888, June 3, 1868.

92. MRP, 7789, June 4, 1868.

93. MRP, 7892, June 7, 1868; 7893, June 9, 1868; 7896, June 9, 1868; 7898, June 12, 1868; 7899, June 13, 1868; 7900, June 14, 1868; 7901, June 14, 1868; 7904, June 19, 1868; Reina, *Rebeliones campesinas*, 67–68.

94. MRP, 7904, June 19, 1868; Reina, *Rebeliones campesinas*, 77–78.

95. Reina, *Rebeliones campesinas*, 69–70, 80–81.

96. MRP, 7290, 1868; Florescano, *Análisis histórico*, 106–7.

97. MRP, 7911, July 7, 1868; 7916, July 27, 1868; 7921, August 4, 1868; 7935, September 10, 1868; 7973, January 3, 1869; 7990, February 3, 1869; 7994, February 16, 1869; 7996, February 22, 1869.

98. MRP, 8048, September 5, 1869; 8065, September 26, 1869; 8109, October 12, 1869; 8111, October 12, 1869; 8150, October 17, 1869; 8154, October 18, 1869; 8181, October 24, 1869; 8331, December 21, 1869; 8347, December 24, 1869; Reina, *Rebeliones campesinas*, 132–35.

99. Similar timing sustained the origins of the Hidalgo revolt in September of 1810.

100. MRP, 8150, October 17, 1869; 8844, September 19, 1870; 8979, December 13, 1870; 9115, February 14, 1871; 9195, May 1, 1871; 9540, October 3, 1871; 9750, December 1, 1871.

101. MRP, 9007, January 2, 1871; 9990, February 19, 1873.

102. Pedrero Nieto, "Estudio regional," 99–150; on Galarza, 127–35.

103. Pedrero Nieto, "Estudio regional," 106, 111, 125–40.

Chapter Nine

1. My understanding of Porfirio Díaz's politics and heartland communities relies on Salinas Sandoval, *Política y sociedad*.

2. This new vision of the Díaz regime and its operation in the state of Mexico began with Reina, "Local Elections," and is now deepened and confirmed in Falcón, *Jefe político*, both focused on the state of Mexico.

3. On the Díaz regime, Guerra, *México*; on liberalism, see Hale, *Transformation of Liberalism*; on railroads, see Coatsworth, *Growth against Development*.

4. Falcón, *Jefe político*.

5. See Barrett, *Sugar Hacienda*; Martin, *Rural Society*; and my syntheses in chapters 2 and 3.

6. Paul Hart, *Bitter Harvest*.

7. The essential study of Porfirian Morelos is Warman, *We Come to Object*, 42–76; it is complemented by Ávila Espinosa, *Origines del zapatismo*; Crespo, "Pueblos de Morelos"; and Tortolero Villaseñor, *Notarios y agricultores*.

8. This analysis synthesizes the pivotal analysis based on documents and interviews in Warman, *We Come to Object*.

9. De la Peña, *Herederos de promesas*, 95–97.

10. PML.

11. PML, 6–10.

12. PML, 7.

13. PML, 17–18, 21–26.

14. PML, 18–19, 21.

15. PML, 25–26, 31, 35, 39.

16. PML, 48, 54, 59.

17. PML, 55, 63–64.

18. Romanucci-Ross, *Conflict, Violence, and Morality*. The anthropologist recorded Filomena's story around 1960, and published the transcript in English as "Filomena's History," 209–13.

19. My calculations of materials in the Memorias of the Estado de México from 1870 to 1900 are presented in the many tables in Tutino, "From Involution to Revolution"; full citations are in an appendix there.

20. On Chalco: Tutino, "Entre la rebelión"; Tortolero Villaseñor, *Máquina de vapor*; and Anaya Pérez, *Rebelión y revolución*. On Tenango, key studies are González Montes and Iracheta Cenegorta, "Violencia," and González Montes, "Trabajo femenino."

21. MCX.

22. Tutino, "From Involution to Revolution," table 1.

23. Tutino, "Entre la rebelión," 377, fig. 2.

24. See chapter 8; for a case near Toluca, see Menegus Bornemann, "Ocoyoacac." On early privatizations, see Salinas Sandoval, *Política y sociedad*, and Salinas Sandoval and Birrichaga Gardida, "Conflicto y aceptación." On the long term, Falcón, *Jefe político*.

25. Tutino, "Entre la rebelión," 379, fig. 4.

26. Pedrero Nieto, "Estudio regional," documents the stability of most estate boundaries; in *Notarios y agricultores*, Tortolero Villaseñor stresses their emphasis of gaining water more than land.

27. Anaya Pérez, *Rebelión y revolución*, vol. 2, 38–42, calculates a vast shift of land from communities and smallholders to estates. But 20,000 hectares are unaccounted between 1893 and 1915. I follow Pedrero's and Tortolero Villaseñor's emphasis on stability in estate land holding—then the claiming of Xico, while privatized lands concentrated within communities.

28. MCX, 49–58.

29. MCX, 54, 56.

30. MCX, 57.

31. MCX, 59–60.

32. MCX, 58–59.

33. MCX, 59–60.

34. MCX, 61–62, 196.

35. As detailed in Anaya Pérez, *Rebelión y revolución*, vol. 2, 32–88, and in Tortolero Villaseñor, *Notarios y agricultores*.

36. This is the essential contribution of Tortolero Villaseñor, *Máquina de vapor*, and *Notarios y agricultores*.

37. *Memoria de la administración pública*, 1894, 339, 655–67.

38. See Huerta González, "Agua, bosques, y capitalismo."

39. Tortolero Villaseñor, *Notarios y agricultores*, 151.

40. Tutino, "Entre la rebelión," 391, fig. 12.

41. *Memoria de la administración pública*, 1894, 339.

42. Camacho Pichardo, "Motines y la centralización."

43. See Hale, *Transformation of Liberalism*.

44. Tutino, "Entre la rebelión," 394–96, figs. 13–15.

45. Tutino, "Entre la rebelión," 398, fig. 16.

46. Milada Bazant, *Busca de la modernidad*; Salinas Sandoval, *Política y sociedad*.

47. Tutino, "Entre la rebelión," 399–401, figs. 17–18.

48. Romero Ibarra, *Manuel Medina Garduño*, 33–64.

49. *Memoria de la administración pública*, 1894, 339, 351–52.

50. *Memoria de la administración pública*, 1894, 351–52, 741–49, 804–6.

51. MCX, 168.

52. González Montes, "Trabajo femenino," 281–99.

53. González Montes and Iracheta Cenegorta, "Violencia."

54. I analyzed state of Mexico crime statistics from 1820 to 1910 in Tutino, "From Involution to Revolution," emphasizing uncertainties before 1870 and probabilities from 1870 to 1900. Here I report key trends.

55. Tutino, "From Involution to Revolution," table 4.

56. Tutino, "From Involution to Revolution," table 5.

57. Tutino, "From Involution to Revolution," table 6.

58. González Montes and Iracheta Cenegorta, "Violencia," 114–15.

59. MCX, 51–52.

60. MCX, 52.

61. MCX, 64–65.

62. Tutino, "From Involution to Revolution," table 7.

63. MCX, 162.

64. Tutino, "From Involution to Revolution," table 8.

65. Parcero, *Condiciones de la mujer*, 121.

66. Tutino, "From Involution to Revolution," table 9.

67. Tutino, "From Involution to Revolution," table 10.

68. Scheper-Hughes, *Death Without Weeping*.

69. See Womack, *Zapata*, and Ávila Espinosa, *Orígenes del zapatismo*.

70. PML, 73–75.

71. PML, 84–91.

72. PML, 92–93.

73. Romanucci-Ross, "Filomena's History," 210–11.

74. PML, 92–102, 119.

75. This is detailed in Pineda Gómez, *Irrupción Zapatista*.

76. This sequence is clear in Womack, *Zapata*, and detailed in Warman, *We Come to Object*.

77. Again, this is clear in both Womack, *Zapata*, and Warman, *We Come to Object*.

78. Romero Ibarra, *Manuel Medina Garduño*, 85–113.

79. The revolution at Chalco is detailed in Anaya Pérez, *Rebelión y revolución*, vol. 2, 110–80, and in Tortolero Villaseñor, *Notarios y agricultores*.

80. Aguilar, *Revolución*, 88, 112.

81. Castro Domingo, *Chayotes, burros y machetes*, 70–90, 178–88; 229–31; wheat production figures are on 76.

82. Castro Domingo, *Chayotes, burros y machetes*, 90–120, 189–204, 229–42.

83. For state government as the revolution escalated, see Romero Ibarra, *Manuel Medina Garduño*, 115–96.

84. Romero Ibarra, *Manuel Medina Garduño*, 264–65.

85. MCX, 69.

86. MCX, 70.

87. MCX, 74.

88. MCX, 74.

89. MCX, 75.

90. MCX, 84.

91. MCX, 78.

92. MCX, 79.

93. MCX, 76.

94. Castro Domingo, *Chayotes, burros y machetes*, 114.

95. All that was also remembered at Xalatlaco; see MCX, 85–151.

Chapter Ten

1. This synthesis is grounded in Womack, *Zapata*; Katz, *Secret War in Mexico*, and *Pancho Villa*; and Knight, *Mexican Revolution*, plus Pineda Gómez, *Irrupción Zapatista*, and Ávila Espinosa, *Orígenes del zapatismo*.

2. On Huerta, Michael Meyer, *Huerta*; on British interests, Garner, *British Lions*.

3. On US opposition to Huerta, see Katz, *Secret War in Mexico*, 156–202; on Veracruz, see Quirk, *Affair of Honor*.

4. Michael Meyer, *Huerta*, 90–91; Knight, *Mexican Revolution*, vol. 2, 45, 77–78, 129–36.

5. Knight, *Mexican Revolution*, vol. 2, 81–87.

6. Womack, *Zapata*; Ávila Espinosa, *Orígenes del zapatismo*; and Pineda Gómez, *Irrupción Zapatista*.

7. This was first detailed and emphasized in Womack, *Zapata*.

8. Womack, *Zapata*, 184.

9. Buve, "Peasant Movements," and "Neither Carranza nor Zapata."

10. This reflects Tutino, *Making a New World*, and the distinctions among silver economies in chapter 1.

11. See Hu-Dehart, *Yaqui Resistance*; Meyers, *Forge of Progress*; and Vanderwood, *Power of God*.

12. On borderland politics, see Wasserman, *Capitalists, Caciques, and Revolution*.

13. Richmond, *Venustiano Carranza*, and Córdova, *Ideología de la revolución*.

14. Richmond, *Venustiano Carranza*, 49–50; Córdova, *Ideología de la revolución*, 195–96; Katz, *Secret War in Mexico*, 128–31.

15. This synthesizes Katz, *Pancho Villa*, and Salmerón, *División del norte*. For a contemporary narrative of life among the Villistas, see Reed, *Insurgent Mexico*.

16. This pivotal turn is detailed in Quirk, *Mexican Revolution*; Hall, *Álvaro Obregón*; Knight, *Mexican Revolution*, vol. 2; and Katz, *Secret War in Mexico*, and *Pancho Villa*.

17. See Quirk, *Mexican Revolution*; Knight, *Mexican Revolution*, vol. 2; and Womack, *Zapata*.

18. Womack, *Zapata*, 206.

19. The key sources are Quirk, *Mexican Revolution*; Hall, *Álvaro Obregón*; Katz, *Secret War in Mexico*, and *Pancho Villa*; Knight, *Mexican Revolution*, vol. 2; and Womack, *Zapata*, as revised by Pineda Gómez, *Revolución del sur*.

20. See Ankerson, *Agrarian Warlord*; Buve, "Peasant Movements"; and Knight, *Mexican Revolution*, vol. 2.

21. Cárdenas, *Largo curso*, 307–8, figs. V.2, V.3.

22. The essential statistics are in Cárdenas, *Largo curso*, 307–25, figs. V.2, V.3, V.5, V.6; the general pattern is clear in Womack, "Mexican Economy"; Haber, *Industry and Underdevelopment*; and Gómez-Galvarriato, *Industry and Revolution*.

23. See Brown, *Oil and Revolution*; Garner, *British Lions*; and Santiago, *Ecology of Oil*.

24. The case is made in John Hart, *Revolutionary Mexico*, 276–303, based on US military records.

25. This, too, is emphasized in John Hart, *Revolutionary Mexico*.

26. See Katz, *Secret War in Mexico*, 270; Lorenzo Meyer, *México y los Estados Unidos*; and Brown, *Oil and Revolution*.

27. The populist moment is detailed in Quirk, *Mexican Revolution*, 152; Córdova, *Ideología de la revolución*, 202–4; Hall, *Álvaro Obregón*, 103–17; Richmond, *Venustiano Carranza*, 68–69; Knight, *Mexican Revolution*, vol. 2, 313–14; and Buve, "Peasant Movements," and "Neither Carranza nor Zapata."

28. On the Constitutionalists and labor, the literature is extensive. See Quirk, *Mexican Revolution*, 183–87; Hall, *Álvaro Obregón*, 110–19; Richmond, *Venustiano Carranza*, 72–73; Ruíz, *Revolución mexicana*, 71–79; and Carr, *Movimiento obrero*, 62–67. Recently, Lear, *Workers, Neighbors, and Citizens*, and Gómez-Galvarriato, *Industry and Revolution*, have focused on workers in the capital and Orizaba, showing limited loyalty to Carranza.

29. Katz, *Secret War in Mexico*, 272; Knight, *Mexican Revolution*, vol. 2, 247–51; Joseph, *Revolution from Without*.

30. Quirk, *Mexican Revolution*, 153–57, 176–78, 213–14; Hall, *Álvaro Obregón*, 114–19; Warman, "Political Project of Zapatismo."

31. As detailed in Pineda Gómez, *Ejército libertador, 1915*; this work ends the presumption that Zapata left Villa to face Obregón alone in the key battles of the revolution.

32. My analysis of Monterrey in 1915 builds on Fernández Martínez, "Revolution and the Industrial City."

33. Again, I draw from Fernández Martínez's essential "Revolution and the Industrial City."

34. Understanding this shift is a key contribution of Katz, *Pancho Villa*.

35. Córdova, *Ideología de la revolución*, 166–71; Katz, *Secret War in Mexico*, 283–85; Warman, "Political Project of Zapatismo."

36. See Womack, *Zapata*, and Katz, *Pancho Villa*.

37. Katz, *Secret War in Mexico*, 187–93; Richmond, *Venustiano Carranza*, 80–81, 114–18, 121–24; on Tlaxcala, Buve, "Neither Carranza nor Zapata," 350–75; on San Luis Potosí, see Falcón, *Revolución y caciquismo*, 96–97.

38. Ruíz, *Revolución mexicana*, 79–82; Carr, *Movimiento obrero*, 72–79; Richmond, *Venustiano Carranza*, 125–32. See Lear, *Workers, Neighbors, and Citizens*, on the turn against labor in Mexico City, and Gómez-Galvarriato, *Industry and Revolution*, on parallels in Orizaba.

39. See Córdova, *Ideología de la revolución*, 214–21.

40. All this is detailed in Cárdenas, *Largo curso*, chap. 5.

41. Hall, *Álvaro Obregón*, 160–83.

42. This pivotal deal is detailed in Womack, *Zapata*.

Chapter Eleven

1. This is detailed in Markiewicz, *Mexican Revolution*, 23–34.

2. This is a key emphasis of Markiewicz, *Mexican Revolution*, which shows that even as Constitutionalists recognized the political necessity of land distribution, they aimed to use it to draw villagers into capitalism—in direct contradiction to the goals of so many Zapatista revolutionaries.

3. Cárdenas, *Largo curso*, 306, 322–23, figs. V.2, V.5, V.6.

4. Rath, *Myths of Demilitarization*, 26.

5. Warman, *We Come to Object*, 133–42.

6. Hall, *Oil, Banks, and Politics*.

7. Brown, "Why Foreign Oil Companies," and Santiago, *Ecology of Oil*, 205–55.

8. Cárdenas, *Largo curso*, 367, fig. VI.4.

9. Friedrich, *Agrarian Revolt*.

10. Markiewicz, *Mexican Revolution*, 180, table 2.

11. Middlebrook, *Paradox of Revolution*.

12. Cárdenas, *Largo curso*, 379.

13. The essential history of a Cristero community is González y González, *San José de Gracia*; Jean Meyer, *Cristiada*, offers a broad study, linking politics and popular movements, across wide regions in Jalisco, Michoacán, Guanajuato, and beyond; Purnell, *Popular Movements*, details how communities, indigenous and ranchero, made decisions about joining the Cristeros.

14. See the classic works of Arnaldo Córdova, *Ideología de la revolución*, and *Revolución en crisis*.

15. Garrido, *Partido de la revolución*, 78–117.

16. Markiewicz, *Mexican Revolution*, 57–62, makes this sequence clear.

17. Rath, *Myths of Demilitarization*, 22–26.

18. Cárdenas, *Largo curso*, 390–402.

19. Again, my interpretation of global dynamics reflects my reading of Findlay and O'Rourke, *Power and Plenty*—in the context of a wide historiography on Europe and the Americas.

20. Cárdenas, *Largo curso*, 406–23.

21. My calculations are based on Markiewicz, *Mexican Revolution*, 180, table 2.

22. Cárdenas, *Largo curso*, 429–40; Markiewicz, *Mexican Revolution*, 59–69, 180, table 2.

23. The rise of Cárdenas and the land distribution numbers are synthesized in Markiewicz, *Mexican Revolution*, 59–81, 180, table 2. The larger history of Cardenismo is the subject of superb studies and endless debates. See Córdova, *Política de masas*; González y González, *Presidente Cárdenas*; Hamilton, *Limits of State Autonomy*; and Gilly, *Cardenismo*. On the cultural conflicts inherent in the Cárdenas project, see Vaughan, *Cultural Politics in Revolution*, and Fallaw, *Religion and State Formation*.

24. Hamilton, *Limits of State Autonomy*, 195–96, 202.

25. On Cárdenas and rise of industry as a leading sector, see Cárdenas, *Largo curso*, 451–88.

26. Vaughan, *Cultural Politics in Revolution*.

27. Cabrera's views and influence on Carranza are in Markiewicz, *Mexican Revolution*, 23–34.

28. Markiewicz, *Mexican Revolution*, 180, table 2.

29. Garrido, *Partido de la revolución*, 299–323.

30. Rath, *Myths of Demilitarization*, 31–53.

31. Lorenzo Meyer, *México y los Estados Unidos*, and Santiago, *Ecology of Oil*. On the negotiations, see Gilly, *Cardenismo*.

32. Cárdenas, *Largo curso*, 527.

33. Hewitt de Alcántara, *Modernizing Mexican Agriculture*, provides the foundation analysis of this shift.

34. Mexico during World War II has received limited study. See Loyola, *Entre la guerra*, for diverse studies; on politics, Medina, *Hacia el nuevo estado*, sets the period in political context. Durand, *Braceros*, is a probing anthology of Mexican workers' experiences in the United States.

35. Cárdenas, *Largo curso*, 495–503, 523.

36. Cárdenas, *Largo curso*, 531, table IX.7.

37. Cárdenas, *Largo curso*, 355.

38. These postwar developments and their global impacts are brilliantly synthesized in McNeill and Engelke, *Great Acceleration*.

39. Rath, *Myths of Demilitarization*, emphasizes the shift of role, arguing that the regime did not become less military, but that it turned the military to social control—a pivotal point.

40. Coral, "Mexico City Middle Class," explores the rise of that key population after 1940, and its diverse sectors' often uneasy relations with a state on which so many depended.

41. Cárdenas, *Largo curso*, 514, 521, 566, fig. IX.5.

42. Cárdenas, *Largo curso*, synthesizes the best of this literature—and provides much data and analysis essential to my critique.

43. Haber et al., *Mexico since 1980*.

44. The best of the political studies is Servín, *Ruptura y oposición*; see also the essays in Servín, Reina, and Tutino, *Cycles of Conflict*.

45. Landes, *Unbound Prometheus*, is the classic analysis. For nineteenth-century Mexico, see Beatty, *Technology*; on late twentieth-century global accelerations, see McNeill and Engelke, *Great Acceleration*.

46. Hobsbawm, *Industry and Empire*, illustrates this sequence.

47. The essential revision is Beckert, *Empire of Cotton*.

48. See Hobsbawm's classic *Industry and Empire*.

49. For very different illustrative analyses, see Cronon, *Nature's Metropolis*, and Prasad, *Land of Too Much*.

50. On persistent, accelerating concentrations, the key study is Piketty, *Capital*.

51. See McNeill, *Plagues and People*; Gereffi, *Pharmaceutical Industry*; and Soto Laveaga, *Jungle Laboratories*.

52. The sustaining link is emphasized in de la Peña, *Herederos de promesas*, and Warman, *We Come to Object*, and is a focus of chapter 12 here.

53. Hewitt de Alcántara, *Modernizing Mexican Agriculture*, is the classic study.

54. Wright, *Death of Ramón González*, offers an essential analysis of this transition.

55. Haber et al., *Mexico since 1980*, 80, fig. 3.8.

56. Padilla, *Rural Resistance*, and McCormick, *Logic of Compromise*, explore this from different perspectives—as I will in chapter 12.

57. Alegre, *Railroad Radicals*.

58. Coral, "Mexico City Middle Class," and Pensado, *Rebel Mexico*.

59. Aviña, *Specters of Revolution*.

60. On post-1968 politics, see Louise Walker, *Waking from the Dream*; on economic challenges, see Cárdenas, *Largo curso*; on the long evolution of the PRI regime, Medina, *Hacia el nuevo estado*, remains a key synthesis.

61. Middlebrook, *Paradox of Revolution*, offers a long-term case history focused on labor; for diverse broader perspectives, see the essays in Servín, Reina, and Tutino, *Cycles of Conflict*.

62. The 1970s and the promise of oil, the escalation of debt, and the collapse in the 1980s are ably analyzed in Haber et al., *Mexico since 1980*, with a focus on the heights of power. Migration numbers are on p. 80, fig. 3.8.

63. Cárdenas, *Largo curso*, 401, 510, 557, 611, figs. VI.17, IX.2, IX.15, X.5.

Chapter Twelve

1. Warman, *We Come to Object*, 133.

2. PML, 120–44.

3. PML, 186.

4. PML, 147–51.

5. PML, 157, 172.

6. MCX, 125–28 (quote 125).

7. MCX, 129–32.

8. MCX, 132–41.

9. Castro Domingo, *Chayotes, burros y machetes*, 121–78, 207–29, 243–61.

10. PML, 181–82.

11. PML, 233, 261.

12. Warman, *We Come to Object*, 161.

13. Warman, *We Come to Object*, 136, 146, 157, 186.

14. Castro Domingo, *Chayotes, burros y machetes*, 141–42.

15. Warman, *We Come to Object*, 184–85.

16. Details come from Padilla, *Rural Resistance*. My larger interpretation builds on that work and McCormick, *Logic of Compromise*. Both are deeply researched and detailed studies that focus on politics.

17. The mass recruitment of cane cutters in Guerrero is emphasized in Lomnitz-Adler, *Exits from the Labyrinth*.

18. Padilla, *Rural Resistance*, focuses on Jaramillo; McCormick, *Logic of Compromise*, sets his politics in context.

19. This section synthesizes materials in Lewis, *Mexican Village*, xi–281, based on local investigations, interviews, and personal encounters; I find less of value in Lewis's turn to psychocultural analysis, 287–448.

20. Lewis, *Mexican Village*, 26–32.

21. Lewis, *Mexican Village*, 118–23.

22. Lewis, *Mexican Village*, 98.

23. Lewis, *Mexican Village*, 130–35.

24. Lewis, *Mexican Village*, 105, 162, 164, 195.

25. Lewis, *Mexican Village*, 174.

26. Lewis, *Mexican Village*, 102, table 19.

27. Lewis, *Mexican Village*, 99.

28. Lewis, *Mexican Village*, 57.

29. Lewis, *Mexican Village*, 137, 261–78.

30. Lewis, *Mexican Village*, 78.

31. Lewis, *Mexican Village*, 227, table 53.

32. In *Conflict, Violence, and Morality*, Romanucci-Ross never names the village; Lomnitz-Adler does in *Exits from the Labyrinth*, 126. As this history has repeatedly demonstrated, location matters.

33. Romanucci-Ross, *Conflict, Violence, and Morality*, 2–20.

34. Romanucci-Ross, *Conflict, Violence, and Morality*, 6.

35. Romanucci-Ross, *Conflict, Violence, and Morality*, 21–23.

36. Romanucci-Ross, *Conflict, Violence, and Morality*, 24–25.

37. Romanucci-Ross, *Conflict, Violence, and Morality*, 35–44, 120–30.

38. Romanucci-Ross, *Conflict, Violence, and Morality*, 46–64, 76–78, 133–36, 154–55.

39. Romanucci-Ross, *Conflict, Violence, and Morality*, 169–81.

40. Warman, *We Come to Object*, 186, 193, 199.

41. Warman, *We Come to Object*, 170, 176.

42. de la Peña, *Herederos de promesas*, 143.

43. This synthesizes Warman, *We Come to Object*, 193–252, and de la Peña, *Herederos de promesas*, 195–252.

44. de la Peña, *Herederos de promesas*, 133.

45. Warman, *We Come to Object*, 216–34.

46. Warman, *We Come to Object*, 260–90.

47. de la Peña, *Herederos de promesas*, 150–52.

48. de la Peña, *Herederos de promesas*, 97–125.

49. de la Peña, *Herederos de promesas*, 126–43.

50. de la Peña, *Herederos de promesas*, 206–16.

51. de la Peña, *Herederos de promesas*, 198–200, figs. 6.1–6.3.

52. de la Peña, *Herederos de promesas*, details all this; the emphasis on patriarchy is mine.

53. de la Peña, *Herederos de promesas*, 254; on one of the few Morelos communities, high on the slopes of Popocatépetl, that retained indigenous identity into the 1960s, see Friedlander, *Being Indian in Hueyapan*.

54. de la Peña, *Herederos de promesas*, 262.

55. de la Peña, *Herederos de promesas*, 271–84.

56. I confess to holding such views at the time. For more from the perspective of Morelos communities, see Hughes, *Mexican Crucifix*.

57. Hughes, *Mexican Crucifix*, 131–70.

58. de la Peña, *Herederos de promesas*, 290–303.

59. de la Peña, *Herederos de promesas*, 295–310 (quote 307).

60. This is detailed for three municipalities in Castro Domingo, *Chayotes, burros y machetes*, 269–464.

61. MCX, 145–49.

62. Castro Domingo, *Chayotes, burros y machetes*, 319–37.

63. de la Peña, *Herederos de promesas*, 313–14.

64. Lomnitz, *Exits from the Labyrinth*, 1974.

65. This synthesis reflects the anthropologists cited here, my experiences visiting Morelos since the early 1970s, and conversations with scholars and others who live there.

66. Padilla, *Rural Resistance*; Lomnitz-Adler, *Exits from the Labyrinth*, 68–69.

67. Lomnitz-Adler, *Exits from the Labyrinth*, 85–93.

68. Lomnitz-Adler, *Exits From the Labyrinth*, 95–108.

Chapter Thirteen

1. López-Alonso, *Measuring Up*.

2. Population figures for Mexico and the Mexico City metropolis are in Tutino, "Americas in the Twentieth-Century," table 1.

3. Nationally, life expectancy rose from under forty in 1940 to over sixty in 1970, to seventy-five by 2000; child-rearing, which held over six per woman in the 1960s and 1970s, fell below three in the 1990s. See María Eugenia Zavala, "Transición demográfica."

4. I drew these figures from Mexico's Instituto Nacional de Estadística y Geografía, diverse tables, accessed November 7, 2016, http://www3.inegi.org.mx.

5. See Illades, *Hacia la república*; Trujillo Bolio, *Operarios fabriles*; Miranda Pacheco, *Tacubaya*.

6. See Aréchiga Córdoba, *Tepito*.

7. This synthesizes Aréchiga Córdoba, *Tepito*; Illades, *Hacia la república*; and Trujillo Bolio, *Operarios fabriles*.

8. Rodríguez Kurí, *Experiencia olvidada*.

9. Miranda Pacheco, *Tacubaya*, 145–65; Rodríguez Kurí, *Experiencia olvidada*, 151–74.

10. Rodríguez Kuri, *Experiencia olvidada*, 92–96.

11. Again, this is detailed in Aréchiga Córdoba, *Tepito*.

12. Again, Aréchiga Córdoba, *Tepito*, is the key source.

13. Francois, *Culture of Everyday Credit*.

14. See Porter, *Working Women*.

15. See Lear, *Workers, Neighbors, and Citizens*; Piccato, *City of Suspects*; and Bliss, *Compromised Positions*.

16. Tutino, "Americas in the Twentieth-Century," table 1.

17. Lear, *Workers, Neighbors, and Citizens*.

18. From Pani, *La higiene en México* (1916), cited in Agostini, *Monuments of Progress*, 149–52.

19. See Miranda Pacheco, *Tacubaya*, and *Departamento del Distrito Federal*.

20. Tenorio, *I Speak of the City*, explores all this and more in wonderful detail.

21. On Cárdenas and the postrevolutionary regime, see Hamilton, *Limits of State Autonomy*, and Gilly, *Cardenismo*. On postrevolutionary industry, see Gauss, *Made in Mexico*; on the limits of Cárdenas's power, see Fallaw, *Religion and State Formation*.

22. Diane Davis, *Urban Leviathan*, is pivotal on this and much more.

23. The classic study is Hewitt de Alcántara, *Modernizing Mexican Agriculture*.

24. See Garza, *Proceso de industrialización*, and Fulwider, "Driving the Nation."

25. CSL.

26. Jesús reports his life in CSL, 3–13, 81–99.

27. CSL, 10, 12.

28. CSL, 31.

29. CSL, 17–87, 157–233, 323–402, for the son's recollections.

30. CSL, 22, 55.

31. CSL, 82.

32. CSL, 82–83.

33. CSL, 277.

34. CSL, 299.

35. CSL, 312.

36. CSL, 312–19 (quotes 316, 319).

37. CSL, 370.

38. CSL, 391.

39. CSL, 403–42 (quotes 442).

40. CSL, 443–77 (quote 452).

41. CSL, 481–99 (quotes 494, 499).

42. This is emphasized in Haber et al., *Mexico since 1980*.

43. Diane Davis, *Urban Leviathan*, shows how city infrastructure projects built debts that helped crash the system.

44. This understanding of city politics depends of Diane Davis, *Urban Leviathan*.

45. See Coral, "Mexico City Middle Class," and Louise Walker, *Waking from the Dream*.

46. Vélez-Ibañez, *Rituals of Marginality*, and Palma Galván, *Participación social*.

47. The approach to urban development that shapes this analysis is explored in greater depth and detail in Tutino and Melosi, *New World Cities*; my emphases are the focus of the Introduction and chapters 1 and 2, with the latter offering a more structural analysis of Mexico City's challenges from 1870 to 2000.

48. See Vélez-Ibañez, *Rituals of Marginality*; Cornelius, *Politics and the Migrant Poor*; and Eckstein, *Poverty of Revolution*.

49. My vision of Mexico after 1980 is shaped by the essays in Servín, Reina, and Tutino, *Cycles of Conflict*. On the economic collapse and its impacts, see Haber et al., *Mexico since 1980*, and Louise Walker, *Waking from the Dream*.

50. The political economy of the crisis and transition are critically detailed in Haber et al., *Mexico after 1980*.

51. See Haber et al., *Mexico after 1980*, 80, fig. 3.8.

52. My understanding of the city after 1980 is shaped by Peter Ward's superb synthesis, first published in English in 1989, revised and updated in Spanish as *México megaciudad*; see also Pacheco Gómez Muñoz, *Ciudad de México*.

53. My sketch of Ajusco depends on Pezzoli, *Human Settlements*.

54. See Hiernaux, "Expansión metropolitana"; Lindón Villoria, *Trama de la cotidianidad*; and Herrera Bautista and Molinar Palma, *Silencio de su soledad*.

55. This is my reading of the research and analysis in Herrera Bautista and Molinar Palma, *Silencio de su soledad*.

56. On self-help and city politics, see Duhau, "Informal City."

57. Rojas, *Paternidad y vida familiar*, 81–83.

58. This is explored in depth in Gutmann, *Meanings of Macho*, and *Romance of Democracy*.

59. On historic patriarchy, see Stern, *Secret History of Gender*, and Tutino, *Making a New World*. On changing patterns of patriarchy and family violence in late twentieth-century Mexico City, see Gutmann, *Meanings of Macho*; Herrera Bautista and Molinar Palma, *Silencio de su soledad*; and Rojas, *Paternidad y vida familiar*.

Epilogue

1. Haber et al., *Mexico since 1980*, provides a strong synthetic analysis of the political economy of the transition, focused on the regime and the institutions it sustained and/or transformed.

2. La Botz, *Mask of Democracy*.

3. de Janvry, Gordillo, and Sadoulet, *Mexico's Second Agrarian Reform*, explores the opening of ejidos.

4. La Botz, *Mask of Democracy*.

5. Warman, *Campo mexicano*.

6. This is my recollection and interpretation of a process I lived as a citizen of the United States and a scholar of Mexico. For a scholarly analysis, see Cameron and Tomlin, *Making of NAFTA*.

7. On the uprising and its ramifications, see Womack, *Rebellion in Chiapas*, and Stephen, *Zapata Lives!*

8. This is explored with greater detail and complexity in Haber et al., *Mexico since 1980*.

9. Haber et al., in *Mexico since 1980*, conclude the same.

10. For revealing case studies, see Espinosa, *Dilemma del retorno*, and Martínez, *Crossing Over*.

11. Lida, *First Stop*, offers a deep and revealing exploration of the city's diversity.

12. Gutmann, *Meanings of Macho*, discusses challenges and adaptations in Mexico City.

13. I first developed this analysis in Tutino, "Revolutionary Capacity."

14. Fitting, *Struggle for Maize*.

15. This synthesizes Wright, *Death of Ramón González*.

16. Wolf emphasized this in *Peasant Wars*, an analysis deepened by Scott in *Moral Economy*.

17. See Williams, *Export Agriculture*, and Paige, *Coffee and Power*.

18. For a powerful set of illustrations, see Mike Davis, *Planet of Slums*.

19. The rise and limits of new urban politics are explored in Tutino and Melosi, *New World Cities*.

20. See the essays in Servín, Reina, and Tutino, *Cycles of Conflict*, on the larger challenges of globalization in Mexico. See Gilly and Roux, *Tiempo del despojo*.

21. I write this on the day of his victory—the road ahead in the United States is uncertain at best.

22. Piketty, *Capital*.

23. This is the focus of Haber et al., *Mexico since 1980*, and the more global vision of Acemoglu and Robinson in *Why Nations Fail*.

24. On the ongoing global transformation, McNeill and Engelke, *Great Acceleration*, is a good place to begin.

25. Desmarais, *Via Campesina*, analyzes a transnational movement that implicitly recognizes that agrarian autonomies are gone—and draws rural women and men seeking to shape new ways forward.

Acemoglu, Daron, and James Robinson. *Why Nations Fail: The Origins of Power, Prosperity, and Poverty*. New York: Crown, 2012.

Agostini, Claudia. *Monuments of Progress*. Boulder: University of Colorado Press, 2003.

Aguilar, José Ángel. *La revolución en el Estado de México*. Toluca: Gobierno del Estado de México, 1987.

Alamán, Lucas. *Documentos diversos (inéditos y muy raros)*. Vol. 1. Mexico City: Editorial Jus, 1945.

———. "Memoria de la Secretaría del Estado . . . 1830." In Alamán, *Documentos diversos*, 163–242. Cited: LAM, 1830.

———. "Memoria de la Secretaría del Estado . . . 1831." In Alamán, *Documentos diversos*, 243–337. Cited: LAM, 1831.

———. "Memoria de la Secretaría del Estado . . . 1832." In Alamán, *Documentos diversos*, 339–433. Cited: LAM, 1832.

———. "Memoria sobre el estado de la agricultura é industria de la república . . . 1843." In *Documentos para el estudio*, 2–85. Cited: LAM, 1843.

———. "Memoria sobre el estado de la agricultura é industria de la república en el año de 1844." In *Documentos para el estudio*, 88–155. Cited: LAM, 1844.

———. "Memoria sobre el estado de la agricultura é industria de la república en el año de 1845." In *Documentos para el estudio*, 157–242. Cited: LAM, 1845.

Alegre, Robert. *Railroad Radicals in Cold War Mexico: Gender, Class, and Memory*. Lincoln: UNP, 2014.

Allen, Robert. *The British Industrial Revolution in Global Perspective*. Cambridge: CUP, 2009.

Anaya Pérez, Marco Antonio. *Rebelión y revolución en Chalco-Amecameca, Estado de México, 1821–1921*. 2 vols. Mexico City: Instituto Nacional de Estudios Históricos de la Revolución Mexicana, 1997.

Anderson, Benedict. *Imagined Communities: Reflections on the Origins and Spread of Nationalism*. London: Verso, 1991.

Andrews, Catherine. *Entre la espada y la Constitución: El General Anastacio Bustamente, 1780–1853*. Ciudad Victoria, Mexico: Universidad Autónoma de Tamaulipas, 2008.

Ankerson, Dudley. *Agrarian Warlord: Saturnino Cedillo and the Mexican Revolution in San Luis Potosí*. DeKalb: Northern Illinois University Press, 1984.

Anna, Timothy. *Forging Mexico, 1821–1835*. Lincoln: UNP, 1998.

———. *The Mexican Empire of Iturbide*. Lincoln: UNP, 1990.

Annino, Antonio. "The Two-Faced Janus: The Pueblos and the Origins of Mexican Liberalism." In Servín, Reina, and Tutino, *Cycles of Conflict*, 60–90.

Archer, Christon. *The Army in New Spain, 1760–1810*. Albuquerque: UNM, 1977.

Aréchiga Córdoba. Ernesto. *Tepito: Del antiguo barrio de indios al arrabal*. Mexico City: Ediciones Unión, 2003.

Arenal Fenocchio, Jaime del. *Un modo de ser libres: Independencia y constitución en México, 1816–1822*. Zamora, Mexico: CMCH, 2002.

Assadourian, Carlos Sempat. *El sistema de la economía colonial: El mercado, regiones y espacio económico*. Lima: Instituto de Estudios Peruanos, 1982.

Ávila, Alfredo. *En nombre de la nación: La formación del gobierno representativo en México, 1808–1824*. Mexico City: Ediciones Taurus, 2002.

———. *Para la libertad: Los republicanos en tiempos del imperio, 1822–1823*. Mexico City: UNAM, 2005.

Ávila Espinosa, Felipe. *Los orígenes del zapatismo*. Mexico City: CMEX, 2001.

Aviña, Alexander. *Specters of Revolution: Peasant Guerrillas in the Cold War Mexican Countryside*. New York: Oxford University Press, 2014.

"Ayutamientos, Alcaldes, y Ciudadanos, 1826." Conde de Santiago Papers. Biblioteca Nacional de México, Mexico City.

Bakewell, Peter. *Miners of the Red Mountain: Indian Labor in Colonial Potosí*. Albuquerque: UNM, 1984.

———. *Silver Mining and Society in Colonial Mexico: Zacatecas, 1546–1700*. Cambridge: CUP, 1971.

Barr, Juliana. *Peace Came in the Form of a Woman: Indians and Spaniards in the Texas Borderlands*. Chapel Hill: UNC, 2007.

Barrett, Ward. *The Sugar Hacienda of the Marqueses del Valle*. Minneapolis: University of Minnesota Press, 1970.

Basave Kunhardt, Jorge. "Algunos aspectos de la técnica agrícola en las haciendas." In Semo, *Siete ensayos*, 189–246.

Bauman, Zygmunt. *Liquid Times: Living in the Age of Uncertainty*. Cambridge, UK: Polity, 2007.

Bazant, Jan. *The Alienation of Church Wealth in Mexico*. Cambridge: CUP, 1971.

Bazant, Milada. *En busca de la modernidad: Procesos educativos en el Estado de México, 1873–1912*. Zinacatepec, Mexico: CNSE, 2002.

Beatty, Edward. *Technology and the Search for Progress in Modern Mexico*. Oakland: University of California Press, 2015.

Beckert, Sven. *Empire of Cotton: A Global History*. New York: Knopf, 2014.

Benson, Nettie Lee, ed. *Mexico and the Spanish Cortes, 1810–1822*. Austin: UTP, 1968.

———. *The Provincial Deputation in Mexico: Harbinger of Provincial Autonomy, Independence, and Federalism*. Austin: UTP, 1992.

Berdan, Frances. *Aztecs of Central Mexico: An Imperial Society*. New York: Wordsworth, 2004.

Blackburn, Robin. *The Making of New World Slavery: From the Baroque to the Modern*. London: Verso, 1997.

———. *The Overthrow of New World Slavery, 1776–1845*. London: Verso, 2011.

Bliss, Katherina. *Compromised Positions: Prostitution, Public Health, and Gender Politics in Revolutionary Mexico City*. State College: Penn State Press, 2002.

Borah, Woodrow. *Justice by Insurance*. Berkeley: UCP, 1982.

Bowser, Frederick. *The African Slave in Colonial Peru, 1524–1650*. Stanford, CA: SUP, 1972.

Brading, D. A. *The First America: The Spanish Monarchy, Creole Patriotism, and the Liberal State, 1492–1867*. Cambridge: CUP, 1993.

——. *Mexican Phoenix: Our Lady of Guadalupe: Image and Tradition Across Five Centuries*. Cambridge: CUP, 2001.

——. *Miners and Merchants in Bourbon Mexico, 1763–1910*. Cambridge: CUP, 1971.

Brading, D. A., and Harry Cross. "Colonial Silver Mining: Mexico and Peru." HAHR 52, no. 4 (1972): 545–79.

Braudel, Fernand. *Civilization and Capitalism*. Translated by Sian Reynolds. 3 vols. New York: Harper and Row, 1982–84.

Breña, Roberto. *El primer liberalismo español y los proceso de emancipación de América, 1808–1824*. Mexico City: CMEX, 2006.

——. *En el umbral de las revoluciones hispánicas: El bienio, 1808–1810*. Mexico City: CMEX, 2010.

Brown, Jonathan. *Oil and Revolution in Mexico*. Berkeley: UCP, 1993.

——. "Why Foreign Oil Companies Shifted Their Production from Mexico to Venezuela in the 1920s." *American Historical Review* 90, no. 2 (1985): 362–85.

Bullock, W. *Six Months' Residence and Travels in Mexico*. 1824. Reprint, Port Washington, NY: Kennikat, 1971.

Burkhart, Louise. *The Slippery Earth: Nahua-Christian Moral Dialogue in Sixteenth-Century Mexico*. Tucson: University of Arizona Press, 1989.

Buve, Raymond. "Neither Carranza nor Zapata: The Rise and Fall of a Peasant Movement That Tried to Challenge Both, Tlaxcala, 1910–1918." In Katz, *Riot, Rebellion, and Revolution*, 338–75.

——. "Peasant Movements, Caudillos, and Land Reform during the Revolution, (1910–1917) in Tlaxcala, Mexico." *Boletín de Estudios Latino-Americanos y del Caribe* 5, no. 18 (1975): 112–52.

Calderón de la Barca, Fanny. *Life in Mexico*. Edited and annotated by Howard and Marion Hall Fisher. New York: Doubleday, 1966. Cited: FCB.

Camacho Pichardo, Gloria. "Los motines y la centralización de las aguas en el Estado de México, 1870–1900." In Zamudio and Camacho Pichardo, *Estado de México*, 173–93.

Cameron, Maxwell, and Brian Tomlin. *The Making of NAFTA: How the Deal Was Done*. Ithaca, NY: Cornell University Press, 2002.

Candiani, Vera. *Dreaming of Dry Land: Environmental Transformation in Colonial Mexico City*. Stanford, CA: SUP, 2014.

Cañeque, Alejandro. *The King's Living Image: The Culture and Politics of Viceregal Power in Colonial Mexico*. London: Routledge, 2004.

Caplan, Karen. *Indigenous Citizens: Local Liberalism in Early National Oaxaca and Yucatán*. Stanford, CA: SUP, 2009.

Cárdenas Sánchez, Enrique. *El largo curso de la economía Mexicana: De 1780 a nuestros días*. Mexico City: FCE, 2015.

Carr, Barry. *El movimiento obrero y la economía de México*. Mexico City: Ediciones Era, 1981.

Carson, Rachel. *Silent Spring*. Boston: Houghton Mifflin, 1962.

Castellanos Suárez, José Alfredo. *Empeño por una expectativa agraria: Expropiación ejidal en el municipio de Acolman, 1915–1940*. Mexico City: Instituto Mexicano de Estudios Históricos de la Revolución Mexicana, 1998.

Castro Domingo, Pablo. *Chayotes, burros y machetes*. Zinacatepec, Mexico: CNSE, 2003.

Castro Gutiérrez, Felipe. *Nueva ley y nuevo rey: Reformas borbónicas y rebelión popular en Nueva España*. Zamora, Mexico: CMCH, 1996.

———. *Los tarascos bajo el imperio español, 1600–1740*. Mexico City: UNAM, 2004.

Cayuela Fernández, José Gregorio, and José Ángel Gallego Palomares. *La Guerra de Independencia. Historia bélica: Pueblo y nación en España, 1808–1814*. Salamanca, Spain: Editorial Universidad, 2008.

Chambers, Sarah. "From One Patria, Two Nations: The Andean Heartland, 1750–1850." In Tutino, *New Countries*, 316–49.

Chassen López, Francie. *From Liberal to Revolutionary Oaxaca: The View from the South, México, 1867–1911*. University Park: Penn State Press, 2004.

Chowning, Margaret. *Wealth and Power in Provincial Mexico: Michoacán from the Late Colony to the Revolution*. Stanford, CA: SUP, 1999.

Clendinnen, Inga. *Ambivalent Conquests: Maya and Spaniard in Yucatán, 1517–1570*. Cambridge: CUP, 1982.

———. *Aztecs: An Interpretation*. Cambridge: CUP, 1991.

Cline, S. L. *Colonial Culhuacan, 1580–1600: A Social History of an Aztec Town*. Albuquerque: UNM, 1986.

Coatsworth, John. *Growth against Development: The Economic Impact of the Railroads in Porfirian Mexico*. DeKalb: Northern Illinois University Press, 1981.

Colín, Mario. *Índice de documentos relativos a los pueblos del Estado de México: Ramo de tierras*. Toluca, Mexico: Gobierno del Estado de México, 1966.

Collins, James. *The State in Early Modern France*. Rev. ed. Cambridge: CUP, 2009.

Connaughton, Brian. "Estudio introductorio." In MEM, 21–76.

Cook, Sherburne, and Woodrow Borah. *Essays in Population History*. 3 vols. Berkeley: UCP, 1971–79.

Coral, Emilio. "The Mexico City Middle Class, 1940–1970: Between Tradition, the State, and the United States." PhD diss., Georgetown University, 2011.

Córdova, Arnaldo. *La ideología de la revolución mexicana: La formación del nuevo régimen*. Mexico City: Ediciones Era, 1972.

———. *La política de masas del cardenismo*. Mexico City: Ediciones Era, 1974.

———. *La revolución en crisis: La aventura del maximato*. Mexico City: Cal y Arena, 1995.

Cornelius, Wayne. *Politics and the Migrant Poor in Mexico City*. Princeton, NJ: PUP, 1975.

Couturier, Edith. *The Silver King: The Remarkable Life of the Count of Regla in Colonial Mexico*. Albuquerque: UNM, 2003.

Crespo, Horacio. "Los pueblos de Morelos: La comunidad agraria, la desamortización liberal en Morelos y una fuente para el estudio de la diferenciación social Campesina." In Espejel, *Estudios sobre el Zapatismo*, 57–120.

Cronon, William. *Nature's Metropolis: Chicago and the Great West*. New York: Norton, 1991.

Crosby, Alfred. *The Columbian Exchange: Biological and Cultural Consequences of 1492*. Westport, CT: Greenwood, 1972.

Cross, Harry. "The Mining Economy of Zacatecas, Mexico, in the Nineteenth Century." PhD diss., University of California, Berkeley, 1976.

Cubillo Moreno, Gilda. *Los dominios de la plata: El precio del auge, el peso del poder— los reales de minas de Pachuca y Zimapán, 1552–1620*. 2nd ed. Mexico City: INAH, 2006.

Curtin, Phillip. *The African Slave Trade: A Census*. Madison: University of Wisconsin Press, 1972.

Dabbs, Jack Autry. *The French Army in Mexico, 1861–1870*. The Hague: Mouton, 1963.

———. *The Mariano Riva Palacio Archive*. 3 vols. Mexico City: Editorial Jus, 1962–72.

Davis, Diane. *Urban Leviathan: Mexico City in the Twentieth Century*. Philadelphia: Temple University Press, 1994.

Davis, Mike. *Planet of Slums*. London: Verso, 2005.

de Janvry, Alain, Gustavo Gordillo, and Elizabeth Sadoulet. *Mexico's Second Agrarian Reform*. La Jolla: Center for US-Mexican Studies, University of California, San Diego, 1997.

de la Peña, Guillermo. *Herederos de promesas: Agricultura, política y ritual en los Altos de Morelos*. Mexico City: CIESAS, 1980.

Delay, Brian. *The War of a Thousand Deserts*. New Haven, CT: Yale University Press, 2008.

Desmarais, Annette Aurelle. *La Via Campesina: Globalization and the Power of Peasants*. London: Pluto Press, 2007.

de Urrutia, Carlos. "Noticia geográfica de Reino de Nueva España y el estado de su población." In Enrique Florescano and Isabel Gil, eds., *Descripciones económicas generales de la Nueva España*. Mexico City: Secretaría de Educación Pública 1973, 68–127.

Díaz Díaz, Fernando. *Caudillos y caciques*. Mexico City: CMEX, 1972.

Documentos para el estudio de la industrialización en México, 1837–1845. Mexico City: Secretaría de Hacienda y Crédito Público, 1977.

Duhau, Emilio. "The Informal City: An Enduring Slum or a Progressive Habitat?" In Fisher, McCann, and Auyero, *Cities from Scratch*, 150–69.

Durand, Jorge, ed. *Braceros: Las miradas mexicanas y estadounidenses, antología, 1945–1964*. Mexico City: Miguel Ángel Porrúa, 2007.

Eckstein, Susan. *The Poverty of Revolution: The State and the Urban Poor in Mexico City*. Princeton, NJ: PUP, 1977.

Elliott, J. H. *Empires of the Atlantic World: Britain and Spain in America, 1492–1830*. New Haven, CT: Yale University Press, 2007.

Enciso Contreras, José. *Taxco en el siglo XVI: Sociedad y normatividad en un real de minas novohispano*. Zacatecas, Mexico: Universidad Autónoma de Zacatecas, 1999.

Escalante Gonzalbo, Fernando. *Ciudadanos imaginarios*. Mexico City: CMEX, 1992.

Escobar Ohmstede, Antonio, ed. *Los pueblos indios en los tiempos de Benito Juárez, 1847–1872*. Oaxaca, Mexico: Universidad Autónoma Benito Juárez, 2007.

Espejel, Laura, ed. *Estudios sobre el Zapatismo*. Mexico City: INAH, 2003.

Espinosa, Victor. *El dilema del retorno: Migración, género y pertenencia en un contexto transnacional*. Zamora, Mexico: CMCH, 1998.

Espinosa de los Monteros, Manuel. *Miscelánea: Curato de Iztacalco, 1831–1832*. Edited and with an introduction by Brian Connaughton. Mexico City: Universidad Autónoma Metropolitana, Iztapalapa, 2012. Cited: MEM.

Estatutos de la Empresa del Ferro-Carril de México a Chalco. Mexico City: Imprenta de J. Abadiano, 1865.

Falcón, Romana. *El jefe político: Un dominio negociado en el mundo rural del Estado de México, 1856–1910.* Mexico City: CMEX, 2015.

———. *Las naciones de una república: La cuestión indígena y el congreso mexicano.* Mexico City: Congreso de la Unión, 1999.

———. *Revolución y caciquismo: San Luis Potosí, 1910–1938.* Mexico City: CMEX, 1984.

Fallaw, Ben. *Religion and State Formation in Post-Revolutionary Mexico.* Durham, NC: DUP, 2013.

Farriss, Nancy. *Maya Society under Colonial Rule.* Princeton, NJ: PUP, 1984.

Fernández, Vicente. *Testimonio del expediente promovido por el Señor Conde de la Cortina . . . por el administrador de sus haciendas Teniente Coronel D. Vicente Fernández, 1816.* Bancroft Library, University of California, Berkeley. Cited: VFT.

Fernández Martínez, Rodolfo. "Revolution and the Industrial City: Violence and Capitalism in Monterrey, Mexico, 1890–1920." PhD diss., Georgetown University, 2014.

Findlay, Ronald, and Kevin O'Rourke. *Power and Plenty: Trade, War, and the World Economy in the Second Millennium.* Princeton, NJ: PUP, 2007.

Fisher, Brodwyn, Brian McCann, and Javier Auyero, eds. *Cities from Scratch: Poverty and Informality in Urban Latin America.* Durham, NC: DUP, 2014.

Fitting, Elizabeth. *The Struggle for Maize: Campesinos, Workers, and Transgenic Corn in the Mexican Countryside.* Durham, NC: DUP, 2011.

Florescano, Enrique, ed. *Análisis histórico de las sequías en México.* Mexico City: Comisión Nacional del Plan Hidraúlico, 1980.

———. *Etnia, estado y nación: Ensayo sobre las identidades colectivas en México.* Mexico City: Taurus, 1997.

———. *Los origines del poder en Mesoamérica.* Mexico City: FCE, 2009.

———. *Precios del maíz y crisis agrícolas en México, 1708–1810.* Mexico City: CMEX, 1969.

Flynn, Dennis, and Arturo Giráldez. "Born with a 'Silver Spoon': The Origins of World Trade in 1571." *Journal of World History* 6, no. 2 (1995): 201–21.

———. "Cycles of Silver: Global Economic Unity through the Mid-Eighteenth Century." *Journal of World History* 13, no. 2 (2002): 391–427.

Fowler-Salamini, Heather. *Working Women, Entrepreneurs, and the Mexican Revolution: The Coffee Culture of Córdoba, Veracruz.* Lincoln: UNP, 2013.

Francois, Marie Ellen. *A Culture of Everyday Credit: Pawnbroking and Governance in Mexico City, 1750–1920.* Lincoln: UNP, 2006.

Frank, Andre Gunder. *ReOrient: Global History in the Asian Age.* Berkeley: UCP, 1998.

Frank, Ross. *From Settler to Citizen: New Mexican Economic Development and the Creation of Vecino Society, 1750–1820.* Berkeley: UCP, 2000.

Fraser, Donald. "La política de desamortización en las comunidades indígenas, 1856–1872." *HM* 21, no. 4 (1972): 618–27.

Friedlander, Judith. *Being Indian in Hueyapan: A Study of Forced Identity in Contemporary Mexico.* New York: St. Martin's, 1975.

Friedrich, Paul. *Agrarian Revolt in a Mexican Village.* Chicago: University of Chicago Press, 1977.

———. *The Princes of Naranja.* Austin: UTP, 1987.

Fulwider, Benjamin. "Driving the Nation: Road Transportation and the Post-Revolutionary Mexican State." PhD diss., Georgetown University, 2009.

García Castro, René. *Indios, territorio y poder en la provincia matlazinca.* Zinacatepec, Mexico: CNSE, 1999.

García de León, Antonio. *Resistencia y utopia: Memorial de agravios y crónica de revueltas y profecías acaecidos en la provincia de Chiapas durante los últimos quinientos años de su historia.* Mexico City: Ediciones Era, 1985.

———. *Tierra adentro, mar en fuera: El Puerto de Veracruz y su litoral a sotovento, 1519–1821.* Mexico City: FCE, 2011.

García Ugarte, Marta Eugenia. *Hacendados y rancheros queretanos, 1780–1920.* Mexico City: Conaculta, 1992.

Garner, Paul. *British Lions and Mexican Eagles: Business, Politics, and Empire in the Career of Weetman Pearson in Mexico, 1889–1919.* Stanford, CA: SUP, 2011.

Garrido, Luis Javier. *El partido de la revolución institucionalizada: La formación del nuevo estado en México, 1928–1945.* Mexico City: Siglo XXI, 1986.

Garza, Gustavo. *El proceso de industrialización en la Ciudad de México.* Mexico City: FCE, 1985.

Gauss, Susan. *Made in Mexico: Regions, Nation, and the State in the Rise of Mexican Industrialism.* University Park: Penn State Press, 2011.

Gereffi, Gary. *The Pharmaceutical Industry and Dependency in the Third World.* Princeton, NJ: PUP, 1983.

Gibson, Charles. *The Aztecs under Spanish Rule: A History of the Indians of the Valley of Mexico, 1519–1810.* Stanford, CA: SUP, 1964.

Gilly, Adolfo. *El Cardenismo: Una utopía Mexicana.* Mexico City: Cal y Arena, 1994.

Gilly, Adolfo, and Rhina Roux. *El tiempo del despojo: Siete ensayos sobre el cambio de época.* Mexico City: Editorial Itaca, 2015.

Giraldez, Arturo. *The Age of Trade: The Manila Galleons and the Dawn of the Global Economy.* Lanham, MD: Rowman and Littlefield, 2015.

Goldstone, Jack. *Revolution and Rebellion in the Early Modern World.* Berkeley: UCP, 1993.

Gómez Galvarriato, Aurora. *Industry and Revolution: Social and Economic Change in the Orizaba Valley, Veracruz.* Cambridge, MA: Harvard University Press, 2013.

González Marín, Silvia. "Chapingo." In Semo, *Siete ensayos,* 19–39.

González Montes, Soledad. "Trabajo femenino y expansión de las relaciones capitalistas en el México rural durante el Porfiriato: El distrito de Tenango del Valle, Estado de México, 1900–1910." In Miño Grijalva, *Haciendas, pueblos y comunidades,* 270–99.

González Montes, Soledad, and Pilar Iracheta Cenegorta. "La violencia en la vida de las mujeres campesinas: El distrito de Tenango, 1830–1910." In Ramos Escandón, *Presencia y transparencia,* 111–42.

González Montes, Soledad, and Alejandro Patiño, eds. *Memoria campesina: La historia de Xalatlaco contada por su gente.* Toluca, Mexico: Instituto Mexiquense de Cultura, 1994. Cited: MCX.

González Navarro, Moises. *Anatomía del poder en México, 1848–1854.* Mexico City: CMEX, 1977.

González Reyna, Jenaro. *Riqueza minera y yacimientos minerales de México.* Mexico City: El Banco de México, 1947.

González y González, Luis. *Los días del presidente Cárdenas*. Mexico City: FCE, 1981.

———. *El indio en la era liberal: El hombre y la tierra, el subsuelo indígena, la escala social*. Mexico City: Editorial Clío, 1996.

———. *San José de Gracia: Mexican Village in Transition*. Translated by John Upton. Austin: UTP, 1982.

Granados, Luis Fernando. *En el espejo haitiano: Los indios del Bajío y el colapso del orden colonial en América Latina*. Mexico City: Ediciones Era, 2016.

———. *Sueñan las piedras: Alzamiento ocurrido en la Ciudad de México, 14, 15, 16 de septiembre 1847*. Mexico City: Ediciones Era, 2003.

Grosso, Juan Carlos, and Juan Carlos Garavaglia. *La región de Puebla en la economía novohispana*. Mexico City: Instituto Mora, 1996.

Gruzinski, Serge. *Man-Gods in the Mexican Highlands: Indian Power in Colonial Society, 1520–1800*. Translated by Eileen Corrigan. Stanford, CA: SUP, 1989.

Guardino, Peter. *In the Time of Liberty: Popular Political Culture in Oaxaca, 1750–1850*. Durham, NC: DUP, 2005.

———. *Peasants, Politics, and the Formation of Mexico's National State, 1800–1857*. Stanford, CA: SUP, 1997.

Guarisco, Claudia. *Los indios del Valle de México y la construcción de una nueva sociabilidad política, 1770–1835*. Zinacatepec, Mexico: CNSE, 2003.

Guedea, Virginia. *La insurgencia en el Departamento del Norte*. Mexico City: UNAM, 1996.

Guerra, Francois-Xavier. *México: Del antiguo régimen a la revolución*. 2 vols. Mexico City: FCE, 1988.

———. *Modernidades e independencias: Ensayos sobre las revoluciones hispánicas*. Mexico City: FCE, 2001.

Guevara Sanginés, María. *Guanajuato diverso: Sabores y sinsabores de su ser mestizo*. Guanajuato, Mexico: Ediciones la Rana, 2001.

Gutmann, Matthew. *The Meanings of Macho: Being a Man in Mexico City*. Berkeley: UCP, 1996.

———. *The Romance of Democracy: Compliant Defiance in Contemporary Mexico*. Berkeley: UCP, 2002.

Haber, Stephen. *Industry and Underdevelopment: The Industrialization of Mexico, 1890–1940*. Stanford, CA: SUP, 1995.

Haber, Stephen, Herbert Klein, Noel Maurer, and Kevin Middlebrook. *Mexico since 1980*. New York: CUP, 2008.

Haber, Stephen, Armando Razo, and Noel Maurer. *The Politics of Property Rights: Political Instability, Credible Commitments, and Economic Growth in Mexico, 1876–1929*. New York: CUP, 2003.

Hadley, Philip. *Minería y sociedad en el centro minero de Santa Eulalia, Chihuahua, 1709–1750*. Mexico City: FCE, 1979.

Hale, Charles. *Mexican Liberalism in the Age of Mora, 1821–1853*. New Haven, CT: Yale University Press, 1968.

———. *The Transformation of Liberalism in Late Nineteenth-Century Mexico*. Princeton, NJ: PUP, 1986.

Hall, Linda. *Álvaro Obregón: Power and Revolution in Mexico*. College Station: Texas A&M University Press, 1981.

———. *Oil, Banks, and Politics: The United States and Postrevolutionary Mexico, 1917–1924.* Austin: UTP, 1995.

Hämäläinen, Pekka. *The Comanche Empire.* New Haven, CT: Yale University Press, 2008.

Hamill, Hugh. *The Hidalgo Revolt: Prelude to Mexican Independence.* Gainesville: University of Florida Press, 1966.

Hamilton, Nora. *The Limits of State Autonomy: Post-Revolutionary Mexico.* Princeton, NJ: PUP, 1982.

Hamnett, Brian. *Roots of Insurgency: Mexican Regions, 1750–1824.* Cambridge: CUP, 1986.

Hart, John. *Anarchism and the Mexican Working Class, 1860–1931.* Austin: UTP, 1978.

———. *Revolutionary Mexico: The Coming and Process of the Mexican Revolution.* Berkeley: UCP, 1987.

Hart, Paul. *Bitter Harvest: The Social Transformation of Morelos, Mexico, and the Coming of the Zapatista Revolution.* Albuquerque: UNM, 2007.

Haskett, Robert. *Indigenous Rulers: An Ethnohistory of Town Government in Colonial Cuernavaca.* Albuquerque: UNM, 1991.

———. "Our Suffering with the Taxco Tribute: Involuntary Mine Labor and Indigenous Society in Central New Spain." HAHR 71, no. 3 (1991): 447–75.

———. *Visions of Paradise: Primordial Titles and Mesoamerican History in Cuernavaca.* Norman: UOP, 2005.

Hassig, Ross. *Trade, Tribute, and Transportation: The Sixteenth-Century Political Economy of Mexico.* Norman: UOP, 1985.

———. *War and Society in Ancient Mesoamerica.* Berkeley: UCP, 1992.

Hemming, John. *The Conquest of the Incas.* London: Macmillan, 1970.

Hernández Jaimes, Jesús. *La formación de la hacienda pública mexicana y las tensiones centro-periferia.* Mexico City: CMEX, 2013.

Herr, Richard. *Rural Change and Royal Finances in Spain at the End of the Old Regime.* Berkeley: UCP, 1989.

Herrrera Bautista, Martha Rebeca, and Patricia Molinar Palma. *En el silencio de su soledad: La reproducción de la violencia intrafamiliar.* Mexico City: Juan Pablos, 2006.

Herrero Bervera, Carlos. *Revuelta, rebelíon y revolución en 1810: Historia social y estudios de caso.* Mexico City: Miguel Ángel Porrúa, 2010.

Hewitt de Alcántara, Cynthia. *Modernizing Mexican Agriculture: Socioeconomic Implications of Technical Change.* Geneva: UN Research Institute for Social Development, 1976.

Hiernaux, Daniel. "La expansión metropolitana y las estructuras regionales: El Valle de Chalco en la actualidad." In Tortolero Villaseñor, *Entre lagos y volcanes,* vol. 1, 575–600.

Hiernaux, Daniel, Alicia Lindón Villoria, and Jaime Noyola Rocha, eds. *La construcción social de un territorio emergente: El Valle de Chalco.* Zinacatepec, Mexico: CNSE, 2000.

Himmerich y Valencia, Robert. *The Encomenderos of New Spain, 1521–1555.* Austin: UTP, 1996.

Hoberman, Louisa. *Mexico's Merchant Elites: Silver, State, and Society, 1590–1660.* Durham, NC: DUP, 1991.

Hobsbawm, Eric. *Industry and Empire: The Birth of the Industrial Revolution*. Rev. ed. New York: New Press, 1999.

Horn, Rebecca. *Postconquest Coyoacán: Nahua-Spanish Relations in Central Mexico, 1519–1650*. Stanford, CA: SUP, 1997.

Hu-Dehart, Evelyn. *Yaqui Resistance and Survival: The Struggle for Land and Autonomy, 1821–1920*. Madison: University of Wisconsin Press, 1984.

Huerta González, Rodolfo. "Agua, bosques y capitalismo: La región de Chalco, 1890–1940." In Hiernaux, Villoria, and Noyola Rocha, *Construcción social*, 65–85.

Hughes, Jennifer Scheper. *Biography of a Mexican Crucifix: Lived Religion and Local Faith from the Conquest to the Present*. New York: Oxford University Press, 2010.

Huitrón, Antonio. *Bienes comunales en el Estado de México*. Toluca: Gobierno del Estado de Mexico, 1972.

Humboldt, Alejandro de. *Ensayo político sobre el reino de Nueva España*. Mexico City: Editorial Porrúa, 1966.

Illades, Carlos. *Hacia la república del trabajo: La organización artesanal en la Ciudad de México, 1853–1876*. Mexico City: CMEX, 1996.

Instituto Nacional de Estadística y Geografía. Diverse tables. Accessed November 7, 2016. http://www3.inegi.org.mx.

Islas Jiménez, Celia. *El real de Tlalpujahua: Aspectos de la minería novohispana*. Mexico City, INAH, 2008.

Israel, Jonathon I. *Race, Class, and Politics in Colonial Mexico, 1610–1670*. Oxford: Oxford University Press, 1975.

Jacobsen, Nils. *Mirages of Transition: The Peruvian Altiplano, 1780–1930*. Berkeley: UCP, 1993.

Jalpa Flores, Tomás. *La sociedad indígena en la región de Chalco durante los siglos VVI y XVII*. Mexico City: INAH, 2009.

———. *Tierra y sociedad: La apropiación del suelo en la región de Chalco durante los siglos XV a XVII*. Mexico City: INAH, 2008.

Jarquín Ortega, María Teresa, and Manuel Miño Grijalva, eds. *Historia general ilustrada del Estado de México*. Vol. 3. Zinacatepec, Mexico: CNSE, 2011.

J. G. "Industria nacional: Su defensa contra los ataques que ha recibido." In *Diario del Gobierno*, no. 3644, June 10, 1845. Mexico City: Imprenta del Águila, 1845. Reprinted in *Documentos para el estudio*, 414–28. Cited: JG.

Joseph, Gilbert. *Revolution from Without: Yucatán, Mexico, and the United States, 1880–1924*. Stanford, CA: SUP, 1982.

Kamen, Henry. *Empire: How Spain Became a World Power, 1492–1763*. New York: Harper Collins, 2003.

Kanter, Deborah. *Hijos del Pueblo: Gender, Family, and Community in Rural Mexico, 1730–1850*. Austin: UTP, 2010.

Katz, Friedrich. *The Life and Times of Pancho Villa*. Stanford, CA: SUP, 1998.

———, ed. *Riot, Rebellion, and Revolution: Rural Social Conflict in Mexico*. Princeton, NJ: PUP, 1988.

———. "Rural Uprisings in Pre-conquest and Colonial Mexico." In Katz, *Riot, Rebellion, and Revolution*, 65–94.

———. *The Secret War in Mexico: Europe, the United States, and the Mexican Revolution*. Chicago: University of Chicago Press, 1981.

Knight, Alan. *The Mexican Revolution.* 2 vols. Cambridge: CUP, 1986.

Konrad, Herman. *Santa Lucía: A Jesuit Hacienda in Colonial Mexico, 1576–1767.* Stanford, CA: SUP, 1980.

Kourí, Emilio. *A Pueblo Divided: Business, Property, and Community in Papantla, Veracruz.* Stanford, CA: SUP, 2003.

La Botz, Dan. *Mask of Democracy: Labor Suppression in Mexico Today.* Boston: South End, 1999.

Lack, Randolph. *The Texas Revolutionary Experience: A Political and Social History, 1835–1836.* College Station: Texas A&M University Press, 1992.

Ladd, Doris. *The Making of a Strike: Mexican Silver Workers' Struggles in Real del Monte, 1762–1775.* Lincoln: UNP, 1985.

Landes, David. *The Unbound Prometheus: Technological Change and Industrial Development in Western Europe from 1750 to the Present.* Cambridge: CUP, 1969.

Langue, Frederique. *Los señores de Zacatecas: Una aristocracia minera del siglo XVIII novohispano.* Mexico City: FCE, 1979.

Lara Cisneros, Gerardo. *¿Ignorancia invencible? Superstición e idolatría ante el Provisorato de Indios y Chinos del Arzobispado de México en el siglo XVIII.* Mexico City: UNAM, 2015.

Lear, John. *Workers, Neighbors, and Citizens: The Revolution in Mexico City.* Lincoln: UNP, 2001.

Lemoine, Ernesto. *Morelos y la revolución de 1810.* Mexico City: UNAM, 1979.

Lempérière, Annick. *Entre Dios y el rey, la república: La Ciudad de México de los siglos XVI al XIX.* Translated by Ivette Hernández Pérez Vertíz. Mexico City: FCE, 2013.

Lerdo de Tejada, Miguel. *Memoria de la Secretaría de Hacienda . . . México, 1857.* Mexico City, 1957.

LeRoy Ladurie, Emmanuel. *The Peasants of Languedoc.* Translated by John Day. Urbana: University of Illinois Press, 1974.

Lewis, Oscar. *The Children of Sánchez: Autobiography of a Mexican Family.* New York: Knopf, 1961. Cited: CSL.

———. *Life in a Mexican Village: Tepoztlán Restudied.* Urbana: University of Illinois Press, 1951.

———. *Pedro Martínez: A Mexican Peasant and His Family.* New York: Random House, 1964. Cited: PML.

Lida, David. *First Stop in the New World: Mexico City, Capital of the 21st Century.* New York: Riverbend Books, 2008.

Lin, Man-Huang. *China Upside Down: Currency, Society, and Ideology, 1808–1850.* Cambridge, MA: Harvard University Press, 2006.

Lindón Villoria, Alicia. *De la trama de la cotidianidad a los modos de vida urbanos: El Valle de Chalco.* Mexico City: CMEX, 1999.

Lipsett-Rivera, Sonya. *Gender and the Negotiation of Daily Life in Mexico, 1750–1856.* Lincoln: UNP, 2012.

Lockhart, James. *The Men of Cajamarca.* Austin: UTP, 1972.

———. *The Nahuas after the Conquest.* Stanford, CA: SUP, 1992.

———. *Nahuas and Spaniards: Post-Conquest Central Mexico in History and Philology.* Stanford, CA: SUP, 1991.

———. *Spanish Peru, 1532–1562.* Madison: University of Wisconsin Press, 1968.

Lockhart, James, and Enrique Otte, eds. *Letters and People of the Spanish Indies: Sixteenth Century*. Cambridge: CUP, 1976.

Lomnitz-Adler, Claudio. *Exits from the Labyrinth: Culture and Ideology in the Mexican National Space*. Berkeley: UCP, 1992.

López-Alonso, Moramay. *Measuring Up: A History of Living Standards in Mexico, 1850–1950*. Stanford, CA: SUP, 2012.

López Austin, Alfredo, and Leopoldo López Luján. *Mexico's Indigenous Past*. Translated by Bernardo Ortíz de Montellano. Norman: UOP, 2005.

López Escudero, Manuel. Papers. Folder 88, files 1–7. García Collection, Benson Latin American Collection, University of Texas at Austin. Cited: MLE.

Loyola, Rafael, ed. *Entre la guerra y la estabilidad política: México en los 40*. Mexico City: Editorial Grijalbo, 1990.

Lynch, John. *Spain under the Hapsburgs*. Vol. 2, *Spain and America, 1598–1700*. London: Blackwells, 1969.

MacLeod, Murdo. *Spanish Central America: A Socioeconomic History, 1520–1720*. Berkeley, UCP, 1973.

Mallon, Florencia. *Peasant and Nation: The Making of Post-Colonial Mexico and Peru*. Berkeley: UCP, 1995.

Mangan, Jane. *Trading Roles: Gender, Ethnicity, and the Urban Economy of Colonial Potosí*. Durham, NC: DUP, 2005.

Markiewicz, Dana. *The Mexican Revolution and the Limits of Agrarian Reform, 1915–1940*. Boulder: Lynne Reinner, 1993.

Martin, Cheryl. *Rural Society in Colonial Morelos*. Albuquerque: UNM, 1985.

Martínez, Rubén. *Crossing Over: A Mexican Family on the Migrant Trail*. New York: Picador, 2001.

Martínez Baracs, Andrea. *Un gobierno de indios: Tlaxcala, 1519–1750*. Mexico City: FCE, 2008.

Martínez Baracs, Rodrigo. *Convivencia y utopía: El gobierno indio y español en "la ciudad de Mechuacán," 1521–1580*. Mexico City: FCE, 2005.

McCormick, Gladys. *The Logic of Compromise in Mexico: How the Countryside Was Key to the Emergence of Authoritarianism*. Chapel Hill: UNC, 2016.

McNeill, John R., and Peter Engelke. *The Great Acceleration: An Environmental History of the Anthropocene since 1945*. Cambridge, MA: Harvard University Press, 2014.

McNeill, William. *Plagues and Peoples*. New York: Doubleday, 1976.

Medina, Luis. *Hacia el nuevo estado*. Mexico City: FCE, 1995.

Melville, Elinor. *A Plague of Sheep: Environmental Consequences of the Conquest of Mexico*. New York: CUP, 1994.

Memoria de la administración pública del Estado de México presentada a la XV Legislatura por el Gobernador Constitucional general José Vicente Villada, cuatrenio de 1889–1893. Toluca, Mexico: Imprenta de la Escuela de Artes y Oficios, 1894.

Menegus Bornemann, Margarita. *Del señorío a la república de indios: El caso de Toluca, 1500–1600*. Madrid: Ministerio de Agricultura, Pesca y Alimentos, 1991.

———. "Ocoyoacac: Una comunidad agraria en el siglo XIX." *Estudios Políticos* 6, no. 18–19 (1979): 81–112.

———. "La organización económica-espacial del trabajo indígena en el Valle de Toluca, 1530–1830." In Miño Grijalva, *Haciendas, pueblos y comunidades*, 21–59.

Meyer, Jean. *La cristiada*. 3 vols. Mexico City: Siglo XXI, 1973.

Meyer, Lorenzo. *México y los Estados Unidos en al conflicto petrolero, 1917–1942*. Mexico City: FCE, 1972.

Meyer, Michael. *Huerta: A Political Portrait*. Lincoln: UNP, 1972.

Meyers, William. *Forge of Progress, Crucible of Revolt: The Origins of the Mexican Revolution in the Comarca Lagunera, 1880–1911*. Albuquerque: UNM, 1994.

Middlebrook, Kevin. *The Paradox of Revolution: Labor, the State, and Authoritarianism in Mexico*. Baltimore: JHU, 1995.

Miller, Simon. *Landlords and Haciendas in Modernizing Mexico*. Amsterdam: Centro de Estudios y Documentación Latinoamericanos, University of Amsterdam, 1995.

Millon, René; Bruce Drewitt, and George Cowgill. *Urbanization at Teotihuacán*. 2 vols. Austin: UTP, 1975.

Ministerio de Fomento. *Anales del Ministerio de Fomento: Industria agrícola, minera, fabril, manufacturera y comercial, y estadística general de la República Mexicana*. Mexico: Imprenta de Escalante, 1854.

Miño Grijalva, Manuel. *Haciendas, pueblos y comunidades: Los Valles de México y Toluca entre 1530 y 1910*. Mexico City: Conaculta, 1991.

Miranda, José. *La función económica del encomendero en los origines del regimén colonial: Nueva España, 1521–1531*. Mexico City: UNAM, 1965.

Miranda Pacheco, Sergio. *La creación del Departamento del Distrito Federal: Urbanización, política y cambio institucional*. Mexico City: UNAM, 2008.

———. *Tacubaya: De suburbio veraniego a ciudad*. Mexico City: UNAM, 2007.

Molina del Villar, América. *Diversidad socioétnica y familias entre las calamidades y crisis del Siglo XVIII*. Mexico City: CIESAS, 2009.

———. *La Nueva España y el matlazáhuatl*. Zamora, Mexico: CMCH, 1998.

———. "Santa María de Guadalupe, Atlacomulco, ante los aciados años de principios del siglo XIX: Conflictos locales, crisis agrícolas y epidemia, 1809–1814." *Relaciones* 31, no. 121 (2010): 109–36.

Moore, Barrington, Jr. *Social Origins of Dictatorship and Democracy: Lord and Peasant in the Making of the Modern World*. Boston: Beacon, 1966.

Mumford, Jeremy. *Vertical Empire: The General Resettlement of Indians in the Colonial Andes*. Durham, NC: DUP, 2012.

Mundy, Barbara. *The Death of Aztec Tenochtitlan, the Life of Mexico City*. Austin: University of Texas Press, 2015.

North, Douglass, John Joseph Wallis, and Barry Weingast. *Violence and Social Orders: A Conceptual Framework for Interpreting Recorded Human History*. Cambridge: CUP, 2009.

Olvera Estrada, María Otilia. *Los tiempos del patrón . . . Danza de mil soles: Los últimos trabajadores de las haciendas en Querétaro*. Querétaro, Mexico: Gobierno del Estado, 1997.

Ortega Soto, Marta. *Alta California: Una frontera olvidada del noroeste de México, 1769–1848*. Mexico City: Universidad Autónoma Metropolitana, 2001.

Ortíz, Tadeo. *México considerado como nación independiente y libre*. Bordeaux: Imprenta de Carlos LaWalle Sobrinos, 1933. Reprint, Mexico City: Miguel Ángel Porrúa, 2010. Cited: TOM.

Ortiz Escamilla, Juan. *Guerra y gobierno: Los pueblos y la independencia de México*. Seville: Universidad de Sevilla, 1997.

Osborn, Wayne. "Indian Land Retention in Colonial Meztitlán." HAHR 53, no. 2 (1973): 217–38.

Owensby, Brian. *Empire of Law and Indian Justice in Colonial Mexico*. Stanford, CA: SUP, 2008.

Pacheco Gómez Muñoz, María Edith. *Ciudad de México, heterogéneo y desigual: Un estudio sobre el mercado de trabajo*. Mexico City: CMEX, 2004.

Padden, Robert C. *The Hummingbird and the Hawk: Conquest and Sovereignty in the Valley of Mexico, 1503–1541*. New York: Harper and Row, 1970.

Padilla, Tanalís. *Rural Resistance in the Land of Zapata: The Jaramillista Movement and the Myth of the Pax Priista, 1940–1960*. Durham, NC: DUP, 2008.

Paige, Jeffrey. *Agrarian Revolution*. New York: Free Press, 1976.

———. *Coffee and Power: Revolution and the Rise of Democracy in Central America*. Cambridge, MA: Harvard University Press, 1977.

Palerm, Ángel. *Obras hidráulicas prehispánicas en el Valle de México*. Mexico City: INAH, 1973.

Palma Galván, Fernando. *La participación social en la planeación del desarrollo urbano: Caso Nezahualcóyotl, Estado de México*. Mexico City: UNAM, 2007.

Pani, Erika. *Para mexicanizar el segundo imperio*. Mexico City: CMEX, 2001.

———. *Una serie de admirables acontecimientos: México en el mundo en la época de la Reforma*. Mexico City: Ediciones Educación y Cultura, 2013.

Parcero, María de la Luz. *Condiciones de la mujer en México durante el siglo XIX*. Mexico City: INAH, 1992.

Parthasarathi, Pranasan. *How Europe Grew Rich and Asia Did Not: Global Economic Divergence, 1600–1850*. Cambridge: CUP, 2011.

Pastor, María Alba. *Crisis y recomposición social: Nueva España en el tránsito del siglo XVI al XVII*. Mexico City: FCE, 1999.

———. *Cuerpos sociales, cuerpos sacrificiales*. Mexico City: FCE, 2004.

Pastor, Rodolfo. *Campesinos y reformas: La mixteca, 1700–1856*. Mexico City: CMEX, 1987.

Payno, Manuel. *Los bandidos de Río Frío*. Mexico City: Editorial Porrúa, 1971. Cited: BRF.

Paz, Octavio. *Sor Juana, or the Traps of Faith*. Translated by Margaret Sayer Peden. Cambridge, MA: Harvard University Press, 1990.

Pedrero Nieto, Gloria. "Un estudio regional: Chalco." In Semo, *Siete ensayos*, 99–150.

Peña, Devon. *The Terror of the Machine: Technology, Work, Gender, and Ecology on the U.S.-Mexico Border*. Austin: UTP, 1997.

Pensado, Jaime. *Rebel Mexico: Student Unrest and Authoritarian Political Culture during the Long Sixties*. Stanford, CA: SUP, 2013.

Pérez Montesinos, Fernando. "Poised to Break: Liberalism, Land Reform, and Communities in the Purépecha Highlands of Michoacán, México, 1800–1915." PhD diss., Georgetown University, 2015.

Pérez Rosales, Laura. *Minería y sociedad en Taxco en el siglo XVIII*. Mexico City: Universidad Iberomericana, 1990.

Pezzoli, Keith. *Human Settlements and Planning for Environmental Sustainability: The Case of Mexico City*. Cambridge, MA: MIT Press, 1998.

Piccato, Pablo. *City of Suspects: Crime in Mexico City, 1900–1931*. Durham, NC: DUP, 2001.

Picketty, Thomas. *Capital in the Twenty-First Century*. Translated by Arthur Goldhammer. Cambridge, MA: Harvard University Press, 2014.

Pimentel, Francisco. *Memoria sobre las causas que han originado la situación actual de la raza indígena de México*. Mexico City: Imprenta de Andrade y Escalante, 1864.

Pineda Gómez, Francisco. *Ejército libertador, 1915*. Mexico City: Ediciones Era, 2013.

———. *La irrupción Zapatista*. Mexico City: Ediciones Era, 1997.

———. *La revolución del sur, 1912–1914*. Mexico City: Ediciones Era, 2005.

Pizzigoni, Catarina. *The Life Within: Local Indigenous Society in Mexico's Toluca Valley 1650–1800*. Stanford, CA: SUP, 2012.

Pletcher, David. *Rails, Mines, and Progress: Seven American Promoters in Mexico, 1867–1911*. Ithaca, NY: Cornell University Press, 1958.

Pomeranz, Kenneth. *The Great Divergence: China, Europe, and the Making of the Modern World Economy*. Princeton, NJ: PUP, 2000.

Poole, Stafford. *Our Lady of Guadalupe: The Origins and Sources of a Mexican National Symbol*. Tucson: University of Arizona Press, 1995.

Porter, Susie. *Working Women in Mexico City: Public Discourses and Material Conditions, 1879–1931*. Tucson: University of Arizona Press, 2003.

Potash, Robert. *El Banco de Avío de México: El fomento de la industria, 1821–1846*. Mexico City: FCE, 1959.

Powell, Thomas G. *El liberalismo y el campesinado en el centro de México, 1850–1870*. Mexico City: Secretaría de Educación Pública, 1974.

Prasad, Monica. *The Land of Too Much: American Abundance and the Paradox of Poverty*. Cambridge, MA: Harvard University Press, 2012.

Presthold, Jeremy. *Domesticating the World: African Consumerism and the Genealogies of Globalization*. Berkeley: UCP, 2008.

Purnell, Jennie. *Popular Movements and State Formation in Revolutionary Mexico*. Durham, NC: DUP, 1999.

Quirk, Robert. *An Affair of Honor: Woodrow Wilson and the Occupation of Veracruz*. New York: Norton, 1967.

———. *The Mexican Revolution, 1914–1915: The Convention of Aguascalientes*. Bloomington: Indiana University Press, 1960.

Rabell Romero, Cecilia, ed. *Los mexicanos: Un balance del cambio demográfico*. Mexico City: FCE, 2014.

Ramírez Melgarejo, Ramón. *La política del estado mexicano y los procesos agrícolas de los Totonacos*. Xalapa, Mexico: Universidad Veracruzana, 2002.

Ramos Escandón, Carmen. *Industrialización, género y trabajo femenino en el sector textíl mexicano*. Mexico: CIESAS, 2004.

———, ed. *Presencia y transparencia: La mujer en la historia de México*. Mexico City: CMEX, 1987.

Rath, Thomas. *Myths of Demilitarization in Postrevolutionary Mexico, 1920–1960*. Chapel Hill: UNC, 2013.

Reed, John. *Insurgent Mexico*. New York: International, 1969.

Regla, Condes de. Papers. Washington State University Library. Cited PCR; PCRb: bound volumes; PCRun: uncataloged items.

Reina, Leticia. "Local Elections and Regime Crises: The Political Culture of Indigenous Peoples." In Servín, Reina, and Tutino, *Cycles of Conflict*, 91–127.

———. *Rebeliones campesinas en México, 1819–1906*. Mexico City: Siglo XXI, 1980.

Reyes García, Cayetano. "Estado general de tributos y tributarios, 1805." *Boletín del Archivo General de la Nación*, 3rd series, 1, no. 3 (1977): 3–43.

Ricard, Robert. *The Spiritual Conquest of Mexico*. Translated by Lesley Byrd Simpson. Berkeley: UCP, 1966.

Richmond, Douglas. *Venustiano Carranza's Nationalist Struggle*. Lincoln: UNP, 1983.

Riley, G. Michael. *Fernando Cortés and the Marquesado in Morelos, 1522–1547*. Albuquerque: UNM, 1973.

Riley, James. *Hacendados jesuítas en México: La administración de los bienes inmuebles del Colegio Máximo de San Pedro y San Pablo de la Ciudad de México, 1687–1767*. Mexico City: Secretaría de Educación Pública, 1976.

Riva Palacio, Mariano. Papers. García Collection, Benson Latin American Collection, University of Texas at Austin. Indexed in Dabbs, *Mariano Riva Palacio Archive*. Cited: MRP.

Rodríguez, Jaime. *"We Are Now the True Spaniards": Sovereignty, Revolution, Independence, and the Emergence of the Federal Republic of Mexico, 1808–1824*. Stanford, CA: SUP, 2012.

Rodríguez Kuri, Ariel. *La experiencia olvidada: El Ayuntamiento de México, política y gobierno, 1876–1912*. Mexico City: CMEX, 1996.

Rojas, Olga Lorena. *Paternidad y vida familiar en la Ciudad de México*. Mexico City: CMEX, 2008.

Romanucci-Ross, Lola. *Conflict, Violence, and Morality in a Mexican Village*. Rev. ed. Chicago: University of Chicago Press, 1986.

———. "Filomena's History." In *Conflict, Violence, and Morality*, 209–13.

Romero Ibarra, María Eugenia. *Manuel Medina Garduño: Entre el porfiriato y la revolución en el Estado de México, 1852–1913*. Mexico City: Instituto Nacional de Estudios Históricos de la Revolución Mexicana, 1998.

Romero Sotelo, María Eugenia. *Minería y guerra: La economía de Nueva España, 1810–1821*. Mexico City: CMEX, 1997.

Rugeley, Terry. *Yucatán's Maya Peasantry and the Origins of the Caste War*. Austin: UTP, 1996.

Ruíz, Ramón Eduardo. *La revolución mexicana y el movimiento obrero, 1911–1923*. Mexico City: Ediciones Era, 1978.

Ruíz de Alarcón, Hernando. *Treatise on the Heathen Institutions that Live Today among the Indians Native to This New Spain*. Translated and edited by Richard Andrews and Ross Hassig. Norman: UOP, 1984.

Ruíz Medrano, Ethelia. *Mexico's Indigenous Communities: Their Lands and Histories, 1500–2010*. Translated by Russ Davidson. Boulder: University Press of Colorado, 2010.

———. *Reshaping New Spain: Government and Private Interest in the Colonial Bureaucracy, 1535–1550*. Translated by Julia Constantino and Paulette Marmasse. Boulder: University Press of Colorado, 2006.

Salinas Sandoval, Carmen, and Diana Birrichaga Garrida. "Conflicto y aceptación ante el liberalismo: Los pueblos del Estado de México, 1856–1876." In Escobar Ohmstede, *Pueblos indios*, 207–51.

Salinas Sandoval, María del Carmen. *Política y sociedad en los municípios del Estado de México, 1825–1855*. Zinacatepec, Mexico: CNSE, 1996.

Salmerón, Pedro. *La División del norte: Los hombres, las razones y la historia de un ejército del pueblo*. Mexico City: Editorial Planeta, 2006.

Sánchez de Tagle, Estéban. *Del gobierno y su tutela: La reforma a las haciendas locales del siglo XVIII y el Cabildo de México*. Mexico City: INAH, 2014.

Sánchez Santiró, Ernest. *Las alcabalas mexicanas, 1821–1857: Las dilemas en la construcción de la Hacienda nacional*. Mexico City: Instituto Mora, 2009.

Sanders, William, and Barbara Price. *Mesoamerica: The Evolution of a Civilization*. New York: Random House, 1968.

Santiago, Myrna. *The Ecology of Oil: Environment, Labor, and the Mexican Revolution, 1900–1938*. New York: CUP, 2006.

Scheper-Hughes, Nancy. *Death Without Weeping: The Violence of Everyday Life in Brazil*. Berkeley: UCP, 1992.

Schroeder, Susan. *Chimalpahin and the Kingdom of Chalco*. Tucson: University of Arizona Press, 1991.

Schwartz, Stuart. *Sugar Plantations and the Formation of Brazilian Society: Bahia, 1550–1835*. New York: CUP, 1985.

Scott, James. *The Art of Not Being Governed: An Anarchist History of Southeast Asia*. New Haven, CT: Yale University Press, 2009.

———. *Domination and the Arts of Resistance*. New Haven, CT: Yale University Press, 1990.

———. *The Moral Economy of the Peasant: Rebellion and Subsistence in Southeast Asia*. New Haven, CT: Yale University Press, 1976.

———. *Seeing Like a State: How Certain Schemes to Improve the Human Condition Have Failed*. New Haven, CT: Yale University Press, 1999.

Semo, Enrique, ed. *Siete ensayos sobre la hacienda mexicana, 1780–1880*. Mexico City: INAH, 1977.

Serrano Ortega, José Antonio, ed. *El sexenio absolutista: Los últimos años insurgentes, Nueva España, 1814–1820*. Zamora, Mexico, CMCH, 2014.

Serulnikov, Sergio. *Revolution in the Andes: The Age of Tupac Amaru*. Translated by David Frye. Durham, NC: DUP, 2013.

———. *Subverting Colonial Authority: Challenges to Spanish Rule in the Eighteenth-Century Southern Andes*. Durham, NC: DUP, 2003.

Servín, Elisa. *Ruptura y oposición: El movimiento henriquista, 1945–1954*. Mexico City: Cal y Arena, 2001.

Servín, Elisa, Leticia Reina, and John Tutino, eds. *Cycles of Conflict, Centuries of Change: Crisis, Reform, and Revolution in Mexico*. Durham, NC: DUP, 2007.

Silva Prada, Natalia. *La política de una rebelión: Los indígenas frente al tumulto de 1692 en la Ciudad de México*. Mexico City: CMEX, 2007.

Simpson, Lesley Byrd. *The Encomienda in New Spain*. Rev. ed. Berkeley: UCP, 1950.

Skocpol, Theda. *States and Social Revolutions: A Comparative Analysis of France, Russia, and China*. Cambridge: Cambridge University Press, 1979.

Smith, Benjamin. *The Roots of Conservatism in Mexico: Catholicism, Society, and Politics in the Mixteca Baja, 1750–1962*. Albuquerque: UNM, 2012.

Soto Laveaga, Gabriela. *Jungle Laboratories: Mexican Peasants, National Projects, and the Making of the Pill*. Durham, NC: DUP, 2008.

Sousa, Lisa, Stafford Poole, and James Lockhart, trans. and eds. *The Story of Guadalupe: Luis Laso de Vega's Huei tlamahuiçoltica of 1649*. Stanford, CA: SUP, 1998.

Spalding, Karen. *Huarochirí: An Andean Society under Inca and Spanish Rule*. Stanford, CA: SUP, 1984.

Stavig, Ward. *The World of Tupac Amaru*. Lincoln: UNP, 1999.

Stein, Barbara, and Stanley Stein. *Crisis in an Atlantic Empire: Spain and New Spain, 1808–1810*. Baltimore: JHU, 2014.

———. *Edge of Crisis: War and Trade in the Spanish Atlantic, 1789–1808.* Baltimore: JHU, 2009.

Stein, Stanley, and Barbara Stein. *Apogee of Empire: Spain and New Spain in the Age of Charles III, 1759–1789.* Baltimore: JHU, 2003.

———. *Silver, War, and Trade: Spain and the Americas in the Making of Early Modern Europe.* Baltimore: JHU, 2000.

Stephen, Lynn. *Zapata Lives: Histories and Cultural Politics in Southern Mexico.* Berkeley: UCP, 2002.

Stern, Steve. *Peru's Indian Peoples and the Challenge of Spanish Conquest.* Madison: University of Wisconsin Press, 1982.

———, ed. *Resistance, Rebellion, and Consciousness in the Andean Peasant World: 17th to 20th Centuries.* Madison: University of Wisconsin Press, 1987.

———. *The Secret History of Gender: Men, Women, and Power in Late Colonial Mexico.* Chapel Hill: UNC, 1995.

Stevens, Donald. " 'Temerse la ira del cielo': Los conservadores y la religiosidad popular en los tiempos del cólera." In William Fowler and Humberto Morales Moreno, eds., *El conservadurismo mexicano en el siglo XIX.* Puebla, Mexico: Benemérita Universidad Autónoma de Puebla, 1999, 87–101.

Strayer, Joseph. *On the Medieval Origins of the Modern State.* Princeton, NJ: PUP, 1970.

Streeby, Shelley. *American Sensations: Class, Empire, and the Production of Popular Culture.* Berkeley: UCP, 2002.

———. "Imagining Mexico in Love and War: Nineteenth-Century U.S. Literature and Visual Culture." In Tutino, *Mexico and Mexicans,* 110–40.

Tavares, David. *The Invisible War: Indigenous Devotions, Discipline, and Dissent in Colonial Mexico.* Stanford, CA: SUP, 2011.

Taylor, William. *Drinking, Homicide, and Rebellion in Colonial Mexican Villages.* Stanford, CA: SUP, 1979.

———. *Magistrates of the Sacred: Priests and Parishioners in Eighteenth-Century Mexico.* Stanford, CA: SUP, 1976.

———. *Shrines and Miraculous Images: Religious Life in Mexico before the Reform.* Albuquerque: UNM, 2010.

Tellez González, Mario. *La justicia criminal en el Valle de Toluca, 1800–1829.* Zinacatepec, Mexico: CNSE, 2001.

Tenorio, Mauricio. *I Speak of the City: Mexico City at the Turn of the Twentieth Century.* Chicago: University of Chicago Press, 2013.

Terraciano, Kevin. *The Mixtecs of Colonial Oaxaca: Ñudzahui History, Sixteenth through Eighteenth Centuries.* Stanford, CA: SUP, 2002.

Thomson, Guy, with David LaFrance. *Patriotism, Politics, and Popular Liberalism in Nineteenth-Century Mexico: Juan Francisco Lucas and the Puebla Sierra.* Wilmington, DE: Scholarly Resources, 1999.

Thomson, Sinclair. *We Alone Will Rule: Native Andean Politics in the Age of Insurgency.* Madison: University of Wisconsin Press, 2003.

Tilly, Charles. *Coercion, Capital, and European States, AD 990–1992.* Oxford: Blackwell, 1992.

Topik, Stephen, and Allen Wells. *Global Markets Transformed, 1870–1945.* Cambridge, MA: Harvard University Press, 2014.

Tortolero Villaseñor, Alejandro. *De la coa a la máquina de vapor: Actividad agrícola e innovación tecnológica en las haciendas mexicanas, 1880-1914.* Mexico City: Siglo XXI, 1995.

——, ed. *Entre lagos y volcanes: Chalco-Amecameca, pasado y presente.* Zinacatepec, Mexico: CNSE, 1993.

——. *Notarios y agricultores: Crecimiento y atraso en el campo mexicano, 1780-1920.* Mexico City: Siglo XXI, 2008.

Trujillo Bolio, Mario. *Operarios fabriles en el Valle de México, 1864-1884.* Mexico City: CMEX, 1997.

Turner, John Kenneth. *Barbarous Mexico.* Chicago: S. H. Kern, 1911.

Tutino, John. "Agrarian Social Change and Peasant Rebellion in Nineteenth-Century Mexico: The Case of Chalco." In Katz, *Riot, Rebellion, and Revolution,* 95-140.

——. "The Americas in the Rise of Industrial Capitalism." In Tutino, *New Countries,* 25-70.

——. "The Americas in the Twentieth-Century World." Chapter 1 in Tutino and Melosi, *New World Cities.*

——. "Creole Mexico: Spanish Elites, Haciendas, and Indian Towns, 1750-1810." PhD diss., University of Texas at Austin, 1976.

——. "De Hidalgo a Apatzingán: Insurgencia popular y proyectos políticos en la Nueva España, 1811-1814." In *La insurgencia mexicana y la Constitución de Apatzingán,* edited by Carolina Ibarra, Marco Antonio Landavazzo, Juan Ortiz Escamilla, José Antonio Serrano, and Marta Terán, 49-78. Mexico City: UNAM, 2014.

——. "Entre la rebelión y la revolución: Compresión agraria en Chalco, 1970-1900." In Tortolero Villaseñor, *Entre lagos y volcanes,* 365-412.

——. "La estructura agraria del Valle de México, 1600-1800." In Jarquín Ortega and Miño Grijalva, *Historia general,* 481-531.

——. "Family Economies in Agrarian Mexico, 1750-1910." *Journal of Family History* 10, no. 3 (1985): 258-71.

——. *From Insurrection to Revolution in Mexico: Social Bases of Agrarian Violence, 1750-1940.* Princeton, NJ: PUP, 1986.

——. "From Involution to Revolution in Mexico: Liberal Development, Patriarchy, and Social Violence in the Central Highlands, 1870-1910." *History Compass* 6, no. 3 (2008): 796-842.

——. "Globalizing the Comanche Empire." *History and Theory* 52, no. 1 (2013): 67-74.

——. "Hacienda Social Relations in Mexico: The Chalco Region in the Era of Independence." HAHR 55, no. 3 (1975): 496-528.

——. *Making a New World: Founding Capitalism in the Bajío and Spanish North America.* Durham, NC: DUP, 2011.

——, ed. *Mexico and Mexicans in the Making of the United States.* Austin: UTP, 2012.

——. *Mexico City, 1808: Power, Sovereignty, and Silver in an Age of War and Revolution.* Albuquerque: UNM, 2018.

——, ed. *New Countries: Capitalism, Revolution, and Nations in the Americas, 1750-1870.* Durham, NC: DUP, 2016.

——. "Power, Class, and Family: Men, Women, and Power in the Mexico City Elite, 1750-1810." *Americas* 39, no. 3 (1983): 359-81.

———. "Provincial Spaniards, Haciendas, and Indian Towns: Interrelated Sectors of Agrarian Society in the Valleys of Mexico and Toluca." In *Provinces of Early Mexico*, edited by Ida Altman and James Lockhart, 177–194. Los Angeles: UCLA Latin American Center, 1976.

———. "Querétaro y los orígenes de la nación mexicana: Las políticas étnicas de soberanía, contrainsurgencia e independencia, 1808–1821." In *México a la luz de sus revoluciones*, edited by Laura Rojas and Susan Deeds. Vol. 1, 17–64. Mexico City: CMEX, 2014.

———. *Remaking the New World: Bajío Revolution, Mexican Independence, and the Transformation of North America, 1800–1860*. Durham, NC: DUP, forthcoming.

———. "The Revolutionary Capacity of Rural Communities." In Servín, Reina, and Tutino, *Cycles of Conflict*, 211–68.

———. "The Revolution in Mexican Independence: Insurgency and the Renegotiation of Property, Production, and Patriarchy in the Bajío, 1800–1855." HAHR 78, no. 3 (1998): 367–418.

———. "Urban Power and Agrarian Society: Mexico City and Its Hinterland in the Colonial Era." In *La ciudad, el campo, y la frontera en la historia de México*, edited by Gisela von Wobeser and Eric Van Young, 507–52. Mexico City: UNAM, 1992.

Tutino, John, and Martin Melosi, eds. *New World Cities: The Challenges of Globalization and Urbanization in the Americas*. Chapel Hill: UNC, 2018.

Vanderwood, Paul. *Disorder and Progress: Bandits, Police, and Mexican Development*. Lincoln: UNP, 1981.

———. *The Power of God Against the Guns of Government: Religious Upheaval in Mexico at the Turn of the Twentieth Century*. Stanford, CA: SUP, 1996.

Van Young, Eric. "Of Tempests and Teapots: Imperial Crisis and Local Conflicts in Mexico at the Beginning of the Nineteenth Century." In Servín, Reina, and Tutino, *Cycles of Conflict*, 23–59.

———. *The Other Rebellion: Popular Violence, Ideology, and the Struggle for Mexican Independence, 1810–1821*. Stanford, CA: SUP, 2001.

Vaughan, Mary Kay. *Cultural Politics in Revolution: Teachers, Peasants, and Schools in Mexico, 1930–1940*. Tucson: University of Arizona Press, 1997.

Vázquez, Josefina. *México al tiempo de su guerra con Estados Unidos*. Mexico City: CMEX, 1997.

Velasco Ávila, Cuauhtémoc, Eduardo Flores Clair, Alma Aurora Palma Campos, and Edgar Omar Gutiérrez López. *Estado y minería en México, 1767–1910*. Mexico City: FCE, 1988.

Velasco Godoy, María de los Ángeles. *Ixtlahuaca: Población y haciendas, pueblos y sistema de trabajo colonial, 1600–1711*, 2 vols. Toluca: Universidad Autónoma del Estado de México, 2012.

Velázquez Gutiérrez, María Elisa. *Mujeres de origen africano en la capital novohispana, siglos XVII y XVIII*. Mexico City: UNAM, 2006.

Vélez Ibáñez, Carlos. *Rituals of Marginality: Politics, Process, and Culture Change in Central Urban Mexico, 1969–1974*. Berkeley: UCP, 1983.

Vilar, Pierre. *A History of Gold and Money, 1450–1920*. Translated by Judith White. London: Verso, 1984.

Vinson, Ben. *Bearing Arms for His Majesty: The Free Colored Militia in Colonial Mexico.* Stanford, CA: SUP, 2001.

Walker, Charles. *Smoldering Ashes: Cuzco and the Creation of the Peruvian Republic, 1780–1840.* Durham, NC: DUP, 1999.

———. *The Tupac Amaru Rebellion.* Cambridge, MA: Harvard University Press, 2014.

Walker, Louise. *Waking from the Dream: Mexico's Middle Class after 1968.* Stanford, CA: SUP, 2013.

Wallerstein, Immanuel. *The Modern World-System.* 4 vols. 1974–2011. Reprint, Berkeley: UCP, 2011.

Ward, Peter. *México megaciudad: Desarrollo y política, 1970–2002.* Zinacatepec, Mexico: CNSE, 2004.

Warman, Arturo. *El campo mexicano en el siglo XX.* Mexico City: FCE, 2004.

———. "The Political Project of Zapatismo." In Katz, *Riot, Rebellion, and Revolution,* 321–37.

———. *"We Come to Object": The Peasants of Morelos and the National State.* Translated by Stephen Ault. Baltimore: JHU, 1980.

Wasserman, Mark. *Capitalists, Caciques, and Revolution: The Native Elites and Foreign Enterprise in Chihuahua, Mexico, 1854–1911.* Chapel Hill: UNC, 1984.

Wells, Allen. *Yucatan's Gilded Age: Haciendas, Henequén, and International Harvester, 1850–1915.* Albuquerque: UNM, 1985.

Wells, Allen, and Gilbert Joseph. *Summer of Discontent, Seasons of Upheaval: Elite Politics and Rural Insurgency in Yucatán, 1876–1915.* Stanford, CA: SUP, 1996.

West, Robert. *The Mining Community in Northern New Spain: The Parral Mining District.* Berkeley: UCP, 1949.

Williams, Robert. *Export Agriculture and the Crisis in Central America.* Chapel Hill: UNC, 1984.

Wolf, Eric. *Europe and the People without History.* Berkeley: UCP, 1982.

———. *Peasant Wars of the Twentieth Century.* New York: Harper and Row, 1968.

Womack, John, Jr. "The Mexican Economy during the Revolution, 1910–1920." *Marxist Perspectives* 1, no. 4 (1978): 80–123.

———. *Rebellion in Chiapas: An Historical Reader.* New York: New Press, 1999.

———. *Zapata and the Mexican Revolution.* New York: Knopf, 1968.

Wood, Stephanie. "Corporate Adjustment in Colonial Mexican Indigenous Towns: The Toluca Region, 1550–1810." PhD diss., UCLA, 1984.

———. "La evolución de la corporación indígena en la region del Valle de Toluca, 1550–1810." In Miño Grijalva, *Haciendas, pueblos y comunidades,* 117–42.

———. *Transcending Conquest: Nahua Views of Spanish Colonial Mexico.* Norman: UOP, 2003.

Wright, Angus. *The Death of Ramón González: The Modern Agricultural Dilemma.* Rev. ed. Austin: UTP, 2005.

Wyllie, Robert Crichton. *México: Noticia sobre su hacienda pública bajo el gobierno español y después de la independencia.* Mexico City: Ignacio Cumplido, 1845. Reprinted in *Documentos para el estudio,* 243–352. Cited: RWM.

Yannakakis, Yanna. *The Art of Being In Between: Native Intermediaries and Local Rule in Colonial Oaxaca.* Durham, NC: DUP, 2008.

Zamudio, Guadalupe, and Gloria Camacho Pichardo. *Estado de México: Experiencias de investigación histórica*. Toluca: Universidad Autónoma del Estado de México, 2002.

Zavala, María Eugenia. "La transición demográfica de 1895–2010." In Rabell Romero, *Mexicanos*, 87–114.

Zavala, Silvio. *La encomienda Indiana*. Mexico City: Editorial Porrúa, 1935.

Zubieta, José. *Sentencia definitiva . . . por el despojo del Monte de las Haciendas de S. Pedro Martír y S. Antonio Abad*. Mexico City: Imprenta Literaria, 1865.

Zulawski, Ann. *They Eat from Their Labor: Work and Social Change in Colonial Bolivia*. Pittsburgh: University of Pittsburgh Press, 1995.

INDEX

Page numbers in italics refer to illustrations

A NOTE ON THE TYPE

THIS BOOK has been composed in Miller, a Scotch Roman typeface designed by Matthew Carter and first released by Font Bureau in 1997. It resembles Monticello, the typeface developed for The Papers of Thomas Jefferson in the 1940s by C. H. Griffith and P. J. Conkwright and reinterpreted in digital form by Carter in 2003.

Pleasant Jefferson ("P. J.") Conkwright (1905–1986) was Typographer at Princeton University Press from 1939 to 1970. He was an acclaimed book designer and AIGA Medalist.

The ornament used throughout this book was designed by Pierre Simon Fournier (1712–1768) and was a favorite of Conkwright's, used in his design of the *Princeton University Library Chronicle*.